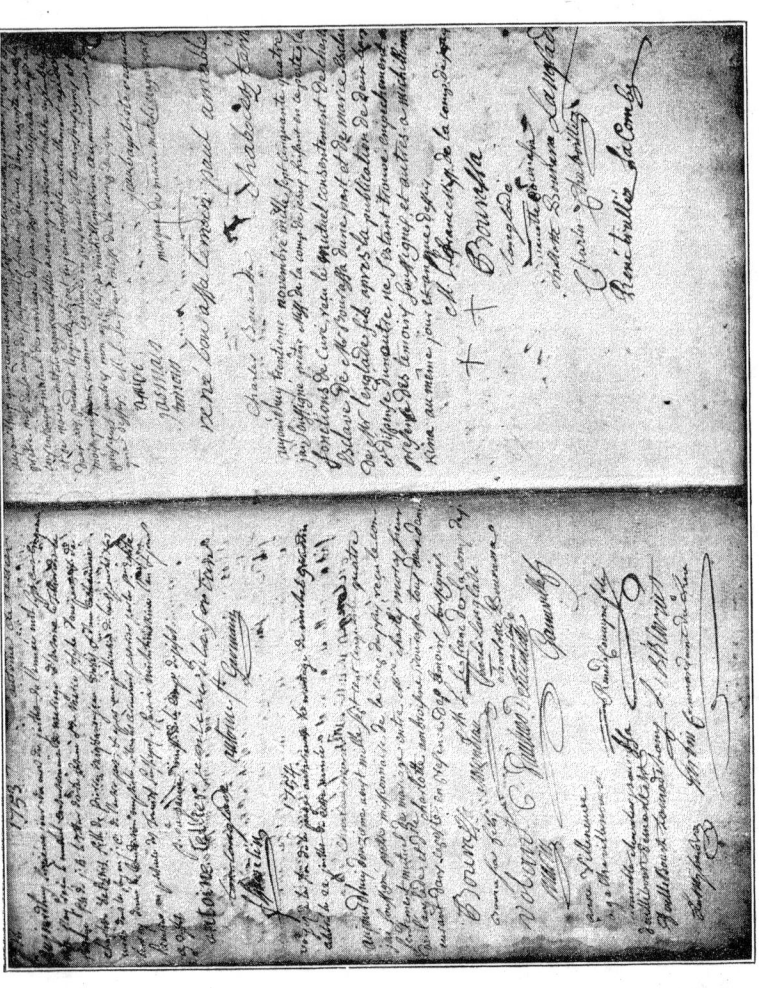

Two pages of the Mackinac Register
Reduced from a photograph of the original

COLLECTIONS OF THE STATE HISTORICAL SOCIETY OF WISCONSIN

VOLUME XIX

Mackinac Register of Baptisms
and Interments—1695-1821

A Wisconsin Fur-Trader's Journal—1804-05

The Fur-Trade on the Upper Lakes—1778-1815

The Fur-Trade in Wisconsin—1815-1817

Edited by
Reuben Gold Thwaites, LL.D.
Secretary and Superintendent of the Society

HERITAGE BOOKS
2009

HERITAGE BOOKS
AN IMPRINT OF HERITAGE BOOKS, INC.

Books, CDs, and more—Worldwide

For our listing of thousands of titles see our website
at
www.HeritageBooks.com

A Facsimile Reprint
Published 2009 by
HERITAGE BOOKS, INC.
Publishing Division
100 Railroad Ave. #104
Westminster, Maryland 21157

Originally published by the Society
Madison
1910

— Publisher's Notice —
In reprints such as this, it is often not possible to remove blemishes from the original. We feel the contents of this book warrant its reissue despite these blemishes and hope you will agree and read it with pleasure.

International Standard Book Numbers
Paperbound: 978-0-7884-1443-5
Clothbound: 978-0-7884-8128-4

Contents

	PAGE
OFFICERS OF THE SOCIETY, 1910	ix
PREFACE	xi

THE MACKINAC REGISTER

1695–1821:	REGISTER OF BAPTISMS OF THE MISSION OF ST. IGNACE DE MICHILIMAKINAK	1
1787:	REGISTER OF MARRIAGES	149
1743–1806:	REGISTER OF INTERMENTS	150
1787–1821:	MISCELLANEOUS NOTES IN THE REGISTER	160

A WISCONSIN FUR-TRADER'S JOURNAL, 1804-05

LETTER TO THE READERS	163
FROM FORT KAMANAITIQUOYA TO THE MONTREAL RIVER	166
LIST OF GOODS GIVEN FOR PROVISIONS AND EXPENSES OF THE FORT OF LAC DU FLAMBEAU	216
STATEMENT OF GOODS SENT TO THE OUISECONSAINT RIVER	221
INVENTORY OF GOODS REMAINING AT LAC DU FLAMBEAU	224
STATEMENT OF THE GOODS GIVEN TO THE SAVAGES FOR NOTHING (three broadsides)	224
ACCOUNT BOOK FOR DROUINE	225

THE FUR-TRADE ON THE UPPER LAKES

1778:	SUPPLIES RECEIVED AND FORWARDED	234
1784:	SALES AT MONTREAL	259
1786:	RETURNS UNSATISFACTORY	261
1789:	SUPPLIES FOR NORTH WEST COMPANY	266
1790:	OUTFITTING AT GREEN BAY	267
1791–92:	CONDITIONS AT MACKINAC	270
1792:	FUR-TRADE UNPROFITABLE	271
1793:	REGULATIONS PROPOSED	273
1793:	DISPUTE WITH EMPLOYÉ	275
1796:	BRITISH EVACUATE DETROIT	276
1798:	FURS CAPTURED BY FRENCH	277
1799:	NEW NORTH WEST COMPANY	

[iii]

1799:	OUTFITTING FOR WISCONSIN	.	.	.	282
1799:	COMPETITION IN THE NORTHWEST	.	.	.	283
1799:	SHIPPING ON LAKE HURON	.	.	.	285
1799:	NEWS FROM MACKINAC	.	.	.	287
1799:	ENGAGÉS DESERT	.	.	.	288
1799:	PRICES FOR PELTRY	.	.	.	289
1800:	RIVALRY IN NORTHWEST TRADE	.	.	.	289
1800:	WISCONSIN ENGAGEMENT CONTRACT	.	.	.	292
1800:	PROVISIONS FOR FUR-TRADE	.	.	.	293
1801:	LICENSES FOR THE FUR-TRADE	.	.	.	295
1801:	MONTREAL EXPORTS OF FURS	.	.	.	297
1802:	SETTLEMENT OF ACCOUNTS; LANGLADE'S LANDS	.	.	.	298
1802:	UNITED STATES REGULATIONS FOR FUR-TRADE	.	.	.	301
1803:	A TYPICAL FUR-TRADE ACCOUNT	.	.	.	304
1804:	TRADE AT MILWAUKEE	.	.	.	305
1804:	PROVISIONS ON UPPER LAKES	.	.	.	306
1804:	UNION OF NORTHWEST COMPANIES	.	.	.	308
1805:	LOCATION OF FUR-TRADE FACTORIES	.	.	.	310
1806:	WISCONSIN TRADERS AND AGENT	.	.	.	311
1807:	OPERATIONS OF DUBUQUE	.	.	.	318
1807:	A TYPICAL INVOICE	.	.	.	321
1807:	INFLUENCE OF TECUMSEH'S BROTHER	.	.	.	322
1808:	WISCONSIN AGENT KILLED IN DUEL	.	.	.	324
1808:	DIRECTIONS FOR FACTORS	.	.	.	326
1809:	MICHILIMACKINAC FACTORY	.	.	.	333
1809:	THE MACKINAC COMPANY	.	.	.	334
1809:	HATTERS' FURS FROM FACTORIES	.	.	.	335
1810:	AMERICANS ABSORB MONTREAL FUR-TRADE	.	.	.	336
1811:	EMBARGO AFFECTS FUR-TRADE	.	.	.	338
1811:	WISCONSIN CARGO CLEARED	.	.	.	340
1811:	TRADERS PURCHASE FROM FACTOR	.	.	.	341
1811:	AVOIDANCE OF EMBARGO	.	.	.	342
1812:	FUR-TRADE ENGAGEMENT	.	.	.	343
1812–13:	WISCONSIN TRADE AGREEMENTS	.	.	.	344
1813:	AMERICAN FUR COMPANY ON THE GREAT LAKES	.	.	.	346
1814:	RUMOR OF PEACE	.	.	.	350
1814:	NORTH WEST COMPANY EQUIP GREEN BAY TRADER	.	.	.	355
1814:	AMERICAN EXPEDITION ON LAKE HURON	.	.	.	357
1814:	BRITISH CONTROL MACKINAC	.	.	.	364
1815:	EFFECT OF PEACE	.	.	.	369
1815:	LAST DAYS OF THE NORTH WESTERNERS	.	.	.	372

THE FUR-TRADE IN WISCONSIN

1815:	AMERICAN MESSAGE TO MENOMINEE	.	.	.	375
1815:	WISCONSIN POSTS RECOMMENDED	.	.	.	376
1815:	UNITED STATES FACTORIES IN WISCONSIN	.	.	.	380

Contents

1815:	USE OF LIQUOR PROHIBITED	395
1815:	DUTY ON FUR-TRADE MERCHANDISE	396
1815:	ORDERS FROM ILLINOIS	398
1815:	INDIAN AGENT AT GREEN BAY	399
1816:	PROHIBITION OF LIQUOR	399
1816:	TRADERS AT MILWAUKEE	400
1816:	BRITISH SUBJECTS IN WISCONSIN FUR-TRADE	401
1816:	AGENTS OF THE SOUTH WEST AND AMERICAN FUR COMPANIES	413
1816:	SEIZURE OF FURS	415
1816:	TROOPS AT PRAIRIE DU CHIEN	424
1816:	LICENSES FOR FOREIGNERS	425
1816:	GREEN BAY TRADERS AND PRICES	428
1816:	TROOPS AT GREEN BAY	430
1816:	FACTORY AT PRAIRIE DU CHIEN	433
1816:	POST BUILT AT GREEN BAY	436
1816:	FACTORY AND LICENSES AT GREEN BAY	440
1816:	LEGAL OPINION ON LICENSES	441
1816:	AFFAIRS AT GREEN BAY	442
1816:	LICENSES TO FOREIGNERS	443
1817:	DIFFICULTIES OF WISCONSIN TRADERS	445
1817:	FACTORY RECEIPTS	447
1817:	AMERICAN FUR COMPANY'S AGENTS	451
1817:	ABUSE OF LICENSING POWER	452
1817:	PRICES FOR FURS	453
1817:	INSTRUCTIONS FOR SHIPPING FURS	454
1817:	WINNEBAGO HOSTILE	455
1817:	PURPOSES OF PRIVATE TRADERS	456
1817:	FOREIGNERS NOT EXCLUDED	457
1817:	NEWS FROM MACKINAC	461
1817:	INSTRUCTIONS FOR WISCONSIN FACTOR	463
1817:	PROCEEDS OF FACTORIES	466
1817:	PROHIBITION OF LIQUOR	466
1817:	BRITISH SUBJECTS AT GREEN BAY	468
1817:	WISCONSIN INDIAN CENSUS	470
1817:	WISCONSIN INDIANS VISIT BRITISH POST	472
1817:	LOCKWOOD AT PRAIRIE DU CHIEN	474
1817:	LICENSES AT GREEN BAY	475
1817:	TRADERS ARRESTED ON THE MISSISSIPPI	477
1817:	LICENSES TO FOREIGNERS	480
1817:	MISSISSIPPI TRADERS ARRESTED	483
1817:	INSTRUCTIONS FOR GREEN BAY FACTOR	484
1817:	LOCAL TRADING INCIDENTS	485
1817:	GREEN BAY AGENT'S REPORT	487
INDEX		489

Illustrations

	PAGE
TWO PAGES OF THE MACKINAC REGISTER. Reduced photographic facsimile . . . . . *Frontispiece*	
ENTRIES IN MACKINAC REGISTER, July 20 and September 10, 1742. Reduced photographic facsimile . . .	8
ENTRY IN MACKINAC REGISTER, March 11, 1749. Reduced photographic facsimile	26
ENTRY IN MACKINAC REGISTER, July 28, 1768. Reduced photographic facsimile	75
AUTOGRAPH LETTER BY FRANÇOIS VICTOR MALHIOT. Reduced photographic facsimile	166
ARTICLES OF CHIPPEWA HANDICRAFT. Selected from specimens in Museum of Wisconsin Historical Society . . .	174
PORTRAIT OF SHINAABAW'OSIN, OR THE FIGURED STONE, CHIPPEWA CHIEF. Photographic reduction of colored lithograph by James Otto Lewis, 1826	208
PORTRAIT OF MAKOMETA, OR BEAR'S OIL, MENOMINEE CHIEF. Photographic reduction of colored lithograph by James Otto Lewis, 1827	208
STATEMENT OF THE GOODS GIVEN TO THE SAVAGES BY MALHIOT FOR NOTHING (July 25–October 4, 1804). Folded broadside	224
THE SAME (October 13, 1804–April 9, 1805). Folded broadside	224
THE SAME (April 11–May 21, 1805). Folded broadside .	224
MAP OF MACKINAC ISLAND, 1910 . . .	234
PORTRAIT OF KEEOTUCKKEE, POTAWATOMI CHIEF. Photographic reduction of colored lithograph by James Otto Lewis, 1827	256
PORTRAIT OF NAHSHAWAGAA, OR THE WHITE DOG'S SON, POTAWATOMI CHIEF. Photographic reduction of colored lithograph by James Otto Lewis, 1827 . . .	256
WINNEBAGO VILLAGE. Reduced from lithograph in Henry R. Schoolcraft's *Indian Tribes* . . .	300
PORTRAIT OF SHOUNKCHUNK, OR THE BLACK WOLF, WINNEBAGO CHIEF. Photographic reduction of colored lithograph by James Otto Lewis, 1827 . . .	320
PORTRAIT OF WAAPALAA, OR PLAYING FOX, FOX CHIEF. Photographic reduction of colored lithograph by James Otto Lewis, 1825	320
PORTRAIT OF RAMSAY CROOKS. From oil painting by E. Saintan, in possession of Wisconsin Historical Society . .	347

Illustrations

VIEW OF BRITISH LANDING, MACKINAC ISLAND. From photograph taken in 1910 362
ARTICLES USED BY WISCONSIN FUR-TRADERS. Selected from specimens in Museum of Wisconsin Historical Society . 375
PORTRAIT OF LEWIS CASS. From oil painting in possession of Wisconsin Historical Society, copied by Lewis T. Ives from original (Detroit 1839) by George A. P. Healy . . 379
PORTRAIT OF ANDREW JACQUES VIEAU. From oil painting (Detroit, 1839) by George A. P. Healy, in possession of Wisconsin Historical Society 400
PORTRAIT OF JAMES H. LOCKWOOD. From oil painting by Samuel M. Brookes, in possession of Wisconsin Historical Society . 474

Officers, 1910

President

WILLIAM WARD WIGHT, M. A. . . . . Milwaukee

Vice Presidents

HON. EMIL BAENSCH	Manitowoc
HON. LUCIUS C. COLMAN, B. A. . . .	La Crosse
HON. BURR W. JONES, M. A. . . .	Madison
HON. JOHN LUCHSINGER	Monroe
HON. BENJAMIN F. MCMILLAN . . .	McMillan
HON. JOHN B. WINSLOW, LL. D. . . .	Madison

Secretary and Superintendent

REUBEN G. THWAITES, LL. D. . . . . Madison

Treasurer

HON. LUCIEN S. HANKS . . . . . Madison

Librarian and Assistant Superintendent

ISAAC S. BRADLEY, B. S. . . . . . Madison

Curators, Ex-Officio

HON. JAMES O. DAVIDSON . . .	Governor
HON. JAMES A. FREAR . . .	Secretary of State
HON. ANDREW H. DAHL . . .	State Treasurer

Curators, Elective

Term expires at annual meeting in 1910

ROBERT M. BASHFORD, M. A.
JAIRUS H. CARPENTER, LL. D.
LUCIUS C. COLMAN, B. A.
HENRY E. LEGLER, ESQ.
HON. BENJAMIN F. MCMILLAN
DANA C. MUNRO, M. A.

WILLIAM A. P. MORRIS, B. A.
REV. J. M. NAUGHTIN
ARTHUR C. NEVILLE, ESQ.
ROBERT G. SIEBECKER, LL. B.
FREDERICK J. TURNER, LL. D.
CHARLES R. VAN HISE, LL. D.

Term expires at annual meeting in 1911

RASMUS B. ANDERSON, LL. D.
HON. EMIL BAENSCH
CHARLES N. BROWN, LL. B.
FREDERIC K. CONOVER, LL. B.
ALFRED A. JACKSON, M. A.
BURR W. JONES, M. A.

HON. ELISHA W. KEYES
HON. JOHN LUCHSINGER
MOST REV. S. G. MESSMER
J. HOWARD PALMER, ESQ.
JOHN B. PARKINSON, M. A.
WILLIAM A. SCOTT, PH. D.

Term expires at annual meeting in 1912

THOMAS E. BRITTINGHAM, ESQ.
HENRY C. CAMPBELL, ESQ.
WILLIAM K. COFFIN, M. S.
HON. LUCIEN S. HANKS
NILS P. HAUGEN, LL. B
COL. HIRAM HAYES

REV. PATRICK B. KNOX
MAJ. FRANK W. OAKLEY
ARTHUR L. SANBORN, LL.B.
HON. HALLE STEENSLAND*
E. RAY STEVENS, LL. B.
WILLIAM W. WIGHT, M. A.

Executive Committee

The curators, the secretary, the librarian, the governor, the secretary of state, and the state treasurer, constitute the executive committee.

---

* Died August 20, 1910.

Preface

The documentary material published in the present volume of our COLLECTIONS continues and supplements that presented in Volume xviii, which closed with the chronicle of marriages in the Mackinac Register. We now publish the remainder of the Register (1695–1821), comprising baptisms, interments, and a few miscellaneous entries concerning parish affairs.

The significance of these mission records of old Mackinac is apparent only when considered as a whole. Their interest is by no means confined to genealogical data concerning the handful of inhabitants dependent on the fur-trade and on the military post long dominating the strait between Lakes Huron and Michigan; in an historic sense, the document is an epitome of life and manners throughout the entire "Upper Country" during the most picturesque period in its history.

Mackinac was the commercial entrepôt for the shores and hinterland of the vast region of the upper Great Lakes; here fur-traders, *voyageurs,* trappers, and aborigines, gathered each summer to buy and sell peltries, and secure goods and necessities for forest life and traffic. In a very practical way, also, it was the social centre of that far-stretching wilderness which included the small Wisconsin settlements of Green Bay, Chequamegon, and Prairie du Chien—official and commercial "dependencies" of Mackinac.

At Mackinac was a church and, during the French regime (1670–1760), a resident missionary priest. Under British rule (1761–1796), ecclesiastical ministrations were less regular, for only an occasional call was expected from some itinerating pastor. On such occasions, nevertheless, word of the priestly visitation was swiftly passed around the lakes and to the inland fur-trade settlements of Wisconsin and Michigan, and whole families (many of them conspicuous in the early annals of our State) at once hastened to Mackinac by batteaux or canoes, to receive churchly sanction for their domestic arrangements. Then were men and women married, and their natural offspring baptized; frequently the mother, if of Indian origin, was also baptized; and often included in the ceremonies were the family servants—domesticated Indians, who cheerfully did the bidding of their masters: classed as *panis* (slaves), they nevertheless were held in the feudal bonds of affectionate interest and reciprocal service.

At these recurring ceremonies in the little wilderness chapel—which at first was on the mainland, but after 1780 on the island—there were not infrequently present, the entire resident population of the Mackinac neighborhood. Sometimes the expected itinerant missionary failed to appear, for distances were great, and many were the exigencies of travel by canoe; but lacking the ecclesiastic, civil ceremonies were substituted, and for that purpose the military officials, together with the resident royal notary, or (under the American regime) a justice of the peace, were pressed into service. Even in the priestly presence, these same civil functionaries, as well as visiting officials of other posts, stood as godfathers for the white and half-breed children, or signed the marriage record as witnesses. Such side-lights on official history are of especial value in the absence of other records. They reveal to us who commanded for the king, not only at Mackinac but at far distant posts in the Upper Country; they inform us as to the rank and position of historical personages; they likewise set forth the official arrangements during interregnums, or periods between different military occupations—particularly after Pontiac's savage conspiracy had expelled from this region every British officer and soldier.

Following the Mackinac Register, we present a series of documents on the fur-trade of the Northwest, between 1778 and 1815. This commerce of the forest profoundly affected early Wisconsin life; indeed, during the first two centuries of our Commonwealth's history, collecting furs for the European market was the only industry that flourished within our bounds. The trade developed a peculiar organism, which widely influenced the social development not only of Wisconsin but of the entire continental interior. Its personal relationships were comparable, in some degree, with those of the Scotch Highlands, under which chieftain and retainer were joined by certain obligations, and an unwritten code of custom. Although this system reached its height of efficiency under the Scotch traders who officered the great trading companies during the most prosperous period of the Northwest fur-trade, it was directly inherited from the French—being a legacy of the semi-feudal seignoirial arrangements of French-Canadian agricultural life, modified by the necessities of wilderness service. The chief trader was the *bourgeois*—governor of pack and train, master of the canoe-brigade, despot of the trading post. Under him were the *commis,* or clerks—gentlemen's sons, apprentices to the business, in arduous training for the responsibilities of a future *bourgeois*. These youth shared the appointments of their chief, slept in his tent, partook of his food, kept his accounts, and wrote his letters; and at his dictation, took charge of subsidiary posts, or of side-expeditions to native villages supposedly rich in peltries. If successful, the *commis* became in course of time a wintering partner in the great company to which he was apprenticed. The third and lowest stratum of the hierarchy was composed of *voyageurs*—young, hardy French-Canadian peasants, or half-breeds, who, rather than work in the narrow paternal fields, volunteered for this free life of the forests and waterways, or were apprenticed thereto by their parents and guardians. Their signed contracts (*engagements*) with the *bourgeois* bound them to obey the latter in all things, to do his will, seek his profit, avoid his damage, and refrain from trading on their own account. Their duties were to propel the canoe, portage the craft and its cargo, provide for the comfort of the *bourgeois,* pitch his tent, and prepare his meals; while at the trading post, they were to hunt, fish, cut wood, beat and pack furs, run the *drouine,* defend the post against hostile attacks, and be on good terms with as many Indians as possible. During his term of probation, the *voyageur* was known as a *mangeur de lard* (pork-eater), a derisive term for a dainty person, unused to wilderness fare and needing to be pampered in food and living—equivalent to the "tenderfoot" of the later American frontier. After one or two seasons the *voyageur* became a *hivenant* (or winterer), able to endure privations and fatigues that would appal the inexperienced.

For the second document in our volume, we publish the journal of a *commis,* stationed at a northern Wisconsin tradingpost. François Victor Malhoit, coming of a good Canadian family and allied by kinship to prominent traders of Green Bay, was in 1804–05 sent to winter at Lac du Flambeau, among the wild Chippewa of that region. His experiences are typical of the annoyances and hardships incident to life at the interior posts. In clear, vigorous language, with an occasional outburst of emotion, he narrates the events of his daily life— rivalry with a neighboring trader, drunken bouts among the savages, transportation of goods over a difficult portage, transmission of small equipments to the camps of the aborigines, scarcity of provisions, isolation and loneliness, tricks to secure large commercial gains. The record seems sordid and degrading enough, yet between the lines one obtains glimpses of the compensations that attracted and held so many civilized men to the wilderness trade—life in the open, lure of the stream and forest, constant opportunity for adventure, independence from conventional restraints.

Following the text of the journal, are given Malhiot's invoices and memoranda, which throw strong light on the economics of the trade, the goods, the peltries, the methods of credit and recovery, the curious terminology, the manner of accounting, and the numerous presents necessary to hold the good will of savage customers.

One of the interesting features illustrated by Malhiot's Jour-

Preface

nal is the competition created by the rivalry of the two great fur-trading companies of his time; and their final coalition into one monopoly. The heyday of the Northwest fur-trade was the period of the formation and growth of these organizations, roughly covered by the dates 1778 to 1815. The documents succeeding Malhiot's account, have been selected as further illuminating this period. As in the preceding three volumes of the COLLECTIONS, and for the same reasons, the Editor has found it impracticable strictly to limit the range of his material to the present boundaries of Wisconsin. It has been necessary to consider the region of the upper Great Lakes as the geographical unit within which Mackinac and Wisconsin traders operated. The district was reached by two principal routes: that of the lower Great Lakes, and that of the Ottawa and French rivers and Georgian Bay. About the close of the eighteenth century, however, there came into common use a third route, via Lake Ontario and the portage from Toronto to the lower arms of Georgian Bay. Detroit was the natural emporium for the lower lakes route, and Mackinac for the two via Georgian Bay. After the latter stronghold fell into American hands, the British entrenched themselves some forty miles to the eastward, on St. Joseph Island. But their fur-traders still resorted to Mackinac, and sent thence canoes to Sault Ste. Marie and the Superior posts, to Green Bay and the Mississippi (via the Fox–Wisconsin portage), to the lesser lake posts at Milwaukee and Chicago, and to trading stations on the Michigan rivers of Grand and Kalamazoo.

The documents herein given consist principally of business and friendly letters, interspersed with a few selected and typical official mauscripts—*engagement* contracts, customs clearances, licenses, and territorial regulations for the trade. These inform us as to the routes of travel, the vast extent of territory over which the trade was scattered, the methods of transportation, and the constant intercommunication between commercial centres in this great Northwest region. It is surprising to see the intimacies which were maintained between members of the trading guild in places so remote from each other as St. Louis and Montreal, Grand Portage and Detroit.

Of first importance, is the information here obtainable, on the organization, management, and methods of the great corporations. From the time of its formation, the North West Company monopolized the field until the vigorous rivalry of the X Y Company bade it look to its laurels. Then followed five or six years of lawless, ruinous competition, terminated only by the union of the two in 1804. Meanwhile, the Michilimackinac Company paralleled the success of the "Nor' Westers," in the lands south of the Great Lakes and along the Mississippi. Shortly after this, a coalition headed by John Jacob Astor began competition with the Michilimackinac concern, and finally bought out a number of the lesser partners of the latter; with them and a few of the chief Canadian traders, he organized (1808) the South West Company. The success of this venture led Astor into the Pacific Fur Company, and the founding of Astoria. Not until after the close of our second war with England did he launch the American Fur Company, which in time profoundly influenced the destinies of Wisconsin fur-traders.

The fur-trading corporations naturally tended toward monopoly. At the portages they secured the right of way; at the emporia, the best of provisions and supplies; among the winterers, they had their choice of men; and the returns of their "brigades" were as valuable as the argosies of the Spanish main. Their influence was felt not only in provincial, but in national parliaments; diplomacy was not seldom exercised on their behalf; and they dictated the terms of several international treaties.

Many of the letters herein published are from early leaders of the Western fur-trade, such as Alexander Henry, Forsyth, Richardson, the Todds, McGills, Frobishers, and MacGillevray of Montreal; and Ramsay Crooks and John Jacob Astor of New York. From this material, we obtain also definite, sometimes illuminating, information concerning certain other per-

Preface

sonalities, whom heretofore we have but vaguely known as actors on the stage of Wisconsin history. Such are Pierre Antaya, credited with being the founder of Prairie du Chien; Julien Dubuque, early lead-miner, and patronym of a neighboring Iowa town; James Aird, whom Lewis and Clark, returning to civilization after their quest of the Columbia, encountered far up on the Missouri; Pierre Grignon the elder, second "father of Green Bay;" and Jacob Franks and the brothers Rocheblave, who traded with tribesmen towards the distant headwaters of the Mississippi and far into the Canadian Northwest.

In addition to exhibiting the methods and scope of their business operations, these letters show the personalities of the men, the ties and amenities of courtesy and friendship between them, the interest they felt in each other's families—particularly in the children, whose education was often conducted in Montreal. Herein are also set forth the personal needs of the Northwest traders—their orders for clothes *a la mode,* for violins, and for table luxuries. In letters from the seaboard, are heard echoes of European complications, of the successes and defeats of Napoleon, of the capture of fur-laden vessels on the high seas. From the interior, come incidental references to the American Revolution, to the War of 1812–15 on the Great Lakes, to the capture and siege of Mackinac (1812–14), to the predatory British expedition to Wisconsin (1814), to the safe passage of the fur-brigade in the same year, and to the immunity generously granted by both contending nations to Astor's agents.

Not until 1800, did the American influence begin seriously to be felt. There was then a slight infiltration of American traders, such as Henry Monroe Fisher at Prairie du Chien, and John and Michael Dousman at Mackinac. The question of American licenses arose; our territorial regulations were found to interfere with established French and British usages; certain of the traders were granted American civil commissions as justices of the peace or as Indian agents—such as John

Campbell and Nicolas Boilvin at Prairie du Chien, and Charles Reaume at Green Bay. Zebulon M. Pike ascended (1805–06) the Mississippi from St. Louis, and warned the British traders against displaying their country's flag on American soil.

Within this period, likewise, the factory system of Government trading houses was extended to the Northwest. Such establishments at Chicago, Mackinac, and the Sauk towns on the Mississippi tended to destroy the equilibrium and profits of the British traders. Moreover, the Embargo Act seriously affected the obtaining of European supplies for the fur-trade. The superintendent of Indian trade at Washington wrote plausible excuses, to be offered by Government factors to their tribal customers; but meanwhile the enterprising Scotch trader, Robert Dickson, a British subject familiar to Northwest Indians, was avoiding the terms of the embargo by conveying goods to his clients in the Wisconsin forests, over a circuitous route of extraordinary length—from Montreal to Pittsburgh, down the Ohio River to its mouth, and thence up the Mississippi to his old posts, which in earlier days he had reached by the convenient Fox–Wisconsin waterway.

During the first decade of the nineteenth century, the Shawnee head-chief, Tecumseh, together with his brother the Prophet, instituted a new religious movement among the tribesmen of the continental interior, which had for its object the expulsion of the white man and all of the curses (including fire-water) which the latter had introduced into the life of the forest. This uprising culminated in the battle of Tippecanoe (1811). Upon the declaration of war by the United States, the succeeding year, most of the tribes and fur-traders of the upper Great Lakes naturally enlisted under the banner of Great Britain. A small knot of American sympathizers at Prairie du Chien were forced to leave the country. Meanwhile, the British fur-trade in our region flourished greatly, yielding enormous profits, but there was always present the risk of capture of fur cargoes by American vessels patrolling the lakes. The American expedition to Mackinac in 1814 sought not merely the recovery of that post from British hands, but the capture of the North West Company's fleet of fur-laden canoes. Consequently, goods from Montreal were detained in reaching their destinations, and the amusing complaints of Jacob Franks reveal that the Canadian traders were much alarmed at the prospect.

With the signing of the Treaty of Ghent (December, 1814) British fur-traders lost their ascendancy on American soil. The important mart of Mackinac was restored to the Americans; the British-sympathizing tribesmen were ordered to bury the tomahawk, and thereafter to submit to the dictates of their American Father. British traders and Indian agents felt that they had been betrayed by their own nation into the enemy's hands. Removing their military posts to the nearest possible sites within British boundaries—Amherstburg, opposite Detroit, and Drummond Island, east of the Mackinac straits—they now began a systematic course of cajolery and present-giving, to counteract American overtures and keep the tribesmen friendly to their former interests; for it was hoped by the agents of the king that the time might not be far distant when some fresh clash between the nations would result in regaining the Northwest for His Britannic Majesty. Such methods naturally caused friction between the agents of the neighboring powers. The indignant letters of William Henry Puthuff, American agent at Mackinac, must be read in this light.

Troublous times now befell the Wisconsin–French traders, who had been among King George's most faithful subjects. The treaty had left them within the American border; but they were allied to the British by every tie of consanguinity, custom, self-interest, and association. Their lot was hard; their status was undefined, for now they were neither British subjects nor American citizens. Living in the so-called "Indian country," they could obtain no titles to the lands which they had inherited from their ancestors, and long had cultivated. Suspected and harassed by officious American agents, their furs were seized, their licenses revoked, and every possible hindrance placed in the path of the business from which they were accustomed to obtain a livelihood for their families. Small wonder that the better class of these old-time inhabitants of Wisconsin at first seriously contemplated removal, with all their goods and chattels, to some site in Upper Canada where they might live in peace, unvexed by Yankee officials.

In this dilemma, the Wisconsin traders were befriended by Astor and his agents. The long association which that astute captain of forest commerce had had with the merchants of Montreal and the Northwest, taught him that the fur-trade was an intricate business, not easily acquired by the inexperienced; he saw that his proposed operations in this region would be more successful if conducted by those accustomed from childhood to traffic with the Indians. When the American Fur Company was organized, it gave immediate employment to the practiced traders of the Wisconsin settlements. Their Americanization, although a slow process, was thenceforth assured.

During the years immediately following the war (1815–17), the Federal Government was likewise cementing its advantage by establishing both posts and trading factories within the borders of Wisconsin. In 1816 Fort Howard was built at Green Bay, and Fort Crawford at Prairie du Chien, with Indian agencies auxiliary to both establishments. The Government factory system was extended to the Northwest, no longer merely as a benevolent institution to benefit the neighboring tribesmen, but as an aggressive movement to diminish the power and influence of British traders. With the inauguration of this policy, a new phase of the fur-trade had begun—no longer was competition limited to rival companies, but hereafter Government agents and private traders competed one with the other for the custom of the tribesmen. Now that the bars were down, the traders themselves were disorganized; a horde of adventurous Americans rushed into the territory, and with new methods and ideals entered the lists against the old established trading families, who were allied to the Indians by intermarriage, and trained in the traditional methods of the Franco-British regimes.

Preface

We propose in our Volume xx, to continue these documents on the fur-trade in Wisconsin, thereby furnishing opportunity for a detailed study of this all-pervading commerce, throughout our entire pre-territorial period (until 1836).

The papers herein published have been obtained from several sources. Aside from the Mackinac Register and Malhiot's Journal, the material has in the main been secured from three repositories: the Federal archives at Washington (except those of the War Department, whose documents are not as yet available to students of American history), the admirable and extensive private library of Clarence M. Burton, Esq., of Detroit, and the library of our Society. The Federal material was obtained through the systematic and efficient co-operation of Dr. J. Franklin Jameson, director of the Bureau of Historical Research in the Carnegie Institution of Washington, and of his capable assistant, Mr. Leo F. Stock. Mr. Burton's generosity in opening to us his collections of Northwestern material, and aiding in the procurement of transcripts therefrom, is most gratefully acknowledged. We are also much indebted to Edward E. Ayer, Esq., of Chicago, for transcripts of documents in his large collections; to Charles Henry Gould, Esq., librarian of McGill University, Montreal, for transcripts of the invoices and accounts accompanying Malhiot's Journal; and to Col. Crawford Lindsay of Quebec, who skillfully Englished the text of that journal. The Hon. Edward Osgood Brown of Chicago, furnished us with a faithful transcript of the Mackinac Register. After this was in type, the original of the document was courteously loaned to us for purposes of textual comparison and photography, by the Right Reverend Frederick Eis, bishop of Marquette, through the medium of its custodian, the Rev. M. C. Sommers, pastor of the parish of Ste. Anne, Mackinac Island. For information on local topography, genealogy, and fur-trade usages, acknowledgments are due to the Hon. James Bardon, president of the Superior Historical Society, the Hon. Samuel S. Fifield, postmaster of Ashland, David H. Grignon of Green Bay, Antoine Grignon of Trempealeau, and

Miss Deborah Beaumont Martin, public librarian of Green Bay. Prof. George Wagner of the University of Wisconsin has aided us in the identification of several zoological references. Mr. Wilberforce Eames, Lenox librarian of the New York Public Library, contributed interesting data relative to the Astor family.

In editing, annotating, and indexing this volume, the Editor has had valuable expert co-operation from Dr. Louise Phelps Kellogg his editorial assistant on the Society's Library staff, who in addition has Englished all of the French documents except the Mackinac Register and Malhiot's Journal. In the difficult work of transcribing and proof-reading, important aid has been rendered by Misses Annie A. Nunns and Daisy G. Beecroft, also of the Library staff.

September, 1910.   R. G. T.

The Mackinac Register

1695–1821: REGISTER OF BAPTISMS OF THE MISSION OF ST. IGNACE DE MICHILIMAKINAK.

[Translation from a transcript of the original, which latter is kept in the parish church of Ste. Anne, at Mackinac.][1]

In nomine patris & filii ✠ *& Spiritus sancti.*

Extracts from the ancient Registers beginning the 28th of April 1695[2]

antoine mainard, son of the late maurice mainard.[3]

---

[1] For a description of this document see *Wis. Hist. Colls.*, xviii, p. 469, notes 95, 96. The records of marriages at Mackinac, from 1725 to 1821, extracted from the register, were reproduced in translation in that volume. We here publish a translation of the remainder of the register—baptisms (1695–1821) and interments (1743–1806).

Lacunæ are indicated by leaders (......). Asterisks (* * *) indicate that the Editor has, for sake of space, omitted portions of the entry. These omissions are mere repetitions of formal phrases, conveying no specific information concerning the event or the persons interested, and are the same for each entry. Liberty has also been taken with the form of the date—the spelled-out style of the original being reduced to briefer numerical form. Further, in our need of saving space in so bulky and repetitious a document, we have eliminated the name of the holy day, where occasionally given in the register.—ED.

[2] The following list of baptisms, giving merely date and name, was copied from an older register into the new one, which latter was apparently begun in 1741. The transcriber, probably a clerical, seems to have freely added remarks of his own, indicating the status of the persons at the time of the copying—e. g., "now madame l'anglade." The few appended dates of deaths were obviously added later.—ED.

[3] Either the date for this entry was omitted, or it was April 28, 1695, the first entry in the old register.—ED.

27 September 1712 daniel, son of daniel villeneuve and of domitille, now madame l'anglade.

12 July 1713 jean l'espérance, then 7 years of age; now become a Savage at la pointe; and antoine, then 4 years old.

8 December 1713 ignace, son of ignace du Rivage.

23 March 1714 coussant, son of ignace vieu and of angélique du Sable.

8 March 1716 Anne, daughter of daniel Villeneuve and of M^{de} l'anglade, the said Anne[4] being now the wife of Sieur guiori.

2 August 1716 michel du Rivage, son of old du Rivage.

3 April 1719 coussante [Chevalier], now wife of Sieur hins.[5]

10 January 1720 marie Louise Therese [Villeneuve], now wife of Sieur gautier.[6]

30 November 1720 louis Therese, son of J. B. Chevalier, etc.

17 May 1721 louis Therese, son of ignace vieu—died at detroit in 1743.

13 May 1722 jean Baptiste villeneuve, son of madame l'anglade.

18 March 1723 josephe marguerite, daughter of J. B. Chevalier etc.

5 February 1724 agathe [Villeneuve], daughter of madame l'anglade, now wife of boishile [Boisguilbert].[7]

12 October 1724 marie (manon) daughter of J. B. Chevalier.

20 October 1724 marie judith, now wife of Gendren—died at St Joseph in 1744.

29 October 1724 marie ursule, daughter of J. B. Amiot, etc.

27 June 1725 judith, daughter of J. B. Reaume, etc.

---

[4] See *Wis. Hist. Colls.*, xviii, p. 136, note 74; also her marriage entry, p. 472, and her death in 1757, *post.*—ED.

[5] The mother of Joseph Louis Ainse (Hins); for her second marriage, see *Ibid.*, p. 478.—ED.

[6] The mother of Charles Gautier; see *Ibid.*, p. 136, note 77.—ED.

[7] For this person, see *Ibid.*, p. 135, note 75.—ED.

14 November 1725 coussant Stanislas, son of madame l'anglade.

1 March 1726 anne Charlotte veronique (nannette), daughter of J. B. Chevalier.[8]

22 April 1726 anne domitille (nanette), daughter of p. parent[9] etc.

5 June 1726 Catherine angelique, daughter of ignace vieu, etc.

10 October 1727 Charles (l'avoine) son of J. B. Chevalier.

13 May 1728 marie françoise (manon), daughter of p. parent.

5 October 1728 joseph maurice, son of J. B. Chevalier etc.

9 May 1729 charles michel, son of monsieur l'anglade,[10] etc.

1 October 1729 charlotte, daughter of p. parent[11] etc.

2 May 1730 Nicolas, son of j. B. amiot, born on the 7th of April.

22 July 1730 louis pascal, son of J. B. Chevalier.

15 October 1730 claude, natural son of claude Caron.

29 September 1731 Rene michel, son of marie, a slave of menard.

28 March 1732 anne Therese Esther, daughter of J. B. Chevalier[12]

20 March 1732 Marie louise, daughter of J. B. Amiot.

9 October 1732 pierre coussant, son of p. parent.

14 January 1733 philippe Bolon, son of gabriel Bolon.

11 July 1733 angelique, daughter of J. B. Chevalier.

2 August 1733 antoine, then 5 years of age, son of one la fortune.

---

[8] For these persons, see *Ibid.*, p. 136, note 80.—ED.

[9] For her marriage record, see *Ibid.*, p. 472.—ED.

[10] For a brief biographical sketch of Charles Langlade, see *Ibid.*, p. 130, note 68.—ED.

[11] Her marriage record is in *Ibid.*, p. 478.—ED.

[12] For her marriage to Etienne Chesnier, see *Ibid.*, p. 479.—ED.

5 April 1733 Charles dominique, 4 years old, son of p. du plassy etc.

4 August 1733 maurice, son of pierre du plasse etc.

16 October 1733 marie anne, daughter of Thomas Blondeau.

1 January 1734 francois Renard, two years old, slave of Mr du Braise.

1 January 1734 marie esther, daughter of augustin l'arche, then one year old.[13]

5 April 1734 marie anne, daughter of J. B. Amiot etc.

19 September 1734 marie Catherine, daughter of Sieur des hêtres, then two years old.

19 April 1735 pierre louis, a slave of Mr de Clignancourt,[14] 20 years of age. (Rocambole, now an apostate and become a Savage at Chicagou).

18 October 1734 joseph, son of p. parent.

14 May 1735 marie madaleine, 4 years old, slave of M^r l'anglade.

22 May 1735 luc, son of J. B. Chevalier.

27 May 1735 jean louis, son of gabriel Bolon.

9 July 1736 Charles jean Baptiste, son of Charles Chabyer.[15]

28 September 1736 michel, natural son of T. Blondeau.

7 October 1736 marie françoise, slave of menard, 40 years old.

26 November 1736 marie anne, daughter of p. parent.[16]

30 November 1736 louis josué, about 2 years old, son of Sieur du lignon, since legitimized.

30 December 1736 Catherine, one year old, daughter of Sieur Rocheveau, since legitimized.

5 January 1737 françoise, then about 20 years old, now

---

[13] Apparently from St. Joseph's—the full name is L'Archevêque. *Ibid.*, p. 476.—ED.

[14] A lessee of the fort at La Baye, 1747-49. *Ibid.*, pp. 7-10.—ED.

[15] For this family, see *Ibid.*, p. 255, note 51.—ED.

[16] For the marriages of this person, see *Ibid.*, pp. 480, 482.—ED.

the lawful wife of Sieur Rocheveau—died at Sault Ste marie, in January 1742.

29 September 1737 marie angelique, about 20 years old, now the lawful wife of Sieur de lignon; died here on the 4th September 1748.

29 September 1737 françoise michelle, one year old, daughter of Sieur du lignon.

13 October 1737 marianne, about 20 years old, now the lawful wife of jean Baptiste, formerly a slave.

21 November 1737 marie, born of a slave of Sieur Chevalier.

3 February 1738 claude charles, son of Sieur Gauthier.[17]

29 April 1738 françoise veronique, two months old, daughter of Sieur Rocheveau.

3 August 1738 ignace, son of pierre parent.

16 August 1738 augustin, son of a negress, then belonging to Sieur marin urtubize.[18]

23 November 1738 pierre pascal, legitimate son of Sieur hamelin, born on the 21st of February, 1735—died at montvert in 1743.

24 November 1738 louis Charles, legitimate son of Sieur hamelin, born in the month of March, 1737.

25 November 1738 jacques, legitimate son of Sieur hamelin, etc., born on the 22nd of January, 1733.

26 November 1738 marianne, legitimate daughter of Sieur hamelin, born on the 10th of January, 1731.

27 November 1738 marie Athanase, about 30 years old, now the lawful wife of Sieur hamelin; died at pointe St ignace in 1745.

27 December 1738 ursule, daughter of J. B. Amiot, etc.

13 July 1739 anne, daughter of Sieur François menard, born on the 18th of November, 1738.

---

[17] For this nephew of Charles Langlade, and his assistant in commanding the Indians in time of war, see *Ibid.*, index.—ED.

[18] This man was killed by a Sioux. *Ibid.*, p. 78.—ED.

14 July 1739 Therese, daughter of Sieur de lignon, etc; born on the 19th of November, 1738.

26 July 1739 augustin, son of Charles Chaboyer etc.

31 July 1739 ignace, from 3 to 4 years of age, given to this church.

27 September 1739 michel, son of a female slave of m^{de} Chevalier.

27 March 1740 jean Baptiste, son of Sieur gautier etc.

13 May 1740 jean Baptiste, born the previous 11th of January, son of Sieur Rocheveau.

19 May 1740 angelique, born on the previous 25th of April, daughter of Sieur du lignon.

4 June 1740 anne josephe, born on the 11th of the previous month, daughter of Sieur Parent.[19]

2 October 1740 marie françoise, born on the 4th of November 1739, daughter of Sieur hamelin.

20 May 1741 marie madelaine, about 5 or 6 years old, slave of Sieur C. gautier.

2 June 1741 louis, son of Sieur j. B. Amiot, born on the 3rd of November 1740.

27 August 1741 jean Baptiste, son of Sieur hamelin.[20]

The Register from which the above summary is taken, Remains in the archives of this mission.

Here follows the new Register:

In the year one thousand seven Hundred and forty-one, on the twenty-fourth of October, I, the undersigned priest and missionary of the society of Jesus in the mission of St ignace at the post of Michilimakinak, did baptize Louis joseph Chaboyer, one day old, son of Charles Chaboiller and of marianne Chevailler, his Wife. The godfather was joseph Ens, and the godmother nannette Chevalier, both residing at the said post, who have signed with me.

---

[19] Her marriage is recorded in *Ibid.*, p. 483.—ED.
[20] Possibly the Cahokia trader of 1780. See *Ibid.*, p. 416.—ED.

Mackinac Baptisms

JEAN BAPTISTE LAMORINIE,[21] missionary of the Society of Jesus.

NANETTE CHEVALIER; JOSEP HAINS.

May 12, 1742.[22] * * * two adults * * * being slaves: one of Mr de Blainville, the officer commanding this post;[23] the other of Sieur hamelin, trader, residing at Sault Ste Marie. The former—whom Reverend father de la morinie wished to hold over the baptismal font and who is about twelve years of age—took the name of jean Baptiste françois; the other, aged about fifteen years took the name of Joseph; his godfather was Charles ange Colet; and his godmother marianne Chevalier, wife of Sieur Chaboyer * * *

P. DU JAUNAY, *miss. of the society of Jesus.*[24]

JEAN BAPTISTE LAMORINIE, of the society of Jesus.

M N CHEVALIER; CHARLES COLLET.

May 19, 1742 * * * I Baptized conditionally[25] marie, legitimate daughter of Sieur gautier, a soldier of the garrison

---

[21] For a biographical sketch of this missionary, see *Ibid.*, p. 474, note 6.—ED.

[22] The preceding entry is given entire, with full formula; commencing with this entry, however, we adopt the method used in the marriage register of modernizing the date form, and omitting repetitions of formal phrases—these omissions being indicated by asterisks. See *ante*, note 1.

[23] Jean Baptiste Céloron, sieur de Blainville, commandant during the absence of his elder brother, Pierre Joseph Céloron. See *Id.*, xvii, p. 367.—ED.

[24] For this missionary see *Ibid.*, p. 370, note 1; xviii, p. 471, note 99.—ED.

[25] The expression "baptized conditionally" indicates that the child has previously received lay baptism, at some time or place where a priest was not available; it is now regularly baptized by one in holy orders. On the margin of the original register, before the first entry for 1747, appears this explanation, apparently an interpellation by some later hand: "S. C. means conditionally (*sous condition*) when the children have been baptized in case of necessity by doubtful means."—ED.

[7]

of this post, and of Therese villeneuve his wife, born at la manistic on the 9th of this month while they were returning from winter quarters, and privately baptized on the same day because she was thought in danger of death. The godfather was Sieur guyori, voyageur, residing at this post; and the godmother m^{de} l'anglade. * * *

      P. DU JAUNAY, miss. of the society of Jesus.
ANTOINE GUILLORY; ANNE VILLENEUVE.

May 20, I solemnly administered holy Baptism to Marie Coussante, legitimate daughter of Joseph hins, master carpenter, residing at this post, and of coussante Chevalier, his wife, born this morning. The godfather was Mr de Celoron, captain, knight of St Louis, Commanding for the King at this post;[26] and the godmother marie françoise alavoine, wife of Sieur Chevalier, voyageur. * * *

      P. DU JAUNAY, miss. of the society of Jesus.
CELORON; JOSEPH HAINS.

I baptized conditionally a child born on the 18th of this month and privately baptized the same day through precaution—the legitimate daughter of Pierre Parent, residing at this post, and of Marianne Chaboyer, his wife. The godfather was françois Joliet; and the godmother anne parant, sister of the child, who gave her the name of Anne Catherine. She declared that she could not sign her name.

Done at michilimakina the 20th of July, 1742.

      C. GOD^e COQUART, M. D. C. J.[27]
FRANCOIS IOLLIETTE.

I solemnly baptized the slave of M Langlade, an adult about

---

[26] For this officer see *Wis. Hist. Colls.*, xvii, p. 207, note 1; xviii, p. 28, note 42. Apparently he had returned to Mackinac between May 12 and May 20, 1742, to resume command.—ED.

[27] The letters indicate "Missionnaire de la Compagnie de Jesu." For a brief biography see *Wis. Hist. Colls.*, xviii, p. 471, note 98.—ED.

ENTRIES IN MACKINAC REGISTER, JULY 20 AND SEPTEMBER 10, 1742

From photograph; reduced about one-half. The date 1743, in lower left-hand corner, precedes the succeeding entry (not here shown)

22 years old. The godfather was Sieur jean Baptiste Marsollete; and the godmother Anne Villeneuve, wife of Sieur guillory, residing at this post, who gave the young man the name of Charles. 10th of September, 1742.

C. God. Coquart, M. D. C. J.

J. B. Marsollete; Anne Villeneuve

Died at la grande Rivière the following winter.

I baptized a daughter of Bon Coeur, a negro, and of Marguerite, a Negress, belonging to Sieur Boutin who is obliged to winter here on his way to illinois. The godfather was Sieur Nicolas Rose, a trader at this post; and [the godmother] Dame Constante Chevalier, wife of Sieur hains, Master Carpenter, who gave the child the name of Veronique. The godfather signed with me; the godmother declared that she could not sign her name. Michilimakina, 19th of January, 1743.

C. God. Coquart, M. D. C. J.

Rose.

June 21 1743, I solemnly baptized in the church of this mission paul amable, legitimate son of Charles Chaboyer, voyageur, and of marianne chevalier, his wife, residing at this post, born this morning. The godfather was Mr Rupalais Clayer; and the godmother agathe Villeneuve, wife of Boisguilbert.

P. du Jaunay, miss. of the society of Jesus.

Agathe Villeneuve; Rupalaist; Charle Langlade;[28] Charles Chaboillez.

June 22, 1743, I solemnly baptized in the church of this mission, marie joseph, natural daughter of Sieur Thomas blondeau and of a female Savage, aged about five years, whom both he and demoiselle marie joseph de Celles, his present lawful wife,

---

[28] This is probably the earliest extant signature of Charles Langlade, then but fourteen years old.—Ed.

residing at this post, undertake to educate. The godfather was Sieur jacques farly, voyageur.²⁹ * * *

      P. DU JAUNAY, miss. of the society of Jesus.
FARLY; MARIE JOSEPH DESELLE.

June 24 [1743], I solemnly baptized in the church of this mission, a young slave about twelve years old who was sufficiently instructed. The catechumen took the name of jean Baptiste. The godfather was Sieur Germain, voyageur; and the godmother nanette parent. * * *

      P. DU JAUNAY, miss. of the society of Jesus.
CD. GERMAIN; NANETTE PARONT.

July 17 [1743], I solemnly Baptized in the church of this mission paul, the legitimate son of Sieur de lignon, voyageur and of angelique, his wife—born at Sault Ste Marie, October 31 last. The godfather was the Sieur de Coulonge; and the godmother anne villeneuve, wife of Sieur guyori, who signed with me. * * *

      P. DU JAUNAY, miss. of the society of Jesus.
COULONGE; DULIGNON; LA GUILLORY.
Died at the Sault in the following autumn.

July 27 [1743], I solemnly baptized in the church of this mission a slave of M. maugres, 13 or 14 years old, sufficiently instructed and desiring holy Baptism, who took the name of pierre Augustin. The Godfather was Monsieur Langlade; the godmother Mlle. marie Catherine de lerige, wife of M. Bourassa.³⁰ * * * C. GOD. COQUART, Miss. de la C. de J.
LANGLADE; M. CATERINE LERIGE.

August 24, 1743, I solemnly baptized in the church of this mission joseph Barthelemi, legitimate son of Sieur Thomas

---

²⁹ For a brief sketch of Farly, later interpreter at Mackinac, see *Wis. Hist. Colls.*, xviii, p. 258, note 54.—ED.

³⁰ For these residents of Mackinac, see *Ibid.*, p. 136, note 78.—ED.

Mackinac Baptisms

Blondeau, voyageur, and of demoiselle marie joseph de Selle, his lawful wife, now residing at this post, born yesterday evening. The godfather was M^r joseph dit carris, voyageur;[31] and the godmother marianne alavoine, wife of j. B. Chevalier, who signed with me. * * *

P. DU JAUNAY, miss. of the society of Jesus.

JOSEPH DE CARIS; MANON LAVOINE CHEVALIER; THOMAS BLONDEAU.

Jan. 6, 1744, I solemnly baptized in the church of this mission Charles, a negro slave of M^r de vercheres commandant of this post,[32] from about 18 to 20 years of age, sufficiently instructed and desiring holy Baptism which he thought he had probably never received and which I administered to him conditionally. The godfather was Mr Charles Chaboiller, voyageur; and the godmother Therese villeneuve, wife of Sieur gautier. * * *

P. DU JAUNAY, miss. of the society of Jesus.

THERESE VILLENEUVE; CHABOILLEZ.

March 25, 1744, I solemnly baptized in the church of this mission Charles antoine, legitimate son of Sieur parent and of his wife, marianne Chaboyer, residing at this post—the said child having been born this morning. The godfather was Sieur Charles Chaboyer; and the godmother Mlle. marie joseph de selle, wife of Sieur Blondeau who signed with me. * * *

P. DU JAUNAY, miss. of the society of Jesus.

CHARLES CHABOILLEZ; MARIE JOSEPH DESELLE.

May 1, 1744, I solemnly baptized in the church of this mission Joseph louis, legitimate son of joseph hains, master carpenter, and of his wife constante Chevalier, now residing at this

---

[31] Consult *Ibid.*, p. 472, note 1.—ED.
[32] For a sketch of this officer see *Id.*, xvii, p. 274, note 1.—ED.

post—the said child having been born this morning.³³ The godfather was louis Chevalier; and the godmother Marianne Chevalier, wife of Sieur Chaboyer. * * *

P. DU JAUNAY, miss. of the society of Jesus.

L. CHEVALLIER; JOSEPH HAINS; M. A. CHEVALIER; LA CHABOILLEZ.

July 12 [1744], I solemnly baptized in the church of this mission françoise angelique, natural daughter of Claude Caron, voyageur, adopted by Sieur Texier, voyageur and farmer of la baye, aged about six years, held over the baptismal font by Sieur pierre Ritchot, voyageur and farmer of la baye; and the widow lacroix, her **godfather and** godmother; also Marie josephe, natural daughter of one l'espérance, an apostate at la pointe, adopted by Sieur l'ecuyer, a voyageur employed by the farmers of la pointe, aged about six years, held over the baptismal font by M^r l'anglade and the wife of M^r l'ecuyer, her godfather and godmother * * *

P. DU JAUNAY, miss. of the society of Jesus.

LANGLADE; PIERRE RICHOTTE; CH. TAXIER; BLONDEAU LECUYE; FRENSOYSE CARDINALLE, VEUVE LACROIX.

July 21, 1744, I supplied the ceremonies of Baptism in the church of this mission to Marie, daughter of marie chevalier and jaques Dumée—which child they acknowledged to be their legitimate child at their marriage celebrated this same day.³⁴ The godfather was M. de Ramesai, Captain of a company of the marine detachment and commandant for the king at Nepigon; and the godmother marie françoise alavoine, wife of Sieur jean Baptiste chevalier, who signed with me. * * *

C. GOD. COQUART, Miss^{re} D L. C. d. J.

MANON LAVOINE CHEVALIER.

---

³³ For a biographical account of this child see *Id.*, xviii, p. 309, note 29. The father was apparently a German named Heins, which was gradually metaphorphosed into Ainse and Ainsée.—ED.

³⁴ For this marriage see *Wis. Hist. Colls.*, xviii, p. 470.—ED.

Mackinac Baptisms

I supplied the ceremonies of Baptism in the church of this mission to René françois, son of René Bourassa and of anne Charlotte véronique Chevalier, born on the 31st of March of this year, which child they acknowledged to be their legitimate child at their marriage celebrated this same day. The godfather was M. Bourassa, Father of René Bourassa; and the godmother marie françoise alavoine, wife of Sieur jean Baptiste chevalier, who signed with me, on the 3rd of August, 1744, at mikilimakina.   C. God. Coquart, M. J.

I solemnly administered holy Baptism in the church of this mission to francoise marianne, legitimate daughter of Sieur du lignon, voyageur, and of angelique his wife—the said little girl having been born yesterday evening. The godfather was m^r dailleboust de la Magdelaine; and the godmother m^{de} de quindre who signed here with me. Done at Mikilimakina this 5th day of August, 1744.

P. du Jaunay, miss. of the society of Jesus.

Dailleboust de la Magdelaine; Dulignon; Beletre de Quindre.[35]

I solemnly administered holy baptism to a young girl Savage, aged about 10 or 12 years, a slave of Boiguilbert, sufficiently instructed and desiring holy Baptism. She took the name of anne; her godfather and godmother were Sieur jean marie Blondeau, voyageur; and domitille, wife of m^r langlade. michilimakina, 27th of September 1744.

P. du Jaunay, Miss, of the Society of Jesus.

J. M. Blondeau; agathe villeneuve, la Guilbau.

Feb. 1, 1745, I baptized in the church of this mission pierre louis, legitimate son of Sieur Charles Chaboyer and of Marianne Chevalier, His wife, residing at this post—the said child

---

[35] This lady belonged to a Detroit family, where her brother was last French commandant of regulars and her husband commandant of militia. See *Ibid.*, p 234, note 14.—Ed.

having been born last night. The godfather was louis chevalier; and the godmother Charlotte parent. * * *

P. DU JAUNAY, miss. of the society of Jesus.
C. CHABOILLEZ; MARIANNE CHABOILLEZ PARENT.

April 30, 1745, I solemnly baptized in the church of this mission Thomas, legitimate son of Thomas Blondeau and of demoiselle marie joseph de Celle, his lawful wife, residing at this post—the said child having been born last Sunday, the 25th of this month. The godfather was M^r· de l'anglade; and the godmother agathe villeneuve, wife of Sieur Boisguilbert who signed here with me. * * *

P. DU JAUNAY, miss. of the society of Jesus.
AGATHE LA BOIGUILBER; THOMAS BLONDEAU.
He died on the 9th of July following.

May 16, 1745, I solemnly baptized (Conditionally, however, because he had been privately baptized the day he was born by a servant) joseph, legitimate son of Gabriel Bolon and of susanne Menard, his wife, now residing at this post—the said child having been born at quiquanamaso, the wintering place,[36] on the 20th of March last. The godfather was Sieur Joseph des Caris, voyageur; and the godmother Agathe villeneuve, wife of Sieur Boisguilbert. * * *

P. DU JAUNAY, miss. of the society of Jesus.
JOSEPH DECARY; AGTHE LABOIGUILBER; GABRIEL BOLLON.

July 11 [1745], I solemnly baptized a young Sauteux woman Savage, Sister of the late marie Athanase, wife of Sieur

---

[36] Quiquanamoso (usually spelled Kikkanamazoo) is the Indian word for the river now corrupted into the form Kalamazoo. The word is said to signify "bubbling or boiling water." Such entries as this and similar ones in the register show how French traders scattered along the shores of the lakes and rivers of the upper country, returned to Mackinac in the summer to traffic for their skins, and brought with them their families for marriage, baptism, etc.—ED.

Charles hamellin, now residing at Sault Ste marie, the said woman being about 30 years old, desiring holy Baptism and being sufficiently instructed; she took the name of Marie Charlotte in holy baptism and was held over the sacred font by Mr Charles du Plessis de Morampont, the Officer Commanding for the King at Camonettiqouia;[37] and by Angelique, wife of Sieur de lignon; the former signed here with me.   *   *   *

P. DU JAUNAY, miss. of the society of Jesus.
DU PLESSIS DE MORAMPONT; COULONGE, witness.

The same day, I solemnly baptized in the church of this mission a young female slave of Sieur Charles hamelin, about 20 years of age, desiring holy Baptism and sufficiently instructed, who took the name of marie Athanase according to the desire of her deceased mistress and was held over the sacred font by Mr de Coulonge, and M^{de} Bourassa the elder who signed here with me.   Done at michilimakina this 11th of July, 1745.

P. DU JAUNAY, miss. of the society of Jesus.
COULONGE; MARIE CTERINNE LERIGE DE BOURASSA.

She died   *   *   *   on January 24, 1748, and was buried in the church the following day beside her deceased mistress.

August 25, 1745, I solemnly administered holy Baptism to Elizabeth louise, legitimate daughter of pierre locat, voyageur, and of josette Chevalier, his wife, now residing at this post. The godfather was Mr de Noyelle, the younger, an officer of the troops, Second in command for the King at this post;[38] and the godmother Manon Alavoine, wife of Sieur Chevalier, voyageur,

---

[37] Charles Denis Duplessis, Sieur de Morampont, was born in 1704 and married in 1742. After his term of service at Kamanistigoya, he was appointed (1749) prevost of the court at Quebec, which office he held until the British conquest. He would appear to have then retired to France, where in 1774 his wife applied for a pension.—ED.

[38] Charles Joseph des Noyelles, for whom see *Wis. Hist. Colls.*, xvii, p. 462. He appears to have retired to France after 1760.—ED.

who signed here with me. The said child was born yesterday morning. * * *

P. DU JAUNAY, miss. of the society of Jesus.

NOYELLE; MANON LAVOINE CHEVALIER.

September 28, 1745, I solemnly baptized in the church of this mission Marianne, legitimate daughter of André Skayamick *dit* landroche, voyageur, and of anne parent, his wife, now residing at this post. The said child was born this morning. The godfather was Sieur jean Marie Blondeau, voyageur; and the godmother Marianne Chaboyer, wife of parent, who signed here with me. * * *

P. DU JAUNAY, miss. of the society of Jesus.

MARIANNE CHABILLES PARANT; J. M. BLONDEAU.

October 3, 1745, I solemnly baptized in the church of this mission joseph augustin, legitimate son of Claude Germain Gautier and of Thérèse villeneuve, his wife, now residing at this post; the said child having been born this morning. The godfather was M^r langlade; and the godmother agathe villeneuve, wife of Boisguilbert who signed here with me. * * *

P. DU JAUNAY, miss. of the society of Jesus.

LANGLADE; LA BOIGUILBER.

March 4, 1746, I supplied the ceremonies of holy Baptism to and baptized conditionally Therese,[39] born on the 2nd of the same month and privately baptized by the midwife because she was considered in danger of death, being the legitimate daughter of Sieur parent, voyageur, and of marianne chaboyer, his wife, residing at this post. The godfather was alexis Sejournée, sergeant of the troops of the garrison of this post; and the godmother Marie françoise, daughter of Sieur parent and sister of the newly baptized infant. * * *

P. DU JAUNAY, miss. of the society of Jesus.

ALEXIS SEJOURNÉ; PIERRE PARANT.

---

[39] She was married in 1763; see *Id.*, xviii, p. 486.—ED.

Mackinac Baptisms

May 4, 1746, I administered holy baptism to marianne marthe, legitimate daughter of Charles chaboyer and of marianne Chevalier, his wife, residing at this post, the said little girl having been born on Friday, the 8th of April on the other side, at the settlement of St pierre and St paul, where they spent the winter. The godfather was noel piquet; and the godmother the wife of Sieur Chevalier, voyageur, who signed here with me. * * *

P. DU JAUNAY, miss. of the society of Jesus.

NOELLE PIQUETTE; MANON LAVOINE CHEVALIER; CHARLES CHABOILLEZ; MARIE ANNE CHEVALIER CHABOILLEZ.

June 14, 1746, I administered holy baptism to louis, legitimate son of amiot and marianne, his wife, now at this post; the said child having been born at the Rivière aux plains [40] near chikago at the beginning of the month of October last. The godfather was M^r. louis de la Corne, Captain Commanding for the King at this post;[41] and the godmother M$^{lle.}$ Catherine la plante, wife of m^r. Bourassa who signed here with me. * * *

P. DU JAUNAY, Miss. of the society of Jesus.

LACORNE; MARIE CATERINNE LERIGE; AMIOT.

June 29, 1746, I Solemnly baptized in the church of this mission a woman Sauteux Savage, Sister of the late françoise, wife of Rocheveau, about 25 years of age, Sufficiently instructed and desiring holy Baptism; who took the name of françoise. The godfather was Mr de Noyelle, second in Command at this post; and the godmother Mlle Bourassa, who signed here with me. * * *

P. DU JAUNAY, miss. of the society of Jesus.

NOYELLE, fils; MARIE C. LAPLATE.

---

[40] Now Des Plaines River, in Illinois. The word is derived from a French term for the soft swamp maple tree.—ED.

[41] On this officer consult *Wis. Hist. Colls.*, xvii, p. 448.—ED.

June 29, 1746, I Solemnly baptized in the church of this mission Elisabeth, daughter of françoise, baptized this morning, and of a French father not yet declared, aged about three years. The godfather was paskal Chevalier; and the godmother Catherine Rocheveau. * * *

P. DU JAUNAY, miss. of the society of Jesus.
LOUIS PASCAL CHEVALIER.

July 3, 1746, I Solemnly baptized in the church of this mission angelique, daughter of a woman savage belonging to Sieur Chevalier, voyageur, whose father the mother declared to be louis fleurs d'épée, born this morning. The godfather was one marcot; and the godmother esther Chevalier, daughter of Sieur chevalier, both of whom declared that they could not sign their names. * * *

P. DU JAUNAY, miss. of the society of Jesus.

September 26, 1746, I solemnly baptized in the church of this mission josephe marguerite, daughter of Thomas Blondeau and of demoiselle marie joseph de selle, his lawful wife; the said child was born last night. The godfather was Mr de Noel, the younger, Commandant of this post, and the godmother Anne Villeneuve, wife of Sieur Blondeau, called nanette.

P. DU JAUNAY, miss. of the society of Jesus.
NOYELLE, fils; ANNE VILLENEUVE; THOMAS BLONDEAU.

October 9, 1746, I solemnly baptized in the church of this mission Agathe, daughter of Marie Charlotte, a woman Savage baptized last year and of a French father not yet declared, born in the month of February last. The godfather was françois jerosme, a Savage; and the godmother agathe Villeneuve, wife of Sieur Boishibert [Boisguilbert] * * *

P. DU JAUNAY, miss. of the society of Jesus.
F. SAUVAGE; AGATHE VILLENEUVE.

March 17, 1747, I supplied the ceremonies of holy baptism to Anne Catherine, daughter of René Bourassa, the younger, and of anne chevalier, his wife, born the day before and privately baptized at once because she was deemed in danger of death. The godfather was Mr Chevalier; and the godmother Mlle Bourassa, wife of Monsieur Bourassa, the elder. * * *

P. DU JAUNAY, miss. of the society of Jesus.
M CATERINE LERIGÉ.

May 7, 1747, I baptized (S. C.) in the church of this mission Therese, daughter of pierre locat and of josephe chevalier, his lawful wife, now residing at Sault Ste Marie,[42] where she was born on the 29th of January last. The godfather was Michel Rocheveau, voyageur, residing at Sault Ste marie; and the godmother the wife of M^r langlade. * * *

P. DU JAUNAY, miss. of the society of Jesus.
MICHEL ROCHEVEAU.

May 23, 1747, I solemnly baptized (S. C.) Charles Stanislas, legitimate son of Mr Caesaire de Quindre d'ouville and of M^{de} françoise marianne Belêtre, his wife, returning from St. joseph and about to start for Montreal. The said child was born at St joseph on April 29, 1746. The godfather was M^r du plessis Morampont, an officer of a company of the marine detachment, commanding for the King at Cammanettigoia; and the godmother the wife of M^r l'anglade. * * *

P. DU JAUNAY, miss. of the society of Jesus.
DUPLESSIS DE MORAMPONT; CESERE DE QUINDRE; BÉLESTRE DE QUINDRE.

June 17, 1747, I solemnly baptized (S. C.) joseph Marguerite,[43] legitimate daughter of Sieur de lignon, voyageur, and of

---

[42] For the marriage of these residents of Sault Ste. Marie, see *Id.,* xviii, p. 470.—ED.

[43] For her marriage see *Ibid.,* p. 485.—ED.

angelique, his wife, residing at Sault Ste Marie. The said child was born at the beginning of the month of May last at the said Sault Ste Marie. The godfather was Mr de Noyel, the younger, commandant of this post; and the godmother d^{lle} Marie joseph de Celle, wife of Thomas Blondeau who signed here with me. * * *

P. DU JAUNAY, miss. of the society of Jesus.
NOYELLE, fils; DE SELLE BONDEAU.

June 20, 1747, I solemnly baptized (S. C.) marie joseph,[44] legitimate daughter of jean baptiste jourdan and of josephe Reaume, residing at la Baye, the said child having been born at la baye in the month of April last. The godfather was Mr de Noyel, the younger, commandant of this post; and the godmother Mlle Bourassa, wife of Mr Bourassa, the elder, who signed here with me. * * *

P. DU JAUNAY, miss. of the society of Jesus.
NOYELLE, fils; MARIE LA PLENTE BOURASSA.

July 7, 1747, I solemnly baptized marie françoise, legitimate daughter of Gabriel Bolon and of Susanne Menard, his wife, residing at this post; the said child having been born yesterday evening. The godfather was etienne auger, voyageur;[45] and the godmother marie françoise la Croix. * * *

P. DU JAUNAY, miss. of the society of Jesus.
ETIENNE AUGER; MARI FRANSOSE LA CRIX; GABRIEL BOLLON.

July 22, 1747, I solemnly baptized in the church of this mission a female neophyte, sufficiently instructed and desiring holy baptism, about 35 years old, born at nipissing, and her two children: the elder about three [thirteen] years, and the younger about nine years of age, both born in the direction of

---

[44] One of the two sisters married July 24, 1764; see *Ibid.*, pp. 486, 487.—ED.

[45] For this person see *Ibid.*, p. 8, note 14.—ED.

matchidock of the aforesaid neophyte and of jean Baptiste Tellier dit la fortune.[46] The neophyte took the name of Marie josephe in holy baptism. Her godfather was Mr de Noyelle, the younger, the commandant of this post; and the godmother d^{lle} de Selles, wife of Sieur Thomas Blondeau, voyageur. The older child took the name of françois Xavier; his godfather was Sieur Baribeau, voyageur;[47] and his godmother Agathe Villeneuve, wife of Sieur Boishibert. The other took the name of René françois; his godfather was René Bourassa, the younger; and his godmother Esther Chevalier, all of whom signed here with me. * * *

                    P. DU JAUNAY, miss. of the society of Jesus.

NOYELLE, fils; F. BARIBEAU; MARIE JOSEPH DE SELLE; AGATHE VILLENEUVE; JEAN TELLIER; RENÉ BOURASSA, fils.

July 22, 1747, I solemnly baptized in the church of this mission, three children of jean Baptiste Tellier dit la fortune and of marie josephe, a Nipissingue woman baptized this morning: the first about six years, the second about three years old, the last one born in the month of February last, all three born in the direction of Matchidock. The godfather and godmother of the 1st were ignace Bourassa and Charlotte Parent who gave him the name of ignace. The godfather and godmother of the second were Antoine St Germain and Susanne Bolon who gave him the name of joseph. The godfather and godmother of the 3rd were Mr de Coulonge and Manon Chevalier, wife of du May who gave her the name of marie joseph—who signed here with me. * * *

                    P. DU JAUNAY, miss. of the society of Jesus.

IGNACE BOURASSA; COULONGE; ANTOINE ST GERMAIN; JEAN TELLIER.

---

[46] For the marriage of these two persons see *Ibid.*, p. 474. In the names and ages of the children the two entries do not agree.—ED.

[47] Possibly the person for whom Baraboo River in Sauk County, Wis., was named.—ED.

July 22, 1747, I supplied the ceremonies of holy Baptism to jean Baptiste, born in the month of March of the previous year of a female slave of Sieur Chaboyer and privately baptized a few days afterward. The said slave, called madeleine, declared that the father of the child was Daniel villeneuve. The godfather and godmother were Charles l'anglade and Angelique Chevalier. * * *

P. DU JAUNAY, miss. of the society of Jesus.
CHARLE LANGLADE.

I, the undersigned, baptized solemnly and according to the rite of our mother, the holy Catholic, apostolic and roman Church, a female slave of m° Marin de la periere. The godfather was M^r de noyelle, the younger, commandant of the post of michilimakina; and the godmother Madame Magdelaine viliers de la pereire. In testimony whereof I have signed on the 1st of September 1747.[48]

JEAN BAPTISTE LAMORINÈE, jesuit
NOYELLE, fils; MAGDELAINE DE VILLIERS LAPERIERRE.[49]

October 25, 1747, I solemnly baptized in the church of this mission a child about a year old, the illegitimate son of one dion, a voyageur, and of a slave now belonging to Catherine, an ylinois woman, the lawful wife of one Cadieu residing at ylinois. The godfather was Mr Bourassa, the elder; and the

---

[48] Note on original MS.: "This entry is badly put down in the register because I was interrupted while writing."—ED.

[49] She was the eldest daughter of Nicolas Antoine Coulon, sieur de Villiers, killed at Green Bay in 1733. Her first husband was François Duplessis-Fabert, the cadet killed with her father (see *Wis. Hist. Colls.*, xvii, p. 189). In 1837 she married Claude Marin, sieur de la Perrière, brother of Capt. Paul Marin, commandant in Wisconsin. Her third husband was Joseph Damours, whom she married in 1754 at Quebec.—ED.

[22]

godmother the aforesaid Catherine, wife of Cadieu, who gave him the name of louis René at the Sacred font. * * *

P. DU JAUNAY, miss. of the society of Jesus.
+ mark of the said CATHERINE; BOURASSA.

On the [blank in MS.] of the month of August, 1747, Reverend father de la morinée Baptized a young child about 3 years old, natural son of Charles Chevalier tallier and of a Sioux slave. The said child was born at lac de la pluye [Rainy Lake]. The godfather was poncelet Batillot dit Clermont, a soldier of the garrison; and the godmother louise Bolon, who gave him the name of pierre in holy Baptism, in the presence of the other witnesses, undersigned, whom I have heard on October 31, 1747 at michilimakina.

P. DU JAUNAY, miss. of the society of Jesus.
PONALET BATILLOT DIT CLERMONT, soldier; COLONGE;[50] BOURASSA.

December 6, 1747, I baptized in the church of this mission pierre Charles, natural son of Charles hamelin and of a female Savage called Catherine, of the Sauteux nation, daughter of the pagan Savage called mouus—born on the 15th of February of the previous year at Sault Ste Marie. The godfather was M^r langlade esquire; and the godmother Anne villeneuve, wife of Sieur Blondeau. * * *

P. DU JAUNAY, miss. of the society of Jesus.
LANGLADE; ANNE VILLENEUVE; BLONDEAU.
Died a few days afterward.

February 1, 1748, I solemnly baptized in the church of this mission a female Saulteux Savage about twenty years old, daughter of the savage called Mouus, mother of the child mentioned above, desiring holy Baptism and being sufficiently in-

---

[50] Coulange signed here by mistake, instead of after the second succeeding entry. This having been noticed, he signed again in the proper place.—ED.

structed, who took the name of Marie Athanasie in holy Baptism.⁵¹ Her godfather was M^r d'ailleboût de Coulonge; and her godmother M^{de} l'anglade. * * *

     PÈRE DU JAUNAY, miss. of the society of Jesus.
COULONGE.

February 28, 1748, I supplied the ceremonies of holy Baptism to jacques, son of jacques du may and of marie madelaine Chevalier, his wife, residing at this post. The said child was born on Sunday last, the 25th, and was privately baptized the same day, being in danger of death. The godfather was M^r jacques le Gardeur de St Pierre, lieutenant in a company of the marine detachment and commanding for the King at this post;⁵² and the godmother demoiselle marie Catherine la plante, wife of Mr Bourassa. * * *

     P. DU JAUNAY, miss. of the society of Jesus.
LEGARDEUR DE ST PIERRE; MARIE CATERINE LERIGE; JACQUE DUMAY.

March 17, 1748, I supplied the ceremonies of holy baptism to Angelique, legitimate daughter of pierre pelletier and of marie françoise parent, his wife, residing at this post. The said child was born January 18 last on the other side where they spent the winter and was privately baptized shortly afterward through fear of unforeseen accidents. The godfather was René provancher; and the godmother Charlotte Parent, her aunt. * * *

     P. DU JAUNAY, miss. of the society of Jesus.
RENÉ PROVANCHE

July 7, 1748, I Supplied the ceremonies of holy baptism to and baptized conditionally Augustin, son of the late Augustin l'archevêque and of Marie Reaumé, his wife, residing at St Joseph. The said child was born at St joseph on January 9,

---

⁵¹ For her marriage see *Wis. Hist. Colls.*, xviii, p. 475.
⁵² This officer's career is noted in *Id.*, xvii, pp. 165, 166.—ED.

1746, and was privately baptized the same day. The godfather was m^r· Augustin moras de l'anglade, esquire; and the godmother m^{lle}· Bourassa, the elder. * * *

     P. du Jaunay, miss. of the society of Jesus.
 Langlade; Marie Catherinne Lerige.

July 21, 1748, I supplied the ceremonies of holy Baptism to and baptized conditionally Catherine, daughter of Charles personne dit la fond, blacksmith, and of Susanne Réaume, his wife, residing at la Baye. The said child was born at la Baye on the 14th of April last and was privately baptized, being considered in danger of death. The godfather was Mr de Coulonge; and the godmother Catherine l'archevêque, wife of Sieur joutras. * * *   P. du Jaunay, miss. of the society of Jesus.
 Coulonge; Catherine lathre [Larche]; Susane reaume

September 8, 1748, I solemnly baptized in the church of this mission, an adult woman sufficiently instructed, about twenty years of age, the slave of Sieur Bourassa, the elder, a former voyageur, desiring holy baptism. She took the name of Marianne and was held over the baptismal font by Mr de Coulonge, her godfather; and by Mlle Bourassa, her mistress and godmother, who signed here with me.

     P. du Jaunay, miss. of the society of Jesus.
 Coulonge; Caterine la plente [Lerigé Bourassa]

January 21, 1749, I solemnly baptized in the church of this mission marie josephe, legitimate daughter of the late joseph Charles hamelin and of marie Athanasie, his lawful wife. The said child was born last month. The godfather was M^r jacques le Gardeur de St pierre, Captain Commanding for the King at this post; and the godmother demoiselle Marie Catherine l'erige de la plante, wife of Sieur Bourassa, a former voyageur, * * *
     P. du Jaunay, miss. of the society of Jesus.
 Legardeur de St Pierre; Marie Catherinne La plante Bourassa.

January 27, 1749, I solemnly baptized in the church of this mission, Blaise, legitimate son of jean Baptiste Amiot, Armorer, and of Marianne, his lawful wife. The said child was born this morning. The godfather was M^r· the Chevalier de Repentigny, the officer second in Command;[53] and the godmother Agathe Amiot, sister of the said child. * * *

P. du Jaunay, miss. of the society of Jesus.
Amiot; Le Gardeur, Ch^r Repentigny.
Died at the beginning of October, 1750

March 11, 1749, I solemnly baptized in the church of this mission, Angelique,[54] born yesterday evening, legitimate daughter of Sieur Alexis Sejournée surnamed Sans Chagrin, a Sergeant of the troops, and of angelique Taro, his lawful wife. The godfather was M^r le Gardeur de St Pierre, Captain commanding for the King at this post; and the godmother Agathe Villeneuve, wife of Sieur boisguilbert. * * *

P. du Jaunay, miss. of the society of Jesus.
Legardeur De St Pierre; Agathe Villeneuve; Sanchagrin.

March 22, 1749, I baptized conditionally an illegitimate child born of Constante Chevalier, widow of the late hins and of a father whom she would not name. The child was privately baptized through fear of accident. The godfather was Antoine janis who gave him his name and signed here with me; and the godmother was esther Chevalier. * * *

The father of the child is M^r· dequindre, according to the declaration of the lady.

P. du Jaunay, miss. of the society of Jesus.
Antoine Janisse; Barthelemi Blondeau.

July 4, 1749, I supplied the ceremonies of holy baptism and baptized conditionally jean Baptiste, legitimate son of jean

---

[53] A note on this officer is given in *Id.*, xviii, pp. 35, 36.—Ed.
[54] This child was married May 4, 1764; *Ibid.*, p. 486.—Ed.

ENTRY IN MACKINAC REGISTER, MARCH 11, 1749

From photograph; reduced about one-half

Baptiste jourdain and of Marie joseph Reaume, his wife, born at la Baye in the month of November last and privately baptized through fear of accident. His godfather was ignace Bourassa and his godmother Agathe Amiot. * * *

     P. du Jaunay, miss. of the society of Jesus.
Ignace Bourassa.

July 17, 1749, I solemnly baptized in the church of this mission a young man about 15 years old, a slave of one Texier dit la vigne, voyageur, who was ill, had been sufficiently instructed previously and desired baptism for a long while. The Catechumen took the name of Antoine in holy baptism. The godfather was M^r· la plante; and the godmother M^{de} Bourassa, his sister, who signed here with me. * * *

     P. du Jaunay, miss. of the society of Jesus.
 Marie Catherinne Laplante; Barthélémi Blondeau; Urbain Texier.

August 29, 1749, I solemnly administered holy baptism to Anne esther and marie josephe, daughters of jean Manian l'esperance and of a Sauteux woman Savage of la pointe;[55] the former about six years and the latter about three years old. The godfather of Anne esther was M^r· Godefroy, an officer of a company of the marine detachment;[56] and the godmother Mlle esther Chevalier. The godfather of Marie josephe was Mr de Coulonge; and the godmother Mlle Angelique Chevalier. * * *

     P. du Jaunay, miss. of the society of Jesus.
 Godefroy; Coulonge; Barthelemi Blondeau.

---

[55] For the marriage of these persons, see *Ibid.*, p. 476.—Ed.

[56] Jean Baptiste Godefroy, member of the younger branch of the same family as the Sieurs de Linctot. He was born in 1723, made second ensign in 1748, first ensign in 1751, and lieutenant in 1757. During the French and Indian War he served on the Ohio in 1756, and the following year accompanied Rigaud's detachment to the reinforcement of Crown Point. He was present at the siege of Montreal in 1760, and went to France with the returning troops. In 1763 he received a passport to return to Canada, where he appears to have died before 1767.—Ed.

August 13, 1749, I Solemnly baptized Alexis, son of jean manian l'esperance, about eight years old, and Rose, a Sauteux woman Savage of la pointe, about thirty-five years old, sufficiently instructed and desiring holy baptism, the mother of the aforesaid Alexis. The godfather of Alexis was M$^{r.}$ Alexis Sejourné dit Sans Chagrin, a sergeant of the troops; and the godmother Agathe Amiot. The godfather of Rose was Mr Bourassa, a former voyageur; and the godmother M^{de} langlade.
* * *   P. DU JAUNAY, miss. of the society of Jesus.

SANSCHAGRIN; BOURASSA

November 19, 1749, I Solemnly baptized in the church of this mission, Angelique, legitimate daughter of Sieur pierre Parent, voyageur and of Marianne Chaboiller, his wife, residing at this post. The said child was born yesterday evening. The godfather was jean Baptiste jasmin, voyageur; and the godmother Charlotte Parant. * * *

P. DU JAUNAY, miss. of the society of Jesus.

J. B. JASMIN; PARANT.

March 17, 1750, I administered holy baptism to Basile, born this month, son of Marianne, a slave of Sieur Bourassa, voyageur, whom she declared to belong to Sieur jasmin, also a voyageur. The godfather was the said Sieur Bourassa; and the godmother M^{de} langlade. * * *

P. DU JAUNAY, miss. of the society of Jesus.

BOURASSA.

March 24, 1750, I administered holy baptism to ignace françois xavier, son of agathe villeneuve amiot, daughter of Sieur Amiot, born this day, whom she declared to belong to Sieur ignace Bourassa dit la Ronde, son of Sieur René Bourassa now wintering at la grande Rivière. The godfather was M$^{r.}$ du plessis faber, Captain, Knight of St Louis, first Captain and

Commanding his majesty's infantry in Canada, Commandant of this post;[57] and the godmother Mlle Bourassa. * * *

P. DU JAUNAY, miss. of the society of Jesus.

MARIE CATERINNE LA PLANTE BOURASSA; DUPLESSIS FABER; AMIOT.

Died on the 17th of July following.

March 28, 1750, I solemnly baptized in the church of this mission Charles, a young man about eighteen years old, a slave of Sieur René Bourassa, sufficiently instructed and desiring holy baptism. The godfather was Sieur Charles langlade, a Cadet in the troops; and the godmother Mlle Bourassa. * * *

P. DU JAUNAY, miss. of the society of Jesus.

April 6, 1750, I solemnly baptized in the church of this mission, jean françois Regis, a young slave about seven years old, given to this mission last year out of gratitude by M[r.] the Chevalier de la verendreye on his return from the extreme West[58]—the said child being well instructed and demanding holy Baptism. His godfather was the Sieur etienne chenier, and his godmother Charlotte parent. * * *

P. DU JAUNAY, miss. of the society of Jesus.

ETIENNE CHENIER; PIERRE DEMAIS; BARTELEMI BLONDEAU.

May 10, 1750, I solemnly baptized in the church of this mission antoine, son of a panise [slave woman] of Sieur Chaboyer, voyageur, and of an unknown father. The said child was born this day. The godfather was Sieur la guerse; and the godmother the wife of the said Chaboyer. * * *

P. DU JAUNAY, miss. of the society of Jesus.

ANTOINE LA GUERECHE; MARIE ANNE CHEVALIER; BARTELEMI BLONDEAU.

---

[57] For this officer, commandant at Mackinac (1750-53), see *Wis. Hist. Colls.*, xvii, p. 17; xviii, p. 61.—ED.

[58] Evidently Pierre Gautier de la Vérendrye junior, for whom see *Ibid.*, p. 213, note 67.—ED.

May 26, 1750, I baptized in the church of this mission marie françoise, born about two months ago of a Scioux female slave, whom she declares to belong to a Frenchman called chevreaux now in the north. The godfather was joseph la Croix dit marantot; and the godmother marie françoise, his sister, wife of Sieur jasmin. * * *

P. DU JAUNAY, miss. of the society of Jesus.
FRANSOISE LA CROIX JACEMAIN; BARTELEMI BLONDEAU.

July 31, 1750, I solemnly baptized in the church of this mission, a child, Marin, legitimate son of Jean manian dit l'esperance and of Rose, his wife, born at the Rivière de vasynagan on the 15th of last month [May]. The godfather was Mr Marin, the younger, commandant at la pointe de Chagouamigouay;[59] and the godmother m^{lle} Bourassa. * * *

P. DU JAUNAY, miss. of the society of Jesus.
MARIN, fils; LA BAPTISTE; BOURASSA.
He died the following winter.

October 12, 1750, I solemnly baptized in the church of this mission Louis Poncelet, legitimate son of jean Baptiste la fatiere dit jasmin and of françoise hubert de la Croix, his wife, residing at this post.[60] The said child was born last night.

The godfather was Sieur poncelet Batillo; and the godmother M^{de} Bourassa. * * *

P. DU JAUNAY, miss. of the society of Jesus.
PONCELET BATILLO DIT CLERMONT; JEAN BAPTISTE LA FAITIER; M. CATERINNE LERIGE.

February 11, 1751, I baptized in the church of this mission Marie Angelique, natural daughter of Constance Chevalier, widow hins, born this month, whose father she did not declare. The godfather was Etienne Chenier; and the godmother the

---

[59] For this officer see *Id.*, xvii, p. 315; xviii, p. 97.—ED.
[60] For the marriage of these persons see *Ibid.*, p. 477.—ED.

wife of Sieur Alexis Sejourné dit Sans Chagrin, Sergeant of the troops. * * *

P. DU JAUNAY, miss, of the society of Jesus.

E CHENIE; MARI ANGELIQUE TARO.

October 8, 1751, I Solemnly baptized in the church of this mission françois hyppolite, legitimate son of Charles Chaboiller and of marianne Chevalier, his wife, residing at this post. The said child was born last night. The godfather was M^r du plessis, the younger, an officer of the troops, second in command at this post;[61] and the godmother angelique Chevalier, the aunt of the aforesaid child. * * *

P. DU JAUNAY, miss. of the society of Jesus.

CHABOILLEZ; DUPLESSIS FABER, fils.

December 10, 1751, I Baptized according to the usages and rite of our mother the holy catholic, apostolic and roman church, marie Anne [daughter of] Chartres and of agnes agathe amiot, married together. Her godfather was nicolas amiot, her uncle; and her godmother marianne Amiot her grandmother. She was ten days old when I Baptized her. In testimony whereof I have signed without a witness.

JEAN BAPTISTE LAMORINIE, Jesuit.

BOURASSA, witness.

February 20, 1752, I, in the absence of the missionary, supplied the ceremonies of holy Baptism to and baptized conditionally veronique Cardin, legitimate daughter of louis Cardin and of constante Chevalier, married together.[62] Her godfather was

---

[61] The son of the well-known Captain Duplessis-Fabert was made ensign in 1741; three years thereafter he was with his father in command at Niagara; in 1746 he led a war-party into Massachusetts, and two years later took part in the attack on Northfield. During the French and Indian War he was actively employed in scouting and similar duties, becoming lieutenant in 1757. Having retired to France, he was in 1767 living at Tours.—ED.

[62] For their marriage see *Wis. Hist. Colls.*, xviii, p. 478.

alexis Sejourné; and her godmother marie françoise a la voine. The said girl was born on the day and in the year above written.
 In testimony whereof I have signed   LAMORINIE, Jesuit.
 The godfather and godmother have also signed with me.
 CARDIN, father of the girl; ALEXIS SEJOURNE; MANON LAVOINE VEUVE CHEVALIER.

February 27, 1752, I solemnly baptized in the church of this mission augustin Laffertiere dit jasmin, legitimate son of jean Baptiste laffetier dit jasmin and of françoise hubert la Croix, his wife. His godfather was Monsieur Augustin langlade; and his godmother francoise Cardinal, his grandmother.
 In testimony whereof I have signed.   LAMORINIE, Jesuit.
 The godfather, godmother and father of the child have also signed with me as witnesses.
 JASMIN; LANGLADE; FRANÇOISE CARDINALE.

This day, the first day of the month of [blank in MS.], 1752, I solemnly baptized agnes, daughter of the slave of Chaboiller, a resident of this post. The godfather was ive ellien; and the godmother Angelique Chevalier.
 In testimony whereof I have signed   LAMORINIE, Jesuit.
 The godfather signed with me and the godmother made the usual mark.
 YVE ELLIEN; ++++

July 3, 1752; Reverend father de la morinie, a missionary of the society of Jesus, solemnly administered the Sacrament of holy Baptism to a young man about thirteen or fourteen years old, natural son of M^r· la plante and of a woman Savage of Cammanettigouia, he being sufficiently instructed and desiring holy Baptism. He took the name of louis at the sacred font. The godfather was M^r· de Gonneville; and the godmother Mlle Bourassa who signed here. * * *
 The child also made his mark of a cross, not being able to sign his name   +   LAMORINIE, Jesuit.
 GONNEVILLE; MARIE DE LA PLANTE.

September 10, 1752, I solemnly administered holy Baptism to a young female slave of M^r· langlade, about fifteen years old, who had been instructed for a long time and greatly desired it. She took the name of mari at the sacred font and afterward had the happiness of making her first Communion. Her godfather was M^r· de Coulonge; and her godmother Mme Langlade, her mistress. * * *

      P. DU JAUNAY, miss. of the society of Jesus.
COULONGE.

September 17, 1752, I solemnly administered holy Baptism to a young child, slave of Sieur Beaubien's wife, about three years old. The godfather was pierre Poulain dit sans gêne; and the godmother Angelique Chevalier who gave her the name of Catherine in holy Baptism. * * *

      P. DU JAUNAY, miss. of the society of Jesus.
PIERRE POLIN DIT SANGENNE.

September 20, 1752, I baptized conditionally and supplied the ceremonies of holy Baptism to Therese Elizabeth, legitimate daughter of joseph Couvret and of Charlotte, his wife, residing at Sault Ste. Marie.[63] The said child was born on the 26th of the month of December last. The godfather was Mr de Beaujeu, Captain Commanding for the King at this post;[64] and the godmother Mlle Bourassa. * * *

      P. DU JAUNAY, miss. of the society of Jesus.
BEAUJEU; COUVRETT; M C^t LERIGE.

October 8, 1752, Reverend father le Franc, missionary of the society of Jesus, solemnly administered holy Baptism to Daniel,[65] legitimate son of Sieur Bourassa, the younger and of

---

[63] For the marriage of the parents see *Ibid.*, p. 476.
[64] For a sketch of this commandant see *Ibid.*, p. 84, note 24.—ED.
[65] This child became an important resident of Mackinac. See *Ibid.*, index.—ED.

his wife, anne Chevalier, now residing at this post. The said child was born this morning. The godfather was M$^{r\cdot}$ de Beaujeu, Captain Commanding for the King at this post; and the godmother M^{de} langlade. * * *

M. L. LEFRANC[66] *of the society of Jesus.*

P. DU JAUNAY, miss. S. J.

BEAUJEU; The godmother declared that she could not sign her name; RENÉE BOURASSA, fils.

January 6, 1753, I, the undersigned priest, missionary of the society of Jesus, solemnly administered holy baptism to a young female slave about seven years old belonging to Sieur Sejourné dit Sans Chagrin, residing at this post. The godfather was Paul Amable Chaboier; and the godmother Marie Angelique taro, wife of the said Sieur Sejourné, who gave her the name of marie Catherine. * * *

M. L. LEFRANC of the society of Jesus.

April 4, 1753, I solemnly baptized in the church of this mission, Charles domitille, legitimate daughter of Sieur Chaboyer, voyageur, and of Marianne Chevalier, his wife, residing at this post. The said child was born this morning at daybreak. The godfather was M^r the Baron de longueuil, the younger, a lieut. of the troops;[67] and the godmother Mlle Bourassa.

P. DU JAUNAY, miss. of the society of Jesus.

LONGUEUIL, fils; LAPLANTE BOURASSA.

April 21, 1753, I solemnly administered [omission in MS.] instructed and desiring it for a long while, who took the name

---

[66] This is the earliest entry in the register, by Father Le Franc. See *Ibid.*, p. 480.—ED.

[67] Charles Jacques le Moyne, third baron de Longueuil, for whom see *Ibid.*, p. 107, note 53. He was sent to Detroit in charge of a convoy in 1752, and as his letter shows, *Ibid.*, pp. 126, 127, was interested in the fur-trade. He was probably in Mackinac on private business, although it is quite possible he went down from there with the spring convoy to Montreal.—ED.

of Catherine. The godfather was M^r langlade; and the godmother Mlle Bourassa. * * *

    P. DU JAUNAY, miss. of the society of Jesus.
LANGLADE; M. CATERINE LAPLANTE.

 June 14, 1753, I supplied the ceremonies of holy baptism to and baptized conditionally Marie josephe, legitimate daughter of jean Baptiste Tellier dit la fortune, voyageur, and of marie josette, his wife, now here. The said child was born on the way while returning from where they spent the winter at fond du lac on the 18th of May last, and was hurriedly baptized privately being considered in imminent danger of death. The godfather was Monsieur nicolas volant, voyageur; and the godmother the wife of Sieur Sejourné dit Sans Chagrin. * * *

    P. DU JAUNAY, miss. of the society of Jesus.
JEAN TELIER DIT LA FORTUNE; VOLANT; MARI TARO.

 July 15, 1753, I administered holy Baptism to Catherine, legitimate daughter of Sieur Beaulieu and of his wife françoise,[68] residing at Sault Ste Marie, born on April 18 last. The godfather was Mr de Beaujeu, Captain Commanding for the King at this post; and the godmother Mlle Bourassa. * * *

    P. DU JAUNAY, miss. of the society of Jesus.
BEAUJEU; JEAN BRIAN DIT BEAULIEU; CT. LAPLANTE.

 July 18, 1753, I supplied the ceremonies of holy Baptism to and baptized conditionally Daniel Augustin, born on August 9, 1751, legitimate son of augustin l'éveillé and of Clotilde girardin, his father and mother, residing at la Baie. The godfather was Mr de Beaujeau, Captain Commanding for the King at this post; and the godmother Mlle Bourassa. * * *

    M. L. LEFRANC, miss. of the society of Jesus.
BEAUJEU; CT. LAPLANTE.

---

[68] For their marriage see *Ibid.*, p. 479.—ED.

July 18, 1753, I supplied the ceremonies of Baptism and rebaptized conditionally Clotilde, legitimate daughter of augustin l'eveillé and of Clotilde girardin, her father and mother, born on the twenty-eighth of January of the present year. The godfather was Mr Marin, an officer of the troops and commanding for the King at the post of la Baiè; and the godmother Mlle Blondeau. * * *

M. L. LE FRANC, miss. of the society of Jesus.
MARIN, fils; ANNE VILLENEUVE

I, the undersigned missionary of the society of Jesus, baptized Louis hubert, aged about three years, a slave of Monsieur the Chevalier de repentigni. The godfather was jacques hamelin; and the godmother Charlotte Bourassa who signed in this register.

Done at Michilimakina, Sept. 14, 1753.

M. L. LE FRANC, miss. of the society of Jesus.
CHARLOTTE BOURASSA; J. HAMELIN.

January 9, 1754, I, the undersigned priest, miss. of the society of Jesus, solemnly baptized Charles Augustin, legitimate son of Charles Chartre dit Chantloup and of Agathe Amiot, his father and mother,[69] born this morning. The godfather was Mr Augustin Amiot; and the godmother Mlle Charlotte Bourassa. * * *

M. LE FRANC, miss. of the society of Jesus.
AMIOT; LANGLADE; CHARLOTTE BOURASSA.

February 13, 1754, I solemnly baptized in the church of this mission a young catechumen about fourteen years old, sufficiently instructed and desiring holy baptism, being a slave of Mr Bourassa, who took the name of ignace in holy baptism. The

---

[69] For their marriage see *Ibid.*, p. 478.—ED.

godfather was the said Mr Bourassa; and the godmother the wife of Sieur Blondeau called Nannette. * * *

    P. DU JAUNAY, miss. of the society of Jesus.
BOURASSA; ANNE VILLENEUVE BLONDEAU

May 5, 1754, I supplied the ceremonies of baptism to and baptized conditionally Marie Charlotte farley born on the twentieth of March of jacques farley and josette du mouchel, her father and mother. The godfather was M^r· Charles de langlade; and the godmother Charlotte Bourassa who signed, as did also the father of the child. * * *

    M. L. LE FRANC, miss. of the society of Jesus.
JACQUE FARLEY; LANGLADE; CHARLOTTE BOURASSA

May 8, 1754, I supplied the ceremonies to and baptized conditionally Charlotte Cardin born this morning of françois louis Cardin and of Constance Chevalier, her father and mother. The godfather was Mr de Beaujeu, Captain Commanding for the King at this post; and the godmother Mlle· Bourassa. * * *

    M. L. LE FRANC, miss. of the society of Jesus.
LAVOIN; LAPLANTE BOURASSA; BEAUJEU

June 9, 1754, I solemnly baptized in the church of this mission a slave of M^r langlade, about twenty years old, sufficiently instructed and desiring holy baptism, who took the name of jean Baptiste. The godfather was M^r· langlade, the younger; and godmother the daughter of M^r· Bourassa. * * *

    P. DU JAUNAY, miss. of the Society of Jesus.
LANGLADE; CHARLOTTE BOURASSA.

July 28, 1754, I, the undersigned, solemnly administered Baptism to an adult slave of Monsieur the Chevalier de la verandrie, about seventeen years old. He was given the name of Joseph. The godfather was M^r· herbin, Captain command-

ing for the King at this post;[70] and the godmother Louise Bolon.
* * * M. L. LEFRANC, Miss. of the society of Jesus.
CH. DE LAVERANDRY; HERBIN; LIZETTE BOULLON.

August 14, 1754, I, the undersigned, administered holy Baptism to jean Baptiste reaume, son of jean baptiste reaume and of matchiouagakouat, whom I am to solemnly Baptize and marry tomorrow.[71] The child is eleven months old. The godfather was pierre le duc;[72] the godmother Anne villeneuve.
* * * M. L. LEFRANC, miss. of the society of Jesus.
ANNE VILLENEUVE; REAUME; + mark of PIERRE LE DUC.

August 14, 1754, I, the undersigned, administered holy baptism to Marie renée Chaboiller, legitimate daughter of Charles Chaboiller and of Marie Anne Chevalier, her father and mother, born this morning. The godfather was rené Bourassa; and the godmother Charlotte Bourassa. * * *
M. L. LEFRANC, Miss. of the society of Jesus.
RENÉE BOURASSA, fils; CHARLOTTE BOURASSA; CHABOILLEZ.

August 15, 1754, I, the undersigned priest, missionary of the society of Jesus, solemnly administered holy baptism to an adult instructed and desiring holy baptism. She is about twenty years old. I named her Marie, her savage name is Matchiougakouat. The godfather was M[r.] Marin, the officer Commanding for the King [at La Baye]; and the godmother Marie joseph du mouchel. * * *
M. L. LEFRANC, Miss. of the society of Jesus.
MARIN; MARIE JOSEPH DE MOUCHELLE FARLEY.

August 18, 1754, I administered holy Baptism to marie migouanounjan, daughter of pierre migouanounjan and of

---

[70] His brief biography is given *Ibid.*, p. 135, note 76.—ED.
[71] For this marriage see *Ibid.*, p. 481.—ED.
[72] For this person consult *Ibid.*, p. 264, note 64.

marie ouakkouaouagan, her father and mother. The godfather was M[r.] Augustin de langlade, Esquire; and the godmother Marie josephe, wife of la fortune. * * *
The child is about 25 days old.

       M. L. LEFRANC, of the society of Jesus.

LANGLADE; The others declared that they could not sign their names.

September 27, 1754, I, the undersigned, solemnly administered holy Baptism to joseph Augustin Couvret, legitimate son of joseph Couvret and of Charlotte, his wife, residing at sault Ste Marie. He was born on the feast of St. Lawrence, the 10th of August. The godfather was Messire augustin de langlade; and the godmother Charlotte Bourassa. * * *

    M. L. LEFRANC, miss. of the society of Jesus.

LANGLADE; CHARLOTTE BOURASSA LANGLADE; J. COUVRETT.

January 18, 1755, I, the undersigned, solemnly baptized Charle louis Bourassa, legitimate son of René Bourassa and of Anne Charlotte Veronique Chevalier, his father and mother. The godfather was M[r.] The Chevalier de Repentigni, the Officer Commanding for the King at the Sault; and the godmother M[de.] de l'anglade. * * *

    M. L. LEFRANC, Miss. of the society of Jesus.

LOUIS LE GARDEUR, CHEVALIER REPENTIGNY; BOURASSA D'ANGLADE.

March 30, 1755, I, the undersigned priest, missionary of the society of Jesus, solemnly administered holy Baptism to two adults: one about twelve or thirteen years old, called piere françois, a panis [slave] belonging to the M[r.] parent; whose godfather was pierre monbron; and whose godmother was Marianne Chaboiller parent; the other marie Charlotte, a panis belonging to M[r.] Monbron, about fourteen or fifteen years old. The godfather was Louis gervais; and the godmother Ciele

Cousin et Monbron. Both were sufficiently instructed and well disposed. * * *

   M. L. LEFRANC, miss. of the society of Jesus.
MARIANNE CHABOILLEZ PARANT; PIERRE MONBRON.

May 17, 1755, I, the undersigned missionary of the society of Jesus, solemnly administered holy Baptism to joseph, legitimate son of pierre Ketchinape and of Angelique nekikkoue, his father and mother. The godfather was Monsieur joseph Amable hubert, merchant; and the godmother Charlotte Bourassa de l'anglade. * * *
This child was born on the 29th December last.

   M. L. LEFRANC, of the society of Jesus.
J. A. M. HUBER; CHARLOTTE BOURASSA LANGLADE.

May 27, 1755, I, the undersigned priest, missionary of the society of Jesus, solemnly administered holy Baptism to Ambroise, whom nicolas amiot acknowledged to be his son, and of oukimakoue, a woman savage, his mother. The godfather was Mr. Amiot, father of nicolas; and the godmother josette Kiouittakigir la fortune. * * *

   M. L. LEFRANC, Miss. of the society of Jesus.
AMIOT; LA FORTUNE.

June 18, 1755, I solemnly administered holy Baptism to pierre, son of achaka ouabeno and of maouemkouens, his father and mother. The godfather was M^{r.} nicolas du fresne, merchant; and the godmother Angelique ouechipoussé, the grandmother of the child. * * *

   M. L. LEFRANC, Miss. of the society of Jesus.
NICOLA DUFRESNE.

June 17, 1755, I, the undersigned, solemnly administered holy baptism to jean baptiste, legitimate son of antoine le tellier and of Charlotte ouetokich, his father and mother, born on the tenth of September of the previous year. The godfather was René Bonaventure Angé; and the godmother marie joseph farle. * * *

M. L. Lefranc, Miss. of the society of Jesus.
Marie Josete Farley; Jean Telier dit la Fortune.

July 11, 1755, I solemnly administered holy Baptism to marie Anne, legitimate daughter of françois brisbé and of mariane parent, her father and mother.[73] The godfather was Messire augustin moras de l'anglade, esquire; and the godmother marie Anne parent. * * *

M. L. Lefranc, miss. of the society of Jesus.
Marianne Brisbé; Langlade; Marianne C. B. Parent; Lagrandeur.

July 13 [1755], I supplied the ceremonies of baptism to Catherine, a slave of M[r.] la fortune, about thirteen years old, whom I Baptized last autumn when in danger. The godfather was M[r.] giasson; and the godmother M[de] de l'anglade. * * *

M. L. Lefranc, of the society of Jesus.
Bourassa Langlade; Giasson.[74]

July 21, 1755, I solemnly administered holy Baptism to Marie Anne, a slave of M[r.] Caron, about sixteen or seventeen years old and sufficiently instructed. The godfather was M[r.] filé, Esquire; and the godmother M[de.] Bourassa. * * *

M. L. Lefranc, miss. of the society of Jesus.
Jan Mari Filé; Marie Caterine Lerige.

July 27, 1755, I solemnly administered holy baptism to Anne, about eleven or twelve years old, a slave of M[r.] St Omer.

---

[73] For the marriage of these parents see *Ibid.*, p. 482.—Ed.

[74] Jacques Giasson was a lessee of the Green Bay post in 1757. *Ibid.*, pp. 197–199.—Ed.

The godfather was M.^r. du fresne; and the godmother M.^de. monbrun. * * *

     M. L. LEFRANC, miss. of the society of Jesus.
NICOLA DUFRESNE.

August 2, 1755, I solemnly administered holy baptism to Albert, legitimate son of jacque farley and of josette Dumouchel, his father and mother residing at this post, born this morning. The godfather was Antoine Janis residing at this post; and the godmother marie josette farly. * * *

     M. L. LEFRANC, miss. of the society of Jesus.
JANIS; MARY JOSETE FARLY; JAC FARLY.

August 17, 1755, I solemnly administered holy Baptism to a Catechumen, about twenty-one years old, desiring that Sacrament and sufficiently instructed, who took the name of susanna. The godfather was M.^r. l'ami hubert, trader; and the godmother M.^de. langlade, the elder. * * *

     P. DU JAUNAY, miss. of the society of Jesus.
BARTHELEMI BLONDEAU; J. AM. HUBER.
Since married to nicolas Amiot.[75]

August 24, 1755, I solemnly administered holy Baptism to a child from a year and a half to two years old, daughter of a daughter of a savage called Misoumanitou, being a slave belonging to mr. de villebon.[76] The godfather was M.^r. the chev.^r. de Repentigny, lieutenant of infantry; and the godmother m.^de. l'anglade, the younger, who gave her the name of Charlotte. * * * P. DU JAUNAY, miss. of the society of Jesus.
LE GARDEUR CHR. REPENTIGNY; CHARLOTTE BOURASSA LANGLADE; BARTHELEMI BLONDEAU.

---

[75] For this marriage see *Ibid.*, p. 482.—ED.

[76] Charles René Desjordy, Sieur de Villebon, was king's officer at Green Bay in 1749–50. See *Ibid.*, p. 64, note 7.—ED.

January 6, 1756, I solemnly administered holy Baptism to a catechumen about eighteen years old, sufficiently instructed and desiring holy baptism, who took the name of Charles. His godfather was M$^{r.}$ langlade; and his godmother the wife of Sieur Bourassa, the younger.

     P. DU JAUNAY, miss. of the society of Jesus.

LANGLADE; NANETTE CHEVALIER BOURASSA; LOUIS PORTELENCE; BARTHELEMI BLONDEAU.

January 14, 1756, I solemnly Baptized a little girl born this morning whose father is Charles and whose mother is marie, both slaves and lawfully married last year, 1754.[77] The godfather was M$^{r.}$ Bourassa, the elder; and the godmother m$^{de.}$ langlade, the elder, who gave her the name of susanne. * * *

     P. DU JAUNAY, miss. of the society of Jesus.

BOURASSA; BARTHELEMI BLONDEAU.

February 4, 1756, I solemnly baptized a little daughter of Sieur Cardin, notary at this post and of Coussante Chevalier, his lawful wife, born yesterday evening at four o'clock. The godfather was M$^{r.}$ langlade, church warden; and the godmother the wife of Sieur Blondeau dit Nanette, voyageur, who gave her the name of marie. * * *

     P. DU JAUNAY, miss. of society of Jesus.

CARDIN; BLONDEAU.

April 17, 1756, I solemnly administered holy Baptism to three Catechumens, desiring the same and sufficiently instructed. The first is a slave of Sieur Bourassa, the younger, about fifteen years old, who took the name of antoine. His godfather was M$^{r.}$ Bourassa, the elder; and his godmother the wife of Sieur Chaboyer. The second is our slave, about eight years old, who took the name of jean. His godfather was la palme.

---

[77] See *Ibid.*, p. 481.—ED.

The third is a slave of Sieur farley, who took the name of Charlotte; she is about seventeen or eighteen years old. Her godfather was M^{r.} langlade; and her godmother the eldest daughter of Sieur farley. All of whom signed this act.

P. DU JAUNAY, miss. of the society of Jesus.

LAPALME; LANGLADE; BOURASSA; BLONDEAU; JOSETTE FARLY; MARIE ANNE CHEVALIER CHABOILLEZ.

April 28, 1756, I, the undersigned, supplied the ceremonies of holy Baptism to Charlotte Catherine [daughter of Monsieur] de l'anglade, Esquire, and officer in the troops of the marine, and of Charlotte Ambroise Bourassa,[78] her father and mother, whom I had privately baptized on the twenty-ninth of January last at la grande rivière, where she was born. The godfather was M^{r.} de l'anglade, the elder; and the godmother M^{de.} Bourassa. * * *

M. L. LEFRANC, miss. of the society of Jesus.

LANGLADE; CTRINNE LERIGE.

May 9, 1756, I solemnly baptized an outaouaise catechumen, daughter of neskes and granddaughter of kinoncharnee, sufficiently instructed and desiring holy baptism, who took the name of marie;[79] the godfather was M^{r.} l'anglade, the elder, and the godmother m^{de.} langlade, the younger. * * *

P. DU JAUNAY, miss. of the society of Jesus.

LANGLADE; CHARLOTTE BOURASSA LANGLADE; JOSEPH BARTHELEMI BLONDEAU.

May 23, 1756, I, the undersigned priest, missionary of the society of Jesus, solemnly Baptized an outaois catechumen, about fourteen years old, son of the late Cardinal, sufficiently instructed and desiring holy Baptism. He took the name of

---

[78] This child, known as Lalotte, was afterwards married to a M. Barcellou, dying the following year. See *Id.*, iii, p. 235.—ED.

[79] Afterwards the wife of Jean Baptiste Marcot. See *Id.*, xviii, p. 484.—ED.

George. The godfather was pierre migouanounjan; and the godmother anne villeneuve Blondeau, who signed with me.

M. L. LEFRANC, miss. of the society of Jesus.

ANNE VILLENEUVE BLONDEAU; AMABLE CHABOILLEZ; RENÉ BOURASSA.

June '5, 1756, I, the undersigned priest of the society of Jesus, solemnly baptized pierre antoine le tellier, legitimate son of antoine le tellier and of charlotte ouetokis, his father and mother,[80] born on the thirteenth of December of the previous year. The godfather was pierre le duc; and the godmother M$^{de.}$ and M$^{lle.}$ Bourassa.

M. L. LEFRANC, Miss. of the society of Jesus.

PIERRE LE DUC; CATERINNE LERIGE BOURASSA.

June 7, 1756, I, the undersigned priest, missionary of the society of Jesus, solemnly administered holy baptism to Magdelaine, a slave of Monsieur Chaboille, about forty-five years old, sufficiently instructed and desiring baptism. The godfather was M$^{r.}$ René Bourassa; and the godmother Marianne Chevalier Chaboillez. * * *

M. L. LEFRANC, miss. of the society of Jesus.

RÉNÉ BOURASSA, fils; MARIE ANNE CHEVALIER CHABOILLEZ.

June 19, 1756, I, the undersigned priest, missionary of the society of Jesus, supplied the ceremonies of baptism and baptized conditionally Marie Catherine guillory, legitimate daughter of joseph guillory and of Marie Louise Bolon, her father and mother. The godfather was M$^{r.}$ hertelle Beau Bassin, an Officer in the troops of the marine and commanding for the King at la pointe,[81] where the child was born on the twenty-

---

[80] For their marriage see *Ibid.*, p. 480.—ED.

[81] The parents of this child were married at Mackinac on Sept. 5, 1747. *Ibid.*, p. 474.

This officer, Pierre Joseph Hertel, Sieur de Beaubassin, was the last French commandant at Chequamegon. A brief biographical sketch is given in *Ibid.*, p. 163.—ED.

second of June of the previous year; the godmother was Mlle. Bourassa. * * *

M. L. LEFRANC, miss. of the society of Jesus.
JOSEPH GUILLORY; BEAUBASSIN; CT. LERIGE.

July 19, 1756, I, the undersigned priest, missionary of the society of Jesus, supplied the ceremonies and baptized conditionally, jean Simon personne, son of Charles personne and of suzanne Reaumé, his father and mother; and hubert personne, son of the same above mentioned; marie josephe, daughter of jean Baptiste jourdain and of marie joseph Reaumé, her father and mother, and Marie magdelaine, daughter of the same— the first boy, six years old, born on the fourteenth of April, 1750; the second born on the 1st of December, 1753; the first girl born on the tenth of October, 1751, the second on the 25th of January, 1754.[82] The godfather of the first boy was jean le febvre; and the godmother marie josette farley; the godfather of the second boy was Mr. Couterot,[83] Lieutenant of infantry; and the godmother Charlotte Bourassa; the godfather of the first girl was jean Baptiste le tellier; and the godmother Marie Anne Amiot; the godfather of the second girl was Antoine janis; and the godmother Marie Angelique Taro.

M. L. LEFRANC, miss. of the society of Jesus.
H. COUTEROT; BOURASSA LANGLADE; JEAN LE FAIBRE; JOSETTE FARLY; JEAN TELIER; ANTOINE JANISE; MARI ANGELIQUE TARO.

October 15, 1756, I, the undersigned priest, missionary of the society of Jesus, solemnly administered holy baptism to marie Renée, daughter of jean Baptiste Cadot and of Catherine, a girl of the nepissing, whom they are to legitimize by their

---

[82] These children were brought from Green Bay to Mackinac for baptism. For the marriages of their parents—the mothers were sisters—see *Ibid.*, pp. 473, 474.—ED.

[83] Hubert Couterot was the last French commandant at La Baye; see *Ibid.*, p. 184, note 28.—ED.

marriage to be performed shortly.[84] The child is about two months old. The godfather was M$^{r.}$ de Couagne; and the godmother M$^{de.}$ Bourassa. * * *

    M. L. LEFRANC, miss. of the society of Jesus.

R. DE COUAGNE, fils; M. C. LERIGE.

I, the undersigned priest, miss. of the society of Jesus, solemnly administered holy Baptism to Charles joseph, son of a female slave of M$^{r.}$ the chevalier de repentigny, born yesterday evening. The godfather was Louis joseph Ens [Ainse]; and the godmother Charlotte Bourassa. At michilimakina January 3, 1757.

    M. L. LEFRANC, miss. of the society of Jesus.

RENÉ BOURASSA; PAUL A. CHABOILLER.

I, the undersigned priest, Miss. of the society of Jesus, administered holy baptism to anne agnes Bourassa, legitimate daughter of René Bourassa and of anne Chevalier, her father and mother. The godfather was M$^{r.}$ de langlade; and the godmother M$^{de.}$ Blondeau. At Michilimakina, March 2, 1757, the day on which the baptized infant was born.

    M. L. LEFRANC, Miss. of the society of Jesus.

LANGLADE; ANNE VILLENEUVE BLONDEAU.

I, the undersigned priest, miss. of the society of Jesus, solemnly baptized, on Holy Saturday of the present year, a young slave belonging to Sieur amiot, armorer, at this post, about twelve years old, sufficiently instructed and desiring holy baptism. The sponsors were Sieur Amiot and his wife. Done at michilimakina, the 9th of April, 1757.

    P. DU JAUNAY, miss. of the society of Jesus.

BARTHELEMI BLONDEAU; PAULE AMABLE CHABOILLER; RENE BOURASSA.

---

[84] For a sketch of this early settler of Sault Ste. Marie, see *Ibid.*, p. 103, note 47. His marriage is registered on p. 483.—ED.

May 16 [1757], I, the undersigned Miss. of the society of Jesus, solemnly baptized Augustin, legitimate son of pierre Kitchinapé and of angelique, his wife, born on the last day of March of the previous year. The godfather was M$^{r.}$ de l'anglade; and the godmother M$^{de.}$ sans Chagrin, the undersigned.
* * * M. L. LEFRANC, Miss. of the society of Jesus.
LANGLADE; MARIE TARO.

May 20, 1757, I, the undersigned priest, Miss. of the society of Jesus, solemnly Baptized marie Anne, legitimate daughter of Claude pellé dit le haie and of Marie Meghissens, her father and mother,[85] born on the tenth of March last. The godfather was M$^{r.}$ Antoine St. germain; and the godmother M$^{de.}$ Anne villeneuve Blondeau, undersigned. * * *
M. L. LEFRANC, of the society of Jesus.
ANTOINE ST GERMAIN; ANNE VILLENEUVE BLONDEU; CLAUDE PELLE.

May 20, 1757, I supplied the ceremonies of baptism to joseph, son of a female slave of M$^{r.}$ jean Baptiste le febre, trader, born on the fifth of April last and privately baptized. The godfather was the aforesaid M$^{ess.}$ le febvre; and the godmother M$^{lle.}$ marie josephe farly, undersigned.
M. L. LEFRANC, Miss. of the society of Jesus.
JEAN BAPTISTE LE FEBVRE; MARIE JOSEPH FARLY.

May 30, 1757, I supplied the ceremonies of holy baptism to and baptized conditionally joseph, legitimate son of jean Baptiste Reaume, interpreter at la Baye, and of Marie joseph, his wife, born at the wintering place of the mississipi on the 7th

---

[85] For their marriage see *Ibid.*, p. 483.—ED.

of May, 1755. The godfather was M^r· Amiot, Armorer of this post; and the godmother M^de· farley, who signed here. * * *

P. DU JAUNAY, Miss. of the society of Jesus.

AMIOT; MARIE JOSEPH DU MOUCHELLE FARLEY; JEAN BAUPTISTE REAUME.

June 1, 1757, I solemnly administered holy Baptism to Marie françoise, legitimate daughter of françois Brisbé and of Marie anne parent, her father and mother, born yesterday evening. The godfather was pierre parent; and the godmother M^de· de l'anglade.

M. L. LEFRANC, Miss. of the society of Jesus.

BOURASSA LANGLADE; FRANCOIE [B]RISBE; PIERRE PARENT.

June 22, 1757, I, the undersigned, solemnly administered Holy Baptism to Antoine, legitimate son of joseph guillory and of Marie Louise Bollon, his father and mother, born yesterday morning. The godfather was M^r· Antoine St germain, trader; and the godmother Mariane Cecile Cousineau Monbron. * * *

M. L. LEFRANC, Miss. of the society of Jesus.

ANTOINE ST GERMAIN.

July 3, 1757, I, the undersigned, solemnly administered Holy Baptism to Antoine, a slave of M^r· St. germain, trader, about fifteen or sixteen years old, sufficiently instructed and demanding Baptism. The godfather was M^r· francois marie hamelin, trader; and the godmother M^de· Bourassa. * * *

M. L. LEFRANC, Miss. of the society of Jesus.

F. HAMELIN; MARIE CATHERINE LERIGE; ANTOINE ST GERMAIN.

July 18, 1757, I, the undersigned, supplied the ceremonies of Baptism to marie Catherine, a slave of M^r· hamelin, seven or eight years old, whom I had privately baptized last winter while ill. The godfather was M^r· St. germain; and the godmother M^de· Bourassa.

    M. L. LEFRANC, Miss. of the society of Jesus.
 ANTOINE ST GERMAIN; MARIE CATHERINE LERIGE; F. HAMELIN.

I privately baptized a little girl who is thought to be the daughter of Rupalais and of a daughter of la Culote. This little girl was about six weeks and sick with small-pox. This 11th of October, 1757.

           LEFRANC, jesuit.

This day I privately baptized a little girl savage about a year old, who is called outeskouiabano. This 15th of October, 1757.

This same day I privately baptized the son of miskoumanitou who desired baptism and was dangerously ill with small-pox.

This day, the 15th of October, I privately baptized the son of Lou ouicheina, whom I buried on Thursday, and kininchioue, both dangerously ill. They eagerly asked for Baptism and promised to get themselves instructed and to live as Christians. Both are dead.

I, the undersigned priest, Miss. of the society of Jesus, solemnly baptized Marie Bichibichikoue (since dead), an adult about twenty-three or twenty-four years old, sufficiently instructed and desiring baptism. The godfather was M^r· janis, trader; and the godmother M^de· Sans chagrin. At michilimakina the 18th of October, 1757.

    M. L. LEFRANC, Miss. of the society of Jesus.
 ANGELIQUE TARO.

I privately baptized the son of neoukima, on the eighteenth. He was dangerously ill with small-pox.

On the 22nd of October I privately baptized a little boy (since dead) of la pointe, about six months old, in danger of death.

On the 27th I privately baptized a female panis [slave] belonging to M$^{de.}$ Blondeau.

On the 28th I privately baptized the daughter of memanghiouinet.

On the 29th, the Sister-in-law of mikisinensa, all dangerously ill.

Eight days previously I had privately baptized Sarasto, a panis [slave] belonging to M$^{r.}$ Sans chagrin.

On the 1st of November I privately baptized a case.

On the 31st of October, I privately baptized the brother-in-law of mikisinensa, who died on the 2nd of November.

On the 2nd of November I privately baptized a little boy, a panis belonging to M$^{de.}$ Blondeau.

On the 3rd a little boy Savage who is at M$^{r.}$ the commandant's, who was abandoned and is said to belong to chambele (since dead) [also] A little panis girl belonging to M$^{r.}$ the commandant.

On the 4th I privately baptized ouabikeki, who died on the 5th and a girl panis of M$^{r.}$ langlade, the younger.

On the 5th I privately baptized two women Savages (since dead) in the Lodge of nanchoukaché or in that of Kaouchimagan (dead); a woman abandoned under a bark shelter near the same place; the wife and a little son of pitatchaouanon, both of whom died the same day.

On the 6th I privately baptized a daughter of mikisinensa (since dead) the son of memainghiouinet (since dead) and la Ronde, a panis of M^r· de langlais, the elder.

On the 7th I privately baptized a little daughter of pittachaouanon. (Since dead.)[86]

On the 17th of November, I privately baptized two nephews (still living) of the wife of mikisinensa; and a little boy called kinonchamon (since dead); and a little boy in the Lodge of the late ouabikiké.

On the 22nd of November I privately baptized the old mother-in-law of nanchoukaché (since dead); and a young man about 17 or 18 years old in the same lodge (since dead); also a little child in an adjacent Lodge, all in great danger.

February 23, 1758, I solemnly administered holy Baptism to Louis joseph, legitimate son of jacques farly and of josette du Mouchel, his father and mother, born this morning. The godfather was M^r· de Beaujour, Captain, commandant; and the godmother. M^{de}· de Langlade. * * *

M. L. LEFRANC, Miss. of the society of Jesus.
JACQUE FARLY; BEAUJEU.

Holy Saturday [March 25], 1758, I supplied the ceremonies of holy baptism to Thomas about twelve or thirteen years old, sufficiently instructed and privately baptized in the month of December last, being in danger of death, son of hyppolite kinonchamee dit Choumen, recently reconciled with the church. His godfather was Sieur farly, interpreter; and his godmother Agathe villeneuve, widow of the late Boisguilbert. * * *

P. DU JAUNAY, miss. of the society of Jesus.

---

[86] Here follows an entry crossed out in the original: "On the 8th I privately baptized a little child (since dead) of neoukima."—ED.

Mackinac Baptisms

April 12, 1758, I, the undersigned, solemnly administered holy Baptism to joseph Laurent, legitimate son of Laurent du Charme and of Marguerite metivier, his father and mother, born yesterday evening. The godfather was M$^{r.}$ Nicolas du fresne, trader; and the godmother M$^{de.}$ Bourassa. * * *

M. L. LEFRANC, Miss. of the society of Jesus.

MARIE CATERINNE LERIGE DE BOURASSA; LAURENT DU CHARME; NICOLA DUFRESNY.

June 12 [1758], I supplied the ceremonies of Baptism to and Baptized conditionally, Marie Angelique, legitimate daughter of Joseph Couvret and of charlotte, his wife, born about three months ago. The godfather was M$^{r.}$ amable de Rivière; and the godmother M$^{de.}$ Angelique Metivier.

M. L. LEFRANC, Miss. of the society of Jesus.

ANGELIQUE METIVIER; AMABLE DERIVIÈRE.

June 29, 1758, I solemnly administered holy Baptism to Marie jeanne, presented by M$^{r.}$ Monbrun, who received her from a woman savage and who took her to bring her up as a Christian. The said M$^{r.}$ Monbrun was godfather; and Madame his wife was godmother. At Michilimakina.

M. L. LEFRANC, Miss. of the society of Jesus.

MONBRON.

June 29, 1758, I solemnly baptized in the church of this mission a Catechumen of the Outaouas nation, the father of a family, over forty years of age, sufficiently instructed and desiring holy baptism; he is called kiniouichatoun and took the name of pierre at the sacred font. His godfather was M$^{r.}$ de Beaujeu, Captain commanding here for the King; and the godmother M$^{de.}$ langlade, the younger. * * *

P. DU JAUNAY, jesuit Miss.

BEAUJEU; BOURASSA LANGLADE.

I, the undersigned priest, Miss. of the society of Jesus, solemnly administered holy baptism to Charles, legitimate son of antoine le tellier and of Charlotte ouetokis, his father and mother. The godfather was M^r· de l'Anglade, an officer of the troops and second in command at this post;[87] and the Godmother M^{de}· his wife. At Michilimakina July 2, 1758.

M. L. LEFRANC, miss. of the society of Jesus.
LANGLADE fils; BOURASSA LANGLADE.

July 13 [1758], I solemnly administered holy Baptism to Marianne, daughter of a female slave of M^r· L'anglade, born on the tenth of March last. The godfather was M^r· the chevalier de Repentigny; the godmother M^{de}· Langlade. * * *

M. L. LEFRANC, Miss. of the society of Jesus.
LE GARDEUR CHE. DE REPENTIGNE; BOURASSA F. LANGLADE.

July 16, 1758, I solemnly baptized a catechumen of the Saulteux nation, sufficiently instructed and desiring holy Baptism. This catechumen is thirty years old and is called tiennotte.[88] She took the name of Marie in Baptism. The godfather was M^r· de Beaujeu, Captain, the commandant of this post; and the godmother M^{de}· de langlade. * * *

M. L. LEFRANC, Miss. of the society of Jesus.
BEAUJEU; BOURASSA LANGLADE.

July 16 [1758], I solemnly Baptized jean Baptiste, born on the 8th of February, 1756, and marie joseph, about two months old, son and daughter of michel Rocheveau and of marie tiennotte, who will this day receive the nuptial benediction and acknowledge the aforesaid Baptized children as legitimate. The godfather of the little boy was jean Baptiste La Douceur; the godmother M^{de}· metivier. The godfather of the little girl

---

[87] For Langlade's appointment as second in command, see *Wis. Hist. Colls.*, viii, p. 213.—ED.

[88] For her marriage to Michel Rocheveau, the same day, see *Id.*, xviii, p. 484.—ED.

was M^r· Sans Chagrin; and the godmother M^{de}· Sans chagrin.
* * * M. L. LEFRANC, Miss. of the society of Jesus.
SEJOURNE; ANGELIQUE TARO.

September 10, 1758, I solemnly baptized a female Catechumen, about sixteen or seventeen years old, sufficiently instructed and desiring Baptism. The godfather was M^r· janis, trader; and the godmother M^{de}· metivier. * * *
M. L. LEFRANC, Miss. of the society of Jesus.
JANISE; MARI ANGELI METIVIER.

October 1, 1758, I supplied the ceremonies of baptism to Charlotte, natural daughter of pierre Souligni, the younger, about two years old. I had baptized her privately about three months previously. The godfather was M^r· de Langlade; and the godmother M^{de}· Souligni.
M. L. LEFRANC, Miss. of the society of Jesus.
LANGLADE; AGATHE VILLENE[UVE] SOULINE.

October 4, 1758, I solemnly baptized marie joseph, born this day of a panis [slave] woman residing with M^r· Souligni, who gave her to le febvre, formerly a clerk at la Baie. The godfather was M^r· Souligni; and the godmother M^{de}· farley.
M. L. LEFRANC, Miss. of the society of Jesus.
J. MARIE JOSEPH DU MOUCHELLE FARLY.

December 17, 1757 [1758], I solemnly Baptized Louis francois xavier, legitimate son of René Bourassa and of anne Chevalier, his father and mother, born last night. The godfather was M^r· de Baujeu, Captain, Commandant of this post; and the godmother Marie Anne Chevalier, widow Chaboiller.
M. L. LEFRANC, Miss. of the society of Jesus.
BEAUJEU; VEUVE CHABOILLEZ; RENÉ BOURASSA fils.

January 30, 1759, I solemnly administered holy Baptism to Louis[e] domitille, legitimate daughter[89] of M$^r.$ Charles de Langlade and of M$^{de.}$ Charlotte Bourassa, her father and mother. The godfather was M$^r.$ de Beaujeu, Commanding for the King at this post; and the godmother M$^{de.}$ langlade. * * *

M. L. LEFRANC, Miss. of the society of Jesus.
BEAUJEU; LANGLADE.

April 14, 1759, I supplied the ceremonies of holy baptism to louise, about eleven or twelve years old, a slave of M$^r.$ de Beaujeu, Commandant of this post, formerly baptized privately by Reverend Father Lefranc, when in danger of death. I also administered holy baptism to Caterinne, about seven years old, a slave of M$^r.$ langlade, the younger. The godfather and godmother of louise were M$^r.$ langlade, the elder; and M$^{de.}$ langlade, the younger; those of Caterinne were M$^r.$ dufrêne, trader; and M$^{de.}$ langlade, the elder. * * *

P. DU JAUNAY, Miss. of the society of Jesus.
LANGLADE; BOURASSA LANGLADE; NICOLA DUFRESNE.

April 30, 1759, I administered holy Baptism to a little bastard girl, born this morning of the panis slave of Constant villeneuve, who accuses herself of having become enceinte by her Master. The child received the name of Charlotte. The godfather was René Bourassa; the godmother Charlotte Bourassa. * * *

M. L. LEFRANC, Miss. of the society of Jesus.
RENÉ BOURASSA.

May 11, 1759, I supplied the ceremonies of holy baptism to Pierre françois, legitimate son of françois Brisbé and of Marianne Parent, his father and mother, born the day before yesterday at la pointe au sable where I baptized him privately yester-

---

[89] For her marriage to Pierre Grignon see *Ibid.*, p. 493.—ED.

day. The godfather was M^{r.} parent; and the godmother M^{de.} farly.

M. L. LEFRANC, Miss. of the society of Jesus.

MARIE JOSEPH DU MOUCHELLE FARLY; PIERRE PARANT; FRANCOIE [B]RISRE.

May 30 [1759], I solemnly baptized augustin, legitimate son of hyppolite kinonchamek and of marianne, his wife, born on the 15th. The godfather was M^{r.} de l'anglade, and the godmother M^{de.} Soulignis. * * *

M. L. LEFRANC, Miss. of the society of Jesus.

AGATHE VILLENEUVE SOULIGNI; LANGLADE.

This day, the feast of pentecost, I supplied the ceremonies of holy baptism to Louis Joseph, a panis slave of M^{r.} farly whom I had privately baptized in 1757 when dangerously ill with small-pox, about 15 or 16 years old. The godfather was Louis desmouchells; the godmother M^{de.} farly. I also solemnly baptized a panis woman, about 20 years old, sufficiently instructed and desiring baptism for a long while. She took the name of Marie xavier. The godfather was M^{r.} janis, trader; and the godmother M^{de.} Sans Chagrin. At Michilimakina June 3, 1759.

M. L. LEFRANC, miss. of the society of Jesus.

MARIE JOSEPH DU MOUCHELLE FARLY; JANIS; ANGELIQUE TARO.

On the same feast of pentecost, I baptized Catherine, daughter of joseph Sans peur and of Michelle, his wife, born last winter. The godfather was Barthelemi janise; and the godmother Catherine parent. * * *

M. L. LEFRANC, Miss. of the society of Jesus.

BATTSE; JANIS.

June 14, 1759, I solemnly administered holy baptism to Antoine, son of pierre kinoncheton and of a pagan woman savage deceased, aged about five or six years. The godfather was M^r· janis; and the godmother M^de· Bourassa.   *   *   *

    M. L. LEFRANC, Miss. of the society of Jesus.
 AT JANISE; CATERINNE LERIGE.

 June 14, 1759, I solemnly administered holy baptism to pierre, son of pierre kinonchaton and of a pagan woman savage, who died in paganism, about ten years old, sufficiently instructed and desiring Baptism. The godfather was M^r. dufresne, trader; and the godmother M^de· Bourassa, the younger.   *   *   *

    P. DU JAUNAY, Miss. of the society of Jesus.
NANETTE BOURASSA; NICOLA DUFRESNE.

 I solemnly administered holy baptism to Nicolas, legitimate son of Antoine le tellier dit la fortune and of Charlotte ouaboki, his wife, born at Matchidack on the sixth of March last. The godfather was M^r· du fresne; and the godmother M^de· la fortune. At Michilmackina, June 24, 1759.

    M. L. LEFRANC, Miss. of the society of Jesus.
NICOLA DUFRESNE.

 August 7, 1759, I solemnly administered holy Baptism [to jean Baptiste born] yesterday, legitimate son of jean Baptiste metivier and of josette parent, his father and mother.[90] The godfather was pierre parent; and the godmother Angelique Metivier.   *   *   *

    M. L. LEFRANC, Miss. of the society of Jesus.
PIERRE PARENT; MARIE ANGELIQUE METIVIER.

 August 17, 1759, I solemnly administered holy baptism to Louis françois, legitimate son of francois Louis Cardin and of Constante Chevalier, his father and mother, born last night.

---

  [90] For their marriage see *Ibid.*, p. 483.—ED.

The godfather was M^r· janis; and the godmother M^ll· Chaboiller.
* * *

M. L. Lefranc, Miss. of the society of Jesus.
Cardin; at. Janis; Manette Chaboiller.

September 30, 1759, I supplied the ceremonies of Baptism to marie, privately baptized by Reverend Father du jaunay, born on the 8th of the present month, legitimate daughter of jean Baptiste marcot and of marie amighissen, her father and mother. The godfather was M^r· de Langlade; and the godmother M^de· Souligni.

M. L. Lefranc, Miss. of the society of Jesus.
Langlade; Agathe la Souligni.

November 6, 1759, I administered holy Baptism to Louis jacques, legitimate son of jacques Gaillard and of Marie jbeau,[91] born last night. The godfather was M^r· de beaujeu, Commanding for the King at this post; and the godmother M^de· de Langlade. * * *

M. L. Lefranc, Miss. of the society of Jesus.
Beaujeu; J. Galliord.

December 4, 1759, I solemnly baptized francois xavier, born yesterday, natural son of Catherine, a panis slave of M^r· Lafortune. The godfather was René Le tallier; and the godmother Marie anne marthe Chaboiller. * * *

M. L. Lefranc, Miss. of the society of Jesus.
Manette Chaboiller; René Letellier.

March 2 [1760], I privately baptized a young girl Savage called kioueiatchiouenoukoue, to whom I gave the name of Charlotte. She is about 14 or 15 years old. Since she has been with antoine la fortune she has always been very assiduous at catechism. She seems to be in danger of death from an abscess in the side.

[91] For their marriage entry see *Ibid.*, p. 484.—Ed.

May 22, I supplied the ceremonies of baptism to and baptized conditionally charlotte, born at Sault Ste. Marie at the beginning of last October, legitimate daughter of jean Baptiste Cadot and of Athanasi, her father and mother. The godfather was Mr. janise; and the godmother M{de.} de langlade. * * *

M. L. LEFRANC, Miss. of the society of Jesus.
BOURASSA LANGLADE; AT JANISE.

May 25, 1760, I solemnly administered holy Baptism to Alexandre Louis, a panis, about 14 years old, of Mr. de Beaujeu; and to genevieve, 9 or 10 years old, a panis of Mr. janis; the two adults being sufficiently instructed and asking for baptism. Monsieur de Beaujeu was godfather and M{de.} Blondeau godmother of the first; Bartholomée janis was godfather, and Mlle. Blondeau godmother of the second. * * *

M. L. LEFRANC, Miss. of the society of Jesus.
BEAUJEU; BARTHELEMI JANISE; MARGUERITE BLONDEAU.

May 26, I supplied the ceremonies of Baptism to josette, a slave of Mr. Bourassa, the elder, about 13 or 14 years old, whom I had privately baptized two years ago when in danger of death. The godfather was Mr. janis, trader; and the godmother M{de.} de langlade.

M. L. LEFRANC, Miss. of the society of Jesus.
MARIE ANGELIQUE METIVIER; AT. JANISE.

June 8, 1760, I administered holy baptism to josette, about 6 months old. She is the daughter of the granddaughter of the old nipissing and of jacques hamelin. As she is always sick, I deemed it advisable to Baptize her. The godfather was René le tellier; and the godmother josette dulignon. * * *

M. L. LEFRANC, miss. of the society of Jesus.
RENÉ LETELLIER.

Mackinac Baptisms

July 16, 1760, I supplied the ceremonies of Baptism to marie Angelique, legitimate daughter of jean Baptiste jourdin and of Marie josephe Réaume, her father and mother. She was born on the last day of February, 1759. The godfather was Mr. de souligni; and the Godmother M{de.} de langlade.

M. L. LEFRANC, miss. of the society of Jesus.
CHARLOTTE BOURASSA LANGLADE.

On the day and in the year above written I solemnly baptized Marie, daughter of jean Baptiste Cottenoire and of marie josephe ouagakouat, her father and mother,[92] born at the beginning of November, 1759. The godfather was Mr. giasson; and the godmother M{de.} de Soulignis.

M. L. LEFRANC, Miss. of the society of Jesus.
JAQUE GIASSON; AGATHE SOULINIE.

September 6, 1760, I administered holy Baptism to Louis and pierre Augustin, legitimate sons of Laurent du Charme and of Marguerite Metivier, his wife, born this morning. The godfather of the first was Mr. de Beaujeu, Commandant; and the godmother M{de.} de Langlade, the younger. The godfather of the second was augustin Chaboiller; and the godmother Angelique Metivier. * * *

M. L. LEFRANC, Miss. of the society of Jesus.
BEAUJEU; BOURASSA LANGLADE; ANGELIQUE CHABOILLER; MARIE ANGELIQUE METIVIER.

I solemnly baptized jacques, natural son of jean Baptiste Sans Crainte by a slave belonging to him, born the day before

---

[92] Their marriage was solemnized Aug. 6, 1758. *Ibid.*, p. 485.—ED.

yesterday. The godfather was jacques Gaillard; and the godmother, his wife. At michilimakina October 9, 1760.

M. L. LEFRANC, miss. of the society of Jesus.

JAQUE GALLIARD; JEAN BAPTISTE SANS CRAINTE; MADELAINE MGULPIN.[93]

November 23, 1760, I solemnly administered holy baptism to andré Vital, legitimate son of Charles farly and of josette de mouchel, his father and mother, born last night. The godfather was M$^{r.}$ Boiser, the elder; and the godmother M$^{dlle.}$ metivier. * * *

M. L. LEFRANC, miss. of the society of Jesus.

MARIE ANGELIQUE METEVIEZ; JAC FARLY.

April 4, 1760 [1761], I solemnly administered holy Baptism to josette Catherinne, legitimate daughter of françois Brisbé and of Marianne Parent, her father and mother, born the day before yesterday. The godfather was joseph saint Aubin; and the godmother Catherine parent. * * *

M. L. LEFRANC, Miss. of the Society of Jesus.

FRANCOIE [B]RISBÉ.

May 13, 1761, I solemnly administered holy baptism to joseph, legitimate son of Antoine le tellier dit La fortune and of Charlotte ouetoukis, his father and mother. The godfather was pierre dugast; and the godmother M$^{lle.}$ Chaboiller. This child was born at the wintering place on the second of March last.

M. L. LEFRANC, Miss. of the society of Jesus.

P. DUGAST; MANETTE CHABOILLEZ; ANTOINE LA FORTUNE.

June 1, 1761, I solemnly administered holy Baptism to Charles jean Baptiste, legitimate son of René Bourassa and of

---

[93] This name was written twice in the original, and both times crossed out.—ED.

Mackinac Baptisms

Anne Veronique Chevalier, his father and mother. The godfather was M$^{r.}$ de langlade, the younger; and the godmother M$^{de.}$ Cardin. This child was born last night. * * *

M. L. LEFRANC, Miss. of the society of Jesus.
LANGLADE fils; RENÉ BOURASSA, fils.

I, the undersigned priest, Miss. of the society of Jesus, solemnly administered holy Baptism to an adult, the natural daughter of francois duclos dit Carignan, sufficiently instructed and desiring holy Baptism. She is 23 years old. She took the name of marie josephe. The godfather was M$^{r.}$ provanché; and the godmother M$^{de.}$ la fortune. At michilimakina this 12th of July, 1761.

M. L. LEFRANC, miss. of the society of Jesus.
FRANÇOIS CARIGNANT; RNE PROVANCHE.

September 3, 1761, I solemnly administered holy Baptism to Charles Louis, legitimate son of Louis Cardin, notary at this post, and of Coussante Chevalier, his wife, born on the twentieth of August last. The godfather was Charles Boyer, voyageur; and the godmother Marthe Chaboyer. * * *

P. DU JAUNAY, Miss. of the society of Jesus.
MANETTE CHABOILLEZ; CARDIN.

September 4, 1761, I solemnly administered holy Baptism to Charles, legitimate son of Sieur michel Boyer, trader at this post and of josephe Marguerite du lignon, his wife;[94] the said child born on the twelfth [second] of this month. The godfather was Sieur Alexis Sejourné, trader, of this post; and the godmother M$^{de.}$ langlade, the younger. * * *

P. DU JAUNAY, Miss. of the society of Jesus.
ALEXIS SEJOURNE; BOURASSA LANGLADE; MICHELE BOYEZ.

---

[94] Their marriage entry is given in *Wis. Hist. Colls.*, xviii, p. 485.—ED.

October 28, 1761, I supplied the ceremonies of holy Baptism to joseph jean Baptiste, legitimate son of jean Baptiste Metivier and of josette parent, his wife, born on the seventh of this same month and privately baptized the same day, being in danger of death. The godfather was jean Baptiste Marchetteau, voyageur; and the godmother Catherine parant. * * *

                P. DU JAUNAY, Miss. of the society of Jesus.

MARCHETAUX; DENOYE.

January 27, 1762, I baptized a girl born yesterday of a slave of Amiot. The mother says that the father of the little girl is a savage. The godfather was René Bourassa; and the godmother Charlotte langlade who gave the child the name of joseph. * * *

                P. DU JAUNAY, Miss. of the society of Jesus.

RENÉ BOURASSA.

March 8, 1762, I baptized a young female slave belonging to M$^{r.}$ Parent, who is ill and, from all appearances will soon die. The godfather was Sieur michel Boyer; and the godmother M$^{de.}$ Parent, the latter undertook to supply what is wanting in the instruction of the girl who may be about twelve years old. * * *

                P. DU JAUNAY, Miss. of the society of Jesus.

MICHELE BOYER; MARIE C. B. PARENT.

April 10, 1762, I solemnly baptized a young negro about twenty years old, belonging to this mission since the day before yesterday, sufficiently instructed to even serve at the holy mass following the baptism, at which mass he made his first communion. He took the name of pierre in holy Baptism. His godfather was M$^{r.}$ jean Baptiste dit noyer, voyageur; and his godmother M$^{lle.}$ Marthe Chaboyer. * * *

                P. DU JAUNAY, Miss. of the society of Jesus.

DESNOYE; MANETTE CHABOILLEZ.

Mackinac Baptisms

April 25, 1762, I baptized in the church of this mission a child born a few hours ago of a slave belonging to Sieur Cardin the younger, being the son of Constant villeneuve according to what that slave said. The godfather was pierre la joye, at present residing with us; and the godmother Constante Chevalier, wife of Sieur Cardin, who gave the child the name of pierre louis. * * *

P. DU JAUNAY, miss. of the society of Jesus.

May 30 [1762], I solemnly baptized in the church of this mission two children; one the legitimate son of pierre kiniouichattouin and of marie, his wife, born at la grande Riviere about two months ago; the other the son of elizabeth nattamanisset, daughter of the said kiniouichattouin, and of one Bissonet, a voyageur, born at la grande Rivière on the 6th of January last, the feast of the Epiphany. The godfather of the first was M^{r.} pierre parent; and the godmother his wife, who gave him the name of pierre ignace. The godfather of the other was Mr. Michel Boyer; and the godmother his wife, who gave him the name of michel. * * *

P. DU JAUNAY, miss. of the society of Jesus.

PIER PARENT; MARIANNE C. B. PARANT; MICHEL BOYER.

June 13, 1762, I baptized conditionally jean Baptiste, legitimate son of jean Baptiste Marcot and of marie, his wife, born in the winter quarters at la pointe de Chagouamigoun on the twelfth of January last. The godfather was joseph St Germain; and the godmother angelique Sejourné. * * *

P. DU JAUNAY, miss. of the society of Jesus.

JOSEPH ST GERMAIN; ANGELIQUE SEJOURNÉ.

June 29, 1762, I solemnly baptized in the church of this mission jean baptiste, legitimate son of jean Baptiste Cadot and of Athanasie his wife, born at sault Ste. Marie on the 25th of October last. The godfather was M^{r.} jean baptiste adhemar;

and the godmother josephe, wife of Sieur Boyer, voyageur.
* * * P. DU JAUNAY, miss. of the society of Jesus.
ADHEMAR; MICHEL BOYER.

July 11, 1762, I baptized conditionally, hyppolite, son of Sieur hyppolite de Rivieres and of Marie, his wife, the said child having been born at Alimipigon on the 19th of December of last year. The godfather was Amable des Rivieres, uncle of the child; and the godmother Marthe Cheboiller. * * *
P. DU JAUNAY, miss. of the society of Jesus.
AMABLE DE RIVIÈRE; HYPPOLITE DE RIVIERE.

July 17 [1762], I privately baptized a little girl, about two years old, in danger of death, daughter of ouindigouich, brother of oulaoue, and of a daughter of the late ouiskentcha called teleiprieoue. I gave the little girl the name of Christine l'esperance, who held her while she was being baptized.

July 17, 1762, I baptized a child born last spring while they were returning from the winter quarters in the direction of la Baye, of a young Christian woman called Charlotte, who lived with antoine La fortune, and of a father not yet named. The godfather was M^r· Lafortune, the elder; and the godmother his wife, who gave him the name of joseph. * * *
P. DU JAUNAY, Miss. of the society of Jesus.
LA FORTUNE.

August 15, 1762, I solemnly baptized a young catechumen about 18 years old, a slave of old Angelique ouechibisse residing at the mission of St ignace, sufficiently instructed and desiring holy Baptism at which he took the name of Antoine. His godfather was Antoine la fortune; and his godmother Charlotte, wife of the said Antoine la fortune. * * *
P. DU JAUNAY, miss. of the society of Jesus.

Mackinac Baptisms

October 16, 1762, I supplied the ceremonies of holy Baptism to René, son of madelaine, a slave of Sieur Laurent du charme and of an unknown father, whom I had privately baptized this morning because he seemed in danger of death. The godfather was Sieur René Bonaventure Auger, voyageur; and the godmother Charlotte Bourassa. * * *

P. DU JAUNAY, Miss. of the society of Jesus.
B. AUGER.

January 12, 1763, I solemnly administered holy baptism in the church of this mission to Gabriel, legitimate son of jean Baptiste metivier and of josette parent, his wife; the said child was born last night. The godfather was Sieur Sejourné dit sans chagrin, residing at this post; and the godmother marianne parent, wife of Sieur [B]Risbé dit le Grandeur. * * *

P. DU JAUNAY, miss. of the society of Jesus.
ALEXIS SEJOURNÉ; MARIANNE PARANT LAGRANDEUR.

May 23, 1763, I administered holy Baptism to two children both born last winter; one at sault Ste. Marie, the other at Saghinau. The first is a son of a woman named Chopin, formerly a slave of M^r· le Chevalier and afterward sold to an English trader called henneri,⁹⁵ who, although not yet baptized, protested, when she offered her child for holy Baptism, that she had never had any other faith than that of the holy Catholic, Apostolic and Roman Church and that her new master had promised her never to force her with regard to her Religious belief. She also declared that the father of the child was one la Mothe, a voyageur, now at la pointe. The second is the legitimate daughter of joseph dit Sans peur and of Michelle, his wife. The godfather of the first was Alexis Chapoton; and the godmother Catherine parent, who gave him the name of joseph. The godfather of the little girl was paul Thomas; and the god-

---

⁹⁵ Alexander Henry, for whom see *Ibid.*, p. 277, note 88. He appears to be the first Englishman mentioned in the register.—ED.

mother Therese parent, who gave her the name of Therese. None of all these can sign their names. * * *

    P. DU JAUNAY, Miss. of the society of Jesus.

 June 30, 1763, I solemnly baptized, with the ceremonies prescribed by the holy Roman Church, ignace, legitimate son of Antoine tellier dit la fortune and of Charlotte Outoukis, his wife, born last winter in the upper ouisconsin,[96] on the 5th of January of the present year. The godfather was Sieur ignace Bourassa dit la Ronde; and the godmother Charlotte Bourassa. * * * P. DU JAUNAY, Miss. of the society of Jesus.
 IG BOURASSA.

 August 22, 1763, I solemnly baptized with the ceremonies prescribed by the holy Roman Church, Marie marguerite, daughter of Sieur Laurent de Charm and of marguerite metivier, his lawful wife, born on the 19th of this month. The godfather was M$^{r.}$ Kerigoufili and the godmother Angelique Metivier, his wife. * * *

    P. DU JAUNAY, Miss. of the Society of Jesus.
 CONSTANT QUIERIGOUFILI; ANGELIQUE METIVIEZ; LAURENT DUCHARME.

 November 29, 1763, I Solemnly baptized in the church of this mission with the ceremonies prescribed by the holy Roman Church, Angelique, daughter of Sieur René Bourassa and of anne Chevalier, his lawful wife, born on the 18th of this month

---

 [96] It is to be noted that this is the first recorded baptism after the Pontiac conspiracy at Mackinac, which broke out June 2, 1763. The English troops, with the traders and escorting Indians, arrived from Green Bay at L'Arbre Croche, July 1. The French traders had doubtless hastened on to Mackinac, where no Frenchmen were molested, and this child, born in Wisconsin, was there baptized. La Fortune (Lafortain) was again trading in Wisconsin the following year; see *Wis. Hist. Colls.*, xviii, p. 267.—ED.

Mackinac Baptisms

here at michilimakina. The godfather was René Bourassa, the younger; and the godmother Angelique Sejourné, daughter of Sieur Sejourné, who signed here with me. * * *

P. DU JAUNAY, miss. of the society of Jesus.

RENÉE BOURASSA; RENE BOURASSA; ANGELIQUE SEJOUR-NELLE.

June 23, 1764, I Solemnly baptized in the church of this mission, with the ceremonies prescribed by the holy Roman Church, Marie Anne, legitimate daughter of michel joseph marchetau dit des noyet and of Therese parent, his wife, born on the same day of this month here at michilimakina. The godfather was M^r· pierre Parent, acting commandant of this post;[97] and the godmother Marie Anne chaboiller, his wife. * * *

P. DU JAUNAY, miss. of the society of Jesus.

PIERRE PARANT; MARIE C. B. PARANT.

August 13, 1764, I solemnly baptized in the church of this mission, michel,[98] legitimate son of jean Baptiste Cadot and of

---

[97] This is an interesting side-light on conditions at Mackinac, and would lead to the belief that the Langlades had removed to Green Bay in the spring of this year, 1764. Capt. George Ethrington, when obliged to abandon his post at Mackinac in June, 1763, had placed it in charge of Lieut. Charles Langlade; see *Ibid.*, pp. 253, 258. The English garrison did not return until September, 1764; *Ibid.*, pp. 270, 271. If the Langlades removed to Green Bay in the spring of 1764, Parent must have held command until the arrival of Capt. William Howard.—ED.

[98] Michel Cadotte became an important Wisconsin trader. With his elder brother, Jean Baptiste, he was early upon the Grand Portage of Lake Superior. By 1784 he was wintering with the Indians at the head of Chippewa River, and had posts on the St. Croix tributaries and upper Mississippi, advancing with the Chippewa, his mother's tribe, in their progress into former Sioux territory. About 1792 he located at La Pointe village, Madelaine Island, whence he frequently went to winter at Lac du Flambeau and Lac Court Oreille, where he had posts. Cadotte was agent for the North West, and later for the

Athanasie, his wife, born at sault Ste Marie on the 22nd of July last. The godfather was jean Baptiste Cauchois; and the godmother Angelique sejournée, his wife. * * *

P. DU JAUNAY, miss. of the society of Jesus.

JEAN BTE CAUCHOID; ANGELIQUE SEJOURNÉ CAUCHOID.

September 13, 1764, I solemnly baptized in the church of this mission Laurant Constant,[99] legitimate son of Monsieur Constant Kerigoufili and of Angelique Metivier,[1] his wife, born on the 8th of this month. The godfather was Laurant du Charme, voyageur; and the godmother Marguerite Metivier, his wife. * * *

P. DU JAUNAY, miss. of the society of Jesus.

LAURENT DUCHARME; MARGUERITE METTEVIER DU CHARME; CONSTANT QUIERIGUEFILI.

On the same day I administered holy baptism to a little girl, born on the tenth of this month of a panise [woman slave] belonging to Sieur Cardin, who declared that the father was Sieur

---

American Fur Company. The Chippewa over whom he had great influence, called him Kichemeshane (Great Michel). In 1818 two New England traders named Warren arrived at La Pointe, and in 1821 they married two of Cadotte's daughters. Two years later he sold his trading post to his sons-in-law, and retired from active life, dying at La Pointe village in 1836. He married the daughter of White Crane, hereditary chief of the tribe at this place. His wife survived him for some years.—ED.

[99] Laurent Fily was well-known to early Wisconsin settlers. His grandfather, Michel Fily de Kerrigou, was a sergeant in the troops, coming to Canada from Brittany. His father Constant was born (1710) in Montreal. Laurent Fily first traded with the Sauk and Foxes on the Mississippi and in Iowa. Later he married into the De Kauray family, among the Winnebago, and was for some time clerk for Jean l'Ecuyer at the Fox-Wisconsin Portage. He was trading at Milwaukee in 1804–05. Having entered the employ of Augustin Grignon, he finally died in 1846 at the latter's home at Grand Kaukaulin (the present Kaukauna).—ED.

[1] Their marriage is recorded in *Wis. Hist. Colls.*, xviii, p. 486.—ED.

la joye. The godfather was pierre amable Roy; and the godmother Charlotte Bourassa, who gave her the name of Marie. Done at Michilimakina, September 13, 1764.

                P. du Jaunay, miss. of the society of Jesus.

Amable Roy.

Died the following autumn.

April 26, 1765, having privately baptized in the morning, because he was considered in danger of death, a child born yesterday, legitimate son of Jean Baptiste Cauchois and of Angelique Sejourné, his wife,[2] I supplied to him the ceremonies prescribed by the holy Roman Church. His godfather was M^r· Sejourné dit Sans Chagrin; and his godmother the wife of Sieur Sejourné, the Grandfather and Grandmother of the child, who gave him the name of jean Baptiste George. * * *

                P. du Jaunay, miss. of the society of Jesus.

Sejourné; Angelique Taro.

June 29, 1765, I solemnly baptized in the church of this mission Marie Charlotte, born on the 27th of the same month of Catherine, a slave of Mr Sans Chagrin, the said Catherine having declared that the said child belonged to M^r pierre Claire. The godfather was Sieur Etienne Campion, voyageur; and the godmother the wife of Sieur Sans Chagrin. * * *

                P. du Jaunay, miss. of the society of Jesus.

Campion; Angelique Taro.

June 13 [30], 1765, I supplied the ceremonies of holy baptism to Antoine, legitimate son of antoine La fortune and of Charles outoukis, his wife, born on the 23rd of January last on the mississipi, above the mouth of the ouisconsin. The god-

---

[2] This marriage is found *Ibid.*, p. 486.—Ed.

father was Sieur Nicolas Marchesseau; and the godmother angelique Sejournée, wife of Sieur Cauchois. * * *

P. DU JAUNAY, miss. of the society of Jesus.

MARCHESSAU; ANGELIQUE SEJOURNÉ.

This child had been privately baptized by Amable Roi.

July 1, 1765, I supplied the ceremonies of Baptism to jean Baptiste, born about the month of February, of the widow of the late hyppolite Kinonchame, and I baptized him conditionally because he who had privately baptized him declared that he had not assured himself of the validity of his action. The godfather was Sieur j. B. Charles Chaboyer, voyageur; and the godmother the wife of Sieur Michel Boyer. * * *

P. DU J'AUNAY, miss. of the society of Jesus.

CHABOILLEZ.

July 3, 1765, I supplied the ceremonies of holy Baptism to and baptized conditionally françois, born at la grande Rivière on the 1st of January, 1764, the natural son of René la fortune and a woman savage called Maccatemicoueoue, daughter of Missoussicoue. The godfather was Sieur Chaboiller, trader; and the godmother the wife of Sieur la Grandeur. * * *

P. DU JAUNAY, miss. of the society of Jesus.[3]

LA FORTUNE; CHABOILLEZ; MARIANNE PARANT.

July 29, 1768, by us, Vicar-General of Louisiana, was Baptized joseph marie, born In the Course of the month of October, 1767 of the Lawful marriage of Jean Baptiste Cadot And of marie mouet his Wife. The godfather was Sieur Jean Baptiste Chaboiller, trader; And the godmother marie anne Viger, wife of Sieur antoine Beauvais, Who signed with us. The mother,

---

[3] This is the last entry in the register, by Father Du Jaunay, who went back to Quebec, where he spent the remainder of his life.—ED.

who was present, Declared that she could not sign her name. The father Was absent.

GIBAULT, Vicar-general.[4]

CHABOILLEZ; MARIANNE VIGE BAUXVES.

July 24, 1768, by us, Vicar-General of Louisiana, the undersigned, was Baptized angelique, born on the [blank in Ms.] 29, 1767 of a slave of M^r· Cardin. The godfather was Sieur pierre Grignon, trader; And the godmother Dem^{elle} Veronique Cardin. The godfather signed with us.

GIBAULT, Vic-Gen.

PIERRE GRIGNON.

July 24, 1768, by us, the undersigned, Vicar-General of Louisiana, was Baptized marie Louise, born about nine months ago, Of the lawful marriage Of Joseph Kakigiguam And Of marie nanjoiquoy, his Wife. The godfather was Sieur Bazile mador; and the godmother marie Louise Gibault. The godfather signed with us. The godmother Declared that she could not sign her name; so did the mother, who was present as well as the father.

GIBAULT, Vic-gen.

BASILE MADOR.

July 25, 1768, by us the undersigned, Vicar-General of Illinois, was baptized marianne, born on February 28, 1767, of the lawful marriage of Gabriel Cotté and Of agate Desjardins, his Wife.[5] The godfather was Sieur nicolas Catin, trader; and the godmother Dame therese Campion, wife of Sieur pierre ignace Du Bois, all of whom signed with us as did also the father who

---

[4] See sketch of Gibault in *Wis. Hist. Colls.*, xviii, p. 292, note 14. Some newly-discovered material on Gibault's connection with George Rogers Clark is published in *Amer. Hist. Review*, xiv, pp. 544–557.—ED.

[5] Their marriage ceremony was performed the same day; see *Ibid.*, pp. 487, 488.—ED.

was present. The mother, who was also present, declared that she could not sign her name.

GIBAULT, Vic-gen.

COTTÉ; CATIN; THERESE CAMPION DUBOIS.

July 26, 1768, by us, Vicar-general of illinois, was baptized marie joseph, born about a year ago, Of the lawful marriage of joseph kakigiguam and Of marie nanjoiquoy, his wife. The godfather was Jean Baptiste Cauchois; and the godmother marie anne Viger, wife of antoine Beauvais, who signed with us. The father and mother, who were present, Declared that they could not sign their names.

GIBAULT, Vic-gen.

MARIANNE VIGE BAUVES; JEAN BTE CAUCHOID.

July 26, 1768, by us, the undersigned Vicar-General of Illinois, was baptized Marie, born about five years ago Of the lawful marriage Of Joseph Kakigiguam And of marie nanjoyquoy, his Wife. The godfather was Sieur Joseph Ains; and the godmother D^{lle} Marie therese Cardin. The godfather signed with us. The godmother, father and mother who were present, declared that they could not sign their names.

GIBAULT, Vic-gen.

JOSEPH AINS.

July 27, 1768, by us, the undersigned Vicar-general of illinois, was Baptized marie Louise, born about two years ago Of the lawful marriage of jean Baptiste pacoacona and of françois marie megonojan, his wife. The godfather was pierre Grignon; and the godmother Marie Louise Gibault. The godfather signed with us, as did also the father. The godmother and mother declared that they could not sign their names.

GIBAULT, Vic. g.

PIERRE GRIGNON; JAN BAPTISTE PACOACONA.

ENTRY IN MACKINAC REGISTER, JULY 28, 1768

From photograph; slightly reduced

July 28, 1768, by us, the undersigned Vicar-general of illinois, was solemnly Baptized marie Josephe about twenty-two years old. The godfather was Sieur Charles Chaboillez, trader; and the godmother dem^elle therese Campion, wife of Sieur Du Bois who signed with us.

GIBAULT, v. g.

CHABOILLEZ; THERESE CAMPION DUBOIS.

I, the Undersigned Royal Notary, the Justice of the peace at Michilimakina, Certify that, in the absence Of the Missionary of the said post, the daughter of Charles Sanguinet and of veronique Cardin, Born on the twenty-seventh of September of this year, was privately Baptized by Sieur Pierre Chaboille

In testimony whereof we have signed these presents on the day and in the year aforesaid at michilimakina September 27, 1770. CARDIN.[6]

CH^le SANGUINED.

June 27, 1775, by us, missionary Priest, the Ceremonies Of holy Baptism were supplied to Laurent,[7] born June 8, 1771, Of the Lawful marriage of Joseph Laurent Bertrand And Of Marie therese Du Lignon, his Wife. The Godfather was Sr Joseph Perinault, merchant; And the Godmother D^me Archange Barthe who signed with us, as did also the Father who was present.

P. GIBAULT, missionary Priest.

PERINAULT; ARCHANGE BARTHE ASKIN;[8] LAURENT BERTRAND.

June 27, 1775, by us, priest and missionary, the Ceremonies of Holy Baptism were supplied to Jean Baptiste,[9] born on June

---

[6] For a sketch of this functionary see *Ibid.*, p. 140, note 83.—ED.

[7] For the marriage of this person see *Ibid.*, p. 498.—ED.

[8] Wife of John Askin from Detroit, for whom see *Ibid.*, p. 309, note 29.—ED.

[9] Jean Baptiste Bertrand married at Mackinac in 1804. *Ibid.*, p. 510.—ED.

24, 1774, of the lawful marriage of joseph Laurent Bertrand and of Marie therese Dulignon, his Wife. The godfather was Sieur pierre Foretier, merchant; and The godmother dame marianne Cardin, Who signed with us as did also the father, who was present.

P. GIBAULT, miss. Priest.

MARIANNE CARDIN; PRE FORETIER; LAURENT BERTRAND.

July 9, 1775, by us, priest and missionary, the ceremonies of holy Baptism were supplied to Bernard, born March 22, 1770, of the lawful marriage of Louis demouchelle and of françoise, a savage, his wife, The godfather was Sieur françois La fontaine; and the godmother D^{me} marianne Cardin, who signed with us. The father, who was present, could not sign his name.

P. GIBAULT, miss. Priest.

MARIANNA CARDIN LA FANTASI.[10]

July 9, 1775, by us, priest and missionary, the ceremonies of holy Baptism were supplied to jean, born January 12, 1772, of the lawful marriage of Louis du mouchelle and of françoise a savage, his wife. The godfather was Sieur pierre foretier; and the godmother Angelique Sejourné who signed with us.

P. GIBAULT, miss. Priest.

ANGELIQUE SEJOURNÉ; PRE FORETIER.

July 9, 1775, by us, the undersigned missionary priest, was Baptized françoise, born May 12, 1774, of the lawful marriage of Louis Dumouchelle and of francoise, a savage, his wife. The godfather was Sieur Joseph perinault, merchant; and the godmother demoiselle felicité Barthe. The godfather signed with us. The father, who was present, declared that he could not sign his name.

P. GIBAULT, miss. Priest.

PERINAULT.

---

[10] For her marriage see *Ibid.*, pp. 488, 489.—ED.

July 10, 1775, by us, Priest and missionary, was Baptized Conditionally Marianne Marcotte, born in the month of September, 1769, Of the lawful Marriage of Jean Baptiste marcotte and of Marianne Neskeek, a savage, his wife. The godfather was hypolitte Campeau, who declared that he could not sign his name; and the godmother Marie angelique Sejourné, who signed with us.

P. GIBAULT, miss. Priest.

MARIE ANGELIQUE SEJOURNÉ.

July 10, 1775, by us, priest and missionary, was Baptized Conditionally Marguerite, born in the month of August, 1771 Of the Lawful Marriage of Jean Baptiste Marcotte and Of Marianne Neskeek, his wife. The Godfather was hyppolite Janis, merchant; and the godmother Agathe, wife of Sieur Coté, who declared that she could not sign her name. The godfather signed with us.

P. GIBAULT, Priest.

H JANIS.

October 3, 1775, by us, the undersigned Priest and missionary in the Illinois Country, was Baptized archange, born the same day Of the Lawful Marriage Of Sieur Jean Askin, King's Commissioner at this post, and Of Dame Archange Berthe, his Wife. The godfather was Sieur hypolite Chaboyer, merchant; and the godmother D^{lle} felicité Berthe who declared that she could not sign her name. The godfather signed with us.

P. GIBAULT, miss. Priest.

H. CHABOILLEZ.

In 1776, Marianne Cardin, wife of fransoi morisse Le fantosie, gave birth to a boy on the 15th of March. He was privately baptized by his uncle, Joseph Ainsse, at six o'clock in the evening.

In the year 1778, marianne Cardin, wife of françois Morise dit La fantizie, gave birth to a boy on June 18. He was privately baptized by his uncle, Joseph Ainsse.

August 13, 1781, was privately baptized Domitille, legitimate daughter of Sieur Charles Gautier and Madelaine Pascal, his lawful Wife, born the same Day at Noon.

JOHN COATES, Notary Public.[11]

I certify you that, according to the due and prescribed order of the Church, at noon on this day and at the above place, before divers Witnesses, I baptized this Child Charlotte Claves.

PATT. SINCLAIR, Lt. Governor, & Justice of the Peace.[12]

Witnesses signed: WILLIAM GRANT; JOHN L MACNAMAA; GEO. Mc BEATH; D. Mc CRAE; GEORGE MELDRUM.

JOHN COATES, Notary Public.[13]

July 15, 1786, I, the undersigned Priest, supplied the ceremonies of Baptism to Magdelaine, aged seven years less about two months, daughter of sieur Charles Gauthier and of Magdelaine Paschal Chevalier, his wife.[14] The Godfather was sieur joseph hains; and the godmother Genevieve Beaubien Cuillerie, dame Barthe, who signed with us, as did also the father.

PAYET, Miss. Priest.[15]

AINSE; C. GAUTIER.

---

[11] For this official see *Ibid.*, p. 434, note 45.—ED.

[12] The preceding entry is written in English by the British commandant. Probably the child baptized belonged to one of the garrison. The witnesses were prominent Mackinac traders. For a sketch of Sinclair see *Id.*, xi, p. 141, note 1.—ED.

[13] Following this in the register is an entry for 1804, which has been placed in its proper chronological sequence.—ED.

[14] For their marriage see *Wis. Hist. Colls.*, xviii, pp. 490-492. This elder daughter, Magdelaine, became the wife of Henry Monroe Fisher, an American resident of Prairie du Chien.—ED.

[15] For this missionary see *Ibid.*, p. 493, note 25.—ED.

July 15, 1786, I, the undersigned Priest, supplied the ceremonies of Baptism to Domitille,[16] five years old, daughter of Sieur Charles Gauthier and of Magdelaine Paschal Chevalier, his wife. The Godfather was sieur Etienne Campion; and the godmother demoiselle felicité Carignan, who signed with us as did also the father.

PAYET, Miss. priest.

FELICITÉ CARIGNANT; ET^{ne} CAMPION; C GAUTHIER.

July 6, 1786, I, the undersigned priest, supplied the ceremonies of baptism to Pierre, about two months old, son of a Negress belonging to monsieur Carignan, Notary public. The Godfather was Sieur Etienne Campion; and the Godmother Susanne hirbou, widow Pelleiter, who declared that she could not sign her name.

PAYET, Miss. priest.

ET^{ne} CAMPION.

July 16, 1786, I, the undersigned priest, supplied the ceremonies of baptism to Augustin, natural son of Augustin Sarasin and of a savage mother, about four years old, adopted by monsieur Charles Gauthier. The Godfather was sieur Louis Carignan; and the Godmother Magdeleine Paschal Chevalier, dame Gauthier, who declared that she could not sign her name.

PAYET, Miss. priest.

L. CARIGNAN.

July 16, 1786, I, the undersigned priest, supplied the ceremonies of baptism to Daniel, born on June 22, 1780, of Sieur Daniel Bourassa and of Marguerite Bertrand, his wife.[17] The Godfather was monsieur Pierre Grignon; The Godmother dame Jean baptiste Barth, who declared that she could not sign her name.

PAYET, Miss. priest.

PIERRE GRIGNON; DL. BOURASSA.

---

[16] For her marriage see *Ibid.*, p. 499.—ED.
[17] For their marriage see *Ibid.*, p. 492.—ED.

July 16, 1786, I, the undersigned priest, supplied the ceremonies of baptism to Marguerite Bourassa,[18] born May 25, 1782, of sieur Daniel Bourassa and of Marguerite Bertrand, his wife. The Godfather was Sieur Jean Baptiste Laframboise; and the godmother Dame Charles Gauthier, who declared that she could not sign her name.

PAYET, priest.

LAFRAMBOISE, fils; DL BOURASSA.

July 16, 1786, I, the undersigned priest, supplied the ceremonies of Baptism to Archange, born March 8, 1784, of sieur Daniel Bourassa and of Marguerite Bertrand, his wife. The godfather was sieur Luc Chevalier; the Godmother Susanne hirbou who declared that she could not sign her name.

PAYET, Miss. priest.

DL BOURASSA; LUC CHEVALIER.

July 16, 1786, I, the undersigned priest, supplied the ceremonies of baptism to jean Baptiste, born June 24, 1786, of Sieur Daniel Bourassa and of Marguerite Bertrand, his wife. The godfather was sieur Charles Danglade; and the Godmother Madame Carignan, who signed with us as did also the father.

PAYET, Miss.ⁿ priest.

LANGLADE fils; PILLET CARIGNAN; DL. BOURASSA.

July 17, 1786, I, the undersigned priest, supplied the ceremonies of Baptism to joseph Marie, born November 1, 1785, the natural son of Joseph Mersier and of a savage mother. The Godfather was Jean Rives; and the Godmother felicité Carignan, who signed with us as did also the father.

PAYET, Miss.ⁿ priest.

JOSEPH MERSIER; JEAN REEVES; FELICITÉ CARIGNAN.

---

[18] She married Guillaume Varin; see *Ibid.*, pp. 506, 511.—ED.

July 17, 1786, I, the undersigned priest, supplied the ceremonies of baptism to Marie, born February 1, 1783, the natural daughter of joseph Mersier and of a savage mother. The godfather was sieur Etienne Campion; and the Godmother Dame jean baptiste Barthe, who declared that she could not sign her name.

PAYET, Miss. priest.

JOSEPH MERSIER; ET^{ne} CAMPION.

July 19, 1786, I, the undersigned priest, supplied the ceremonies of Baptism to Michel, about two years old, natural son of Michel Labat and of a savage mother. The Godfather was Pierre Grignon; and the Godmother dame Bourassa who declared that she could not sign her name.

PAYET, Miss.ⁿ priest.

MICHELL LABATT; PIERRE GRIGNON.

July 19, 1786, I, the undersigned priest, supplied the ceremonies of baptism to Marie Magdelaine, about three years old, natural daughter of a stranger, called Jean Waters, and of a savage mother. The Godfather was Sieur Etienne Campion; and the Godmother Dame Gauthier who declared that she could not sign her name.

PAYET, priest.

J. BTE LAFRAMBOISE, fils[19]; ET^{ne} CAMPION.

July 19, 1786, I, the undersigned parish Priest, supplied the ceremonies of Baptism to Marie, about seven years old, natural daughter of Antoine Guillory and of a savage mother. The Godfather was Sieur Etienne Campion; and the Godmother Madame Gauthier who declared that she could not sign her name.

PAYET, Miss.ⁿ priest.

ET^{ne} CAMPION; ANTOINE GUILLORY.

---

[19] In the margin was written: "Marie Waters adopted by Jean Baptiste Laframboise the younger."—ED.

July 19, 1786, I, the undersigned priest, supplied the ceremonies of Baptism to Charles, about fifteen months old, natural son of Sieur danglade, the younger,[20] and of a savage mother. The Godfather was pierre Joseph hains; and the Godmother dame jean baptiste Barthe who declared that she could not sign her name.

PAYET, Miss.[n] priest.

AINSSE; C. LANGLADE fils.

July 20, 1786, I, the undersigned priest supplied the ceremonies of Baptism to Joseph, born April 17, 1782. The godfather was Sieur Joseph hains; and the godmother Madame Gauthier who declared that she could not sign her name. The child is the issue of Monsieur Luc Chevalier and of a savage mother.

PAYET, Miss[n.] priest.

AINSSE; LUC CHEVALIER.

July 20, 1786, I, the undersigned priest, supplied the ceremonies of Baptism to Jean baptiste, born February 14, 1785. The Godfather was Monsieur Louis Chaboyer; and the Godmother madame Daniel Bourassa who declared that she could not sign her name. The child belongs to Monsieur Luc Chevalier and a savage mother.

PAYET, Miss[n.] priest.

LUC CHEVALIER; L. CHABOILLEZ.

July 20, 1786, I, the undersigned priest, supplied the ceremonies of Baptism to Marguerite, born December 23, 1778. The godfather was Monsieur Carignan, Notary Public; and the Godmother felicité Pillet, his wife, who signed with us. The child is the issue of Monsieur Luc Chevalier and of a woman

---

[20] In the margin appears: "Charles, an added word, correct. Payet, Priest." For this person see sketch in *Wis. Hist. Colls.*, xviii, p. 495, note 29.—ED.

savage, his marriage with whom he proposes to have ratified in the manner prescribed by our mother the holy church.

            PAYET, Miss$^{n.}$ priest.

 PILLET CARIGNAN; L. CARIGNAN; LUC CHEVALIER.

July 20, 1786, I, the undersigned Priest, supplied the ceremonies of Baptism to joseph, born October 8, 1778, of Laurent Bertrand and the late Marie Therese Dulignon, his father and mother, in lawful marriage. The Godfather was Sieur Joseph [Jean] Rives; and the Godmother Madame Bourassa, sister of the child, who declared that she could not sign her name.

            PAYET, Miss. priest.

 LAURENT BERTRAND; JEAN REEVES.

July 20, 1786, I, the undersigned priest, supplied the ceremonies of Baptism to Eustache, born at midnight September 20, 1782, of the lawful marriage of Laurent Bertrand and Marie T. Dulignon. The Godfather was M$^{r.}$ Louis Cardin; and the Godmother Madame Gauthier.

            PAYET, Miss$^{n.}$ priest.

 LAURENT BERTRAND; LOUIS CARDIN.

July 22, 1786, I, the undersigned priest, supplied the ceremonies of Baptism to Rosalie, about six years old, daughter of a Negro called Joas Bongas and of Marie Jeanne, a Negress, living with monsieur Robertson, Captain, Commandant of Michilimakinac and dependencies.[21] The Godfather was Monsieur Antoine Barthe; and the Godmother Madame Jean baptiste Barthe, who declared that she could not sign her name, as did also the father.

            PAYET, Miss$^{n.}$ priest.

 ANTOIN BARTHE.

---

 [21] For Capt. Daniel Roberstson, see *Ibid.*, p. 436, note 50.—ED.

July 22, 1786, I, the undersigned Priest, supplied the ceremonies of Baptism to Joachim born in the month of June, 1776, of the lawful marriage of Louis Dumouchel and françoise of the nation of the courtes Oreilles. The Godfather was M$^{r.}$ Alexis Campion; and the Godmother M$^{ce.}$ Gauthier, who declared that she could not sign her name, as did also the father.

PAYET, Miss. priest.

A. CAMPION.

July 22, 1786, I, the undersigned priest, supplied the ceremonies of Baptism to Josephte, born December 26, 1777, of the lawful marriage of Louis Dumouchel and françoise of the nation aforesaid. The Godfather was Sieur Pierre Thierry; and the Godmother M$^{de.}$ Bourassa, who declared that she could not sign her name.

PAYET, Miss$^{n.}$ priest.

P. THIERRY.

July 22, 1786, I, the undersigned Priest, supplied the ceremonies of Baptism to Magdelaine, born August 7, 1784, of the lawful marriage of Louis Dumouchel and françoise, of the nation above mentioned. The Godfather was M$^{r.}$ Jean Rives; and the Godmother M$^{de.}$ Carignan, who signed with us. The father declared that he could not sign his name.

PAYET, Miss$^{n.}$ priest.

PILLET CARIGNANT; JEAN REEVE.

July 22, 1786, I, the undersigned Priest, supplied the ceremonies of Baptism to Gabriel, born February 17, 1783, a natural son of Gabriel hattinas dit Lavio[le]tte and of a savage mother. The Godfather was M$^{r.}$ Etienne Campion; and the Godmother Dame Jean Baptiste Barthe, who declared that she could not sign her name.

PAYET, Miss. Priest.

GABRIEL HATTINA; ET^{ne} CAMPION.

Mackinac Baptisms

July 22, 1786, I, the undersigned Priest, baptized Marguerite, two years, four months and six days old, natural daughter of Barthelmi chevalier and of a savage mother. The Godfather was M^r· jean Baptiste Chevalier; and the Godmother Madame Bourassa, who declared that she could not sign her name, as did also the father.

PAYET, Miss. Priest.

J. Bap^te· Chevalier.

July 22, 1786, I, the undersigned priest, supplied the ceremonies of Baptism to Genevieve, sixteen months and some days old, born of the lawful marriage of Louis Dufau and of Marie Louise of the sauteux nation. The Godfather was M^r· hypolite Derivière; and the Godmother dame Jeanne Baptiste Barthe who declared that she could not sign her name, as did also the father.

PAYET, Miss. Priest.

HYPOLITE DERIVIERE.

July 30, 1786, I, the undersigned Priest, supplied the ceremonies of Baptism to françois, about a year and a half old, natural son of françois Roy and of a savage mother. The Godfather was Monsieur Etienne Campion; and the Godmother Madame Carignan, who signed with us, the father declaring that he could not sign his name.

PAYET, Miss^n· priest.

PILLET CARIGNAN; ET^ne CAMPION.

August 1, 1786, I, the undersigned Priest, solemnly baptized a Savage Chief of the courts Oreilles or Outaois nation to whom the name of Charles was given. The Godfather was Monsieur Charles Viarville Gauthier, King's interpreter; and the Godmother Madame Daniel Bourassa, who declared that she could not sign her name.

PAYET, Miss^n· priest.

C. GAUTIER.

August 1, 1786, I, the undersigned Priest, solemnly baptized a Panis (belonging to Madame, widow hiacinte Amelin) about twenty years old. He received the name of francois Xavier. The Godfather was Monsieur Paul Lacroix; and the Godmother Susanne hirbou, who declared that she could not sign her name.

PAYET, Miss$^{n.}$ priest.

PAUL HUBER LA CROIX.

August 1, 1786, I, the undersigned Priest, baptized Therese, about ten years old, daughter of Sieur Jean Baptiste Marcot and of Thimotée, of the Outaois nation, his lawful wife.[22] The Godfather was M$^{r.}$ Jean Baptiste Chevalier; and the Godmother M$^{d.}$ Carignan, who signed with us.

PAYET, Miss$^{n.}$ priest.

PILLET CARIGNAN; J. BAP^{te} CHEVALIER.

August 1, 1786, I, the undersigned Priest, baptized Magdelaine,[23] about six years old, legitimate daughter of Sieur Jean Baptiste Marcot and of Thimotée of the Outaois nation. The Godfather was Sieur Antoine Barthe; and the Godmother Madame Charles Gauthier, who declared that she could not sign her name.

PAYET, Miss$^{n.}$ priest.

ANTOIN BARTHE.

August 13, 1786, I, the undersigned priest, baptized Magdelaine, born March 17, 1782, natural daughter of Dominique Chévaré and of a savage mother. The Godfather was Sieur

---

[22] This entry gives another form for the Ottawa wife of Jean Baptiste Marcot, spoken of in preceding and later entries as Marie Nesketh. Her daughter Thérèse, whose baptism is here recorded, became first the wife of Pierre Lasalière, later of George Schindler. See *Id.*, xiv, p. 17, note; xviii, p. 508.—ED.

[23] She married Joseph la Framboise; see *Id.*, xi, pp. 373 374; xiv, pp. 38-40; xviii, p. 507.—ED.

Carignan, Notary public; and the Godmother demoiselle Carignan, who signed with us.

           PAYET, Miss$^{n.}$ priest.
 L. CARIGNAN; FELICITÉ CARIGNAN.

August 13, 1786, I, the undersigned Priest, baptized Etienne, born on February 5, 1785, natural son of Dominique Chévéré and of a savage mother. The Godfather was Monsieur Etienne Campion; and the Godmother M$^{de.}$ Daniel Bourassa, who declared that she could not sign her name, as did also the father.

           PAYET, Miss$^{n.}$ priest.
 Et^{ne} CAMPION.

August 15, 1786, I, the undersigned priest, Baptized a Panis, about nine years old, belonging to monsieur Jean baptiste Barthe. The Godfather was monsieur Jean baptiste Laframboise, the younger; and the Godmother mademoiselle Carignan, who signed with us.

           PAYET, Miss$^{n.}$ priest.
 FELICITÉ CARIGNANT; J. B^{te} LAFRAMBOISE.

August 15, 1786, I, the undersigned priest, baptized a female panis slave of Monsieur Jean baptiste Barthe, about twenty years old. The Godfather was Sieur Gabriel Coté; and the Godmother madame Jean baptiste Barthe, who declared that she could not sign her name.

           PAYET, Miss$^{n.}$ priest.
 G. COTTI.

August 18, 1786, I, the undersigned Priest, baptized Louis, born this morning of the lawful marriage of Louis Maur and of Marie Moran, his wife. The Godfather was françois Duquet; and the Godmother demoiselle Carignan, who signed with us. The father declared that he could not sign his name.

           PAYET, Miss$^{n.}$ priest.
 FELICITÉ CARIGNANT; FRANÇOIS DUQUÉTE.

July 26, 1787, by us, the undersigned priest, was baptized Pierre, born seven months ago, legitimate son of Louis Dufaux and of a savage mother, called Marie Louise of the Sauteurs nation. The godfather was Pierre Thierry; and the godmother felicité Pilet, madame Carignan, both of whom signed. The father declared that he could not sign his name.

PAYET, Miss. priest.

P. THIERRY; FELICITÉ PILLET CARIGNAN.

July 31, 1787, by us, the undersigned priest, was baptized Marie, about three months old, natural daughter of a female panis slave of M^r· Barthe. The godfather was Jean Rives; and the Godmother Magdelaine Chevalier, dame Gauthier, who declared that she could not sign her name.

PAYET, Miss. priest.

JEAN REEVES.

August 3, 1787, by us, the undersigned priest, was baptized Domitille, born four months and thirteen days ago, legitimate daughter of Pierre Grignon and of Louise Domitille Langlade, his wife. The godfather was Sieur Alexis Laframboise; and the Godmother Genevieve Beaubien Cueillieré, dame Barthe, who declared that she could not sign her name.

PAYET, Miss. priest.

AL. LAFRAMBOISE; PIERRE GRIGNON; DOMITILLE LANGLADE.

August 5, 1787, by us, the undersigned priest, was baptized Antoine, about six years and four months old, natural son of Antoine Guillory and of a savage mother. The godfather was Paul Tenier; and the Godmother dame Daniel Bourassa, who signed with us, as did also the father.

PAYET, Miss. priest.

ANTOINE GUILLORY; PAUL TENIER.

August 5, 1787, by us the undersigned priest, was baptized conditionally Pierre Antoine,[24] born October 21, 1797 [1777], son of Pierre Grignon and of Domitille Langlade, his wife. The godfather was Sieur Gabriel Cotté; and the godmother Magdelaine Chevalier, who declared that she could not sign her name.

PAYET, priest.

G. COTTE; PIERRE GRIGNON.

August 5, 1787, by us the undersigned priest, was baptized Jean baptiste, born on November 25, 1783, natural son of Antoine Guillory and of a savage mother. The godfather was Nicolas Marchessau; and the Godmother felicité Pilet, dame Carignan, who signed with us, as did also the father.

PAYET, Miss. priest.

MARCHESSAU; ANTOINE GUILLORY.

August 6, 1787, by us, the undersigned priest, was baptized conditionally Charles, born June 14, 1779, son of Pierre Grignon and of Louise Domitille Langlade, his wife. The godfather was Charles Langlade, maternal uncle of the child; and the godmother Marie souligni, who declared that she could not sign her name.

PAYET, Miss. priest.

C. LANGLADE; PIE.[25]

---

[24] This was the eldest son of the Grignon family, known as Pierre the younger, or "Fanfan." After his father's death he became head of the family, dying at Green Bay, March 4, 1823; see *Id.*, vii, pp. 178, 242, 243, and *post*.—ED.

[25] The signature of the father, Pierre Grignon, begun and for some reason not completed. This son Charles lived at one time on the site of Oshkosh; previous to this he had lived in Canada for some years. *Ibid.*, p. 349; xv, pp. 19, 20; and *post*.—ED.

August 6, 1787, by us the undersigned priest, was baptized conditionally Augustin,[26] born on June 27, 1780, son of Pierre Grignon and of Louise Domitille Langlade, his wife. The godfather was Sieur Joseph Ainse; and the Godmother dame Daniel Bourassa, who declared that she could not sign her name.

PAYET, Miss$^{n.}$ priest.

PIERRE GRIGNON; AINSSE.

August 6, 1787, by us the undersigned priest, was baptized conditionally Louis,[27] born on September 23, 1783, son of Pierre Grignon and of Louise Domitille Langlade, his wife. The Godfather was Sieur Alexis Laframboise; and the Godmother dame Carignan, who signed with us.

PAYET, Miss$^{n.}$ priest.

FELICITÉ PILLET CARIGNAN; PIERRE GRIGNON; ALEXIS LAFRAMBOISE.

August 6, 1787, by us the undersigned priest, was baptized

---

[26] Augustin Grignon became a well-known character in early Wisconsin history. Like his forbears, he early engaged in the fur-trade, wintering in northwest Wisconsin for several years. He then undertook for a time the business of transportation at the Fox-Wisconsin portage. His later home was at Kaukauna, where he lived in patriarchial fashion, with Indian, half-breed, and white relatives and employees. About 1830 he removed to the village of Butte des Morts in Winnebago County, where in 1857 he was interviewed by Dr. Lyman C. Draper, and the results embodied in "Seventy-two Years' Recollections of Wisconsin," in volume iii of the *Collections* (see his portrait in the reprint edition). In his reminiscences he describes this visit to Mackinac to be baptized by the priest Payet. He notes the commandant's name as Robinson (Robertson, in fact); see *Id.*, iii, p. 261. He died in 1860.—ED.

[27] Louis Grignon (1783–1839) was one of the most progressive and intelligent of the French settlers at Green Bay. An early patron of schools, he had his children educated and made his home a centre of hospitality and culture. See *Id.*, vii, p. 244.—ED.

conditionally Jean baptiste,[28] born July 23, 1785, son of Pierre Grignon and of Louise Domitille Langlade, his wife. The godfather was monsieur Etienne Campion; and the godmother demoiselle felicité Carignan, who signed with us, as did also the father.

PAYET, Miss$^{n.}$ priest.

FELICITÉ CARIGNAN; PIERRE GRIGNON; ET^{ne} CAMPION.

August 7, 1787, by us the undersigned priest, was baptized conditionally Magdelaine, about seven years old, natural daughter of hypolite Larrivée and of a savage mother. The Godfather was Sieur hyppolite Deriviére; and the godmother dame Jean Baptiste Barthe, who declared that she could not sign her name, as did also the father.

PAYET, Miss$^{n.}$ priest.

HYPOLITE DERIVIERES.

August 8, 1787, by us the undersigned priest, was baptized conditionally Paul, about eleven years old, natural son of Joseph Bouché and of a savage mother. The godfather was Sieur Paul Tenier; and the godmother madame Carignan, who signed with us.

PAYET, Miss$^{n.}$ priest.

FELICITÉ PILLET CARIGNAN; PAUL TENIER.

In 1787, by us the undersigned priest, was baptized conditionally Louise, about eleven years old, natural daughter of Joseph Roc and of a savage mother. The godfather was Sieur Antoine Barthe; and the Godmother madame Gauthier, who declared that she could not sign her name, as did also the father.

PAYET, Miss. priest.

ANTOIN BARTHE.

---

[28] Jean Baptiste Grignon was still living in Green Bay as late as 1832. Less progressive than his brothers, he occupied his time with farming, and was employed by the British in the War of 1812-15.—ED.

August 8, 1787, by us the undersigned priest, was baptized conditionally, Angelique, nine years old, natural daughter of Joseph Roc and of a savage mother. The godfather was Sieur Louis Chaboiller; and the godmother madame Carignan, who signed with me.

PAYET, Miss. priest.

FELICITÉ PILLET CARIGNAN; L. CHABOILLIEZ; ANTOINE BARTHE.

August 8, 1787, by us the undersigned priest, was baptized conditionally Charlotte, six years old, natural daughter of Joseph Roc and of a savage mother. The godfather was Sieur Pierre Thierry; and the godmother madame Daniel Bourassa, who declared that she could not sign her name, as did also the father.

PAYET, Miss^n· priest.

P. THIERRY.

August 8, 1787, was baptized Augustin, seven months old, natural son of Joseph Roc and of a savage mother. The godfather was monsieur Joseph Ainse; and the godmother madame Barthe, who declared that she could not sign her name, as did also the father.

PAYET, Miss. priest.

AINSSE.

August 9, 1787, by us the undersigned priest, was baptized Antoine, two years old, natural son of Antoine Guigère and of a savage mother. The godfather was jean Alexis Campion; and the godmother madame Gauthier, who declared that she could not sign her name.

PAYET, Miss^n· priest.

FILOGIGERE; A CAMPION.

August 12, 1787, by us the undersigned priest, was baptized Pierre, about three years old, natural son of one Charles Valé and of a savage mother. The godfather was Sieur Alexis Laframboise; and the godmother madame Carignan, who signed with us, the father being absent.

PAYET, Miss$^{n.}$ priest.

FELICITÉ PILLET CARIGNAN; A. L. LAFRAMBOISE.

August 15, 1787, by us the undersigned priest, was baptized Marie, four and a half years old, legitimate daughter of Amable Chevalier, a savage of the Outaouais nation, and of Catherine kimiouenan of the same nation. The godfather was monsieur Ainse; and the godmother madame jean baptiste Barthe, who declared that she could not sign her name, as did also the father.

PAYET, Miss$^{n.}$ priest.

AINSSE.

August 15, 1787, by us the undersigned priest, was baptized Amable, thirteen years old, natural son of Pierre Grignon and of a savage mother.[29] The godfather was Sieur Antoine Tabeau; and the godmother mademoiselle Carignan, who signed with us as did also the father.

PAYET, Miss$^{n.}$ priest.

A. TABEAU; FELICITÉ CARIGNAN; PIERR GRIGNON.

August 19, 1787, by us the undersigned priest, was baptized conditionally Josephete Lesable, about fifty years old, a Sauteux woman savage. The godfather was Sieur Etienne Campion; and the Godmother M$^{de.}$ Jean baptiste Barthe, who declared that she could not sign her name.

PAYET, Miss. priest.

L. HAMELIN;[30] ET^{ne} CAMPION.

---

[29] This child died while at school in Montreal; *Id.*, iii, p. 242. The younger Amable Grignon was born in 1795.—ED.

[30] The margin informs us that she was the wife of Louis Hamelin, who signed the register.—ED.

[93]

August 19, 1787, by us the undersigned priest, was baptized conditionally, Josette,[31] born August 4, 1769, natural daughter of Louis hamelin and of Josephete Lasable. The godfather was Sieur Pierre Grignon; and the godmother M$^{de.}$ Carignan, who signed with us.

PAYET, Miss$^{n.}$ priest.

PIERRE GRIGNON; FELICITÉ CARIGNAN; L. HAMELIN Father.

August 19, 1787, by us the undersigned priest, was baptized conditionally Charlotte, born October 15, 1771, natural daughter of Louis hamelin and of Josephte Lasable, her father and mother. The godfather was Sieur Charles Courtois; and the godmother Madame Gauthier, who declared that she could not sign her name.

PAYET, Miss. priest.

CHARLE COURTOIS; L. HAMELIN Father.

August 19, 1787, by us the undersigned priest, was baptized conditionally Jean baptiste, born January 24, 1774, natural son of Louis Hamelin and of Josette Lasable, his father and mother. The godfather was Sieur Carignan; and the godmother Madame Grinon, who signed with us, as did also the father.

PAYET, Miss$^{n.}$ priest.

L. CARIGNAN; MADAME GRIGNON; L. HAMELIN Father.

August 19, 1787, by us the undersigned priest, was baptized conditionally Catherine, born on June 17, 1776, natural daughter of Louis hamelin and of Josette Lesable, her father and mother. The godfather was Sieur Charles Langlade; and the Godmother mademoiselle Carignan, who signed with us, as did also the father.

PAYET, priest.

L. HAMELIN Father; C. LANGLADE; FELICITÉ CARIGNAN.

---

[31] Married in 1797 to André Charlebois; *Wis. Hist. Colls.*, xviii, p. 499.—ED.

August 19, 1787, by us the undersigned priest, was baptized conditionally Augustin, born February 7, 1779, natural son of Louis hamelin and of Josephte Lasable, his father and mother, a savage of the sauteurs nation. The godfather was monsieur Jean baptiste Barthe; and the godmother madame Daniel Bourassa, who declared that she could not sign her name.

PAYET, Miss$^{n.}$ priest.

J. B. BARTHE; L. HAMELIN Father.

August 25, 1787, by us the undersigned priest, was baptized Louise, natural daughter of Jacques Levasseur and of a savage mother,[22] about six months old. The godfather was françois souligni; and the godmother madame Carignan, who signed with us, the father being absent.

PAYET, Miss. priest.

FELICITÉ PILLET CARIGNAN; F. SOULIGNY.

August 25, 1787, by us the undersigned priest, was baptized françois Louis, twenty months old, natural son of françois Souligni and of a savage mother. The godfather was Monsieur Carignan; and the godmother Mademoiselle felicité Carignan, who signed with us, as did also the father.

PAYET, Miss. priest.

FELICITÉ CARIGNAN; L. CARIGNAN; FRS SOULIGNY.

September 1, 1789, in the afternoon, by the undersigned notary, was privately baptized Marie Louise, daughter of Amable Chevalier, a Savage, and of Catherine Chenier, another savage, both Baptized. The child is about 7 months old.

L. CARIGNAN.

---

[32] The parents were not married until 1799; see *Ibid.*, p. 503. For her marriage to Joseph Gautier *dit* Caron, see pp. 504, 507.—ED.

September 29, 1792, was born and privately baptized by me, the undersigned, on the Thirtieth, Michel, son of M^r· Daniel Bourassa and of Dame Marguerite Bertrand his father and mother, born in lawful marriage. * * *

C. GAUTHIER.

October 21, 1792, by me the undersigned, was privately baptized Therese Victoire, born this day, of the lawful Marriage of M^r· Jean Baptiste Barthe and of Dame Geneviève Beaubien. * * *

ADHEMAR ST MARTIN.

February 7, 1793, I, the Undersigned, privately baptized Etienne, son of a woman savage called Veronique, belonging to M^r· J. B^{te} Barthe. The said child was born this day. * * *

ADHEMAR ST MARTIN J. P.

August 12, 1793, by M^r· Etienne Campion, was privately baptized Alexis, born this day, at half-past one o'clock in the morning, of the lawful Marriage of Sieur Alexis Laframboise and of Dame Josette Adhemar, his wife.[33] In the presence of the said Sieur Laframboise and of Dame adhemar St. martin, who have signed.

ALEXIS LAFRAMBOISE; BLONDEAU ADHÉMAR.

February 6, 1794, I, the Undersigned, privately baptized Marguerite, about twenty years old, belonging to Monsieur Alexis Laframboise, In the presence of the witnesses who have signed. * * *

ADHEMAR ST MARTIN J. P.

G. YOUNG; ALEXIS LAFRAMBOISE; T. POTHIER; ANGELIQUE ADHEMAR; ADHEMAR LAFRAMBOISE.

April 7, 1794, I, the undersigned, privately baptized Alexandre, born March 19, last, of the lawful marriage of Sieur

---

[33] For a reminiscence of these people see *Id.*, xiv, p. 20.—ED.

Daniel Bourassa and of Madame Marguerite Bertrand, his wife; In the presence of the witnesses who have signed with us. * * *

ADHEMAR ST MARTIN J. P.
DL. BOURASSA; ALEXIS LAFRAMBOISE.

April 7, 1794, I, the Undersigned, privately baptized Regis, born on the [blank in MS] of the month of March last, of a panis woman belonging to Mr. Daniel Bourassa, In the presence of the witnesses who signed with us. * * *

ADHEMAR ST MARTIN J. P.

May 4, 1794, I, the undersigned priest, apostolic Missionary, Religious of the order of St Dominic, supplied the ceremonies of Holy Baptism to Charlotte, a free negress, eight years old, legitimate daughter of Jean Bonga and of Janne, her father and mother, privately baptized by the Midwife. The godfather was Alexis Laframboise; and the godmother genevieve Blondeau who signed below in testimony thereof.

LE DRU,[34] apostolic Miss.

BD. ADHEMAR.

May 11, 1794, I, the undersigned priest, apostolic Missionary, French Dominican religious, supplied the ceremonies of holy Baptism to therese Victoire, born October 21, 1792, of the lawful marriage of Mr. Jean B^{te} Barthe and of genevieve Beaubien, her father and mother, privately baptized by M^{r.} antoine adhemar. The godfather was the aforesaid M^{r.} antoine adhemar, royal Notary at this post of Michilimakina; and the godmother dame genevieve Blondeau, wife of M^{r.} ant. adhemar, who have signed beneath in testimony thereof.

LE DRU, apostolic Miss.

ADHEMAR ST MARTIN; BLONDEAU ADHÉMAR.

---

[34] For this priest see *Id.*, xviii, p. 497, note 32.—ED.

May 11, 1794, I, the undersigned priest, apostolic Missionary, French Dominican religious, baptized marie Anne, born in The Woods of an Outhawa woman savage and of george Cown, an american,[35] about nine years old. The godfather was Mr. Antoine Adhémar; and the godmother Marie felicité Carignan. * * *

LE DRU, apostolic Miss.

ADHEMAR ST MARTIN; MARIE FELICITÉ CARIGNAN.

On the day and in the year above written, I supplied the ceremonies of holy Baptism to ursule, six years old, born in The Woods, natural daughter of a woman Savage of the nation of the Sotteurs and of joseph marie mercier, privately baptized at La Baie Des Renards. The godfather was philippe françois Souligny; and the godmother Suzanne hirbourg who signed beneath in testimony thereof.

LE DRU, apostolic Miss.

S. HIRBOUR; FR. SOULIGNY.

June 1, 1794, I, the undersigned, supplied the ceremonies of holy Baptism to marie magdaleine, two and a half years old, natural daughter of a woman savage of the nation of the Sotteurs and of Jerome Blot, privately baptized by Mr. Charles Gauthier. The godfather was Louis Amelin; and the godmother marie felicité Carignant. * * *

LE DRU, apostolic Miss.

L. HAMELIN; MARIE FELICITÉ CARIGNANT.

June 15, 1794, I, the undersigned, supplied the ceremonies of holy Baptism to Jean antoine, born in The Woods, of a woman savage and of George Cown. The said natural child, about twelve years old, had been privately baptized by Sieur Daniel Bourassa. The godfather was Toussaint antoine ad-

---

[35] For a letter of this trader, see *Ibid.*, pp. 435, 436.—ED.

hemar, Royal Notary and justice of the peace; and the godmother genevieve Blondeau.   *   *   *

LE DRU, apostolic Miss.

ADHEMAR ST MARTIN; BLONDEAU ADHEMAR.

June 15, 1794, I, the undersigned, Baptized Antoine and marie Magdelaine, natural children of a woman savage of the nation of the Sotteurs and of Antoine Soud, a Canadian. The boy is two and a half years old and the girl twenty-three days. The godfather of antoine was philippe Soud *dit* martin; and the godmother marie felicité Carignan. The godfather of Marie Magdelaine was jean Baptiste Laborde; [and the godmother Marguerite Chevalier], only one of whom signed; the others, being unable to write, made their usual mark in testimony thereof.

LE DRU, apostolic Miss.

MARIE FELICITÉ CARIGNAN; PHILIPPE SOUD + his mark; J. BAPT BERTRAND + his mark; MARGUERITE CHEVALIER + her mark.

June 18, 1794, I, the undersigned, supplied the ceremonies of holy Baptism to pierre, natural son of a woman savage of the nation of the courtes oreilles, and of joseph roy, who had been privately baptized by M^r. Gautier. The godfather of the child, who is a year old, was phillippe Soud dit martin; and the godmother Marguerite Sans regret who declared that they could not sign their names when thereunto requested by me.

LE DRU, apostolic Miss.

June 18, 1794, I, the undersigned, supplied the ceremonies of holy Baptism to angelique, five years old, natural daughter of a woman savage of the nation of the courtes oreilles, and of joseph roy, who had been privately baptized by M^r. Gautier. The godfather was Nicolas Loisel; and the godmother Magdelaine Chevalier, wife of M^r. Charles Gauthier de vierville, who

declared that they could not sign their names when thereunto
requested by me.

LE DRU, apostolic Miss.

June 22, 1794, I, the undersigned, baptized conditionally
marie, five years old, natural daughter of a woman savage, nation unknown, and of André Roy. The godfather was Nicolas
frerot; and the godmother Marie Josephte Poitrat.   *   *   *

LE DRU, apostolic Miss.

NICOLAS FRÉRAUT; M. JOSEPH POITRA.

June 25, 1794, I, the undersigned, baptized Marie Josephte
and henry, the former a woman Savage of the nation of the
courtes oreilles, about thirty years old; and the latter, twelve
years old, the natural son of the said marie Josephte and of
Monsieur henry Bostick [Bostwick].³⁶   The godfather of Marie
Josephte was Antoine Adhemar; [and the godmother madame
Adhemar] wife of Monsieur Alexis Laframboise. The godfather of the boy called henry was Monsieur Louis hamelin; and
the godmother Barbe felicité pillet, widow Carignan.   *   *   *

LE DRU, apostolic Miss.

ADHEMAR ST MARTIN; VEUVE CARIGNAN; ADHEMAR LAFRAMBOISE; L. HAMELIN.

June 29, 1794, I, the undersigned, supplied the ceremonies of
Baptism to Eloy, Magdelaine, and Alexandre, all three born of
the lawful marriage of Daniel Bourassa and of Marguerite Bertrand, their father and mother, privately baptized by M$^{rs.}$ Campion, carignant, and adhemar. The godfather of the 1st, that is
of Eloy, was Etienne Campion; and the godmother angelique
adhemar. The godfather of the second, that is of Madeleine
was Dominique Ducharme; and the godmother Magdelaine
Gautier. The godfather of the third, that is of Alexandre, was

---

³⁶ For this trader, see a sketch in *Ibid.*, p. 238, note 22.—ED.

Nicolas frerot; and the godmother josephte Poitra, some of whom signed and the others, being unable to write, made their usual marks.

LE DRU, apostolic Miss.

ET^{ne} CAMPION; ANGELIQUE ADHEMAR; DQ. DUCHARME; MAGDELEINE GAUTIER + her mark; NICOLAS FRERAU; M. JOSPH POITRA.

June [July] 5, 1794, I, the undersigned, Baptized Alexandre, natural son of a woman savage of the nation of the courtes oreilles and of george Couwn. The godfather was Alexandre Colbert; and the godmother marianne cown. * * *

LE DRU.

ALEX. CUTHBERT.

July 6, 1794, I, the undersigned, Baptized apoline, four years old, natural daughter of a woman of the nation of the courtes oreilles and of françois Souligny. The godfather was Monsieur Maurice Mougrain; and the godmother Louise dubois, who signed beneath in testimony thereof.

LE DRU, Miss.

MAU^e MOUGRAIN; D. B. SOLOMON.

July 6, 1794, I, the undersigned, supplied the ceremonies of holy Baptism to Charlotte, eighteen months old, natural daughter of Marguerite Marcotte and of Charles Wagacoucher, privately baptized by M^r· Charles Chandonnet. The godfather was the aforesaid Charles Chandonnet; and the godmother Elizabeth Solomon. * * *

LE DRU, Miss.

CHARLES CHANDONETT; ELIZBETH SOLOMONS.

July 9, 1794, I, the undersigned, supplied the ceremonies of holy Baptism to Marie Louise, legitimate daughter of Amable Chevalier and of Catherine, a woman savage, privately baptized by M^r· Louis Carignan, Royal Notary at this post. The godfather was M^r· Etienne Campion; and the godmother Mlle felicité Carignan. * * *

LE DRU, Miss.
ET^{ne} CAMPION; MARIE FELICITÉ CARIGNANT.

August 24, 1794, I, the undersigned pierre Gamelin, privately baptized Genevieve, daughter, issue of the lawful marriage of Sieur Alexis Laframboise and of madame Josephte Adhemar. * * * The said girl was born yesterday, the 23rd instant.

PIERRE GAMELIN, J. P.
G. COTTI J. P.; ALEXIS LAFRAMBOISE; D^n CAMERON; ADHEMAR ST MARTIN; JOSEPH LA FRAMBOISE; BD ADHEMAR; FRANCOIS LA FRAMBOISE; ANGELIQUE ADHEMAR.

October 26, 1794, I, the undersigned, privately baptized Charlotte,[37] a female sauteux savage, in the presence of the undersigned witnesses. The said girl is seventeen years old.

ADHEMAR ST MARTIN J. P.
Witness: ROBT. CAMPBELL; ROBERT M^{c}KENZIE; ALEX SHAW.

October 27, 1794, I, the undersigned, privately baptized Josette, legitimate daughter issue of the lawful marriage of Sieur Nicolas freraux and of Dame Josephte Poitras, his wife, born this day half an hour after midnight. * * *

ADHEMAR ST MARTIN
NICOLAS FRERAU.

September 23, 1795, I, the undersigned, privately baptized a girl named Angelique, born of the lawful marriage of joseph Vaillancourt and of Marie Elizabeth Bourgoin, born this day. * * *

ADHEMAR ST MARTIN J. P.

---

[37] Married the same day; *Ibid.*, p. 497.—ED.

Mackinac Baptisms

February 16, 1796, I, the undersigned, privately baptized a girl born the day before yesterday of the lawful marriage of Jean Baptiste La borde dit Sans regret and of Marguerite Machar Chevalier.[38] * * *

ADHEMAR ST MARTIN J. P.

March 25, 1796, I, the undersigned, one of his Majesty's Justices of the Peace, privately baptized a girl born yesterday about half past ten in the evening, of the lawful marriage of Sieur Alexis La framboise and of madame Marie Josephte adhemar, In the presence of the undersigned witnesses. * * *

ADHEMAR ST MARTIN

ALEXIS LAFRAMBOISE; GUILLAUME LA MOTHE; BD. ADHEMAR.

July 26, 1796, I, the undersigned, supplied the holy ceremonies to her [Angelique Vaillancourt]. The godfather was Sieur antoine reithe, trader,[39] of St Louis; and the godmother M^{de} angelique adhemar, who signed with us.

LEVADOUX, Vic.-general.[40]

A. REITHE; ANGELIQUE ADHEMAR.

July 27, 1796, we, the Undersigned, grand Vicar of Monseigneur the bishop of baltimore, baptized Louis, about four years old; angelique, about nine years old; genevieve, eighteen months old, all children of Louis roi and of a Sauteux woman savage. The godfather of louis was M. alexis laframboise; and the godmother M^e louise dubois Solomon: the godfather of angelique was M. françois laframboise; and the godmother josephe adhemar laframboise: the godfather of genevieve was M. jean

---

[38] For the marriage of these persons see *Ibid.*, p. 494.

[39] The name is commonly spelled Reilhe. He was a resident of St. Louis for many years; see *Ill. Hist. Colls.*, ii, index.—ED.

[40] For this priest see *Wis. Hist. Colls.*, xviii, p. 498, note 33.—ED.

rives; and the godmother genevieve Blondeau adhemar, all of whom Signed with us.

LEVADOUX, V. g.

FRANÇOIS LAFRAMBOISE; ALEXIS LAFRAMBOISE; JEAN REEVES; A. LAFRAMBOISE; D. B. SOLOMON; BD ADHEMAR.

July 27, 1796, We, the Undersigned, grand Vicar of Monseigneur the bishop of Baltimore, Baptized marie anne, natural daughter of [blank in MS.] and of a woman Savage. The godfather was françois Bouthiller;[41] and the godmother Me Angelique adhemar, who Signed with us.

LEVADOUX, V. g.

F. BOUTHILLER; AG ADHEMAR.

July 28, 1796, We, the Undersigned Vicar-general of Monseigneur the bishop of Baltimore, Baptized alexandre Clark, about Six years old, and julienne Clark, about four years old, and supplied the ceremonies of Baptism to louise Clark, about two years old, all born of jacques Clark and of a Sauteux woman Savage. The godfather of Alexandre was Charles Mayet; and the godmother Sophie Solomon: the godfather of julienne was Toussaint pothier; and the godmother angelique adhemar: the godfather of louise was Guillaume la mothe; and the godmother Louise [Dubois Solomon] all of whom signed with us.

LEVADOUX, Vic-gen.

GUILLAUME LA MOTHE; CH^r MAITTE; JAMES CLARK; T. POTHIER; SOPHIE SOLOMON; ANGELIQUE ADHEMAR; D. SOLOMON.

July 28, 1796, We, the Undersigned, vicar-general of Monseigneur the bishop of baltimore, supplied the ceremonies of Baptism to Sophie, natural daughter of Guillaume Solomon and

---

[41] For this early Wisconsin resident, see *Ibid.*, p. 463.—ED.

of a Sauteux woman Savage. The godfather was elias petit;
and the godmother louise dubois who signed with us.

LEVADOUX, Vic.-gen.

D. SOLOMON; E. PETIT.

July 28, 1796, We, the Undersigned, Vicar-general of Monseigneur the bishop of Baltimore, supplied the ceremonies of Baptism to rose,[42] born of the lawful marriage of jean Baptiste laborde and of Marguerite Chevalier. The godfather was Gabriel Cerré; and the godmother josephte adhemar.

LEVADOUX, Vic.-gen.

AD. LAFRAMBOISE; CERRÉ.[43]

July 29, 1796, We, grand Vicar of Monseigneur the bishop of Baltimore, supplied the ceremonies of Baptism to alexis, about three years old; genevieve, about two years old; and josephte, four and a half months old, all born of the lawful marriage of alexis laframboise and josephe adhemar, already privately baptized after their birth As recorded in the present register. The godfather of alexis was françois laframboise; and the godmother genevieve adhemar: the godfather of genevieve was joseph la framboise; and the godmother angelique adhemar: the godfather of joseph was antoine adhemar; and the godmother louise dubois, all of whom signed with us.

LEVADOUX, Vic.-gen.

JOSEPH LAFRAMBOISE; FRANÇOIS LA FRAMBOISE; ANGELIQUE ADHEMAR; BD. ADHEMAR; DB SOLOMON; ADHEMAR ST MARTIN.

---

[42] Probably Rosalie Laborde, who became Mrs. John Dousman; *Ibid.*, p. 512. About 1824 the family removed to Green Bay, where Mrs. Dousman was placed in charge of the Catholic school for Indian girls. This school was removed to the Menominee reservation at Keshena, and there for many years Mrs. Rosalie Dousman and her daughters labored to instruct the Menominee children. The school was finally broken up, between 1869 and 1871, and Mrs. Dousman died during the interval.—ED.

[43] Gabriel Cerré was a prominent resident of the Illinois country; see *Ibid.*, p. 415, note 20.—ED.

July 29, 1796, We, the Under Signed, Vic. general of the bishop of Baltimore, Supplied the ceremonies of Baptism According to the rite of the roman church to jean Baptiste, about eight years old, and joseph about six, both children of alexis laframboise and of a Sauteux woman Savage. The godfather of jean Baptiste was M. pierre isidore la Croix; and the godmother josephe adhemar: the godfather of joseph was patrice adhemar; and the godmother Louise dubois. They were privately baptized, according to the evidence and in the presence of their father, by Mr Campion.   *   *   *

LEVADOUX, Vic.-gen.

ISIDORE LACROIX; ALEXIS LAFRAMBOISE; AD LAFRAMBOISE; PATRICE ADHEMAR; SOPHIA SOLOMON.

Marie Madelaine, about three years old, natural daughter of joseph courtois and of a Sauteux Savage mother, was baptized by us August 1, 1796. The godfather was joseph laurant Bertrand; and the godmother barbe felicité pilette, who signed with us.

LEVADOUX, Vic.-gen.

BARBE FELICITÉ PILLETT; LAURANT BERTRAND.

Magdaleine, about Seven years old, born of louis de bouriess and of a Sauteux woman Savage, was by us, the Under Signed, baptized August 1, 1796. The godfather was antoine brisbois; and the godmother Magdelaine gautier who declared that she could not Sign her name, on being thereunto requested.

LEVADOUX, Vic.-gen.

L. D BOURIECE; ANTOINE BRISBOIS.

August 2, 1796, We the Undersigned, Vic.-gen. of the bishop of baltimore, supplied the ceremonies of baptism to a girl, about two years old, born of the lawful marriage of nicolas frerot and josephine Poitras, already privately baptized by Monsieur Adhemar. The godfather was Nicolas Marchenaux; and the godmother genevieve blondeau adhemar, who signed with us. I approve the addition.

LEVADOUX, Vic.-gen.

MARCHENAU; BD. ADHEMAR.

August 3, 1796, We the Under Signed, Vicar-general of Monseigneur the bishop of baltimore, Supplied the ceremonies of baptism to françois regis, about two and a half years old, son of an unknown father and of a woman Savage belonging to M. Bourassa, already privately baptized by Mr Adhemar. The godfather was joseph laurent Bertrand; and the godmother barbe felicité pillet, who signed with us. I approve the addition.

LEVADOUX, Vic.-gen.

L. BERTRAND; PILLET BERTRAND.

August 8, 1796, We the Under Signed, vicar-general of Monseigneur the bishop of baltimore, administered baptism to françoise, about six years old, born of joseph lafortune and of a Sauteux woman Savage. The godfather was patrik adhemar; and the godmother marianne Cowen, who Signed with us.

LEVADOUX, Vic.-gen.

PATRICE ADHEMAR; NANCY COWEN.

August 8, 1796, We, the Undersigned vicar-general of Monseigneur the bishop of baltimore, baptized Catherine, born of antoine martin and of a Sauteux woman Savage. The godfather was patrik adhemar; and the godmother marie anne Cowen who signed with us.[44]

PATRICE ADHEMAR; NANCY COWEN.

---

[44] The viçar-general's signature is lacking in the register.—ED.

October 4, 1796, was privately baptized angelique, about seventeen months old, natural daughter of hypolite Vaudette and of a woman savage.

ADHEMAR ST MARTIN J. P.

August 8, 1797, I, the undersigned privately baptized a boy, born on the third Instant of the lawful marriage of Joseph Vaillancourt and of marie Elizabeth.

ADHEMAR ST MARTIN.

October 18, 1797, I, the Undersigned, privately baptized a boy, about four years old, and a girl about sixteen or seventeen months old, natural son and daughter of Sieur fr. La framboise.

ADHEMAR ST MARTIN J. P.

November 7, 1797, I, the Undersigned, one of the justices of the Peace of the United States, privately baptized a girl Savage, of the Sauteux nation, called Inaououoiskamoquoy,[45] about seventeen years old, at Michilimakinac, on the day and in the year above written. The Godfather was M[r] alexis Laframboise; and the godmother Mad[me] Mitchell[46] who declared that she could not sign her name and made her mark. The godfather signed with us.

ADHEMAR ST MARTIN J. P.

ALEXIS LAFRAMBOISE; MAD[m] MITCHELL + her mark; F. BOUTHELLIER, witness; G. E. YOUNG; E. MOITH; DL. BOURASSA.

November 19, 1797, I, the Undersigned, one of the justices of the peace of the United States, privately baptized a girl, born this day about two o'clock in the morning, of the lawful marriage of Sieur Alexis Laframboise.

G. E. YOUNG J. P.

---

[45] For her marriage to Michel La Bruyere, see *Wis. Hist. Colls.*, xviii, p. 500.—ED.

[46] For an account of Madame Mitchell, a prominent resident of early Mackinac, see *Id.*, xiv, pp. 35–38.—ED.

Mackinac Baptisms

September 2, 1798 I the Undersigned, one of the justices of the peace, privately baptized a girl about a year old, daughter of the female panis of Mr· D. Bourassa.. * * *

ADHEMAR ST MARTIN J. P.

June 30, 1799, jean baptiste, born October 16, 1797 of an Outawas woman called Minanaconaton and of jean baptiste Desfonts, who acknowledged the child and signed with us, having been privately baptized by Olivier—was solemnly baptized and received the ceremonies of baptism from us the undersigned priest.[47] The godfather was Antoine Adhemar St martin, Justice of the peace; and the godmother Genevieve Blondeau, who signed with us.

ADHEMAR ST MARTIN.

BD ADHEMAR; J BST DEFOND.

July 7, 1799, the ceremonies of baptism were supplied to josette,[48] born on September 24, 1795 of joseph Laframboise and of Madelaine, of the nation of the courtes oreilles. The godfather was Isidore Lacroix; and the godmother josette Adhemar, wife of Alexis Laframboise, who signed with us.

GABRIEL RICHARD, priest.

A. LAFRAMBOISE; JOSEPH LAFRAMBOISE; ISIDORE LACROIX.

July 7, 1799, the ceremonies of baptism were supplied by us, the undersigned priest, to Marguerite, born November 8, 1797,

---

[47] The signature of the priest is lacking. The baptism was performed by Father Gabriel Richard, who in 1799 visited the island; see *Id.*, xviii, p. 302, note 40.—ED.

[48] The father of this child was killed in 1809 near Grand Rapids, Mich. His wife continued his business of trading with the Indians, in which she was very successful. She sent her daughter to Montreal to be educated. Upon her return she met and married Capt. Benjamin K. Pierce of the American garrison, brother of the future president of the United States. The wedding occurred in 1817. The bride dying four years later, was buried in the Mackinac church. See *Id.*, xiv, pp. 36–43.—ED.

of the lawful marriage of Alexis Laframboise and of josette Adhemar. The godfather was Claude Laframboise; and the godmother Angelique Adhemar, who signed with us.

GABRIEL RICHARD, priest.

ANGELIQUE ADHEMAR; ALEXIS LAFRAMBOISE; CLAUDE LAFRAMBOISE.

July 8, 1799, by us the undersigned priest, the ceremonies of baptism were supplied to josette—about five years old, born of Joachim L'Agacé and of Elizabeth, a Courte Oreille—privately baptized by Antoine martin. The godfather was françois Bouthilier; and the godmother Josette Adhemar, wife of Alexis Laframboise, who signed with us.

GABRIEL RICHARD, priest.

F. BOUTHILLIER; A. LAFRAMBOISE.

July 8, 1799 by us the undersigned priest, the ceremonies of baptism were supplied to Henri, born October 23, 1797, of Guillaume Solomon and of Agibicocona of the Sauteux nation, and privately baptized by Antoine Adhemar St. martin. The godfather was Ezechiel Solomon; and the godmother Marie anne Cowen, who signed with us as did also the father.

GABRIEL RICHARD, priest.

GUILLAUME SOLOMON; EZEK¹ SOLOMON; NANCY COUN.

July 8, 1799, by us the undersigned priest, the ceremonies of baptism were supplied to Marie Louise, born April 7, of the same year of Guillaume Solomon and of Agibicocona, a Sauteux woman, privately baptized by Louise Dubois. The godfather was Joseph Baily;[49] and the godmother Louise Dubois, wife of Ezechiel Solomon, who signed with us.

GABRIEL RICHARD, priest.

D. SOLOMON; Jʰ BAILLY.

---

[49] For this Mackinac trader see *Ibid.*, pp. 43–45.—ED.

Mackinac Baptisms

July 9, 1799, by us the undersigned priest, the ceremonies of baptism were supplied to marie judith, born October 10, 1790, of the lawful marriage of Daniel Bourassa and of Marguerite Bertrand, residents of this parish of Ste Anne. The Godfather was Joseph Bailly; and the godmother Marie Anne Cown, who signed with us.

GABRIEL RICHARD, priest.

NANCY COWN; J^h BAILLY.

July 9, 1799, by us, the undersigned priest, the ceremonies of baptism were supplied to joseph, born August 27, 1797, of the lawful marriage of joseph Vaillancourt and of Marie Elizabeth Bourgouin, residents of this parish. The godfather was françois Bouthilier; and the godmother angelique adhemar, who signed with us.

GABRIEL RICHARD, priest.

JOSEPH VAILLANCOUR; F. BOUTHILIER.

July 9, 1799, by us the undersigned priest, the ceremonies of baptism were supplied to Nicolas, born August 20, of the previous year of the lawful marriage of Nicolas frereau and of josette Poitras, residents of this parish. The godfather was françois Bouthilier; and the godmother Angelique Adhemar, who signed with us, as did also the father.

GABRIEL RICHARD, priest.

NICOLAS FREREAU; ANGELIQUE ADHEMAR; F. BOUTHILIER.

July 9, 1799, by us, the undersigned priest, the ceremonies of baptism were supplied to Léon, born October 9, of the previous year of the lawful marriage of Daniel Bourassa and of Marguerite Bertrand, residents of this parish. The godfather was Antoine Guillory, who signed with us; and the godmother Marguerite Bourassa,[50] sister of the child, who declared that

---

[50] For her marriage see *Id.*, xviii, p. 511.—ED.

she could not sign her name when thereunto requested. The father signed with us.

Dl Bourassa; ANTOINE GUILLORY.

July 9, 1799, by us the undersigned priest, the ceremonies of baptism were supplied to jean baptiste, born December 27, of the previous year of the lawful marriage of joseph Vaillancourt and of Marie Elizabeth Bourgouin, residents of this parish. The godfather was jean baptiste Gatien; and the godmother Archange Bourassa who declared that she could not sign her name when thereunto requested. The father signed with us.

Gabriel Richard, priest.

J^n B^{te} Gatien; JOSEPH VAILLANCOURT.

July 9, 1799, by us the undersigned priest, was baptized marie Louise, born of a woman savage of the Sauteux nation called manitowa and of an unknown father. The child is about two years old. The godmother was Louise Dubois, wife of Ezechiel Solomon, who signed with us.

Gabriel Richard, priest.

D. Solomon.

July 10, 1799, by us, the undersigned priest, was baptized conditionally Michel, born on September 6, 1787, of Michel Cadot and of a Sauteux woman. The Godfather was Hubert Lacroix; and the godmother Louise Dubois, wife of Ezechiel Solomon, who signed with us.

Gabriel Richard, priest.

D. Solomon; H. la Croix, fils.

July 10, 1799, by us, the undersigned priest was baptized conditionally Marguerite, born December 15, 1788, of Michel Cadot and of a Sauteux woman. The Godfather was Nicolas frereau; and the godmother Geneviève Blondeau, wife of Antoine Adhemar, who signed with us.

GABRIEL RICHARD, priest.

NICOLAS FREREAU; BD ADHÉMAR.

July 14, 1799, by us, the undersigned priest, was baptized Louis, born December 29, of the previous year, of Antoine Martin and of Kinicona, a Sauteux woman. The Godfather was Jean Baptiste Gautier, who signed with us; and the Godmother Marguerite Bourassa, who declared that she could not sign her name when thereunto requested.

GABRIEL RICHARD, priest.

JN B^{te} GAUTIER.

July 26, 1799, by us, the undersigned priest, the ceremonies of baptism were supplied to Alexis, born May 23, 1797, of Samuel Solomon and of Marie of the Sauteux nation. The father, who was present, signed. The godfather was Alexis Laframboise; and the godmother Elizabeth Dubois, who signed with us.

GABRIEL RICHARD, priest.

DU SOLOMON; ALEXIS LAFRAMBOISE; SAM^l SOLOMON.

July 26, 1799, by us, the undersigned priest, the ceremonies of Baptism were supplied to joseph, born August 8, 1797, of jacques Le Vasseur and of Madelaine of the Courte Oreille nation. The father was present and signed. The godfather was André La Chêne; and the godmother Susanne Hirebour, who declared that they could not sign their names when thereunto requested.

GABRIEL RICHARD, priest.

ANDRE LA CHÊNE mark +; SUSANNE HIREBOUR mark +; JAC. VASSEUR.

Joseph Le Vasseur was legitimized and acknowledged by his

father and mother on the day of their marriage before the church August 5, 1799.[51]

GABRIEL RICHARD, priest.

July 20, 1799, by us, the undersigned priest, the ceremonies of Baptism were supplied to Henry, born June 10, 1797, of the lawful marriage of Patrice McGulpin and of Madeline Crequé, residents of this parish. The Godfather was Simon Champagne; and the godmother Marguerite Chevalier, who declared that they could not sign their names. The father was present and signed.

GABRIEL RICHARD, priest.

PATT. M:GULPIN; mark of + SIMON CHAMPAGNE; mark of + MARGUERITE CHEVALIER.

July 28, 1799, by us, the undersigned priest, the ceremonies of Baptism were supplied to Elizabeth, born February 12, 1798, of the lawful marriage of Patrice McGulpin and of Madeleine Crequé, residents of this parish. The father was present and signed with us. The Godfather was pierre Lacroix; and the godmother Marie McGulpin, wife of the aforesaid Pierre Lacroix,[52] who declared that they could not sign their names.

GABRIEL RICHARD, priest.

PATT. MCGULPIN; mark of + PIERRE LACROIX; mark of + MARIE MCGULPIN.

July 28, 1799, by us, the undersigned priest, the ceremonies of baptism were supplied to Giles, born April 7, of the same year of the lawful marriage of Patrice McGulpin and of Madeleine Crequé, residents of this parish. The father was present

---

[51] See *Ibid.*, p. 503.—ED.
[52] Their marriage had occurred on July 22, 1799; *Ibid.*, p. 502.—ED.

and signed with us. The godfather was jean baptiste Gautier; and the godmother Marie anne Cowen. * * *

GABRIEL RICHARD.

PATT. M: GULPIN; NANCY COWN; Jⁿ Bᵗᵉ GAUTIER.

August 1, 1799, by us, the undersigned priest, the ceremonies of baptism were supplied to Catherine, born in May, 1792, of Louise, a Panis [slave] of Daniel Bourassa and of an unknown father. The Godfather was Patrice Adhémar, who signed with us; and the godmother Marguerite Chevalier, wife of jean baptiste Laborde, who declared that she could not sign her name.

GABRIEL RICHARD, priest.

PATRICE ADHEMAR; mark of + MARGUERITE CHEVALIER.

August 3, 1799, by us, the undersigned priest, the ceremonies of baptism were supplied to josette, born November 18, 1797, of the lawful marriage of André Charlebois and of Josette Ammelain, residents of this Parish.[53] The Godfather was Alexis Laframboise, who signed with us. The godmother[54] declared that she could not sign her name, when thereunto requested.

GABRIEL RICHARD, priest.

ALEXIS LAFRAMBOISE.

August 5, 1799, by us, the undersigned priest, was solemnly baptized Madeleine of the Outawas nation, about thirty years old.[55] The godfather was Pierre Quéri[sic], and the godmother Genevieve Blondeau, wife of Antoine Adhémar, who signed with us.

GABRIEL RICHARD, priest.

P. THIERY; BD ADHEMAR.

---

[53] See their marriage record, *Ibid.*, p. 499.—ED.
[54] The godmother's name is not given in the original.—ED.
[55] Married the same day to Jacques Vasseur; *Wis. Hist. Colls.*, xviii, p. 503.—ED.

August 11, 1799, by us the undersigned priest, the ceremonies of Baptism were supplied to Marie, privately baptized by Louis Carignan about the age of eight years when in danger of death, born April 15, 1787, of Joseph Taillefer and of the late Louise of the Sauteux nation. The father was present. The Godfather was Augustin Hamelin; and the godmother Angelique Adhemar, who signed with us.

GABRIEL RICHARD, priest.

ANGELIQUE ADHEMAR; AUGUSTIN HAMELIN.

August 11, 1799, by us the undersigned priest, the ceremonies of baptism were supplied to Louise Taillefer, privately baptized by Louis Carignan when about three months old, born April 17, 1790, of Joseph Taillefer and of the late Louise of the Sauteux nation. The father was present. The Godfather was Patrice adhemar, who signed with us. The godmother was Archange Bourassa, who declared that she could not sign her name when thereunto requested.

GABRIEL RICHARD, priest.

PATRICE ADHÉMAR; mark of + ARCHANGE BOURASSA.

August 15, 1799, by us, the undersigned priest, the ceremonies of baptism were supplied to jacques, privately baptized by Monsieur Cattillan a month after his birth, born January 8, 1799, of jacques Vasseur and of Madeleine, an Outawas woman, his lawful wife. The father was present and signed. The godfather was Alexis Laframboise; and the godmother josette adhemar, his wife, who signed with us.

GABRIEL RICHARD, priest.

JAC VASSEUR; ALEXIS LAFRAMBOISE; A. LAFRAMBOISE.

August 15, 1799, by us, the undersigned priest, the ceremonies of Baptism were supplied to Louis, privately baptized by Louis duquet, born June 15, 1790, of jacques Vasseur and of Madeleine, an Outawas, his lawful wife. The Godfather was Nicolas freraut; and the godmother josette Poitras, who signed with us.

GABRIEL RICHARD, priest.

NICOL FREREAU; JAC VASSEUR.

August 15, 1799, by us the undersigned priest, the ceremonies of Baptism were supplied to Genevieve, privately baptized by Laurent Bertrand, born July 2, 1792, of jacques Vasseur and of Madeleine, an Outawa, his lawful wife. The father was present and signed with us. The godfather was Antoine Adhemar St Martin; and the godmother Genevieve Blondeau, his wife, who signed with us.

GABRIEL RICHARD, priest.

JAC VASSEUR; BD. ADHEMAR; ADHEMAR ST MARTIN

August 18, 1799, by us the undersigned priest, was baptized Jean Baptiste, ten years old, born of the late Charles Agacouchin of the potowatowmis nation, and of Marguerite of the Outawas nation, the mother being present. The Godfather was Michel La croix; and the godmother marianne Cown, who signed with us.

GABRIEL RICHARD, priest.

NANCY COWN; M. LACROIX.

August 18, 1799, by us the undersigned priest, the ceremonies of Baptism were supplied to Marie Anne,[56] about nine years old, privately baptized by jean Baptiste La Douceur, born of Pierre La Salière and of Therese of the Outawas nation, married before witnesses at St Joseph, the mother being pres-

---

[56] Marienne Lasalière, daughter of Thérèse Marcot Lasalière-Schindler, became the wife of Henry Monroe Fisher of Prairie du Chien, and mother of Mrs. Henry S. Baird, an early settler at Green Bay.—ED.

ent. The Godfather was jacques Giason; and the godmother Angelique Adhemar, who signed with us.

GABRIEL RICHARD, priest.

ANGELIQUE ADHEMAR; J. GIASSON.

August 18, 1799, by us the undersigned priest, the ceremonies of baptism were supplied to Louis joseph, fourteen months old, privately baptized by Charles Chandonnet, born of Louis of the Potowatowmis nation and of Marguerite of the Outawas nation, the mother being present. The Godfather was Jean Baptiste Le Moine; and the godmother Josette Adhemar, wife of Alexis Laframboise, who signed with us.

GABRIEL RICHARD, priest.

J. B^{te} LIMOINE; A. LAFRAMBOISE.

September 23, 1799, by us the undersigned priest, was baptized Antoine of the nation of the Mandanes[57]—in the service of Charles Langlade, who signed with us—about twenty years old. The Godfather was jacques Giasson; and the godmother signed with us. * * *

GABRIEL RICHARD.

A. LAFRAMBOISE; CHARLES LANGLADE; J. GIASSON.

January 19, 1800, by us the Undersigned, one of the justices of the peace of the United States, was privately baptized Marie Louise of the Saulteux nation.[58] The godfather was Sieur f^r Catin; and the godmother Geneviève Plessey, wife of M$^{r.}$ Bourdon. The godmother signed with us in the presence of the undersigned witnesses.

ADEHEMAR ST MARTIN J. P.

J. GIASSON, witness; GENEVIEVE PLAISSEE; ALEXIS LAFRAMBOISE, witness.

---

[57] For the Mandan Indians, see *Wis. Hist. Colls.*, xviii, p. 450, note 72. This is probably the earliest recorded baptism of any of that nation.—ED.

[58] Married the same day to Louis Hamelin; *Ibid.*, p. 503.—ED.

Mackinac Baptisms

March 21, 1800, by me the Under signed, was privately baptized Marie, born yesterday evening of the lawful Marriage of sieur alexis Laframboise and of Dame Joseph Adhemar, In the presence of adhemar St martin and of the said Sieur Laframboise, who signed with me. * * *

ADHEMAR ST MARTIN.

ALEXIS LAFRAMBOISE; J. GIASSON.

April 20, 1800, I, the undersigned, one of the justices of the Peace of the United States privately baptized angelique, an adult woman of the Sauteux nation.[59] The Godfather was M^r· jacques Giasson; and the godmother Mme· Mitchell, who signed with us. * * *

ADHEMAR ST MARTIN J. P.

J. GIASSON; MAD^{me} MITCHELL her mark +.

October 21, 1800, I the Undersigned, one of the justices of the Peace, privately baptized Charles, son of Charles Maillet, issue of his lawful Marriage with Elizabeth McDonald,[60] born this day about one o'clock in the afternoon. * * *

ADHEMAR ST MARTIN J. P.

October 21, 1800, I the undersigned, one of the Justices of the Peace of the United States, privately baptized a natural daughter born of M^r· Wheley and of Genevieve McDonald. * * *

ADHEMAR ST MARTIN, J. P.

October 11, 1801, I the undersigned, one of the justices of the peace of the United States, privately baptized a boy, the natural ·son of Simon Champagne and of a woman savage of the Sehiouse nation, born yesterday about six o'clock in the evening. * * *

ADHEMAR ST MARTIN J. P.

---

[59] Became the wife of Jacques Chauvin; *Ibid.*, p. 504.—ED.
[60] For their marriage entry see *Ibid.*, p. 502.—ED.

June 9, 1804, we the Undersigned Roman Catholic priest and missionary, Baptized conditionally joseph, about five years old, and born of jean Baptiste flamand and of a woman Savage called Marie. The father was present. The godfather was joseph Letard; and the godmother Louise Vasseur, who declared that they could not sign their names, when thereunto requested.

J. DILHET, miss. priest.[61]

June 12, 1804, we, the undersigned, supplied the ceremonies of baptism to hubert Solomon—son of Guillaume Solomon[62] and of a woman savage who are not married—born December 5, 1800, and privately baptized the same day. The godfather was hubert Lacroix; and the godmother Louise Dubois. The father being present, all of whom signed with us.

DILHET, miss. priest.

WILLIAM SOLOMONS; J. H. LACROIX.

June 13, 1804, we, the undersigned, baptized conditionally, joseph, born March 20, 1802, of joseph Gauthier dit Caron and of Louise Vasseur, married according to the law of the state.[63] The father who was present, was unable to sign his name. The godfather was Patrice adhemar; and the godmother josephe adhemar, who signed with us.

J. DILHET, miss. priest.

P. ADHEMAR; JOSEHPTE ADHEMAR LAFRAMBOISE.

---

[61] For a brief biography of this priest see *Ibid.*, p. 506, note 43.—ED.

[62] William Solomon was the son of Ezekiel, for whom see *Ibid.*, p. 254, note 50. He afterwards married a daughter of John Johnston of Sault Ste. Marie, by whom he had ten children. William Solomon was government interpreter for the British during the War of 1812-15; at its close he removed to Drummond Island, and thence in 1828 to Penetanguishene, Ontario. His youngest son Louis, was living at the latter place in 1900. See Ontario Hist. Soc., *Papers and Records*, iii, pp. 126–137.—ED.

[63] For their civil marriage, see *Wis. Hist. Colls.*, xviii, p. 504; July 1, 1804, they had the religious ceremony performed by Dilhet.—ED.

Mackinac Baptisms

June 16, 1804, we the undersigned priest, miss^y at Michilimakina, supplied the ceremonies of baptism to Marie Marguerite, daughter of Alexis Laframboise and of joseph adhemar, about five years old. She was privately baptized after her birth. Her godfather was Gabriel Coté the younger; and the godmother Marguerite adhemar, the mother being present; who all signed with us.

J. DILHET, miss. priest.

JOSETTE ADHEMAR; GAB. COTTÉ; MARGUERITE ADHEMAR.

On the same day and at the same time we, the undersigned, Baptized according to the rite of the holy Roman Church, Mathilde, born August 28, of the previous year of Benjamin Lockwood and of Marianne Pelletier. The Godfather was jacques Giasson; and the godmother josephe adhemar, the father and mother being present; who signed with us.

J. DILHET.

MARIAN LOCKWOOD; B. LOCKWOOD; J. GIASSON.

June 17, 1804, we the undersigned priest, miss. at Michilimakina, supplied the ceremonies of baptism to Marie, born April 18, of the previous year of joseph Gautier dit Caron and of Louise Vasseur, the father being present. The godfather was pierre thyerri; and the godmother Marie Angelique adhemar, who signed with us.

DILHET, miss. priest.

P. THIERRY; MARGUERITE ADHEMAR.

June 17, 1804, we, the Undersigned priest, miss. at Michilimakina, supplied the ceremonies of baptism to Agathe, born May 16, 1802 of Daniel Bourassa and of Marguerite Bertrand, married, the father and mother being present. The godfather was Augustin hamelin; and the godmother Agathe Dubois, who signed with us.

J. DILHET, priest.

D. SOLOMON; DL. BOURASSA; AUGT HAMELIN.

June 17, 1804, we the undersigned, at Mikilimakina, baptized conditionally Charles Michel, born October 10, 1801, of Simon Champagne and of a woman savage. The father was present. The godfather was Charles marley; and the godmother josephe Vaillancour, who signed or declared that they could not sign their names.

J. Dilhet, miss. priest.

On the same day and in the same year, 1804, we, the undersigned, Baptized conditionally Marguerite Louise, born October 6, 1803, of Simon Champagne and of a woman savage. The father was present. The godfather was pierre Lacroix; and the godmother Louise Vasseur, who declared that they could not sign their names.

J. Dilhet, miss. priest.

June 17, 1804, we, the undersigned, baptized conditionally Jean Baptiste,[64] four years old, born of Jean Baptiste Laborde dit Sangrais [Sans Regret] and of marguerite machard. The father and mother were present. The godfather was jean baptiste Toussaint pothier; and the godmother angelique adhemar who signed with us.

J. Dilhet, miss. priest.

T. Pothier; Angelique Adhemar; J. Bte la Borde.

On the same day, in the same year and at the same hour, we, the Undersigned, Baptized conditionally, Elizabeth, three years old on June 4, born of jean Baptiste Laborde Sangrais and of Marguerite Machard, both present. The godfather was Monsieur hubert Lacroix; and the godmother Louise Dubois, who signed with us.

J. Dilhet, miss. priest.

J. H. Lacroix; D. Solomon; J. B^t la Borde.

---

[64] Jean Baptiste Laborde afterwards became a resident of Green Bay, where he had a farm on the southwest side of Fox River.—Ed.

Mackinac Baptisms

On the same day and in the same year, we, the Undersigned, Baptized Catherine, born on May 12 previous, of jean Baptiste Laborde Sangrais and of Marguerite Machard, both present. The godfather was Antoine Duprés; and the godmother magdaleine mongolpine, who signed or declared that they could not sign their names.

J. Dilhet, miss. priest.

Antoine Dupré; J. B^{te} la Borde.

June 19, 1804, we the undersigned, parish priest and miss. at Michilimakina, baptized conditionally pierre, born February 10, 1802, of pierre La Croix and of Marie Mongolpine, married.[65] The father and mother were present. The godfather was André La Chaine; and the godmother, josephe Vaillancourt, who declared that they could not sign their names when thereunto requested.

J. Dilhet, missionary priest.

On the same day, in the same year and at the same hour, we the undersigned priest at Michilimakina, baptized conditionally André, born November 28, 1803, of pierre La Croix and of Marie Mongolpine, married. The father and mother were present. The godfather was pierre thieri; and the godmother, josephe adhemar who signed with us.

J. Dilhet, miss. priest.

P. thierry; Josette Adhemar.

On the same day and in the same year, 1804, we, the undersigned priest, missionary at Michilimakina, baptized conditionally, Magdelaine, born April 16, 1800, of pierre Lacroix and of Marie Mongolpine, married. The father and mother were present. The godfather was Isidore Lacroix; and the

---

[65] For their marriage record, see *Wis. Hist. Colls.*, xviii, p. 502.—Ed.

godmother Magdaleine Mongolpine, who signed or declared that they could not sign, when thereunto requested.

J. DILHET, miss. priest.
ISIDORE LACROIX.

June 20, 1804, we the Undersigned priest, missionary at Michilimakina, Baptized According to the rite of the holy Roman Church our mother, jacques, about seven years old, born of joseph Mercier and of a Sioux woman. The godfather was jacques giasson; and the godmother Marguerite Adhemar, the father being present; who signed with us.

J. DILHET, miss. priest.
J. GIASSON; MARGUERITE ADHEMAR; JOSEPH MERCIER.

On the same day, and in the same year, we, the undersigned missionary priest, baptized According to the rite of the holy Roman Church our mother, marie angelique, about five years old, born of joseph mercier and of a Sioux woman. The father was present. The godfather was Etienne Lamorandiere; and the godmother marie angelique adhemar, who signed with us.

J. DILHET, miss. priest.
ETIENNE LAMORANDIERE; ANGELIQUE ADHEMAR; JOSEPH MERCIER.

June 20, 1804, we, the Undersigned parish priest and missionary at Michilimakina, baptized conditionally Jean Baptiste, born March 15, 1803, of Louis Chevalier and of a Sauteux woman. The father was present. The godfather was isidore Lacroix; and the godmother Marguerite Bourassa, who signed with us.

J. DILHET, missionary priest.
MARGUERITE BORASSA; ISIDORE LACROIX.

On the same day and in the same year, we, the Undersigned, baptized, Archange, born May 15, 1800, of Louis Chevalier and of a Sauteux woman. Her father was present. The godfather was jean Baptiste Le Moine; and the godmother Archange Bourassa, all of whom signed with us.

          J. DILHET, miss. priest.
ARCHANGE BOURASSA; J. B^{te} LAMOINE.

June 23, 1804, we the Undersigned priest, missionary at Michilimakina, supplied the ceremonies of Baptism to Alexandre, fifteen years old, privately baptized two years ago, born of pierre Laurent and of a woman Savage. The father was present. The godfather was Nöel Rocheblave; and the godmother Marguerite Adhemar, who signed with us.

          J. DILHET, missionary priest.
N. ROCHEBLAVE;[66] MARGUERITE ADHEMAR.

June 24, 1804, we the Undersigned priest, missionary at michilimakina, Baptized conditionally Michel, about six years old, born of michel Detrainville and of a woman Savage. The father was present. The godfather was Patrice adhemar; and the godmother Louise Dubois, who signed with us.

          J. DILHET, missionary priest.
P. ADHEMAR; D. SOLOMON.

On the same day, and in the same year, we the Undersigned priest, missionary at michilimakina, Baptized conditionally julie Nadau, about six years old, born of René Nadau and of a woman Savage. The father was present. The godfather was andré Lachaine; and the godmother Louise Dubois, who signed with us.

          J. DILHET, missionary priest.
RENÉ NADEAU; DU SOLOMON.

---

[66] On this trader see *Ibid.*, p. 462, note 84.—ED.

On the same day and in the same year, we the Undersigned priest, missionary at michilimakina, baptized according to the rite of the Holy Roman Church our mother, joseph Numainville, born the day before yesterday of jean Baptiste Numainville and of a woman Savage. The father was present. The godfather was joseph Ricard; and the godmother Marie taillefer, who declared that they could not sign their names when thereunto requested.

       J. DILHET, missionary priest.

On the same day and in the same year, we the undersigned priest, missionary at michilimakina, Baptized according to the rite of the Holy Roman Church our mother, Marie, about four years old, born of jean Baptiste numainville and of a woman Savage. The father was present. The godfather was francois Laventure; and the godmother Marie mongolpin, who declared that they could not sign their names when thereunto requested.

       J. DILHET, missionary priest.

June 29, 1804, we the undersigned priest, missionary at michilimakina, Baptized conditionally Paul, born on January 16 previous of jacques jauvan and of angelique Roi.[67] The father was present. The godfather was pierre Lacroix; and the godmother genevieve Blondeau, who signed with us.

       J. DILHET, missionary priest.

AD BLONDEAU ADHEMAR.

June 29, 1804, we the undersigned priest, missionary at michilimakina, Baptized Conditionally magdeleine, born on April 1, 1802, of jacques jauvan and of Angelique Roi. The father was present. The godfather was joseph Couzineau; and the godmother Josephe Vaillancourt, who declared that they could not sign their names when thereunto requested.

       J. DILHET, missionary priest.

---

[67] They were later married by the same priest; *Ibid.*, p. 508.—ED.

On the same day and in the same year, we the undersigned priest, missionary at michilimakina, Baptized Conditionally marguerite,[68] born on December 26, 1802. The godfather was Ezechiel Solomon; and the godmother Louise Dubois, who signed with us.

J. DILHET, missionary priest.

EZECHIEL SOLOMON JR.; D. SOLOMON.

June 30, 1804, we the Undersigned priest, missionary at michilimakina, Baptized Conditionally Charles, born August 10, 1802, of Antoine martin and of a Sauteux woman. The father was present. The godfather was Pierre Gausselin; and the godmother Magdelaine mongolpine, who declared that they could not sign their names when thereunto requested.

J. DILHET, missionary priest.

July 7, 1804, we the undersigned priest, missionary at Michilimakina, Baptized Conditionally Angelique Roi, twenty years old, daughter of joseph Roi and of Marguerite, a folle avoine.[69] The godfather was hubert Lacroix; and the godmother Louise Dubois, who signed with us.

J. DILHET, miss. priest.

H. LACROIX; D. SOLOMON.

On the same day and in the same year, we the undersigned missionary priest, Baptized Conditionally Charlotte Roi, nineteen years old, daughter of joseph Roi and of Marguerite, a

---

[68] On the margin is written "Marguerite Solomon," which is a probable indication of the identity of this person.—ED.

[69] This was a well-known Green Bay family, the father Joseph Roy having settled there before 1785. He was still living in 1818, and by his marriage with the Menominee woman Marguerite had two sons and four daughters. One son, François, settled at the Fox-Wisconsin portage, and became well-known to early Wisconsin travellers. This daughter Angelique was married nine days later to Jacques Jauvan; see *Wis. Hist. Colls.*, xviii, p. 508.—ED.

folle avoine. The godfather was jean Coursol; and the godmother Louise Dubois, who signed with us.

J. DILHET, miss. priest.

JEAN COURSOLL; D. SOLOMON.

July 8, 1804, we the Undersigned priest, missionary at Michilimakina, Supplied the ceremonies of baptism to ignace chichet, privately baptized a year ago, eight years old, and born of jacques plomondone and of a woman Savage. The godfather was Charles Chadonnet; and the godmother Mariane la Valière [Salière]. The adopted father was present. They signed with us.

J. DILHET, miss. priest.

C. CHANDONNETT; IGNACE CHICHETT.

July 9, 1804, we, the undersigned priest, missionary at michilimakinac, Baptized Conditionally Elizabeth, eight years old, born of George Cowens and of Marianne Kinonchamut, an outaouais. The father was present. The godfather was jacques portier [Porlier];[70] and the godmother Angelique Adhemar, all of whom signed with us.

J. DILHET, missionary priest.

JCQ. PORTIERE; GEO. COWN.

On the same day and in the same year, we, the undersigned priest, missionary at michilimakina, supplied the Ceremonies of Baptism to Marie, two years old, born of augustin Bonneterre and of a woman Savage. The father was present. The godfather was Patrice adhemar; and the godmother Marianne Cowen, who signed with us.

J. DILHET, miss. priest.

ANN. COWN; P. ADHEMAR; WILLIAM J. PICHET.

---

[70] For this well-known resident of early Wisconsin see *Ibid.*, p. 462, and his letters, *post.*—ED.

Mackinac Baptisms

On the same day and in the same year, we, the undersigned, Baptized julie, born thirteen days ago of augustin Bonneterre and of a woman Savage. The father was present. The godfather was jean Baptiste Barthelot; and the godmother josephe adhemar, who signed with us.

J. Dilhet, miss. priest.

Josette Adhemar; J. B^{e.} Berthelot; Piere lacrox; J. Pichet.

July 14, 1804, we the Undersigned priest, missionary at michilimakina, Baptized Marguerite Kodeckoi (le soleil) daughter of manitou Koursseur of the Sauteux nation, who was sufficiently instructed and preparing to be married, according to the rite of the Church, to jean Baptiste Bertrand.[71] The godfather was Charles Chandonnet; and the godmother josephe adhemar, who signed with us.

J. Dilhet, miss. priest.

Josette Adhemar; C. Chandonnette; Jean Baptiste Bertrand.

On the same day and in the same year, we the undersigned priest, missionary at michilimakina, Baptized Conditionally Marie Angelique gravelle,[72] seventeen years old, daughter of joseph gravelle, deceased, and of josette Saint Raisin. The godfather was Charles Chandonnet; and the godmother Marie Angelique Adhemar, who signed with us.

J. Dilhet, miss. priest.

Angelique adhemar; C. Chandonnett.

July 14, 1804, we, the undersigned priest at michilimakina, Baptized conditionally Marie Archange, fifteen months old, daughter of françois grignon[73] and of Marie Angelique gravelle.

---

[71] Their marriage record is found in *Ibid.*, p. 510.—Ed.

[72] Married two days later to François Grignon, *Ibid.*, p. 509.—Ed.

[73] Not of the Grignon family of Green Bay; probably a nephew of the elder Pierre Grignon.—Ed.

The godfather was jean Baptiste maranda; and the godmother Charlotte Roi, who signed with us.

           J. DILHET, miss. priest.
 B. MARANDA.

On the same day and in the same year, we the undersigned priest, missionary at michilimakina, Baptized conditionally Charlotte, about three years old, born of Noel Rocheblave and of an otawas woman. The godfather was pierre thierry; and the godmother Anne Cowen, who signed with us.

              J. DILHET.
 ANNE COWN; THIERRY.

July 16, 1804, we, the undersigned priest, missionary at michilimakina, Baptized conditionally Thomas, son of Stephen Hogan and of josette hamelin, about three years old. The godfather was michel Lacroix; and the godmother anne Cowen, who signed with us.

           J. DILHET, miss. priest.
 M. LACROIX; NANCY COWN.

On the same day and in the same year, we, the undersigned priest, missionary at mikilimakina supplied the ceremonies of Baptism to josette,[74] about forty years old, daughter of an unknown father and mother. The godfather was Noel Rocheblave; and the godmother josette adhemar, who signed with us.

              J. DILHET.
 JOSETTE ADHEMAR; N. ROCHEBLAVE.

On the same day and in the same year, we the undersigned missionary priest, Baptized Louis, four months and a half old, born of isidore Lacroix and of a woman savage. The godfather

---

[74] Probably the mother of Marie Taillefer, married June 30, 1804; *Wis. Hist. Colls.*, xviii, p. 506.—ED.

was michel Lacroix; and the godmother marianne La Saliere, who signed with us.

          J. DILHET, miss. priest.
M. LACROIX.

July 16, 1804, we the undersigned priest, missionary at michilimakina, Baptized françois, about three years old, of an unknown father and of a woman Savage. The godfather was jean Baptiste Le moine; and the godmother magdelene maiculpin.

          J. DILHET, priest.
J. B^e LEMOINE.

On the same day and in the same year we, the undersigned priest, Baptized according to the rite of the Holy Roman Church our mother, jean Baptiste, son of Letourneau, son of kiminoucam (La pluie) and of ouassimigueso (La porcelaine claire) an Otawais woman, about twenty years old, sufficiently instructed. The godfather was Jean Baptiste Bertrand; and the godmother Louise Vasseur, who signed with us.

          J. DILHET, priest.
JEAN BAPTIS BERTRAND.

July 18, 1804, we the undersigned priest, missionary at michilimakina, supplied the ceremonies of Baptism to Marie angelique Vaudet, eight years old, born of hyppolite Vaudet and of a Sauteux woman. The godfather was pierre jolifour; and the godmother Marie maiculpin who declared that they could not sign their names when thereunto requested.

          J. DILHET, priest.

On the same day and in the same year, we the undersigned priest at michilimakina, baptized conditionally andré, two years old, born of jacques vasseur and of madeleine ouiouiskoin (vessie), married.[75] The father was present. The godfather was François grignon; and the godmother angelique Roi, who signed with us or declared that they could not sign their names when thereunto requested.

J. DILHET, priest.

JAC VASSEUER.

On the same day and in the same year, we, the undersigned missionary priest, Baptized conditionally jean Baptiste, three years old, born of jacques vaisseur and of Magdeleine ouiouiskoin, married. The father was present. The godfather was joseph Caron; and the godmother Louise vasseur, who signed or declared that they could not sign their names when thereunto requested.

J. DILHET, priest.

JAC VASSEUER.

Marie M^cculpin, born November 2, 1819, of Guillaume Mc Gulpin and of Madelene Bourassa, married by the justice of the peace,[76] was Baptized conditionally by us the undersigned, parish priest of Ste Anne du Detroit, on August 4, 1821.[77] The father and mother were present. The godfather was Alexandre Bourassa; and the godmother Marie Judith Bourassa, who signed with us.

GABRIEL RICHARD, parish priest of Ste Anne.

ALEXANDRE BOURASSA; MARIE BOURASSA.

---

[75] For their marriage see *Ibid.*, p. 503. André was younger than the children there legitimized. The Vasseur family removed to Drummond Island, and later to Penetanguishene. Andrew was a land-owner at the latter place, and died at Bruce Mines. See Ontario Historical Society *Papers*, iii, p. 165.—ED.

[76] Their religious marriage occurred a few days later; *Wis. Hist. Colls.*, xviii, p. 512. The names and dates of the births of the children do not correspond with this baptismal register.—ED.

[77] No baptisms are entered in the register between 1804 and 1821, possibly because no priest visited the island in that long interval; although the entry in *Ibid.*, p. 512, would indicate the presence of a priest at Mackinac in 1818.—ED.

Ursule M^{c}culpin, born April 4, 1821, of Guillaume Mc Culpin and of Magdelene Bourassa, married by the justice of the peace, was baptized by us the undersigned, parish priest of .Ste Anne, August 4, of the same year. The godfather was Eloy Bourassa; and the godmother Marie, his wife, who declared that she could not sign her name.

    GABRIEL RICHARD, parish priest of Ste Anne.

Marie Bourassa, born April 30, 1821, of the lawful marriage of Eloy Bourassa and of Marie Atten, was baptized by us, the undersigned priest, August 4 of the same year. The godfather was Antoine Dequindre; and the godmother Archange Bourassa.

    GABRIEL RICHARD, parish priest of Ste Anne.
ANTOINE DEQUINDRE.

Eusèbe Bourassa, born September 3, 1819, of Eloy Bourassa and of a woman Savage, was Baptized conditionally by us the undersigned parish priest of Ste Anne du Detroit, on August 4, 1821. The father was present and signed with us as did also the godfather Antoine Dequindre; and the godmother Archange Bourassa.

    GABRIEL RICHARD, parish priest of Ste Anne.
ANTOINE DEQUINDRE; ARCHANGE BOURASSA.

Therese Bourassa, born March 26, 1805, of the lawful marriage of Daniel Bourassa and of Marguerite Bertrand, was Baptized conditionally by us the undersigned, parish priest of Ste Anne du Detroit, on August 4, 1821, the mother being present. The godfather was Antoine Dequindre, who signed with us; and the godmother Madeleine la framboise who declared that she could not sign her name.

    GABRIEL RICHARD, parish priest.
ANTOINE DEQUINDRE.

Amable Bourassa, born on May 20, 1809, of the lawful marriage of Daniel Bourassa and of Marguerite Bertrand, was Baptized conditionally by us, the undersigned parish priest of Ste Anne du Détroit, August 4, 1821, the mother being present. The godfather was Alexandre Bourassa, who signed with us; and the godmother Therese Bourassa, the sister of the Baptized boy who declared that she could not sign her name.

     GABRIEL RICHARD, parish priest of Ste Anne.
ALEXANDRE BOURASSA.

 Lucille Tannor, born July 17, 1820, of John Tannor[78] and of a woman savage, was Baptized conditionally by us the undersigned, parish Priest of Ste Anne du Detroit, August 4, 1821. The godfather was Etienne Dubois; and the godmother Marie Anne Fisher, who signed with us.

        GABRIEL RICHARD, priest.
MARIANNE FISHER.

 Louis Carboneau, born April 13, 1814, of Louis Carboneau dit Provençal[79] and of a woman Savage of the Sioux nation,

---

 [78] John Tanner, known as the "white Indian," was captured at his father's home in Kentucky by Saginaw Chippewa when a boy of nine years of age. Later he lived on Red River of the North, and after nearly thirty years of absence returned to American settlements to visit his white kindred, bringing with him to civilization his half-breed children. He reached Mackinac in 1820, and persuaded Madame George Schindler to adopt his infant child Lucy, or Lucille, into her own family. She was at first privately baptized—see *Wis. Hist. Colls.*, xiv, p. 52—and next year by the priest. She was finally drowned by the foundering of a schooner in Lake Michigan. After two or three years among the settlements, her father returned to Sault Ste. Marie, where he was employed as interpreter until his disappearance in 1846. He was accused of the murder of James Schoolcraft, but the later confession of an army officer proved Tanner's innocence of this crime. Tanner's case attracted much attention and his life was written by Edwin James, *Narrative of the Captivity and Adventures of John Tanner* (New York, 1830). A good recent sketch of his life and character is found in *Mich. Pion. and Hist. Colls.*, xxii, pp. 246–254.—ED.

 [79] One of this family was an early inhabitant of Green Bay; *Wis. Hist. Colls.*, ix, 241, 242, 259; x, 138, 139.—ED.

was Baptized conditionally by us the undersigned, parish priest of Ste Anne du Détroit, August 4, 1821. The godfather was Etienne Dubois; and the godmother Marie Anne fisher, who signed with us.

GABRIEL RICHARD, priest.

MARY A. FISHER.

Antoine Carboneau, born December 12, 1816, of Louis Carboneau dit Provençal and of a woman Savage of the Sioux nation, was Baptized conditionally by us the undersigned, parish Priest of Ste Anne du Detroit, August 4, 1821. The godfather was Etienne Dubois; and the godmother Marie Anne Fisher, who signed with us.

GABRIEL RICHARD, priest.

MARY A. FISHER.

Archange Carboneau, born October 29, 1818, of Louis Carboneau dit Provençal and of a woman Savage of the Sioux nation, was Baptized conditionally by us the undersigned, parish Priest of Ste Anne du Detroit, August 4, 1821, the father being present. The godfather was Etienne Dubois; and the godmother Mary Anne Fisher, who signed with us.

GABRIEL RICHARD, priest.

MARY A. FISHER.

Joseph Carboneau, born December 22, 1819, of Louis Carboneau dit Provençal and of a woman Savage of the Sioux nation, was Baptized conditionally by us, the undersigned parish Priest of Ste Anne du Detroit, on August 4, 1821, the father being present. The godfather was Etienne Dubois; and the godmother Marie Anne Fisher, who signed with us.

GABRIEL RICHARD, priest.

MARY A. FISHER.

Hariette, born April 26, 1820, of Marie Vaillancourt, known under the name of Madame Steven Hogan (dead or absent)[80]

---

[80] For this marriage see *Id.*, xviii, p. 505.—ED.

and of an unknown father, was Baptized conditionally by us, the undersigned parish priest of Ste Anne du Detroit, August 6, 1821. The godfather was Clement Hudon; and the godmother Marguerite Basile, wife of Fr. Albert, who signed with us.

GABRIEL RICHARD, parish priest.
MARRETT BASILL; FRANÇOIS ALBERT.

Alexandre Fraser, born January 22, 1820, of Alexandre Fraser[81] and of Ursul leblanc who say they were married by Messire Cerinaud, parish priest of Kingston in Upper Canada, was Baptized conditionally by us, parish priest of Ste Anne du Detroit, undersigned, August 6, 1821, the father and mother being present. The godfather was Joseph Gueret, who declared that he could not sign his name when thereunto requested; and the godmother Marie Anne fisher who signed with us.

GABRIEL RICHARD, priest.
MARY ANNE FISHER.

Marie Bourassa, born May 22, 1821, of Dominique Rousseau and of Marguerite Champagne, privately baptized by Etienne Dubois, received the solemn ceremonies of Baptism from us, the undersigned parish priest of Ste Anne du Detroit, August 6, 1821, the father and mother being present. The godfather was françois Albert; and the godmother Marguerite Basil who signed.

GABRIEL RICHARD, priest.
MARGUERITTE BASILLE; FRANÇOIS ALBERT.

Sophie Rousseau, born April, 1821, of Dominique Rousseau and of a woman Savage, was Baptized by us, the undersigned

---

[81] Alexander Fraser, serving as a clerk in the North West Company, was on the Columbia in 1814, and with Semple at Red River in 1816. He probably was a relative of Simon Fraser, discoverer of the river bearing his name, whose home was in the neighborhood of Kingston. Alexander Fraser is said to have been killed in a quarrel in 1829, at Paris.—ED.

parish priest of Ste Anne du Detroit, on August 6, of the same year, the father and mother being present. The godfather was Charles Rousseau; and the godmother Marie Anne Fisher, who signed with us.

GABRIEL RICHARD, priest.

MARIE ANNE FISHER; CHARLES ROUSSEAU.

Joseph Louson, born June 10, 1820, of Joseph Louson and of Nancy Pilot, very probably not baptized and married by the civil magistrate, was baptized conditionally by us the undersigned parish Priest of Ste Anne du Detroit, the father and mother being present. The godfather was François Albert; and the godmother Marguerite Basile, his wife, who signed with us, August 6, 1821.

GABRIEL RICHARD, priest.

MARGUERITTE BASILLE; FRANÇOIS ALBERT.

Isabelle Nicole, born November 17, 1820, of Jean Nicole and of Marguerite Beaubin, not baptized and married by the civil magistrate, was Baptized conditionally by us, the undersigned parish priest of Ste Anne du Detroit, August 6, 1821, the father and mother being present. The godfather was françois Albert; and the godmother Marguerite Basile, his Wife, who signed with us.

GABRIEL RICHARD, priest.

MARETTE BASILLE; FRANÇOIS ALBERT.

Marie Anne Cowen, born May 22, 1815, of Pierre Cowen and of an Outawa woman, was Baptized conditionally by us, the undersigned parish Priest of Ste Anne du Detroit, August 6, 1821, the father and mother being present. The godfather was Dominique Rousseau; and the godmother Marie Anne Fisher, who signed with us.

GABRIEL RICHARD, priest.

DOMINIQUE ROUSSEAU.

Anne Cowen, born January 28, 1820, of pierre Cowen and of an Outawa woman, was Baptized by us, the undersigned parish priest of Ste Anne du Detroit, August 6, 1821, the father and mother being present. The godfather was joseph dechamps who declared that he could not sign his name when thereunto requested; and the godmother Agathe Gotrie who signed with us

GABRIEL RICHARD, priest.

AGATHE GATTRIS.

Amable Cowen, born August 6, 1820, of Pierre Cowen and of an Outawa woman, was baptized conditionally by us, the undersigned parish priest of Ste Anne du Detroit, August 6, 1821. The godfather was Amable Turpin; and the godmother Ursule Leblanc who declared that they could not sign their names.

GABRIEL RICHARD, priest.

Julie Mata, born March 3, 1819, of Maurice Mata and of Jeane Die, married by the civil judge, was baptized conditionally by us, the undersigned parish priest of Ste Anne du Detroit, August 6, 1821, the father and mother being present. The godfather was Jean W. Fillon; and the godmother Ursule Leblanc, wife of Alexandre fraser who declared that they could not sign their names when thereunto requested.

GABRIEL RICHARD, priest.

Josephete Bertrand, born July 2, 1819, of the lawful marriage of Jean B. Bertrand and of Marguerite Ouigouisence, was baptized conditionally by us, the undersigned parish priest of Ste Anne du Detroit, August 6, 1821, the father and mother being present. The godfather was Alexandre Bourassa, who signed with us; and the godmother Therese Bourassa who declared that she could not sign when thereunto requested.

GABRIEL RICHARD, priest.

ALEXANDRE BOURASSA.

Joseph Philippe Christy, born June 5, 1821, of Philippe Christy and of Juli Moses, married by the minister of the Anglican Church, was Baptized conditionally by us, the undersigned parish priest of Ste Anne du Detroit, August 6, of the same year. The father and mother were present. The godfather was Joseph Lemoine, who signed with us; and the godmother Charlotte parant, wife of Antoine La Branche who declared that she could not sign her name when thereunto requested.

GABRIEL RICHARD, priest.

JOSEPH LEMOINE.

Elisabeth Therêse Fisher,[82] born April 24, 1810, of Henri Monroe Fisher[83] and of Marie Anne Lasallière, married by the civil judge, privately baptized by Jean Marie Auger, received the solemn ceremonies of Baptism from us, the undersigned

---

[82] She became Mrs. Henry S. Baird, one of the early settlers of Green Bay. For her reminiscences of early life at Mackinac, see *Wis. Hist. Colls.*, xiv, pp. 17-64.—ED.

[83] Henry Monroe Fisher was born of Scotch parentage, somewhere near Lake Champlain, probably upon the Canadian border, although often spoken of as an American. He was educated at Montreal, where he became acquainted with the Todds, and early embarked in the fur-trade, coming West about 1790. At first employed by the North West Company, he later set up an independent trade with headquarters at Prairie du Chien. There he prospered, and upon the organization of Indiana Territory was appointed Aug. 19, 1802, a captain of militia, and on Nov. 26, 1803, as justice of the peace. Lieut. Zebulon M. Pike, on his visit to Prairie du Chien in 1805, speaks in terms of praise of Fisher's ability and hospitality. In 1809 Fisher married for his second wife Marienne Lasalière of Mackinac. When their daughter, whose baptism is here recorded, was two years old, Mrs. Fisher returned to Mackinac for a visit; but the War of 1812-15 breaking out, Fisher was unwilling to take part against the Americans, so he retired to the Red River country and entered the Hudson Bay Company, not returning to Prairie du Chien for over ten years. In 1827 he died at this place, from the effects of fever. He was a man of great physical strength and comeliness, and acquired a powerful influence over the Indians.—ED.

parish priest of Ste Anne du Detroit, August 9, 1821, the mother being present. The godfather was Joseph Rollet;[84] and the godmother Madeline la framboise, who declared that she could not sign her name when thereunto requested. The godfather signed and so did the person Baptized.

GABRIEL RICHARD, priest.

ELIZABETH THARESA FISHER; JOSEPH ROLETTE.

Marguerite Choret, born April 16, 1805, of Simon Choret and of Marguerite, an Otchipwas woman, was Baptized conditionally by us, the undersigned parish priest of Ste Anne du Detroit, August 9, 1821. The godfather was Etienne Dubois; and the godmother Mary Anne Fisher, who signed with us.

GABRIEL RICHARD, priest.

ETIENNE DUBOIS; MARY ANNE FISHER.

Josephte Choret, born March 18, 1807, of Simon Choret and of Marguerite, an Otchipwas woman, was Baptized conditionally by us, the undersigned parish priest of Ste Anne du Detroit, August 9, 1821. The godfather was Etienne Dubois; and the godmother Marie Anne Fisher, who signed with us.

GABRIEL RICHARD, priest.

ETIENNE DUBOIS; MARY ANNE FISHER.

---

[84] Joseph Rolette was the most prominent citizen of Prairie du Chien. Born in Canada in 1781, he was educated for the priesthood but preferred the Indian trade. He came to Prairie du Chien about 1806, where he was at first agent for Murdock Cameron. During the War of 1812–15, he sided with the British, assisting at the capture of Mackinac in 1812, and that of Fort Shelby in 1814. With the return of the Americans, Rolette found himself, because of his pro-British activity, out of favor with the officers at Fort Crawford, but was reinstated through the efforts of John C. Calhoun. Afterwards (1823), he became a naturalized American citizen. He had large business interests and was quite progressive, being a partner in the first sawmilling enterprise in western Wisconsin. Rolette had in 1819 married a half-sister of Elizabeth Thérèse Fisher. Mrs. Baird speaks of him as her godfather in *Wis. Hist. Colls.*, xv. pp, 219, 220. He died at Prairie du Chien in 1842.—ED.

Mackinac Baptisms

Sophie Bailly, born March [blank in MS.], 1807, of Joseph Bailly and of Angelique McGulpin, was Baptized conditionally by us, the undersigned priest, August 9, 1821. The godfather was Eloy Bourassa; and the godmother Marie Judith Bourassa, who signed with us.

GABRIEL RICHARD, priest.

MARIE JUDITH BOURASSA; E. BOURASSA.

Marie Beaubien, born March 22, 1821, of Charles Beaubien and of Marie, an Otchipwas woman, privately baptized by Josephine Lagacé,[85] received the solemn ceremonies of Baptism through us, the undersigned parish priest of Ste Anne du Detroit, August 9, 1821. The godmother was Ursule Leblanc, Wife of Alexandre Fraser who declared she could not sign her name when thereunto requested.

GABRIEL RICHARD, priest.

CH. BEAUBIEN; FRANCOIS PAGET.[86]

Josephte Chevalier, born September 8, 1807, of Louis Pascal Chevalier and of Josephte, an Otchipwas woman, privately baptized by Jean B. Laborde, received the solemn ceremonies of Baptism through us, the undersigned parish priest of Ste Anne du Detroit, August 10, 1821, the father being present. The godfather was Léon Bourassa who signed with us; and the godmother Archange Bourassa who signed with us.

GABRIEL RICHARD, priest.

LEON BOURASSA; ARCHANGE BOURASSA.

---

[85] Josephine (Josephette) Legacé was an important person in both the Mackinac and Drummond Island settlements. She was tall and of commanding presence, and an accomplished violinist, much in demand for her music at all balls and parties. She married Louis Deschenaux and removed to Penetanguishene; see Ontario Hist. Soc. *Papers*, iii, p. 159.—ED.

[86] The godfather's name is omitted in the record; probably this is his signature.—ED.

Elizabeth Vaillancourt, born December 27, 1808, of the lawful marriage of Joseph Vaillancourt and of Marie Bourgouin, privately baptized by André la chene, received the solemn ceremonies of Baptism through us, the undersigned parish priest of Ste Anne du Detroit, August 10, 1821. The father was present and signed with us. The godfather was Etienne Dubois, who signed with us; and the godmother Marie Isabelle Hogan who declared that she could not sign her name when thereunto requested.

GABRIEL RICHARD, priest.

JOSEPH VAILLANCOURT; ETIENNE DUBOIS.

Marie Judith Lusignan, born May 15, 1811, of François Lusignan and of Agathe Langlade[87] who say they were married before two witnesses at Green Bay, privately baptized by Charley Reaume,[88] received the solemn ceremonies of Baptism

---

[87] Apparently the daughter of Charles Langlade junior. His granddaughter Angelique said that one of her grandfather's daughters married and lived at Mackinac. Consult Ontario Hist. Soc. *Papers*, iii, p. 148.—ED.

[88] Charles Réaume, the well-known Green Bay justice of the peace, was born in La Prairie, opposite Montreal, and after receiving some education embarked in the fur-trade. In this he was unsuccessful, and sought the upper country to recoup his losses. He came to Green Bay in 1792, and the following winter traded on St. Croix River. Later he setted at Green Bay, and had a good farm on what was later known as Dutchman's Creek. An Illinois acquaintance recommended Réaume to Governor Harrison of Indiana Territory, as a proper person to be appointed justice of the peace in the French settlement at Green Bay, whereupon a commission to that effect was drawn Nov. 26, 1803. Acting on that commission, Réaume was the sole representative of civil authority at Green Bay until 1818, when he was commissioned associate justice by Governor Cass. Many amusing stories were told of Réaume's methods and eccentricities. His only knowledge of law appears to have been drawn from the single volume of Blackstone that constituted his library; but as he could scarcely read English, his decisions were based on the customs of the country. As magistrate he likewise officiated at all weddings

through us, the undersigned parish priest of Ste Anne du Detroit, August 10, 1821, the father being present. The godfather was William McGulpin who signed with us; and the godmother Marie Judith Bourassa who signed with us.

                    GABRIEL RICHARD, priest.
WIL. GULPIN; MARIE JUDITH BOURASSA.

Pierre Lusignan, born July 2, 1808, of François Lusignan and of Agathe Langlade who say they were married before two witnesses at Green Bay, privately baptized by Charley Reaume, received the solemn ceremonies of Baptism through us, the undersigned parish priest of Ste Anne du Detroit, August 10, 1821, the father being present. The godfather was Etienne Dubois; and the godmother Marie Anne Fisher, who signed with us.

                    GABRIEL RICHARD, priest.
ETIENNE DUBOIS; MARIANNA FISHER.

Charles Marly, born November 9, 1805, of the lawful marriage of Charles Marly and of Josephte Vaillancourt,[89] received the solemn ceremonies of Baptism through us, the undersigned parish priest of Ste Anne du Detroit, August 12, 1821. The godfather was Etienne Dubois; and the godmother Marie Anne Fisher who signed with us.

                    GABRIEL RICHARD, priest.
[E]TIENNE DUBOIS; MARIANNE FISHER.

Luc Marly, born May 2, 1807, of the lawful marriage of Charles Marly and of Josephte Vaillancourt, privately baptized by Patrice Adhemar, received the solemn ceremonies of Bap-

---

and baptisms, for which he received fixed fees. His decisions were seldom controverted, and upon the whole were generally equitable. Judge Réaume sold his farm in 1815, and not long thereafter removed to Little Kaukaulin, where he died in 1822. The Society's manuscript collections include many of Réaume's papers.—ED.

[89] For their marriage see *Wis. Hist. Colls.*, xviii, pp. 506, 511.—ED.

tism through us, the undersigned parish priest of Ste Anne du
Detroit, August 10, 1821, the father being present. The godfather was Etienne Dubois; and the godmother Marie Anne
Fisher who signed with us.

GABRIEL RICHARD, priest.

ETIENNE DUBOIS; MARIANNA FISHER.

Théotis, born November 17, 1805, of Catherine Govreau and
of François Baudoin, was baptized conditionally by us, the undersigned parish priest of Ste Anne du Detroit, August 12,
1821, the mother being present. The godfather was pierre
Crepeau; and the godmother Ursule leblanc, wife of Alexandre
Fraser, who declared that she could not sign her name when
thereunto requested.

GABRIEL RICHARD, priest.

PIERRE CREPEAUX.

Pierre, born September 19, 1818, of Catherine Govreau and
of François Baudoin, was baptized conditionally by us, the undersigned parish priest of Ste Anne du Detroit, August 12,
1821. The godfather was Jean Fillon, who signed with us;
and the godmother Ursule leblanc, wife of Alexandre fraser,
who declared that she could not sign her name.

GABRIEL RICHARD, priest.

Celeste Reed,[90] born in 1799 of N. Reed and of a woman
Savage of the Manomini nation, was baptized conditionally by
us, the undersigned parish priest of Ste Anne du Detroit,
August 13, 1821. The godfather was Pierre Cowen; and the
godmother Marie Anne Fisher, who signed with us.

GABRIEL RICHARD, priest.

PIERRE COWNE; MARIANNA FISHER.

François Cadot, born yesterday of Augustin Cadot and of
l'amainbile an otchipwas woman, was baptized by us, the under-

---

[90] Married François Paget; see *Ibid.*, p. 513.—ED

signed parish priest of Ste Anne du Detroit, August 13, 1821, the father being present.⁹¹ The godfather was Francois Paget who signed with us; and the godmother Marguerite Chovret who was unable to sign her name.

GABRIEL RICHARD, priest.

FRANÇOIS PAGET.

Louis Paquin, born December 2, 1816, of Pierre Paquin and of Marie Campbell, married by the civil judge, was baptized conditionally by us, the undersigned parish priest of Ste Anne du Detroit, August 13, 1821. The father was present. The godfather was Maurice Mata; and the godmother Ursule Leblanc, the wife of Alexandre Fraser, who declared that they could not sign their names when thereunto requested.

GABRIEL RICHARD, priest.

Catherine Paquin, born September 11, 1819, of Pierre Paquin and of Marie Campbell, married by the civil judge, was Baptized conditionally by us, the undersigned parish priest of Ste Anne du Detroit, August 13, 1821. The father was present. The godfather was Maurice Mata; and the godmother Ursule Leblanc, wife of Alexandre Fraser, who declared that they could not sign their names when thereunto requested.

GABRIEL RICHARD, priest.

---

⁹¹ Augustin Cadot, here named, was probably a son or brother of Joseph Cadot, who was interpreter at Fort St. Joseph as early as 1808, when he is mentioned by Col. William Claus on the journey of that year for the Indian Department. In 1810 he was highly commended for his conduct—see *Mich. Pion. and Hist. Colls.*, xxiii, pp. 59, 281. Joseph Cadot was lieutenant during the War of 1812-15, and at its close received a lot on Drummond Island, where he settled. Descendants removed to Penetanguishine, where they were living recently. See Ontario Historical Society *Papers*, iii, p. 152.—ED.

George Smith Dousman,[92] born September 21, 1820, of John Dousman and of Rosalie Laborde, his lawful wife, was baptized by us, the undersigned parish priest of Ste Anne du Detroit August 13, 1821. The father and mother were present. The godfather was William McGulpin; and the godmother Madeline Laframboise who declared that she could not sign her name. The godfather signed with us.

GABRIEL RICHARD, priest.

W. McGULPIN; ROSALIE DOUSMAN; JOHN DOUSMAN.

William d'Alcantura Gordon,[93] born December 6, 1820, at Drummond Island,[94] of George Gordon and of Agathe Landry, was baptized by us, the undersigned parish priest of Ste Anne du Detroit, August 13, 1821, the mother being present. The

---

[92] Removed June 14, 1836, to Milwaukee, where he was city clerk for five terms (1860–68), president of the county board (1869–72), and auditor for Milwaukee County for one term. He died in Milwaukee May 31, 1879.—ED.

[93] George Gordon was the son of a Colonel Gordon of Montreal, who was killed in the West Indies. The son entered the service of Hudson's Bay Company, and settling on Drummond Island married Agatha (Agnes) Landry. In 1825 he removed to Penetanguishene, where he built the first house on the site since called Gordon's Point. His second wife was Marguerite Langlade, great-granddaughter of Charles Langlade of Wisconsin. Gordon died at his Penetanguishene place in 1852. His eldest son, William D., whose baptism is here recorded, was lost in the woods at the age of twelve; fifteen years later his skeleton was discovered, and buried with his father's remains.—ED.

[94] When the British retired from Mackinac in 1815, after the conclusion of the Treaty of Ghent, their commandant was ordered to establish a post as near Mackinac as possible, in order to keep control of the Indian trade. Accordingly the post was built on Drummond Island, opposite the Strait of Detour, now a part of the state of Michigan, and then supposed to be within British territory. There, until 1828, a considerable establishment was maintained, consisting of a garrison, barracks, officers' quarters, and many traders' houses. See description in S. F. Cook, *Drummond Island* (Lansing, 1896). The boundary survey, in which Drummond Island was conveyed to the United States, was not concluded until 1822. The arrangements

godfather was John Dousman; and the godmother Rosalie La
Borde, his wife, who signed with us.

                                    GABRIEL RICHARD, priest.
JOHN DOUSMAN; ROSALIE DOUSMAN.

Marie Anne Clermont, born May 20, 1819, of Jeremie Clermont and of a woman Savage of the Potowatamies nation, privately baptized by J^s Crevier des Chênau,[95] was baptized conditionally by us, the undersigned parish priest of Ste Anne du Detroit, August 15, 1821, the father being present. The godfather was William McGulpin, who signed with us; and the godmother Marguerite Bertrand.

                                    GABRIEL RICHARD, priest.
W. McGULPIN.

Jean Romain, born about June 20, 1818, of a woman Savage of the Outawa nation, called Mayamo and of an unknown father, was baptized conditionally by us, the undersigned parish priest of Ste Anne du Detroit, August 16, 1821, the mother being present. The godfather was françois Paget, who signed

---

for transferring the post were dilatory, so that not until 1828 did the garrison remove to Penetanguishene, on Matchedash Bay, having for thirteen years maintained a British post on American territory, and subsidized the Indians that resorted thither. Many of the former inhabitants of Mackinac, preferring British to American affiliation, went with the garrison to Drummond Island, and there maintained a considerable connection and traffic with their former friends and neighbors at Mackinac.—ED.

[95] Joseph Crevier's name first appears in the records of the Church of the Assumption at Sandwich, opposite Detroit, in November, 1816. He was then clerical assistant. In 1825 he became priest in charge of the parish, and so continued until after 1832. He frequently officiated in Detroit. The church at Sandwich was originally the Huron mission, for which see *Wis. Hist. Colls.*, xviii, p. 32, note 48. Father Crevier is mentioned in *Ibid.*, p. 512.—ED.

with us; and the godmother Marguerite Chauret, who declared that she could not sign her name when thereunto requested.

GABRIEL RICHARD, priest.

FRANCOIS PAGET.

Charles Alexandre, born on March 15, 1818, of an Outawas woman called Abitagowinan, and of an unknown father, was baptized conditionally by us, the undersigned parish priest of Ste Anne du Detroit August 6 [16], 1821, the mother being present. The godfather was Louis Généreux[96] who declared that he could not sign his name; and the godmother Elizabeth Therese fisher, who signed with us.

GABRIEL RICHARD, priest.

ELIZABETH THARESA FISHER.

Pierre Laurent, born March 27, 1817, of Alexandre Laurant and of an Otchipwas woman called Chingwacok, was baptized by us the undersigned parish priest of Ste Anne du Detroit, August 16, 1821, the father being present. The godfather was Antoine Minard; and the godmother Marguerite Bertrand, wife of Daniel Bourassa, who declared that they could not sign their names.

GABRIEL RICHARD, priest.

Francois Samuel Lasselay, born about April 15, of Samuel Lasselay and of an Outawas woman savage called Abitagowinan, was baptized by us, the undersigned parish priest of S^{te}

---

[96] Louis Généreux was a half-breed, well-known to the early American settlers of Ionia County, Michigan. He had a trading-house on Grand River not far from Ionia, and was sentenced to state's prison for burning his father-in-law in a drunken bout. He there learned the shoemaker's trade, and when pardoned settled in Kalamazoo County, at Gull Prairie. He was probably with Colonel McKay in Wisconsin, in the War of 1812-15.—ED.

1787] Mackinac Marriages

Anne du Detroit, August 6, 1821, the mother being present. The godfather was François Paget who signed with us; and the godmother Marguerite Chauret who declared that she could not sign her name when thereunto requested.

GABRIEL RICHARD, priest.

FRANÇOIS PAGET.

1787: REGISTER OF MARRIAGES

[The following entry was omitted, through clerical oversight, from the list of marriages given in our volume xviii.]

August 20, 1787, after granting dispensation of bans between Louis hamelin, son of Sieur Charles hamelin and of the late Awaci, a sauteux savage, his father and mother, of the government of Montreal, of the one part; and Josette Le Sable, a savage of the Sauteux nation, residing at the old fort of Michilimakina, of the other part—I, the undersigned priest, administered the sacrament of matrimony to them, after receiving the mutual consent they had already pledged one another many years ago in the hope of having their marriage ratified by an approved priest and before several witnesses, also according to the ordinances of our mother the holy church and as testified below by the signatures of messieurs J. B^e Nolen; L. Carignan, Notary public, witnesses, who Signed with us, as did also the husband; the wife declared that she could not sign her name.

PAYET, Miss$^{n.}$ priest.

L. HAMELIN.

1743–1806: REGISTER OF INTERMENTS

[Source, same as preceding document.]⁹⁷

Died August 10, 1743 [Marie Coussante, daughter of Joseph Hins]; she was the first one buried in the new church built by her father, under the holy water font.⁹⁸

She [Marie Athanase, slave of Charles Hamelin] died fortified with all the sacraments, on January 24, 1748, and was buried in the church the following day beside her deceased mistress.

Died [Jacques, son of Jacques Dumay, baptized February 1, 1748] a few days afterward and was buried in the church near the little hins girl.

---

⁹⁷ The register of interments was evidently not as carefully kept as those of marriages and baptisms. The following first four entries have been abstracted from the baptismal register, being entered after the records of baptisms on the death of the child previously baptized. The record kept by Father Le Franc, beginning in 1754 and continuing through 1760, is continuous, and entered in one portion of the register, headed "Registre des morts depuis le 1ᵉʳ aoust 1754" [Register of deaths after August 1, 1754]. The remaining entries were scattered miscellaneously among the marriages and baptisms. but have here been assembled in chronological order.—ED.

⁹⁸ Pond describes the church in 1774 as a "Commodious Roman Catholic church;" see *Wis. Hist. Colls.*, xviii, p. 327. Henry, in 1761, also mentions the church. There is a tradition that this building was taken down, and the materials transported to the island and re-erected there. Sinclair writing in 1780 to his superior says: "Could I have completed the church (on the island) the whole garrison would have been over."—*(Mich. Pion. and Hist. Colls.*, ix, p. 579). Father Richard, in 1799, describes the island church as 25 x 45 feet, built of cedar, and very old. The first church on the island was on the site of the old cemetery south of the Astor House; some dispute arising over the land-title, Madame Laframboise gave a lot for the church, which was removed and rebuilt with a large addition. This served the parish of St. Anne of Michimilimackinac until 1874, when the present parish church was erected.—ED.

The child [Augustin Laffertiere dit jasmin, baptized February 27, 1752] died 2 or 3 months afterwards and is buried in the cemetery on the left hand side on entering.

August 1, 1754 was interred in the cemetery of this mission the body of jean Bapt. gourn dit Champagne, about forty-five years old. He had received the holy Viaticum and extreme unction; the prayers for the dying were said for him. He was married and was returning to the ilinois with his wife. He was interred after the celebration of a *requiem* high mass by me the undersigned priest, missionary of the society of Jesus, performing the duties of parish priest.

In testimony whereof I have signed beneath.

M. L. LEFRANC, miss. of the society of Jesus.

August 2, 1754 was interred in the cemetery of this place the body of jean Bapt. rocheleoi, fourteen years old. He had received extreme unction as he had not made his first communion. The prayers of the church for the dying were said for him. He died yesterday evening and was interred this evening with the usual ceremonies. * * *

M. L. LEFRANC, miss. of the society of Jesus.

August 11, 1754 was interred in the cemetery of this place the body of joseph tellier dit la fortune, ten or eleven years old. He received extreme unction.

M. L. LEFRANC, miss. of the society of Jesus.

In the same year, and on the twenty-third of the month aforesaid, I interred in the cemetery joseph Marie le tellier, brother of the above, nearly eight years old, with the same ceremonies. I had interred Marie josephe, their sister, a year and a half old, at the end of the month of July; I am not sure of the day.

Moreover, four men whose names I do not know died last winter at nipigoung, and one at the detour[99] this month.

M. L. LEFRANC, miss. of the society of Jesus.

September 14, 1754, was buried in the cemetery of this mission jean baptiste a slave of M[r.] guion whom I had privately baptized fifteen days ago. He was about eleven or twelve years old. M. L. LEFRANC, miss. of the society of Jesus.

In the evening of the same day was interred in the same place françois le tellier, about twenty years old, after having received all the sacraments and been assisted with the prayers of the church.

M. L. LEFRANC, miss. of the society of Jesus.

In the same year as above on the 15th of the same month, was interred in the same place Antoine des Coteaux, about twenty years old, after receiving all the sacraments and having been assisted with the prayers of the church.

M. L. LEFRANC, jesuit.

I have learned that the panis [slave] of M[r.] Rocheveau died at the Sault about five weeks ago. I had privately baptized him shortly before.

December 10, I interred the panis of Monbrun whom I had privately baptized August 29, 1754.

LEFRANC, jesuit.

I interred Marie françoise Brisbé in the cemetery of this place. She was born June 1, of the present year. At michilimakimak August 30, 1757.

M. L. LEFRANC, miss. of the society of Jesus.

---

[99] The Detour is the southeastern point of the upper peninsula of Michigan; so called because of the abrupt change of direction made by a boat in rounding this point.—ED.

Mackinac Interments

I interred in the cemetery of this place October 11, 1757,[1] joseph parent, aged twenty-three years, after having received all the succors of the church.

Lefranc, jesuit.

I interred in the same place on the 13th, the brother of Kigesse whom I had privately baptized on Monday.

On the 14th I interred ouichema whom I had privately baptized the previous night.

I interred kininchioue and the son of ouichema whom I had privately baptized yesterday.

I, the undersigned, interred in the cemetery of this post Catherine, a slave of Monsieur Bourassa who died yesterday evening in the most Christian sentiments. This 26th of October, 1757.

M. L. Lefranc, of the society of Jesus.

In the same year and month I interred in the same place Louis Amiot, twelve years old, and a little panis girl belonging to Sieur Bourassa, the younger, whom I had privately baptized October 28, 1757.

Lefranc, jesuit.

---

[1] This was the beginning of the great smallpox epidemic, that was brought to Mackinac and all the upper country by the Indians returning from the Lake Champlain expedition of 1757. During the siege of Fort William Henry, smallpox broke out among the garrison and several died. Not content with breaking the capitulation, and beginning an indiscriminate plundering and massacre among the surrendered troops, the barbarous Indians of the North exhumed the recently-buried members of the garrison in order to scalp the corpses, and thus add to their ghastly trophies. In this wise they themselves caught the contagion, which they carried with them to Mackinac and beyond. See F. B. Hough, *Journals of Major Robert Rogers* (Albany, 1833), p. 78; Francois Pouchot, *War in America, 1755-60* (Roxbury, Mass., 1866), i, pp. 91, 92. The latter says that the Potawatomi were almost extinguished. See also *Wis. Hist. Colls.*, xviii, pp. 203, 205.—Ed.

November 4, I interred in the same place ignace Parent, 19 years old. On the same day and in the same place I interred a little girl savage whom I had privately baptized yesterday.

November 8, of the said year, I interred anne Villeneuve, wife of Monsieur Blondeau, in this place, who died yesterday.

LEFRANC, jesuit.

I interred the son of memamghiouinet, who died on the 7th.

I interred in the cemetery of this post, in accordance with his last wishes, jacque Michel hamelin, trader, of the parish of Grondines, who died yesterday. At Michilimakinak, this November 15, 1757.

M. L. LE FRANC, of the society of Jesus.

On the same day I interred Charlotte, a panis of M$^{r.}$ Bourassa, the younger, in the same place.

This day, November 19, I interred in the church of this post Charles Chaboillez,[2] and marie joseph farly.[3]

LE FRANC Miss. of the society of Jesus.

On the 22nd, I interred in the cemetery a little boy slave of M$^{r.}$ Cardin.

November 26, I interred a woman savage whom I had privately baptized.

December 10, I interred ignace, a slave of M$^{r.}$ Bourassa.

December 15, I interred Claude Peletier dit la haie, voyageur, after having administered the sacraments to him and said the prayers for the dying.

M. L. LE FRANC, Miss. of the society of Jesus.

---

[2] This was the father mentioned in *Ibid.*, p. 255, note 51.—ED.

[3] Either wife or daughter of Jacques Philippe Farly, for whom see *Ibid.*, p. 258, note 54.—ED.

Mackinac Interments

February 27, 1758, I interred in the cemetery of this place Louis joseph farly, three days old.
>LE FRANC, Miss. of the society of Jesus.

August 16, 1758, I interred in the cemetery of this post Marie Anne, wife of M^r. Amiot[4] who died yesterday after receiving all the the sacraments of the dying and the suffrages of the church.
>M. L. LE FRANC, miss. of the society of Jesus.

October 5, I interred in the cemetery of this post marie joseph, born and baptized yesterday.
>M. L. LEFRANC, miss. of the society of Jesus.

October 27, 1758, I interred in the cemetery of this post [blank in MS.] a soldier, whom M^r. Giasson had brought back ill from the west, and who died suddenly last night. I had given him absolution last Monday and he was found dead although it was thought he would linger.
>M. L. LE FRANC, Miss. of the society of Jesus.

October 19, 1759, I interred in the cemetery of this post françois Louis Cardin born on August 17, last.
>M. LE FRANC Miss. of the society of Jesus.

August 22, 1760, I interred in the cemetery of this post Antoine St amand, who died yesterday after having received extreme unction.
>M. L. LE FRANC, Miss. of the society of Jesus.

---

[4] For an account of Jean Baptiste Amiot, who was blacksmith at Mackinac, not Green Bay, see *Id.*, iii, pp. 202, 203; vii, pp. 127, 128. See also mention of Amiot and his wife, *Id.*, xviii, p. 483. She was of Ottawa descent, and they were married in 1715.—ED.

June 13, I interred nicolas St medard, who died after having received the last sacraments.

>M. L. LE FRANC, Miss. of the society of Jesus.

She [young female slave of Mr. Parent, baptised March 8, 1762] died on the 17th and was buried on the 18th of the same month.

August 4, 1773, was interred Jean Baptiste Metivier,[5] who died yesterday, with public prayers in the absence of a Missionary.

>CARDIN, notary.

August 7, 1787, by us the undersigned priest, was buried (with the usual ceremonies) in the cemetery of this parish,[6] the body of Jean Baptiste Bourbonniêre who died yesterday (after receiving the sacrament of Penance), about fifty years old, husband of Manon Drouin, residing on the river of l'Assumption in the government of Montreal. There were present: messieurs Etienne Campion, Jean Baptiste Barthe, and Louis Carignan, who signed with us, besides a large concourse of various persons who can neither write nor sign their names.

>PAYET, Miss. priest.

L. CARIGNAN; J. B^{te} BARTHE.

December 13, 1791, about seven o'clock in the morning, Jean Louis Carignan, Esquire, superintendent of inland navigation

---

[5] For his marriage in 1757 see *Ibid.*, p. 483.—ED.

[6] The old French cemetery on Mackinac Island, after the removal of the post thither, was on Water street, west of the present John Jacob Astor House. Most if not all of the remains were removed to the modern cemetery, in order to make room for the growth of the business section of the village. The present Grand Hotel occupies the site of the Indian burial ground of early days, and bones are still exhumed on the hotel property. It is presumable that many half-breeds were buried in the Indian cemetery, while others found resting places in the French burying-ground on the lower level.—ED.

at Michilimakina and notary Public of the said Post, was drowned in Lake Michigan while going to fish with his hired man, Jean B^{te} Dubois, who was saved as well as several persons who were unable to give him assistance.[7]

January 6, 1795, was interred felicité Carignant, about twenty-two years old. She died yesterday about seven o'clock in the morning and was interred in the church of Michilimakina.

GABRIEL RICHARD, priest.

January 22, 1795, was interred in the cemetery of this post Jean Bongas,[8] a free negro—who died the day before yesterday evening about nine o'clock—with public prayers in the absence of a missionary.

ADHEMAR ST MARTIN J. P

August 2, 1796, was interred in the cemetery of this parish, a child born yesterday, son of Charles Spinard and of a savage mother, by us, the undersigned.

LAVADOUX, Vic.-gen.

July 10, 1799, was interred in the cemetery of this parish Marie Louise, a Sauteuse child, about two years old, baptized the previous day and who died during the night—by us the undersigned priest.

GABRIEL RICHARD, priest.

---

[7] Jean Louis Besnard *dit* Carignan was born in Canada in 1737; in 1770, at Montreal, he married Felicité Pillet of Lachine. It would appear that they did not remove to Mackinac until during the Revolutionary War, but they speedily became prominent citizens, the husband being notary public, churchwarden, and clerk of the court of inquiry held in 1787. His tragic drowning was a serious loss to the small community.—ED.

[8] For his marriage notice see *Wis. Hist. Colls.*, xviii, p. 497.—ED.

July 17, 1799, was interred in the cemetery of this Parish a male child about two months old, born of André Charlevoix and of josette Ammilain, his lawful wife.[9]

GABRIEL RICHARD, priest.

July 27, 1799, I interred in the cemetery of this parish the body of josette Ammelain, wife of André Charlevoix who died yesterday. * * *

GABRIEL RICHARD, priest.

October 4, 1799, about three o'clock in the afternoon, Mr. Paul Lacroix died and was interred in the cemetery of McKinac in the afternoon of the following day.

April 2, 1800, Sieur Alexis Laframboise, Esquire,[10] Captain of Militia, died suddenly about 3 o'clock in the afternoon and was interred in the church of McKinanc on the fourth of the said month.

ADHEMAR ST MARTIN

---

[9] For their marriage see *Ibid.*, p. 499.—ED.

[10] Alexis Laframboise was a native of Canada, where the family name was Fafard. His father, Jean Baptiste Fafard *dit* Laframboise, married Geneviève Bissonière in 1769. Alexis was probably born about 1763, being the second son of the family. At what time he came to the Northwest is not known, but he is supposed to have traded at Milwaukee about 1784–85. In 1792 he married at Mackinac Josette Adhemar; see *Ibid.*, pp. 494, 498. Milwaukee was his wintering place for several years. Later, he sent his brother François to take charge of his goods at that point; but François was improvident, and after wasting his property was finally killed by Winnebago Indians. He left a considerable family by a Potawatomi wife. His daughter Josette was with the Kinzies in the Chicago massacre of 1812, and afterwards became the wife of Jean Baptiste Beaubien, an early Chicago pioneer. Claude, Joseph, and Alexis Laframboise, who also were settlers of early Chicago, were probably sons of François, and went thither from Milwaukee. The senior Alexis, who died as here recorded, is not known to have left descendants.—ED.

Mackinac Interments

July 13, 1801, Mr. Eustache Légal dit Sans Cartier died and was interred in the cemetery of this Post in the morning of the fifteenth.

July 11, 1804, we the undersigned priest, the missionary at Michilimakina, buried with the usual prayers of the Roman church, jacques St Germain who died at the age of forty-two years.

J. Dilhet.

November 22, 1804, Sieur Adhemar St martin[11] died, at three quarters past 6 o'clock in the morning, and was Interred in the Church of McKinac on the 23rd of the said month.

Ant^{ne} Dupré, Witness.

January 2, 1806, at two o'clock in the afternoon, Charlotte Chandonette[12] died and was Interred in the cemetery of McKina on the third of the said month.

Dav^d Mitchell, Witness.

---

[11] Toussaint Antoine Adhémar *dit* St. Martin was born in Montreal, Sept. 10, 1740. Sometime before the Revolution he removed to Detroit, where a branch of his family had settled at an early date. He was educated for a physician, and is known to have been at Fort Miami in 1773. Several years were passed at Detroit, and at the close of the Revolution he appears to have settled for a time at Vincennes, Ind., receiving while there, from the British authorities, a commission as justice of the peace. Shortly after this, he removed to Mackinac, where as notary and justice of the peace he was an important functionary. Upon the Americans assuming control, St. Martin was appointed (Sept. 1, 1801) as justice of the peace by Governor Harrison of Indiana Territory. He married (probably at Montreal) Geneviève Blondeau. One of their daughters married Alexis Laframboise, and another, Angelique, taught the first girls' school at Mackinac.—Ed.

[12] Charlotte Chandonnet's marriage is cited in *Wis. Hist. Colls.*, xviii, pp. 495, 509. Her adopted son, Jean Baptiste, was clerk for John Kinzie at Chicago, at the time of the Fort Dearborn massacre (1812), where he was instrumental in saving the life of Mrs. Nathan

MISCELLANEOUS NOTES IN THE FOREGOING REGISTER.[13]

July 22, 1787,[14] after invoking the enlightenment of the Holy Ghost, we, the undersigned, elected by a majority of votes, as church wardens of the church of Ste. Anne de Michilimakina, messieurs Ch. Chaboillé[15] and Daniel Bourassa, who formally promised and undertook to care for the interests of the Said Church as their own and on their soul and conscience.

Heald, wife of the commandant. In 1814 he arrested a number of British traders at St. Josephs River, and it was on that occasion that he killed his uncle, who had been serving with Robert Dickson as British agent in Wisconsin, and had been sent for information to St. Josephs. This explains the seeming anomaly noted in *Wis. Hist. Colls.*, x, pp. 112, 113, where the then Editor thought that the younger Chandonnet was in Dickson's service, because he places the altercation and consequent shooting of the elder Chandonnet at an earlier date. The time is fixed as 1814 by a letter in our Draper MSS., 4T8, which accounts for the fact that the elder Chandonnet did not return to Dickson, as noted in his letter of March 15, 1814. Jean Baptiste Chandonnet married Marie Chapoton of Detroit, who visited Mackinac in the winter of 1815-16, and joined her husband at Chicago the following year; see *Wis. Hist. Colls.*, xiv, pp. 24-27. Chandonnet interpreted for the United States at Greenville in 1814, and at Portage des Sioux in 1815. In 1831 he visited the Healds in their Missouri home, on his way to Kansas to select lands for the Potawatomi. He was at the Chicago treaties of 1832 and 1833, but died soon thereafter, somewhere in Michigan.—ED.

[13] In the original these are scattered through the register, in the neighborhood of entries on other subjects. They are here brought together under one head.—ED.

[14] A parish meeting was held July 23, 1786, wherein Jean Baptiste Barthe and Louis Carignan were elected churchwardens. As this was, in the original, entered among the marriages, it will be found in *Wis. Hist. Colls.*, xviii, p. 493.—ED.

[15] Charles Chaboillez was a prominent trader, with large interests in Lake Superior. He appears to have retired with the British to St. Joseph's Island, possibly as early as 1788 (see next entry), in anticipation of their removal. In 1802 he was appointed storekeeper at the post and in that capacity served several years.—ED.

[1743–1806] Mackinac Interments

In testimony whereof they have signed with us.

PAYET, missionary priest.

CHLES CHABOILLEZ; DL. BOURASSA; BTE. GUILLORY;[16] MARCHENAU; J. B. BARTH; L. CARIGNAN; PR. GRIGNON; ETNE CAMPION; JEAN REEVES; G. COTTE;[17] LAURENT DUCHARME; P. THIERRY; AL LAFRAMBOISE; BTE. TABEAU; P. TABEAUX.✠

Note—In the Notarial Register of Monsieur Adhemar, page 164, 13th August 1788, is an Acknowledgment by Charley Chaboiller, residing at fort St Joseph, or the new fort, for the sum of sixty livres belonging to the church of Ste Anne de Mikili Makina.

GABRIEL RICHARD, missionary priest.

1813, 4 February.[18]

---

[16] The Guillory (Guyari) family were of long-standing and well-known at Mackinac, coming originally from Montreal. Joseph was married at the former place in 1747; *Wis. Hist. Colls.*, xviii, p. 474. Antoine was in Lake Superior in 1738 (*Id.*, xvii, p. 290), and married (1735) Anne Villeneuve, eldest half-sister of Charles Langlade. Antoine had died before 1745. Of the second generation, Jean Baptiste appears to have been most prominent. In 1778 he was a St. Joseph's trader, and the same year signed a petition to the governor-general for a missionary at Mackinac. A man of the same name was interpreter for the troops, and lieutenant in the Indian department during the War of 1812–15, and accompanied Anderson to Prairie du Chien; see *Id.*, ix, p. 234 et seq.—ED.

[17] Gabriel Coté (Cotte) belonged to a well-known Canadian family of Kamouraska, and came out early to the Northwest, where he was married in 1768; see *Wis. Hist. Colls.*, xviii, p. 487. He seems to have traded largely in Lake Superior and the far Northwest. In 1783 he took charge of an expedition to the country north of Lake Superior, wherein four of his men perished, and he found the Indians dying of hunger; see L. R. Masson, *Les Bourgeois de la Compagnie du Nord-Ouest* (Quebec, 1889), i, p. 13. In 1800 Coté removed his home from Mackinac to the British post on St. Joseph's Island, where he was recommended by the Commandant for a magistracy. Voyageurs of the name of Coté reside in Tiny, Ontario—probably his descendants; Ontario Hist. Soc. *Papers*, iii, p. 152.—ED.

[18] The circumstances of this entry at this date do not appear from the register, nor is it known that Father Richard was in Mackinac

This day, the 5th of the month of August 1821, the Inhabitants of the Parish of Ste Anne du Michilimakinac, assembled in the usual manner, appointed as Church-wardens of this Parish, to remain in office until a new nomination: Mr William McGulpine, Mr Eloy Bourassa[19] and M$^{r.}$ Joseph Rollet. They were specially instructed to take care of the movable property of the Parish consisting chiefly of Church linen, vestments, &c &c. and to take an inventory of the same.

In testimony whereof we have signed

GABRIEL RICHARD, parish priest of Ste Anne du Detroit, president of the meeting.

JOHN DOUSMAN; E. BOURASSA.

This day, the 15th of the month of August 1821, the inhabitants of the parish of Ste Anne de michilimakina, assembled in the usual manner, having learned that Mr de Rollet has refused to accept the office of Church-warden, appointed as third church-warden Mr John Dousman received into the catholic church on the 13th of the same month. And the church-wardens are instructed to get a petition signed asking Congress for a lot East of the village, on which to build the church of stone.

GABRIEL RICHARD, parish priest of Ste Anne du Detroit.

JOHN DOUSMAN; E. BOURASSA.

N. B. The second meeting was held on the 10th of the month of August, 1821.

---

in 1813. The entry stands on the second page of the register of baptisms, directly after the title.—ED.

[19] Eloy, younger scion of the prominent Bourassa family of Mackinac, was an employee of the American Fur Company, trading in 1818 to the island of La Cloche, in Lake Huron, at an annual salary of $3,000.—ED.

A Wisconsin Fur-Trader's Journal, 1804-05

By François Victor Malhiot

Letter to the Readers

GENTLEMEN[20]—It would be too venturesome a task for me to undertake to write a full and formal journal; my education is too inadequate. * * * It is true that, in the earlier years of my childhood, I could read, but no sooner had I reached the

---

[20] Addressed to the partners of the North West Fur Company. This organization was one of the most important in the history of the North American fur-trade. It was the successor to the French trade of the Northwest, which began to revive in 1766 at the close of Pontiac's conspiracy. In 1769 the first British trader penetrated to points beyond Lake Superior, going as far as Fort Bourbon, and returning the next year with a rich harvest of furs. For the next ten years this trade continued with increasing vigor, and was extended by the efforts of Peter Pond to the Athabasca region. In 1780 the Indians conspired against the traders, several posts were attacked, and many traders' lives might have been lost, had it not been for an epidemic of smallpox that raged for two years among the natives. Meanwhile, unrestrained competition had wrought great evils, the Indians were debauched, and the traders, being without legal restraints, grew lawless. Several times, interests were pooled for a brief period. Finally, in the winter of 1783-84, a sixteen-share company was formed for five years at Montreal, of which the Frobisher brothers and Simon McTavish were agents; the other, or wintering, partners dwelt at their posts in the far Northwest. The general rendezvous was at the Grand Portage, on Lake Superior. In 1787 the partnership was renewed for nine years, with twenty shares,

age of reason than idleness and pleasure prevented my going further and I have remained within my limited sphere. I write because I am ordered to write and out of submission and respect for the person who has given me the order.[21]

These are notes rather than a journal. No sooner did anything happen during the course of my journey, than I at once scribbled it down anyway; sometimes in bad French, sometimes in Canadian patois. I have described the character of the principal Savages of the place to the best of my ability. I have praised the post of Lac au Flambeau and have said all I thought of every person with me.

You may perhaps find me severe in my ideas and inconsistent in my judgments, especially with regard to the Savages, and you may say that it is the effect of my hatred and bad humor. But no! May God preserve me from wishing ill to any one on earth, and I declare before Heaven that all that is written in

---

thus admitting some former rivals to the partnership. Under the new impetus of combination, the association grew very prosperous, trebled its capital in eleven years, and controlled not only the trade, but the entire destiny of the Northwest country. Under its auspices vast explorations were made—Alexander Mackenzie discovering in 1789 the river that bears his name, also the Arctic Ocean; in 1793 he crossed the Rocky Mountains, and reached the Pacific by land. In 1798, the association was re-formed, with forty-six shares, some of the old partners retiring, and clerks being promoted to partnership. At this time there were employed fifty clerks, seventy-one interpreters, 1120 voyageurs, and thirty-five guides. The company's operations continued until 1821, when after a nine-years' struggle with the Hudson's Bay Company, the North West sold out to the former in that year. Its successor on American soil was the American Fur Company, organized by John Jacob Astor in 1809.—ED.

[21] It was the policy of the North West Company to require the clerks in charge of a post to keep a journal of proceedings therein. L. R. Masson, formerly of Montreal, made a large collection of these journals and letters, many of which he has published in *Les Bourgeois de la Compagnie du Nord-Ouest* (Quebec, 1889). We translate and present to our readers this journal of life at a Wisconsin post in 1804–05, taken from his work, i, pp. 223–263.—ED.

this book, is true and on the honor of a thoroughly honest man. *Honni soit qui mal y pense!*

I remain, Gentlemen, Your very humble and very obedient servant.

F. VT. M. L. O. [FRANÇOIS VICTOR MALHIOT][22]

---

[22] François Victor Malhiot was a French-Canadian of good family, the "son of a respectable gentleman, rich in sentiment and honor." Two of his brothers were known in the service of their country— Lieut.-Col. Pierre Ignace Malhiot, who entered the army and served in Canada, and Hon. Xavier Malhiot, representative in the Canadian parliament, who died at Boucherville in 1855. François was born in 1776, being scarcely fifteen years of age when he became an articled clerk to the North West Company. At the time of Malhiot's apprenticeship, the young clerks were required to serve five years for their expenses and £100. Since Malhiot speaks of thirteen years of travelling and eleven years of wintering, it is possible that he spent two years in coming to the upper country for the summers only, serving in the Montreal house during the winters. It is probable that his experiences were in many ways comparable to those of Gurdon Hubbard of Chicago, who has described in his *Autobiography* the life of a fur-trade apprentice some twenty-five years later (1818-23).

In 1796 Malhiot received his appointment to the upper Red River department, where apparently he remained for eight years, and where in 1799 his annual salary was £240. This was the department of Assiniboine River, which unites with Red River of the North at Winnipeg; and Malhiot was under John MacDonnell, wintering partner of the North West Company (1796–1815). The principal fort was on River Qu'appelle, with several subsidiary posts. See MacDonnell's journal in Masson, *Bourgeois*, i, pp. 267–295.

At the summer meeting of the partners in 1804, it was decided to promote Malhiot and send him to take charge of a post to the south of Lake Superior, where complaints of the clerk in charge, Charles Gauthier, seemed of sufficient importance to make some change necessary. Malhiot's experiences during the succeeding winter are here related by himself. He repaired and rebuilt the post, and his reports were sufficiently promising to cause his return to the same place for the next year, and apparently for the succeeding one.

In 1807, having become tired of the fur-trade, Malhiot determined to retire, and resigned his position with the company. During his residence in the interior he had, in the fashion of the country, married an Indian woman. This occurred August 8, 1800, at the fort at

FROM FORT KAMANAITIQUOYA TO THE MONTREAL RIVER

July 9, 1804 I left Fort Kamanaitiquoya[23] at 4 o'clock with an outfit of eleven assorted bales, twenty kegs of rum double strength, four kegs of powder, five bags of shot and bullets, half

---

the mouth of Winnipeg River. See Daniel W. Harmon, *Journal of Voyages and Travels* (Andover, 1820), p. 49. "This evening," he says, "Mons. Mayotte [Malhiot] took a woman of this country for a wife, or rather concubine." Upon leaving the interior, Malhiot left his Indian wife with her own people, but took with him his half-breed son, François Xavier Ignace (named apparently for himself and his own two brothers). Settling at Contrecœur he educated his son, and lived there until his death in 1840.

Malhiot was familiarly known to his relatives and intimates as Erambert. He was a cousin of Jacques Porlier of Green Bay, and for a short time after his return from the Northwest, lived with the latter's maiden sisters at Verchères. He is frequently mentioned in the family letters, and several letters from him to Porlier are in the Wisconsin Historical Library; i. e., Wisconsin MSS., 3B28, 4B52, 13B42, 2C57, 90.—ED.

[23] This word has had many spellings. The accepted form is Kaminiatiquia, and is said to signify "river with many islands" or "river that flows around"—the Kaministiquia entering Lake Superior by three mouths. It is one of the oldest sites on that lake. Radisson and Grosseilliers are supposed to have passed here in the middle of the seventeenth century. Duluth built the first trading post on this site in 1678, probably at the point where the later posts were found, on the north side of the north branch, a half mile above the mouth. The second French post was established here in 1717, by Zacherie Robutel, sieur de la Noue, who remained in command until 1721. Thenceforward it became an important station, both as gateway to the farther West, and for the amount and quality of furs secured. In 1743 the post was leased for 3000 livres. In 1757 the price had increased to 4000 livres, and every year it sent out from sixty to seventy packs of fine furs. About this period Kaministiquia was abandoned, and when the English reopened the fur-trade on Lake Superior, Grand Portage, sixty miles to the southwest, became their headquarters. After the American Revolution, it was found that the North West Company's post at Grand Portage was on American territory, and attempts were made to open various routes to the interior waters. It was not until 1798 that Roderick McKenzie rediscovered the Kaminis-

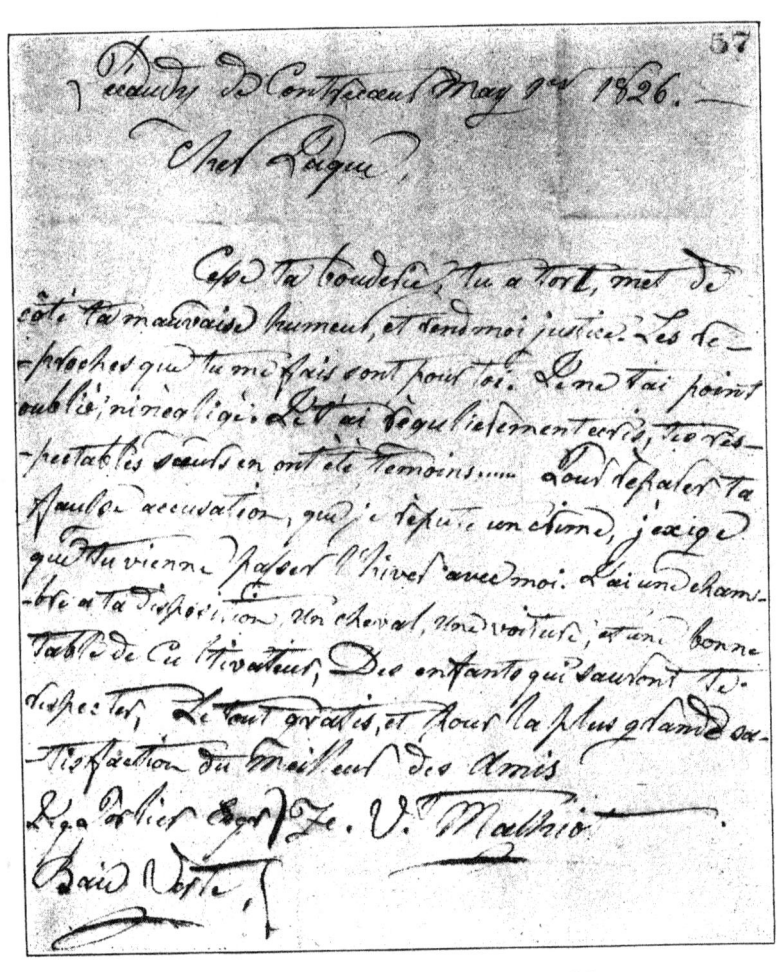

AUTOGRAPH LETTER BY FRANÇOIS VICTOR MALHIOT
Photographic reduction of original, in Wisconsin Historical Library

[1804–05] **Malhiot's Journal**

a bale of kettles, a case of guns, twelve traps and four rolls of tobacco,[24] the whole entrusted to my care by Mr William Mac Gillivray[25] to be traded for furs in the Department of Montreal

tiquia route, and thereupon it was decided to remove headquarters thither. The new fort was begun in 1801, and in the summer of 1804, when Malhiot was present, was about completed.

The name Fort William was not bestowed upon it until 1807. Fort William was for twenty years the centre of Western activity. It covered an area of fourteen acres, was surrounded by high pickets, and contained many buildings, chief of which was the great hall where the partners met and dined. Thither the agents of the company came each year from Montreal, to meet the wintering partners from the far interior. There the business of the year was transacted, the accounts made out, assignments arranged for the ensuing year, and outfits put up for clerks and partners. The classic description of Fort William is found in Washington Irving's *Astoria*. After the amalgamation with the Hudson's Bay Company in 1821, the glory of Fort William departed. It was, however, still maintained as a post, and around it was a small settlement of retired employees. This is now a town of 7000 inhabitants, one of the stations on the Canadian Pacific Railway. Vestiges of the old fur-trade post and its buildings are yet to be seen.—Ed.

[24] Compare the outfit of Alexander Henry the younger, described in his journals in Elliott Coues, *New Light on the Early History of the Greater Northwest* (New York, 1897), p. 7.—Ed.

[25] William McGillevray was at this time one of the chief agents of the North West Company resident at Montreal. He had served his apprenticeship in the field, going out first as clerk, and becoming a wintering partner in 1790, after buying out the interest of Peter Pond. His aptitude for the business was so great, that in 1797 he became one of the agents, and it was his duty to visit the upper country every year, and make the settlements and assignments for the succeeding year. For this purpose he had a special canoe of his own, manned by expert voyageurs who took pride in passing all brigades on the Ottawa River. McGillevray was popular with his colleagues and employees, and was very successful in keeping up the efficiency of the company. After 1804 he was its recognized head, and as such was frequently consulted by the government, especially after the War of 1812–15, in regard to new posts in the Northwest. In 1814 he was appointed legislative councillor, and having amassed a considerable fortune was one of the prominent men

River.[26] Moreover, I was supplied with as many French provisions as a proprietor might have wished for, * * * four hundred pounds of flour, two barrels and a half of pork, forty pounds of biscuit, a Keg of shrub (rum), a Keg of high-wines, two of sugar, four pounds of tea, a ham, bread, butter, etc. etc. The heavy wind compelled me to land at the entrance of Lake Superior; there I found Corbin,[27] one of Mr Cadotte's[28] clerks. My toothache got worse.

11th Wednesday. My people took only 2 Dorés in their nets.[29] I left my camp after we had cooked a meal. At half

---

of Montreal. But his sympathies turned to his native land, and in 1818 he bought an estate in Argyleshire, where he retired from active life, dying in 1825 from the effects of hardships endured in the Northwest trade.—ED.

[26] The term Department of Montreal River appears to be a new one in the North West Company's nomenclature. In the assignments of 1799, all the southern border of Lake Superior is classed together. Malhiot's expedition is apparently a new venture on the company's part—there had been trading here before, but not in charge of a person of the grade of clerk, who reported directly to headquarters.—ED.

[27] The author means that he got no farther than the mouth of Kaministiquia River, where he was storm-bound.

Jean Baptiste Corbin, a young Canadian of good family, born in 1776, had received some education before entering the employ of the North West Company in 1796. He was assigned to the Lake Superior department and entered the service of Michel Cadotte, who in 1800 sent him to establish a post on Lac Court Oreille. There he married a Chippewa woman, and had much influence with his Indian neighbors. In 1808, during the excitement caused by the efforts of Tecumseh and the Prophet, Corbin's post was plundered, he being obliged to flee through the woods to Chequamegon. This was partly due to an indiscretion on his part. He soon after returned, and passed the remainder of his life at this place. In 1818 he was taken into the employ of the American Fur Company, and in 1824 aided in suppressing hostilities on the part of the Indians. He was living at Lac Court Oreille as late as 1852. See *Minn. Hist. Colls.*, v, index.—ED.

[28] Michel Cadotte of La Pointe; see *ante*, p. 69, note 98.—ED.

[29] Elliott Coues identifies this fish, known to the French as *poisson doré*, as the wall-eyed pike-perch (*stizostedion vitreum*).—ED.

past five, after traveling two hours the wind compelled me to camp. * * * By all the devils, my toothache will not leave me.

12th Thursday. I started this morning at four o'clock. At eleven o'clock I met an unloaded canoe of X Y but could not find out where it was going.[30] At noon I passed the Grand Portage[31] where X Y's schooner was weighing anchor. A

---

[30] The great success of the North West Fur Company provoked rivalry and emulation. In 1798 a company was formed to oppose this powerful monopoly, but it was only by dissension within the ranks of the Nor' Westers themselves that efficient opposition could succeed. In 1799 much dissatisfaction was expressed with the haughty bearing and tyrannical methods of the chief agent, Simon McTavish. Accordingly, Alexander Mackenzie withdrew from the company, and going to England published his book of travels. For the discoveries therein recorded he was knighted, and received much honor. Returning to Canada in 1801 he formed a partnership with the North West Company's rivals, Richardson, Forsyth & Co. of Montreal, and Phyn, Inglis & Co. of London, to carry on the fur-trade. This company was usually spoken of as the X Y Company, probably because these letters succeeded in the alphabet the W of the North West Company's name. It was sometimes known as the New Company, and often as Alexander Mackenzie's. For three years the competition was severe, the X Y employees following the Nor' Westers, placing forts beside theirs, securing Indian favor and trade by various means, and vastly damaging the trade monopoly. Further in this journal, we shall see results at Lac du Flambeau. In July, 1804, McTavish died, and occasion for the opposition having ceased, in November of the same year the two companies united, to the satisfaction of all parties concerned. See the agreement in Masson, *Bourgeois*, ii, pp. 482-499.—ED.

[31] The term Grand Portage was first applied to the nine-mile carry between Lake Superior and a point on Pigeon River above its falls. Gradually, however, the name came to be applied only to the landing place on the shore of the lake. This is situated in a bay, too shallow for landing vessels of considerable burden. The place was well-known during the French regime, but the Kaministiquia route was more frequently used. At the beginning of the British regime, however, Grand Portage became an important centre of the fur-trade. Carver found many traders there in 1767; eight years later, Alexander Henry started thence for his tour to the interior,

moment afterward I saw her outside the islands sailing in the direction of Sault Ste. Marie.[32] At half past one o'clock, I saw Chorette[33] and his aide-de-camp Lalancette,[34] two employees of

and found it the scene of harmful competition. Thence, until the removal (1801–04) to Fort William (see *ante*, note 23), Grand Portage was the headquarters of the entire North West fur-trade, and here the company of that name built an important post. After the removal to the new fort, Grand Portage gradually sank into obscurity, having only a local importance. It is now a small post village, and fishing resort of a few whites and half-breeds, in Cook County, Minnesota. For further particulars see *Wis. Hist. Colls.*, xi, pp. 123–125, in which, however, Neill's statements are inaccurate.—ED.

[32] The earliest sailing vessel on Lake Superior would appear to have been that of La Ronde, used for developing his copper-mining interests; see *Id.*, xvii, pp. 310–313. A similar enterprise under British auspices was inaugurated in 1770–71; see James Bain, *Alexander Henry's Travels and Adventures* (Boston, 1901), pp. 220–229. Sailing vessels for the fur-trade do not appear to have been used until the formation of the North West Company, which in 1784 petitioned for the privilege of building barks on Lake Superior. The first vessel, built in 1785, was appropriately named "Beaver," and cost £1843. Unfortunately she could not be passed above Sault Ste. Marie, so the company had to build upon Lake Superior, where in 1787 they had a schooner of about fifty tons burden—with two others on Lake Huron, transporting goods and supplies from Detroit. See Alexander Mackenzie, *Voyages* (London, 1801), pp. xxxix, xl. The X Y Company had likewise their vessel, as appears by this passage.—ED.

[33] Simon or Simeon Chorette (Chaurette, Charrette) was a North West Company employee in the region south of Lake Superior at the close of the eighteenth century. He joined the opposition X Y Company, and as will be seen, proved an efficient rival of Malhiot at Lac du Flambeau throughout the season. After the amalgamation, he again became a North West employee. In 1818 he had entered the American Fur Company, by whom he was given charge that same year of the Lac du Flambeau post on a salary of $1200, with goods to the amount of $5100. The same year, his wife was the Company's trader at Keweenaw Cove. Later, Chorette retired to Green Bay, where he was engaged with the Grignons and Porlier in the fur-trade as late as 1832.—ED.

[34] Antoine Lalancette was taken into the service of the North

X Y for the Montreal River: they were camped and seemed to have three baggage outfits and three canoes. I camped here at la Rivière Brulée[35] and had my nets set. My toothache will not leave me.

13th Friday. My men took up their nets this morning and caught two trout and a white fish. At six o'clock we started after taking a meal. At 11 o'clock the Savages of M. Mi[chel] Cadotte caught up to me and told me they had seen Chorette; who had told them one of the three canoe-loads was for the Rivière des Sauteux,[36] one load and a half for the Montreal River, and the other half load for La Pointe. At three o'clock

---

West Company after amalgamation in 1804. In 1818 he was clerk at Lac du Flambeau for the American Fur Company.—ED.

[35] Not the well known Bois Brulé River of Wisconsin, part of the famous portage route through the St. Croix to the Mississippi, but a small stream in Cook County, Minn., not far from Grand Portage.—ED.

[36] For the early history of Chippewa River (Rivière des Sauteux), see *Wis. Hist. Colls.*, xviii, p. 79, note 18. The source of its western branch has been known for many years as Ottawa Lake, or Lac Court Oreilles, practically synonomous terms. This name was given because the Ottawa refuged there in their flight from the Iroquois in the middle of the seventeenth century; although only remaining a brief while they seem to have often returned to the stream for hunting. The Ottawa acquired the name of Court Oreilles (short ears) some time in the eighteenth century; not, as often stated, because they clipped their ears, but because they left them in the natural condition—that is, the lobe was not distended, or lengthened, by ornaments or weights. The Chippewa did not take possession of this region until well into the middle of the eighteenth century; their first permanent settlements appear to have been about the beginning of the British era.

Trade was first carried among them by the Cadottes, Jean Baptiste II entering this region about 1792. In 1800 Michel Cadotte had a post at Lac Court Oreilles. The clerk in charge thereof for many years was Jean Baptiste Corbin. In 1818 the American Fur Company opened trade at this place, with Corbin still in charge. By 1824 it was placed in the hands of Lyman M. Warren, who maintained the post for ten years. The reservation for the tribe was established in 1854, and there a considerable band yet dwell.—ED.

in the afternoon I camped at the Grand Marais[37] because the Savages told me I should have good fishing there.

14th Saturday. We caught in the nets four fine trout, three large ciscaouettes, and a white fish.[38] At five o'clock I had the canoes put in the water; at noon I met a canoe from Fond du Lac, on its way to Kamanaitiquoya loaded with bark. That night I camped at Collin's winter quarters[39] * * *

16th Monday. Yesterday the wind compelled us to camp at la Roche debout and this morning I started at 4 o'clock. At two o'clock in the afternoon I had to put ashore owing to the great violence of the wind. My toothache was so bad last night that, after trying every imaginable remedy and taking fifty drops of opium without any effect, I decided to take some rum. I swallowed at one gulp half a pint of the raw spirit, which took effect in a quarter of an hour and made me sleep until morning. My body feels broken, my jaw is tender, and I have a sensation of nausea, but my toothache has departed with the half pint of spirits.

19th Thursday. The day before yesterday I started with sails set, but at one o'clock in the afternoon I was obliged to put in at Petite Pêche because it was blowing too hard. The wind and rain continued all day yesterday, and I was unable to leave camp before 4 o'clock in the afternoon. I arrived here, at the

---

[37] Grand Marais is now the seat of Cook County, Minn., with a population of about 300. It has a fine harbor, and is still an excellent place for fishing.—ED.

[38] The trout was that known to the Great Lakes as Mackinac trout, *cristivomer namaycush;* the ciscaouette (now called siskowit) was a fat variety of the same species, now properly called *cristivomer namaycush siscowet*. This was first described by Louis Agassiz in his *Lake Superior* (Boston, 1850), p. 333. The whitefish was the common whitefish of Lake Superior, *coregonus clupeiformis*. For this information, thanks are due to Prof. George Wagner of the University of Wisconsin.—ED.

[39] Probably a free trader, as no person of that name seems to have been in the North West Company employ in 1804.—ED.

entrance of the river of Fond du Lac,[40] at one o'clock in the morning. At 4 o'clock I went to Mr Sayer's[41] Fort. I found him still in bed and had the honor of breakfasting with him.

---

[40] Fond du Lac was a term applied not only to the end of Lake Superior, westward from Chequamegon, but also to the district drained by St. Louis River and the other tributary streams of the region. In fur-trade parlance, the Department of the Fond du Lac embraced the upper waters of the Mississippi, and the posts upon Red Cedar, Leech, and Sandy lakes. By mounting the St. Louis, there was an easy portage, via the Savanna Rivers, to Sandy Lake, a tributary of the upper Mississippi. The fur-trade took this route during the French period; just how early the British began operating upon this waterway, does not seem to easy to determine. Jean Baptiste Perrault was here with Alexander Kay in 1784, and found a North West wintering post on St. Louis River. Jean Baptiste Cadotte II was given charge of the Fond du Lac Department about 1790. He built a permanent post on the bay, where in 1796 two Indians were executed for murdering a white man. The North West Company's post was probably on the same site. Local tradition has given the place the name of "old fort;" it was at the base of Connor's Point, not far from the present gas-works of Superior. (We are indebted for this information to James Bardon, president of the Superior Historical Society.) There the early pioneers of the present city found the remains of a considerable post—several hundred feet of stockade, and the ruins of a dock of cedar logs. A visitor of 1807 describes the place as having an enclosure of several acres, surrounded by a cedar picketing; two horses and several cattle were kept, also a garden wherein was raised on three acres 200 bushels of potatoes. There were one or more Chippewa villages in the vicinity—one on the Minnesota side of the bay was designated in 1789 as a "band of robbers." The importance of the post did not consist, however, in the trade of the vicinity. It was a source of supply for the entire Fond du Lac Department, and being located on the portage between Superior and St. Louis bays, was well adapted to its purpose. This North West post was abandoned after the law of 1816 forbidding British trading-houses on American soil. The American Fur Company located their post at the present village of Fond du Lac, Minn. The remains of the old post at Connor's Point were noted by Schoolcraft and Doty in 1820; the former says that it was abandoned about six years previous to his visit. See H. R. Schoolcraft, *Narrative Journal* (Albany, 1821), p. 203.—ED.

[41] John Sayer had long been connected with the fur-trade, as well

He did me the favor of giving me a keg of sugar for a keg of gum, which had been given me at Kamanaitiquoya instead of a keg of sugar. At nine o'clock, I took leave of him and rejoined my men at the entrance of the river.

20th Friday. I was unable to leave the River of Fond du Lac yesterday because a heavy wind arose just as I was about to embark. I did not start until this morning and had the sails up all day. This evening we camp at the River Ciscaouette.[42]

22nd Sunday. I was detained by rain and wind at my same camp the whole of the day before yesterday, of yesterday, and until noon today, and I was unable to have the canoes put in the water before three o'clock, because the lake was too rough for a long while. I went as far as Rivière à la Framboise;[43] I slept

---

as with the Fond du Lac Department. In 1780 he was at Mackinac, agent for Joseph Howard of Montreal, and the following year presented claims for goods seized for the St. Louis expedition; see *Wis. Hist. Colls.*, xviii, pp. 404–410. In 1784 Perrault found him at Fond du Lac. In 1797–98 he was at Cass Lake, Minn., and the following year with Jean Baptiste Cadotte on the Mississippi. In the summer of 1802 he was at Leech Lake, and by the time Malhiot met him had become a wintering partner in the North West Company, whose agreement with X Y in 1804 he signed by attorney. Sayer appears to have resided some time at Fond du Lac. A half-breed son, Guillaume Sayer, lived in the Red River country, and in 1849 his arrest caused an outbreak among the half-breeds of that region.—ED.

[42] This stream is now known as the Siskowit (English for *ciscaouette*). It is about fifty-five miles east of Duluth, in the present Bayfield County, Wis. It was much used as a "loaded canoe" harbor, since at its entrance there is a small slough that made a safe harbor. The fine sand beach on the eastern side of the bay was a favorite camping-ground of the Chippewa. Its Indian name was Kahpukmekah, and at this place occurred the tragedy to the family of Biauswa, when killed and captured by the Outagami; see *Minn. Hist. Colls.*, v, p. 127. The new town of Cornucopia is at the mouth of the Siskowit. For this information, the Editor is indebted to Hon. Samuel S. Fifield of Ashland.—ED.

[43] The first mention that we have thus far seen, of this stream, now known in translation as Raspberry River; it enters into a small bay just east of Point Detour, about seventeen miles from Ashland. Bayfield's chart of Lake Superior applies the name to what is now

ARTICLES OF CHIPPEWA HANDICRAFT

Selected from specimens in Museum of Wisconsin Historical Society

there and started this morning at 4 o'clock. At 11 o'clock I arrived here at La Pointe, M.ʳ Cadotte's Fort.⁴⁴ I decided to

---

Sioux River, entering the bay just west of Madelaine Island. Doty, however, in the account of his voyage in 1820, mentions this stream (see *Wis. Hist. Colls.*, xiii, p. 201) in the same location given by Malhiot, and doubtless this was the name usually given to it by voyageurs. It is also found on a map of 1830.—ED.

⁴⁴ Cadotte's fort lay upon Madelaine Island, the largest of the archipelago known as the Twelve Apostles—a title apparently suggested by Father Charlevoix, on whose maps it first appears (1744). Madelaine had a title of its own, of older origin, having been named St. Michel, apparently by the early Jesuits in the seventeenth century. This name persisted until the nineteenth century, when in 1820 Schoolcraft calls it "Michael's Island," doubtless thinking it had taken its name from Michel Cadotte. Several other titles for this island are found on early maps; see *Wis. Hist. Colls.*, xiii, p. 410, note 2. The appellation Madelaine, not in use until the nineteenth century, is said to have arisen from the Christian name of Cadotte's wife, daughter of an important Indian chief of the neighborhood. The site of Cadotte's trading establishment was on the south end of the island, at what is now known as "Old Fort." The earlier French fort, so long commanded by Denis de la Ronde, lay about three-quarters of a mile northwest; see Thomas L. McKenney, *Sketches of a Tour to the Lakes* (Baltimore, 1827), p. 265.

The first trading or wintering post in this region was probably built in 1659 by Radisson and Groseilliers, but this was on the mainland, to the southwest. The removal to the island was doubtless due to its good harbor and protected position. It was a prominent post under the French regime, being usually called Chequamegon or La Pointe du Chequamegon. The last French commandant was Hertel de Beaubassin, for whom see *ante*, p. 45, note 81. The British government never rebuilt a fort at this place. The first British trader was Alexander Henry, who came in 1765 and built his house on the shore of the mainland, opposite the island; see Bain, *Henry's Travels*, p. 191. Jean Baptiste Cadotte was Henry's partner, and his sons re-established trade at this place. At what date Michel Cadotte began his island trading post, is not certain. John Johnston was here in the latter part of the eighteenth century, but his post was on the mainland, at the village of Waubojeeg, whose daughter he married. Michel Cadotte resided permanently on Madelaine Island as early as 1800; probably some years before this. At first an inde-

spend the remainder of the day there to give the men time to make themselves shoes for crossing the portage. I obtained eighteen white fish from the Savages in exchange for tobacco. I expressly forbade my people to trade their corn for fish.

24th Tuesday. This morning I started at 9 o'clock and at 11 I camped at Mauvaise Rivière[45] because the wind was too strong to allow of my continuing my journey. The son-in-law of "Les

pendent trader, he became associated with the North West Company, and later with the South West, or American Fur Company. Selling out in 1823 to his sons-in-law, the Warrens, the latter removed the post about 1832 to the site known as "New Fort," on the western side of the island. Around this grew up a considerable village which took the name La Pointe. It was the county seat until 1872, when that was removed to Ashland. The island is now much resorted to by summer cottagers.—ED.

[45] Mauvaise (Bad) River is still known by that name, which it acquired from the difficulties of its navigation. The Indian name was Muskeego. It is about a hundred miles in length, and from its upper waters easy portages are made to the Namekagan branch of the St. Croix, and to the headwaters of the Chippewa; see Doty's map in *Wis. Hist. Colls.*, vii, p. 204. John Johnston describes this stream in his "Lake Superior," in Masson, *Bourgeois*, ii, p. 167. He speaks of the small sandy bay at its mouth, and the shore line thence to Chequamegon Point (now an island), from which it is about six miles to the river's mouth. In 1831 Schoolcraft, accompanied by Douglass Houghton and Lieut. Robert E. Clary, ascended this stream to its source. See Schoolcraft's description in *Thirty Years with Indian Tribes* (Philadelphia, 1851), pp. 363–370. His official account is in *House Ex. Docs.*, 22nd Cong., 1st sess., vol. iv.

In 1845 Rev. L. H. Wheeler, Protestant missionary at La Pointe, planned an agricultural settlement near the mouth of Bad River. There the Indians had for many years been accustomed to make spring gardens, and Wheeler taught them the rudiments of civilized life. He named the settlement Odanah, and in 1854 it was set aside as an Indian reservation. Later, the Roman Catholic mission on Madelaine Island was likewise removed to the Bad River reservation, where in 1906 there were 1174 resident Indians. Considerable money has been spent in improvements, including road- and bridge-making, and the Indians receive a good income from the lease of logging privileges.—ED.

Grandes Oreilles," called Rémond, told me that they are camped at the Montreal River[46] and that "Le Genou" will not start for Lac au Flambeau for some days. There are many pigeons here. I killed 24.[47]

25th Wednesday. I started at half past 4 o'clock this morning from Rivière Mauvaise and arrived here, at the Portage of the Montreal River[48] at three quarters past nine o'clock. There

---

[46] The name for this river is one of the oldest on the map of Lake Superior, and probably was assigned to it by Duluth or some of the Jesuits that preceded him. It is found on a map of 1688, and may have originated from a fancied resemblance between the bluffs at the mouth and the mountain at Montreal. Its Indian name seems to have been Kawasidjiwong. A considerable falls occurs a few yards above the mouth, which is masked by high clay banks. Above the falls there is a succession of rapids, not navigable even for canoes. Montreal River came into prominence during the boundary adjustment between Wisconsin and Michigan. It is said to have been first suggested as a boundary line by Senator William C. Preston of South Carolina, during the committee hearings on the admission of Michigan. According to the map used by Preston, Montreal River took its rise in Lac Vieux Desert, and very near the source of Menomonee River of Green Bay. Upon survey in 1840 this was found incorrect (see report of surveyor T. J. Cram in *Senate Docs.*, No. 151, 26th Cong., 2nd sess., vol. iv). In 1847 W. A. Burt, deputy surveyor, was sent out by the federal land office to complete the survey and mark the boundary. See *Wis. Hist. Colls.,* xi, pp. 471 et seq.; *Mich. Pion. and Hist. Colls.*, xxx, pp. 253-261.—ED.

[47] These birds were the *ectopistes migratorius*, or passenger pigeons, which formerly migrated in such great flocks that they darkened the air, and with their weight broke the branches of trees on which they roosted. McKenney, in his *Tour of the Lakes* (Baltimore, 1827), p. 353, says that thousands perished every year in attempting to cross Lake Superior, where its width was sixty miles. Although so plentiful in the West, even up to forty years ago, the bird has now become rare, due to these accidents and the wholesale operations of pot-hunters.—ED.

[48] The Montreal River portage trail commenced on Lake Superior, east of the mouth. After proceeding six or seven miles, over the river's eastern bluff, it reached the stream at a point above the falls; here crossing the river, the path continued up the southwest (left) bank, at some distance back from the stream, apparently in order

I found old "Les Grandes Oreilles" and "le Genou." The latter told me he was greatly dissatisfied with the X Y's Fort. There is not a single grain of corn to eat, no ammunition, and pigeons are killed with sticks. I think, from what he said, that he must have done something wrong to Chorette, or at least have robbed him, for he said [of him], "Dog! you will be an object for pity." The last words mean many things.

I heard from one of "le Genou's" brothers, who left Lac au Flambeau a week ago, that the Savages have been on the warpath, that they are now hunting and that our people who spent the summer in the interior were to start four days ago to come and meet us.

I gave old "Les Grandes Oreilles" seven chopines of mixed rum for nothing, because every spring he gives quantities of fish to our people, when they come from the interior and moreover, he is devoted to the North-West.

26th Thursday. I ordered the men to get ready to enter the portage tomorrow. I gave each one a double handful of flour, a pound of pork and a drink of rum as a treat. * * * I gave "le Genou" 16 plus credit,[49] after many supplications and

---

to head some of the smaller tributaries. It ended at what was then known as Portage Lake, and there the canoes were kept *en cache*. Portage Lake was probably that now known as Long Lake, in the northeastern portion of Oneida County. The best description of the portage is that given by James D. Doty, who accompanied Cass's party to Lake Superior in 1820. His journal of the trip is given in *Wis. Hist. Colls.*, xiii, pp. 163-219. A letter written to Governor Cass on his return to Detroit is printed in *Id.*, vii, pp. 195-206, accompanied by a map. The trail is also indicated on a map published in 1883 by the Wisconsin Geological Survey.—ED.

[49] "Plus" was a term expressing the monetary unit of the fur-trade, and represented one good beaver skin; see Masson, *Bourgeois*, i, p. 7. Malhiot therefore intends to say that he gave the Indian "le Genou" (the Knee) goods on credit which were worth sixteen beaver skins. The credit system was deeply entrenched in the fur-trade, and the source of much trouble, as will be seen later in this narrative.—ED.

fine promises to work for us next winter. I gave nearly as much to his brother, "La Pourceline."

27th Friday. Our people from Lac au Flambeau, Tremblé Martineau, and Le Beau,⁵⁰ arrived here at six o'clock yesterday evening with their baggage, decided to go on to Mr Cadotte at la Pointe if they had not found another clerk to replace Gauthier.⁵¹ They are thin and emaciated like real skeletons. They say they were more ill-treated than ever by Gauthier; that half the time they had nothing to eat, while he never passed a single day without having a good meal; that he is resolved to go and work for the X Y if he is replaced by another; further, that he has sworn to kill Racicot for having written against him, and that there would be murder before he left Lac au Flambeau; that he is resolved to pull up all the clearings, that is to say the potatoes and corn he had planted or caused to be planted; finally, that he is like a wild beast, and not a day passes without his swearing, storming, and inveighing against those who wintered with him last year. He has got only three packs of furs at the most, besides one he traded for his own goods.

I will not undertake the portage today because these men from the interior ask a day's rest. How weak they are! ! * * * I gave each of them a drink of shrub, two double handfuls of flour, and two pounds of pork and they began to eat with such avidity that I was twice obliged to take the dish away from them, and, notwithstanding this, I feared for a long while

---

⁵⁰ Nothing more is known of these voyageurs than is here narrated. Martineau's name was Ambrose.—ED.

⁵¹ Charles Gauthier was probably a son of the interpreter and Revolutionary participant mentioned *ante*, p. 5, note 17. The elder Gauthier had sons by a Winnebago wife who were older than his daughters, whose baptisms are recorded *ante*, pp. 78, 79. This son had had some education, and was employed by the North West Company before 1799 as clerk and interpreter; little is known of him, however, beyond what is recorded in this journal. He married into the Chippewa tribe, and many of the name of Gauthier still reside on Lac du Flambeau reservation and at old Fond du Lac; see Frank A. Flower, *Eye of the Northwest* (Superior, 1890), p. 43.—ED.

that injurious consequences would result; fortunately they all escaped with slight twinges of colic.

28th Saturday. I started this morning from Lake Superior with seven of my men to proceed at once to Lac au Flambeau. I took with me a bale of merchandize, a roll of tobacco, 20 pounds of shot, 20 pounds of bullets, three quarters of a sack of corn, a barrel of rum double-strength, and all my baggage. Today we did forty pauses.[52] I left the remainder of my things under the care and charge of Racicot. Durocher,[53] who has been poisoned with poison-ivy, is also with him; otherwise he would have come with me with a load. * * * My toothache is beginning again as bad as ever. * * * I gave my people a small drink of shrub.

29th Sunday. Today we did only 20 pauses because I suffered too much from toothache last night, and had to get my head sweated this morning which soothed the pain a little. It is now 4 o'clock in the afternoon and we are camping because several of the men are complaining greatly of pains in their legs and it is necessary to spare them. My toothache is a little better than it was in the morning. I feel weak at times, owing to my being unable to take any food. I gave my men a drink of shrub.

---

[52] During the fur-trade period, distances in the Northwest were measured by the number of pauses (pronounced *pozes*), or times that the voyageurs stopped to rest. A single pause was computed at from 600 yards to a half mile, but this depended very largely upon local conditions—the difficulty of the path, etc.; in hilly or swampy country, the pauses were shorter. They had, however, become fixed by constant usage, and each portage was spoken of as consisting of so many pauses. The long Montreal River portage was reckoned at 120 pauses, or about forty-five miles. The load of each voyageur was two packs, each of eighty to ninety pounds weight.—ED.

[53] Jacques Racicot was probably from a Boucherville family of that name, in which the name of Jacques was frequent. Urbain Durocher (Desroches) was probably from l'Epiphanie, since one of that name returned thither, having married Malhiot's abandoned Indian wife, whom he brought with him from Lac du Flambeau. After the death of Durocher, she married one Pelletier.—ED.

Malhiot's Journal

31st Tuesday. We started at seven o'clock this morning and at last, at one o'clock in the afternoon, we reached the end of the Portage;[54] the people were somewhat tired, and Bourbon had severe pains in his legs. I sent them at once to get the canoes that were cached, to have them gummed, and I made them make paddles so as to be able to start tomorrow morning.

August 2nd Thursday. I started at 4 o'clock this morning and arrived here at Fort du Flambeau at 3 o'clock in the afternoon.[55] I found Gauthier quite disconcerted, trembling, and not knowing what to say. I read him the letter from Mr William McGillivray which frightened him still more and made him shed tears. I gave him all the messages from M^r McGillivray and Mr Sayer, remonstrated with him in every way, after which he admitted his errors.

I have just made out a statement of everything that might

---

[54] See *ante*, note 48.

[55] The dates of the journal show that two days were spent in the canoe journey from Portage (Long) Lake to Lac du Flambeau. The party first made their way by a network of streams and lakes to Turtle Lake, in northwestern Vilas County; thence by short portages they reached Manitowish River (which Doty confuses with the outlet of Lac Vieux Desert); they went eighteen miles down stream to the Flambeau River, and up the last-named twenty-four miles to Lac du Flambeau. The fort stood on the north side of the lake, probably near the present Indian village, on the Lac du Flambeau reservation. This reservation, although provided for by the treaty of 1854, was not laid out and surveyed until nine years later.

Lac du Flambeau, or Torch Lake (Wauswagnining), took its name from the custom of spearing fish by torchlight. It is not one, but a group of connected or adjacent lakes. Apparently it was occupied by the Chippewa before the close of the eighteenth century. The central village and first chief of the band dwelt on this lake, which has ever since been a continuous Indian residence. In 1908, Lac du Flambeau was segregated from La Pointe, and made a separate agency; the population that year was 784, of whom the major portion lived on allotted lands. They have a day school on the reservation, and several villages, and are making progress in the arts of civilization.—ED.

[181]

belong to the company[56] and taken possession of the garden produce. I calculated that there were three packs of furs; besides these were thirty deer, six beaver, one otter, one bear and twenty-four muskrat skins (which he says he traded for with his own goods). These I took possession of, but he will trade them at the store if he decides to pass the winter with me and will behave as an honest man should.

We are here without bread or biscuit and wait on Providence.

3rd Friday. This morning I proposed to Gauthier to go and winter at Latonagane.[57] I told him I would give him a small

---

[56] The following list was not with the journal of Malhiot, but was found by Masson among the papers of Roderick McKenzie:

"List of goods received from Gauthier, August 2, 1804: 1 chief's coat, 1 linen shirt, 1 cotton shirt, 2 ornamented caps, 1 silk handkerchief, ½ piece of ribbon, 1 looking glass with paper border, 3 large knives, 2 dozen horn combs, 1 pack of cards, 3 pairs of scissors, 2 men's collars, ½ lb. vermilion, 3 doz. awls, 5 steels for striking fire, 12 wormers, ½ box wire for snares, 2 [boxes] medicine, 1 hat.

"*Furs* 4 bear skins, summer, 4 otter skins, summer, 6 marten skins, summer, 218 musk-rat skins, 20 lbs. beaver-skins, 100 red deer skins.

"Tools and utensils of the Fort: 4 old axes, 3 augers, 7 old kettles, 1 hand-saw, 1 plane, 1 hatchet-hammer, 1 piercer, 1 funnel, 1 old spigot, 2 old quart measures, 2 old half-pint measures, 1 old gill measure, 5 tomahawks, 1 pair spear-heads, 1 old grenadier gun, 1 pistol, 1 old Bank line, 6 old nets only one of which can be used, 2 old rasps, 2 old files, 1 mattock, 1 hammer. Three old bark canoes fit only for carrying sand or earth.

"(Signed) F. Vt. Malhiot."

[57] Ontonagon River is one of the best-known streams on the south shore of Lake Superior. Rising in the small lakes of the interior, near the watershed between the Mississippi and Lake Superior drainage basins, it collects numerous tributaries into two branches, which unite eighteen miles above the lake, into which the river pours a considerable volume of reddish, turbid water. It is navigable for canoes for over thirty miles in high water, and connected by easy portages with the source of Wisconsin River. In Malhiot's day, a comparatively small, insignificant village of Chippewa dwelt at its mouth, and was closely connected with the Lac du Flambeau band, so that the trade was usually conducted from that point.

The early fame of Ontonagon River was due to the copper found upon its banks; although the first known mention of the stream al-

outfit without rum, but he would not consent because he says there will be too much hardship there. He asked me to send

ludes to the large sturgeon fishery near its mouth. As early as 1665 reports of copper mines were sent out from Lake Superior by voyageurs and Jesuit missionaries. In 1668 a considerable nugget was sent first to the intendant Talon, and later to the king in France. Hence, on one of the earliest maps, the river is designated "Nantononagon or Talon," but the latter name soon disappeared. Aside from the nuggets of copper found, there was a large boulder of virgin copper lying upon the banks of the Ontonagon, some twenty-five miles above its mouth. This caused the French to believe that a copper mine might be discovered in the near vicinity. In 1735 Denis de la Ronde, then commandant at Fort Chequamegon, asked the French government for experts to aid in locating these mines; see report of one Corbin in *Wis. Hist. Colls.*, xvii, pp. 237-240. Three years later, two German miners, father and son, named John Adam Forster, explored this vicinity at the instance of La Ronde, and made favorable reports thereon; *Ibid.*, pp. 306-315. But a fierce Indian war and the subsequent death of La Ronde, ended the mining projects of the French in the Lake Superior district. The earliest English attempt was that of Alexander Henry and his partners in 1772; see Bain, *Henry's Voyages*, pp. 225-229. Douglass Houghton, in his famous geological report of 1841, alludes to this effort, and the lack of scientific knowledge shown in making locations. From Henry's time until the advent of Americans upon Lake Superior, no further effort was apparently made to explore for copper mines. Cass's expedition of 1820 ascended Ontonagon River to the "copper rock," as is graphically described by Schoolcraft in his *Narrative*, pp. 171-188; Governor Cass lost his way, however, and did not reach the rock. Schoolcraft appends a view of the rock and the river banks at this place. In 1841-43 an enterprising merchant of Detroit succeeded in removing the rock from its place and carrying it down the lakes. He purchased permission for this enterprise from the Ontonagon Chippewa, whose chief he denominates as Okondokon. The government made claim to the rock, however, and it was removed to the Smithsonian Institution at Washington, where it now rests. In 1842 the Chippewa disposed of their land on Lake Superior to the government, and mining claims upon the Ontonagon River at once began to be filed. The later history of copper-mining in this vicinity is well-known. The modern town of Ontonagon, with 1600 inhabitants, now lies at the mouth of the stream, on the site of the old Indian village.—ED.

him to the River des Sauteux to work against La Lancette, but I told him he would get no goods from me for that purpose, and that I had other persons to send there. He then told me he would go and winter with his wife's relatives and would obtain goods from Little Mi[chel] Cadotte.[58] I am to give him a small canoe with food and ammunition to enable him to go there. He complained very much of my having taken possession of the garden produce.

I have just sent Bazinet to a place three hours' march from here where some of X Y's Savages are who have provisions. My men are resting today; tomorrow they will start to carry the things over the portage. All the clearings I have been able to see, look well. I got all the meat and furs Chorette's brother-in-law could have, and my men learned there was a rumor that the Savages wanted to go on the war-path.

4th Saturday. Bazinet arrived this morning with old *Plat Côté* who gave me some quarters of deer-meat and some deer-skins in exchange for rum. My people start at once for the Montreal portage. George Yarns will command the march and Racicot have charge of the goods. Today I am sending Bazinet to Ouiseconsaint[59] to try and get the Best skins from the Savages and also a small quantity of wild rice. He takes with him a small assortment of goods and three fourths of a keg of rum,

---

[58] Michel Cadotte Jr. was born at his father's trading post on Chippewa River, just above Chippewa Falls, in 1791. During the War of 1812–15 he served with the British forces, especially acting as guide and interpreter in the capture of Mackinac in 1812. He was afterwards in the battle of the Thames, where he was wounded and lost one arm. He continued in the Indian trade, and in 1843 Alfred Brunson met him at his brother-in-law's post on the Chippewa River. He was living at La Pointe as late as 1852. His nephew, William Warren, in *Minn. Hist. Colls.*, v, pp. 372–377, tells an interesting story of young Cadotte interpreting for the chief Keeshkenum (his grandfather) at Mackinac, when the latter asserted his adherence to the American cause, but desired to remain neutral in the war.—Ed.

[59] Probably somewhere in the vicinity of Tomahawk Lake, the nearest point on the Wisconsin River to Lac du Flambeau. The form Ouisconsaint is a rare phonetic spelling for this stream.—Ed.

double strength. I am sending Bourbon with him because he has pains in his legs and is unable to do his duty in the portage, and I remain to keep the fort with Beaulieu, a Montreal man, who has decided to spend the winter with me, after promising me not to drink any rum, to work like an honest man, and not to set foot on the X Y premises during the winter.

5th Sunday. Yesterday evening I got twelve deer skins from old *La Pierre à affiler* in exchange for some rum. He assured me had had nothing more and would have nothing to give his son-in-law Chorette if he came. I am sending Gauthier and Beaulieu to one of the sons of old *La Chouette* to get what furs and provisions he may have. I remain alone in the Fort and my loneliness may be imagined.

6th Monday. Gauthier returned last night without having been able to see the Savages. This morning I got the meat of a bear from old La crémaillère.

Bazinet and Gauthier made me pass with the Savages as M^r McGillivray's brother and as one of the proprietors of the Company. This has had a very good effect so far, for they never call me anything but their "Father." I am inclined to think they will respect me more than they would otherwise have done, and will deem it an honor to trade with me next winter. Therefore, far from reprimanding Bazinet and Gauthier and forbidding them to say such things, I approved of what they had done and I have reason to hope that the gentlemen will find nothing wrong in it and not be disgraced by my temerity, for it is in their interest. My only object in this is to obtain good returns and not the glory of passing for what I am not. Moreover, if I deem myself honored by passing as the brother of the chief agent of the North and the partner of his partners, they, on the other hand need not consider their dignity in any way disgraced or vilified, for I am the son of a respectable gentleman and rich in sentiment and honor.

8th Wednesday. The wife of old "La Chouette" came last evening and made me a present of four pieces of dried meat. I am sending a brasse of tobacco to her husband to distribute among his children and his people.

Until now, owing to lack of time and to sickness, I have been unable to make any observations on the country and the Savages, but as I am better today I will begin by saying that of all the spots and places I have seen in my thirteen years' of travels, this is the most horrid and most sterile. The Portage road is truly that to heaven because it is narrow, full of overturned trees, obstacles, thorns, and muskegs. Men who go over it loaded and who are obliged to carry baggage over it, certainly deserve to be called "men."

This vile portage is inhabited solely by owls, because no other animal could find a living there, and the hoots of those solitary birds are enough to frighten an angel or intimidate a Caesar.

As to Lac du Flambeau it is worthier of the name of swamp than of lake and at this season it would be easier to catch bullfrogs in the nets than fish. I have had the nets set three times since my arrival without catching a fish. Today I am sending Gauthier to cast his nets in another lake; perhaps we shall get some craw-fish. With regard to the river I will never call it anything but a small stream, because in many places a mouse could cross it without wetting its belly. * * * All the Savages I have seen so far seemed to me to be good providers;[60] another time, when I shall have seen them all, I will speak of them more at length.

9th Thursday. *Le Petit Forgeron*, a Savage from the Vieux Désert[61] came here yesterday evening. I traded with him and

---

[60] The French is, "faire de bon *Besthia*." This must be a local word. Not one of our dictionaries (including those of Canadian, Breton, and Norman patois) has it. It may come from *bestial, bestiaux*, cattle. I have translated it good providers (i. e., good cattle, or useful people for us). Further I translate the same word as "Brutes." This is of course but conjecture.—CRAWFORD LINDSAY, translator.

[61] The term Vieux Désert has often been mistranslated as Lake of the Desert, "the old deserted place," etc. Doty was more nearly correct in speaking of it, as "Old Plantation;" see *Wis. Hist. Colls.*, vii, p. 202. The term in Canadian-French means an old clearing, and was a translation in its turn of the Indian term *Gete Kitigan*—old land under cultivation. The remains of cultivation can still be seen on the principal island in this lake, upon which the Wisconsin-Michigan

got 4 beaver, 2 otter, one beaver and two dressed moose skins. I gave him on credit five plus of ammunition and tobacco and he is not to return until autumn. At last we have caught five carp and a Masquinongé[62] in our nets this morning; but Gauthier had to stay out all night with Beaulieu, my Montreal man. They killed four partridges.[63] What a miracle!

---

boundary line impinges. Lac Vieux Désert is one of the oldest sites on the map of Wisconsin. It was there that in 1661 Father René Ménard waited two weeks for the Huron who had deserted him, only later to lose his life upon Wisconsin River which issues from this lake; see Henry Colin Campbell, "Father Ménard," in Parkman Club *Papers*, No. 11. The name first appears on a map of 1718 prepared by Guillaume de l'Isle from the memoirs of those who had visited this country; it is, however, there erroneously made the source of one branch of the Chippewa (or "Bons Secours") River, and it was so represented throughout the French period. In 1820, Doty makes it the source both of one branch of the Chippewa, and the Menominee of Green Bay. The map used by the makers of the boundary between Michigan and Wisconsin gave Lac Vieux Désert as the source of the Montreal, and it was thus made a cardinal point in the northeast boundary of Wisconsin. It was not until Cram's survey of 1840 that the true position of this lake as the source of Wisconsin River was determined. Thence it was made the starting point of the survey of 1847 that finally marked the boundary. The Indian village was apparently on the north side of the lake; Cram calls it "Katakitakon." While engaged in his survey, the chief of this band, whom he names Cashaosha, opposed his progress until given a written promise that the right of way should be purchased by the government. In reality the land had all been sold to the United States by the treaty of 1842; but the chief again threatened to oppose Burt's survey of 1847, until mollified by valuable presents. In 1854 a treaty at La Pointe allotted a considerable reservation for this band, then spoken of as large and important. It is now consolidated with the band of Anse Keweenaw, living on a reservation at the latter place, on the upper peninsula of Michigan.—ED.

[62] Masquinongé is the Chippewa form of the word now usually given as muskallunge, or maskalonge. Its significance is great pike, or pickerel, and is applied to the fish known to science as *esox nobilior*, a frequenter of the northern Wisconsin lakes.—ED.

[63] The "perdrix," here translated as partridge, must have been one of two birds: the Canadian spruce grouse, *canachites canadensis canace*,

The squirrels are doing much damage in the corn fields; they ate 77 ears last night.

11th Saturday. Old "Lachouette" came here last night with his band. I gave him a small keg of four pots for nothing.

We had a great deal of trouble last night owing to the liquor. They quarreled among themselves; we quarreled with them and almost came to blows. For a trifle I would retract, did I not fear to be inconsistent, and I would say they are very bad rascals. All the Savages I had seen before them were reputed bad, knavish, and addicted to thieving; I found them gentle, well-behaved, polite and docile. These last passed for being good, affable, and interested in the Fort, and I found them detestable. Nevertheless, they made many apologies to me in the morning, saying that such a thing had never happened to them, that they were too drunk—the usual excuses of such black dogs! I threatened old "La Chouette" telling him I would not give him his flag, and I made Gauthier deliver him a harangue suited to his conduct. I am very sorry to be obliged to note here that I did not find Gauthier resolute enough with the Savages as a man should be.

13th Monday. Providence has been pleased to succor us for this morning, we caught in our nets twenty-eight carp and four sun-fish.[64]

I am quite decided, if I am destined to winter at this post next year, to ask M[r] William M[c]Gillivray for a good Sauteux interpreter, an honest man and resolute in dealing with the tribes. The interests of the Company absolutely require it because, every autumn, rum must be given to get provisions. And what are two men to cope with sometimes forty or fifty Savages under the influence of liquor and inclined to evil deeds. Were it pos-

---

Linn.; or, the ruffled grouse, *bonasa umbellus*, Linn. Both are common in the pine districts, where not exterminated, and both are commonly called partridge. There is no basis to determine which of these the traders killed.—PROF. GEORGE WAGNER.

[64] The French word for this fish is *crapaix*, i. e., crapets, sunfish, *lepomis gibbosus*.—CRAWFORD LINDSAY, translator.

sible to gather all the French of the post together at such moments, there would be nothing to fear, but unfortunately they are still in the portage, and, during this time of calamity, Bazinet is sometimes in one village, sometimes in another trying to get a sack of wild rice.[65]

"But," you may say, "how does he manage?" I answer that he runs no risk because he arrives at a village, I suppose, with a keg of rum. He finds the Savages sober; he gets from them 10 or 11 sacks of wild rice for which he gives his keg, then he leaves at once and is rid of them, but it is different at the Fort.[66]

14th Tuesday. Durocher, one of my men, came here at three o'clock in the afternoon with the youngest son[67] of M^r Mi[chel] Cadotte, whom I asked of his father at Fort Kamanaitiquoya. He comes to spend the winter with me to learn to read, and

---

[65] While having a wide habitat in the United States, wild rice (*zizania aquatica*) is particularly a plant of northern Wisconsin and Minnesota, and a staple food with the Indians of that region. It was probably due to this prevalence that so large an Indian population dwelt on the headwaters of the Mississippi, St. Croix, Chippewa, and Wisconsin rivers. On this and the method of harvesting the grain, see Albert E. Jenks, "Wild Rice Gatherers of the Upper Lakes," in American Bureau of Ethnology *Report*, No. 19. Jenks gives a chapter to the use of this product by the whites, and shows how dependent the fur-traders were upon its purchase. It is still used by whites, and forms an article of commerce in the northern Wisconsin towns, but is always garnered by Indians. The sacks in which it was placed were usually made from the skin of some small animal, such as a fawn, but were often woven from rushes. The price of a bushel was usually a plus, or about $2. One Indian family can harvest, cure, thresh, and winnow from five to twenty-five bushels in the early autumn, mostly during September, which is known as the "wild rice moon," or month. The fur-traders called the Chippewa who used this grain, Folles Avoine (Wild Oats) Sauteurs; and the territory between the St. Croix and Lac du Flambeau was early known as the Folles-Avoine district.—ED.

[66] Intoxicating liquor was lavishly dispensed during the struggle with the X Y.—MASSON.

[67] Probably the person mentioned *ante*, p. 184, note 58.—ED.

serve me as interpreter when necessary. If I teach him French, he will teach me Saulteux in return. His father came himself to bring him to the Portage with Mr Léon St Germain,[68] who went on to Latonaganne to get wild rice.

Racicot sent me a keg of rum double strength, by Durocher, foreseeing that I should need it. He wrote to tell me that General Chorette arrived at last on the 8th instant at the Portage with his aide-de-camp Lalancette and ten men hired to work. They have sixty packages of trade goods destined for this post. Racicot says he counted them. They fired small shot at Mr Cadotte when he passed near them on Lake Superior, but I presume they were intoxicated at the time.

From all appearances, I think none of them entered the River des Sauteux, and I am sorry for it, because the more their goods are scattered the more they would waste and the less we should have to fear them. All that the Savages told me about Mr. Cadotte [Chorette] on the subject, while I was on the lake with them, is altogether untrue, for the three canoe loads are entering here, and one Lamarche has arrived from the Grand Portage with another canoe load to work against Mr. Cadotte at la Pointe. This morning I sent back Durocher to rejoin his traveling companions. We caught nothing this morning in the nets. * * * One day of abundance and ten days of famine!

16th Thursday. Today I gave Gauthier some goods for the furs he had in the store. I cannot send him to set the nets because his wife is being confined. He told me yesterday evening that he would never go to Fort Kamanaitiquoya if he thought he would not find Mr Sayer there; that he hoped for everything

---

[68] During this period there were in the Northwest several traders named St. Germain. Possibly the one here mentioned was he who served as Chippewa interpreter during the War of 1812-15. He visited Grand Portage, endeavoring to enlist the Chippewa of Lake Superior in the contest. He was commended for keeping his detachment from plundering. Leon St. Germain entered the American Fur Company in 1819, being employed at Lac du Flambeau at a salary of $2400. He was closely associated with the Cadotte family, having married a daughter of the elder Michel.—ED.

from that gentleman; protection etc. etc, and would rather descend the River des Sauteux in the spring in the hope of meeting people from Michilimakinac[69] there, and obtaining an outfit from them. I calmed him down and made him take other resolutions, telling him that if he acted thus it would be a manifest proof that he was guilty, and that the proper thing for him to do was to go to Fort Kamanaitiquoya, and explain to our Gentlemen all that had occurred, etc. etc. In the end he agreed with me and resolved to go there and ask pardon.

17th Friday. The heat is excessive, such as we have not had this summer, and, strange to say, there is frequently frost at night, which, in my opinion is not very good for the crops; and we could easily dispense with sickness, having famine. O! wretched people of Lac du Flambeau, everything is against you! Little to eat, much work to do; sometimes ill, uncertain of obtaining returns, with reproaches to be dreaded from the Partners, anxiety about the goods out of the fort, Savages to satisfy, and adversaries to watch. What a life!! "Poor Malhiot, when will you be relieved of such a heavy burden? I have cast your nativity."[70] If he who has always protected you so far and has been a second father to you, kindly continues his good graces and covers you with his mantle, you will be sheltered from the weather and will soon be rewarded for all your labor and discomfort."

19th Sunday. Bazinet arrived from Ouisseconsaint yesterday

---

[69] A company of traders against whom the bourgeois [of the North West Company] were competing to the south of Lake Superior. That company joined Mr. John Jacob Astor some years later.—MASSON.

Comment by Ed.—This was the Mackinac Company, whose history is briefly sketched in *Wis. Hist. Colls.*, xviii, pp. 339, 340. Their headquarters were at Mackinac, with a secondary rendezvous at Prairie du Chien. They sent traders up the Chippewa, although it is not known that they had a post thereon. The Mackinac Company traded largely with the Sioux, from whom they secured their best returns. The North West Company had very little Sioux trade.

[70] The French is "tirer ton horoscope", that is, have your future predicted by astrology.—ED.

evening at 6 o'clock. His returns are not what I had expected, but if all the goods I send out between now and the spring yield as good returns I shall not have much to complain of. He reports that the Savages stabbed one another during the drinking bout, and that he would have been killed had it not been for "l'Outarde." He never ceases praising that good Savage to me, saying that he would not touch the rum; and, during the whole time the Savages were intoxicated, he remained armed and walked to and fro in front of the tent door.

Not one devil among them intends to give three deer hides for a plus, and, to avoid displeasing them, I am obliged to do like my adversary who takes two for a plus. We have just heard several gun-shots in the direction of Chorette's fort[71] which leads us to presume that His Lordship has just landed.

20th Monday. The wife of old "La Chouette" and one of his daughters came this morning. I got some deer skins and 2 bear skins from them. Two hours after their arrival they went to Chorette's but were thrown out by Lalancette who was then as drunk as a hog. He said to them: "Go away! Go to your Father, *the Great Trader.* Let him give you drink; as for us, we are slaves and have no rum." * * * Poor Brutes![72] do they think, like the Savages, that I am really one of the partners of the North West Company!

23rd Thursday. Yesterday evening at eight o'clock, Chorette passed here and told Bazinet he had been unable to see the Savages; we think the wounded are dead and that is why they delay. I think I will send some one to meet them tomorrow to make sure of the little provisions they have. I learned this morning from several Savages that one L'étang[73] had entered

---

[71] There does not seem to be any data to determine the site of the X Y Company's post. As it was abandoned upon the consolidation of the companies, or over one hundred years ago, its site is probably now unmarked.—ED.

[72] The French word is here the unknown term "Besthias," referred to *ante,* p. 186, note 60.—E*d.*

[73] This person, whose name is also spelled Le Temps, but was prob-

the River des Sauteux with one canoe load. This completes my conviction that the 60 packages Chorette has with him are intended for this post.

24th Friday. Gauthier, having been asked by Chorette to go and see him, went there with my permission to ascertain what he wanted. At the same time, I wanted to test him and see whether he would drink, but I have the consolation of being able to say that he came back quite sober and I like to think that he will keep the promises he has made me.

We are threatened with a famine because the Savages absolutely want to go on the war-path; consequently they will put the greater portion of their rice in caches, and we shall find ourselves with very little, which we shall have to purchase at its weight in gold.

25th Saturday. Thirty canoes arrived here at noon. Chorette's Savages made me a present of 3 sacks of wild rice for which I gave them a large keg of rum and a brasse of tobacco. I gave "le Muffle d'Orignal"[74] a coat and harangued him as follows:

"*Kinsman*—I am quite willing to forget what thou didst last year and to believe it was not thy fault that we did not get all thy furs, but do not act in the same way in future. The coat I give thee today will show thee the path thou must follow. * * * I rely on all thy promises; be not double-faced. I would like to have not only thy furs but also thy corn. I have many children to feed. Moreover it would soil thy body to carry a single grain of corn to the other fort. My orders from our

---

ably identical with the Canadian-French name L'Estang, was an opposition trader on Red Lake, in the present Minnesota, in 1798. He appears to have settled finally in that state, although a family bearing a similar name resided during the eighteenth century at Cahokia.—ED.

[74] "Le muffle d'Orignal" (moose's muzzle) must have been the chief known as Mozoboddo (Monsobodouh), who succeeded his father Keeshkenum, one of the noted Chippewa chiefs, the first settler at Lac du Flambeau. Keeshkenum was still alive in 1827, but very old, and died soon thereafter, when Mozoboddo was invested with the chieftainship. He in turn died about 1832, and was succeeded by White Crow.—ED.

Father at Kamanaitiquoya were for thee as for all the others. I was to give thee nothing this autumn and to wait until I knew thee. But, from what thou hast just told me and from what the French have told me, I am obliged to act as I am doing. Take courage therefore and think of thy Fort."

I gave 4 kegs, of four pots and one of six to these various savages for nothing, because they are devoted to the Fort and are good hunters.

27th Monday. I sent Bazinet to meet my people in the Portage with two of his brothers-in-law, to bring me 4 kegs of rum, double strength.

28th Tuesday. Several of Chorette's Savages came here last night to get rum and to use violence. For a long while I may say, making use of an expression among the lower orders in Canada, that *"I did not know whether I was eating pork or pig"* * * * I was alone with Gauthier and they were at least 15 rascals all armed; those who had no knives or spears, had sticks or stones. Fortunately we all got off with calling one another names and threatening one another. "Le Taureau" came and told us that "l'Outarde" would soon arrive.

30th Thursday. The Savages were making medicine all night and never stopped smoking for war.[75]

31st Friday. At last "l'Outarde" arrived at noon with a following of 15 canoes of his people. I had not a drop of rum to offer him. He asked me where Bazinet was and I told him he had gone to the Portage, and would not be back until tonight or tomorrow night because he was afraid to pass the village of Lac du Flambeau in the day time lest he might be robbed; that we

---

[75] A large literature exists on the subject of "making medicine," or the religious and magic rites of the Chippewa. An interesting early description of the consultation with their tutelary spirits is found in Bain, *Henry's Travels*, pp. 66–69. The entire subject of what the Jesuit missionaries called sorcery, and others name jugglery, as well as the great religious society found among the Chippewa, is discussed in Walter J. Hoffman, "The Midewiwin, or Grand Medicine Society, of the Ojibwa" in U. S. Bureau of Ethnology *Report*, vii, pp. 149–299.—ED.

had been nearly killed, etc. He rushed out at once and delivered the following harangue: "What have you done, you people of Lac du Flambeau? Why have you come to worry my Trader, and have you threatened to kill him and steal his goods? I did not ask him to come here to be the sport of Savages or to be compelled to feed or treat you. You have your own Trader; get what you want from him. He has rum; let him give you some, and make him give you some. He has some etc. etc." I looked at him while he was speaking. He looked like a soldier. He re-entered a moment afterward and said to me: "No, no, Bazinet will not be robbed," and he at once commanded with authority three young men to go and meet him.

September 2nd Sunday. "L'Outarde" told me yesterday he would do all in his power to prevent the Savages from going on the war-path, because if they went I should get no furs. It has been raining since noon yesterday, and Bazinet has not turned up. The Savages find the time longer than I do.

3rd Monday. Bazinet arrived at 4 o'clock yesterday afternoon with the goods he had gone to get. I gave a coat to "l'Outarde" and also his flag, and one to "la Grande Loutre." I gave a laced capot to "le Grand Canard," and another to the Lieutenant of "La Loutre," and to each his share of rum. I delivered the following harangue to "l'Outarde."

"*Kinsman*—The coat I have put on thee is sent thee by the Great Trader; by such coats he distinguishes the most highly considered persons of a tribe. The Flag is a true symbol of a Chief and thou must deem thyself honored by it, because we do not give them to the first comers among the Savages. One must do as thou dost to get one, that is: love the French as thou dost, watch over their preservation and enable them to make up packs of furs.

"My orders were to give thee nothing this autumn, and to wait until the spring that I might know thee, but, on account of all the good things I have heard of thee from the French, I did not hesitate a moment to make thee glorious, for I am convinced thou wilt always be the same for the Fort; that thou wilt take care of my young men, that no dog may bite them,[76] and that they will never come back ashamed when they go to thy lodges.

"As first chief of the place, thou must make every effort so that all the Savages may come and trade here in the spring; it will be a glory to thee to send the canoes full to the Grand Portage.[77]

"Remember that the name of the Great Trader[78] is on the flag. Wherever thou mayest go, to no matter which one of his Forts, thou wilt be received with open arms, and he cannot give thee a greater token of his friendship. He has listened to thy complaints and is very sorry Gauthier drank thy rum last year. I can assure thee, comrade, that it will be different this year.

"And ye, all of ye, look at me. See the Trader who is sent to you! I am he whom you asked for. This summer, I received three messages from three chiefs of the prairies[79] to go back and winter in their lands, but I refused in order that our Great Trader might speak truly, who wished to send me here to do you a charity and not to be despised. Nevertheless I have no reproaches to address you because this is the first time I see you. Be devoted, therefore, to your Fort; take care of it; guard its doors and next spring I will send good news of you to our Father."

4th Tuesday. We had quarrels all day with the Savages of Lac du Flambeau;[80] spears, knives, hatchets, etc, all were

[76] A figure to express the desire that no misfortune shall happen to them.—ED.

[77] Used to indicate the general rendezvous, which had long been at Grand Portage, but was in process of removal to Kaministiquia. See *ante*, p. 166, note 23.—ED.

[78] The head of the North West Company, William McGillevray.—ED.

[79] Referring to his previous post on Assiniboine River; see sketch of Malhiot, *ante*, p. 165.—ED.

[80] The village of Lac du Flambeau would seem, by inference from this relation, to have been attached to the X Y Company; while Malhiot, for the North West Company, relied upon the trade of the outlying villages. This description of a drunken fray is characteristic of the fur-trade journals, especially during the period of great competition. See J. Long, "Voyages," in Thwaites, *Early Western Travels* (Cleveland, 1904), ii.—ED.

brought into play. They made a breach in the Fort, broke one of the doors and had it not been for the aid of "l'Outarde," of "l'Epaule de Canard," and two or three young men who were quite sober at the time, there would certainly have been bloodshed and even somebody killed on one side or the other. "L'Outarde" had his head cut open with a blow from a stick, and so had one of his young men. I thanked God he had no knife during the fight, for he would assuredly have killed somebody. There were 5 or 6 at him, and I expected every moment to see him pass from this world to the other. He really looked like a madman, uttering yells that would frighten any one and calling out to me from time to time: "Take courage, Father! Strike everywhere— hit! kill!" After a two hours quarrel we succeeded in getting those wild beasts out of the Fort.

5th Wednesday. The Savages of Lac du Flambeau finished their noise only at nine o'clock last night, and to sign the treaty of peace I gave them a keg of four pots and a brasse of tobacco. "L'Outarde" was only half pleased at this and he wanted very much to begin the fight again. Today all is calm. They are sleeping soundly. These Savages of Lac du Flambeau do not belong to "l'Outarde's" band.

6th Thursday. I sent Bazinet to distribute a keg of rum among the lodges. "L'Outarde" and 5 of his young men are continually in the Fort, quite sober, and so is "l'Epaule de Canard," to prevent and stop all quarrels that might arise.

7th Friday. The end of this drinking bout was very quiet; we slept from one o'clock until this morning; we greatly needed it for we had not lain down since the 3rd instant.

10th Monday. The Savages are beginning to leave. May they all be gone soon! "L'Outarde" started yesterday with his young men to gather wild rice at lac de la Truite where his village is.[81]

---

[81] Trout Lake (Lac de la Truite) is in Vilas County, just east of the Flambeau reservation. It is said that when the Chippewa moved down into the interior of the country, somewhere near the middle of the eighteenth century, they tarried awhile at Trout Lake, before passing to Lac du Flambeau on the west.—ED.

12th Wednesday. A band of the rascals who are camped here near the Fort have gone to camp at the village of Lac du Flambeau, until my people come.

14th Friday. Yesterday I got 4 sacks of rice from Folle Avoine for which I gave him half a keg of rum and half a brasse of tobacco. The rum was drunk last night at the lodges of Lac du Flambeau, notwithstanding all I could do and say, for I hoped that devil of a Savage would have taken it to his own grounds as he had promised me. Fortunately, drunk as they were, they did not come and ask me for more. A Great Miracle!

16th Sunday. Three of old "Lachouette's" young men arrived here yesterday at four o'clock in the afternoon, and four others, from Lac de la Folle,[82] from whom I got 3 sacks of rice. The wind blew and rain fell to an extraordinary degree today. The Savages overwhelm us; we cannot set our nets, and we constantly eat our rice with water only. A fine and good dish! dogs would get thin on it.

21st Friday. It rained from Sunday until noon yesterday. This morning Chorette arrived with four of his men carrying loads and he told us the portages were horribly bad.

23rd Sunday. I received a letter from my people this morning; they are still in the great Portage. Through their laziness they ran short of food and went to trade for some at la Tortue's village.[83] I sent Bazinet to meet them and hurry them on and I wrote them the following letter,

"*Racicot,*—I have just received your letter by "La Loche" and I am surprised at its contents. What! people with fourteen and fifteen hundred livres wages take two months to come

---

[82] An abbreviation for *Lac de la Folle Avoine,* or Wild Rice Lake. Jenks, *op. cit.*, pp. 1115–1126, enumerates fifteen or more lakes in northern Wisconsin named for the rice growing therein. There are several in Vilas County alone; the nearest to Lac du Flambeau that now keeps the name is Little Rice Lake, in township 42 north, range 7 east, northeast of Trout Lake.—Ed.

[83] Probably on the lake known as Turtle Lake, on the Montreal River portage.—Ed.

through the Montreal Portage! Children that ye are! people on whom no reliance can be placed.[84] Men coming from Montreal this year could have done as much as you! You have not enough sense to know the injury you are doing the Company by your delay. Now you find yourselves in bad roads and whose is the fault? Say, say that your hearts are not in the right place and that you did not wish to do your duty.

"You, Racicot, who were about to be promoted and enter into office, why did you not command the others and make them push on by force or by gentle means? No doubt you were very glad to sleep with your face to the sun like the others. If you have been without food, it is your own fault also, and what would you have to say now, if I made you pay for the rum you gave to purchase food! You ask me for Durocher; work a miracle, cure him and he will go and warm your beds!

F. Vt. M. l. o."

26th Wednesday. The Savages pester me and my provisions are disappearing like straw in the fire. I am eager to have Bazinet come so as to get rid of them. The rascals are so crowded together in my house, especially in the last five or six days, that they have given me vermin and the more I change my shirt the more vermin I have. It is the same with Gauthier. We hardly have time to put a kettle of rice on the fire before 50 of those dogs are around us asking for some even before it is boiled. Our beards will soon be as long as billy-goats; and we are devoured by farcy.

27th Thursday. "L'Epaule de canard" has just arrived with 30 beaver skins; the traps he got from me a few days ago are broken.

28th Friday. My people came in at last at 4 o'clock yesterday evening. No sooner were the goods put in the store than I began to unpack them and to give some on credit to the Savages of the Vieux Désert who started at one o'clock this morning.

---

[84] The original French reads, "gens de peu de fiate," a local French-Canadian expression, implying that no reliance can be placed in such a person or such a thing.—CRAWFORD LINDSAY.

"L'Aigle"[85] left me his pipe-stem with a porcelain collar to be handed to Mr MacGillivray in the sppring, and he told me he was a straightforward man and left his pipe-stem at the Fort as a token of his sincerity. I gave him a large keg and made the following speech to him:

"*Kinsman*,—It affords me much pleasure to smoke with thy pipe-stem and to receive thy word. Our Great Trader at Kamanaitiquoya will, I hope, receive it in the spring with satisfaction and will send thee a token of his friendship if thou continuest to do well. * * * Take courage therefore; be but one with us and look at the Fort of the X Y only from afar if thou wishest to obtain what thou desirest."

I also gave a laced capot to Barsaloux with a half keg of rum and a large keg to "l'Outarde" to be distributed in his village in exchange for rice.

I forgot to state above that while Bazinet was passing through la Tortue's village with all the goods, he gave away two large kegs of rum there for which he got only two sacks of rice. My cask of shrub was stolen from him and he gave two quarts of rum, double strength, to get it back. He also gave goods on credit to several Savages to whom I would not have given a needle.

I shall take this opportunity to speak of Bazinet according to his merits and to say that he is truly an honest man, as careful as possible of goods on a journey, eager to push on, taking the interests of the Company, working to excess in a fort, a famous hand at going out to meet the Savages and trade with them,[86] but too timid with them, for if a rascal were to look somewhat fixedly at him, he could make him give up his trousers. Such being the case, I maintain that he would be very capable under an-

---

[85] Perhaps this was the chieftain known as Gitshee Migeezee (Great Eagle), who signed the treaty of 1826, and was said to be from Ontonagon.—ED.

[86] The French phrase, a common one among fur-traders, is "courir la drouine," which means to go with the savages to their winter hunting grounds and trade with them there, instead of waiting for their return to the post.—ED.

other, but would be useless as head man of a post. He is a good hand at going out to meet the Savages and trade with them because the quantity of goods is never great and he always manages to defend himself on the person who employs him.

29th Saturday. Barsaloux came back this morning and so did "la Grue Blanche." They say they were wrecked, and I am obliged to give them fresh goods on credit so as not to lose all. They left me their collars as pledges. Today I obtained from the son of "La Pierre à Affiler" four sacks of rice for which I gave him a half keg of rum. I gave my people a feast.

30th Sunday. My people got very drunk yesterday and, through fear, the Savages stopped drinking. Today I sent three of my men to Lac de la Truite to get rice and two others to old "La Chouette's" for the same purpose. Chorette left this morning to go and rejoin his people in the Portage.

October 3rd, Wednesday. Old "La Chouette" arrived here yesterday with his band. I obtained from him the promise that they would not drink in my Fort. He left this morning quite pleased with his Flag and so were all his followers. A number of Savages of Lac du Flambeau were at the water's edge where he embarked and, at my request, he did not give them a single dram.

4th Thursday. I have just sent off Bazinet for Ouisseconsaint with an outfit of 3½ pieces of cloth, 4 kegs of rum, double strength, one of powder etc., etc. I am sending Racicot with him because the majority of the Savages to whom I have given credit are to winter there and he will be only too necessary there, as he can read, to make out all the credits and also to help Bazinet when the Savages are in liquor, for, I repeat it with regret, the poor devil has no more resolution than a child.

5th Friday. I have just taken an inventory of the furs I have traded since my arrival here and I counted: 528 deer skins, 840 musk-rat skins, 107 lbs. Beaver, 44 otter skins, 16 bear skins, 7 marten skins, 1 mink skin—the whole making probably sixteen packs. This autumn trade has greatly reduced my stock of goods so that I am unable to send any into the country of the River of the Sauteux. Without exaggeration it would certainly have required the assortment of 16 pieces of cloth to cope with my adversaries and crush them, and I would venture to bet that Chorette would not get ten packs for all his goods had I the necessary stock to send out and compete with him in the country of the River of the Sauteux.

11th Thursday. "L'Outarde" came here last Monday very late at night, as he was to start the next day. He told me that "l'Epaule de Canard" had started to go and join Bazinet in his winter-quarters. Instead of leaving, "l'Outarde" got drunk at Chorette's and did not get sober until today. To get rid of him and not lose the advances I had made him I gave him another half keg of rum for nothing for himself and his band, and he started with many presents from Chorette. That man never should have had a coat and still less a flag. He is a slave to liquor; he is too importunate and half a canoe load would not suffice to satisfy him. The Savages stole a half keg of rum, double strength, from Chorette last night and "l'Outarde" was at their head.

13th Saturday. Two young men from the Lakes,[87] sent by old "La Chouette" arrived here yesterday morning. I got one hundred and ten musk-rat and two beaver skins from them. I am sending to him George Yarns, his father-in-law, to get the kegs he has belonging to me and to take him ammunition and a few goods he asks for the purpose of trading on commission with the Savages of the Lakes.

14th Sunday. All is calm at last. * * * All those black faces have gone and entered their winter-quarters. May God guide them! We shall therefore begin fishing again and have some fish to season our rice. It is time, for my stomach was getting weak.

15th Monday. Having no more credit to give, I took an in-

---

[87] Probably Pelican Lakes, not far from Rhinelander, in Oneida and Lincoln counties. The Lac du Flambeau band had, towards the close of the eighteenth century, spread into this region.—ED.

ventory of the remaining goods this morning. They consist of 3½ pieces of common cloth, and assortment; 1½ Roll of tobacco; 6 kegs, double strength; 1½ keg of powder; shot, bullets etc.

Had I but as much again, I could have sent to compete against Chorette in the country of the River of the Sauteux. Were I to divide what remains in two, it would spoil the trade.

17th Wednesday. My men have just arrived from Chorette's; they tell me he has started for the Rivière des Sauteux with two bastard[88] canoes and has 6 engagés with him. They say they saw 3½ bales of goods.

18th Thursday. I am despatching Durocher to la Pointe to inform Mʳ Cadotte that I cannot send any one to compete against Chorette at the Rivière des Sauteux; that he must send himself and have him followed step by step and even have him accompanied thus until the spring. I am also asking for a two handed saw to replace the sawn lumber of my fort and protect myself against attack another year.

30th Saturday. Hitherto I have been too busy to speak of the Savages with the exception of an occasional allusion and only in a very imperfect manner; and, so that I may not forget what I have to say about them, I return to the subject. Let us therefore make use of the oil while there is some in the lamp.

"L'Outarde" is very far from perfect. I cannot say he is a rogue and that his heart is black, but he is on the way to it, and I hope, for the public good, both on account of the Savages and of ourselves, and for the benefit of the North West Company, that the flag I gave him will serve as his winding-sheet.

Old "La Chouette" is improving and works with interest for the Fort, but he was lacking in courage to deserve the flag he got.

"L'Epaule de Canard" is the only Savage who deserved a flag and he was not given one! He is a sober, brave Savage, liked by the others, liking the French, capable of sacrificing himself for them; a good man for errands; he does not ask for things, is satisfied with everything that is given him and is a famous

---

[88] The smallest transport canoe of the Northwest.—MASSON.

hunter. I thought I had found another man like him in Bazinet's brother-in-law called "La Loche," but he is not a hunter and is still young. He told me one day he hoped to become as good a man; I answered that many qualities were needed to entitle one to be clothed with a coat, etc; that the position of chief was hard to keep, and that a man must be reckless of his life to be a chief. He then told me he could do everything, etc. I thought proper to answer that the ladder was a very long one, that he had only mounted the first round and had a long way to go before reaching the top.

There are some others whom I might include in the number of good Savages, but, as a rule, if I could put them all in a bag and know that Lucifer wanted them, I would give them all to him for a penny. * * * If they were lambs formerly, today they are rabid wolves and unchained devils. As a rule they possess all the vices of mankind and only think they are living well, when they live evil lives.

After saying what I think of those wretches, I will now deal with the French. I have said what I had to say about Bazinet; as to Gauthier it would be very wrong of me to complain of him. He no longer drinks and behaves like an honest man. At the first drinking bout the Savages had this autumn he weakened a little and seemed lacking in firmness, but it has been quite different since; he is doing his best and if he be expelled from the Company, three fourths of the people may be banished from the Synagogue.

All the other men under me behave like good fellows and are much more polite, much more submissive, and take a little more interest than the people of the North.[89]

November 6th, Tuesday. My men have finished chopping their firewood and tomorrow will begin squaring the pickets for the fort.

* * * * * * *

---

[89] Malhiot is contrasting his employees with those on the company's roll, north and west of Kaministiquia, called collectively "people of the North."—ED.

December 20th, Thursday.[90] Two of the Savages went last night in spite of me to Lalancette's to ask him to sell them some twine for nets. They came back at half past three and told me Lalancette had gone after my people. I sent Martineau today to their lodges with a kettle and two silk handkerchiefs which they asked me to trade to them.

21st Friday. Martineau and Bruno arrived at five o'clock in the evening and brought furs to the value of 24 plus, most of them being beaver skins. George, Durocher and Little Cadotte remained at the lodges. Martineau told me that Lalancette had given a kettle, the first of the nest[91] for two and a half plus; he also gave a new net for twenty muskrat skins and another for the damaged skin of a bear cub. The Savages also ask for provisions, shot and some other small articles.

Lalancette was so intoxicated the day before yesterday that he was obliged to sleep on the road and did not reach the lodges until noon; my people had arrived during the night. Martineau swore to me that Lalancette had fallen at least twenty times, and had wandered as much and broken as much underbrush as a moose that has remained a long time in the same place.[92]

23rd Sunday. At last my people have all arrived and have brought some beaver skins. They say that Lalancette spent a four pot keg of rum, double strength, in the lodges without being able to get a single marten skin, and had it not been for his kettle and his two nets, he would have gone back empty-handed, for the Savages waited a day thinking I would send them some.

Little Cadotte is very clever with the Nations [tribes], al-

---

[90] The part of the journal omitted from Nov. 7 to Dec. 20 contains nothing interesting. The men in the fort lived on a scant allowance of food, catching barely enough fish to season their wild rice or corn [bled].—MASSON.

[91] The smallest kettle of a series fitting one within the other, in order to economize space.—MASSON.

[92] The French phrase is "ravage d'orignal." Our hunters call a ravage of a moose or caribou the place where the animal has eaten moss or twigs, broken the underbrush, etc.—CRAWFORD LINDSAY.

though he is very young. My men say that he gave himself an extraordinary amount of trouble. He got hold of the greater portion of the Savages' Furs as soon as he saw Lalancette come on the lake, and he said to them before Lalancette himself: "Do not trade with him; he knew you were starving and he did not deign to bring you a single grain of rice; he is a hog; he makes a god of his belly. He would see the Savages die rather than give them a glass of water, etc. etc." I take this opportunity to say that the child promises well; his sentiments are very good; he is polite, steady, saving etc. When he came here in the autumn he did not know a single letter of the alphabet, and could barely pronounce a few words in French, and now he can read as well as a child who has been 4 years at school. He knows his prayers and his catechism; but one step more and he will be a prodigy.

* * * * * * *

February 4th, Monday.[93] Chorette came to pay me a visit; I made him stop and have supper with me. He told me that "La Pierre à affiler" and his young men intend to kill me in the spring; to be on my guard against them; that he was sure of their plot. I asked him why, and he said it was because Bazinet had told them I had given them all to the Master of life and they would all die before the spring.[94]

---

[93] The journal from December 23 to February 4 contains nothing interesting. Fishing was a complete failure.—MASSON.

[94] This indicates the superstitions of the Indians, which were largely shared by the French voyageurs. Malhiot means that the Indians believed he had cast some kind of charm or spell upon them, by an appeal to the Great Spirit, for whom they frequently used the term "Master of Life." Nothing more appears of this plot against Malhiot's life; probably the warning given by his rival trader was sufficient to thwart it. The chief whom Malhiot calls "La Pierre à affiler" was the celebrated Keeshkenum, head chief of the Lac du Flambeau band. He was Chorette's father-in-law, and therefore in the interests of the X Y Company. He was a chief of great influence, first founder of the Lac du Flambeau band, descendant of Shadawish, great chief of Sault Ste. Marie in 1671. Keeshkenum was of the totem of the crane, and claimed pre-eminence over all the interior villages of

March 1st, Friday.⁹⁵ I arrived here four hours after nightfall after an absence of two days at old "Lachouette's" whence I brought back 10 beaver skins, also 7 maskinongé for which I gave a keg of rum of 4 pots. Today we caught enough fish for one meal,

I learn from two young men who have just arrived that "le Muffle d'Orignal," one of the Savages I gave a coat to last autumn, starved to such an extent that he had to eat his pack, his dogs, and ever his gun-cover; and that "le Chef des Oiseaux," who found him by accident, gave him assistance. I sent a carrot⁹⁶ of tobacco to "le Chef des Oiseaux."

9th Saturday. "La Tête Grise" arrived and camped near the fort with the whole of his band. When Gauthier's wife went this morning to Chorette's to get her snow-shoes that a Savage had taken from her, Lalancette said so many insulting things to her that the woman came back in tears. Gauthier went there at once and I sent two men with him. He found Lalancette hidden in the garret of his house, but shame compelled him to come down when Gauthier seized him and beat him to such an extent that he cannot see. My two men took off their coats and challenged the remainder of the men in the house, but the challenge was not taken up.

13th Wednesday. Tonight, at a very late hour, "le Gros Aigle,"⁹⁷ a Savage of the Vieux Désert, arrived here. He came to get us to go and collect my advances. He has just told me

---

Wisconsin. In 1808 he sharply rebuked the Lac Court Oreille band for their sympathy with Tecumseh. It is claimed that in 1812 he declared his alliance with the Americans. See *Minn. Hist. Colls.*, v, pp. 372-375. It would seem by that recital that Michel Cadotte Jr. was his grandson—probably his grand nephew, as the Indians did not distinguish between these degrees of consanguinity. He was living in 1827, but soon after died.—ED.

⁹⁵ The journal from February 5 to March 1, contains nothing of interest; it speaks only of the savages starving and the sufferings of the French, who have no fish.—MASSON.

⁹⁶ Two or three pounds of tobacco.—MASSON.

⁹⁷ Probably the same Indian noted *ante*, p. 200, note 85.—ED.

that Tremblé whom I sent with them last autumn with over 90 plus worth of goods, had left their lodges after trading the goods and had gone to Roy's at l'Anse,[98] with a fine pack and that they had not seen him since. That Tremblé must have left his Savages about the 2nd or third of January.

14th Thursday. I am sending Gauthier with Durocher to

---

[98] François Roy was North West Company clerk at l'Anse as early as 1801–02. The name was not uncommon among fur-trade employees. Probably the Indian interpreter of 1812 at Detroit, was the Roy from l'Anse, since he accompanied other Lake Superior traders. From that time he disappears from our knowledge.

L'Anse was the French term for the small bay at the bottom of Keweenaw Bay, and was frequented by the Indians from very early times. It was at an Indian village on this site that Father Ménard spent the last winter before his death (1660–61), laboring among fugitive Ottawa. It soon came, however, to be Chippewa territory. Ménard had given the bay the name of St. Thérèse, but it soon reverted to the aboriginal form. L'Anse was not visited by the ordinary traveller on Lake Superior, since it lies fifteen miles south of the Keweenaw portage. A considerable Indian village at this point, however, induced trading, and the post became an auxiliary of that of La Pointe. When the American Fur Company began trade in Lake Superior in 1816–17, l'Anse was one of their first posts, being managed by John Johnston, from the Sault. In 1826, William Holliday was clerk in charge. A mission for the Indians at l'Anse was begun in 1832, by Methodists from Canada. John Sunday, a converted Chippewa, came out and spent seven months at this place. In the autumn, ten Indians from l'Anse were baptized at Sault Ste. Marie by the well-known Christian chief, Peter Jones. Later, the mission was transferred to the care of the church in the United States. It proved to be quite successful, and by 1848 had 300 civilized Indians dwelling in houses and assuming citizenship. A reservation was laid off in 1859 for the l'Anse band, just north of the American town. The Catholic mission at l'Anse was founded by Father Baraga in 1843, in the township called by his name. There he dwelt for ten years until created bishop, and there prepared his well-known grammar and dictionary of the Chippewa language. L'Anse thus became a noted mission centre; but the invasion of miners and prospectors after 1845, brought to the Indians whiskey and demoralization. Their progress towards civilization has, however, continued, and in 1903 they were reported as self-supporting, partially educated, and living much like their white neighbors.—ED.

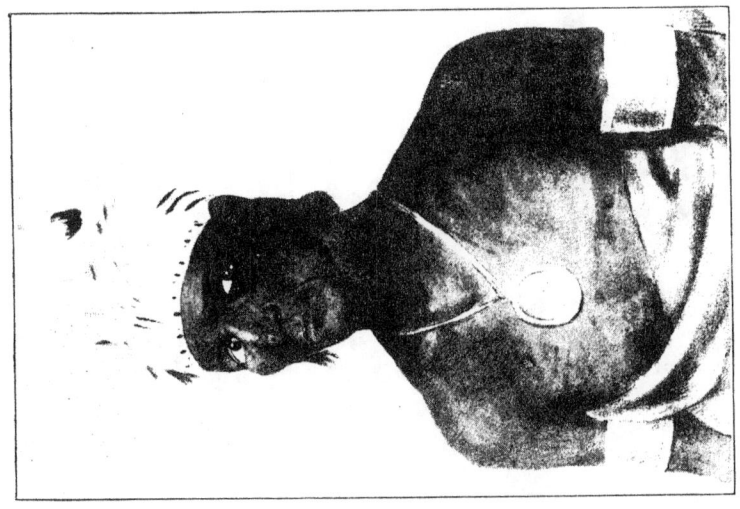

MAKOMETA, OR BEAR'S OIL.
Menominee chief. From colored lithograph by James Otto Lewis, 1827

SHINGGAABAW'OSIN, OR THE FIGURED STONE.
Chippewa chief. From colored lithograph by James Otto Lewis, 1826

the Vieux Desert to collect my advances and to trade. All the Savages of that place starved more than the others and have almost nothing; they will hardly be able to pay one fourth of their advances. I am sending Martineau and Beaulieu to l'Anse with a Savage to whom I am giving 20 plus worth of goods for his trouble. I am giving orders to those three men to try and bring Tremblé back and, if they cannot succeed, to at least seize the pack. This rascally trick does me great harm; it takes two men away from me for at least 20 days and my Fort is kept back. Nevertheless, I do not despair of having the pickets planted before I leave, but the absence of those two men during twenty days will make me lose many plus.

16th Saturday. "L'Outarde" arrived here with two loads of meat which he gave me as a present. I gave him six pots of rum. A moment afterward his brother-in-law arrived thinner than I have ever seen any man and so weakened by starvation that he could hardly put one foot before the other. "Le Genou" arrived later; he told me he had killed three moose and three bears and to send for them; unfortunately, I have only one man and he is ill. Lalancette is to go and get the meat. "Le Genou" will keep the bear skins for me. I forgot to say that on the 17th we had a great deal of thunder and lightning.

April 17th Wednesday. My people have finished planting the pickets of my Fort and it is the finest of all the savage departments. "Long live the North West Company!" "Honor to Malhiot!"

Old La Chouette who has just arrived made me a present of 4 pieces of meat for which I gave him 5 chopines of rum. His son "Le Brulé" repaid me his advance and gave me a bear-skin; I made him a present of half a keg of rum; I gave him another half keg on commission, also some ammunition and tobacco to trade with the people of the Lakes. I also gave his father the same quantity of ammunition. Those Savages are working very well for the Fort. * * * How scarce such people are!

15th Thursday. My men are sawing planks to cover the bastion of the Fort. Chorette gives a brasse of cloth for a bear skin. Rum flows like water on both sides, but Chorette is beginning to complain and I still have seven kegs of mixed rum. I have hardly any more tobacco and fear I shall have none at all before I leave. My supply of goods will also fail. * * * For eleven years that I have been wintering among the Savages I have never known a competitor trade as cheaply as Chorette. I think Lucifer brings him his goods from London as he needs them.

26th Friday. The son of "La pierre à Affiler," Chorette's brother-in-law, came here last night and made me a present of an otter skin, 15 musk-rat skins and 12 lbs of sugar for which I gave him 4 pots of rum. He went to drink it at Chorette's with "l'Ours" and "La Petite Racine." When they were quite drunk they cleared the house, nearly killed Chorette, stabbed Lalancette and broke into the store-room.. They took two otter skins, for which I gave them some more rum this morning not knowing that they had stolen them. All this row happened because Chorette had promised them rum for their skins and had none to give them.

They came here tonight intending to get me to give them liquor, but we drove them away by striking them with poles from the top of the Fort. In their fury they went for their guns but did not venture to fire them and went away with the shame of not having succeeded in doing anything.

I thank God every day for having inspired me with the idea of making so good a fort, impregnable to bullets and to all attacks.

May 2nd, Thursday. St Germain has just arrived from la Pointe. He told me, but too late, that the two Companies now form but one.[99] I have engaged my men!

---

[99] For the union of the two companies, North West and X Y, see *ante*, p. 168, note 30. It was arranged at Montreal Nov. 5, 1804, and the agreement then drawn up remained in force until, in 1821, the North West merged into the Hudson's Bay Company. This settlement of 1804 was of immense advantage to the trade; competition was practically abolished; "scenes of violence in the interior ceased, the sale of

10th Friday. The war party that arrived here the day before yesterday to the number of 17, went to Chorette's, killed his dogs and, this afternoon, are feasting on the same dogs. After making me eat some, they left us, to my great satisfaction, for my provisions are diminishing rapidly. Today I am sending 3 men to Chorette's to get my canoe. He is always extravagant as usual, and gives a brasse of cloth for one otter or two beaver skins.

I am expecting another war party from day to day. God grant they may not be so long in importuning me. I also expect Bazinet from day to day. He alone detains me here and I think the fort I ordered him to make is the cause of his delay. I am alone to guard the Fort with Gauthier. My people have not had a day's rest since my arrival here last autumn. Of all the men who may be in the upper country I do not think there are any who have worked as hard as mine: a house twenty feet square, of logs placed one on the other made by four men; 70 cords of fire-wood chopped; pickets sawn for a fort; a bastion covered; a clearing made for sowing 8 kegs of potatoes; and all the journeys made here and there ! ! !

23rd Thursday. We finished the packs at noon; I had the canoes gummed and started from the Fort at half past five in the afternoon after taking stock of what I left in Gauthier's charge. Fine weather; all my people in good health. * * * God be with us throughout our journey!

24th Friday. On the way I met Chorette who was coming back from Lake Superior with half a keg of rum he was taking to his father-in-law. Tremblé took advantage of the opportunity to come to me. The poor fellow gave me very bad reasons

---

liquor was considerably diminished, and commerce was carried on in a more regular and equitable fashion." When Malhiot says that the news has come "too late," he means too late for the reduction of salaries that followed the coalition. The competition of the two companies had increased wages over twenty-five per cent. These were almost immediately lowered, but the employees of both companies were retained.—ED.

as excuses and I fear for him at the Grand Portage. Roy wrote me about him, and also about the trade. He is very wrong to complain because I did not send Tremblé to trade with his Savages, but with mine who obtained goods on credit at my Fort last autumn, and those same Savages are sending a pipe-stem to Mr MacGillivray so that I may send them more goods another year. Mr Cadotte writes me also and informs me he was unable to forward my letter to Mr MacGillivray etc.

26th Sunday. Yesterday we crossed the Portage des Six Poses and that of the village of la Tortue and, at one o'clock this afternoon we reached the Grand Portage of the Montreal River[1] where my canoe was broken, and we are obliged to camp in order to allow four packs to dry that got wet. The two portages we crossed are exceedingly bad and the Savages tell me this one is still worse.

27th Monday. It rained all last night and we could not begin to portage before ten o'clock. Nevertheless, we did a good day's work having come to camp at the Petite Rivière, this side of the Rivière des Pins.[2] The portage was never so bad and the flies are eating us up.

29th Wednesday. My people did sixteen pauses today although the water was frequently up to their knees, and they

---

[1] See *ante*, p. 181, notes 54, 55.—ED.

[2] Rivière des Pins was probably the present Pine River, flowing from Pine Lake and by its union with Balsam River forming the East branch of the Montreal. This was the point chosen by T. J. Cram in 1841 as the headwaters of Montreal River, and from here was accordingly run the boundary line to Lac Vieux Désert. In recent years, Michigan surveyors have claimed that this is not the true headwaters of the Montreal; that the West branch is the larger and real headwaters, and that its source in Island Lake should be the starting point for the boundary line. Were the interstate boundary thus rectified, Hurley and all the lands between the east and west branches of the Montreal would come under Michigan jurisdiction. The matter has proceeded no further, however, than newspaper agitation. The Northwestern Railway station of Sand Rock is on Pine River, not far from the old Portage Crossing.—ED.

complained a good deal. We are camping at the Rivière des Sapins.³

30th Thursday. My people fortunately finished carrying early, for they were beginning to get tired. The road is so bad and there are so many overturned trees that I was lost for an hour, and should still be so, had I not had a gun.

31st Friday. "L'Epaule de Canard" came to us last night; he is coming to the Grand Portage to see Mr MacGillivray. Today we were obliged to make a small raft to cross the Rivière du Milieu,⁴ and we are camped there. I have not seen the water so high for a long time and I am greatly surprised to see my people hold out so long.

June 2nd, Sunday. The rain prevented us from carrying. We have done only seven pauses since Friday. There are billions of flies! We are weak owing to bad food, and we shall have none at all unless the weather changes.

3rd Monday. After I had written yesterday, the weather became fine and we did ten pauses with one half the baggage. Today, it is raining hard and we are completely weather-bound.

4th Tuesday. "Le Canard" started this morning for Lake Superior because we have provisions only for two days more with great economy, and also to tell the Savages of the Mauvaise Rivière to bring us some fish, if they have any.

The weather is still cloudy; drops of rain fall from time to time. Nevertheless, my people are carrying, but they take the precaution to cover the packs with their blankets at every trip. The only food remaining is ten quarts of corn not treated with lye.⁵

---

³ Probably the stream now known as Balsam River, a tributary of the Montreal in northeastern Iron County; see preceding note for its significance in the boundary question. For an ampler report see that of Captain Cram in *Senate Docs.*, 27th Cong., 2nd sess., No. 170.—ED.

⁴ Rivière du Milieu (Middle River) was without doubt the West branch of Montreal River, which was about half way from Long (or Portage) Lake to Lake Superior. Some of the early maps give the Indian name of this stream as Gogogashugun.—ED.

⁵ The French expression is "bled non lescivé (lessivé)." To soften

5th Wednesday. Today we are in sight of Lake Superior, my people having done 21 pauses yesterday and 20 today. Tonight we are eating our last corn cakes, and tomorrow noon we hope to be at the end of the portage.

6th Thursday. We have at last finished the portage at a quarter past twelve, all very tired. I shall not start from here before tomorrow to give my people a rest. I was lucky enough to get four sturgeon from the Savages today, which will, I hope, last me to la Pointe, where I left a sack of corn in a cache[6] last autumn. Mr Cadotte's eldest son[7] arrived here at three o'clock in the afternoon with a letter from his father informing me of Mr Latour's death.[8]

8th Saturday. I started today from the Montreal River and arrived at la Pointe, Mr Cadotte's fort. While walking beside the lake I found a white fish half eaten by the eagles and half rotten, but not sufficiently so to prevent my eating it after roasting it on a spit.

10th Monday. I had my canoe prepared yesterday to start in company with the Messieurs Cadotte. Their people came from

---

the grains of Indian corn, make the husk break open, and the kernel floury, French-Canadians put a small quantity of lye in the water while boiling the grain. After that treatment, the corn is known as "lyed corn." It is eaten boiled with pea soup or with milk and sugar.—CRAWFORD LINDSAY.

[6] For an explanation of the term cache, see *Wis. Hist. Coll.*, xviii, p. 279.—ED.

[7] Jean Baptiste Cadotte III was called "Gros Cadotte," to distinguish him from his brother, "Petit Cadotte." He seems to have been in the fur-trade with his father, and in 1812 went to the aid of the British and fought in several battles. In the Battle of the Thames he was severely wounded, and thereafter received a British pension. He was employed by the American Fur Company in 1819 as a voyageur on the upper Mississippi, and was living as late as 1852. It was perhaps in his honor that the town of Cadott was named in the present Chippewa County, Wis.—ED.

[8] Probably this was Charles Latour, a clerk of the North West Company stationed in 1799 at Rainy Lake. An employee of the same name was in the Western country as early as 1789.—ED.

Malhiot's Journal

the Rivière Mauvaise with a canoe load of sturgeon so we could not run short. This did very well, and today at 10 o'clock we left la Pointe to come and camp at the Rivière Ciscaouette in the evening.

15th Saturday. At 3 o'clock in the morning on Tuesday we left the Rivière Ciscaouette and camped the same evening at Fond du Lac where, being detained by wind and rain, Mr Cotton[9] was good enough to assist us with a sack of corn and a brasse of tobacco. On Thursday we left Fond du Lac to go and camp at the Rivière aux Groseilles.[10] On Friday we camped at the Rivière à la Framboise,[11] and today, after a long day under sail we are camped in sight of Ile du Grand Portage.

---

[9] Cotton, who in 1799 is listed as Jean Coton, belonged to the Fond du Lac Department for several years. In 1802 William Morrison found him at Fond du Lac as he passed through. During the winter of 1803-04 Cotton was in charge of a fort on Red Lake River, probably at the mouth of the Clearwater, where Alexander Henry the younger visited him. He seems, however, to have been in the Fond du Lac Department, and to have entered and returned via Lake Superior. Apparently he left the fur-trade soon after this meeting with Malhiot, since his name is not given among the list of employees after the coalition.—ED.

[10] The name for this small river in Lake County, Minn., not far above Encampment Island, has had a curious history. It is first marked upon Coronelli's map of 1688 as Rivière des Groseliers, being probably so named in honor of the early fur-trader and explorer Médard Chouart, sieur de Groseilliers, who with his confrère Radisson was, so far as we know, the first white man in this region. The name persists on the maps with various spellings throughout the eighteenth century, but apparently was corrupted by the voyageurs into Rivière aux Groseilles; so, when Bayfield surveyed Lake Superior in 1823, he gave to it the English translation of the French word, Gooseberry River. Such it remains to the present.—ED.

[11] Modern maps indicate no Rivière à la Framboise, or Raspberry River, between Gooseberry River and Grand Portage. Possibly the stream called Indian Camp River is meant; it is about as far from Gooseberry River as the latter is from Fond du Lac.—ED.

LIST OF GOODS GIVEN FOR PROVISIONS AND EXPENSES OF THE FORT OF LAC DU FLAMBEAU[12]

1804		Plus
August 3rd	Gave old La pierre à affiler for the meat of a deer and four other quarters of meat, A keg of four pots[13] of mixed rum	5
4th	To old Plat coté for ten quarters of meat, a keg of six pots	6½
6th	to old Lacramailliere, for the meat of a bear, seven chopines[14] of rum	2
	To Bazinet, a Double handful of Powder	1
	a Handful of shot	1
	two Brasses[15] of tobacco	4
	Malhiot, a Brasse of tobacco	2
8th	To Gauthier, one do	2
11th	To one of the children of old La chouètte for ten quarters of meat, a keg of four pots	5
18th	To Brulé and Petit Bled for going and bringing me a package each in the Portage, a keg of four pots	5
	two double-handfuls of powder	2
	two Handfuls of shot	2
	half a Brasse of tobacco	1
22nd	To old Plat coté for a sack of wild rice, a keg of four pots	5
23rd	To La Petite Racine, for half a sack of wild rice and one of pumpkins, seven chopines of rum	3
25th	To La vielle Française, for a quarter of meat and a dish of wild rice, half a brasse of tobacco	1
25th	To the Savages of Lac du Flambeau, for three sacks of wild rice, a large Keg and a Brasse of tobacco	22

---

[12] The following lists were found among the Masson MSS. in the library of McGill University, Montreal. They evidently accompanied Malhiot's journal of events at Lac du Flambeau, and give interesting sidelights on the economics of the fur-trade.—ED.

[13] "Pot" is an old French measure for liquids, containing somewhat less than two litres, and equivalent in English measure to about two quarts. The "keg of four pots" was thus a two-gallon keg.—ED.

[14] "Chopine" is an ancient measure for liquids, containing about one fourth of a pot, and nearly equivalent to an English pint.—ED.

[15] "Brasse" is a French linear measure, equivalent to 5.318 English feet, something near a fathom. There is evidence, however, that in the middle of the eighteenth century a "brasse" was used for a shorter measure, about the length of the fore-arm. Probably this was the one here meant. The tobacco was braided or twisted into long strands, and then measured by the brasse.—ED.

Malhiot's Journal

	To Barceloux for four quarters of meat, a keg of four pots	5
	To Bazinet's brother-in-law, for a sack of wild rice, seven bottles[16]	3
	To the mother-in-law of La Chouette's son, for a sack of wild rice, seven chopines of rum	3
27th	To the wife of Petit Jour, for two dishes of wild rice, thirty branches of porcelain beads[17]	1
	To Gauthier, a brasse of tobacco . . .	2
September 3rd	To L'Epaule de Canard, for a sack of wild rice, a keg of six pots	6½
	To La Grande Loutre, for three sacks of wild rice, half a Keg of rum	10
	To the son of La moitié de Chef, for three sacks of Corn and one of wild rice, a large Keg	20
	To Le Petit Canard, for three quarters of Meat, seven chopines of rum . . .	3
	To Various Savages, for wild rice, ¼ lb vermilion[18]	1½
	To L'Outarde, to stop him from going on the war-path, a large Keg and a Brasse of tobacco	22
	Gave to the mother of Le Canard, for half a sack of wild rice, a piece of Braid . .	2
	To three young men, for four Dishes of wild rice, Three knives and a looking-glass .	2
5th	To La Feuille, for a Bastard Canoe,[19] Three Brasses of Common cloth @ 4 plus each	12
	Two blankets, two points, @ 3 do do	6
	A Capot of 4 ells @ 4 do	4
	A do 3 do @ 3 do	3
6th	To old La Chouette, a large keg to be traded for provisions	20
	To Bazinet, another do . . .	20
	To the son of La moitié de Chef do . .	20
	To Petit Jour, a Keg of 4 pots for the same purpose	5
	A large Keg given by myself for provisions	20
	Sent to ⸻ ᴄ de la Truite by L'épaule de Canard, a large keg to be traded for provisions	20
	Sent by Le Taureau to the village of La Tortue, a large keg . . .	20

[16] The French word is "fiolles," a popular term for a glass flask or bottle.—Ed.

[17] "Branche de rassade" is the phrase in the original, indicating the strings or bunches of porcelain beads which were put up for the fur-trade.—Ed.

[18] Vermilion was much used in the fur-trade, for the savages bought it for ornamentation of both face and body. It was powdered, and sold in small flat packages; examples are shown in the museum of the Wisconsin Historical Society.—Ed.

[19] For this expression, see *ante*, p. 203, note 88.—Ed.

[217]

9th	Gave Gauthier Two Cotton Shirts	6
	A Brasse of tobacco to smoke	2
	Malhiot do do	2
	Bazinet do do	2
12th	To Several women for husking five sacks of Corn, ½ lb Porcelain beads and ½ a Brasse of tobacco	2
13th	To Folle Avoine, for four sacks of Corn, half a Keg and a Brasse of tobacco	12
28th	To La Grande Loutre, for a small Fishing Canoe, a piece of Braid	2
	To La Feuille, for a sack of Corn, a keg of four pots	5
	To Le Mufle d'orignal for two sacks of Corn, a keg of six pots	6½
	To Barceloux, for five sacks of corn, half a keg and half a Brasse of tobacco	12
	To Le Gros Egle, for six sacks of corn, half a keg and a brasse of tobacco	12
	Sent By L'outarde to Lac de la Truite a large keg	20
29th	To Le Chef des oiseaux, for four sacks of Corn, half a Keg and half a brasse of tobacco	11
	To Gauthier, a Brasse of tobacco to smoke	2
	To Bazinet do do do	2
	Gave le Mufle d'Orignal, for two sacks of corn, a keg of four pots	5
	To La Feuille for a sack of Corn, a keg of two pots	3
October 1st	To Le Petit-Jour for seven maskinongé, six ducks, and four musk-rats, a Keg of four pots	5
6th	To the men, a file for the use of the fort	1
	To an Old woman for having scraped six Deer skins, six Brasses of braid and a comb	1
	Six Deer skins used for the windows[20]	2
15	To Gauthier, one Brasse of tobacco to smoke	2
	To Malhiot do do	2
	Expended, by drams, from the third of August to this date, two and a half large Kegs of mixed rum	50
18	To Durocher, a double handful of powder and a handful of shot	2
	To Gauthier and Little Cadotte, each as much	4
	To Barceloux, provided he will give Tremblé food all winter, A keg of four pots	5
	Sixty bullets	2
	Two double-handfuls of powder	2
24	Gave Martineau, for his engagement feast, half a Brasse of tobacco and a deer skin	1

---

[20] Windows were usually made of parchment, scraped thin enough to be translucent.—ED.

26	To old La Chouëtte for the meat of thirty musk-rats, two outardes,[21] and six ducks, five pots of rum . . .	6
27	To Brunot and Beaulieu, on their engagement, half a brasse of tobacco and a deer skin each	3
Nov. 4th	To an old woman, for some Corn, a Brasse of cloth	4
	For two rolls of bark, a box with a burning glass	2
10	To Gautier, a Brasse of tobacco . . .	2
26	To the Brother-in-law of la Chouette's son, for one hundred white fish, twelve bottles of rum	6
	half a brasse of tobacco	1
	Malhiot, a Brasse of tobacco	2
	To the men, one file	1
December 10	To an old woman, for dressing six deer skins, one Pair of leggings	2
	To the same old woman for lacing four pairs of snow-shoes, one pair of sleeves . .	2
25	To the same old woman, for cutting a doe skin into thongs, a foot and a half of tobacco	½
30	To Gauthier, one Brasse of tobacco . .	2
1805 January 1st	To my men, as a new year's present, five chopines of high-wines . . .	5
	A Brasse of tobacco	2
	To the men of X Y, a chopine of high-wines[22]	1
15	Malhiot, a Brasse of tobacco	2
25th	To Gauthier do do . . .	2
February 28	To Gauthier do do . . .	2
	To Le Canard, for 15 lbs of bear's grease, 4 plus worth of ammunition . . .	4
	To L'outarde do do do	4
	To La Chouette do do do	4
March 1st	To old La Chouette, for 7 maskinongé and 4 lbs of grease, 1 Keg of 4 pots . .	5
10	To the son of old La chouette for ten maskinongé, a small Keg of 4 pots . .	5
14	To L'Egle for seven quarters of meat, three gallons of rum and ½ brasse of tobacco	9
	To The sister of L'Epaule de canard, for half a sack of corn, two double handfuls of powder and 60 Bullets	4
	Gave an old woman, for Lacing two pairs of snow-shoes, a looking glass and ½ Brasse of tobacco	2

---

[21] Outarde is the French-Canadian term for the wild-goose (*bernicla canadensis*).—ED.

[22] See Alexander Henry's description of the New Year's feast at his Red River post, in 1801. Coues, *Henry's Journals*, p. 162.—ED.

	To La Grue Blanche, for guiding my men to Roi's at L'Anse,[23] 4 pots of rum	5
	a Brasse of tobacco	2
	For ammunition	4
16	To L'outarde for two loads of fresh meat, a keg of six pots	8
	To Gauthier a brasse of tobacco to smoke	2
	To Malhiot do do do	2
26	To L'Epaule de Canard, for the meat of a bear, a two-gallon keg	5
29	To L'Epaule de Canard, for the meat of two Moose and of two bears, a large keg	20
27th	Gave old La Chouette, for one half of the meat of a bear and for 4 quarters of meat, 4 pots of rum	5
28	To Barceloux, for 7 quarters of meat, 4 pots of rum	5
April 6th	To the son of Le cioux for going to get George Yarns at his Father-in-law's, 4 plus on his credit	4
	3 chopines of rum	1
9	To Le Chef des Oiseaux, for half a keg of Sugar[24] 6 pots of rum	6
15	To Gauthier, a Brasse of tobacco to smoke	2
	To Malhiot do do	2
17	To Old La Chouette, for four quarters of meat, five chopines of rum	4
25	To the son of La Pierre à affiler for fifteen pounds of sugar, a pot of rum	2
May 7	To Old La Chouette for a Northern canoe,[25] a large keg of rum	20
8th	To the war-party, for an old canoe, a double handful of powder and thirty bullets	2
11	To the son of old La Chouette for a fishing canoe, 10 plus from his credit	10
18	To the young men of J Chouette, for 3 quarters of meat, 2 double handfuls of powder and 30 Bullets	3
	Gauthier, a brasse of tobacco	2
	Malhiot	2
		688½ Plus

---

[23] See the journal for March 14, 1805, *ante*.—ED.

[24] Maple sugar, which the Indians had just been making.—ED.

[25] The Northern canoe was the largest made and used on the northern lakes. A fine description, with illustration, is found in Henry R. Schoolcraft, *Narrative Journal of Travels* (Albany, 1821), pp. 68-70. He says they were thirty-five feet in length by six in width, and capable of carrying four tons.—ED.

Malhiot's Journal

STATEMENT OF THE GOODS SENT TO THE OUISECONSAINT CONFIDED TO THE CARE AND CHARGE OF J. BT. BAZINET AND J. Q. RACICOT BY FR. VT. MALHIOT.

LAC DU FLAMBEAU, OCTOBER 4TH 1804.

October 4th, 1804

Qty	Item			@	Price	Plus		Plus
3	Pieces common Cloth, blue			@	40	Plus the piece		120
3	Brasses	do	H. B.[26]	@	4	do the brasse		12
4	do	do	Scarlet	@	6	do do		24
4	do		Calico	@	2	do do		8
2	Blankets	3-	points[27]	@	4	do each		8
11	do	2½	do	@	3	do do		33
6	do	2	do	@	2	do do		12
6	do	1½	do	@	2	do do		12
6	do	1	do	@	1	do do		6
3	Capots	4	ells	@	3	do do		12
3	do	3½	do	@	3½	do do		10½
3	do	3	do	@	3	do do		9
4	do	2½	do	@	2½	do do		10
1	do	1½	do	@	1½	do do		1½
4	do	1	do	@	1	do do		4
8	Rolls of braid			@	2	plus each		16
3	Skeins of wool			@	2	do do		6
2	Laced caps			@	2	do do		4
1	Chief's coat							8
1	Chief's shirt							2
2	Hats			@	2	plus each		4
1	Plume for hat							1
3	Small children's shirts			@	1	do do		3
2	Black silk handkerchiefs			@	2	do do		4
3	Packages of White porcelain beads			@	4	do do		12
1	Dozen large knives			@	4	for one plus		3
6	Fine knives			@	½	a plus each		3
1	Dozen of Steels for striking fire			@	6	for a plus		2
2	Dozen Awls			@	1	dozen for do		2
3	Dozen Wormers[28]			@		do do		3
1	Dozen horn combs			@	6	for do		2
6	Box-wood Combs			@	3	for do		2
½	Roll of wire for snares							3
3	Packs of cards			@	1	plus each		3
2	Boxes with burning glass			@	2	do do		4
2	pieces of ribbon			@	3	do do		6
3	Looking-glasses			@	1	do do		3
3	Steel boxes			@	1	do do		3
50	Needles			@	25	for 1 plus		2

[26] Probably a kind of cloth manufactured especially for the Hudson's Bay Company and their trade.—ED.

[27] For the explanation of this term, see *Wis. Hist. Colls.*, xvi, p. 400, note 2.—ED.

[28] A wormer was a small coil of iron or steel, used in cleaning a gun.—ED.

Silverware

40 Pairs Small Earrings	@ 10	prs for a plus	.	.	4
40 Pair, medium sized do	@ 10	prs do do	.	.	4
50 Large brooches	@ 15	do do	.	.	3
100 Small do for the hair	@ 20	do do	.	.	5
3 Large double crosses	@ 2	plus each	.	.	6
6 medium-sized do	@ 1	do do	.	.	6
1 Pair Large Armlets	.	. . .	.	.	6
1 Pair medium-sized do	.	. . .	.	.	4
1 Pair do do	.	. . .	.	.	3
50 Branches of porcelain beads	@ 10	branches for a plus	.		5
24 large beads[29]	@ 3	for do	.	.	8
1 Silver shell . . .	.	. . .	.	.	1

Entire Pieces

4 Kegs, double strength	@ 40	plus each	.	.	160
1 do Powder	.	. . .	.	.	50
1 sack of bullets	.	. . .	.	.	40
½ do beaver shot	.	. . .	.	.	25
1 Roll tobacco for snuff	.	. . .	.	.	60
1 gun . . .	.	. . .	.	.	10
2 traps	@ 5	plus each	.	.	10

Ironmongery

1 Pair of spear heads	.	. . .	.	.	1
2 half axes	@ 2	plus each	.	.	4
5 Tomahawks	@ 1	do do	.	.	5

Utensils & Tools

2 Large axes	@ 3	plus each	.	.	6
1 Auger . . .	.	. . .	.	.	1
1 Hoe	.	. . .	.	.	1
1 Padlock .	.	. . .	.	.	1
1 Spigot .	.	. . .	.	.	1
1 Quart pot .	.	. . .	.	.	1
1 do of a chopine					
1 do of a half-chopine		. . .	.	.	2
1 Gill measure					
1 dram measure[30]					
1 Brass kettle .	.	. . .	.	.	7
1 Tin do .	.	. . .	.	.	3

Provisions

18 Bushels of Corn	@ 4	plus per bushel	.	.	72
1½ do wild rice	@ 5	do do	.	.	3

---

[29] The French phrase is "Noyaux porceline." We are informed by a former Indian trader that this refers to a large coarse bead prized by the tribesmen.—ED.

[30] The French word is "miserable," which is argot for a small glass of spirits.—CRAWFORD LINDSAY.

100 lbs flour
½ Barrel of Pork
1   do   Sugar
½ lb of Pepper
6 Quarts of salt
½ lb of Tea

The 22nd February 1805—The following articles

		Plus
4 Blankets, 3 points	@ 4 plus each	16
2 do 2 do	@ 2 do do	4
1 Capot 3½ ells		3½
1 do 3 do		3
2 Rolls of braid	@ 2 plus each	4
1 Brasse cloth H. B.		4
3 do do, common	@ 3 plus each	9
1 do do, scarlet		6
10 Verges [31] ribbon	2 verges for a plus	5
36 Flints		2
18 Pairs Earrings		2½
7 Clusters [of beads]		2
1 Pair Armlets		4
4 pots of rum, double strength		10
		980½

May 18th
1 Sack of Corn 3
                                       ─────
                                       983½

Return

		Plus
May 21, 1805		
69 Large bear skins	@ 2 plus each	138
18 Small do do		18
47 Deer Skins	@ 2 for a plus	23½
327 Musk-rat skins	@ 10 do do	32¾
68 Beaver skins, making		58
3 Lynx skins	@ 2 plus each	6
20 Otter skins	@ do do	40
5 Fisher skins		5
100 Marten skins	@ 2 for a plus	50
½ a Moose skin		1

Goods Brought Back

1 Capot of 3½ ells 3½

Silverware

3 Large double crosses 3
8 Pairs of earrings 1½
30 Small brooches for the hair . 1

Utensils

1 Large brass kettle 7
1 Small tin do 3
2 Large axes 4

[31] "Verge" is a French linear measure, equal to an English ell.—Ed.

1 Quart pot	1
1 Chopine do	1
1 half-chopine do	1
1 Small do	2
1 Spigot	1
1 Funnel	1
1 Padlock	1
1 Northern canoe	30
5 Brasses of bark	2½
1 Keg of gum [32]	10
	445¾

INVENTORY OF THE GOODS REMAINING AT LAC DU FLAMBEAU AFTER THE CREDITS GIVEN, AND WHAT WAS SENT TO OUISSECONSAINT AND THE AUTUMN TRADE

15th October 1804
3 Pieces common cloth
8 Brasses Blue cloth H. B.
4   do   Scarlet do
6   do   rough[33] do
7 Verges calico
2 Blankets 3   points
19   do   2½   do
8   do   2   do
2   do   1½   do
6   do   1   do
5 Capots of 4   ells
3   do   3½   do
3   do   3   do
4   do   2½   do
2   do   1½   do
3   do   1   do
14 Rolls of braid
2 Dozen Large knives
½ Dozen Small do
½ Dozen fine   do
1½ lb Vermilion
4 Small shirts
5 Skeins of wool
6 kegs of rum, double strength
1½ do of powder
2 sacks of Bullets
½ do of Shot
1 Roll of tobacco
18 Carrots do

[32] Both bark and gum were used in the repairing of canoes, and were necessary for any extended voyage.—ED.

[33] The French term is "drap motton," i. e. mottoné—rough, like Irish frieze.—CRAWFORD LINDSAY.

INVENTORY OF THE FURS OF THE AUTUMN TRADE

5th October 1804—LAC DU FLAMBEAU

528 Deer skins
 16 Bear do
840 Muskrat
 44 Otter
  7 Marten
  1 Mink

Provisions

40 minots[34] of Corn and wild rice.

ACCOUNT BOOK FOR DROUINE[35]

LAC DU FLAMBEAU 4th August 1804

August 4th, 1804   Plus
Sent to Ouisconsaint by Bazinet, the following goods:[36]

1 Piece common Blue cloth			.	.	.	.	50
3 Blankets 3 points	@	5	plus each	.	.	.	15
9 do 2½ do	@	4	do do	.	.	.	36
2 do 2 do	@	3	do do	.	.	.	6
2 do 1½ do	@	2	do do	.	.	.	4
2 Capots of 4 Ells	@	5	do do	.	.	.	10
2 do 3½ do	@	4	do do	.	.	.	8
1 do 2½ do	@	2½	do do	.	.	.	2½
1 do 2 do	@	2	do do	.	.	.	2
1 do 1½ do	@	1½	do do	.	.	.	1½
3 Rolls of braid	@	2	do do	.	.	.	6
1 Package of porcelain Beads		3	plus	.	.	.	6
1 lb Vermilion		3	do	.	.	.	3
1 silk handkerchief		2	do	.	.	.	2

---

[34] A minot is an old French measure of capacity, containing somewhat more than a bushel; see *Wis. Hist. Colls.*, xvii, p. 252.—ED.

[35] For the significance of this term see *ante*, p. 200, note 86. The methods of the traders are clearly indicated by this book, each of the voyageurs and interpreters being entrusted with a small outfit, and sent out to a winter camp of some Indians supposed to have furs. In the original account book the outfits are entered upon one page and the returns opposite; for purposes of comparison we have made the return from each drouine follow the outfit entry. The outfit sent to Wisconsin (Ouisconsaint) by Bazinet and Racicot is practically a part of this book for drouine; but being so much more considerable, is given a separate entry.—Ed.

[36] This would seem to have been a brief trial trip, followed by that of October 4, entered *ante*, pp. 221–224.—ED.

1 Piece of ribbon	5	do	5
1 Dozen Large Knives	@ 4	for 1 plus	3
15 lbs. Beaver Shot	@ 1	plus per lb	15
10 lbs. bullets	@ 1	do do	10
18 Brasses of tobacco	@ 2	plus per brasse	36
2 Carrots do	@ 5	plus each	10
2½ kegs of mixed rum	@ 10	do do	25
6 lbs. of powder	@ 1	do do	6
			259

Return

			Plus
August 10th, 1804			
222 Deer skins	@ 2	for 1 plus	111
1 Bear skin			2
90 Muskrat skins	@ 10	for 1 plus	9
3 Otter skins	@ 2	plus each	6
1 Beaver skin	1		1
For meat pounded for pemmican[37]			5
For quarters of meat			5
Given on credit to various Savages for			15
Given a commission for			50

Goods brought back

3 Blankets of 3 points	@ 5	plus each	15
			219

			Plus
October 15th			
To the Vieux Désert by Rèmie Tremblé			
1 Blanket of 3 points			4
2 do 2½ do			6
1 Capot of 4 ells			4
1 do 3½ do			3
1 do 3 do			3
1 do 2½ do			2
2 Brasses of common cloth	@ 3	plus each	6
1 Pair Scarlet leggings			2
1 Piece of braid			2
2 Black silk handkerchiefs	@ 2	plus each	4
1 Carrot of tobacco			5
3 Brasses do	@ 2	plus per brasse	6
1 Tobacco box			2
1 Breech-clout			1
6 Horn combs and 4 of Box-wood			2
6 Packages of porcelain beads			6

---

[37] Pemmican is a food much used in northern latitudes. It consists of equal parts of dried meat, pounded or pulverized, and some kind of fat or tallow. When properly made, it will keep for many months, and formed a staple food in the fur-trade. It is still prepared for Arctic regions. See account in "Franchère's Narrative" in Thwaites, *Early Western Travels*, vi, p. 380.—ED.

1804-05] Malhiot's Journal

1 Small child's shirt and one small do Capot	2
3 Dozen rings	3
1 Dozen awls and 1 Dozen wormers	1
For wool	5
1 Fine knife	1
3 Small knives and one flint	1½
9 Double handfuls of powder	9
300 Gun bullets	10
	90½
Return	Plus[38]

November 2nd, 1804	Plus
Sent to la Puise by Gauthier	
1 keg of 4 pots of mixed rum	5
1 Brasse of common cloth	3
1 Blanket of 2½ points	3
½ Brasse of tobacco	1
½ Roll of braid	1
For porcelain beads	1
	14

Return	
November 5th, 1804	Plus
2½ Sacks of corn @ 3 plus per sack	7½
4 Muskrats and for dry fish	1
Goods brought back	
1 Blanket of 2½ points	3
½ Piece of braid	1
	12½

December 20th	Plus
To Lake Superior by George Yarns and Cadotte	
2 Brasses of Blue cloth H. B.	8
2 do common do	6
1 Blanket of 3 points	4
1 do 2½ do	3
1 do 2 do	2
1 do 1 do	1
1 Capot of 4 ells	4
2 Rolls of braid @ 2 plus each	4
1 Verge calico	1
3 Double handfuls of powder	3
100 Gun bullets	3
For porcelain beads	3
3 Black silk handkerchiefs @ 2 plus each	6
2 Large and 2 small knives	1
3 lbs shot	3
3 Sacks of corn @ 3 plus each	9
1 Kettle	5½
	66½

[38] There were no returns, because Tremblé went on to the post at l'Anse. See *ante*, pp. 207-209.—Ed.

Return

December 23rd — Plus
- 30 Beaver skins, making — 16½
- 4 Otter skins @ 2 plus each — 8
- 7 Marten skins @ 2 for a plus — 3½
- 6 Mink skins @ 2 do do — 3
- 8 Musk rat skins — ½

Goods brought back

- 1 Blanket of 3 points — 4
- 1 do 2 do — 2
- 2 Brasses of cloth H. B. — 8
- 2 Rolls of braid — 4
- 1 Silk handkerchief — 2
- For porcelain beads — 2
- 100 Gun bullets — 3
- For beaver shot — 2

58½

February 18th, 1805 — Plus
To the lodge of le Genou By George Yarns
- 1 Brasse of cloth H. B. — 4
- 1 small wide-mouthed kettle — 2
- 15 Pairs of Earrings — 2
- 10 Common brooches — 1
- 100 Hair do 30 for 1 plus — 3
- 3 large beads — 1
- 9 Branches of porcelain beads — 2
- 1 Black silk handkerchief — 2
- 1 Pair Scarlet leggings — 2

18

Return

February 19, 1805 — Plus
- 4 Beaver skins, making — 2½
- 2 Otter skins @ 2 plus each — 4
- 12 Marten skins @ 2 for a plus — 6

Goods brought back

- 1 Black silk handkerchief — 2
- 3 large beads — 1
- 9 Branches of porcelain — 1
- 10 Common brooches — 1
- 83 Hair do — 2

19½

February 19th — Plus
To The Lodge of Les Grandes Oreilles by little Cadotte
- 1 Brasse of cloth H. B. — 4
- 1 do common do — 3
- 1 Pair Scarlet leggings — 2
- 2 Rolls of braid — 4
- 1 Black silk handkerchief — 2
- 2 chopines of rum — 1

16

Return

February 23rd   Plus
- 2 Beaver skins 2
- 3 Marten skins 1½

Goods brought back

- 1 Brasse of cloth H. B. 4
- 1 Pair Scarlet leggings 2
- 2 Rolls of braid 4
- 1 Black silk handkerchief 2

     15½

February 20th, 1805   Plus
Sent By Gauthier and George Yarns to old La Chouette, Le Canard, and L'Outarde
- 1 Brasse cloth H. B. 4
- 2 do Common do 6
- 1 Blanket 2½ points 3
- 1 do 2 do 2
- 1 do 1½ do 2
- 1 do 1 do 1
- 2 Pairs Scarlet leggings 4
- 2 Double handfuls of powder 2
- 60 Bullets 2
- 2 Half axes 4
- 1½ Brasse of tobacco 3

     33

Return

February 21st, 1805   Plus
- 2 Bear skins @ 2 plus each 4
- 1 Small do 1
- 6 Beaver skins, making 5
- 2 Mink skins 1½
- 9 Muskrat skins.

Goods brought back

- 1 Blanket 2½ points 3
- 2 Pairs Scarlet leggings 4
- 60 Bullets 2
- 2 Double handfuls of powder 2
- Given on credit for 5

     27½

February 26th   Plus
By George Yarns to the lodge of La Moitié de Chef
- 2 Brasses common cloth 6
- 1 Pair Scarlet leggings 2
- 2 Pieces Braid 4
- 2 Blankets 2½ points 6
- 1 do 2 do 2
- 1 Child's shirt 1
- 1 Dozen rings 1
- ½ Brasse of tobacco 1

     23

Return

February 26th — Plus
- 1 Bear skin 2
- 3 Otter skins @ 2 plus each 6
- 4 Marten skins @ 2 for one plus 2
- 1 Small Beaver and 4 Muskrat skins 1
- 6 Deer skins @ 2 for one plus 3

Goods brought back

- 1 Blanket of 2 points 2
- 2 Pieces of braid 4
- 1 Pair Scarlet leggings 2

.... 22

March 4th, 1805 — Plus
By George Yarns to the Lodge of Le Vieux Sorcier
- 1 Brasse of cloth H. B 4
- 1 do common cloth 3
- 1 Pair of Scarlet leggings 2
- 1 Roll of braid 2
- 1 Carrot of Tobacco 5
- 1 Blanket of 2 points 2
- 4 Pots of rum 5

.... 23

Return

March 8th — Plus
- 2 Bear skins @ 2 plus each 4
- 2 Marten skins 1

Goods brought back

- 1 Brasse of common cloth 3
- 1 Pair of Scarlet leggings 2
- 1 Roll of braid 2
- 1 Carrot of tobacco 5
- 1 Blanket of 2 points 2

.... 19

March 14 — Plus
Sent to the vieu Désert by Gautier
- 1 Brasse of common cloth 3
- 1 Blanket of 2½ points 3
- 1 do 1½ do 2
- 1 Pair Scarlet leggings 2
- ½ Carrot of tobacco 2
- ½ Brasse do 1
- 7 large beads 2
- For wool 2
- For porcelain Beads 1
- For ammunition 2
- 1 Silk handkerchief 2
- 4 Pots of rum 5

[27]

Return

March 20   Plus
- 12 Marten skins @ 2 for one plus   6
- 30 Muskrat skins @ 10 for one plus   3
- 1 Fisher[39] and one raccoon   1
- ½ Moose skin   3

Goods brought back

- 3 Skeins of wool   1½
- 1 Package of porcelain beads   ½
- 1 Black silk handkerchief   2
- 6 large beads   2
- ½ carrot of tobacco   2
- 4 Quarters of meat   2

             23

March 25th
Sent to Lac de La Truite by Gautier
- 4 Pots of rum   5
- 40 Small sleigh-bells   3
- 1 Foot of tobacco   ½

          8½

Return

March 26
- 1 Bear's meat   3
- For grease   1
- 2 Moose muzzles   ½

Goods brought back

- 25 Small sleigh bells   2

          6½

March 27th
Sent by Gautier to Lac de la Truite
- 1 Keg of mixed rum   20

          20

Return

March 29
- 2 The meat of two Moose   12
- 2 The meat of two Bears   8

          20

---

[39] Fisher, called by French-Canadians "pecan," is the largest of the weasel family in North America. It is sometimes called black fox. The name fisher is a misnomer, since it does not fish, but will eat fish caught by others. Its scientific name is *mustela pennanti;* it is rare in Wisconsin.—Ed.

March 27, 1805 — Plus
Sent by George Yarns to The people of the Lakes

1 Blanket of 3 points	4
2 do 2½ do	6
1 do 2 do	2
1 Brasse cloth H. B.	4
1 do common do	3
1 Pair Scarlet leggings	2
2 Rolls of Braid	4
1 Carrot of tobacco	4
1 Capot 2½ ells	2½
For ammunition	6
6 Pots of rum	6
	43½

Return

April 12 — Plus

2 Large bear skins @ 2 plus each	4
1 Small do	1
7 Otter skins @ 2 plus each	14
3 Fisher skins	3
3 Beaver skins	3
4 Marten skins	2
20 Muskrat skins @ 10 for a plus	2
For grease	−2

Goods brought back

1 Blanket of 2 points	2
1 Breech-clout	1
60 Bullets	2
	36

April 30 — Plus
Sent by Gauthier to Portage de la Tortue

2 Brasses common cloth	6
1 do H. B. do	4
1 do Scarlet do	5
2 do Calico	4
2 Skeins of wool	3
1 Blanket of 2½ points	3
1 do 2 do	2
2 Medium-sized Armlets	3
50 Brooches for the hair	2
½ Brasse of tobacco	1
2 Packages of porcelain beads	2
6 Pots of rum	8
	43

Return

May 2 — Plus

4 Beaver skins	2½
1 Otter skin	2
15 Muskrat skins	1½
1 A Mocock of sugar[40]	4

[40] The French word is "makague," evidently a rendering of the Indian term mocock. The mococks were large vessels of birch bark, into

Goods brought back

1 Brasse Scarlet cloth	5
1½ do common do	5
1 do H. B. do	4
2 do Calico do	4
2 Medium-sized Armlets	3
50 Brooches for the hair	2
2 Pots of rum	2
	35

May 13
Sent by Gauthier to Portage de la Tortue — Plus

½ Keg of rum	10
1 Carrot of tobacco	4
1 Piece of Braid	2
1 Calico shirt	2
1 Skein of wool	1
	19

Return

May 14

1 Otter skin	2
10 Muskrat skins	1
1 Large bear skin	2
1 Skin of a bear-cub with the meat	2
2 Marten skins	1

Goods brought back

½ Carrot of tobacco	2
7 pots of rum	7
	17

May 18
Sent by Martineau to Lac de la Folle

2 Brasse of common cloth	6
1 Blanket of 2½ points	3
1 Small Capot	1
1 Piece Braid	2
1 Carrot of tobacco	4
For ammunition	8
90 Brooches for the hair	3
For porcelain beads and large beads	2
½ Brasse tobacco for snuff	1
	30

Return

May 21
To all the goods brought back — Plus [30]

which maple sugar was packed, each holding from thirty to eighty pounds. See Mrs. Baird, "Early Days at Mackinac," in *Wis. Hist. Colls.*, xvi, pp. 29–33, on sugar-making and its utensils.—ED.

Fur-Trade on the Upper Lakes
1778-1815

1778: SUPPLIES RECEIVED AND FORWARDED

[Letters of John Askin to fur-traders at Montreal and Detroit, and on Lake Superior.[41] Original MS. letter-book in library of Clarence M. Burton, Detroit.]

[41] The business of forwarding supplies of provisions and liquors to the traders in the Northwest had its headquarters at Michilimackinac, and at this time (1778) was largely in the hands of John Askin. Provisions in Indian corn, bears' tallow, etc., were picked up around the lakes, while the liquors came up from Montreal by two routes: that of the Ottawa (Grand River), and that of Niagara and Detroit. The former was more expensive, because light boats had to be used, on account of the many portages; the latter more uncertain, especially in times of war.

The following letters from John Askin's letter-book, which now rests in the Burton Library, Detroit, reveal the names of traders engaged in the traffic, the predominance of the North West Company, and the difficulties of the business; they also incidently throw much light on conditions along the upper lakes during the Revolution, the state of shipping, and the interference with trade due to the progress of the war.

For a brief sketch of John Askin see *Wis. Hist. Colls.*, xviii, p. 309, note 29. To that should be added the information that he came West soon after the treaty of Paris (1763); that his wife was Archange Barthe of Detroit; and that after the transfer of the posts to the United States in 1796, he elected to remain a British subject, and removed to the Canadian side of Detroit River, where he died in 1817. His relations with the early traders continued friendly throughout their lives; and among his papers (in the Burton Library) are many letters from Isaac Todd, Alexander Henry, the McGills, and other founders of the Canadian fur-trade.—ED.

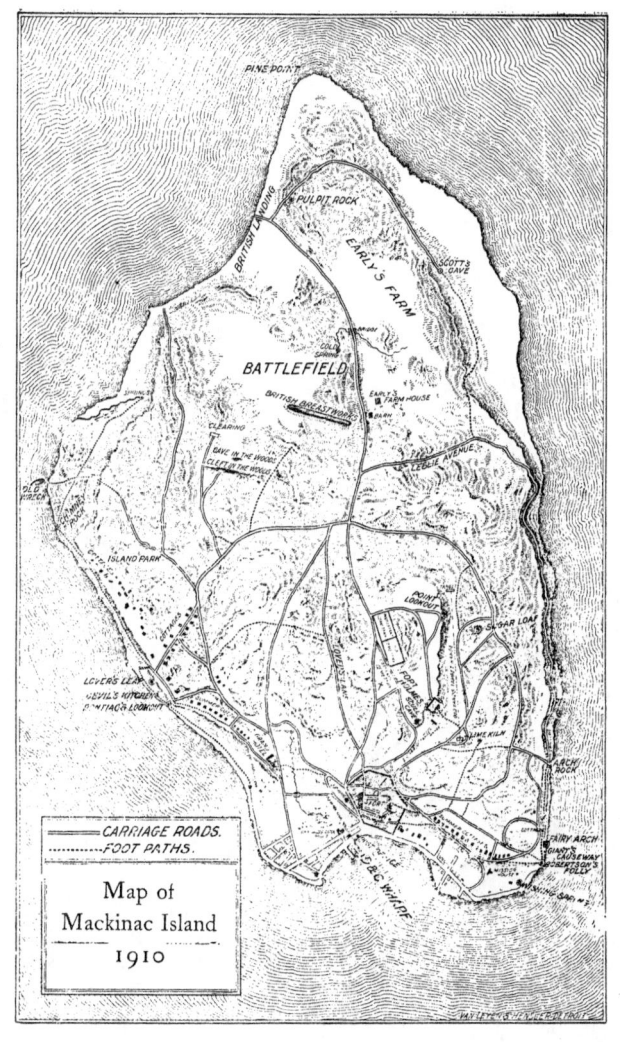

By courtesy of Detroit & Cleveland Navigation Company

Fur-trade on Upper Lakes

MICHILIMACKINAC, April 28th, 1778.

Messrs. McGill, Frobisher, and Patterson at Montreal.[42]

I take this opporttunity to acquaint you that I'm taking every precaution and hope to prevent your meeting with any disapointment in what I'm to furnish you. As I found that no part of the great quantity of Liquors which I had on the Road arrived, I attempted to purchase some at Detroit, but the Price being far from 26s to 30s N. Y. Curr^y: the Gallon and little certainty of getting it here, made me drop the Scheme. I'm to have 80 kegs of W[est] I[ndia] Rum of 8 G^s· each from Mons. Barth,[43] at 150$^{lvs·}$ the Keg, this with about 100 Bushells of hulled Corn, shall go off very early for the Portage. Corn in all probability will be as hard to be got as Rum. I'm informed from Detroit that it will cost 26s. the Bushell Unhulled

---

[42] For a brief biographical notice of James McGill see *Ibid.*, p. 326.

This was Benjamin Frobisher. The three brothers of that name, Thomas, Joseph, and Benjamin, were among the earliest British traders in the Northwest. Benjamin appears to have been the youngest, and to have entered the fur-trade as early as 1766. Joseph and Thomas were the original founders of the firm of Frobisher Brothers, but Thomas retired about 1778, and Benjamin succeeded him. Joseph and Benjamin were very active in the formation and conduct of the North West Company, acting as their chief agents in Montreal. Benjamin died before the reorganization of 1790. The Benjamin Frobisher who met a tragic death in 1819 during the struggles of the North West and Hudson's Bay companies was a nephew of the elder Benjamin.

Charles Patterson was likewise one of the early traders. He was with the Frobishers in the Northwest by 1775, and being one of the founders of the North West Company was active in its management. In 1788 he and his entire crew were drowned in Lake Michigan, some sixty miles from Mackinac, at a place since known as Patterson's Point.—ED.

[43] Jean Baptiste Barthe, son of Charles, one of the early colonists of Detroit, was born at that city in 1753. He was a brother-in-law of John Askin, and at this time employed in the shipping business with headquarters at Sault Ste. Marie. After some difficulty with British officers, he left the Sault and in 1782 was settled at Mackinac. Later he returned to Detroit, and in 1796 elected to remain a British subject; whereupon he removed to Upper Canada, which he made his home during his last years.—ED.

& without Bags, but that's not the worst, how to get it here now the Vessels are stopt, the Kings Vessel will come as usual perhaps, but besides King's Stores, she has to carry for so many persons, that each can have very little on the Board, I myself could [fill] her twice. from all this you may judge, how difficult it is to fullfill contracts, however don't be discouraged if money or Industry will answer, you shall not be disapointed. Rum I expect for a Certainty by the Grand River & and I shall send a Vessell to Millwakee in search of Corn. I have 150 Bushells already there & hope for more. I have about 200 here & I shall send a Batteau to Detroit that will bring me at least 120 Bushells this with my chance in the Vessels, I hope will answer my demands, my principle motive for giving you this information was, least the public Report of a Scanty [supply] might make you uneasy. I'm well provided with all the necessary Voytures to pass your effects from hence to the Portage[44]

[JOHN ASKIN]

MICHILIMACKINAC, May 8th, 1778.
Gentlemen of the N. W. Co. at Montreal.[45]

I wrote you the latter end of last month, since which Lieut Bennett[46] with Messrs McBeath & Rankin[47] are arrived here in

---

[44] "Voiture" was the French-Canadian term for any vehicle of transportation; here, it evidently includes both canoes and small sailing vessels. The Portage referred to is Grand Portage, headquarters for the traders of the Northwest interior. For a description see *ante,* p. 169, note 31.—ED.

[45] Askin here refers to the company formed this year (1778), which was the precursor of the North West Company. See *Wis. Hist. Colls.,* xviii, p. 314, note 39; and *ante,* p. 163, note 20.—ED.

[46] For Lieut. Thomas Bennett see *Id.,* xviii, p. 375, note 4.—ED.

[47] George McBeath was a prominent Mackinac trader, being one of those who formed the sixteen-share company of 1780. In 1782, being employed by Governor Sinclair to supply provisions for the post, he became involved in financial difficulties. Capt. Daniel Robertson, however, continued him in government employ, and in 1783 sent him to restrain the Western Indians from further hostilities and from com-

Boats, they say that we cannot expect any Vessells from Detroit before news gets from Montreal there, but what concerns you & me much more is, a Report that perhaps neither Flour, Corn or Rum will be suffered to come from that Post to this, this Season. (I mean for People in Trade) its certain that those who left Detroit this Spring were not suffered to bring but a very small quantity nor could they get a positive answer whether or not these articles would be Suffered to come at all or not.

I have applied to Major De Peyster who will make known to Governor Hamilton[48] the bad consiquences of laying an Imbargo on Provisions & without which it is impossible that trade can be Supported. You may depend on everything that's possible being done to prevent Disapointments. when the Vessel arrives, I will be able to write you with more certainty, therefore this warning is only to yourselves.

I send off the first of your things for the Portage in three days Consisting of Rum, Corn & what's most necessary, I shall at same time write your Clark [clerk] to provide some place to receive L[t.] Bennett & the Troops with him, until some of Your Co. Arrives. Your Canoes are Ready.

[JOHN ASKIN]

[Translated from the French.]

MICHILIMACKINAC, May 18, 1778.

{*Mr. McDonnell.*}

Give my Compliments to Madame M[c]Donnell.[49] There is nothing new I have not written her. Send the Baggage of Mr.

---

ing to Mackinac. He held at Prairie du Chien a great council, whose effects were beneficial. See documents in *Id.*, xi, pp. 165–174. McBeath continued in government employ until 1785, when he left Canada.

David Rankin was a Mackinac merchant who had connections with Detroit. In 1781 he was a witness to the deed for the purchase of Mackinac Island.—ED.

[48] For De Peyster and Hamilton, governors respectively of Michilimackinac and Detroit, see *Id.*, xviii, pp. 344, 371.—ED.

[49] McDonnell was clerk and forwarding agent for Askin at Sault Ste. Marie. We have not been able to identify him; although he may have

howard to Mr. Charles Boyez.[50] I ought to furnish for Mr. henrie 20 sacks or minots of large corn [gros Blé] 20 minots of lyed corn and 2 Hundred weight of flour. I will put these articles in the Vessel if there is time, if not they will go at another time. However if any one asks you in Mr. henrie's name for these articles before I can send them, have the kindness to give him this amount from your own stores. We must try to find a man to go in Pomp's place after the first voyage. I cannot get on without him. I have no one at present among all my men, one of whom is ill. You will deliver the goods of Mr. Henrie to Mr. Cadott[51] and take a receipt. You will find perhaps some articles in your account very dear. I assure you that everything is scarce & dear here and that it cannot be otherwise, and I reckon that the price will increase instead of dimin-

---

been the John McDonnell who was clerk (1793-95), and later (1796) partner, of the North West Company, whose journal is published by Masson, *Bourgeois*, i, pp. 267-295.—ED.

[50] Joseph Howard was one of the first traders under the British regime, being in the firm with Bostwick as early as 1763. He had large connections in Montreal, and was suspected of sympathy with the American cause, although active in repelling the invasion of 1775. He aided American prisoners to escape from Montreal, and in 1779 was arrested for going to trade in the Upper Country without a license. In 1781 he complained to the authorities that his interests suffered from his not being allowed to visit Mackinac, whereupon he received a permit to adjust his affairs the following year. He is known to have been trading as late as 1790, for John Sayer was his representative at that time on Lake Superior.

Charles Boyer would seem to have been one of Alexander Henry's clerks. In 1780 he was with a trader named Bruce on the Assiniboine River, when they were attacked (in the spring of 1781) by a numerous band of Indians, but saved the fort after an heroic defense. In 1787 Boyer went out to Peace River, where be built Fort Vermilion, near an affluent of that stream, still known as Boyer River.—ED.

[51] This was the well-known trader Alexander Henry the elder, for whom see *Wis. Hist. Colls.*, xviii, p. 277. Henry was not at this time in the Northwest, having but recently returned from a voyage to England; see *post*. He was an intimate personal friend of John Askin, whose papers contain many of his letters. J. B. Cadotte was his partner; see *Ibid*, p. 103.—ED.

ishing. Beef at Detroit is from 30^{lvs} to 40^{lvs} a pound & Pork in proportion. As the quantity of sacks with each mark is not mentioned in the account, only the number of minots, you will find the sacks containing two minots marked 2, those of one and a half 1½, and the others according to their quantity. You will find somethings on your account furnished for Boulon and La Voine last autumn; if you have not deducted these articles from their wages, do so.

[JOHN ASKIN]

[Translated from the French.]

MICHILIMAKINA, May 18, 1778.

Monsieur Beausoleille.

SIR—I am sending off from here a Bark loaded with goods for the grand portage, there will also arrive at Saut Ste marie the Loading of the other Bark which is on Lake Superior. I send you inclosed The account of what belongs to the great Company embarked in the two Vessels; however As that which is above the Saut is much more than that which is to ascend, I have written to Mr. Barthe to divide equally between the two Barks the Baggage that each can carry, it being sure that all will arrive a long time before the Gentlemen of the Company need it. They say that the Liquor & provisions that should come from Detroit will be stopped. I assure you therefore that it will be necessary to take great care of what you already have. Both are very dear. Grain will sell here at 30^{lvs} to 40^{lvs} the minot. There are in the Vessel some things with a letter for Mr. Chaboilliez the elder.[52] I beg you to receive both

---

[52] Not of the Chabollier family of Mackinac. Charles Jean Baptiste was born in 1742 at Three Rivers, son of François Chabollier. He began his career in the Northwest at an early age, and was one of the few French-Canadians who became a partner in the North West Company. For several years he had a fort at Pembina; but finding (1796) that his post was in United States territory, he destroyed it, and built farther north. In 1804 he was head of the Assiniboine district, and planned the expedition to the Missouri which encountered Lewis and

for him and keep them until he arrives, as there is no one at Grand Portage in his interest. You will have an officer and several soldiers to pass the summer at Grand portage. I beg you to try and have a house ready to receive them so that it may be let to them. The place must have a Chimney. You will have the goodness to have 200 pickets forty feet long made by your men and erected as a barrier between the old fort and yours. It will be the great Company's duty to furnish a dwelling for the officer and his soldiers. What I have taken the liberty to suggest to you, On the subject will be approved by them I am very sure.

I need two pretty Slave girls from 9 to 16 years old. Have the goodness to ask the Gentlemen to procure two for me.

I am &ca.

[JOHN ASKIN]

By Mr. McDonald

MICHILIMACKINAC, May 28, 1778.

Messrs. Todd & McGill, Montreal.

The foregoing is the copy of a Letter I wrote you by the way of the lakes the 8th Instant, I forgot to mention that there was inclosed in it a small memord. for some things & affidavids about the Martens that were missing last year. I here inclose you the Copy of the Memord. but not the Copies of the Affidavids, nor bill of sale of the Land, I hope the Originals will not miscarry, you have with this a Copy of my letter dated the 28th of April last which left this with my other Dated the 8th of May. Your Acct Currt with me I here inclose which comprehends every acct I received of Yours before the 1st of January last, since which I have received one amounting to (£) 1023 11', 7¼ Halifax, which I have credited your new Acct with. Capt Bannerman arrived here a few days ago in their small Vessells from Detroit with some corn & Rum for the North Trade, he had permition to bring it forward on making

---

Clark among the Mandan. In 1805 he retired, and died four years later at Terrebonne.—ED.

Oath, that no part of it was for any other use. I think he says that the whole flour Allowed for the North Trade & this Post is thirteen thousand W. not half what I want alone, so that I'm almost certain there will be a Disapointment in this Article, but as to all the others I hope not provided you send me the three Canoeloads of Rum. I have sent off two Vessell load for the Portage of what I thought was most wanted, for those I have contracted with.

Capt. Robertson[53] got to Detroit in three days he was to return as soon as a Vessell arrived from Niagara, the Angelica was on the Bar on lake Sinclair on her way here, but not yet arrived, think of Maj. De Peyster's Situation with the Indians about him & not for one Shilling come for him this year, I believe five Kegs of Rum is the whole Stock of this Post, private Stores even counted, & its reported there is none on board the Angelica. Please inform the Gentlemen of the N. W. Co. what relates to them. Mons. Hypolite Chaboulliez[54] proposes to leave this to morrow with the Indians, you'll receive this by him

The things I ordered from London last fall I suppose will get to Montreal about the time this letter does & as some part of them cannot come by the way of the Grand River, they must

---

[53] Samuel Robertson was from his youth bred a sailor, and in 1774 was sent to Detroit by the London firm of Phyn & Ellice to command a small vessel for some of the merchants trading to Mackinac. He sailed on Lakes Michigan and Huron until the government forbade private vessels on these lakes. He was part owner of two small vessels, besides an establishment at Sault Ste. Marie, in partnership with John Askin and Jean Baptiste Barthe. In 1779 Robertson was commissioned by the governor to voyage around Lake Michigan in search of corn, and to secure the wavering Indians of that region to British authority. For an account of that voyage, see his journal in *Wis. Hist. Colls.*, xi, pp. 203-207. The following winter he was engaged in building a wharf and several houses on Mackinac Island, preparatory to the removal of the fort thereto. Having had the misfortune to displease Governor Sinclair, he was arrested, and sent to Montreal for a trial. In 1782 he was still at Quebec, awaiting trial, soon after which he died, leaving his family resident at Niagara.—ED.

[54] For this person see *Id.*, xviii, p. 255.—ED.

be risked the other way, I here inclose you a Copy of that memord, the Articles that have no mark in the Margin, are to come by the grand River, those marked L by the way of the Lakes, there is others marked as per example 5 Ct. [hundredweight] of Powder 3 by L which means that 3 Ct. of it is to come by the lakes & the remainder by the Grand River, other things in the same way—of the Barrells of Pitch & Tarr, there must be three Kegs of the former & 1 of the latter sent by the Grand River, as also of the Cordage, there must also a Coil of Inch & another Coil of half Inch Roap be made up the weight of a Peice, each of them & sent by the same way. These things I can no longer do without, I dont know how Roap is measured in Canada, but those I mean are for Running Riging such as Halliers [halyards] &c. of small craft. In my memord. of the 8th Instant I made a mistake ordering 2 Doz. of womans Shoes & afterwards 12 pairs for Mrs. Askins, omit the 2 Doz. the 12 pairs is Sufficient. I owe Kitty[55] her wedding Gown, as there was nothing here fit for it Please have one made for her the french fashion, of a light blue Sattin. I will for certain this Season send a Vessell & perhaps Establish a house at the French River to take things from thence here. I wish you could engage men to there only, provided the Vessell meet them, or so much more if obliged to come here, the agreement should be Conditional to prevent Accidents or disapointments.

[JOHN ASKIN]

MICHILIMACKINAC, June 4, 1778.

Mr. John Hay, Detroit.[56]

The two Vessells, the first Canoes from Montreal & the Ottawa Indians going to war all arrived Yesterday, the latter is now

---

[55] "Kitty" was Askin's daughter Catharine, who had recently been married to Capt. Samuel Robertson, noted above. After Robertson's demise she married Robert Hamilton of Niagara, for whom see *post*, note 74.—ED.

[56] Possibly this may be Maj. Jehu Hay, later lieutenant-governor of Detroit. He had a son John in the Indian trade, but in 1778 the latter was hardly old enough to be the recipient of this letter.—ED.

1778-1815]   Fur-trade on Upper Lakes

dancing at my door, my things coming on Shore in the greatest confusion & the Angelica preparing to Sail. all this shall not deprive me of the pleasure of writing you a few lines in answer to your obliging letter by Robertson. The news is that Gen. Clinton below Albany fought and beat Gen. Gates, in which 7000 of the Enemy & their Gen. fell, before this reaches you perhaps you'll have the Acct. more fully by Niagara. great numbers of Canoes are on their way here from Montreal. Lieut. Bennett left this a few days ago for the grand Portage. I must take some other opportunity of writing you, for at present it is next to impossible. Mrs. Askin & Mrs. Robertson presents their best Compliments to Mrs. Hay.

[JOHN ASKIN]

MICHILIMACKINAC, June 6, 1778.
Mr. [Benjamin] Frobisher, Montreal.

I will attempt writing you by these Indians but cant say I will get through, having three Vessells to fit off now, your Canoes & my Public employment.[57]

St. Cir arrived last night. I have delivered him the Canoes, all your Corn, Sugar, Gum, Bark & Watap now remaining here shall be delivered him to Day, all the rum coming up in the Canoes he shall also have (I expect they will arrive today). I have this Spring got about five Barrells of Spirits up, which is now a Drawing off & shall be sent, this with 60 Kegs of W. I. Rum I borrowed of Mr. Barth is all the Liquors I can possibly muster. I dont keep two Barrells for myself. I have not had one pound of Flour this Season, Lt Governor Hamilton would not Suffer more than thirteen thousand W. to leave detroit & that only to such persons as were on the Spot, or had others to make oath that it was for the N. W. Trade. Mr. Sterling[58] has

---

[57] Askin means his duties as commissary to the garrison at Mackinac.—ED.

[58] James Sterling came to America during the French and Indian War, acted as commissary during the Oswego campaign (1759), and at its close removed to Detroit. There he married Angélique Cuille-

fourteen thousand W. purchased for me, my Vessells is just now going to Sail in order to fetch it & and what Rum I may have arrived at Detroit, which without one moments loss of time shall be forwarded to the Portage. I'm in great hopes from what Major De Peyster has wrote Lt. Governor Hamilton with the other precautions I have taken, that not only the 14 Thousand but even more may come for me if Ready. I dare say by this time the Spring News from Canada has got to Detroit (which was not the case when the last Vessell left it) So that Governor Hamilton will now see that there is now no necessity for Stoping the provisions in that settlement. Your Canoes shall be loaded with what's here & at St. Mary's as nearly conformable to your orders as possible & I believe it will make about their Loading. I have sent some flour forward and will now send about a thousand W. more, so that I still hope there will not be the least disapointment. I wish Messrs. Todd & McGill had sent me by the Grand River the 1700 Gallons they wrote me they would, I in many letters warned them not to depend on the Liquors comeing the other way, & that I had none. I know it was their great desire not to [be at] too much expences, prevented them, but I asure you nothing hurts me so as any persons being disapointed who depend on me, tho not my fault. I have wrote you the most necessary [things] & must refer the rest for an other opportunity.

Your Brothers Letter from St. Mary's which you [will receive] with this will inform you further

As it's impossible for me to write any other at Montreal by this opportunity, please make my excuses to Madam Chaboullier, I will do myself the Honour to write her in a few Days, for the present please let her know, I will execute her orders for the Additional Quantity of Corn she has ordered. The Rum

---

rier *dit* Beaubien, and became identified with the French habitants, speaking their language and instructing their militia. He became one of the prominent merchants, but during the Revolution was suspected of sympathy with the Americans; about the time Askin is writing, he was arrested and sent to Canada for safe-keeping. It does not appear that he ever returned to Detroit.—ED.

I cannot promise untill I have fullfilled my engagements, let her know also that her Canoes was the first men here this Spring & took (with what was sent before) everything that Mons. Chaboulliez was to get, except 10 Kegs of Rum & 5 bags of Flour which shall go with the rum and Flour I'm now sending to Detroit for. I know no person so well of in the North Trade as he is.

Please excuse my not writing to Mr. McGill, also by this oppertunity, I mean make my excuse to him.

Mrs. Askin & Mrs. Robertson presents their best compliments & believe me most truly,

[JOHN ASKIN]

P. S. St. Cir goes off tomorrow with the small Canoes & whats here & leaves two large Canoes to take my Rum thats coming by the Grand River.

MICHILIMACKINAC, June 13, 1778.

Messrs. Jos. Frobisher & Jno. McGill,[59] [Grand Portage or Sault Ste. Marie].

As I'm informed that you two have to transact the business of the N. W. Co. this Season, I take this oppertunity of Mr. McBeth to inform you that by letter I Received from Montreal to day, I'm asured that there is on the way for me about 150 Kegs of Rum & Spirits all which quantity or more if it arrives you shall have by the two Canoes St. Cir left for the purpose,

[59] Joseph Frobisher was one of the most distinguished explorers and traders of the early British forces in the Northwest. As early as 1772 he had passed beyond Lake Superior, and by 1774 penetrated to Churchill River, whence on his return (1775) he met Alexander Henry. It is said that he never again wintered in the interior, but came up to Grand Portage each year to superintend his affairs. He was one of the first founders of the North West Company, and very active in its management. In 1798 he retired, having made a considerable fortune, and thereafter lived at Montreal, occupied in civic service and hospitality.

John McGill was embarked with his brother James in the fur-trade. He died at Montreal, December 1, 1797, aged fifty-one years.—ED.

or what part of it they may not be able to take with them shall go by the first Vessell, the Grease your Mr. Jo. Forbisher ordered shall also go by the Canoes & if in my power I will furnish the additional quantity of Rum he wrote me about, however it will first be necessary to send what I have already engaged to find you. I hope the return of my Vessells from Detroit will put it in my power to send you the remainder of your Rum & Flour. My Liquors that's comeing up this [month] I'm informed was to leave Deer Island the 10th of last Month in a Vessell that was ready to take them on Board, I imagine that you got by the first trip of the Vessells, all that was forwarded to you, except what your own Canoes took, for tho I mean to serve others, yet my intention is by all means that you have the Preference, indeed I mean to allott one of the two small Vessells purely for your Services, only when you cannot load her of course others may put on board, the other I mean for the use of such other Gentlemen as may choose to ship in her. when I have the Pleasure of seeing you here we will settle all them matters.

I have not as yet heard from your Mr. John McGill who I'm told is gone to the Saut St. Mary's some time ago, you have only 50 Bushells of Corn more to receive of me, which I was ordered to leave at the Saut for the Canoes that go down, except the 40 lately ordered. I am very [truly]

[JOHN ASKIN]

Per Mr. McBeth

MICHILIMACKINAC, June 14, 1778.

Messrs. Todd & McGill, Montreal.

I hear Mr. Howard intends sending a Canoe for Montreal tomorrow, I will therefore write you as much as time will permit for the present & the remainder by some other oppertunity. I have Received five letters from you this Season, dated the 21st & 28th April, the 9th, 11th, & 16th May, the two first Received the 5th. and the three latter the 13th. Instant, I believe there is some others from you for me, but Mr. John McGill having taken them to St. Mary's with him, prevents their coming by several days so soon as they otherwise would. I'm very sorry you should make yourself so unhappy about the return of my Rum last fall, I'm sure I never blemt you for it, on the contrary I'm well persuaded when anything under your directions miscarry, the same would happen were I there in person, I do asure you I'm under many obligations to you for the pains you have taken about my things, I now have great hopes of seeing them soon & tho I may reap a great benefit by it in the sale of some of them, what pleases me most is the having it in my power to furnish the Gentlemen of the N. W. Co. the remainder of their Liquors after what I sent them & what is in my Canoes, which is not yett arrived. The very clear account you have sent me of the furrs shipt on my account as well as my Liquors etc. in their different Situations deserves my thanks, as I see you have not spared pains to make everything very clear to me. I have already sent you all the proofs I can give about the Martens that are missing, if they do not answer they must of cource be lost. I approve of your plann of sending me Rum whether ordered or not, if it can get up, I can never Suffer by having a quantity, besides I can then contract with much more Safety to myself & others. I shall not for some time be able to examine our Accounts.

I have wrote Mr. Steadman to send me Rum in lieu of what he took of mine, this will be more advantagious to me by much. You forgot inclosing the Gentlemen of Garrison Accounts as you mention, you have only noted the Sum. however, I believe this will answer for me to get payment from them, Lieut. Bennett had already desired me to charge him his, he knew and told me the amount, when I see my Canoes and hear from St. Marys, I will let you know exactly what Rum & Spirits is come for me in my own & the N. W. Canoes. I wish you had been more plain in letting me know whether they were to go to St. Mary's or come here first, as I have kept two large Canoes of the Co.'s here in order to take the Rum that is in mine. Old Francois is not yett arrived, but I expect him daily, I shall pay due attention to what you say respecting his going into the North, I'm sure he shall not with my consent & I dare say he will not without. I asure you that tho' I now supply several others, besides the great Co. I have a certain inclination to forward their interest preferable to any other & tho' I would not take any unfair means to prevent Gentlemen in that concern doing well, yett no profit should induce me to undertake anything that could in the least hurt a concern where so many of my friends are interested. I'm determined never to undertake Canoes for any but them, & one Vessell shall be sole[l]y at their disposal, so far as they can make use of her. As to the supplying of others with Rum, Corn etc. after I have made sure of what will be wanted for the great Co. (as we must now term them for distinction Sake) it can be a matter of no consiquence to that concern, for if I do not do so others would. I'm therefore sure it would be rather pleasing than otherwise to my friends to hear I made money. I Received 240$^{lvs.}$ from Major DePeyster for the Rum & Bisket taken by Mr. Ainse[60] from Roi, & the N. W. Co. has credit for it in their last years accounts the 28th of June. I Received from Amable Roi[61] & Lafevre £9:6:8 N. Y. C^y· last Year which I omitted advising you of, charge me with that sum, it's all I have been able to collect on acct. of you & and your Brother John.

Before Lieut. Bennett left this I did what I thought was necessary in order that your Co. at the Portage should still pass for what it actually is, the most respectable as to proprietor & amount. Nous Sommes fort sur Le Dernier Gout de Londres [we are very interested in the latest London fashions], you may judge of Mrs. Askin & Mrs. Robertson by other ladys, for in certain matters women are almost all alike. I believe Capt. Robertsons Marriage will make him consent to pass some years in this Country, I have not yet talked to him on the Subject,

---

[60] For Joseph Ainse see *Wis. Hist. Colls.*, xviii, p. 309.—ED.

[61] Little is known of Amable Roy, an early settler of Green Bay. He was born in Montreal, came early to the Northwest, married a stepdaughter of the elder Langlade, and had a small farm at the Green Bay settlement. Having no children of their own, Roy and his wife adopted Louis Grignon, who inherited their property after their deaths, about the beginning of the nineteenth century.—ED.

however had there been anything entered into on his account, you should not have been disapointed, he has too much sentiment to suffer it, we have time to see more in these matters, he could have the Command of King's Vessell on these lakes, but it realy is not worth his acceptance nor will he take it.

I hope to hear much news from you after Mrs. Todd's Arrival from England. don't be plagueing me at this busy time with an account of my having drawn the £2000. I shall not make you any remittances until my own Canoes go down.

I believe I mentioned to you in my last that Robison is looking out for the best harbour that can be found nearest the french River & that I intend to build a Store there.

Please pay Mr. Benj. Frobisher one hundred Livres for me. Mrs. Askin presents her Compliments to Mrs. McGill.

Mr. Howards Canoe has Slipt off. I wait an other Oppertunity.

[JOHN ASKIN]

MICHILIMACKINAC, June 15, 1778.

Mr. Benj. Frobisher, Montreal.

In my last dated the 6th Instant I wrote you pretty fully about everything relative to your North Concern, for the present I have only to add on that head, that I every day expect my Vessells every day with the Rum & Flour to compleat your Co's quantity which shall be forwarded with the greatest expedition, my Canoes from Montreal are not yet arrived but I expect them to morrow, as Capt. Robertson on his way from taking a view of the french River, saw three which must be them.

Mr. John McGill has got to St. Mary's several days ago if I may judge from where Mr. Morrison[62] left him, but I have not

---

[62] Charles Morison was of Scotch origin and came to Mackinac to reside, about 1789. He there served as magistrate, until after the British surrender. As a merchant he trafficked to Lake Superior, but as an independent trader, not connected with the North West Company. He died in 1802 on his way to Montreal, and was buried at Niagara. See Ontario Historical Society *Papers*, vi, p. 29. See also his letters, *post.*—ED.

as yet received the letters etc. he brought up for me. In all your new undertakings I wish you Equal sucess to that you have had in the North & the continuance of that also. I think it very just that the young sett should now take the same pains the old have done, it's true equal success can hardly be expected from such a change, added to the number of adventure[r]s being Augmented, if anything I can do here exclusive of what I'm obliged to do, can be of Service to the concern, it never shall be wanting.

This place affords no news which I can send you in return to your's, which I thank you for.

I received the hundred Livres Galliard owed you & have wrote to Messrs. Todd & McGill to pay you that sum, as we have no other account open with each other to my knowledge. I return you thanks for the Printed engagements you were so kind as to send me, they will be very serviceable & prevent some trouble. I have this day promoted a very necessary Ordinance, which is, that no person can hire an Engagé without seeing a proper discharge from his former Master, or a Certificate from the Commanding Officer why he has none, & what strenthens this is all the Merchants having Signed it & invested the Commanding Officer with Authority to make such agressor pay 1000$^{lvs.}$ without the power of afterwards sueing for it, there is something more to prevent carrying from any place persons in Debt who are not hired, the like is to take place at the Portage, so that I hope things will soon be on a better footing.[63]

[JOHN ASKIN]

MICHILIMACKINAC, June 17, 1778.

Mr. John Hay, Esq., Detroit.

As a true Irishman I want to tell you that at this present time I have nothing to say, or rather that is worth your hear-

---

[63] These plans for the better regulation of voyageurs or engagés are very interesting. A number of the engagements of this period are in the Wisconsin Historical Library, and samples thereof will be given *post.*—ED.

ing, all the Spring news from Montreal you must have had. Your last canoes from Montreal left about the 16th of May, at which time there was not any Vessels Arrived from London, or any part of Europe at Quebec.

Messrs. Langlade & Gotiez are on their way from LaBay here with above two hundred Warriors who are going down the Country.[64]

Mr. Charles Morrison is with us & gives a much better Account of the Rebbels behaviour respecting what they call justice than any I have heard, as to public matters he was kept in the dark as much as if he had not been in the Country, he got twenty eight of their paper Dollars for a half Joe before he came away, judge the repute their Currency is in.

This is my buisy time, I. shall therefore conclude by presenting Mrs. Hay & Family with Mrs. Askin & my Compliments I am etc.

[JOHN ASKIN]

MICHILIMACKINAC, June 22nd, 1778.

Messrs. Todd & McGill, Montreal.

My Canoes are now arrived & have brought everything in good order & agreeable to the invoice, except in Bale N°. 7: a small white Shirt in lieu of a large one Ruffled, Bale N°: 3 wants a Shirt of Russia Sheeting, a pair of Russia Trousers & a pair of Oxhide Shoes, N°. 4 also wants a Shirt of Russia Sheeting.

The things from England are really well choose & please me much, however a fiddle which I had mentioned in that memor^d. is left out, & tho' such an omition can be of no consiquence to persons who can supply the want at the next Shop, it is so different here, that I would not for ten Guineas it had not come, please purchase one for me at Montreal without fail, let the price be about £6 Hallifax, I sent you a memord. this Spring in which a fiddle was mentioned, that one is also to come, its for

---

[64] For this expedition see *Wis. Hist. Colls.*, xviii, pp. 368, 369, with accompanying notes.—ED.

an other person, please not to forget a quantity of strings with the fiddles.

I approve much of your plann of forwarding Rum as soon as you received it, no matter what Quantity if it gets on, for except I have it here before hand, I will not make any more positive contracts, the freight of what came in my Canoes will I dare say cost as much as I get for the whole Rum, but this is not what gives me the greatest uneasyness it's the fear of the N. W. Co. not receiving the whole of the Quantity in time. during these troubles I know of no other way of contracting with them, but fixing a price on what of the rum comes by the Lakes & letting them have that by the Grand River at first cost & Expences (I want no profit on it) they must allow me Commissions for purchasing their Corn, flour etc. for the Bushell of Corn this year costs me 32sh. & I furnish it for 24sh.

I received my shirts by Mr. Soloman[65] who arrived here in eighteen Days.

I have no time at present to examine the Accounts, but shall as soon as more at leisure, [as] I intend sending off my Canoes in about ten days time, I cannot, there is above three hundred Warriors going down. Robertson has been detained with my Vessells untill they go off.

Mrs. Askin presents her compliments to Mrs. McGill in which I join with all my heart   I am etc.

[JOHN ASKIN]

Per Campau

MICHILIMACKINAC, June 23rd, 1778.
Messrs. Todd & McGill, Montreal.

Looking over the letters yet unanswered I find yours of the 25th. Ult°. to which I made no reply in my Yesterdays letter I'm very glad that there is so great a likelyhood of my Rumm arriving so soon. I daily expect the Angelica & the Vessells I sent for the flour here, perhaps my Rum may be on board. the Tarr & Kettles are not pressing articles, I can do without them

---

[65] For this trader see *Ibid.*, p. 254, note 50.—ED.

Fur-trade on Upper Lakes

some time, provided the pitch gets safe here, & as to the cheese please replace it with another Hamper this Year. The Canadian Pork & loaf Sugar which you mention being Short of my order of the 18th, Sep. 1777, I can well do without, but the covering Nails & common Wine are both very Saleable articles, however as there is a large Quantity of the former of these articles comeing or come out for me, it will be needless to purchase others at Montreal. Old Francois goes for Detroit he intends living there. I shall send a Young Brother in law of mine[66] to take his place at Millwakee as much on acct of the Corn to be got there as the Peltry. I am under many obligations to you for the Uncommon pains you have been at in order to insure the speedy passage of my things by the Lakes. I will be attentive to what you mention respecting the time of payment of such drafts as I shall draw on You. I am in such want of Waistcoats & Breeches that I beg you will have immediately purchased for me six or eight Yards of fine white Cloth, which with sutable trimings please send me by the very first oppertunity, hardly any person will refuse to embark so small a Bundle on being paid for so doing, the kind of Buttons I would choose is plain double gilt with eyes if to be had, if not with Ivory buttons, but eyes answers best as they can be taken off when washing.

The want of Breeches makes me dwell so long on the Subject, in order to insure their coming   I am etc.

[JOHN ASKIN]

Per Campau

MICHILIMACKINAC, June 23rd, 1778.

Mr. Alex. Henry, Montreal.

I suppose by this time you are returned from England & of cource expect to hear from your old Acquaintances.

---

[66] No doubt this was Louis (called Louison) Barthe, born in 1760, and living in his latter years at Amherstburg, near Detroit. During the War of 1812-15 he was employed as interpreter, and accompanied Robert Dickson and others on the Prairie du Chien expedition (1814).

I sent your Corn & flour to St. Mary's agreeable to your letter to me on that Subject. I did not go to Detroit last fall as I intended when I seen you last, these troublesome times causes many disputes in which A man often gets involved, not withstanding his great desire to the contrary. I therefore thought it most prudent to stay where I'm sure to live in peace.

I'm building a new house out of the Fort and intend to make use of it untill the present warr is at an end, & then shall change my Quarters, but where to I know not as yet. Lyons wintered with us here & Bostwick[67] went to the Illinois, he is returned with a large Bag Diamaonds & other precious Stones. Kitty is Married to Capt. Robertson and joins with Mrs. Askins in compliments to you   I am as usual

[JOHN ASKIN]

Per Campau

MICHILIMACKINAC, June 29th, 1778.

Messrs. Todd & McGill, Montreal.

I have answered the last of your letters in two I wrote you by Mr. Campau, the 22. & 23. Instant, their Copies you shall have by this oppertunity if time will permit.

Your Clerks or some other have made a very great mistake in the Tea they sent me, it is not only the most common sorts of green Tea, but so bad besides that I would prefer the Bohea to it ten to one, besides its comeing in Paper in a bale has still done it some damage by bruising it into powder. I shall send you a Sample of it which will be the best proof of its quality, Please Credit me the difference of price, it's charged 15s Hallifax. My Canoe goes to morrow, not all loaded with my own

---

It is not probable that he remained long at Milwaukee, as during the winter of 1779–80 he was assisting Samuel Robertson on the island of Mackinac.—ED.

[67] Benjamin Lyons appears to have been in partnership with Askin, the firm being mentioned in 1780 as Askin, Lyons & Bostwick. He was at Mackinac as early as 1776 and as late as 1800. Both De Peyster and Sinclair used him in aid of the government.

For Henry Bostwick see *Wis. Hist. Colls.*, xviii, p. 238.—ED.

Packs, as I have not yet had any from St. Mary's, I will take some for Mr. Lyons & he will take as many for me. The Strouds you now send are the worst I ever have seen, those to Mr. Lyons excepted, it hurt his trade I know & as he would be perhaps delicate about complaining, I thought proper to mention it you.

You will doubtless send me some Canoes with the part of my things that comes from England, which I have mentioned was to come by the Grand River, you may hire them for certain to come to the entrance of the lake only, as I will send People in a few days to Build there as I would choose however that all was examined it will be necessary to send an account of the contents of each Package, directed to the person acting for me there & if you could without too much trouble send the account of the Packages both in french & english, so much the Better, however, I mean to send an Englishman.

I here inclose you a list of what goods I shall want for that place for the Winter of which please send me a separate Invoice as they are for Mr. Lyons & me, half the amount of which to be charged to each of our account separately. In about eight days I will be able to send you some remittances in Bills etc.

No Vessell yet from Detroit, you'll be surprized when I tell you that we have not heard from Niagara this Year, so of cource we got no letters that are come by the way of the lakes we have no news worth communicateing. Pray dont forget the white cloth for my Breeches & the trimings. Mrs. Askin joins in Compliments to Mrs. McGill. I am etc.

[JOHN ASKIN]

MICHILIMACKINAC, June 30th, 1778.
Messrs. Holmes & Grant[68] [*Lake Superior*].

I received a letter for your Mr. Wm. Holmes this morning which I now send you, no news here of Vessells yett Arrived at

---

[68] William Holmes was one of the early British traders in the far Northwest. In 1776 he was in the interior with Alexander Henry and

Quebec, there is now full liberty for Provisions to come from Detroit, owing to a large Quantity on the Road for the Crown. The Provisions for your Canoes that go down shall be at St. Mary's in good time. I'm sorry to inform you of an Accident that happened poor James, fireing the Cannon on board he had the most part of his hand blown off, nothing but the thumb and part of the fore finger remains, I hope he may recover, but cannot say anything for certain yet. I most truely pity the poor lad. Mrs. Askin presents her Compliments, I shall conclude by wishing you much Success. I am

[JOHN ASKIN]

MICHILIMACKINAC, July 2nd, 1778.

Messrs. Todd & McGill, Montreal.

Mons. Thierry[69] goes off to day in a light Canoe well maned, which makes me think his passage will be short & you will receive this before several others I wrote you some time ago. I received Yours of the 7th. Ult° & am sorry to hear Beaver is fallen, did I know any certain price I could give for furrs, I could have purchased some parcells.

Tho the Vessells from Europe are long a comeing, yet I dare say nothing has happened them, its necessary they now take more precaution than formerly. Mr. Lyons suffers much by his goods not comeing, he is obliged to keep men whose provisions are now very dear, corn will not be had for $30^{lvs.}$ in a few days, added to all this had they come up in the Spring he could have Sold them to government. with this I send you the

---

Charles Patterson; and in 1780 was, with his partner Grant, a stockholder in the North West Company. In 1790 he sold his share to John Gregory. Which one of the numerous Grants was his partner, cannot be determined. James Grant was a Montreal outfitter in 1778 and 1782; John, Charles, and William Grant were all traders to the Northwest in 1786.—ED.

[69] Pierre Thierry was born in Montreal in 1750. His occupation was conductor of canoes, which he brought up the Grand (Ottawa) River to Mackinac. He was frequently at the latter place, and signed the register of marriage as late as 1804.—ED.

NAHSHAWAGAA, OR THE WHITE DOG'S SON
Potawatomi chief. From colored lithograph by James Otto Lewis, 1827

KEEOTUCKKEE
Potawatomi chief. From colored lithograph by James Otto Lewis, 1827

Fur-trade on Upper Lakes

Copy of a Letter I wrote you the 29th. Ult°· as also a memord. for some Goods for Mr. Lyons & me for the trade at the entrance of the french River, and as there is several things in this Memord. to be made up at Montreal, it cannot get to you too soon. Three Canoes loaded with furrs will set off this evening, or to morrow morning.

I write the N. W. Co. by this oppertunity, I'm so hurryed that I can only add that I am etc.

no news of Lorty yett

[JOHN ASKIN]

MICHILIMACKINAC, July 2nd, 1778.

Gentlemen of the N. W. Co., Montreal.

I wrote you formerly that I had sent a Vessell of mine to Detroit for flour & Rum for you, at her arrival Governor Hamilton did not think proper to suffer any provisions, I mean flour, to leave the Settlement, however a Vessell arriving from Niagara with some provisions & bringing an acct. that there was great quantities on the way, there was an order published that every person with permition might send what Quantity they thought proper, but this served no great purpose as my Vessell was ordered along side of the Kings & what clothing, Liquors etc. for this garrison were put on board her, & not only that, but merchants had permission to put things on board as well as myself. I asked the Master of the Vessell if he represented to the Governor that the Vessell was not in the Service & therefore not subject to carry for every person, he says he did & even mentioned that after he had taken the King's things on board, he desired that he might make up the rest of the loading with mine, & that the Governor told him I could not have any preference over others. If what he says be true, I realy think it a hardship. I imagine Major DePeysters letter to Governor Hamilton explained fully his reasons for letting my Vessells go to Detroit. I dont want there should be any complaints about these matters, I only mean to show you that I or no other person in these troublesome times can asure you about Provisions, or anything Else, all I received was four thousand of flour & 48 Kegs of Rum which I dispatched immediately for the Portage. I expect more in a few days, as it comes here I will forward it till I at last get your quantity or more. I am etc.

[JOHN ASKIN]

MICHILIMACKINAC, 2nd July, 1778.
Richard Dobie,[70] Esq., Montreal.

I have only time to inform you that I have received the thirty otters remaining due me. Messrs. Hippolite Chaboulliez & Co. wrote to you & as I had sent you back the note the 22nd. Ult., I gave them a Receipt which you will please take up when you deliver the note. I mentioned that the otters were not choice, since which I got good ones in their Stead, as least such as pass for good here, the Quantity I had to choose from was not great. By my Canoes that leave this to morrow you will receive the whole of the Beaver & otters made up in three Packs. Kitty is now at Detroit. Mrs. Askin joins in Compliments to Mrs. Dobie, I am with esteem etc.

[JOHN ASKIN]

MICHILIMACKINAC, July 3rd, 1778.
Messrs. Todd & McGill, Montreal.

I here inclose you an Acct. of 42 Packs the contents of each pack seprately, the amount of the whole in their supposed value amounting to 10303 Livres or ancient Shillings, the guides were present when each pack was made up & seen their contents. There is three packs also belonging to Mr. Dobie & 3 of Mr. Perinaults[71] the Acct. of which I send them, the Guides also were present when they were made up, as to six

---

[70] Richard Dobie was a well-known Montreal merchant, being in business there as early as 1763. He was, however, not among the founders of the North West Company.—ED.

[71] Very little is known of this trader, who is mentioned as "trading to Lake Superior," in *Mich. Pion. and Hist. Colls.*, xx, p. 280.—ED.

for Mr. Alex. Ellis⁷² & 54 which Mr. Lyons sends, their contents are unknown to the Guides. You have likewise inclosed the men's Acc^t in so plain a manner as will not admit of any dispute, by it you'll see there is a ballance due them of 51|16^{lvs} for remainder of wages, Equipments etc. which You'll please charge me with.

There is one man named Couroy in your list to whom you advanced 74^{lvs} I can hear of no such person, or no other in his stead. You'll please receive 90^{lvs} from Mr. Dobie & as much from Mr. Perinault, for freight of their Packs, Mr. Lyons & McBeath, I settle with here for freight of theirs.

Since Settlement I sold the guide for 110^{lvs} which please deduct from what is due him.

I dont know if I before mentioned to you to charge the Gentlemens Acct. of this Garrison to me, I mean Lieutenants Bennett, Clows,⁷³ & Doctor Mitchell.⁷⁴ I am Dear friends etc.

[JOHN ASKIN]

1784: SALES AT MONTREAL

[MS. in Burton Library, Detroit, vol. 1, p. 109.]

MONTREAL 11 October 1784.

DEAR SIRS—We now enclose you copies of the different Sales of Furs shipped last year for your account, on which it is pleasing to remark there arrises a very handsom profit vizt

---

⁷² Alexander Ellice, born at Knockleith in 1743, was a Scotch merchant of good family, who had emigrated to New York and laid the foundation of a considerable fortune. Being a Loyalist he removed at the beginning of the Revolution to Montreal, where he founded the firm of Inglis, Ellice & Co. About 1780 he returned to England as head of the London house, leaving his brother Robert as manager of the Montreal business. Alexander's son Edward became prominent in the fur-trade, effected the union of the North West and Hudson's Bay companies, and became a member of the British cabinet.—ED.

⁷³ For this person see *Wis. Hist. Colls.*, xviii, p. 393.—ED.

⁷⁴ Doctor Mitchell is noted in *Ibid.*, p. 496.—ED.

on those of mark (B)	£794. 1. 7.
on do mark (A) } if purchased from MᶜComb.	34. 6. 2d.
on do I A A	41.19. 5
on do I A–T. W. C.	752.12. 3
on do I B A (Barthe)	349.11. 3
	£1972′10″8 Sterling

equal to £2191.14. 1 Currency carried to the credit of your Account. It would afford us satisfaction could we hold out to you similar hopes against another year. but we fear much for deer Skins, as the quantity going home greatly exceeds that of last year & we are sorry to remark that those from the Messrs. MaCombs[75] turn out a very inferior quality, nor are the Racoons of this parcle any thing so good as those of last years and to add to these untoward circumstances there is yet near to 400 packs not come down, on which we fear an additional premium of 2 per cent must be paid as there remains but small hopes of our being able to get them a board the vessels which are to sail from Quebec on the 25th. Inst.

Ever since the arrival of our Mr. Todd our time has been so much taken up with baling Furrs & providing Funds to answer the heavy drafts from above that we have not looked into the accounts he brought down & we must now deferr it until all the shipping are gone.

We have now nearly made provision to get through the business this year with the same regard to your drafts as heretofore,

---

[75] The Macombs, Alexander and William, were Irish born, coming while quite young to America, with their parents, and settling (1755) at Albany. About 1772 they removed to Detroit, where the sons became the most prominent merchants of the town, and acted as government agents during the Revolution.

Alexander married Catherine Navarre in 1773. In 1785 he removed to New York City, where on Broadway he built a palatial home, which was rented to President Washington as the first executive mansion. The son of Alexander, bearing the same name, entered the United States army and arose to eminence. The father died in 1831 at Georgetown, D. C.

William Macomb, brother and partner of Alexander, remained in Detroit, where he died in 1796, leaving three sons.—ED.

that is, that no man can say he has ever called twice for money that was due. we think we may now flatter ourselves with things going on more smoothly in future & that we shall be more free from perplexity & anxiety than has been the case for two or three years past.

We have hitherto as you may have observed declined making any charge for our Trouble of shipping Furrs to England, tho' most certainly it creates more employment than importing Goods, nor is it our intention to make any charge on what is past, but on all future Shippments as well as on those of this year we mean to make charge of One & a half per cent, which we dare say you will think reasonable for that kind of Agency. The Merchants at home charge 2½ per ct. altho' they never see a Skin, whilst we are obliged to do everything ourselves & we assure you it is not a small business to go properly through with. We are with much esteem, Dear Sirs your sincere Friends

TODD & M^cGILL

Messrs. John Askin & Co.

1786: RETURNS UNSATISFACTORY

[Source, same as preceding document, but p. 167.]

MONTREAL 12 April 1786

DEAR ASKIN—I must not let the first opportunity of the Spring slip over without my personal Respects & I hope they will find you well in your health & a fair prospect of plentiful Returns from the Indian Country.

The Firm having wrote you on business; leaves me nothing further to say on that head than to enjoin you by every turn of friendship to leave no stone unturned in order to make remittances, for on this Summer depends even our existance as much of Character & Credit. The very scanty payments we made last year, has left us indebted with our Friends in England, so largely that Todd writes us he was under the necessity of relinquishing every Scheme of business except the shipping a few dry Goods & some Rum, being afraid to run further in debt and perhaps even met with a refusal of further Credit. This situation I must not tell you the cause, least it should have an appearance of reproach, your own feelings will dictate what must be wise. I have no occassion to say more than that I depend confidentially on your acting in consequence. Do not suppose that, because I have been complaining for years past, the necessity is not greater than it was the case is much altered— a bad trade here, a scarcity of money & no doubt the sum owing us from above; but why should I detain you with the exposition of affairs, knowing that you will leave nothing undone that may be in your power to accomplish. I forsee & know that very few Goods will be sent to Detroit this Season & it might have been a good year to push, but it is out of our power, therefore I advise you to husband well your dry Goods & if you order any that you may be as sparing as possible. Michilimakinac will be greatly overstocked, insomuch that it would not surprise me were goods sent from that Post to Detroit.

I cannot yet say anything certain to you about the price of Furrs, but I am pursuaded deer skins have sold badly & I fear Bear & otter have had a tumble. I advise you strongly to change all your late fall & winter deer Skins for Racoons & Picheux [lynx] but Foxes are really worth no more than 4sh. york a good Raccoon large size is better & two Raccoons or one Picheux as they were of more value than a deer skin, except it be a good red, very short blue [?] or parchment Buck.

Your Friends of the Northwest are making a larger outfit this year than they did the last & are going to build a small vessel at the Portage.[76] their great success last year enables them to undertake anything & I make no doubt they will continue successful, which on some of their accounts I most sincerely wish.

It is generaly thought that Sir Guy Carleton who is expected early to be our Governor[77] will permit small vessals of private property on the Lakes, should that be the case you will

---

[76] For early vessels on Lake Superior see *ante*, p. 170, note 32.—ED.

[77] For a brief notice of Carleton see *Wis. Hist. Colls.*, xviii, p. 288, note 10.—ED.

no doubt wish to have one, but it will be prudent to wait till his determination is known & so soon as we do know it, you shall hear from us.

I hope you will push Barthe to convert everything into Returns this Season, he says he intends it as well to pay you as us, the Balance he owes is very near to 70000$^{lvs.}$ Houses and lands can never produce much benefit to Merchants & it may be the properest time to sell them before the final determination of Government is known respecting the Posts. excepting a House for my business I would not wish to have any dead property in a country where for want of Courts of Justice, Tenures must be very insecure.

Your daughter Madelion is in perfect health & when a proper opportunity offers, It is my intention to fulfil Mrs. Askin's & your wish by sending her up & I am pretty certain you will find her "bien entendue dans le menage"[78] insomuch that I fancy you will not keep her many years Madamoiselle. I expect Todd from England early & as there will be little to do here, he may probably pay you a visit, taking Madelion with him.

Mrs. McGill requests Mrs. Askin with your good self & Family to accept her best Complements and believe that I am, Dear Askin Your affectionate Friend

JAMES M^{c}GILL.

[Source, same as preceding document, but p. 185. Translated from the French.]

DETROIT June 30, 1786.

Monsieur Durand

SIR—I do not reproach you for the past, that is no use. I only say to you, that I have supported you As well as many

---

[78] "Well-taught in the art of housekeeping." Madeleine Askin married Dr. Robert Richardson, a surgeon of Amherstburg, Ont., who was appointed to the Indian department during the War of 1812-15. While acting as surgeon for the British, he was captured by Perry's fleet, but was later released, and in 1815 was acting as clerk of court at Sandwich. His wife died young, leaving small children, one of whom, Maj. John Richardson, afterwards became a well-known novelist and traveller.—ED.

others, when I can scarcely support my self to day. Monsieur Vigoe[79] seems to be among your friends, and assures me that you will do me justice for the loss so I content myself for the present. It gives me much pain that when I could serve you, you have detached yourself from me. I hope that you will see that it will be for your interest to return and I believe that I will not have any difficulty in getting for you Merchandise from our Company. There were 226 of your Deer skins with several Bears that were so bad that I have them here yet. In this regard I have done for the best, for the bad Skins have not brought enough to pay for half the expense. The 27 of Sept, 1784 I sent you your account by Mr. Vigoe amounting then to 26,279^{lvs} 17^s & at present it makes the sum of 2210£ 11^{sh} New York Currency, without interest, and all that you have sent me credited as you will see by the Account & I can assure you that I have lost well by the Sale of your Peltries, as on those of others as I can prove. However that is not your fault. I only have to add, that I have not yet lost hope for you, and that you will have a Good Opportunity This year to recoup all that you have lost. I am Sir your Servant

[JOHN ASKIN]

Mr. Jean Durand[80]

[Source, same as preceding document, but p. 187.]

MONTREAL 16 July 1786.

DEAR SIR—Since ours of the 8th July, we are favored with your letters of the 22^d & 27 ult and as our Mr. Todd will we dare say be with you when this gets to hand, it is the less necessary for us to write you at length. But we cannot help expressing much uneasiness that on the 22d of last month you were still unacquainted how, many of your Customers had made out, for we have allways thought that at so advanced a time of

---

[79] For Vigo see *Wis. Hist. Colls.*, xviii, p. 466, note 91.—ED.

[80] Jean Durand appears to have traded to the Illinois, where in 1780 he was sued at Cahokia. The same year he was at Mackinac, and offered to guide Langlade's forces to the Illinois River.—ED.

the year it was in every bodys power to tell pretty nearly the prospect of their returns, and from your silence on that head we are really concerned.

The Person gone off, whose name you do not mention, we suspect to be Lorimier,[81] should that be the Case we fear you suffer greatly by him, having recollection of your saying in a former leter that he owed you largely.

In sending off the last boats from La Chine a few barrels of Rum were put into them not charged in the Invoice, from our suppossing enough of other things to load the Battoes, and as they may reach you before a regular Invoice is furnished, we shall note their numbers and Contents at Bottom.

Part of the Packs A B being come to hand we cannot help taking nottice to you of this apparently inferior quality, they appear all to be long hair Skins, which are of all the others the

---

[81] Louis Lorimier, son of the trader Peter, was born in 1748 at La Chine, near Montreal. In 1769 the father and son came to the Western country and established their trading house on the portage between Great Miami and Maumee rivers, on the creek which has since been known as Laramie's. They acquired large influence with the Shawnee of the neighborhood, and during the Revolution acted as British agents. Either father or son accompanied the expedition that in 1778 captured Daniel Boone. In 1782 the Kentuckians raided the Miami, captured Lorimier's store, and plundered and burned the goods. The owner barely escaped with his life, and never again returned to the site, establishing instead a temporary encampment upon the Maumee. Louis Lorimier removed to Spanish territory in 1786 or 1787; it is his contemplated removal thither, to which reference is here made. He attracted to his neighborhood a considerable band of Shawnee and Delaware Indians, and in 1793 received a grant from the Spaniards at Cape Girardeau. He was likewise made captain of militia and commandant. His journal for the year 1793-94 was found among the Louisiana papers in the archives of Seville. In 1796 he revisited the United States as Spanish agent to attract still more Indians to the west of the Mississippi. He expressed great regret at the cession of Louisiana to the United States, and in 1804 entertained the retiring Spanish commandant at the "Red House," Lorimier's homestead at Cape Girardeau. In 1806 he was one of the commission to lay out the town, where in 1812 he died, leaving a large estate and several children, one of whom was educated at West Point, and entered the United States Army.—ED.

worst; insomuch that a Battoe load of them is not worth the expense of sending for them to St Dusky were they to be got on the Beach. now that you have got into a Company at Detroit, if you do not adopt some measure to prevent the Traders from taking such trash, ruin must insue infallibly. we request of you also to advise that the Chuck Skins tho mostly in good Season, are exceedingly unfit for the London Market, owing to the manner in which they were stretched and altho' Mr. Vigoe may be of opinion that the Skins are not the less good, we can assure you that their value is much inferior at that Market by which we must all be regulated. Some part of the V Packs being baled up before your letter desiring them to be baled apart came to hand we cannot now follow your directions, but that you may see the difference in the G. A, we shall make them up under a separate mark. In hopes that your next advices may bring us more satisfactory accounts, we are with Sentiments of friendship and esteem, Dear Sir Your sincere Friends

TODD & M^{c}GILL

Mr. John Askin.

1789: SUPPLIES FOR NORTH WEST COMPANY

[Source, same as preceding document, but p. 321.]

SIR—Yours of this date with proposals for Supplying the North West Company with a Certain Quantity of Hulled Indian Corn & Flower during the Space of Three years, in answer to Which, I do Hereby Accept of the Proposal therein Contained, for the quantity of Each Article & at the Prices therein Specified—the Payment for which Shall Be Made in Montreal p^r Messrs. McTavish Frobisher & Co. on the fifteenth day of October After the Delivery. I am Sir, Yours most H^{bl} Ser^t

JOHN GREGORY[82]

Agent for the North West Company

DETROIT 26th Septr 1789.
John Askin Esq.

---

[82] John Gregory was in the Northwest by 1778 as partner of James Findley, his brother-in-law. Gregory was one of the founders of the

1778-1815] **Fur-trade on Upper Lakes**

1790: OUTFITTING AT GREEN BAY

[Letters from Pierre Grignon to Pierre Antaya. MS. in Wisconsin Historical Library, Grignon letter book, pp. 66-68. Translated from the French.]

LA BAIE 25th August, 1790.

To Mr. Antaya at la prairie.[83]

SIR—I hope that your health has been good since you left me to follow the fortune which certainly should await you, if the vows that I have made on your behalf are listened to. You have begun your task under very advantageous circumstances, and I do not doubt in spite of the ambitious measures of certain people, that you will succeed. I congratulate you in advance, and request you to await the invoice that I am sending to the prairie. I believe you are too honest to wish to take advantage of my confidence, and although things have been said of you at Michilimakinack of which I shall send you the details when I send my consignment, I have abated nothing of

---

North West Company, and made his headquarters in Montreal, going up to Grand Portage each year. In 1791 he had two shares in the concern, having bought out the interest of William Holmes. In 1804 he signed the agreement for union with the X Y Company, and seems to have retired soon thereafter.—ED.

[83] Pierre Pelletier *dit* Antaya has long been recognized in Wisconsin history as one of the founders of the village of Prairie du Chien, but little has been known of his personality. These letters addressed to him by Pierre Grignon of Green Bay make it possible to estimate Antaya's standing as a trader. He was probably a native of Canada, but removed early to the Illinois country, where the family is known to have settled as early as 1751. The registers of Ste. Geneviève frequently contain this name; and a granddaughter of Antaya, who died in 1902 at Prairie du Chien, asserted that her mother was born in St. Louis in 1775. The tradition is that the Antaya family came to Prairie du Chien in 1781, possibly with a desire to be under British rather than Spanish or American protection. The following letters indicate Antaya's close connection with the traders at Mackinac. He appears to have had relations with the Fox Indians, and his wife is reported to have been of that race. He probably died before Pike's visit in 1805, and his immediate descendants were daughters who married into the La Pointe and Fraser families.—ED.

[267]

my belief in you, since I allowed you to make your choice from among my Goods. There is no doubt that if you had succeeded, they would have made you many offers, but do not allow yourself to be surprised, and distinguish between the one who serves you as a friend, and those whose only view is to make a profit by fawning upon you. For you should not Doubt that the one who trusts in your probity will still believe therein if you do your best, and try to work for our mutual advantage. I have never wasted my Goods, and I do not think I am doing so now in trusting to you. You ought therefore to have a just idea of this and strive to justify my confidence. It is your place now to respond thereto. Believe me I pray, Yours &c
[Pierre Grignon]

I cannot go myself to see you, you yourself see the impossibility, but I send to you in my place, one who will give you what you need, and will arrange everything for the best. Wait for him I beg you. Without turning aside from what you have done you may prove to me by this, that I am right in being your servant and good friend.

La Baie 12 Sept. 1790.

To Mr. Antaya at la prairie.

Sir—I repeat the greeting I have already sent to you, and within six days I will send you the proof of my remembrance, persuaded that you will render me one in return. I extend it also to what you have told me and to what I have written you myself. Do not be impatient at the delay, I do not Think that it can be prejudicial to you, and when [the goods] arrive, I beg you to notice that I have done for you as well as I can, but not what I would wish. I think that we shall be ready as soon as the others, and it will be enough for you at present to know that the Goods that I have promised you will not be wanting, and that you will not fail to receive them. Once en route you may believe they will not be slow in reaching you. It is your duty after that to respond to my good faith. I have treated you with all possible frankness, persuaded that you will take account thereof, and that I make no mistake in trusting you. Do not make an arrangement with anyone else, and do not believe them; as I have already said, their offers may be advantageous for the moment, that the desire for your furs influences them. I do not think that you have had occasion to complain of the Beginning, keep to the same arrangement in the future, and it may be even more advantageous for you.

Believe me to be one who is with Sincerity your Servant

P. G.

LA BAIE 24 Sept. 1790.

To Monsieur Antaya at La prairie.

SIR—I fulfill my engagements with you, and send you the Canoe that I have promised. I trust that you will likewise keep your promise, therefore I do not diminish the invoice except by what may be necessary in case of the foundering of the merchandise itself, for fear of giving you useless expense. Supposing that you are not without provisions, I have sent the voyageurs off with what will last only until they meet the Savages, from whom they must get enough to last as far as la prairie. My preceding letters have sufficiently advised you of my Sentiments since I cannot Doubt the successful result of my Confidence in you, and now I expect return therefor. I should never do the same again if you should deceive me. You see yourself the Damage you can Cause me. A Canoe without provisions in an advanced season is not one to enter the wintering country. Besides it is the articles you have requested of me, that have caused this to go out unassorted, unlike a Canoe I should send into winter quarters. It goes under your name, I hope that you will be prompt, and that you will have a good journey in order to give me the pleasure of seeing you again next Spring. In that hope I am Your &c.

P. G.

1791-92: CONDITIONS AT MACKINAC

[Source, same as preceding document, but pp. 70, 76. Translated from the French.]

To Mr. Cotté

LA BAIE [June 25, 1791].

SIR—I received your last which leads me to think that your health is good, since you do not speak of it. It is not true of my own of which I have nothing good to say. Nothing new in our little Country. There are few events that can disturb your province and some fortunate ones that you may suppose I am not a little interested in. I cannot but be charmed with your share, and congratulate you on the successful return of your traders to Quebec, as well as to Makinack. I cannot leave as early as you Wished. I shall not embark for six days, but that need not retard you at all. Do your business, I have no Choice to make in your Goods, and what is left will be all right for me, so you may depart for le pick[84] without 'waiting for me. We will have time to see one another on your return. Adieu, Sir, I have performed your Commissions, do likewise for me. Persuading you that I am &c.

P. G.

Monsieur Gabriel Cotté.

LA BAIE [June 16, 1792].

SIR—I have had the pleasure of learning by your Canoe that you have safely arrived at Makinac in good health. I wish that it may continue to be the Best possible. I Thank you for the interest you take in mine. It is good enough,

---

[84] Le Pic was a trading post on the north shore of Lake Superior, about 200 miles from Sault Ste. Marie. It was not founded until after the beginning of the English regime. Probably it belonged to Cotté, who was an independent trader and did not join the coalition. Later, the post passed into the hands of the North West Company, and for many years was maintained by Hudson's Bay Company people. The Canadian Pacific Railway now crosses Pic River near its mouth, and not far from the site of the old fur-trade post.—ED.

I have nothing to complain of at present. I yield to your desires in regard to the House,[85] and against my own interests. After having refused five thousand livres for it, for fear of harming you, I offer it to you for three thousand five hundred in order to conclude with you in good friendship, all the more since you do not intend to Return any more.[86] I hope, Sir, that for your part, you will be gallant enough not to trouble me in the choice of Goods, it is with that expectation that I do not wish to disturb Mr. Billon[87] in the Clauses of the transfer. I entered into a bargain with this Gentleman to sell you my Peltries, but he has not been willing to give me my Price, which however was not Large considering the quality of the Peltries, which I can say is of the Best. My wife Thanks you very much for what you sent her and prays you to believe that she is very grateful therefor, and as for me, I have the honor of being Yours

[Pierre Grignon]

1792: FUR-TRADE UNPROFITABLE

[MS. in Burton Library, Detroit, vol. 2, p. 58.]

London 10th Augst, 1792.

Dear Askin—I wrote you by the Spring Ships Since which I am favored with yours of the 20 May. Mr. McGill has been so employed in forwarding Goods &c that hitherto he has com-

---

[85] For the lot that was granted Pierre Grignon upon the island of Mackinac, see *Wis. Hist. Colls.*, xviii, pp. 432–434. Many of the older traders kept a house in Mackinac for use during the summer trading season, even while making their homes elsewhere.—Ed.

[86] It would seem from this letter that Cotté intended to leave the Upper Country in 1792; but see the evidence *ante*, p. 161, note 17.—Ed.

[87] Bartholemi Billon, a friend of Grignon, lived in Montreal, and made trading trips to Mackinac. To his care was entrusted the education of Grignon's sons, when they were sent to Montreal to school. Wisconsin MSS., 29C2, in the Wisconsin Historical Library, contains an account (dated 1793) for the schooling of Amable, Pierre, and Charles Grignon, made out in favor of Billon.—Ed.

municated little to me on Business. I am extremely sorry to hear your Indian Trade has been generally bad and that you are among the unsuccessfull. I agree with you that pushing that trade answers no good purpose, I have strongly recommended to the House to curtale & Lessen our connections in that Trade, for when I considered the uncertainty of our retaining the Posts, the Warr between the Indians & Americans, and the evident fall on furs I am convinced it is an unsafe & unprofitable business, and will continue so for two or 3 years. I am certain there will be a fall in Furrs at this Market this year of 15 to 20 pr. Ct. and every apperance they will continue falling for 2 or 3 years which has ever been the case, therefore untill matters comes back to the old standard those who do least will do best. I am certain there is this year double the quantity of Goods intended for that trade that it can pay for, I trust your New Goverm^s: may open some advantagious Trade that may answer your purpose better.[88]

I am happy in hearing you and Family enjoy good health Long may it continue, I enclose a letter for Miss Therese[89] to which I reffer you for family [news] Mr. Robertson[90] is now here he talks of paying you a visit in the Spring, which I have my doubts off unless his business at Detroit gos wrong, he is

---

[88] The reference here is to the act for the division of Canada and the organization of a separate government for the upper province, which passed parliament May 14, 1791.—ED.

[89] Thérèse Askin married Capt. Alexander McKee, son of the Revolutionary Loyalist of the same name. He made his home about a mile below Sandwich, Ontario, and served under Proctor in the War of 1812-15.—ED.

[90] William Robertson, brother of Samuel (noted *ante*, p. 241), came to Detroit in 1782, and for two years acted as clerk or agent for a local firm. Going into business for himself, he acquired a competence and a large landed property about Detroit. In 1789-90 he served on the landboard of the district of Hesse, Upper Canada, having refused a judgeship for the same district. Some time in 1790 he retired to England, and thereafter made but occasional visits to Detroit. He died early in the nineteenth century, leaving much of his property to his nephew William, of Queenston, Ontario.—ED.

[1778-1815]   **Fur-trade on Upper Lakes**

Surprised at not hearing from any of his friends this Spring. Please remember me kindly to the Commod^r:[91] as I suppose the Naval business will be immediatly under Govr: Simcoe[92] it will make it more pleasant and easy for him and put more in his power to serve his Friends, I hope to hear often from you, and with Kind Respects to Mrs. Askin & family believe me ever yours Sincerely.

ISAAC TODD

Mr. John Askin.

1793: REGULATIONS PROPOSED

[Source, same as preceding document, but p. 94.]

SIR—With the Utmost Submission and Defferance to your Excellencys better Judment I beg leave to Suggest a mode of Carrying on the Indian Trade to the Westward by means that would in the first Instance in a great measure Secure the Lives & property of the Traders, in the Second procure a greater Consumption of Goods & larger remittances in Furrs, & in the third furnish the Indians with what Commodities they might want on the Frontiers and by that means prevent them retiring

---

[91] The reference is to Commodore Alexander Grant, a brother-in-law of John Askin, for whom see *Wis. Hist. Colls.*, xviii, p. 311, note 33. In addition to that sketch, it should be said that Grant was for many years a member of the executive council of Upper Canada; and in 1805, when serving as president of the council, was *de facto* governor of the province during the interregnum between Governors Hunter and Gore.—ED.

[92] John Graves Simcoe was an English soldier, born in 1752 and educated at Eton, and Merton College, Oxford. In 1771 he was commissioned in the 35th infantry, served throughout the American Revolution, and surrendered with Cornwallis at Yorktown (1781). In 1790 he entered parliament, and next year was appointed lieutenant-governor of Upper Canada, where he arrived in the summer of 1792. After four years of governorship, he was granted leave of absence and sent (1796–98) to manage affairs at San Domingo. He never returned to Canada, dying in England in 1806.—ED.

from the best Hunting Grounds & leaving that part of the Country free & oppen to the Encrochments of new Enemies.

That the Fidelity & good Character of Each person desirious to Trade with the Indians beyond the foot of the Rapids be Assertained to the Satisfaction of the Commanding officer, Coll. McKee[93] & such others as they may think Worthy of Trust after which such person to be Admitted as a Joint Partner in all the Indian Trade carried on beyond the Afors^d: Place he conforming to the regulations made for that Purpose which regulations before Carried into Execution to be Transmitted to you by the Commanding Officer of the Post for your Excellencys Approbation.

That all the Trade of that Country should be carried on by a Company to consist of Persons of the forgoing Characters. That no Traffic should be carried on but in Stockaded Trading Forts nor less than Twenty four men Exclusive of the Trader & his Interpretor in Each Fort which men should take the oath of Allegiance & by there Agreement be Obliged to mount Guard & do Duty as Soldiers so far as necessary for the Preservation of the Lives & property of the People in it. That These men should be Commanded by a Person of Fidelity & Prudance Approved of by the Commanding Officer.

I beg your Excellency will Excuse my want of method in conveying my Ideas & Suffer me to say that I have no wish so at Heart as that of promotating the wellfare of his Majestys Goverment Under your directions & should it Please your Excellency to Enact any Laws for the regulations of the Trade on the Frontier and that any Information I'm possessed of would on that occasion be necessary, I will with much Chearfulness

---

[93] Governor Simcoe built (1794) a British fort on American territory at the foot of the rapids of the Maumee. Probably, however, Askin here refers to the commanding officer of Detroit, Col. Richard England, and the agent for the Western Indians, Col. Alexander McKee, whose store and buildings were on the south side of Maumee River, opposite Fort Miami. For these two persons see *Wis. Hist. Colls.*, xviii, pp. 434, 443 respectively.—ED.

go to Niagara[94] for that purpose and Always, think myself greatly Honored in Executing your Commands.

I am with Great Submission Your Excellencys Most Obedient & very Humble Servent

[JOHN ASKIN]

Detroit February the 22 1793.
Governor Simcoe.

1793: DISPUTE WITH EMPLOYÉ

[MS. in Wisconsin Historical Library; Pressmark: Wisconsin MSS., 60B1. Translated from the French.]

We the arbitrators named by the Parties in the Case between Sieur Charles Reaume and Ambroise Dubeau his Clerk,[95] have found, after the Depositions taken that the Said Ambroise Dubeau has not followed the orders of the said Charle Reaume his Bourgeois, and Declarations showing that he has done his work badly on Several occasions, that he ought to lose his Wages at la prairie Du Chien.

April 20, 1793.

J^m EALING
J. BLEAKLEY
J. GIASSON
JAM$^{s.}$ AIRD[96]

---

[94] Niagara, at the mouth of the river on its west side, was the seat of the government of Upper Canada under Governor Simcoe. He arrived there July 26, 1792, and made headquarters at Navy Hall, built during the Revolution by Haldimand, for the accommodation of the naval officers on Lake Ontario. Simcoe had this repaired, and made it his official residence. There, in the summer of 1793, he entertained the United States commissioners who were endeavoring to obtain peace with the Indians. See Gen. Benjamin Lincoln's journal in *Mass. Hist. Colls.*, 3d series, vol. v.—ED.

[95] For Charles Reaume see *ante*, p. 142, note 88. Ambroise Dubeau had wintered in 1786–87 on St. Peter's River, apparently as clerk for James Aird.—ED.

[96] These were traders in the Mississippi valley, and probably all members of the Mackinac Company.

Josiah Bleakley was in 1783 storekeeper and clerk for the Indian de-

1796: BRITISH EVACUATE DETROIT

[MS. in Burton Library, Detroit, vol. 3, p. 208.]

DETROIT 2 July 1796.

DEAR ASKIN—I leave in your care 64 packs Musk^t M[arked] No. 1 to 64, which I request you will send to Fort Erie[97] as soon as possible either in the Kings Vessels or any other sending with them an acc^t to Mr. Warran and Mr. Hamilton,[98] there is allso 17 packs that Mr Hands has & a like number with Mr Dufresne[99] if you can assist in Getting them down, I wish you

---

partment at Mackinac; in 1785-86 he wintered on the upper Mississippi. He appears to have been associated with Porlier on the lower Mississippi in 1812, and at Montreal signed an invoice as late as 1814.

Jacques Giasson was son of the trader mentioned in *Wis. Hist. Colls.*, xviii, p. 197, note 52. Born at Montreal in 1747, he was active in the trade of the Upper Country from his youth until his death in 1808. In the letter given in facsimile in *Ibid.*, p. 462, the name erroneously transcribed "Grayson" should be Giasson.

For Aird, see *Ibid.*, p. 437, note 51.—ED.

[97] Fort Erie was erected in 1764 by Capt. John Montressor at the entrance to Niagara River, on the west bank. This was a preliminary to Bradstreet's expedition to Detroit of the same year. During the Revolution it was maintained chiefly as a depot of supplies, and rebuilt at various intervals (1778, 1790, 1807). In the War of 1812-15 Fort Erie played an important part in the campaigns around Niagara. In July, 1814, it was seized by the Americans, who successfully defended it during a severe siege of nearly two months. Upon the retirement of the American army, in November of the same year, the fort was blown up, and its ruins are still to be seen.—ED.

[98] John Warren was at Fort Erie as early as 1780, and for many years acted as assistant commissary. He was in the transportation business, and died at that place in 1832.

Robert Hamilton was the founder of Queenston, on Niagara River. For a portrait and sketch, see Buffalo Hist. Soc. *Publications*, vi, pp. 73-95.—ED.

[99] William Hands was an early Detroit merchant, who elected to remain British in 1796 and removed to the east side of the river. He, or a son of the same name, was sheriff at Amherstburg in 1818.

Louis Dufresne was from Montreal, coming to the Upper Country about 1795. In 1796 he was recommended for the post of government blacksmith at Fort St. Josephs, where he was in service as late as 1804.—ED.

1778-1815]   **Fur-trade on Upper Lakes**

would as they are for us   I think by going to the mouth of the River with Col^n[1]. England[1] you might Get him to leave an order or at Least a request with the Command^r. there to give you the first Kings Vessels that returns from F^t. Erie to take packs, this on Account of freight owing you, and on this assurance you might be ready to send the packs down   I am Yours Sincerely

ISAAC TODD

John Askin Esq.

Endorsed: Col. England wrote from Fort Erie to John Askin about July 18th–20th 1796.

1798:   FURS CAPTURED BY FRENCH

[Source, same as preceding document, but vol. 5, p. 11.]

MONTREAL 21th April 1798.

DEAR SIR—We are your debtors for favors of the 23d & 31st Jan^{ry} and of the 13th Feb^{ry} ulto and pay attention to their contents   the only matters in your first that require particular answer seem to be respecting the Men you wish should be engaged, a Miller & the Invoice of Goods forwarded last Fall. To the first, out of Six for you & Mr. Anderson,[2] we have met with but two as Miller, & we find by an invoice remaining here of a Bale dry Goods & Roll of Tobacco, it must have been omitted to be endorsed and we now hand it to you, ammount £57. 9. 10 Cy. at your debit in October 1797.   The Silver works order'd for Mr. Anderson & your own order for Smiths Utensils, we have put in Hand of a Silver smith to get done & order'd

---

[1] For a reference to Col. Richard England, see *Wis. Hist. Colls.*, xviii, p. 443, note 60.   England was leaving Detroit, after having delivered it into the hands of the Americans.—ED.

[2] John Anderson was a trader who had formerly lived near Pittsburgh, and removed to the Detroit country about the close of the Revolution. He was closely connected in business with Askin, and appears to have traded in northern Ohio. Probably the Col. John Anderson of the militia (1805), afterwards justice of the county court, and auditor of public highways, was his son.—ED.

yours from Quebec, the first will be got down but we are not yet informed respecting the smiths Tools &c. as to the expence of going in a Boat, it will no doubt come much higher than by Vessel.

We are doing everything in our power to get the Winterers & if they can be had may go up in Mr Parks[3] Boat or in two that we are sending for Mr McGregor.[4] You will probably have heard by the States that one of our Annual Fur Ships was captured & carried into Bourdeaux by the French and your parcel was shiped in her what effect the loss of so great a Supply will have on the London Market seems to be very uncertain & people are divided in their opinion because one of our great outlets for Skins & Furs was Germany & the goods will of course be had in France at less expense & perhaps price too. Mr. Todd & our prior have seen your letter of the 13th Feb^{ry}. Having nothing more interesting, We remain very truly Dear Sir Your most obd^t servt

JAMES & A. M^{c}GILL

John Askin Esq.

Memorandum: Ship Ariadné, E. Boyd taken, value on board of yours N Y 1391.8.6.

---

[3] William Park was one of the early merchants of Detroit, being there as early as 1780, when he acted as representative of James Sterling. The next year the firm was William Park & Co.; a few years later, Meldrum & Park. The latter was spoken of as desirable for a magistrate of the new British government of 1792, and in 1796 elected to remain a British subject. He was still living in 1807, although apparently no longer in active business.—ED.

[4] Gregor McGregor was an early British merchant of Detroit, being mentioned as early as 1774. Four years later he was made captain of militia in the place of James Sterling, and in 1788 served the district of Hesse, Canada, as sheriff and superintendent of inland navigation. Later he became major and colonel of local British militia. Although in 1796 he elected to remain a British citizen, he had a place at Grosse Point, where he resided as late as 1808.—ED.

1778-1815]   **Fur-trade on Upper Lakes**

[Source, same as preceding document, but p. 17.]

MONTREAL 27 April 1798.

John Askin Esq.

DEAR SIR—We wrote you on the 21st inst and the present serves chiefly to hand statements of Accounts up to 10th instant agreeable to custom; in your acct appears a balance of £725.7.9 & in that under title of John Anderson & Co of £426.18.1 of both Currency & in our favor which we trust you will find right Last night we had advices from England with Sales of deer Skins on 3 Feby which we are very sorry to say is 20% worse than last year & it falls particularly on the heavy Skins; the general average of Detroit Deer Skins does not exceed 5/6 Stg. & the Charges on Skins are not less than 1/3 Stg. from which you may judge of their value with you. as to Peltries we can say nothing certain but fear for them also, the Sales of them was fixed for 8 March; [we] certainly regret the capture of your Furs, but we are at this moment inclined to think that it has saved you from a greater loss. As at present it is not possible to say when the Trade Ships may arrive & those Goods are not ordered for your account from England we suppose that after seeing how payments are likely to come in that you will have modelled an order to answer your Trade, we mean your own for [the goods for] Anderson & Col. Gouin[5] have been ordered from England. we do not wish you to be without Goods but we wish you at all times as old Friends to weigh the means of payment to the undertaking that in advanced years the pressure of Engagements may not annoy & aid to bind down.

We can meet with no Miller at your price and had few Engagés against the time however of sending up Mr. Andersons

---

[5] Charles Gouin belonged to a prominent French family in Detroit, being born at that city in 1752. He long retained vivid recollections of the siege of Pontiac (1763), for many of its scenes he witnessed from his father's house; he related them for publication in 1824 (see *Mich. Pion. & Hist. Colls.*, viii, pp. 344–351). At the latter date he occupied the parental homestead, after having had an adventurous career as trader and militia officer. Gouin lived to an old age, being still alive in 1834.—ED.

Goods some may be had, which we presume will answer his purpose. We are Dear Sir Your very obd{t}. Sevt{s},

JAMES & AND. M{c}GILL

P. S. Under cover are your two notes to I. Todd & J. M. McGill omitted to be returned in winter

J. A. M.

1799: NEW NORTH WEST COMPANY.

[Source, same as preceding document, but p. 169.]

MONTREAL 25 January 1799.

DEAR ASKIN—I received your several letters, and observed what you say respecting Trade at your post it is nothing new when money is gaind one or two years in a post they must loose five business is much the same here all Trades overdone from your information, I have alter'd my plan and sold off all my importations at cost & Charges so I am again free living on stock which goes very fast, and [what] the next will be cannot say. the New North West Company is going on it will be a considerable struggle but I know who will gain.[6] The one party is a new rais'd corps without discipline, the other old veterans I cant find one man of experience that has the least knowledge in the North concern'd Forsyth does the business here and Sharp[7] at the portage, I thank you for the memorandum &c, you sent me, I did not mean that my Nephew[8] should

---

[6] Referring to the corporation usually known as X Y Company. See *ante*, p. 169, note 30.—ED.

[7] Probably George Sharp, a prominent fur-trader, who in 1786 was in the Southwest Company, giving information to the British commandant at Detroit. In 1790 he reported upon American movements in Ohio, and is noted as declaring for British citizenship in 1796. He died, as per letter published *post*, in 1800.—ED.

[8] This is Alexander Henry the younger, whose journals were edited by Elliott Coues (New York, 1897). He is known to have been with his uncle at Montreal in 1787. In 1799 he entered the fur-trade, wintering until 1808 at several posts on Red River, whence he reported upon the expedition of Lewis and Clark. For three years he

have settled at Sagana or the Indian Country but at Detroit. he is going to the North West—With the old Company. I am informed that Sheipland was at Philadelphia with the Indians from Detroit but cannot know what has been done, but can guess that Isaac Todd was there at the Time but has not returned I supose you will have the News—such as Never was known—Admiral Nelson with 13 Ships of the line attacked the Toulon fleet, which took Boanaparte to Egypt and took Eleven of the french the Beys or Generals in Egypt has killed the greatest part of her army,[9] Nelson's fleet also destroyed 300 Transports

Admiral Warran has Taken & Destroyed the Brest fleet going to Ireland with troops. The french Landed a number of troops there sometime before these, but they were all taken or killed. The Turks has declar'd war against france, and it is supos'd Germany Russia & all the world will do the same. America talks big, they feel Bold. all this good news has rais'd our spirrits furs in England will sell, by the best Information I can get far less than last year Beaver very great fall Deer about the same as last year Bear much less Raccoons a fall Muskratts will sell here 20 coppers good, no small ones —to 22—that is if those shiped for England [this] fall, sells for that in London p^r Cwt if for less they will return to America and *over stock* the market, then a fall. I expect Todd up soon with all the news. he like myself growing old always complains. one of your old friends General Christie[10] took his

---

was at Saskatchewan posts, being in 1813 sent to Columbia River, where, with Donald McKenzie, he took over the charge of Astoria when that post was surrendered by the Americans. In April, 1814, both traders were drowned in the mouth of the river by the overturning of a small boat.—ED.

[9] The battle of the Nile, fought in Aboukir Bay, August 1, 1798.—ED.

[10] Gen. Gabriel Christie was a veteran of the British army, having had the rank of colonel as early as 1762. He does not appear to have come to America until 1768, when he was lieutenant-colonel of the 60th (or Royal American) regiment for ten years. Probably it was at that time that Askin formed his friendship. In 1787 he returned to Canada after an absence of several years, and was until his

departure for the other world a few days, ago, old standards diminishes very fast. there is not more than five [or] six remaining in Montreal which are Dobie, John Neagles, Major Hughs, James Morrison, and myself Tod came sometime after the conquest, we have lost that number in about two years—so we may keep a sharp look out. Tell my old friend Com'odore Grant that I received a letter from Doctor Wright Barbados 24 August Mrs. Wright[11] and the children is well, they have an adition of one to their family since they left this. as the time is so very short for us, we should endeavor to meet once more, which you may do this summer and bring Mrs Askin with you. I have tired your patience with so much stuf, So when you are half through lay this by for another time, and believe me ever, with my wishes & that of my family for the Happiness of you and your family Your affectionate friend

ALEXANDER HENRY

John Askin Esquire Detroit Mich.

1799: OUTFITTING FOR WISCONSIN

[Source, same as preceding document, but p. 226.]

DETROIT 6 Mar. 99.

DEAR SIR—The Bearer hereof Mr. Ebenezer Allen[12] has applied to me to know If there is any merchant who I think

---

death (1799) colonel-commandant of the above regiment. He was promoted from major-general (1781) to lieutenant-general (1793), and finally to general (1798). His death occurred at Montreal.—ED.

[11] The eldest daughter of Commodore Grant married a Doctor Wright of the English army.—ED.

[12] Ebenezer Allen was an American from Vermont, possibly the son of Maj. Ebenezer Allen, who was a Revolutionary soldier serving at Bennington and Fort Ticonderoga. In 1791 he was in correspondence with Joseph Brant, who speaks of his influence with the Indians. In 1795 Allen, with two associates, formed a plan for securing a large land grant from Congress—it is said, by questionable means. He induced Askin and some other Detroit merchants to embark in this scheme, which in the end came to naught. Nothing further is known regarding his proposed fur-trading expedition to Wisconsin.—ED.

1778-1815] **Fur-trade on Upper Lakes**

would advance a Small Indian Cargo on getting Security for the payment. as I think you wrote me last year of having ordered out goods of that kind, and perhaps have not disposed of them, I mentioned you to him he says his plan is to go to the Ouisconsin, on or near the fox River and he will acquaint you with the rest of his Scheme of this, or the place of Trade I am no judge you are so much better yourself. I therefore have no advice to give respecting the intended trade, nor must you consider me as answerable in any respect, should matters not turn out well. my intentions are to serve both. Mr Allen is not my debtor, nor to my knowledge does he owe any merchant here. I have seen his deed, from Government for between two & three Thousand acres of Land, a part of this he has sold for £3000 and I believe little or no payment is made yet, nor has he given Deeds, as I understand for what he sold but intends to do so, and take Mortgages which mortgage I suppose is to be the Security for the payment of the goods he may get of you or any other. I have heard that there is a grist & a saw mill on his lands & an excellent pinery therefore must be valuable, & have only to add that Mr. Allen is as active and enterprizing a man as any in the province & perfectly Sober. I have now stated the business fair on both sides so far as is come to my knowledge therefore do as you think fit.

[JOHN ASKIN]

Endorsed: John Askin to Mr. Alex⁽ᵈ⁾ Henry of Montreal.

1799: COMPETITION IN THE NORTHWEST

[Source, same as preceding document, but p. 245.]

MONTREAL 8th May 1799.

DEAR ASKIN—I received your favor of January am Happy to find your Health and spirits are so good for me my Health is not so good as usual and I have symptoms of old age advancing rappid, so much that unless I see you this summer I am affraid I never will. but I have no reason to complain since on calculation since my time there has been Two Thousand Million buryed a few years can make no difference, if we can only approve of our conduct while here we need fear nothing hereafter Hope and reliance on Providence is all we can do. there is no fear of being worse treated than others. I seem to be more anxious to know if you and I will ever meet there, than anything else. our old friend Todd is going to Niagara and expects to meet you there was it not for a voyage to New York which I must make I would go also was it only to see you I am informed the President has ordered a Council to be held in Detroit this summer to hear the Complaints of the Indians. but I think nothing will do. Congress is selling the Lands on Lake Erie to the Westward of the N England Grant[13] William Robinson[14] is here busy nursing his child and taking care of his wife by Gentlemen who this day arrived from London in February bring Ammount of Deer Skin Sale, they did very well much the same as last but bad appearance fore Raccoons, dont you send any here if Possible for they will sell badly. good Muskratts will bring from 20 to 22 sols here— there is no accounts of other furs. if Raccoons sells badly Detroit Trade must be much injured, and the N W Company on

---

[13] "New England grant" is the term used to designate the Connecticut Western Reserve, which was retained by that state when in 1786 its Western land claims were ceded to the United States. This reserve extended westward 120 miles from the Pennsylvania boundary; that is, as far as the present western boundaries of Huron and Erie counties. West of that, was territory guaranteed to the Indians by the treaty of Greenville (1795). The Indian title to a portion of this land was extinguished in 1806. Before that date, no sale thereof by Congress could have been legal. It is difficult, therefore, to determine what Henry here refers to. Possibly he was speaking of what were known as the "Firelands," a reserve (made in 1792) of 500,000 acres in the western portion of the Connecticut tract, for the benefit of the sufferers by British aggression during the Revolution. In 1799, the Connecticut legislature passed an act incorporating the proprietors of this tract into a body politic. However, no actual sales were made therein until after 1806; but there was considerable speculation in these lands, titles to which were to be granted after the survey of the tract. Henry may refer to this activity.—ED.

[14] Probably this was the elder William Robertson, for whom see *ante*, p. 272, note 90.—ED.

1778-1815]   Fur-trade on Upper Lakes

account of opposition it is said intends to send quantitys of Goods to Detroit & Makinac to sell at cost and Charges, because Forsyth & Co interfers with their trade in the North. the War seems to have commenced between them, like the french Derectory they will not allow any kings but themselves.

as for Politics, things seems not to stand so favorable as they did at the close of the last year, the french has obliged the king of Naples to leave his Kingdom of which they have Possession. Boanaparte still seems to have Possession of Egypt, and it [is] supos'd the french will not stop until they have taken all the continent of Europe. the Idea of Liberty and equallity, is still gaining ground. England is intending to make a Union with Ireland which will I expect be a bad business before it is settled, as the Irish is much against it, and even our friend Isaac [Todd] disaproves of the English craming the Irish with what they dont like.

I am sorry I have nothing to ammuse you further my family is all well and joins in best wishes for yours dont forget my best respects to Mrs. McKee who I would be glad to see, and remain while there is a spark remaining your sincere friend

ALEXANDER HENRY

John Askin Esquire at Detroit.

1799: SHIPPING ON LAKE HURON

[Source, same as preceding document, but vol. vi, p. 754. Translated from the French.]

MICHI MAKINAC 5 June 1799.

MONSIEUR—I have received your letter dated April 30th and thank you for your attention. You said that "le Saquinaat" ought to leave May 20 but it appears she did not, for she should be here. I beg you if you receive any articles for me to send them to me by any Boat whatsoever that may come, for I much fear that My Goods coming up this spring will be late, which will do me much harm. I am Sir with Consideration Your very humble servant

J. GIASSON & Co.

Addressed: John Askin Esquire Detroit favor of Mr McKinsay to be placed on the "Charlotte"

Endorsed: Mich. June 5, 1799 Messrs Jacque Giasson & Co. to Jno Askin. rec'd the 17th

---

[Source, same as preceding document, but p. 94.]

DETROIT 11 June 1799.

DEAR SIR—Your Sundry favors of the 4th, 10 & 16 of May reached me some time ago, Since which until now I have not had an opportunity to reply. your Account is right, I had thought it would have been reduced to £3000 York, which would have been the Case, had I received, or you or me from Mr Todd what I then expected with the Bill I sent you.

Under cover herewith I send you the Copy of an Account I sent Mr Giasson ammount 351£-2-11, added to which I paid in august last freight for him to the Ammount of 24-2-0 as I suppose more will be added to this account before the Season is over and he give an order on you for payment it is needless to add at present. I am sorry to learn that Racoons are so low, yet I do not believe that there is a very great number in John Anderson & Co's Packs; when he comes in which will be soon we will answer your Letter to him in w^h the account is covered I suppose very right. Notwithstanding our best endeavors the "Saguinaw" will only be ready to sail tomorrow downward for all the freight to McKinac is gone I am glad to find I may expect Winterers and If only one Boat comes I will be necessitated to purchase another to Raft Hay and transport wood for really, there is hardly any Money to be got accept [except] for whats wanted by either of the Governments which is Hay, wood, timber, Bricks etc. and I wish by every means in my power to make you the best payments I can, but as I before wrote the best will be bad I am Sure, and those who have imported lose Cargoes must Suffer, yet whilst a man is in trade, he Should have an assortment but the quantity Small and well chosen and not so over loaded as to have to trust where the payment is very doubtful. there is so many Vessels and so little for them to do that I cannot think Mr Giasson will be at the least loss to get down your Packs. I am sorry, both on your account and our own that the "Saguinaw" could not have been sent up but that, Messrs. Meldrum & Park could not agree to unless you or Mr Giasson would allow for her going up empty as If loaded, and I had no instructions of the kind from either of you. his Boats are arrived to day, and as Soon as Biscuit is ready they will proceed.

My Eyes having been weak for Some time past, that I'm obliged to write no more than what's necessary, I have only to add that I'm with real regards

J. ASKIN

Endorsed: Detroit 11 June 99 John Askin to James & And. MGill

1799: NEWS FROM MACKINAC

[Source, same as preceding document, but p. 100.]

MICHILIMACKNAC 17th June 1799.

DEAR SIR—Your much esteemed favor of the 28th Ult°. I had the pleasure of receiving some days ago.

Please accept of my best thanks for your kind attention in taking the earliest Oppor^y of writing me,

I am very Sorry to find that you are troubled with a weakness in your eyes. I hope by this time you are perfectly recovered. I am happy to learn that Madam Askin & the rest of your family are Well,

We have Nothing New in this part of the World, The Spring here has been Very cold & backward, Ice were floating in the Lakes here the 16th ult°. We have now several Canoes from Montreal, but they bring nothing new. The traders are also coming in from the Westward. The Skin Merchants has not as yet begun to make any purchases. As Corn & flour is Only Arrived, I cannot say what the price Will be here this Summer, there were No Want of either here during the Winter. Please make my best respects to Madam Askin & all your family. And believe me to be Dear Sir Your well wisher & Very Hum^b. Servant.

CHARLES MORISON.

John Askin Esq. Detroit per the Schooner "Thomas."

1799: ENGAGES DESERT

[Source, same as preceding document, but p. 131. Translated from the French.]

MICHILIMAKINAC July 5, 1799.

John Askin Esquire,

MONSIEUR—I forgot to write to you yesterday for a man who deserted fifteen days ago, a winterer, who came up in the canoes. His name is Pierre Turcotte[15] and as he has taken the route to Detroit, and as I believe that you can find him there, these are the advances which have been made him and his engagement contract. He received at Montreal 94^{lvs} and here 2^{lvs} 4 and his equipment which amounted to 64^{lvs}. If you can take him, secure what he owes me, or if he cannot pay, ship him back to me by the first vessel.

I send you also the account and engagement contracts of the Three Lafontaines dit Marion, who deserted last year, one at Niagara, and the other two at Detroit. They say that they wintered at the Miamis. If you can take them, do so and make them pay the accounts and the damages if possible. I am Sir with consideration Your very humble Servant

J. GIASSON & Co.

Addressed: John Askin Esquire at Detroit

Endorsed: Michilimackinac July 5th, 1799 Messrs Jacques Giasson & Co. respecting his Engages who run away Recd & Answered 8th July

---

[15] In 1818, an employé of this name served the American Fur Company at Fond du Lac (of Lake Superior) at an annual salary of $600. It was not uncommon for young homesick engagés to desert, and afterwards to return to their posts and become useful and able winterers.—ED.

Fur-trade on Upper Lakes

1799: PRICES FOR PELTRY

[Source, same as preceding document, but p. 176.]

MICHILICKINAC 27th July 1799.

DEAR ASKIN—Your favor of the 10th Instant came to hand Sum days ago. I am glad you are pleased with the Exchange I made of your flour and Sugar, I can assure you, that no exchange has been made for that Article Since, On the same terms.

By an express Canoe lately from Montreal to the Grand Portage, We learn that Beaver, Otters & Bears Sold high, the former is said to have Averaged 12 sh. Sterling, And that about the 15th of last Month, 27 Sail of Ships from England arrived at Quebec,

We have nothing new in this part of the World. Please make my best Respects to Madam Askin & the rest of your family, And believe me to be, Dear Askin, Your well wisher & H. Sev^t.

CHARLES MORISON.

John Askin Esq. Detroit.

1800: RIVALRY IN NORTHWEST TRADE

[Source, same as preceding document, but vol. 7, p. 221.]

MONTREAL 18 January 1800.

DEAR ASKIN—I wrote to you by the last boats since which I have received a few lines saying you was well which you know always gives me great pleasure, but much more could I see you which never will happen in this world. I have been laid up since last october with a complication of disorders, so that I have kept the House, and a great part my Bed, but at present am mending and as soon as I can get strength suficient will make a trip to the Balls Town spring, which renews ones age. I wish you was there. Mr Todd is going with me he is always complaining when his intestines are empty, but after Dinner recovers wonderfully. I observe what you say respecting hireing young men for three or four years, the opposition to N West has raised the price so very high that I dont think they can be got without giving much more than they may be got for at Detroit boys asked me seven & eight hundred livres and would engage only for one year. the Old N West Company is all in the Hands of M{c}Tavish Frobisher, and M{c}Kensey[16] is out, the latter went off in a pet, the cause as far as I can learn was who should be the first—M{c}Tavish or M{c}K. and as there could not be two Ceasars in Rome one must remove.

by the last accounts from England there is very bad appearance of furrs selling well. they say most of the furr buyers are bankrupts owing to several Houses in Hamburg failing, which has bankrupt all the foreign Houses in London, and several in New York. Seaton Maitland & Co who had all the China business in hand of M{c}Tavish & Co is shut. I suspect it will fall heavy on them. Muskratts is the only article which may keep at 24—good—and this is owing to Astore[17] and me

[16] This refers to Sir Alexander Mackenzie, whose connection with the founding of the X Y Company is outlined *ante*, p. 169, note 30. He was born in the Scotch Highlands about 1755 and came to Canada in 1779, entering the merchant house of Gregory & McLeod at Montreal. In 1784 he made his first voyage West, as far as Detroit. The following year he became a partner in the organization opposing the North West Company, and went up as wintering partner to English River. The opposition having united with the older concern, Mackenzie was sent in 1788 to the Athabasca region, where the following year he made a trip to the Arctic Ocean, discovering the great river that bears his name. In 1791 he visited London, and returning to the Northwest, equipped for further discovery, made (1792–93) his famous journey across the northern Rockies, reaching the Pacific Ocean in July of the latter year. This was the limit of his discoveries and trading in the interior. In 1794 he finally left the Northwest, but continued active in the fur-trade. His journal appeared in England in 1801, and the next year he was knighted. After 1804, Sir Alexander was frequently in Canada, serving in the provincial legislature about 1806. In 1812 he settled permanently in Scotland, dying there in 1820.—ED.

[17] It is interesting to see what a marked effect the fur-buying operations of John Jacob Astor had in Montreal at this early date. Born in Waldorf, Germany, in 1763, Astor had come to America in 1783

being in opposition, if you can sell yours for that I think you ought, as you may have buyers there, for should Astore & me agree they will fall—unless they should sell high in London, there is only 10,000 Shipt from Quebec, not one from this. Astore & me bought the whole, from 20 to 24, some small parcels at auction from the spirrit of opposition sold 26 to 27. I bought 700 Bear Skins at auction when the ammount [of] sales incouraged us, very high. that article I am informed will fall one half, and if some new place is not found [for] Raccoons they will go badly. the yankeys will trade Rum for Raccoons should you have any I would recomend you to do it they may not be worth here 6^s another cause has happened contrery to our expectation 50,000 men from England landed in Holland the Duke of York commanded all the Dukes fleet surrendered—the army within a few miles from Amsterdam was drove back to their Landing great numbers killed, and to save the remainder was obliged to make some kind of a convention or Treaty, one of the articles is we are to deliver 8,000 prisoners without exchange. they say there are other stipulations not known. Robinson is well. General Washington Dead My family all join in praying for the Happiness of yours and remain your affectionately

ALEXANDER HENRY

Rum is selling 5^{sh}. Spiritts high, proof Mr Sharp Died yesterday of an inflamation of the Bowells, which shall be a great loss to Leath.[18]

John Askin Detroit.

---

and embarked in the fur-trade; first as an employee, but after 1786 on his own account. He early began buying at Montreal and shipping to London. His first venture in the China trade occurred in 1800. Astor was quick to take advantage of the surrender of the Northern posts to the United States, and in 1808 founded the South West Company, which later bought out the Mackinac Company—see documents *post*. His Astorian enterprise and the Pacific Fur Company have been graphically described by Washington Irving. The American Fur Company will be noted in connection with later documents. Astor retired from its presidency in 1834, and died at New York in 1848.—ED.

[18] George Leith was a British merchant of Detroit and vicinity,

1800: WISCONSIN ENGAGEMENT-CONTRACT

[MS. in Wisconsin Historical Library. Pressmark: Wisconsin MSS., 56B2. Translated from the French.]

In the Presence of Witnesses was present at La Baye[19] Charles Tason, who has voluntarily engaged and by these presents engages himself to M^r. Jacob Franks[20] Merchant here present, and agreeing at his first requisition to leave La Bay in the capacity of a winterer in one of his Canoes or Batteaus, in order to make the Journey, both ascending and descending, to winter in the dependencies of Michilimakinac, to do the duty of a man, to be released at the departure of Jacob Franks from La Baye. Also to take good and due Care along the route, and in the said places of the Merchandise, Provisions, Peltries, Utensils and everything necessary for the Voyage, to Serve, obey and execute faithfully all that the said Sieur Jacob Franks or all others representing him shall lawfully and honestly order him to do, to Consider the Latter's profit, avoid his damage, notify him if anything comes to his knowledge, and in general to do all that a good winterer ought and is obliged to do, without trading in his own account, nor absenting himself from nor leaving the said service, under the penalties imposed by the ordinances, and the loss of his wages. This Engagement thus made for and in consideration of the sum of Seven Hundred Livres or Shillings, ancient Currency of this province, will be acquital of all obliga-

---

who was in that neighborhood before 1784 and was reputed in 1798 to have rapidly made a fortune. About the time of this letter, he had a store and considerable establishment at Amherstburg.—ED.

[19] This is selected from a large number of like documents, both written out and in the form of printed blanks, preserved in the Wisconsin Historical Library, and is here presented as a typical engagement for a general voyageur or "hand." This particular document is somewhat unusual, from having been drawn up in the "Indian country" (so called), instead of in Montreal as customary.—ED.

[20] For a brief sketch of Jacob Franks, see *Wis. Hist. Colls.*, xviii, p. 463, note 85.—ED.

tion, which shall be paid and I hereby oblige myself to release and pay it to the said engagé one month after his return to Michilimakanac; and also in the beginning to furnish him the ordinary Equipment.

For thus &c. Promising &c., obliging &c. Renouncing &c.[21] Done and passed at the said La Bay in the year One thousand eight hundred the eighth of May before Noon, and they have signed with the exception of said engage, who having declared on enquiry being made that he did not know how, made his usual mark after having the above read.

The said Engagé agrees to carry at the portages, and cut wood, and will be furnished with tobacco, shoes, and food.

CHARLES TASON + his mark

Witnesses: JOHN LAWE   J. DUCHARME[22]

1800: PROVISIONS FOR FUR-TRADE

[Source, same as preceding document, but 1B1.]

DETROIT 29 May, 1800.

SIR—Your boat[s] arrived late last eve^g I have provisioned them from this day, for twenty days, should they arrive in a shorter time they will have to account to you—with respect to

---

[21] A customary notarial formula for all deeds and contracts. See *Ibid.*, p. 139, note 82.—ED.

[22] For a brief biographical sketch of John Lawe, whose papers as published *post* will furnish much additional information, see *Id.*, vii, p. 250. Lawe states in Wis. MSS., 63B25, that he first settled at Green Bay in June, 1799.

Joseph Ducharme was the eldest son of Jean Marie, noted in *Id.*, xviii, p. 161, note 4. He was probably born at Lachine, and does not seem to have settled permanently at Green Bay until the latter part of the eighteenth century. He had a large homestead on the east side of Fox River, on the site of the later Shantytown. In 1831, Ducharme gave the land on which the Catholic church was built. He was known as "Colonel," and possibly served in the Canadian militia. His wife was of Indian extraction, and they had four sons, all of whom had musical tastes.—ED.

the Duties, which may be laid on at Mackinac, you will no doubt get every information there. I shall write you by the next Boats   I am sir your H^{ble} Ser^t

M. DAVID.[23]

10 O'Clock A M

200^{lb} Pork   300^{lb} Bisquet   1½ Bush Corn

Addressed: Mr. Jacob Franks Mackinac
Endorsed: Letter from Detroit from Mr Moses David Dated 29th May 1800.

[MS. in Burton Library, Detroit, vol. 9, p. 151.]

MICHILIMACKINAC 10, Feby 1801.

DEAR ASKIN—I embrace the present Opportu^y to inform you that I am well, And am in hopes that this few lines Will find you & family in perfect health. We have Nothing new in this Part of the World. I am afraid there has been but an indifferent Deer hunt last fall, as we had No Snow here that lay Until the 13th of last month, And the Ice only closed the 22d   Mr Fraser had to Stay at Mr Campbells 15 Days before he got Over here, Which was on the 24th Ult°.

Flour & Corn is here in pleanty, but in No Demand. Please make my best Wishes to Madam Askin & all your family, and believe me to be with much esteem, Dear Sir, Your Very Hum^{bl} Sev^t

CHARLES MORISON

John Askin Esq. Detroit

---

[23] Moses David probably belonged to the David family of Montreal, whose ancestor, Lazarus, born in England about 1734, came in with Amherst's army. His is the first recorded burial (1776) in the Jewish cemetery of Montreal. One son, David David, was a prominent merchant, and director of the first bank of Montreal. Moses David of Detroit was pro-British during the War of 1812–15, and some goods being sent up for him were seized in 1812 by the American General Hull.—ED.

Fur-trade on Upper Lakes

1801: LICENSES FOR THE FUR-TRADE

[MS. in Wisconsin Historical Library. Pressmark: Wisconsin MSS., 60B4.]

WAYNE COUNTY the first day of March 1801.
Territory of the United States north west of the Ohio.

This certifies that Jacob Franks is authorized to vend Merchandize within this territory for one year from the date hereof, the said Jacob Franks having this day, paid to me Matt^w Ernest Treasurer of the Said County of Wayne[24] the sum of ten Dollars, it being the annual tax imposed on Retailers of Merchandize by a Law of this territory.[25]

MATT^w. ERNEST
Treas^r. W. C.

[Extract from a letter dated at Michilimacinac May 19, 1801. MS. in Burton Library, vol. 10, p. 15. Translated from the French.]

N. B. They have told us here that for the Grand River, St Joseph River of the Illinois, one must have Permits from the Post[26] to go to those places, but knowing nothing of this I beg

---

[24] Matthew Ernest was the first collector for the United States at the port of Detroit. His appointment dated from 1799, with a salary of $200 and fees, but he was not confirmed by the senate until Jan. 6, 1800. He seems to have been county treasurer (from 1801–05), quartermaster general, colonel of militia, and justice of the peace. He had a considerable farm near Detroit, at what is known as Springwells. In 1805 Ernest's accounts were found to be in confusion and he was requested to resign, whereupon he disappeared from official life.—ED.

[25] At this time Wayne County was a part of the Northwest Territory. The law to which this refers is to be found in *Laws of Northwest Territory*, chap. xxxii, sec. 6; it imposed a tax of $10 on all retailers within the territory, of merchandise other than the produce or manufacture of said territory. The county treasurer was required to give a receipt therefor. In 1805 this tax was raised to $20 per annum.—ED.

[26] Mackinac and all the country west of a line drawn due north from Fort Recovery to the international boundary was set off on May 7, 1800, as Indiana Territory. Its capital was Vincennes, then commonly known as "Au Poste," "Opost," or (as here) simply "the Post." Li-

you to give me some information thereon. I fear it will be difficult for us to get the permits from the Post and not knowing of this and not perhaps acting with sufficient caution in that regard, I flatter myself that you will be good enough to inform me on this subject. We have large interests in these places and if it is necessary to have these permits if possible send me a Blank for the names and places. I beg you to have some four sent us. we receive every year for those that wish to take them a permit from the Commandant and besides we paid last year a license for the privilege of selling, but fearing this is not enough we leave it to you to do what is necessary & beg for a response on this matter by the first Bark.

I am Sir with consideration Your very humble Servant

JACQUE GIASSON & Co.

[Reply made to Monsieur Giasson, June 4, 1801, in English.]

MR. GIASSON—I have arranged with Mr. Henry to have him send by Monsieur William Henry of Michilimacinac[27] four licenses of which you will have the Choice. All you have to do

---

censes for trading with the Indians had been required from the inception of the United States government; the law now in force dated from March 3, 1799, under chap. 46, sec. 7 of "An act to regulate trade and intercourse with Indian tribes," etc. These licenses could be secured of any Indian agent, or of any army officer commanding a post. They cost but $2, and were indiscriminately given. See letter of William Burnett in H. H. Hurlbut, *Chicago Antiquities* (Chicago, 1881), pp. 71–74. The writer of this letter evidently supposed that the new governor of Indiana Territory would exercise authority over these permits—a reform which he later attempted.—ED.

[27] The first "Mr. Henry" is James, a Detroit merchant and tanner. He was in 1803 a justice of the peace, and member of the board of commissioners for Wayne County. Two years later he was a delegate from the same county to the Indiana territorial assembly, and seems to have died before the War of 1812–15.

William Henry of Michilimackinac was probably not the one noted in *Wis. Hist. Colls.*, xviii, p. 505; but apparently was the brother of James, commander of a vessel on Lake Huron, and very likely an American.—ED.

[1778-1815]   Fur-trade on Upper Lakes

is to sign a Bond with two sureties. I would have done that here, but you cannot be embarrassed to find them at your place. I have paid for the licenses here & his brother the Captain who takes the licenses does not know the price I am Sir Your very humble Servant

[JOHN ASKIN]

1801: MONTREAL EXPORTS OF FURS

[Source, same as preceding document, but p. 92.]

MICHILIMACKINAC 30 June 1801.

DEAR ASKIN—By your favor of the 1st Instant, I am happy to learn that your health were Restored, May you long enjoy it.

We have Nothing New in this part of the world. A great Number of Packs are come in & many of them are already sent off to Montreal. This year the Skin Merchants are making no purchasses here, Corn & flour are in good pleanty, So that Bread is Sold by the single loaf at 15 sols. My best wishes waits on Madam Askin & the rest of your family, and am sincerely your Well Wisher & H^e. S^t.

CHARLES MORISON

John Askin Esqr.

[Source, same as preceding document, but vol. 11, p. 24.]

DETROIT Nov. 5th 1801.

Mr Askin's Compliments to Colonel Hamtramck[28] & sends

---

[28] John Francis Hamtramck was a native of Quebec, his father having emigrated in 1749 to Canada, from Luxembourg, and married a Canadian-Frenchwoman. Born in 1756, the younger Hamtramck embraced the American cause with enthusiasm, and in 1776, before attaining his majority, joined Montgomery's army at the siege of Quebec. Having served throughout the Revolution in Hazen's corps, the young Canadian continued his career as a soldier, being appointed (1785) a captain in the United States infantry, and the next year major. Upon the reorganization of the army in 1789, Hamtramck became major of the 1st infantry, stationed at Cincinnati. He was a trusted subordinate of Wayne, and in the battle of Fallen Timbers

him under cover the paper he promised by which it appears that the Exports from Quebec in Furrs, Skins & Castor [Beaver] in 1800 Ammounted to £209614 Halifax Cur. or 838,456 Dollars two Thirds of which sum he believes are the proceeds of the North and founds his oppinion from his having been many years Ago in that Trade & afterwards an Agent to those who now carry it on so Extensively, also his constant residence Either at Mich[ilimackinac] or this Post since 1764 & being concerned most of the Time in the furr Trade.

1802: SETTLEMENT OF ACCOUNTS; LANGLADE'S LANDS

[Source, same as preceding document, but p. 135.]

MONTREAL 15 April 1802.

DEAR SIR—We wrote you a Short Letter on the 23 of March acknowledgeing your favor of the 26 December and to give our consent for the late Company of J. & A. M°Gill to the disposing of your property, payable by installments & we now confirm the same. By this opportunity we cannot inclose continuation of Acc't up to the 10th Current, but we shall forward it soon, mean time your Acc^t. against Messrs J. Giasson & Co has been settled with very little exception which will be pointed out in transmitting your A/C curr^t.

You may be assured it was our wish to throw every thing in your way which we could, but Mr. Giasson now acting for himself thought proper while at Detroit to change Correspondents and when arrived here we could not prevail on him to return to you, which has really pained us, tho he has agreed to employ the Messrs MacGregors being our Correspondents. The

---

(1794) commanded the right wing. The same autumn he took command at Fort Wayne, continuing there until ordered to take possession of Detroit (1796) for the Americans. He was in command at Detroit until his death, April 11, 1803. Being a Catholic, and speaking French as his native tongue, Hamtramck was popular with the older French-Canadian families. He was said to have gone into partnership with James Abbott, a successful merchant, but death cut short his useful career.—ED.

Fur-trade on Upper Lakes

Accounts from the Sale of Furs are very favorable; it was the same at the close of last war, but the year following, both you & the writer have cause to recollect   we are Dear Sir Your obed^t & very hbl Sev^{ts}

JAMES & AND. M^{c}GILL

John Askin Esqr. Detroit

[Source, same as preceding document, but p. 140.]

MONTREAL 24 April 1802.

John Askin Esqr

DEAR SIR—Our last respects were of the 15th Inst. and since these we are without any of your favors

Accompanying the present you will find State of Acc^t Currt. up to the 10 of the month as is our usual practice, balance in our favor £1981. 4. 2 Currency, which we hope you will find right   as it has diminished something within the last year, we hope you may be enabled to continue the diminution so as shortly to prevent the accumulation of Interest   It would have afforded us much satisfaction had Messrs. Giasson now doing business for himself only continued to employ you; he has done otherwise but the Packs of J. G. & Co are to be put on board the "Saguinau" by preference if at MaKinac when they are ready for shipping.

In one of your accounts there is a charge for duties you were bound to pay, we think about £20 york, will you have the goodness to mention if you have paid it and inform us also if Bunnells protested draft has been paid to you.

Having an Interest in 3000 Acres of Land in your District belonging to Langlade of La Baye, which he has authorised Mons. Rocheblave to sell under a very informal Power of Attorney[29] & it being necessary to have a proper Power for con-

---

[29] For the letter accompanying this power of attorney, and a note of Noel Rocheblave, see *Wis. Hist. Colls.*, xviii, pp. 462, 463. The power of attorney given to Rocheblave and Porlier is in the library of Edward E. Ayer, Chicago, who has kindly furnished us with a copy. See also the next document.—ED.

veying fixed Property in your Provence, we have had one made out & also a memorial of the Power in your name and Mons. Giasson is to send one of the witnesses interested to see them executed to La Baye; and afterwards to send him to you with these two Papers that you may have them registered; and as we presume they will be sufficient to authorise you to dispose of the Lands, we shall now or some time after transmitt you the Patents, in order to your disposing of these Lands at the best price for ready money you can obtain; but previous to your selling them let us know what you think of their value & [arrange] by Advertisement such time for selling them & before a Notary at Malden as may enable us to return you an answer. wishing you health & comfort, we are Dear Sir Yours most Sincerely

JAMES & AND. M^{c}GILL

John Askin Esq. Detroit

[MS. in possession of Edward E. Ayer, Chicago. Translated from the French.]

LA BAY 8 May 1802.

Mr. Adhemar St. Martin, Esquire.

SIR—I have charged Mr. Rocheblave to deposit My Inventory in the Record office, thus Signing in my name the renunciation that I make to the community of goods[30] that I had with Mr. de Langlade for Maintaining my Rights. I hope that you will be good enough to receive this in my Stead.

I beg you to present my respects to the Ladies and believe me with Consideration Sir, Your Very h. Servant

THE WIDOW LANGLADE

Addressed: Adhemar St. Martin, Esquire, at Makinac

Endorsed: Letter on Langlade's business, with his Notes. Rec'd from Mr. McGill 21st May, 1803. True copy from the original, placed at McKinac 29 august, 1802. Adhemar St. Martin Notary Public

---

[30] See the marriage contract in *Ibid.*, pp. 135–140.—ED.

A WINNEBAGO VILLAGE
Reduced from lithograph in Henry R. Schoolcraft's *Indian Tribes*, ii, p. 80

1778-1815] **Fur-trade on Upper Lakes**

1802: UNITED STATES REGULATIONS FOR FUR-TRADE

[MS. in Wisconsin Historical Library. Pressmark: Wisconsin MSS., 1B4.]

PEORIAS the 20th of May 1802.

M^r. *Arundel* [31]

D^r SIR—I lately received a letter from the Attorney General of the Indiana Territory, concerning the Indian trade and as you are now about going to a Country where the opinion of the Attorney General may be of use as well to your Self as to some of your Friends upon this Subject I have taken the liberty to give you an extract of his letter which is as follows, I apprehend that you have taken up a wrong idea of the restrictions contained in the Licenses, from carrying goods &c, to trade with the Indians to trade at their Hunting Camps. the intention of this clause I am authorized to Say was solely to prevent traders from following small parties on their *mere Hunting expeditions* for a few days, and that without their families and not to prohibit selling them their necessaries at any camp which the indians might think proper to form, and in which their wives and children accompany them; their camps from my small Knowledge of the indian trade, are in one winter season changed three or four times, it would therefore in my opinion be very detrimental even to the indians themselves to construe the restrictions so as to prevent traders from furnishing them their Goods on the Spot, and would therefore oblige them to carry their Peltries to the Traders at their fixed Stations, often at a considerable distance and as often without a

---

[31] William Arundel was of Irish birth, and came to Detroit before the Revolution. During that time he had a large establishment at Lower Sandusky, where he rescued prisoners, entertained the Moravian missionaries, and was spoken of as a kind, humane, and generous man. After the Revolution he removed westward, and by 1787 was established at Cahokia, where he seems to have acted as agent for the Michilimackinac Company, which traded between the two posts by way of Prairie du Chien and the Wisconsin River. He became a useful citizen of Illinois, where he acquired a large landed property, and served in various local offices. He died at Kaskaskia in 1816, at an advanced age.—ED.

sufficient number of horses, saying nothing about the loss of time in the most precious seasons. From what I have said it will occur to you that no trader at any one of these camps can be permitted to follow a detached party from thence on their hunting expeditions for a few days or to purchase their peltries befor the indians return to their main body I believe these restrictions were inserted in consequence of Complaints from the chiefs Stating that traders followed these small parties and before their return for very small trifles purchased the skins when green, and often tempted them to do so with Liquor.[32]

The above is the Opinion of Mr Jones[33] upon the existing regulations relative to the indian trade. You may now figure to Yourself how much mistaken many traders have been, and how much they now suffer in consequence of that Mistake.

---

[32] This opinion was given in reference to a proclamation issued by Gov. William H. Harrison, Aug. 31, 1801, in which that official states that frequent complaints had been made by the Indians of the mischief caused by traders frequenting their hunting camps. The governor therefore notifies them that a regulation has been made by the executive of the United States, whereby the licensed traders are expected to confine themselves to the towns, and not follow the Indians to their hunting grounds; in the future, this regulation will be strictly enforced. See reprint of "Executive Journal of Indiana Territory, 1800-16," in Indiana Historical Society *Publications*, iii, No. 111, p. 103.—ED.

[33] John Rice Jones was born in Wales, Feb. 11, 1759. After being educated at Oxford, and practicing law in London, he came to America in 1784, and located for a few months at Philadelphia. Having decided to seek the West, Jones established himself at Louisville, where in 1786 he joined George Rogers Clark's expedition into the Indian country. About this time he settled at Vincennes, where he formed a warm friendship with Harrison, who appointed him (Jan. 29, 1801) attorney-general of Indiana Territory. Jones served in this capacity until 1808, when having a political disagreement with Harrison, he resigned, and removed to Kaskaskia, where he had previously spent some years. About 1810 he emigrated to Missouri, and engaged in mining and smelting lead at Mine à Breton (now Potosi). He was a member of the Missouri constitutional convention (1820), and served as justice of the state supreme court until his death at St. Louis in 1824.—ED.

I wish you a pleasant voyage, and hope that you will not forget to write me upon every occasion that presents as I promise on my part to do the Same.

I am, Sir, with much respect & Esteem Your Sincere friend and most obedient Servant

I. DARNIELLE[34]

Addressed: William Arundel Esquire McKinac
Endorsed: A true Copy from the Original. William Arundel

[MS. in Pension Office, Washington. Pressmark: Indian Office Letter Book "A", p. 276.]

WAR DEPARTMENT 14th. September 1802.

Circular to all Indian Agents

SIR—The chiefs of many of the Indian Nations having applied to the President of the U. States for the suppression of the sale of ardent Spirits in their several Nations and Congress having authorised the President to comply with the request. It is therefore the wish of the President that you adopt such measures, as will as soon as practicable; with due regard to particular circumstances, prevent the sale of any ardent spirits to the Natives. In order therefore to effect this object, no trader should be allowed to vend any Goods, to the Indians, who shall cary ardent Spirits into their Country for sale or other purposes, and such as are now trading under former licenses should be restricted in like manner. I am etc.

[HENRY DEARBORN]

On margin: Benjamin Hawkins, Govr. St. Clair, Governor Harrison, Silas Dinsmoor, Return J. Meigs, John Johnston, William Wells, Samuel Mitchell, Jona. Halstead, John W. Hooker, Robert Munroe, Joseph Chambers, Thomas Peterkin.

---

[34] Isaac Darnielle arrived in Illinois from Maryland, apparently about 1794, the second professional lawyer in the territory. He was a classical scholar and of polished manner, but something of a rake, and is said to have eloped from Cahokia to Peoria with a married woman. In later life he became reduced in circumstances, and taught school in western Kentucky, where he died about 1830, in poverty and neglect.—ED.

1803: A TYPICAL FUR-TRADE ACCOUNT.

[MS. in Wisconsin Historical Library. Pressmark: Wisconsin MSS., 1A2. Translated from the French.]

Account of Peltries sold to Messrs. J. Giasson & Berthlotte,[35] N Rocheblave & Porlier By Charles Sanguinaitte.[36] Namely

1803
August 13

  For 245 bear skins ⎫
    90 cubs   ⎪
    26 Otters   ⎪
    11 lynx   ⎪
    30 muskrats ⎬ for 18,000.0
    1 mink   ⎪
    500 lvs. beaver ⎪
    434 cat skins ⎪
    133 deer skins ⎭

  In addition
    For 7 cubs 20   140
    " 10 lvs. beaver 8 80
    " Cats   3
               ———
               223

  To deduct
    1 Otter   20
    6 deer skins 30 50   173".0
          —   ═   ———
                    18,173.0

---

[35] Jean Baptiste Berthelot was a prominent trader in Wisconsin between 1800 and the second war with England. Anderson mentions him as being in opposition (1801) in the Sauk villages, and he appears to have had also an establishment at Prairie du Chien. After the War of 1812–15, Berthelot seems to have established himself on Drummond Island, where in 1816 he was granted a lot of land. He long maintained his friendship with Wisconsin traders, and many of his letters to the Grignons, Rolette, Porlier, and others are in the manuscript collections of the Wisconsin Historical Library.—ED.

[36] Charles Sanguinet was a wealthy merchant of St. Louis. He was born at Quebec in 1740, and coming West first settled in Detroit. About 1775 he removed to St. Louis, where he married Marianne Condé, and became allied to the prominent French creoles of that place. Being a free lance in the fur-trade, he opposed the estab-

1778-1815]   Fur-trade on Upper Lakes

1803
August 11
    On the account of Messrs.
    N. Rocheblave [and] Porlier
    presented this day   320.10

Balance due to
  Ch. Sanguinet   17,852.10
Save errors or omissions

McKinac 16th of August 1803   Ch^{les} Sanguinet

Received payment at Michilimakinac 17th of August 1803
                               Ch^{les}. Sanguinet.

1804: TRADE AT MILWAUKEE

[Source, same as preceding document, but 1B8. Translated from the French.]

                           Milwaki May 18, 1804.

Sir—I received your account but there are some articles which are not in the invoice that I hope you will have the Kindness to remit, as Mr. Anderson[37] will tell you.

I send you my account which you will find very just and wish that you may send me the Balance by a similar occasion. Sir I am surprised that you do not wish to pay the Account of Mr. Charles Chadonette[38] when he was your clerk, and the

---

lished companies and won a large competence, dying at St. Louis in 1818.—Ed.

[37] Thomas Anderson was born in Sorel in 1779, his father being a Massachusetts Loyalist. In 1795 he was apprenticed to a Kingston merchant, with whom he remained until 1800, when he came West to enter the fur-trade. For his own description of his experiences, and his life at Milwaukee (1803-06), see *Wis. Hist. Colls.*, ix, pp. 137-206. After serving in the War of 1812-15, he finally settled on Drummond Island, and retired with the British to Penetanguishene in 1828. For thirty years thereafter he was Indian agent for that vicinity, and died at Port Hope, Feb. 16, 1875. Many of his papers and letters are in possession of the Wisconsin Historical Library.—Ed.

[38] Charles Chandonnet was born at Quebec in July, 1763. His marriage is recorded at Mackinac in 1792; see *Wis. Hist. Colls.*, xviii,

20   [305]

wages of J. B^t. Lajeunesse[39] that he has well earned. Sir I am your Very humble Servant

F^r Laframboise[40]

I am much obliged to you for the Messages that you have promised

Addressed: To Jacob Franks merchant at Makinac.

1804: PROVISIONS ON UPPER LAKES

[MS. in Burton Library, Detroit, vol. 13, p. 13.]

Montreal 20 July 1804.

Dear Sir—We are indebted for your favors of 29 May which we might have answered sooner but having Knowledge that Mr Hamilton would soon return up the Country we postponed until he should so far be the bearer of our respects.

To your proposal of our furnishing your sons with Goods & taking payment next year in whiskey and Flour at Michilimackinac we have to observe that as we have not any direct interest in the Trade to that Post, we have no occassion whatever to buy either whiskey or Flour for exporting other Goods, we therefore do not wish to begin a Trade, in which agents must be employed & who would for their trouble get all the profit; indeed we do not at present wish to extend our Trade in your part of the Country & therefore must decline supplying the Goods you have wished for.

You wish us to try some other House, but really we Know not of any to whom the proposal would be suitable; and we fear

---

pp. 495, 509. He seems to have been at Milwaukee frequently after 1800, and was employed during the War of 1812-15 by Robert Dickson. For his death in 1814, at the hands of his nephew and adopted son, see *ante*, p. 159, note 12.—Ed.

[39] Over thirty French-Canadian families bore the surname of "La Jeunesse." There was likewise one prominent Illinois family of the same name. To which of these the engagé here mentioned belonged, had not been ascertained. Probably he was the same person whom Pike met in 1806 with Louis Grignon on the upper Mississippi.—Ed.

[40] For François Laframboise, see *ante*, p. 158, note 10.—Ed.

that our declining it might prove a sufficient reason to other Houses not to take up the business; you had better therefore not count on the memorandum being fulfilled.

We note the price you were to charge for flour on Acc^t of J & And. McGill, it is higher than at this place or Quebec, but as others pay the same, we are satisfied except the five per cent Commission which we think wrong since the flour is on Account of a debt & taken from you to facilitate payment. The Flour was to be addressed to Mons. Giasson and we think at the time of proposing such mode of payments, we mentioned him to you as the Comm's'ner. Our Fleet is but lately arrived at Quebec & God knows when the Goods may reach this place. as there are a great many Packs this year we think your vessel the "Saguinau" must get at least one load down, and if she can be back there by 15 Sept at latest we are of opinion she might get a second   we are Dear Sir   Your very obedt Servents
JAMES & AND. M^{c}GILL

[*John Askin*]

[Source, same as preceding document, but p. 26.]

MICHILIMACKINAC Augt. 24 1804.

DEAR SIR—As I am just setting out for the Mississippi and I leave a young man to pass the winter at this place finding that you have a quantity of whisky—for sale here—please direct to Patrick Adhemar[41] informing him of the lowest price and enclose an order on Jaques Giasson with whom it is stored for what quantity he may want for which I will be accountable & write you the amount next spring.   My best respects to Mrs Askin & family.   Wishing the full enjoyment of health,   I am Dear Sir, Your very Obd^t & very hbl Servant
R. DICKSON[42]

John Askin Esq. Detroit

---

[41] Probably a son of Toussaint Antoine Adhemar St. Martin, noted *ante*, p. 159, note 11. Patrick was witness for several marriage contracts (1792–96), and apparently is the trader who proposed to build in 1799 at St. Josephs Island.—ED.

[42] An early letter of Robert Dickson, the famous Scotch trader and British partisan. See his biography by Ernest A. Cruikshank in

1804: UNION OF NORTHWEST COMPANIES

[Source, same as preceding document, but p. 86.]

MONTREAL 8th Decemb. 1804.

William Park, John Askin, Alex^r Harrow[43] Esquires

GENTLEMEN—A coalition being affected between the N. W. Companies, it becomes necessary that a valuation should be made of the "Nancy,"[44] "Caledonia" and "Charlotte," with their respective Rigging and Materials whether in use or spare. The transfers will be made the 1st of April. The Parties interested have here jointly agreed, to nominate you to make the Valuations, and we hope that you will be good enough to undertake the Charge. Previous to your fixing said Valuations, it is meant that a Survey should be held upon each of the Vessels by three Carpenters, viz. Messrs Connolly, Baker and Nelson, and a Report made by them to you thereon. In confiding this business to you, we are satisfied that the object of the Interested will be attained, without favor, affection or prejudice to either. There is a Store House, House, and Warff belonging

---

Wis. Hist. Colls., xii, pp. 133–153. It will be a surprise to those knowing his later career to learn that he received an American commission as justice of the peace in August, 1802; see *Executive Journal of Indiana Territory*, cited *ante*, p. 302, note 32.—ED.

[43] Alexander Harrow began his career on the lakes as early as 1777. During the Revolutionary period he commanded on Lake Huron, and as late as 1794 was still in charge of a vessel. Sometime before 1796 he bought a large tract of land on St. Clair River, where he settled near the modern town of Cottrellsville. He rescued a white captive girl from the Indians of the vicinity, and married her. He died before 1821, and his descendants live in St. Clair County, Mich.—ED.

[44] On the building of the "Nancy," see letters of John Richardson in Ontario Historical Society *Papers*. vi, pp. 22, 27–32. The schooner was built at Detroit in 1789, of the best materials and plan possible at the time. She was in the service of the X Y Company until the amalgamation in 1804. During the War of 1812–15 she was hired as a transport by the government, and destroyed by her crew (Aug. 14, 1814) to prevent her falling into the hands of the Americans.—ED.

to the Owners of the "Nancy" of which we wish for a separate Valuation from the Vessel and her Materials, according to what you may think the fair present worth of said Houses and Wharff.

Excuse the Trouble we hereby give you, and believe us with much esteem   Gentlemen Your very Humble Servents

FORSYTH RICHARDSON & Co.[45]

P. S. Mr. Duff & Capt. Mills will represent the Interested in the "Nancy," and Mr. Jas. MacIntosh those in the other Vessels.

Addressed: William Park Esq. Sandwich

[Source, same as preceding document, but p. 88.]

MONTREAL 10 December 1804.

DEAR ASKIN—I forwarded, the papers, which by the opinion of the Lawyers here was sufficient to prevent Mr Williams[46] from geting possession of the Estate, without paying the Debts

---

[45] The firm of Forsyth, Richardson & Co. was one of the most important mercantile houses of Montreal. It was formed in 1790 by John Forsyth and John Richardson, both from Aberdeenshire, Scotland. They soon began to oppose the North West Company as represented by McTavish, McGillevray & Co. After 1795 this became an open war, in which Forsyth, Richardson & Co. represented the interests of the X Y Company. After the union of 1804, both firms continued to conduct the business of the amalgamation until the combination surrendered (1821) to the Hudson's Bay Company. For a sketch of John Richardson, who died in 1831, see *Ibid.*, pp. 20, 21.—ED.

[46] The reference is to John R. Williams of Detroit, who in 1804 attempted to have himself appointed sole administrator of the estate of his father Thomas, who had died in 1785, indebted to several Montreal merchants. John R. Willams was born in 1782 at Detroit. In 1800 he was appointed a cadet in the United States army, but resigned in 1802, to enter business at Detroit. In 1804 he was one of the trustees of the town, and in 1824 served as its first mayor under the charter, being re-elected for the years 1825, 1830, 1844–46. He also served in the militia, being in 1829 a major-general, and in 1832 having the conduct of an expedition towards Chicago. He died in 1854, and many of his papers are in the Burton Library, Detroit.—ED.

first, since which I have not heard from him, or you. as the Winter is come on and you have time to write, hope you will not forget to send me a few lines, for you seem to be lasey, and remind Mr Brush[47] to write what is doing in the business. the best way for Williams is to give security to pay me a fix^d sum of money which may be agreed thereon for which I will discharge him from Murray Samon & Co, David White, R. Cruickshanks, & Kay—which is the greatest part of the Creditors. The others he may easily settle with. we have nothing New here. Todd laid up with the Rumatism, the two N. West Companys joined. it is said the New Company have lost £70,000, since their comencing the opposition. it will be some time before they bring up that sum. Nothing new from Europe. we are all well with best wishes for you & yours remain sincerely ever your old friend

A. HENRY

I cannot procure a pair of Boots for you in this province—they are made in New England

John Askin Esq. Detroit

1805: LOCATION OF FUR-TRADE FACTORIES

[MS. in Pension Office, Washington. Pressmark: Indian Office Letter Book "B." Secretary of War to William Davy.]

WAR DEPARTMENT Dec: 30, 1805.

SIR—I have lately heard of Mr. Peterkin at Wheeling a little below Pittsburg. He was confined for a considerable

---

[47] Elijah Brush was one of the earliest Americans to settle at Detroit, having arrived there before 1799, probably from Vermont. He was prominent in the conduct of affairs before and during the War of 1812–15. In that war he served as colonel of the rifle corps, and in that capacity signed the capitulation of Detroit in 1812, although this was much against his will. He was a lawyer of repute, county treasurer (1806–13), United States attorney (1811–14), and (1806) mayor of the village by appointment of the governor. He married Adelaide, daughter of John Askin, and left several sons who became prominent in the early years of Detroit and Wisconsin history.—ED.

time at Lancaster by sickness; and was waiting for the water of the Ohio to rise.

I very much doubt the expediency of removing our Factories, from Fort Wayne and Chikago to Michilimackinac. We should by such a measure, deprive the Indians generally, who have become our friends and depend on our supplies, of any means of procuring goods, except by small British traders; and only supply such as are very distant; and who are and would be principally supplied by the British Companies.[48] There are very few Indians in the vicinity of Michilimackinac; the head of Green Bay would be a more eligible situation than that; but, at present, neither would be equal to Chikago. I am very resp. Yr. Obt. Sert.

[HENRY DEARBORN]

On margin: Wm. Davy

1806: WISCONSIN TRADERS AND AGENT

[MS. in Wisconsin Historical Library. Pressmark: Wisconsin MSS., 53B76. Translated from the French.]

6 January [1806]

I wish that you may begin the year 1806 with the best of Health, and that you may so Continue until its close. I have

---

[48] The factory system of the United States was an attempt to conduct the Indian trade by government agents, and to give the Indians the benefit of fair dealing, and of goods at cost prices. The system was highly recommended by Washington, who in several messages urged its adoption upon the attention of Congress. In 1795 an appropriation of $50,000 was made for testing the system, and two houses or "factories" were established among the Southern Indians. Nothing more was done until Jefferson induced Congress in 1802 to pass a bill to revive the scheme, and four new "factories" were begun— those at Detroit and at Fort Wayne being for the Northern tribes. In 1804 an additional appropriation was made, in order to extend the system to Louisiana. That same year, the Detroit establishment was discontinued and its effects moved to Chicago, where a military station had just been erected. The factory system was extended to Mackinac in 1808. For further materials on its location and management, see documents and notes *post*.—ED.

received your two letters in due time and I Must compliment you on your exactness. I have not had the advantage of sending you a Reply, not having Known any opportunity since their Arrival, I do not know yet whether I shall find any [opportunity] to send you the present letter. I write you in advance as I am preparing for a journey from which I do not expect to come back until about the 25th of the month. You can arrange matters above not to come to see me until about that time, so that I may not be deprived of the pleasure of your visit. I have done my best to keep them from visiting you. I am strongly of the opinion that they should not run the Derouine but I have gained nothing except to retard things a little. I have myself made only one little excursion that has been very unsuccessful. Pichipieca whom I went to see gave me nothing, his son in law nearly a third of the amount of his Credit. Kiotom has made little hunt but he is rather old. Mr Kaokitte denies that he had Credit for a cotton shirt. I plan to return there in a little while, I do not know whether I shall succeed any better. I have made some headway with vieu, the gros puant has made a good hunt, he has as yet given me on his Credit only some meat, fortunately however, for without that I should have had very little to eat. I have been very short of provisions up to these Last Days when providence willed that I should meet him at the lodge one day when he had killed eleven Deer of which ten came to me, that gives me hope of not enjoying lent all winter.

You appeared to me In your Last letter uneasy in regard to what you Ought to do and you Ask me to tell you what you should do. I will reply to you as I have above, that you should come here. I do not pretend to take you under my tutelage, moreover, being on the spot you know better than I what you should do, and Moreover when one has done for the best that is what is asked of him, therefore calm yourself, do the best you know how and I am persuaded that all will be well, for the little you can do you always will do better than I, therefore be consoled. I have as yet in my storehouse only 30^{lvs} of Beaver & 60 deer skins. Adieu, have good courage, try to salt down the meat. I only hope you will live through till spring. Give an occasional dram to the other savages but recommend to Master Antoine not to drink with them as they say he did on the Ste. Croix. Nothing more except the pleasure of being your servant and friend,

JQ. PORLIER.[49]

I shall be charmed if you will keep an exact account of what you receive from our creditors and if you will let me share it. I have just received from the son of la biche 20 deer skins 9 male and 9 female 2 in bad shape.

Addressed: Monsieur L. Grignon On la Riviere a l'eau de vie.[50]

---

[49] The preceding letter of Jacques Porlier to Louis Grignon needs some explanation. It will be seen by reference to a biographical sketch of him in *Wis. Hist. Colls.*, xviii, p. 462, that Porlier had acted as tutor to the young Grignons. The accompanying letter is written by the elder to the younger man at his wintering post, on the upper Mississippi. Porlier gives Grignon (for whom see *ante*, p. 90, note 27) some friendly advice, the gossip of the trading-post, news of the Indians' movements, etc. The letter incidently epitomizes conditions at some of the small interior wintering places. Porlier's post was located at the mouth of Crow River, near the present Dayton, Minn. It seems to have been located on an island. Lieut. Z. M. Pike stopped there on his descent of the river, four months after the penning of this letter. Pike met Porlier himself while visiting at Dickson's wintering post, some miles farther up. Porlier had wintered there in 1797; but he clearly locates his own post below, where no doubt the present letter was written. The district was a hunting-ground for the Menominee Indians, with whom Porlier and Grignon traded.—ED.

[50] "La Rivière à l'eau de vie" was Rum River, outlet of Lake Mille Lac. It was first visited by Father Hennepin, when in 1680 he was carried captive to the Sioux village. He calls it in his narrative, St. François River; afterward it was known by many names, of which the most frequent was either River "du Lac" or "Issati;" until Carver gave it (1781) the title of Rum River. The French form of this name was "L'eau de Vie;" see Elliott Coues, *Pike's Expeditions* (N. Y., 1895), p. 356. This is probably the origin of the term "Audevie Creek" that appears on the map accompanying the Biddle edition of the Lewis and Clark Journals, published in 1814; although Rum River likewise appears.

Pike's map places traders' houses on the south side of the Mis-

[MS. in Pension Office, Washington. Pressmark: Indian Office Letter Book "B". Secretary of War to Nicolas Boilvin.[51]]

WAR DEPTMT. Ap. 10, 1806.

SIR—You having been appointed an Assistant Indian Agent, will make the Sacque Village, at the Rapids of the Mississippi, above the mouth of the River Lemoin,[52] your principal place

---

sissippi, opposite the mouth of Rum River. This may have been the site of Louis Grignon's wintering place.—ED.

[51] Nicolas Boilvin was a native (1761) of Canada, whither his father had emigrated from France in 1748. The son came to Spanish Louisiana in 1774. In 1784 he was living in Ste. Geneviève District, and in 1797 was entrusted with a diplomatic message to visit Boston, as special agent of the Spanish commissioner, Don Carlos Howard; see *Amer. State Papers, Public Lands*, iii, p. 592. For this service he received from the Spanish government a grant of land three miles from Grand River; and there married (1802) Hélène, daughter of Hyacinthe St. Cyr. A persistent tradition notes that Boilvin's father aided a young American officer in Canada during the Revolution; young Boilvin met the latter in St. Louis, and was recommended by him for the post of Indian agent. The appointment here noted is for 1806. On the death of John Campbell, Boilvin removed to Prairie du Chien, and performed the former's duties until regularly appointed in 1811 as his successor. During the War of 1812-15 Boilvin used his utmost endeavors to maintain the Indians in the American interest. These failing, he was obliged temporarily to retreat to St. Louis. Returning in 1815, he maintained his agency until 1827, when he died while descending the Mississippi. Having been appointed in 1808 justice of the peace of St. Clair County, Indiana, Boilvin was one of the first American officials to exercise his duties at Prairie du Chien.—ED.

[52] This village was situated on the site of the present town of Montrose, Iowa, and was known as the "Lower Sauk Town." It seems to have been in existence as early as 1781, when Spaniards from St. Louis established a garrison at this place to maintain the Sauk in their alliance; see *Wis. Hist. Colls.*, iii, p. 504, xi, p. 169, xii, p. 66, xviii, p. 422. This alliance was maintained, as a rule, throughout the Spanish occupation. See Black Hawk's *Autobiography*, where he speaks of the last time he visited his Spanish father in 1804. British traders, however, were at the Mississippi villages previous to 1801; see *Wis. Hist. Colls.*, ix. Occasionally a delegation would seek the British at Amherstburg, Ontario—*Id.*, xviii, p. 460. In 1804, Gov-

Fur-trade on Upper Lakes

of residence, but will occasionally visit other Towns and places, particularly the Iawe [Iowa] Towns on the Lemoin, the other Sacque Towns, and the Prairie due Chien.

You will make every exertion in your power to conciliate the friendship of the Indians, generally, towards the United States, and to encourage a peaceable and friendly disposition among themselves; to prevent any acts of hostility on red or white people, and to cause proper punishment to be inflicted on such individuals as may be guilty of any hostile acts. You will, by all the means in your power, prevent the use of ardent spirits among the Indians. No Trader should be allowed to sell or dispose of any ardent spirits among them; nor be allowed to have any at their trading stations.

You will, by precept and example, teach the Indians such of the arts of agriculture and domestic manufactures, as your situation will admit. You will give all the aid in your power to Mr. Ewing,[53] who has been placed among the Sacques, for the purpose of instructing them in the arts of husbandry. You should early procure Garden seeds, peach and other fruit stones, and apple seeds. A Garden should be established for the most useful vegetables, and nurseries planted with fruit trees;

---

ernor Harrison treated with a small delegation at St. Louis, and secured from them a large grant of land, which was repudiated by the majority of the tribe. In this treaty a promise was made of a government trading house, and part of Pike's duty in 1805 was to choose a site therefor. It was probably in pursuance of this policy that Boilvin was commissioned as sub-agent at this village.—ED.

[53] William Ewing had been sent out in 1805, apparently by Governor Harrison, to instruct the Sauk in agriculture and civilization. He was under the superintendency of Chouteau, and had an annual salary of $500 from the United States. Pike found him, with his interpreter Louis Honoré, on the Illinois side of the Mississippi, about where the Mormon town of Nauvoo was later placed. Pike had small opinion of Ewing's fitness for this task, and General Wilkinson spoke of him as "a young man of innocence, levity, and simplicity, without experience or observation." In 1807, Clark made against him graver charges of incapacity and even of dishonesty; see Coues, *Pike's Expeditions*, i, pp. 15, 222, 293. He appears to have been removed soon after Clark's report.—ED.

for the purpose of distributing the most useful seeds and trees among such of the Chiefs as will take care to cultivate them. You should also instruct them in the art of cultivating and preserving the fruit trees and garden vegetables.

The cultivation of Potatoes ought to be immediately introduced into your own Garden;—and the Indians should be encouraged to cultivate them, as an important article of food, and the substitute for bread.

As soon as practicable, you will be furnished with a Blacksmith to make and mend the hoes and axes, and repair the Guns of the Natives. Ploughs should be introduced, as soon as any of the Chiefs will consent to use them. I am, respectfully, Sir, Yr. Obt. Ser^t.

[HENRY DEARBORN]

On margin: Nichl. Boilvin

[MS. in Wisconsin Historical Library. Pressmark: Wisconsin MSS., 1B15.]

St LOUIS 7 June 1806.

Dr FRANKS—As the Boats are just going I have only time to write you a few Lines   I was much surprised at not Receiving a line from you Since we Parted as you have had repeated opportunities of writting me   I would have wrote you last fall but the State of my health was so bad that I could not hold a pen   D^r. Jack you cant Imagine the trouble I have had since I saw you last but it is not Necessary that [I] write to you the particulars as you must have been inform'd of it all by this time.   I had a letter from my Robert[54] including an advice to me that I should never consent to any particular payments being made To any one and I mention it to you hoping that you will agree in opinion with me that all the returns we have will be Equally dividede among our Creditors.   God knows all wont be near Enough but it is our duty to act honorably and honestly

---

[54] Probably Robert Aird, mentioned in *Wis. Hist. Colls.*, **xviii**, p. 437.—ED.

Toward all men and not get discouraged nor dispirited for one bad Year. the returns from the Missouri are certainly bad but no worse that I expected when I found I was detained at Illinoix to the month of Octr. I was convinced the season was over for me to do Any thing considerable however I still hope to mend them a little this Summer I intend leaving this in three days to proceed up to the River plate [Platte] where I left the Goods and if I can dispose of them Between this and the month of Augt I intend comming down To meet the goods and bring down the pack that I may thare make[55] I beg you will not Neglect writting me as often as opportunity offers I beg you will not get discouraged but keep up your spirits and I think we have a fair Chance of overcoming all our difficulties. Excuse hast and Believe [me] to be Dr Jack Your Sincer Friend

JAMES AIRD

Addressed: Mr Jacob Franks Michillimackinac.

[Source, same as preceding document, but 1B17. Translated from the French. Date, about 1806 or 1807.]

MY DEAR SIR—I flatter myself that you have been long enough alone this summer to profit by it and that you will find yourself in a condition to resist your neighbors banded together against you. You will need to put every thing in shape to resist the storm, and I hope from your activity and your talents that they will not hinder you from making your returns

---

[55] Aird's difficulties had not all ended; in July he lost a boat, sunk in the Missouri during a serious storm. He therefore determined to continue farther up the river, where (Sept. 3, 1806) he encountered the return expedition of Lewis and Clark; see Thwaites, *Original Journals of Lewis and Clark Expedition* (N. Y., 1905), pp. 374-376. Aird was the first person met by the explorers after their own absence of over two years from the settlements. They eagerly questioned him for news, of which he made a considerable report. He was preparing, so Clark tells us, to form an establishment among the Yankton Sioux, not far from Vermilion River, S. Dak.—ED.

although I recommend to you to hold the price until the Last Moment. That is not to say that you should allow the others to make it. You should conform to the price and when it becomes too low, allow the others to fix it and try and incite them always to Make it lower. But if there is any Means of accord that will be preferable.

I recommend you to try for good peltry, especially deer skins; get as many rats [muskrats] also as possible. Do not neglect the fat. Adieu I have good hope for your affairs. Keep well. I am your Servant and Friend

JQ. PORLIER, Agent

Mr. A. Grignon Wisconsing

1807: OPERATIONS OF DUBUQUE

[Source, same as preceding document, but 1B21. Translated from the French.]

DE LA PRERYE DA CHIENTS 3 June 1807.

M^{srs} *Rochebléve & poollier & Co^y*

SIRS—by Mr Brisebois[56] you will receive twenty eight packs and four ditto for Mr. Berthelotte all together making thirty two packs whose invoice is enclosed, and which you will receive and send on to be sold on the account I owe you

I have drawn on you for the wages of only one man to whom is due 689^{lvs}. the rest I have drawn for Mr. Brisebois which I suppose will only be to transfer it from one leaf to another of your books.

Probably you will be astonished at so small returns this year. It is true, but consider the circumstances which have caused this small result. For seeing the fine appearances of last autumn I arranged with 8 men to trap Beaver on the Missourrye

---

[56] For a brief sketch of Brisbois, see *Wis. Hist. Colls.*, xviii, p. 495, note 29.—ED.

Fur-trade on Upper Lakes

I had sent them An Outfit [?] to make their Entrance into the village and entrench it etc. When they had gone ten days journey or had camped ten times they met the Sioux of Des Moins river, and had a little Broil with them. They all gave up the enterprise and came to pass the winter opposite their village eating up their maize since they had no meat to eat. This spring they came to return to me what remained, their guns, traps and Kettles, and I refused to accept them only replying that the loss was total. I told them that these credits remained for another year, which they must make up. But this Misfortune makes me wish to give up trading and I will really quit it when affairs have become settled up.

I pray you not to be apprehensive for the Balance that remains against me—it is true that I am on the wrong side of the account But when I die I have funds that belong to me that will more than equal the Balance owing you. For all the small debts that I owe you I would much prefer to pay in peltry than to draw on you for money.

I inform you that I have waited in vain since I had the honor of receiving a letter from you last Autumn and for information of the inheritance that I charged you to recover. I do not know the result, but whatever it may Be I always await with Great impatience whatever you may have to tell me.

I had hoped to go to Makinac this year but an alarm spread among the Savages renders my presence necessary in my locality and I must postpone my journey until next year.

As for the Accounting that you ask me for, I make it the same as to what I owe you as you and every one does. But there are some small differences in regard to the price made on sugar, rum, and powder; and after these are settled, I will adjust the Balance whenever you wish.

Since we have learned from you that I have had my lands confirmed, I await a favorable opportunity to sell a portion of them to satisfy those that I owe, and to have left sufficient to live on the remainder.

I am, awaiting the honor of one of your letters, and the

pleasure of seeing you afterward, one who has the honor to be, Messieurs, Your very humble and very affectionate Servant

J. Dubuque[57]

Addressed: Messieurs M^ers Rochebleve & porlier C^o. Merchants at Mackinac

Endorsed: J Dubuck 1807

---

[57] Julien Dubuque, who seems to have been the first permanent white settler of Iowa, who has left behind him a record of his life, was born in Lower Canada, Jan. 10, 1762. His mother was a Malhiot, and he was probably a kinsman of Victor Malhiot and Jacques Porlier. His inclination led him into the fur-trade, and by 1785 he was at Prairie du Chien, having a trading house on the Iowa side. There he came in contact with the Sauk and Foxes, and learned of the lead mines in their territory which they rudely worked. In 1788 he secured an important concession from these tribesmen to work the mines at what he called the "Spanish diggings," near the site of the city now bearing his name; see *Wis. Hist. Colls.*, xiii, pp. 279–283. In 1796 the Spanish government gave him some kind of title to his lands, which became the basis of a law-suit, that was not terminated until (1853) the Iowa supreme court decided against the assignees of Dubuque's title. The inheritance of which he speaks in this letter, is probably a Canadian claim on the estate of some of his relatives. On his voyage of 1805 Pike met Dubuque and found him evasive and non-committal concerning his mining interests. He died in 1810, and his grave on a high bluff below Dubuque was long an object of interest to travellers. Contrary to the ordinary belief, he was at the time of his death much indebted to St. Louis and Mackinac traders. Many letters in the manuscript collections of the Wisconsin Historical Library relate to the settlement of his estate. For a considerable biography of Dubuque, see *Annals of Iowa*, 3d series, vol. ii, pp. 329–336.—Ed.

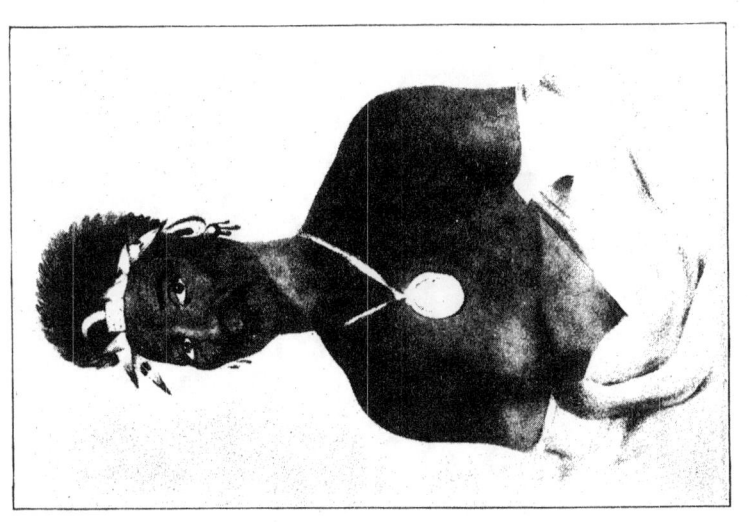

WAAPALAA, OR PLAYING FOX

Fox warrior. From colored lithograph by
James Otto Lewis, 1825

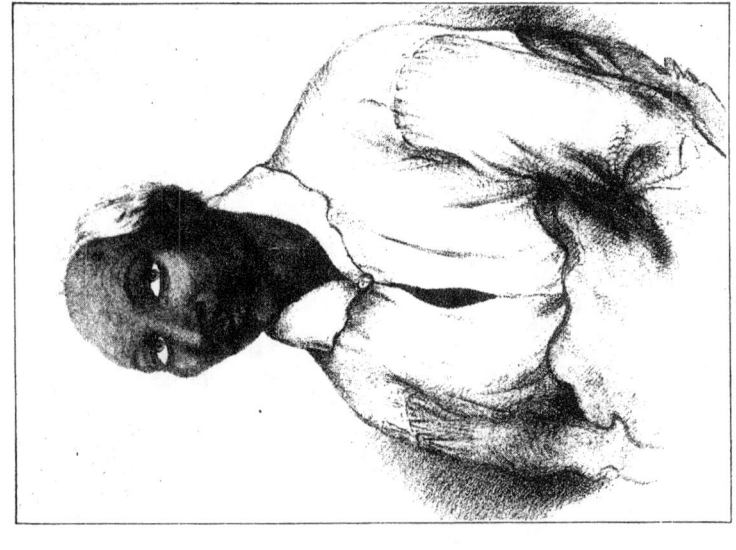

SHOUNKCHUNK, OR THE BLACK WOLF

Winnebago chief. From colored lithograph by
James Otto Lewis, 1827

1778-1815] Fur-trade on Upper Lakes

1807: A TYPICAL INVOICE

[Source, same as preceding document. Pressmark: Account Book 22. Translated from the French.]

1807	Returns of Oliva [58] Invoice			
June 8	By different articles of clothing		294	12
	By diverse Merchandise		868	12
	Advances made to the men		1004	15
	3 bearskin coverings	10	30	
	483 female deerskins	4.10	2173	10
	154 male do	6	924	
	70 fisher	9	630	
	26 Red Foxes	7	182	
	62 Martens	6	372	
	8 Otters	20	160	
	1 made into a sack	18	18	
	6 lynx	4	24	
	14 fine bearskins	50	700	
	6 Common Do	36	2 16	
	4 bear cubs	24	96	
	27 lvs of Beaver	16	432	
	1466 muskrats	1.10	2199	
	510 wildcats	3	1530	
	100 mink	4	400	
	2 dressed deerskins	10	20	
	1 " doe skin	12	12	
	1 green do	10	10	
	100 lvs of Suet or Fat	1.10	150	
	1000 lvs of Sugar	.10	500	
	36 lvs of feathers	1.10	54	
			13000	9

[58] Frederic Oliva's father came to Canada from Hesse Cassel, after the English conquest. The son was in the fur-trade during the early years of the nineteenth century, and during the War of 1812-15 acted as government agent at Mackinac. He died in 1819.—ED.

1807: INFLUENCE OF TECUMSEH'S BROTHER

[MS. in Burton Library, Detroit, vol. 15, p. 50.]

ST. JOSEPH'S [59] 1st Sept. 1807.

MY DEAR FATHER—I avail myself of the opportunity of Mr. Boucharville[60] who leaves this tomorrow for Makina in order to embark on board of the "Adams" for Detroit. We are continually on the look out for the "Genl. Hunter" in hopes of hearing from you & all our freinds in your Quarter. This place is destitute of News since the Montreal Canoes have done plying. All the Ottawas from L'arbe au Croche adhere strictly to the Shawney Prophet's[61] advice they do not wear Hats, Drink or Conjure, they intend all to Visit him this Autumn, which will occasion a great scarcity of corn at this post & Makina. The Merchants will suffer by it as they have not provided themselves with that Article Whisky & Rum is a Drug, the Indians do not purchase One Gall^n. per month. I saw upwards of 60 of them at one time together spirits, rum & whisky was offered for nothing to them if they would drink but they refused it with disdain. The Chiefs reply to the officer Commanding

---

[59] For this post see *Wis. Hist. Colls.*, xviii, p. 447, note 68.—ED.

[60] Possibly Pierre Amable Boucher, Sieur de Boucherville (1780-1857), who was several times in the upper country; once in 1813, when aide-de-camp to General Prevost. See *Id.*, xii, p. 145.—ED.

[61] The Shawnee Prophet was a brother of Tecumseh, his name being Tenkswatawa, or Elkswatawa. About 1805 he assumed the character of a prophet, and began a course of religious instruction that spread from the Indians of Florida to those of Saskatchewan. Among the tenets of the new doctrine was abjuration of the white man's dress and the white man's "firewater." This is interesting testimony to his success among the tribes of the North. In 1811, in Tecumseh's absence, the prophet brought about the Battle of Tippecanoe. When defeated, the prophet's influence waned. He did not fight with the British in the War of 1812-15, but removed to Canada with his fellow tribesmen. After Tecumseh's death, the prophet sunk into obscurity, and in 1827 removed with his tribe to the trans-Mississippi, where in 1834 he died. On the popularity of his religious impulse, see James Mooney, "Ghost Dance Religion," in U. S. Bureau of Ethnology, 14th *Report*, chaps. iii, iv.—ED.

Fur-trade on Upper Lakes

when he offered them some of his milk was That when they were young & had no teeth to eat they could not get any of their Fathers milk & used to beg constantly for [it] to suck, but now that they were grown up & had good teeth they didn't see why their Father should be so generous with offers of giving them some, especially as they could eat all the provissions he might give them. A number of Old men who knew you at Makina addressed me as the Commissarys son. One of the Chimneys of the House you built at Old Makina fell down only last Summer. Several large trees have grown upwards of a fathom in Cercumferance about the Garden. I'm led to believe that they are Pickets which you planted for enclosures which have taken root as they are populars they could not have grown to that size since you left it.[62] The following persons arrived this day from Makina on their way to Montreal—Tous^t Pothier,[63] Campbell, Giasson, Dav^d Mitchel Jr.[64] Pothier &

---

[62] Old Mackinaw is on the south side of the straits, and near the site of the French and British forts of 1713-80. Askin removed with the troops to Mackinac Island in 1781.—ED.

[63] Toussaint Pothier was the son of a fur-trader of the same name, who was one of the North West associates. The younger Pothier was born in Montreal in 1770, and entered the company's employ in 1790. He became one of its most prominent supporters, and in 1812 was in charge of the trading post at St. Joseph's Island. There he organized a corps of 160 voyageurs, and aided in the capture of Mackinac from the Americans. He was afterwards major of militia, member of the legislative council, seignior of Ste. Marie de Lanaudière, and died at Montreal Oct. 25, 1845.—ED.

[64] Probably John Campbell, who was a Scotch-Irish trader on the upper Mississippi as early as 1792. It it not yet apparent how, about 1802, he secured the appointment of United States Indian agent at Prairie du Chien. The same date he, together with Robert Dickson, was appointed a justice of the peace for Indiana Territory. It was said that he performed marriages at Prairie du Chien, his fee being 100 pounds of flour; see *Wis. Hist. Colls.*, ii, pp. 120, 121. Pike met him on his Mississippi voyage in 1805, and speaks favorably of his character. For his death in a duel at Mackinac, see documents *post*.

David Mitchell, Jr., was probably a son of Dr. Mitchell, noted in *Id.*, xviii, p. 496, note 30. The son appears, however, to have had about this time a business house in Montreal.—ED.

that poor simple man J. Bleakly all members or Partners in the South West Co. I intend to send down so much Cedar Bark as will cover my Farm House & Barn as soon as I can [get] them embarked I'm told they make verry good Covering far superior to any other bark. I have not seen half a Doz^n. of white fish since my arrival this is most barron place I believe in the whole Western Country. Doc^t Richardson praised this place most on Account of Ducks Rabbits Hares & pheasants but they must have all been eat by him, for I have not cast my eyes on any yet.

Madelaine and the Children are well. She presents her love to you & my Dear Mother. Please assure Mr & Mrs Barthe of our best wishes for their welfare & family & hope they have not been visited by the fever this year

Accept my sincere wishes for your & my Dear Mothers Health Respects to my Brothers & Sisters. I remain Dear Father yr Dutiful son

JNO. ASKIN JR.[65]

John Askin Esquire, Strabane Near Sandwich

1808: WISCONSIN AGENT KILLED IN DUEL

[Source, same as preceding document, but p. 164.]

ST. JOSEPHS 17th Augt. 1808.

MY DEAR FATHER—My letter per the "General Hunter" was very short, owing to the Business I had on hand which consisted of Report of Survey etc & my mind wholely taken up with the narrow escape I had of my being supersceded without any reasons assigned for the same. I entertain hopes that my

---

[65] John Jr. was the eldest son of John Askin, and had a home at Amherstburg. In 1807 he received the appointment of storekeeper and interpreter at St. Joseph's Island. Thence he led the Indians in the capture of Mackinac (1812), and it was largely due to him that no massacre occurred. During the war he was active in furnishing supplies, etc. Later he returned to Amherstburg, where he died about 1823.—ED.

Fur-trade on Upper Lakes

Enemies will let me alone after they have been so compleated frustrated on their operations. Count Chabot will I'm persuaded speak to the Governor in Chief in my behalf, thats to say he will give His Excellency an Account of my Character & Ability. No doubt you have been informed of the unfortunate meeting between Mr. Redford Crawford of the Mississippi & Mr J Campbell Agent of Indian Affairs for the United States of the Ouisconsan. it appears a misunderstanding took place over the Bottle, a Challange took place, they met & were prevented from accomplishing their ends by the Makina Justice but agreed to meet some place along Lake Huron near or about the Detour (the place I cannot assertain exactly) where poor Campbell received a Mortal Wound. he was brought to this in a Canoe mann'd by American Soldiers, who put him ashore & immediately returned to the American Side. the infortunate man Died the Second day after his arrival & his corps was taken back to Makina, agreeable to a wish he had expressed on his arrival. Redford Crawford & his second immediately went back to Makina, from the place where the Duel took place w^h. his Second Robert Dickson. As its probable that Mr Crawford & Dickson will return to the country where this mans family resides, I'm approhensive that they will meet with a great deal of difficulty & its the general Oppinion that they will loose what property they may take in that Country.

I send Mr. J. & Mrs Barthe Senr a Mocouts of Sugar addressed to your Care. One for Mr Badishon w^h Madelain & my Comp^s, a Mocouts marked I P for Mr Peltier[66] & a Bundle. You'll receive One Mocouts Sugar, a Bundle of Mats, & a mocout of dryed Huckleberrys which you'll please accept of. The sugar is very clean I believe having received it from a clean woman.

Madelaine & the Children are well & all join me in Sincere wishes for your & My Dear Mothers Health & prosperity Our

---

[66] Jacques Peltier (Pelletier) was the father-in-law of John Askin. The family was prominent in early Detroit history, and many of their descendants yet live in the vicinity.—ED.

Love to Charles, James, Alex, Alice, Nelly & Brush & Patterson [Pattinson].[67]   I remain My Dear Father

JNO. ASKIN JR.

[P. S.]   Comp^s to Mr L. Barthe inform him I have not forgot him but cannot procure at present what Stone he wants for pipes.

An Indian by the name of Rayshay mekoquan from Saging a place where the "Weasel" was lost informes me that he found an Anchor at that place & that Jn. Marice Bobien[68] claimed it as yours & rec^d. it, but afterward told the Indians that it was not yours, but it had been lost by Mr. L. Barthe when commanding a Kings Vessel & that it was to be ret'd to the King, this happened three years ago that Beaubien got the Anchor.

John Askin Esq. Strabane.

1808: DIRECTIONS FOR FACTORS

[MS. in Pension Office, Washington. Pressmark: Indian Office Letter Book "A," p. 231. Instructions to Mathew Irwin and Jos. B. Varnum.[69]]

OFFICE OF IN: TRADE, GEO TOWN, WASH: 9 Sept. 1808.
Mathw. Irwin Esq Chicago

SIR—Having been appointed agent of Indian Trade at Chicago, by direction of the Secretary of war, I now transmit the Instructions which are to govern your conduct.

---

[67] These were brothers and sisters of the writer; the last two, brothers-in-law.—ED.

[68] Probably Jean Marie Beaubien, a well-known French-Canadian of Detroit, born in 1745. He was a captain of militia, and held several offices in the early city.—ED.

[69] For a sketch of the career of Maj. Matthew Irwin, see *Wis. Hist. Colls.*, vii, pp. 269, 270, 475. The following document shows that his appointment as factor at Chicago was made two years earlier than there stated.

Joseph Bradley Varnum was a son of the Massachusetts general of that name, who was in the house of representatives (1795-1811), its speaker for two terms, and United States senator (1811-16).

Fur-trade on Upper Lakes

1st. The principal object of the Government in these establishments being to secure the Friendship of the Indians in our country in a way the most beneficial to them and the most effectual and economical to the United States, you will avail yourself of every proper means and opportunity of impressing these People favourably toward the Government; let every transaction with them be so conducted as to inspire them with full confidence in its honor Integrity and good faith and in that of its agents; let no imperfect goods be passed on them, without a previous notice of and allowance for such imperfection; and you will strictly require from them and encourage them to the same conduct; all attempts on their part at Fraud, Trick or deception should be discountenanced and prevented if possible, and when such things do happen, they should be reproved in the most instructive and dignified manner; you will nevertheless be conciliatory in all your intercourse with the Indians and so demean yourself towards them generally and toward their chiefs in particular as to obtain and preserve their Friendship and to secure their attachment to the United States.

2nd. The prices you put on the Goods you have on sale must necessarily vary according to circumstances, but that which you will consider as the standard advance on the price charged in the Invoices received from this Office, will rate from 66 2/3 to 100 per centum and this you will consider as the estimate to cover the cost of transportation and to yeild such profit only as will indemnify the establishment for the expences at your Trading House and on the returns made by you to bring round

---

Through his influence, Joseph Varnum was appointed factor at Chicago, and continued there until transferred to Mackinac (1808). In the early part of 1812 he was at Detroit because of illness, therefore escaped capture at Mackinac. However, he was made a prisoner at Hull's surrender, but was soon afterwards released at Toronto because of illness. After recovering health at his Massachusetts home, Varnum was assistant postmaster for the army on the Niagara frontier. After the close of the war, he acted for two years as Astor's agent; but abandoning the fur-trade about 1817, he returned to New York, and became a wholesale dry-goods merchant. There he died in 1867, leaving a considerable estate.—ED.

the sales of Furs and peltries without loss, as to the prices allowed to Indians for the Skins you will be governed generally by those to which they have been accustomed and at which you can obtain them without giveing them dissatisfaction but after all much must be left to your discretion and prudence so to reduce or raise your prices as compared with the standard advance and with the rate you may be obliged to allow for Skins as to enable us to pay all charges and to avoid sinking money, to enable you to judge of which the rate of sales of the Skins will be occasionally furnished you.

3rd. The goods to be sent you from time to time are intended for sale to the Indians (and it is the express direction of the secretary of war that) no white persons are to be considered as having any right to be furnished with Factory Goods and except in very particular and pressing cases, no sales should be made to white persons of any description whatsoever and in no case but for prompt pay and at an advance of 10 per cent on the Indian Prices and you will be held accountable for the payment of all articles sold to white People on credit excepting (to the U. S. Army officers, and soldiers, under direction, or orders for the officers).[70] Credits may however be given to Principal cheifs of good character. If a professed white Trader wants goods you are not to sell him at any price any article you may possibly be in want of for the Indians If you have a surplus of others you may useing great caution sell them but then only at an advance of 10 per cent on the current prices.

4th. A suitable guard will be furnished you (by order of the Secretary of war) by the Officer commanding the Garrison near you, you will however be absent as little as possible from the Store, an Interpreter when necessary will be furnished you and it is of importance that he should be a person of sober discreet and temperate habits and attached to the Interests of the United States.

---

[70] The portion in parentheses was inserted in the original draft, in pencil.—ED.

5th. You are restricted by Law from carrying on any Trade commerce or Barter on your account or any other, except for the United States as you will observe by the Law establishing Indian Trading Houses *passed on the 21st. April 1806.*[71]

6th. The sale of ardent spirits is most strictly prohibited.

7th. You will furnish me once a year with your list of articles wanted for the succeeding year and as early in the season as possible and not later than the 1st. of Octr. it being of great advantage to have ample time to make purchases   let your lists be full clear and explicit in description as to each article and always bear in mind that good supplies must depend upon adequate remittances.

8th. You will take the greatest possible care to ascertain and examine the quality of the Furs and Peltries you receive to see that their quality is fairly proportioned to the price allowed, that their condition is good to preserve them with attention while in your possession and to send them off in good order carefully and safely packed and so time their departure as that they arrive early in Spring or late in Fall that by avoiding the warm weather on the route they may be saved from the worm.   particularly you are to be watchfull to avoid the imposition of private Traders who may attempt to make instruments of the Indians or otherwise to put off on you bad Skins and to get hold of your goods for the purposes of their Trade   take[72] in as small a proportion of Deer Skins as you can with propriety do and forward whatever you receive as returns (Cash, Notes and drafts excepted) to Genl. Peter Gansevoost Jr. military agent for the United States at Albany, forward to me the Invoices respectively as you send of the articles to Albany and a duplicate to him.

9th. All remittances of Bills notes or Cash must be made to me and under my direction and you are to correspond with take orders on all commercial operations from and keep all your

---

[71] The fourth and fifth articles of instruction are crossed through, as if for erasure.—ED.

[72] All of the remainder of this paragraph was crossed out in the original draft.—ED.

accounts with me If any communication of a civil or Political nature be necessary you will make them separately and in a direct correspondence with the Secretary of War. If any of the Officers of Government who are well known to you want Cash you may take their drafts for it on any of the Departments at the Seat of Government.

10th. You will keep correct accounts of every transaction in a Day Book, Journal, and Ledger and Cash Book, In they Day Book every thing must be recorded you will also keep an Invoice Book and a Letter Book, you will render me quarter yearly accounts of all money goods and property whatsoever which shall be transmitted you or which shall come into your hands and you shall transmit duplicates of your accot. to the Secretary of the Treasury of the, U. S. these accounts you will make up to the last days Inclusively of March, June, Septr. and December in each year they will comprise abstracts of your acct. Books balanced up to and includeing those days respectively as to Sales recpts. expenditures and stock on hand, the stock on hand you will detail clearly and accurately by Inventory this point as to makeing up to the given day and transmitting regularly your accounts and Inventory is so essential that it must not be dispensed with in any Instance and you must be as early as possible after the time to which made up in sending them off.

Assureing you of my prompt attention to all your communications and with best wishes for the success of your Trading House,[73] I am very Respectfully

[JOHN MASON] Supr. In: Tr.[74]

Endorsed: A copy of the foregoing was sent to Jos: B. Varnum Esq at Michilimackinac

---

[73] In original, this final paragraph was crossed out with pencil.—ED.

[74] John Mason was the fourth son of George Mason of Gunston Hall. Born in 1766, John entered the mercantile profession and lived some years at Bordeaux, France. After his father's death, he settled on his estate near Georgetown and in 1806 was appointed superintendent of Indian Trade, according to the law of that year authorizing such an appointment. During the War of 1812-15 he was commissary-general

[1778-1815] Fur-trade on Upper Lakes

[Source, same as preceding document, but p. 224.]
OFFICE OF INDIAN TRADE GEORGE TOWN (WASHINGTON)
10th. Septemr. 1808.
Joseph B Varnum Esqr. Agent for the United States at Michilimackinac

SIR—It having been determined to establish a Factory for Indian Trade at Michilimackinac, I have the pleasure to inform you, that you have been appointed by the Secretary of War to take charge of that establishment and Matthew Irwin Esqr. of Philadelphia who will hand this and other dispatches for you, has been appointed to succeed you at Chicago The absence of the Secretary from the Seat of Government at this time prevents the issuing of your Commission, on his return, next month, it will be forwarded you, when a new Bond and oath of Office from you will be required—of this I shall write you in due time.

I hand you under cover an Invoice of 172 Packages [of] Goods intended for the new trading house at Mackinac Post including a sett of Books and stationary for the use of the Factory, the assortment and qualities have been obtained from a person well skilled in the Trade of that part of the Country, and on whose judgment and information we had reason to believe dependence could be placed—so that I trust they will be found to answer well, and as the amount is considerable, I flatter myself you will be able to open the New establishment to considerable advantage. When the goods are opened and examined, and you shall have made yourself acquainted with the fashion and quality of the Articles in de-

---

of prisoners; hence the courtesy title, "General" Mason, by which he was usually known. He continued to superintend the Indian trade until 1816, being then replaced by Thomas L. McKenney. The remainder of his long life was spent on his estates. He lived in his later years at "Clermont," in Fairfax County, where he died in 1849. His son James was Confederate commissioner to England in 1861; his daughter was the mother of Gen. Fitzhugh Lee. On taking office, McKenney commented on the accuracy and the systematic care which his predecessor had used in the business of the department.—ED.

[331]

mand in that quarter by the Indians, you will be pleased [to] remark particularly on such (if any) as may not suit—and describe accurately which will, and where description cannot well carry a correct idea of the thing in question send us Samples.

I have directed Mr. Irwin who has charge of these goods to store them at Mackinac safely and subject to your order as he passes that place, there to await your arrival which I hope will be very soon after he reaches Chicago, as it is extremely desirable that you should be located at Mackinac and have the new Establishment opened before winter sets in, for which I calculate there is yet full time—if Mr. Irwin should be fortunate to meet with no unforeseen delay, I have urged on him every possible exertion to reach you quickly and must beg on your part, that nothing be left undone to Inventory and give up to him all the Goods and other public property at the Factory at Chicago including those Goods now Invoiced for that place forwarded by Mr. Irwin and addressed to you, and to repair to Mackinac and open the New Trading House there with the least possible loss of time. Should it however unfortunately happen, that he does not get to Chicago in time as to Frost, for you to repair safely to your destined station—in that case, and in that case only, you will continue at Chicago 'till the Spring, as principal, and Mr. Irwin will, act there as your assistant, and he is instructed accordingly, and you will give up to him the Factory at Chicago and remove to Mackinac as early in Spring as practicable. it was to provide against such a possible state of things that in writing to [you] yesterday as agent at Chicago, I addressed the present Invoice of Goods for that place to you. A dwelling House and Stores at Mackinac suitable for the intended Factory have been rented as long ago as December last, by the Secretary of War, of a Mr. Campbell, as you will see by the inclosed Letters (Copies) which passed between them on 16th. December, Certified from the War Office and which I hope will be found sufficient to enable you to get immediate possession. As I presume Mr. Campbell must immediately after the engagement have directed his agent there to deliver the Stores to the United States Factor when called for. In the absence of the Secretary, I have annexed an order for them which I presume will be sufficient, in case of a necessity of Communicating with him. Mr. Campbell resides at Prarie des Cheins on the upper Mississippi and has lately been appointed Indian Agent there for the United States. The rent is to be paid by you from time to time, at the stipulated rate, say $150 p^r an: when it is to commence must depend on circumstances,—if Mr. Campbell has held the house empty to our Order, it ought to be paid from the time it was so ready to be delivered to us; otherwise only from the time you get possession.[75]

Referring for all that relates to your accounts and Agency at Chicago to my Letter of yesterday, I am Sir very respectfully Your Mo obt Servt

J. M. Supr. Ind. Trade.

P. S. In the present Invoice there are only 171 Packages, one to go from New York and some additional charges will be stated in my next J M

1809: MICHILIMACKINAC FACTORY

[Source, same as preceding document, but Letter Book "B", p. 434.]

WAR DEPARTMENT 26 April 1809.

SIR—Your letter of the 18th. of February last addressed to my predecessor in office has been received. I have also been favored by Genl. Mason with a perusal of your letter to him under date of the 12th. of March.

Having maturely considered the subject, it is thought best, both as it respects yourself and the public Interest that you should be charged with the Factory at Michilimacinac; to which place you will immediately repair on the Arrival of Mr. Irwin at Chicago, to whom you will make over all the public property

---

[75] It is evident that the authorities at Washington had not yet learned of the death of Campbell, as mentioned *ante*, p. 325.—ED.

at that Place, now under your direction, with such Advice as may be useful to him in conducting the business as your Successor.

Should the building at Michilimacinac mentioned in your Letter to Genl Mason, appear on examination to be well calculated for a public Store, you will please to consult with the Officer commanding at that Post, on his relinquishing of it, for some other Situation, whitch it is hoped may be procured, that will equally well accommodate him. I am etc.

[WILLIAM EUSTIS]

Addressed: J. B. Varnum, Jr.

1809: THE MACKINAC COMPANY

[MS. in Wisconsin Historical Library: Pressmark: Wisconsin MSS., 60B27.]

Know all Men by these presents that we James McGill, Francis Desrivieres and Thomas Blackwood, trading under the Firm of James & And^w McGill & Co. of Montreal Merchants,[76] have made, constituted & ordained, and by these presents do make, constitute & ordain Jacques Porlier, and Jean Baptiste Berthelot, jointly & severally, our true & lawful Attornies for the special purpose of appearing for & representing us, in the General Council or Councils to be held at St Josephs or elsewhere, conformable to the Articles of Agreement of the Michillimakinac Company, and in every such Council or Councils for us, and in our name to vote & give their opinion for us, as fully & amply as if we were personally Present, hereby ratifying & approving of whatever our Said Attornies may do in the premises. And this Power shall be in force and continue until the tenth day of April now next ensuing and no longer.

In Witness whereof we have set our Hands & Seals at Mon-

---

[76] Andrew McGill died in 1805. For James McGill, see *Wis. Hist. Colls.*, xviii, p. 326. François Desrivières was son of an early trader of that name, and a stepson of James McGill. Thomas Blackwood was a well-known Montreal merchant, who in 1812 was officer in the local militia and in 1821 one of the founders of the General Hospital.—ED.

treal this 15th day of May in the Year of our Lord 1809. At Montreal aforesaid where no Stamps are used

       JAMES McGILL [Seal]
       FRANᶜ. DESRIVIERES [Seal]
       THO. BLACKWOOD [Seal]

Signed Sealed and delivered before John Grant Junior;
         PETER HARKNESS

1809: HATTERS' FURS FROM FACTORIES

[MS. in Pension Office, Washington. Pressmark: Indian Office Letter Book B, p. 63. Extract from a letter of John Mason Supt. to Gen. Henry Dearborn, Boston, dated Georgetown, Oct. 9, 1809.]

I am sorry to say that so miserable has been the trafic of our Factories on the lakes for the last year, that they furnish no Hatters furs worth dividing—or which it would be proper to send further for a market than New York the place where they are first landed on the Sea Board—the whole quantity (of the kinds you mention as wanting in Boston) not exceeding about 10,000 Racoon skins, 3,000 muskrat skins and 40 or 50 of Beaver & no old Coat—the Mackinac Factory has not yet got into operation

  * * * * * * * *

The factors complain of the hard winter and give this as a reason why the Indians hunted much less than usual—should we be more fortunate another season on the lakes as I trust with the assistance of the Michilimackinac Factory we shall—the applications from the Boston Hatters shall not be forgotten. I shall take pleasure in recommending that a trial be made of some of the Furs in that market.

1810: AMERICANS ABSORB MONTREAL FUR-TRADE

[MS. in Burton Library, Detroit, vol. 16, p. 50.]

MONTREAL 26 February 1810.

MY DEAR OLD FRIEND—I received a letter from you last fall and wrote to you the same time which is very extraordinary that you did not recieve it. there is no safty in writing otherwise than by post, as the Boatmen is very careless. I also this day had the pleasure of receiving yours of the 13th January and am Happy to find that you and yours are in good Health, which is one of the greatest blessings Providence can bestow on us poor Mortals, also that you are exempt from the many troubles, vexations, and disapointments attending those who are in commerce, for my part I have had a severe Bileous Fever which I got in Lake Champlain, which was near puting an end to our friendly intercource, however it pleased providence to Lengthen out my span, for sometime longer, I wish when it was in my power to have retired from active live to have done as you did, when we are young we do not feel the effects of misfortune, so much as when we grow old, however when I look arround I find many worse than myself which is a consolation. our old friend Todd is in New York and has been there all winter, which has been a loss to our Sociaty, especially to me, he being the only old friend, except Mr. Frobisher, who has not changed their dispositions, some from geting rich others from having obtain'd places—& has raised them in their own imagination above their old acquaintance, and I am sorry to say your friend M°Gill is one of that number. the poplation of this city within this two years exceeds all imagination, the whole trade of the Country is carried on by Americans, and their agents, and I expect the Indian Trade will fall into their Hands, as Mr Astore offerd to purchase out the Makenau Co. he has a Charter from Congress to an exclusive right to the Indian Trade, and I understand he is to be conected with the N W Company to make settlements on the North West coast of America, to communicate with the inland N W Trade. Mr

Fur-trade on Upper Lakes

MGillavray is now in New York & Mr Richardson on that business.[77]

I hope your reading this Letter will not give you the blues, it is a bad rainy day that has affected my spirrits, the next I hope will be better, we have had a disagreeable winter, more sickness in the Country & Town than ever was known. I have not heard from Mr Brush this 12 Months. let me know whether he is dead, or no. Mrs. Henry and my Daughter are all I have of my family, two of my boys in the N West, one on board of a Man of Warr. my paper is almost full therefore I must close (is it possible we will never meet in this world) Mrs Henry Etc., Join in wishing you & Mrs Askin every Happiness this world can give   remain Dear Askin your old friend

ALEXANDER HENRY

John Askin Esquire, Strabane Detroit

[MS. in Wisconsin Historical Library. Pressmark: Wisconsin MSS., 1B34.]

MONTREAL, June 8, 1810.

Mr. Jacques Porlier

SIR—This will be delivered by Messrs. Gillespie[78] and Pothier, who carry up ample powers for the purchase for the whole of the Interest of the Wintering Partners in the Concerns of the late Mich^a. Co., or for winding up the business according to the original agreement.

Notwithstanding the favorable Sales of Deer & Beaver, we

---

[77] This refers to Astor's plans for the founding of Astoria. In 1808 he obtained a charter for the American Fur Company and in 1810 bought out the Mackinac Company, uniting it with the former and denominating it South West Company. In his plans for the Pacific trade, Astor made overtures to the North West partners, which were later rejected. Whereupon he managed the company on his own account—a measure that ultimately led to the failure of the enterprise.—ED.

[78] George Gillespie, a prominent Montreal merchant who had in 1798 been in charge of the house of the North West Company at St. Joseph's. In 1808 he went to Washington to remonstrate against the embargo.—ED.

do not see that a loss on the whole business of the Comp^y can be avoided, unless the Returns of this year should be great, and the Sales very favorable.

Whatsoever you may determine upon in respect to a continuance of your own Interest in the present years Outfit or not, we hope that you will alike be disposed to give your best aid towards making the most of matters for those who may run the risk, whosoever they may be; because if you *sell out*, a fair consideration for your services will be allowed. And even if what the Attornies of the four Houses may offer you *in such case* should be considered by you too small, we would readily credit to the account of your late Firm or your part of it, such Sum as would make up the difference between your ideas of the allowance for services *if you sell out*, and what the said Attornies may offer you. The Sales MK [Mackinac] in London have been.

Deer Skins	Gro:	average about	7 sh.	2^d	per skin
Beaver	"	"	13 "		per skin
Otter	"	"	16 "	3^d	per skin
Fisher	"	"	7 "		per skin
33 Bear	"	"	20 "	"	"
21 Swanskins	"	"	30 "	"	"

The Racoons & Minks are still unsold   We remain, Sir, Your most Obed^t Servants

FORSYTH RICHARDSON & Co.

Endorsed by Porlier, in French: 1810 Letter of Mr. Richardson mentioning the dissolution of the Company of MKa. and the compensation allowed to the proprietors of the interior.

1811: EMBARGO AFFECTS FUR-TRADE

[MS. in Pension Office, Washington. Pressmark: Indian Office Letter Book "C", p. 75. Circular Letter to Indian agents.]

WAR DEPARTMENT April 15th. 1811.

SIR—It is possible (indeed it has been intimated) that in consequence of the operation of the late Law prohibiting the importation into the United States of British Goods,[79] the British Agents and Traders with the Indians, may attempt to excite in their minds, prejudices and hostile dispositions towards the United States, insinuating, that as the British Goods intended for their trade, will not be permitted to enter and pass the American posts on the Western Frontier, this act, which has been dictated as a measure of general policy in relation to Great Britain, was intended as an act of hostility against the Indians. You will be on your guard; and use all proper means to anticipate and frustrate any such attempts: Explaining to the chiefs of the several Tribes as occasion may offer, that the Government of the U. S. has been compelled by long continued injuries and violations of their rights on the part of Great Britain for which no satisfaction or redress has been had, to interdict their trade rather than make war against them: That as the White people have it is expected the Red people will, submit to an inconvenience which it is in the power of Great Britain to terminate, by returning to a sense of right and pursuing a course of Justice.

In resisting such endeavours and conciliating the disposition of the Indians, your vigilance and exertions are expected: And in case it should become necessary to extend indulgencies and to make presents exceeding the usual allowance, your discretion is confided in, to act as circumstances may require.

The Agents at the Several factories will receive instructions on the Subject, from the Superintendent of Indian trade. Respectfully,

[WILLIAM EUSTIS]

Addressed: Gov Wm. Hull, Gen. Wm. Clark, Charles Jouett, Erastus Granger, John Johnston[80], Nichs. Boilvin, J. B. Varnum, Ind. Agents.

---

[79] The non-importation act, passed by Congress March 2, 1811, after a period in which the embargo had been temporarily suspended.—ED.

[80] As governor of Michigan Territory, William Hull was *ipso facto* Indian agent.

Gen. William Clark at St. Louis had been since 1807 Indian agent for Louisiana, which embraced all of the purchase, except that afterwards erected into the state of Louisiana.

1811: WISCONSIN CARGO CLEARED

[MS. in Wisconsin Historical Library. Pressmark: Wisconsin MSS., 60B38.]

DISTRICT OF MICHILIMACKINAC
PORT OF MICHILIMACKINAC

These are to certify that Lewis Grignon Commander of a Barge bound to Green Bay and having on board the following Cargo, Viz. Five Barrel Sundries, two Cases Merchandize, two bales merchandize, two kegs Pork & Gum, Four Pots, One keg powder, three bags Corn, together with the necessary Sea Stores for the Voyage, Hath here entered and cleared his said barge as the law directs

Given under my hand and Seal of office this 18th day July A. D. 1811.

[Seal] SAMUEL ABBOTT[81]
Collector

Charles Jouett was of Virginia birth (1772). In 1802 he was chosen Indian agent at Detroit, and three years later was removed to Chicago. In 1811 he resigned his agency and settled in Kentucky, whence in 1815 he was again summoned to occupy the Chicago agency. After his resignation from this office he was a judge (1819–20) in Arkansas Territory, and in 1834 died at Lexington, Ky.

Erastus Granger was brother of Gideon, postmaster-general in Jefferson's cabinet. Erastus was agent for the Six Nations, with headquarters at Buffalo, where he died in 1823.

John Johnston (1775–1861) was Indian agent at Fort Wayne until 1812, when he removed to Upper Piqua, where he kept his agency until 1829.—ED.

[81] For Abbott see *Wis. Hist. Colls.*, xviii, p. 512, note 46.—ED.

Fur-trade on Upper Lakes

1811: TRADERS PURCHASE FROM FACTOR

[Source, same as preceding document, but 1A158.]

Messrs. Porlier & Bartlet [Berthelot] to the U. S. Factory M^r
Dr.

2	Pieces stroud				35.00	70.00
15¼	yards Crimson Molton				75	11.62½
18	Pairs Blankets 3½ Point				9.00	162.00
20	do	do	3	do	8.00	160.00
12	do	do	2½	do	6.30	75.00
3	do	do	2	do	4.00	12.00
19	do	do	1½	do	3.00	57.00
6	Calico Shirts				2.00	12.00
1	Doz: Papercase Looking Glasses					1.50
4	do Scalping Knives				2.00	8.00
4	Padlocks				62½	2.50
1	Gross Gartering					3.50
2¼	Pounds Worstead				2.50	5.62½
30¾	do Vermillion				2.25	69.19
4	do Cotton wick				1.00	4.00
800	Gun flints				1.00	8.00
6	small axes				75	4.50
6	Hoes				75	4.50
75	Pounds Powder				1.00	75.00
10	Pairs Blankets 3½ Pt.					90.00
10	do do 1½ "					30.00
5	do do 2 "					10.00
6	Hoes					4.50
						891.04

Rec.ᵈ Wm. Howards Draft
for   612.76
Gold   234.24½
Paper   40.00
Silver   4.05¾
                       $891.04

J. B. VARNUM
U. S. Factor.

Endorsed: Invoice of August 14, 1811, with receipt.

1811: AVOIDANCE OF EMBARGO

[MS. in Burton Library, Detroit, vol. 456, p. 194.]

St. Josephs 25th Augt. 1811.

My Dear Father—Tho I have not any of your favors before me to answer yet cannot let this opportunity slip without letting you know that we are all well. The constant arrival of Canoes for some days past from Michilimakinac and Boats from Montreal *via* the Lakes has kept the place alive The non-importation act will effect the S. W. Furr Company much for their Goods must remain here this winter unsold. Messrs Gillispie, Pothier, Berthelet and many others are expected in tomorrow they are to remain some time in hopes that the Act will be repealed. Mr. Robert Dickson intends going to Queenston *via York* from Queenston to Buffaloe from B. to Fort Pitt down the Ohio to the Mississippi then up the last mentioned river to the head thereof amongst the Siouxs. Johnney has made his agreements w^t. Mr Lewis Crawford[82] and is to winter at Lake de Flambeaux, Superior, he only gets £50 Hf. (tho little) its better than to be Idle. Madelaine, John & the children join me best wishes for your & my Dear Mothers Health & Happiness & our Love to My Brothers & Sisters & am My Dear Father Your dutiful Son

Jno Askin Jr.

Have the goodness to tell my D^r mother that I have not forgot her about the Buffaloe Skin

John Askin Esquire Strabane

---

[82] Lewis Crawford was a member of the North West Company. In 1812 he headed a body of Canadian volunteers engaged in the capture of Mackinac. In 1814 he was on the island when the Americans landed, and aided in their repulse. His services having been commended by the British authorities, he was in 1816 recommended for a magistracy, but by that time had left the country. He was a brother of Redford Crawford, who, as related *ante*, p. 325, killed John Campbell in a duel.—Ed.

[1778-1815] Fur-trade on Upper Lakes

1812: FUR-TRADE ENGAGEMENT

[MS. in Wisconsin Historical Library. Pressmark: Wisconsin MSS., 56B30. Translated from the French.]

Before the undersigned Notaries residing in the town of Montreal,[83] in the Province of Lower Canada appeared [Charles S^t. Antoine dit Vacher of Maskinonge] who voluntarily is engaged and by these presents engages himself to the Company of Michilimackinac, [T. Pothier Montreal agent] here present and accepting, to depart at their first requisition in the capacity of middleman in one of their Canoes or Batteaux, in order to make the voyage in ascending and also to winter [three] years in the dependences of St. Joseph Island, Michilimakinac, Mississippi and Missouri [and to descend after the said three years]. Also to take good and due Care on the route and while at the said place of the Merchandise, Provisions, Peltries, Utensils and all things necessary for the voyage; to serve, obey, and faithfully execute all that the said Sieurs his Bourgeois or all others representing them to whom they may transfer the present engagement, shall lawfully and honestly order him to do; without trading on his own account, nor absenting himself from nor leaving the said service, under the penalties imposed by the Ordinances, and the loss of his wages. This engagement thus made, for and in consideration of the sum of [twelve Hundred] livres or shillings ancient currency of this province, that they promise and oblige themselves to release and pay to the said [Engagé] one month after his return to this town; and at the beginning to furnish him one 3 point Blanket, 3 ells of cotton, one pair of shoes and one collar, and to pay in advance [forty eight livres and he shall also receive on his Departure twenty four livres currency. Joseph St Antoine de Vacher his uncle of the said town of Maskinongé enters into Bond for the said Engagé]. He agrees to contribute one

---

[83] The following engagement is printed in French, with blanks for filling in; the words within the brackets are written. This is a typical engagement contract for Canadian voyageurs—one of the forms used for many years with but slight variation.—ED.

[343]

percent of his wages for the fund for voyageurs; the said bourgeois will be bound to feed the said engagé in such places as he may be during the present engagement, only with Indian corn or such other food as there is ordinarily to be found among the savages. For thus &c. promising &c. obliging &c. renouncing &c. Done and passed at the said Montreal in the Notary's Office in the year one thousand eight hundred and [Twelve] the [fourteenth of March] at noon; and they have signed with the exception of the said engagé who, having declared on being asked that he does not know how, made his usual mark after having had read to him [what is in the draft of these presents]

L^s. CHABOILLEZ

Endorsed: Engagement of Charles St. Antoine dit Vacher 1200lvs for three years.

1812–13: WISCONSIN TRADE AGREEMENTS

[Source, same as preceding document, but 1B51. Translated from the French.]

ST. JOSEPH July 4, 1812.

Robert Dickson Esquire

As I see that it is impossible to terminate our business because of the sale of Peltries and other critical circumstances, I am obliged to yield to you my part of all Peltries, merchandise, Debts belonging to us under the following conditions, namely 1st that you will exonerate me from my proportion of the debt owed by us to the S. W. Company by M^{rs}. Pothier. 2nd that you will pay me in the month of May next the sum of two thousand four hundred livres ancient Quebec currency. 3^d that you will discharge my individual account in the books, including the charges that have been made and shall be made in the following accounts against me, namely S. W. Company at Prairie du Chien for Mr Oliva, Nich^s Jarrot,[84] Fr^s. Boutheiller,

---

[84] Nicolas Jarrot was a native of France, whence he emigrated to America during the early part of the Revolution. Landing at Baltimore he visited various parts of the United States, finally settling in 1794 at Cahokia. There he embarked in the fur-trade on the upper

Fur-trade on Upper Lakes

M. Brisbois & L[t]. Grignon,[85] as well as assuring me that you will remit the money due to Nich[s] Jarrot, either in merchandize or otherwise according to his bargain with us, as I have given him my note, also to retire my notes at Michillimakinac in the hands of Ja[s]. Reid and Michael Dousman,[86] as they appear on our books, also to liquidate all small Accounts that I may have made on our Account that have escaped my memory, also to give me the Barge or boat on which I came to Makinac. Moreover I obligate myself to arrange the accounts of the men at your demand. I am your obedient Servant

Jo[s]. ROLETTE

ST JOSEPH July 6, 1812. I accept the above Conditions.

R. DICKSON & Co.

[Source, same as preceding document, but 2A21.]

Franks and Co. Dr. To Alexis Reaume.[87]

To account Render[ed]	83
To Mr. John Law accot'	130
To Mr. T: Anderson	50
	263

Credit—By 190 musrat in Full of all demand To This day July 10th 1813

ALEXIS REAUME

Endorsed: Paid A. Reyaume 263 10th July 1813.

Mississippi, and had large dealings at Prairie du Chien, where Pike found him in 1806. During the War of 1812-15, Jarrot was pro-American and aided Boilvin in rallying the inhabitants for the United States; see *Wis. Hist. Colls.*, xi, pp. 290, 295. He made his home in Cahokia, where he had a fine house and was magistrate for St. Clair County. He died there in 1823, leaving a large fortune.—ED.

[85] For François Bouthillier see *ante*, p. 104, note 41. Lieutenant Grignon is Louis Grignon.—ED.

[86] Michael Dousman is sketched in *Wis. Hist. Colls.*, xviii, p. 506, note 42.—ED.

[87] Alexis Reaume may have been a nephew of Judge Charles Reaume of Green Bay. He carried on business between Detroit and Mackinac, and is said to have been the first to arrive at the latter place in 1815, with news of the peace.—ED.

[Source, same as preceding document, but 2B6.]

SANDWICH 18 Augt 1813.

DEAR SIR—M^r. Franks arrived here two days ago & is in good health. the Bearer of this is Thomas[88] who has conducted himself with the greatest propriety.

You will please cloathe his Wife & Children & I will return you the goods this Fall—it is also M^r. Frank's wish that you should do so. I will write you more fully. Yours sincerely

R. DICKSON

N. B. Mr Franks tell you to give [Thomas some] Flour.

J. FRANKS

Addressed: Mr. John Lawe, La Baye

1813: AMERICAN FUR COMPANY ON THE GREAT LAKES

[Transcripts in Burton Library, Detroit. Letter Book of Ramsay Crooks.]

BUFFALO 21st. October, 1813.

John Jacob Astor,

After a very dissagreeable ride I reached this place the night before last in good health, since when I have made every enquiry respecting the prosecution of my journey and find I must either go on horseback by way of Presque Isle or on board the Schooner "Chippewa" that was stranded a little below this place a few days ago. By land it will be a trip of ten or twelve days and an expense of about $100—while by water the charges will be comparatively trifling—but the very advanced state of the season and the uncertainty of the Vessels being soon repaired & got off are great objections to trusting this mode of conveyance however I shall see both the Schooner and Captain to-morrow & if convinced that she will sail in a few days I shall engage my passage in her. Since the evacuation

---

[88] This was Tomah, the Menominee chief, for whom see *Wis. Hist. Colls.*, i, pp. 53–58; iii, pp. 269–283; xviii, p. 446, note 65. Tomah was then returning from the sieges of Forts Meigs and Stephenson.—ED.

RAMSAY CROOKS
From oil portrait by E. Saintain, in possession of
Wisconsin Historical Society

of Malden[89] many of those who fled from Detroit during the reign of Terror have returned, and among the others a Mr. Ten Eyck[90] who I understand has about ninety Packs of Skins he had concealed previous to the trouble—he left this village sometime ago but wheather with the intention of bringing his property here immediately it is impossible to ascertain. I shall endeavor to meet him somewhere. A Mr. William Baird of this place will act as our agent here, he is industrious and attentive and is allowed to be a man of the strictest integrity. You will consequently address any Communication you may make me to his care—to-morrow will determine when and in what manner I shall leave Buffalo with which you shall be made acquainted by next mail. I am &c

[RAMSAY CROOKS][91]

---

[89] Malden was evacuated by General Proctor Sept. 27, 1813, on the approach of General Harrison. Although Proctor and his van had left some days previous, the rear-guard had only departed an hour before the victorious Americans entered the town, where the burned remains of Fort Malden and its several storehouses were yet smoldering.—ED.

[90] Conrad Ten Eyck was a native of Albany, where he was born in 1782. When nineteen years of age he came to Detroit and engaged in mercantile business, having for a partner his brother Jeremiah. Their establishment was destroyed by the fire of 1805, but they began anew only to be banished from the place in 1812 by Proctor. After his return, Ten Eyck became a prominent citizen; he was treasurer of Wayne County (1816–25), trustee of the village (1818), and member of the militia (1836–38). Being an active Democrat, he was appointed federal marshal by Van Buren. Having purchased a large farm west of the city he removed thereto, and kept a tavern, which became well known to west-bound emigrants. There he died in 1847.—ED.

[91] Ramsay Crooks was a native (1787) of Greenock, Scotland. Several members of his family migrated in 1792 to America and settled on the Canadian side of Niagara River. Thence young Crooks, at the age of sixteen, came West with Robert Dickson and was in Wisconsin as early as 1806. The next year he left the North West Company, and at St. Louis formed a partnership with one of Wayne's veterans, Robert McClellan, for a fur-trading expedition up the Missouri. This, however, was frustrated by the hostility of the Teton Sioux. In 1811 Crooks joined the Pacific Fur Company, and was one of the over-

NEW YORK 1 Nov. 1813.

DEAR SIR—I have just now your letter of 21 Oct. and am glad to see you have got so far. I hope you will get the skins of teneyck as well as all others particularly Raccoon, Beaver, Martin and Mink which are all much wanted here, if you are obliged to give a little more than the price stated never mind it.

I request you again give no information Whatsoever to any person as to our Columbia River Buisness. the "Beaver" arrived at Canton.

Yours J. J. A[STOR]

P. S. Send some of the furrs as soon as you can that we may have the best of the market

---

BUFFALO 1st. Decem. 1813.

DEAR SIR—On the 17th Ulto., I had the pleasure of enclosing you a list of Indian Goods necessary for the trade of Michilimakinac. Since when your favor of the 15th Nov. has come to hand.

Although the journey by land on this side of Lake Erie to Detroit, has always been deemed a perilous undertaking, and

---

land Astorian expedition headed by Wilson Hunt. In that journey Crooks endured almost incredible hardships, eventually reaching Astoria May 12, 1812, and starting homeward the 28th of June following. The return journey was accomplished with nearly as great difficulties as the outward, the party being attacked and robbed by hostile Indians; after wintering on the upper waters of the Platte, they reached St. Louis in April, 1813. There Crooks first heard of the declaration of war between England and the United States. He at once proceeded to New York, whence he was sent, as the accompanying documents show, to aid Astor in his fur-trade along the Great Lakes. Crooks remained in Astor's employ until, in 1817, he was made a partner in the American Fur Company, and each year made a visit to Mackinac and the upper country in the interests of that corporation. In 1834, upon Astor's retirement, Crooks became its president. He died at New York in 1859, leaving a reputation for business integrity. He was interested in the founding of the Wisconsin Historical Society, and presented his portrait to its museum; see article thereon in *Wis. Hist. Colls.*, iv, pp. 95–102.—ED.

is at this moment peculiarly so, from the removal of the few scattering inhabitants, as a space of nearly Two Hundred miles (in which there are several unfordable streams) has thereby been left destitute of even one solitary Cabin to shelter the Traveler or furnish a bite of fodder for his famished Horse. Yet these difficulties I would not have considered insurmountable had the object in view required incountering them, and warranted my incurring the expense incident to such an enterprize.

No person has gone from hence to Detroit since my arrival, and as the British are said to have abandoned Burlington Heights, look on my departure as at hand, and all hope to see Mr. Ten Eyck in all this month.

According to your request, I have relinquished all idea of going to St. Louis, and to insure my being early at Mackinac and St. Joseph, I purpose going in the Fleet which transports the Troops destined for the reduction of those places, and shall exert myself to the utmost in bringing to a happy termination every part of the business with which you have intrusted me.

I am sorry to hear of the difficulties in obtaining Goods as it is far from certain that Montreal will be in possession of our armies this winter, but as I said in my last, I think enough to answer the present exigence may be got in New York and Philadelphia.

If the success of your application to import, depends in the least on the Indians Supplicating the Government for supplies, I must acknowledge my apprehentions of the result for unfortunately these savages entertain ideas bordering on Conviction that their Father is like any other Trader who will find it his interest to furnish them with Merchandize as heretofore by the factories. An illusion which will never loose the force of a reality, until the United States totally abandon that species of monopoly, and I trust that before long the gentlemen who vote appropriations to carry on a traffic of no real benefit to our tawny neighbors, and bemeaning to the Government, will discover how fallacious were their expectations when by such Establishments they promised themselves the Philanthropic satisfaction of Meliorating the condition of the Indians and attaching them unalterably to the United States. Since it is a fact notorious to all the world that those very Tribes who experienced in the greatest degree this fostering care of the Executive were the first to raise the Tomahawk against the American Settlements. in short as the Officer who concluded the late Armistice with the Hostile nations at Detroit, assured them that on applying at Fort Wayne Ammunition &c. would be issued according to their wants.[92] I see no reason why they should be when their necessities are thus gratuitously relieved without intercession. I shall be glad of the letter to Genl. Cass and if another can be obtained for Captain Elliot of the Navy,[93] I am confident they will be of great use to Dear Sir Your most ob servt

RAMSAY CROOKS

John Jacob Astor Esq. New York

1814: RUMOR OF PEACE

[MS. in Wisconsin Historical Library. Pressmark: Wisconsin MSS., 2B47. Translated from the French.]

MICHILIMACKINAC the 29 March, 1814

Mr. Louis Grignon

MY DEAR FRIEND—I welcome the reception of your letter dated the 1st instant, which came to me the 25th, the courier

---

[92] Before General Harrison left Sandwich, in pursuit of Proctor's troops, he was sought by chiefs of the Chippewa and the Ottawa, who asked for peace. He referred them to Gen. Duncan McArthur, left in command at Detroit, who concluded a temporary armistice. This was on his return, renewed by Harrison, who wrote to the secretary of war (letter in the Draper MSS., vol. 4X) that he was obliged to promise the hostile tribes occasional supplies of provisions in order to prevent their preying upon the inhabitants and thereby inciting fresh hostilities.—ED.

[93] Gen. Lewis Cass was appointed by Harrison as civil and military governor of Michigan Territory, and left in charge at Detroit. Lieut.

was delayed to await the mail from York which arrived here day before yesterday, and brought Favorable News.

It appears that we are to have a General peace, so that America will be drawn into it. Bonaparte has lost already 150 thousand men, and according to the address which he made to his ministers in France he admits that he is no longer Capable of Sustaining the War, that he has too much misfortune, and Mr. Madison seeing Bonaparte falter and tremble in his boots has regret for having declared War and has Cut it short as you will see by the Gazettes sent by Mr. Dickson.

I received a letter from Mr. Forrest dated 27 January that gives me this information. There is no Merchandise at Montreal for the Comp^y Mr. Pothier comes up merely to regulate the formal business of the Co. He tells me that a Mr. Crawford sends up a little merchandize that he bought for ready money at Montreal, and which is very badly assorted, and probably that Mr. Rousseau[94] will bring some up, and that he thinks merchandise will sell here at 150 pr Cent.

It seems likewise that troops to the number of 300 men are coming to this post with nine officers, a Major, and one Doctor with 40 Boatloads of provisions.[95] Mr. Crawford was at York to see that all was in order for Spring.

He did not speak of the value of Peltries, it appears however that it is not large, nevertheless, it is to be hoped that they will become more valuable some future day.

Jesse D. Elliott (1785-1845) was second in command of Perry's fleet. He rendered efficient service on the lakes, capturing two British vessels (Oct. 8, 1812) and aiding in the assembling of the Lake Erie fleet. After the victory of 1813 Congress voted him a gold medal, and assigned him to the command of an ocean sloop-of-war.—ED.

[94] Jean Baptiste Rousseau was in the Indian department at St. Josephs as early as 1808. He was probably the father of Jean Baptiste and Charles Rousseau, employees of Hudson's Bay Company, who removed from Drummond Island and settled at Penetanguishene.—ED.

[95] This reinforcement was under the command of Lieut-Col. Robert McDouall. For the orders of Sir George Prevost in relation to this re-inforcement, see *Mich. Pion. and Hist. Colls.*, xxv, pp. 573, 575, 578,

If you have any provisions I advise you as a friend to try and sell them to Mr. Dickson always on the condition that he will take them and that his money is good.

Not having anything more particular to communicate than that I wish you all possible prosperity Believe that I am thy sincere friend and Servt

FRED^k OLIVA

If you come here this spring I shall have a House for you, fanfan[96] and Augustin. Keep well. I expect constantly to obtain the canoe of merchandise that I sent to Montreal for.

Addressed: Lieut. Louis Grignon La Bay.

[Transcript in Burton Library, Detroit. Letter Book of Ramsay Crooks.]

PITTSBURG 17th April 1814

DEAR SIR—On the 10th. and 14th. Instant, I had the pleasure of addressing you, and have now to reply to your favors of the 5th. and 9th. of this month recently come to hand.

It affords me real satisfaction to learn that our industry and enterprise are no longer to be cramped and that goods will next spring be procured for the Indian trade

The memorandum I formerly sent you, I shall reexamine; for as it was submitted under the impression of its being intended only as a temporary supply to be extracted from sources by no means abundant: I think it may be somewhat imperfect, so I shall revise and transmit it in a short time should my alterations be found necessary.

In the event of Peace or the conquest of the upper Country putting us in possession of the trade of Mackinac, we will for at least the first year, be compelled to content ourselves with the boatmen already engaged in the trade and what few can be

---

583. McDouall arrived at Mackinac May 18th, after nineteen days on Lake Huron.—ED.

[96] Fanfan was the nickname for Pierre Antoine Grignon. See *Wis. Hist. Colls.*, vii, p. 242.—ED.

had in the Detroit Strait to carry on the business East of the Mississippi, and on that River above the Prairie du Chien: and for that portion comprising the Saaks, the Winnebagoes of Rock River and the Missouri Tribes, I am almost certain a sufficient number are to be found in and about St. Louis.

Your obtaining a vessel to proceed to Mackinac on the promulgation of the Armistice will be an object of primary importance, for even should the Commanding Officer of that Post, now allow your property to be transported to the United States, it can hardly be supposed he will prevent its being sent to Montreal, and without a vessel specially appointed for the service. I am apprehensive no oppertunity of visiting Michilimackinac will offer, untill the season is so far advanced as to render the completion of your business (in time) very uncertain. Besides if the Vessel is not permitted to return with a Cargo, she will be usefull in conveying from Detroit whatever Furs may be obtained in that quarter.

As you last fall confided to me the transacting of all your private affairs at Mackinac, I am a good deal surprised to find you intend sending out a special agent for that purpose. Believe me had I ever thought the addition of your business could have made the undertaking so very complex and of such magnitude as not to be completely within the powers of even my circumscribed abilities, I would without hesitation or reluctance have declined the proffered honor, but confident as I am of not having undertaken more than I can execute I must feel agrieved in the step you are about to take until I am convinced your concerns are far more extensive and intricated than I apprehended them to be, or that my incompetency is demonstrated beyond all possibility of doubt.

The offer came spontaneously of yourself and I cannot consider it fair, thus to withdraw your confidence in so important a branch of the enterprise without assigning the most cogent reasons for so doing.

If you do send an agent, I suppose he will bring the order for the vessel so it will be best for him to come to Erie, where the requisition must necessarily be presented to the Commadore.

I feel particularly greatful for your permission to draw for the amount I owe Mr. Philipson but shall not avail myself of it unless I am ultametly obliged to visit St. Louis

Without loss of time I shall proceed to the Lake, where, if I find not any immediate conveyance, I will wait a few days in hopes trusting the order for the vessel will there overtake me, and in expectation of hearing from you very soon, I remain Dear Sir Respectfully Your most ob. Servant.

RAMS^y CROOKS

P. S. Continue to address my letters to the Care of Mr. Wilt

[MS. in Library of Congress. McArthur Papers. An order signed by George Prevost.]

All Officers or others commanding or employ'd in His Majestys Troops Vessels or boats or in the Indian Department on the shores or in the Waters of Lake Erie or of Lake Huron are hereby enjoined and directed to allow the Vessel bearing the Flag of Truce and proceeding upon the Voyage and for the account within mention'd and on board of which this passport shall be found to pass free from all molestation and annoyance to Isle du bois blanc in the Vicinity of Michilimackinac in Lake Huron where she is to come to Anchor and be immediately reported to the commanding Officer of that Post she will afterwards receive on board from such place as the said commanding Officer shall appoint the skins and furs within mention'd of which Mr Touissant Pothier the Agent of the within named John Jacob Astor at Michimackinac or the Agent of Messrs McTavish McGilivray and Compy or Forsyth Richardson and Compy at that place shall furnish a correct list under his signature to the said commanding Officer a copy of which list is to be given to the Officer having the charge of said flag of Truce and with which cargo the said flag of Truce is to be permitted to pass unmolested from Lake Huron to Black rock or Buffalo as

1778-1815]   Fur-trade on Upper Lakes

shall be designated by the Passport to be furnished for that purpose by the Officer commanding at Michilimackinac[97]

HEAD QUARTERS MONTREAL 9 June 1814

GEORGE PREVOST[98]
Com^r of the Forces

By his Excellencys Command

NOAH FREER,
Mil'y Secretary.

1814: NORTH WEST COMPANY EQUIP GREEN BAY TRADER

[MS. in Wisconsin Historical Library. Pressmark: Wisconsin MSS., 2B61. Translated from the French.]

SAULT Ste MARIE 14 July 1814

MY DEAR SIR—An opportunity offering for La Baie at the moment of my arrival at Michilim^k. I wrote you a few hasty lines sending you at the same time by Mr. Ducharme the family letters entrusted to me with two small packages

Having finished my business at Michilim^a. I came here to do likewise after which I propose to continue my route to Montreal.

Mr. Barthelot offered me your Peltries which I bought. I

---

[97] In the spring of 1814 Astor went to Washington, where he obtained permission for a private vessel to proceed to Mackinac to bring away the goods of the South West Company that were there stored, which were in part the property of British subjects. He then sent his brother, George Astor, to Montreal, to obtain a permit from the British authorities, of which this document shows the result. After Ramsay Crooks reached Detroit on his return from the unsuccessful voyage to Mackinac with the American fleet, he found that George Astor had arrived with the schooner "Union," on which they proceeded to Mackinac, and brought away the company's furs.—ED.

[98] Sir George Prevost (1767–1816) was the son of a Swiss officer in the British army. He himself early adopted the profession of arms, and won distinction in the West Indies, whereupon he was in 1805 created baronet. As lieutenant-governor of Nova Scotia (1808-11), he served acceptably, and was promoted to the chief command in Canada, in which post he served throughout the war.—ED.

[355]

hope you will believe that I gave you the highest price consistant with the present situation, therefore I am persuaded you will be satisfied therewith.

I believe that the expedition that you have Joined for the Prairie[99] will succeed without the necessity of fighting, it seems to me that the number of Savages ought to be sufficient to Chase the enemy or at least divide them and make them yield.

The determination that you have taken regarding Merchandise was prudent, but at the same time I should like to discuss the outlook for the future with you. The general Peace in Europe will change the entire face of affairs in this Country and from my point of view Commerce will have advantage therefrom for some time.

As soon as there is the least Security against Enemies in this Countrey it is the intention of the Houses of McTavish & Co. & of Forsyth & Co. to unite to Equip at McKinac such persons as deserve their confidence, you may be assured that I shall interest myself upon your behalf.

I believe that you were informed last year that I propose to discontinue Commerce in this Country; although I am still of that purpose I hope that I shall have the satisfaction of news from you, and believe that I am very glad to be of use to you and continue your friendship. I remain with sentiments of sincere attachment Your friend & Servant

T. POTHIER.

Jacques Porlier Esquire

Endorsed by Porlier: Letter of Ts^t Pothier Esq. announcing the 2 Houses of the N West for equipment after the peace 1814.

---

[99] Referring to the expedition headed by Capt. William McKay for the capture of the American fort at Prairie du Chien. Porlier did not go in person, but his son Joseph Jacques was a lieutenant in this campaign. See *Wis. Hist. Colls.*, ix, xi, xii, *passim*.—ED.

1778–1815]   Fur-trade on Upper Lakes

[Source, same as preceding document, but 2A83. Translated from the French.]

Statement of Peltries of Mr. Jac Porlier Sold by the Undersigned to Mons. Pothier

1814 July 4

838	Cats	50	2095
47	Otters	22	1034
77	Mink	50	192.10
5	red foxes	2	10
6	lynx [pichou]	2	12
29	bear cubs	5	145
18	bear skins	24	432
5	"	15	75
1670	muskrats	30	2505
104½	Liv. Beaver	20	2092
29	fishers	6	174
123	martens	4	492
2	lynx [loup cervier]	3	6
1	virgin fox	2	2
74	Deer Skins	5	370
		Livres	9634

66   Little muskrats unsold

BERTHELOT

Endorsed [MS. marred] with a sale of peltries on the back, July 11, 1814.

1814: AMERICAN EXPEDITION ON LAKE HURON

[Source, same as preceding document, but 1C11.]

LAKE HURON 7 Agust 1814

MY DEAR JOHN—I arrived near the Entrance of Lake huron on the fourth of this month on my way to Mackinac where I was in great hopes of meeting with all my friends once more. But found an Express arrived there from the Sault Ste maries warning all the Canoes not to proceed [to Mac] kinac as the expedition of the Americans [MS. torn] communication with the Iland but to proceed to [MS. torn]. I came withe M^r

Lamothe[1] in one of his light Canoes two days march in lake huron to try if we could get further Information but getting none we thought proper to return I Shall wait in the french river 4 or 5 days & then Shall proceed to Machedach & try & dispose of my goods at yorck. I should have made a good profit on them if I had got Safe to Mackinac as I have an excellent asortment a mounting to 1327^{lb} H. Cr. I shall be obliged to make a Sacrifice of them at york but what can I do what greaves me the most is that I am prevented from Seeing you & my other friends Mr Aird & anderson & all those that I have ben so many years living in friendship with in that country. I Shall remain at york till late in the fall in hopes of being able to get in to Mackinac with my old friends if it does not fall and if in case that it unfortunately Should fall in the americans hands I shall be obliged much against my will to go Back to montreall.

This canoe that I am bringing up is in company with Mr P. I. Lacroix[2] but I intended to dispose of his half to Mr Aird & Anderson which would have answered them very well & the other half would have served for the retail at Mackinac or la Bay as you would have thought proper. I had allso made a purchase [MS. torn] that is allready at Mackinac [MS. torn] hands belonging to a M^r [MS. torn] which I Should have made out verry well with & I think I Should have mad Verry handsome profits this year if I could have got in to Mackinac & at the Same time bin of Some Service to my friends. I was not liable for that Canoe loade untill I receaved the goods & have a letter to Mr Askin mention^g the business but as I cannot get in to Mackinac of course I cannot receive the goods. when I met Mr Pothier he told me he had 500 or 700 £ in his hands he did not recollect which & he told me that you or me Could draw on him for that amount but not for more now as you have had the Settlement of all this Business I shall not draw on

---

[1] A distant relative of the person noted in *Id.*, xviii, p. 442; probably Joseph Maurice Lamotte, a well-known Montreal merchant.—ED.

[2] Pierre Ignace Lacroix, of a Montreal family related to the Porliers and Malhiots.—ED.

him for one Farthing but shall leave it all to you. I owe to Mr G. Plot of montreal 260 £ H. Cr. which he was good Enough to lend me to enable me to get this half Canoe of goods & which I never would have bin able to have procured without his generous assistance. Therefore I must beg of you to draw on Mr Pothey in my Favor for that amout so that I may be able to return him his money by the 1^s of October which I Fairly promised him & you will allso draw on Mr Pothey for the remainder of the money that you have deposited in his hands in my Favor [MS. torn] to live in Montreal [MS. torn] John I shall not make any Bad [MS. torn] you may See by my not owing more than 260 £ [MS. torn] half canoe Load I was bringing you I hope you have paid Mr Crofford & dupuy I had not time to Informe myself of Mr Pothey as I onely Saw him but a few minutes in passing If Anderson Insists in getting his money you will draw on Mr Pothey for it Mr Forrest will let you know the amount as it was to him I paid the different moneys for Anderson I beleve it is a little Better than one hundred pounds that is coming to him But Anderson would oblige me much if he would leave it with me for I Shall be in much want if I am obliged to return to Montreal I Should bring him up goods for it next year if we can get to mackinac O I am in a most wretched & deplorable Sittuation at Present in not being able to get to you at Mackinac I will remain at York & machedach till the last Season & if an opportunity Should offer I will certainly Try & get to you. I cannot Bear the Idea of being so long a time from you & my other friends I did not pass a pleasant winter, far from it in montreal. I beg my Dear John you will assist me as much as you possibly can as I shall be in great distress you can [MS. torn] favor of me for your pay that [MS. torn] in want of it yourself. [MS. torn] for you a number of small articles [MS. torn] have pleased you much I got 30 £ for your share of the prise money at Mackinac

Do not fail to write me by the first opportunity to york or Machedash or if an opportunity offer very soon for the French River as I Shall remain there Some time in hopes of getting news from Mackinac & if good news I shall risk all for all & try & get in to Mackinac

Do not forget to send me a draft on Mr Pothey for all the money that you have left in his hands as I have that Debt to pay to Mr Plot which I would not fail of doing on any a/c & I assure you I Shall be much in want for my Self Adeu my Dear John & belive me your Affectionate unckle

J. FRANKS

O how I regret my not being able to get to you after a long Tedious voiage of 31 Day & every day rain exceting 4 Days Remember me kindly to Mr Dickson, Mr Aird & Anderson

---

[Source, same as preceding document, but 2A101.]

MICHILIMACKINAC 22 Augt. 1814.

Messrs. *Aird & Lawe Bought of Jacob Franks.*

One Canoe-load of merchandize marked F. L. now in La Rondes Bay—they incurring all Risks of damage, charges &c. in bringing them here—reserving the canoe 1 kettle, 1 Sail, 1 axe, 1 oil cloth and one Towing Line for £1500.

H. Curr^y £1500.

N. B. Should the Property fall into the hands of the Americans before its arrival at this place, then Messrs. Aird & Lawe are only to pay the original amount of the Montreal Invoice of these Goods.

J. FRANKS.

Received Michilimackinac 5th Oct of Messrs Aird & Lawe the above amount in full

J. FRANKS.

Endorsed: Aird & Lawe £1500 Makana 22^d Augt. 1814.

[Transcript in Burton Library, Detroit. Letter Book of Ramsay Crooks.]

DETROIT 21st. Augt. 1814.

DEAR SIR—Having but a few moments notice to repair on board, on the 3rd. of July, I was constrained barely to advise you of my drawing on you that day for Two Hundred Dollars in favor of Mr. Ten Eyck, at ten days sight which by the annexed statement of my finances, you will perceive was an act of absolute necessity.

On entering Lake Huron we shaped our course for Machedash, but this part of the navigation being imperfectly known, the Commodore was after sometime spent in fruitless search of the Bay induced to steer for St. Josephs, there the Schooner Mink, belonging to the North West Company laden with Two Hundred and thirty Barrels of Flour for St. Mary's was captured and the Fort and Store Houses redused to ashes.

A Company of Regulars and some Sailors were next dispatched to St. Mary's where the company's Store houses were burned. there fine Schooner Perservance destroyed and a quantity of dry goods sugar and spirits said to belong to a Mr. Johnson[3] taken and brought to the fleet.

---

[3] The raid against Sault Ste. Marie was headed by Maj. Arthur H. Holmes, who fell at the attack on Mackinac a few days later. The attack on the North West Company was in retaliation for the activity of its agents in arming and conducting its voyageurs against the American posts, and in inciting the Indians against the frontiers.

John Johnston was born in 1763 at Craignear, Giant's Causeway, Ireland. Coming to America in 1792 he at once entered the fur-trade, and was stationed at La Pointe du Chequamegon, where he took to wife the daughter of a prominent Chippewa chief. In 1794 Johnston established himself at Sault Ste. Marie on the southwest (American) side. There he had a large domestic establishment, a fine library for those days, and such of the products of civilization as might be obtained in that then far frontier post. His children were interesting and well-educated; one of the daughters married Henry Rowe Schoolcraft, another an English clergyman. Johnston had held an American commission as justice of the peace, and collector of the port. In the War of 1812-15, however, he sympathized with the British and was regarded by the Americans as a renegade. One son was in the British fleet, being wounded in the battle of Lake Erie. Johnston himself had gone at the head of a party of his own employes, to the number of 100, to the defense of Mackinac. In his absence his property was burned and his goods confiscated. After this raid he rebuilt his dwelling, and lived there until his death in 1828. He hospitably re-

Off Mackinac we lay a considerable time and only saw a few Indians to skirmish with occasionaly, till in the afternoon of the 4th Instant the troops were landed on the west side of the Island, and at some distance from the beach, were vigoriously attacked by Indians[4] and others in ambush, aided by four pieces of artillery planted on elevated spots—a charge made the enemy fall back, but he soon returned to the work of death which lasted until a number fell, when owing to the total impractability of penetrating to the Fort through the woods and finding every position of any strength on the road in possession of the British it was judged most advisable to return to the Vessels, which was effected without opposition, and all the well and wounded were re-embarked before sunset.

Understanding early on the 6th. that we were about to weigh anchor, and supposing thereby the expedition abandoned, I waited on the Commodore requesting permission to go ashore and ascertain whether the commandant of Mackinac would allow your property to be brought away, but was answered that from information obtained the day previous there was no doubt he would but as the future movements of the forces were not determined on, it was thought improper to suffer any communication with the Island. We soon after sailed again to St. Joseph's, anchored one night, and then came down to an Island about one hundred miles from Mackinac;[5] where Commodore Sinclair[6] delivered me a letter from Mr. Forrest agent for the

---

ceived General Cass and his party in 1820, and the vigilance of Mrs. Johnston averted a hostile attack upon them by the Indians.—ED.

[4] Tomah (for whom see *ante.* p. 346, note 88) was on this occasion the leader of the Indians.—ED.

[5] One of the objects of the expedition, aside from the attempt to recover Mackinac, was to secure the furs of the North West Company's flotilla, then coming from Fort William on Lake Superior. In this, likewise, the expedition was a failure, for the flotilla, worth over $1,000,000, managed to elude the Americans and enter French River in safety. See "Franchère's Narrative," in Thwaites, *Early Western Travels*, vi, pp. 393-397.—ED.

[6] Capt. Arthur Sinclair, of the United States navy, entered as a mid-

BRITISH LANDING, MACKINAC ISLAND

From photograph, 1910

Fur-trade on Upper Lakes

late South West Company (a copy of which is subjoined) telling me at same time that as the object of the enterprise could not be attained with the force on board, I was at liberty to visit Mackinac; and the Captain Dexter[7] who was going to Erie with the Lawrence, Caledonia, and Mink would grant the necessary passports at Detroit.

Here I arrived four days ago, and am happy to inform you that Mr. George Astor[8] entered the river yesterday with a vessel of about 90 tons, he chartered at Grand River 70 miles above Erie. I have not yet seen him, neither has he wrote me, but he certainly must be up the first fair wind.

I have your favor of 2nd. July from Washington and observe what you say of Racoons and Muskrat.

The season is now pretty far advanced, but with moderate luck we can get back from Mackinac before the weather becomes boisterous—to ensure which, you may rest satisfied not a moment will be lost.

For the Vessel I should suppose he has the necessary papers from the Naval Commandant on Lake Erie, but to make all sure in the event of his not arriving before Captain Dexter

---

shipman in 1798. In 1807 he was commissioned lieutenant, and in 1812 master commandant. On the outbreak of war he was in command of the "Argus." After Perry's retirement he was given command of the fleet on the upper lakes, and took charge of the unsuccessful expedition to Mackinac. In 1815 he was in command of the "Congress," and served actively until his death in 1831.—ED.

[7] Daniel S. Dexter was appointed midshipman in the United States navy in 1800, lieutenant in 1807, and commander in 1814. He died in 1818.—ED.

[8] George Peter Astor, the eldest brother of John Jacob Astor, was born in 1752 at Waldorf, Germany. Early in life he went to London, and became partner in the firm of Broadwood & Company, piano makers. He came to America during the War of 1812–15, and had a store on Water Street, New York, where he was engaged in the fur-trade. He died in 1832. His name appears in the New York directories from 1816–32; and several real estate transfers are entered in his name. For this information the Editor is indebted to Mr. Wilberforce Eames of the Lenox branch, New York Public Library.—ED.

leaves this, I will go down till I meet him. I am Dear Sir Your most ob Servant

RAMS^y CROOKS

John Jacob Astor Esq. New York

1814: BRITISH CONTROL MACKINAC

[MS. in Wisconsin Historical Library. Pressmark: Wisconsin MSS., 60B46.]

By Robert McDouall Esqr Lieutenant Colonel of His Majestys Glengarry Light Infantry and Commandant of the Post of Michilimackinac and Dependencies, &c.[9]

Permission is hereby granted to Louis Beaupré[10] to depart from hence and winter at Green Bay and Dependencies with a Barge containing the Packages as specified on the other side and navigated by one Man they behaving as becometh

Given under my Hand and Seal at the Post of Michilimackinac October 19th. 1814

RT McDOUALL Lt. Col.
Commanding

[Seal]

Endorsed: Loading of the Barge: 3 Barrels Sugar 7 Bales Merchandize, 2 Kegs Powder 4 Ditto Rum 3 Ditto Merchandize, 4 Bags Shot & Ball 3 Casettes Merchandize And the necessary Provisions &c.

---

[9] For a brief sketch of Lieut.-Col. Robert McDouall of the British army (1796–1848), see *Wis. Hist. Colls.*, ix, p. 193.—ED.

[10] Louis Beaupré was a well-known Green Bay fur-trader and *habitant*. He is said to have been in the West as early as 1797, when he wintered with John Lawe near Fond du Lac. In 1798, Beaupré began a farm on the east side of Fox River, that which was in later years known as "private claim No. 13;" see *Amer. State Papers, Public Lands*, iv, pp. 703, 858. In 1810–11 he ...tered on Lemonweir River, and in January of 1814 was with Dickson at Lake Winnebago. He is said to have assisted in 1814 at the defense of Mackinac. A person of his name (possibly his son) was employed in 1831 at the shot-tower at Helena. The elder Beaupré is mentioned as a householder at Green Bay in the census of 1836, and died there in the summer of 1838.—ED.

1778-1815]   Fur-trade on Upper Lakes

[Source, same as preceding document, but 1C16.]

[MONTREAL, winter of 1814–15][11]

Col. McDouall is appointed Superintendent of all the Indians to the westward & William McKay[12] is appointed Superintendant for Michilimackinac Mr Dickson will I believe be confined to the Mississipy as Superintendant to the Indians their   William McKay is I believe disposed to Serve me as much as lies in his power he has lent me 300£ Yk C. [York currency] through the hands of a nother person but do not mention this as he does not wish it to be nown.   You cannot conceive the high price of Goods in montreal & I consider my Self verry happy & Succesfull in procuring the assortment I have got through the means of my friends here—goods will be verry

---

[11] This document is undated; but its contents show that it must have been written during the winter of 1814–15, probably late in the season.—ED.

[12] William McKay was one of three brothers who entered the North West Company, and traded in the upper country. His brother Alexander was killed on the "Tonquin" near Astoria. Donald was known as "Mad McKay," because of his impetuous temper. William began trading in Wisconsin in 1793, on Menominee River; the following winter he passed at Green Bay, and then entered the far Northwest, wintering 1794–95 at Portage la Prairie. He was at the Grand Portage rendezvous in 1797 and 1798, and the next year was stationed on Lake Winnepeg. In 1804 he was a wintering partner of the North West Company. When the War of 1812–15 broke out, he joined the volunteers, and in 1813 was made major of the Michigan Fencibles. In 1814 he was selected to command the expedition to capture the American fort at Prairie du Chien—see *Wis. Hist. Colls.*, ix, xi, xii, index. His regiment was disbanded at Mackinac in the summer of 1815, he receiving the appointment of Indian superintendent, first at Mackinac, later at Drummond Island. Thereafter McKay made his home at Montreal, coming up for the autumn months to transact business with the Indians. He married in Montreal a daughter of Judge Davidson, and his son Robert became a judge. William McKay continued his official duties until the removal of the post from Drummond Island in 1828. He died in 1832 of cholera, at Montreal. He was a tall, strong man, severe with his inferiors and the Indians, but possessed of ability and integrity.—ED.

[365]

high at Mackinac as they cost so very high here but they will not be so Scarce as last year as Michell la Croix[13] is going up with 6 Canoe loads Mr Roch Blave[14] with 8 & Bailley[15] with 2 Boat loads by the way I am going Mr Derivier is sending Mr Barthelotte his goods by the grand River I hope I shall be

---

[13] Michel Lacroix was a Canadian of good education, who early in the nineteenth century, settled at Peoria. There he built a good house, and took for his wife Catharine Dubuque, a cousin of the famous Julien. In 1812, Lacroix went to Canada with a convoy of furs. During his absence war began, and in the raid of Captain Craig his house at Peoria was burned, and his family carried off to Cahokia. He thereupon joined the British army, and served as an officer. At the close of the war he returned with goods for trading, found his family, and settled with them at Cahokia. After Lacroix's death in 1821, his widow married Gov. John Reynolds of Illinois.—ED.

[14] Pierre Rastel, sieur de Rocheblave, was a son of Philippe François, British governor of Illinois, who was captured in 1778 by George Rogers Clark. In *Wis. Hist. Colls.*, xviii, p. 214, note 70, it is stated that Pierre and Noël (noted *Ibid.*, p. 462, note 84) were nephews of the elder Rocheblave. Recent information from family descendants proves that they were in truth his sons, of whom the elder—Noël, once partner of Jacques Porlier—died in Montreal in 1805. Pierre entered the fur-trade before the close of the eighteenth century, and was by 1801 a partner of the X Y Company, and in 1803 wintered in the Athabasca region. In 1804 he signed the agreement, by attorney, for the union of the two companies. Upon the re-assignment in 1805, Rocheblave took charge of the Assiniboine district, where he was met by Alexander Henry the younger. Rocheblave was prominent in the reorganized company, and from 1812–14 officered a voyageur company raised to protect the North West Company's property. In 1816 he retired from active wintering and acted as managing agent of the company, each summer going up to Fort William. He was active in opposition to Lord Selkirk and in 1817 secured the arrest of the latter. Feb. 9, 1819, Rocheblave married at Montreal Elmire Bouthillier. After the union of his company with the Hudson's Bay (1821), he devoted himself to public service, as member of the legislature and council, and as local magistrate. He died at Montreal in 1840. One of his daughters was living in 1908. See also his letters, *post*.—ED.

[15] For a reference to Joseph Bailly, see *ante*, p. 110, note 49. When the American expedition visited Drummond Island in 1814, Bailly was one of three who were captured. He was taken to Detroit, and afterwards exchanged.—ED.

able to dispose of a great part of my goods at Mackinac to enable me to fulfill my Engagements here, I mean afther you & Aird has got your full Supplies I am pretty Confident their will be a great deal of goods wanted at Mack.

Their is no appearance of peace with the Americans as yet it appears that G[en.] Proctor intends to carry on the Ware Vigourously we are Building a 40 Gun Frigate in lake huron Say Machadach Bay. Their is Every appearance of our present governor Sr George Provost being recalled & a new governor appointed for the Canadas it is Said that the people in england are verry much displeased with his conduct at Platsburgh & cry out much against it Their is an immense number of Troupes to be Sent out here earely in the Spring which will assist in making [up] all the loss of all the Merchants in Montreal I hope a few will benefit by it in our poor Quarter of the world. you must reserve as much provisions as will be necessary for the men to come with the Boats as fare as holland River & as much As will Support you at Mackinac untill I arrive you can get Beauprey & Chaque[16] to accompany Mr Aird to meet me at holland River[17]

---

[16] Stanislaus Chappu was known to have been a clerk, before 1800, at the Milwaukee post, where he seems to have remained until about 1805. By 1813 he was a clerk for John Lawe; and being at Mackinac in 1814, assisted in its defense. He likewise was at this post in 1816, when he acted as pilot to the American troops coming to build a fort at Green Bay. He remained in Lawe's employ for many years. In later life, his post was on the Menominee River, where he took up a farm, dying thereon about 1854. He was a typical trader, and in the documents given *post* much will be found of his activity.—ED.

[17] Franks was planning to come up via the Toronto portage, which was much used during the War of 1812-15. In 1793 Sir John Simcoe, governor of Upper Canada, made an excursion from Toronto (then Little York) northward along the route that he had laid out in subsequent years (1794-96). This road, thirty miles in length, was known as Yonge Street; its northern terminus was on Holland River, an affluent of Lake Simcoe. Holland River was explored in 1791 by Maj. S. Holland, surveyor-general of Upper Canada, and to it was given his name, upon a large manuscript map now in the crown land office of Ontario. There were two landings, a mile and a half apart—

My Sister Becky is at York   I saw her last fall as I passed their.   Mr Kemble is paymaster to the Incorporated Melissia of upper Canada.   Try and make as much peltries as possible they will be of value   I wish you could get parish griginon[18] to Buy his assortment from me next Summer as he will have a good deal of peltries as well as money & I Shall have a good deal more goods than you & James will want   Make a long a/c with goverment & Supply them with all they may want in your Quarter & I hope James Aird will have a long a/c against goverment allso.   I think it would be well to retain powell[19] in your employ next year but you are the best Judge of that   do as you think proper

I think it would be well for James to try & get Some one to winter in the yancton country as I Suppose Anderson will continue in goverment employ & an Equiptment with the Yanktons will answer well on account of the Beaver & Buffalo Robes. I am much affraid that Goverment will Take all the provisions belonging to Individuals a bout york as the person I contracted with made that reserve that if goverment Seized the provisions he would not be obliged to deliver them to me & of course I would [MS. torn] pay for them   on my Arrivall here I went

---

the upper being for canoes and vessels of light draft, the lower for larger craft. The government erected warehouses at this point, to be used in the transport to the naval station at Penetanguishene. At present there is a small village here, known as Holland Landing.—ED.

[18] Perische Grignon was a son of Pierre the elder, by a Winnebago mother. He was brought up with the Grignon family, and during the War of 1812–15 acted as interpreter, accompanying the Indian contingent that went to the siege of Fort Meigs. He had a homestead on the west side of Fox River, which in 1823 was confirmed to him by the federal land commissioners. Later he removed to the Fox-Wisconsin portage, where he married a daughter of a Winnebago chief. He was living at the portage as late as 1836.—ED.

[19] Peter Powell was a well-known Wisconsin trader, who was a lieutenant in McKay's expedition against Prairie du Chien (1814), and was commended for courage and activity. He seems to have settled near Butte des Morts, whence in 1832 a letter (Wisconsin MSS., 3C132) was written by him to friends in Green Bay. He died in the latter part of the year 1837.—ED.

to M^rs McDougalls to Board but all the Beds were taken up & it was a difficult matter to find lodgings in montreal I am Boarding with the Miss Levys where I am very well off. I have Settled with La Croix but he made Some fus & Noise here about my Selling the goods to you & James & threatened to prosecute me about it but all is Settled Amicably now. I have rented a room in Mr Platts Store to place my goods in & am verry offten at a loss[20]

[JACOB FRANKS]

1815: EFFECT OF PEACE

[Transcript in Burton Library, Detroit. Letter Book of Ramsay Crooks.]

NEW YORK 14. Feb. 1815

DEAR SIR—You will have heard of the word of Peace this will not lessen the value of the Muskrat Skins. At sametime I wish that you could sell them all, and come on here, as I shall probably engage in the Indian Trade.

I expect some goods in about two months, when you come, I hope you will bring M [1000] pounds of the Muskrat skins with you.

Ginseng ought to be here by first of May Value same as before, I expect now all the Bank Notes will be in value much the same so that you may take Philadelphia or Baltimore notes which I hope will facilitate the sales I am truly yours,

JOHN JACOB ASTOR

[Source, same as preceding document.]

BROOKLYN 21st. March 1815

DEAR CROOKS—Long ere now you must have chalked me down in your *Black Buke* for a most ungrateful, lazy dog, but my dear fellow you must no longer remain under that surly impression, for be it known unto you, that almost ever since you last heard from me I have been *Campaigning* it between this and the *Canadian lines,* partly for myself and particularly

---

[20] The manuscript here ends abruptly, a portion being lost. It is in Franks's handwriting.—ED.

for an old *friend* of *ours;* the result of this peregrination &c. you shall have at full length when we meet, which I hope you will accelerate as much as circumstances may permit. I am now in the full bustle of preparation for Albany, where business calls me for a few days, therefore have only time to give you the purport of a short tete-a-tete I had with the old Cock this morning, Viz—

That he is digesting a very extensive plan for establishing all the Indian Countries within the line of demarkation between G. B. & the U. S. and the probability is that a considerable time may elapse before that object can be brought to full maturity, as he wants an exclusive grant or privelege &c. &c. he added that it would be a pity, we should in the meantime be altogether inactive, therefore as he expects a parcel of Indian goods out in the Spring it is his wish that (*Lob Man*) you and myself would come to some arrangement either to purchase the goods and try the S. W. on our own Acct, or take them to Mackinac and give him a certain share of the profits, (as might be agreed upon)

These are the general outlines, from which you can very easily draw your conclusions regarding his views, which I really believe are as friendly toward us all, as his own dear interest will permit, for of that you are no doubt aware, he will never loose sight *until some kind friend will put his or her fingers over his eyelids.*

If something like this plan would meet your ideas, it will give me much pleasure for on your judgement I can entirely rely, knowing you are perfectly conversant in every branch of that business, and there is no mortal living, I would prefer being concerned with, of this I have no doubt you are perfectly convinced. On your arrival at New York have the goodness to come to Brooklyn before you wait on the old man as I would *much like* to have the first *confab* with you. Fat McKenzie[21] is here for the third time since his arrival in the

---

[21] No doubt a reference to Donald McKenzie, who was a distant relative of Sir Alexander McKenzie, and brother of Roderick. He had

Fur-trade on Upper Lakes

white man's country, he pesters the old Tyger's soul out to employ him again, but he dislikes him very much, sometimes says that if he enters into the business upon the meditated large scale that he should like to give him a situation in some retired corner where he could do no mischief &c. &c.

I am glad that he did not propose him as one of our party as I think it would break up the concern. Keep these affairs to yourself and hasten to meet your sincere friend

ROBERT STUART[22]

All the good folks of this family desire me to rem. them very kindly to you—I no sooner told the old Lady that I expected you soon, that she began to *scour her little pot, and called for the supper to be got ready* for her *poor Scotchman*. I really think the old lady has some design upon you; and whether you are to become my father, brother or son-in-law, you will always find me yours truly

R. S.

N. B. Betsy is so glad at the near prospect of your coming amongst us, that if I did not depend much on my own *qualifi-*

---

been a clerk in the North West Company, and in 1809 joined the Astoria enterprise, proceeding overland from St. Louis to the Columbia. He returned in 1814, and later re-entered the North West Company. After the coalition of that concern with the Hudson's Bay Company, he served the latter corporation several years, acting as governor for the Red River colony. Retiring in 1833, he settled at Mayville, N. Y., where he died in 1851.—ED.

[22] The career of Robert Stuart was remarkable for adventure and vicissitude. Born in Scotland in 1784, he was educated at Paris. In 1806 he came to Montreal, where his uncle, David Stuart, was engaged in the fur-trade. Both uncle and nephew entered Astor's Pacific Fur Company, and in 1810 sailed for the Columbia in the "Tonquin." On that famous voyage he showed the resolution and resource that afterwards characterized his career. In July, 1812, Stuart was placed in charge of the overland party, of which Ramsay Crooks was a member; after severe hardships, it reached St. Louis the following April. After reaching New York, Stuart married, and the next year began operations in behalf of Astor, being in 1819 stationed as manager at Mackinac. There, Stuart was one of the chief personages of the island, and after 1829 was a member of the mission church. About

cations I assure you, it staggers my faith not a little. Magee desires his best wishes to you, but is too devilish lazy to write, but promises to make up for it in *chat* when you meet.

Addressed: Ramsy Crooks Esq. care of Messrs Brown McDonell & Co. Pittsburg Pennsylvania

Endorsed: Brooklin 21st. March 1815 Robert Stuart Recieved 17 April 1815 Answered 24 April Ditto Rec'd 17th, answered in part same day Do in full 24th. April

---

1815: LAST DAYS OF THE NORTH WESTERNERS

[MS. in Burton Library, Detroit, vol. 457, p. 1.]

MONTREAL 9th May 1815

MY DEAR OLD FRIEND—It is three days since I had the pleasure of receiving yours of the 21 February, where could it have been so long on the road—I think before this we should have a regular post to your place, but you have been so long separated from us that your place is forgoten, however we are blessed with another peace, which I hope may continue, as long as I live, but we live in a time that such wonderfull things happen, that we cannot say what may come to pass. Boneparts return to France, will cause another General War in Europe, which I am afraid will extend to America, as they do not approve of the peace, I received a letter a few day ago from our old friend Todd, he was then at Bath taking the Mineral Waters, and says if his leg gets better he will return to this Country, as he has no friends in any other,—I expect he will come by New York. It is not only him whom old age deprives of friends. I must say that I experience every day the want of Old acquaintance. they are all Dead. there is only one alive in Montreal that was here when I came. I know but very few—what do you think of our Beaver Club which commenced in 1786 and consisted of 16 members—and I the

---

1833 he retired from active business, making his later home in Detroit, where he served as state treasurer (1840–41) and federal Indian agent (1841–45). He died in 1848, while visiting Chicago.—ED.

Fur-trade on Upper Lakes

only one alive.[23] our late Friend McGill was the last, and a great loss he was to Montreal, he allways continued friendly to the last. and was much regreted, I was happy to hear he was so friendly to you, his sudden Death deprived him of doing more good to those who wanted it,[24] several who he mentioned to me shortly before his death—for he had no Idea of going off half an hour before he died. Mrs. McGill is left comfortable, but young Deriviere will it is said have £60,000. My dear friend are me never to meet in this world I think it would do you much good to Come down. Could I be spared from business I would go on purpose, to say we Meet once more, old Age should not prevent me having that pleasure, but necessity at my time of life obliges me to be attentive in procuring Necessarys. Mrs. Henry & my Daughter Julia has enjoyed uncommon Health, I have only one Daughter & one son living one was kiled in the North West[25] the other died in the West Indeas, being a Mid-

---

[23] It has usually been supposed that the famous Beaver Club of Montreal was founded in 1785, and flourished until 1824—see Masson, *Bourgeois*, i, pp. 92-94—but Henry would appear to know. Probably he means that he is the last of the original members. The regimen and entertainments of the Beaver Club rendered it famous. No one could be admitted until he had served apprenticeship in the upper county. The motto of the club was "Fortitude in Distress," and this was engraved on gold medals, some of which are still existing. The meeting place was known as Beaver Hall, and during the winter fortnightly meetings were held. Here the difficulties and dangers of a fur-trader's life were recounted, the recital being the more graphic by contrast of wilderness conditions with the luxurious surroundings of the club house.—ED.

[24] The best-known of McGill's benefactions was the bequest which he made for an educational foundation. This consisted of £10,000 in money, and a valuable suburban estate. This institution had been planned some time before his death, and according to the terms of the will was to be established within ten years after his decease. Accordingly a charter was granted in 1821, but actual teaching was not begun until some years later. In 1852, McGill University of Montreal was reorganized, and is at present the most prosperous educational institution in Canada. Founder's Day is still celebrated each year at the university.—ED.

[25] Alexander Henry, second son of the writer, was murdered by a

shipman in the Navey we are subject to many misfortunes in the World—but our hope is that we will be more happy in the next. the great Ruler of the World orders all for the Best. we must depend on him and hope for our support in this life, and hope for his protection in the Next, where you & I may meet in those regions of Happiness in the Next. that period must soon come. it gives me great pleasure to hear you and Mrs Askin enjoy Health and that you have Escaped the ravages of War poor Mrs McKee[26] suffered much while she was here with her unfortunate Husband. he had no command over himself. continually deranged with Liquor, if he had lived, Goverment could have no relyance on him. I wish she was with you. I sent by Mr McIntosh a Keg with some Tea Coffee & Sugar for you, and have never heard from him what he has done with it, I wish you would enquire of him as I supose he sold it not suposing while the war continued to be able to convey it to you   as the communication is now open I hope to hear from you frequently. with the most sincere wishes & prayers of me & Mine for you Mrs Askin & all yours—remain ever My dear Askin your old friend

ALEXANDER HENRY

N B   enclose a News paper with all the News.

John Askin Esquire Sandwich

---

party of natives while at Fort Nelson, on the Liard River, in the Athabasca district. The son still living was William, for whom see *Wis. Hist. Colls.*, xviii, p. 505, note 41.—E<small>D</small>.

[26] For this person see *ante*, p. 272, note 89.—E<small>D</small>.

ARTICLES USED BY WISCONSIN FUR-TRADERS
Selected from specimens in Museum of Wisconsin Historical Society

The Fur-Trade in Wisconsin
1815-1817

1815: AMERICAN MESSAGE TO MENOMINEE

[MS. in Wisconsin Historical Library. Pressmark: Wisconsin MSS., 3B33. Translated from the French.]

LA BAY VERTE 17 June 1815

Monsieur Louis Grignon

MY DEAR LOUIS—I write this line to inform you of the small returns in Peltry that are being sent you, But hope that they will Sell well. There are only 680 rats & 12 bears 18 cats 2 Martens 3 skunks 19 American martens, 3 otters 2^{lvs} beaver 12 deerskins 5 bear cubs 4 not very good obliged to make them cheap. They were 21 days in transit so you will see that no further Returns may be expected. I transfer to Pollitte[27] your half except one of the 2^{lvs} of beaver and 1 otter, 1 bearcub skin and 1 deer skin which remain with me to give you your half.

---

[27] This was the brother of Pierre and Louis Grignon. His baptismal name was Hippolyte, but he was usually called "Pollitte" or "Paul." Being born at Green Bay Sept. 14, 1790, he was next to the youngest son. He was in the fur-trade with his brothers, and about 1818 wintered at Milwaukee. After the death of his eldest brother Pierre (1823), he was administrator for the estate. In 1825 he entered into a trading partnership with his younger brother Amable, which continued for some years. He finally settled in the neighborhood of Appleton. His first wife was a Menominee woman, by whom he had several daughters. Afterward he married Lizette Chorette, for whose father see *ante*, p. 170, note 33; Simon and Joseph Grignon of Appleton were their sons, and Mrs. James Knaggs and Josette de Crenier of Oshkosh, their daughters. Paul Grignon was at Portage in 1836, when Pauquette was killed; see *Wis. Hist. Colls.*, vii, p. 385.—ED.

Inclosed are three notes that I request you will hand to Monsieur Bertelotte to get from him money if he can furnish it. There is nothing going on here, Pollitte is in charge as usual. I send the Peltries for Gravelle,[28] and note that there are 3 Martens, 1 skunk, 1 Deerskin, 68 Rats. His Pay about equals the expense A message from the Americans W. Clak [Clark] & A. Chouteau[29] having Come addressed to the Chief and Warriors of the Folle Avoines I have sent it to you by Monsieur Porlier, he will give you an idea of it I am with Esteem & consideration Your Brother & friend

P. GRIGNON.

Try and make tomas do his duty they say he wishes to give a favorable reply to the Americans Tell him to take care.

1815: WISCONSIN POSTS RECOMMENDED

[MS. in Pension Building, Washington. Pressmark: Indian Office, Book 204. Letter Book 1, p. 101; Lewis Cass to Secretary of War.]

DETROIT June 20th. 1815.

SIR—I had intended by this time to have submitted to you a general view of the state of Indian affairs in this Country and of the measures necessary to be adopted, to secure permanent tranquility upon the frontiers.

But so much of my time is engaged by applications and visits from the Indians that I find it impracticable to effect this object immediately. I am only able to submit to you the accompanying propositions, which are the result of my enquiries and which if adopted will I trust cause a salutary reform in the state of our Indian relations.

The privilege which British traders have heretofore enjoyed

---

[28] Louis Gravelle was an early Canadian-French settler and voyageur of Green Bay. He had a farm on the west side of Fox River, which was confirmed to him by the land commissioners, and there he was living as late as 1832.—ED.

[29] For a sketch of Auguste Chouteau, see *Wis. Hist. Colls.*, xviii, p. 412, note 18.—ED.

of carrying on a lucrative commerce with the Indians is a subject, which will doubtless engage the attention of the Govt., To this source may be traced most of the difficulties we have experienced in our intercourse with them, I have every reason to believe that the Indian Department opposite to us are about to adopt the same systematick course of measures, which they have so long and so successfully pursued but with renewed activity and increased exertion. A deputation of one influential Chief from each of the different tribes left Malden shortly since for the lower province and another follows in a few days. What their precise object is we have not yet been able to ascertain, but such enquiries are making as will soon disclose it to us, There is little doubt however of its relating to a general, systematick and vigorous organization of their Indian Department. In the mean time a large quantity of goods have arrived at Malden to be distributed as presents and the Agents and subordinate officers are more numerous than at any former period, These unerring indications give us timely warning that the same measures are to be adopted, the same lying system continued (pardon the epithet, could all the facts be presented to you, you would say no milder term could be used) and the same plan of filling our Indian Country with the agents and Interpreters and traders which have at all former periods kept the North Western frontiers in a state of feverish alarm.

I am aware that the Government are compelled to view the whole ground and it may become necessary to grant to the British the privileges heretofore held among the Indians in order to secure to our Country commercial rights more important to the nation at large. It is with a view to such a possible event, that I submit these propositions to you. Their adoption will be found to counteract in a very considerable degree causes which have heretofore operated without any check.

Should it be found necessary in a treaty of commerce to make such a stipulation, the evil would be diminished by allowing to British subjects this privilege under the same restrictions it is granted to American Citizens. This will secure to us the right of recalling them, when we find their machinations injurious or when their obvious purpose of trading is to cover a p[olicy] for scattering disaffection among the Indians.

There are three great channels of communication, by which traders may introduce the goods into the Mississippi and Mississouri Country from the British dominions, One is by the way of Chicago, and down the Illinois. Another by the way of Green Bay up the Fox River and down the Ouisconsin. This has been the great thoroughfare along which goods have been taken. Immense quantities have been smuggled to the Mississippi and it is calculated that not more than one third part of those sold in the Indian Country, every [year] pay duties. The establishment of a post at Green Bay and at Prairie du Chien will close this line of communication. Another at Chicago will effect the same object upon the Illenois. There will then remain a route to be taken, which has heretofore been little used. It is up a small river which enters lake Superior near the Grand Portage and along a number of small lakes with portages to heads of the Mississippi. I am informed by intelligent men that this is the only route, after closing those by Chicago and Green Bay which is practicable.

If the British traders are eventually to be excluded, a post near the Grand Portage will be necessary to effect this object. Should other considerations render their admission proper the post would still be necessary to ensure a collection of the duties and to enforce the regulations proper to be adopted. A display of the power of the United States in that remote quarter would be productive of salutary effects upon the minds of the Indians. Should it be deemed proper to establish a post in that Country the previous arrangements should be made this fall, in order that we may be ready to proceed at the opening of the navigation.

I am inclined to believe if these posts are all established and proper regulations adopted at the various agencies, that British traders may be admitted without very serious inconvenience. Certain I am that their admission will not be attended with the same evils, which have heretofore been Experienced.

Mr. Jouett the Agent for Green Bay has arrived here, he has

LEWIS CASS
From oil portrait, in possession of Wisconsin Historical Society, copied by Lewis T. Ives from original (Detroit, 1839) by George A. P. Healy

been long acquainted with Mr. Kinzie[30] whom I recommended to you for the appointment of Agent at Chicago, I have requested Mr. Jouett to address you upon the subject. Very Respectfully Sir I have the honor to [be] Yrs. etc. etc.

[LEWIS CASS][31]

Hon. A. J. Dallas Actg. Secty. of War.

---

[30] John Kinzie was the son of John McKenzie, a British surgeon of the Royal American regiment. Kinzie was born at Quebec, Dec. 3, 1763, and in early life removed with his mother and stepfather, William Forsyth, to New York City. At the age of ten, John ran away from home, and finding his way to Quebec learned the trade of silversmith. His family having removed to Detroit, he began at the age of eighteen the career of a fur-trader, and was known to the Indians as Shawneeawkee, or "Silver Man." During his fur-trading adventures in Ohio and Indiana, he met Margaret McKenzie, an American captive, whom he married in Indian fashion. After her return to Virginia at the close of the Indian wars (1795), Kinzie married (1798) at Detroit, Eleanor Lytle, widow of a British officer, Capt. Daniel McKillip. In 1803, Kinzie removed his family to Chicago, where Fort Dearborn was about to be built, and this place became his future home, his house being just west of the river's mouth, on the north bank. In 1812 the Kinzie family were saved from the general massacre by the friendship of the Indians, taken to Detroit, and surrendered as prisoners of war. In January, 1813, Kinzie was paroled by General Proctor. In August of the same year, he was arrested for treasonable correspondence with the Americans, and carried captive to Quebec, where he was finally released as being a United States citizen. In 1816 he returned to Chicago, where he resided until his death in 1828. For a more extended notice, see Eleanor Lytle Kinzie Gordon, *John Kinzie* (Savannah, Ga., 1910).—ED.

[31] Lewis Cass (1782–1866) was an important agent in the development of Michigan and Wisconsin territories. After an active part in the War of 1812–15, he was in 1813 appointed governor for the territory, an office which he filled until 1831, when he was called to the presidential cabinet. During his governorship he was superintendent of Indian affairs for the Northwest region. The agents of Mackinac, Green Bay, and Chicago reported to him; while those of the Mississippi region were under the charge of Gen. William Clark.—ED.

1815: UNITED STATES FACTORIES IN WISCONSIN

[Source, same as preceding document, but Indian Office Letter Book "C," p. 223.]

The Acting Secretary of War has the honor to represent to the President of the United States—

That the menaces of the Indians throughout the Indian countries, require immediate attention; and among the means which are proper for restoring harmony, preserving peace, and defeating the arts employed by intrusive traders to generate Indian hostilities, it is recommended that there be immediately established an Indian agency on the Fox river, in the neighborhood of Green bay, upon the following principles:—

1. That the agent shall make a competent establishment upon a site to be selected by him, and approved by the major general commanding the division of the north, at which an armoury proper for the accommodation of the Indians, shall be maintained under the charge of the agent.

2. That the establishment, so formed, shall be a military station, to be occupied by two companies of the troops of the United States, or such other force as the commanding general shall deem competent for its defence and support.

3. That a factory shall be connected with the establishment, so formed, to be provided with a competent supply of suitable merchandise for the Indians, to be distributed, or disposed of, in such manner as the department of War shall, from time to time, direct.

4. That notice of this arrangement be given to the major generals of divisions,—to the commanding officers of the troops of the United States at Michillimackinac, and to the superintendant of Indian factories, for the benefit of their immediate co-operation.

5. That Mr. Charles Jouett be appointed the Indian agent for the proposed establishment, to repair to the station, forthwith, having arranged with general Mason, for procuring and transporting an immediate supply of goods, to be distributed

Fur-trade in Wisconsin

in presents to the Indians, until a permanent factory be provided.

6. That the Secretary of the Navy be requested to issue orders for the co-operation of the public vessels on lake Erie, in forming the proposed establishment, in transporting troops or supplies,—and in impressing the Indians with the naval force of the government in that quarter, by navigating lake Michigan.

7. That the Indian agent shall receive as a full compensation for his services, a salary of one thousand dollars, payable quarterly, with an allowance of six rations per diem, or an equivalent in money, according to the price at the nearest military post.

All which is respectfully submitted.

A. J. DALLAS.

DEPARTMENT OF WAR, 19th. June, 1815.
June 20, 1815, Approved JAMES MADISON.

Endorsed: Report to the President of the United States.

[Source, same as preceding document, but p. 225.]

DEPARTMENT OF WAR, June 20th. 1815.

SIR—Inclosed herewith, you will receive a commission as agent of Indian affairs, to be stationed at Fox river, in the neighbourhood of Green bay. Should you accept the appoinment, you will please to repair to Detroit, forthwith, and report yourself to governor Cass, thro' whom your communications will be made to this department.

Your compensation will be at the rate of one thousand dollars per annum, and six rations a day, to commence at the time of your departure to take possession of the agency, of which you will please to notify this department. I am, Sir, very respectfully,

A. J. DALLAS.

Addressed: Charles Jouett.

[Source, same as preceding document, but p. 366.]

INDIAN OFFICE GEO:TOWN 21 June 1815

Jos. B. Varnum Jr. Esq, now at Albany

SIR—It has been determined by the Department of war to establish a military Post and an Indian military agency forthwith on the Green bay of Lake Michigan at or near where the fox River—or the streight between Lake Winebago falls into the Green Bay, and at this office to place a Factory at the same spot—as you gave me to understand when I had the pleasure to see you some time agoe that you would willingly again accept an agency in this Department and in some of your former letters while employed at Michilimackinac you expressed an opinion that the place now contemplated would be a proper location for a trading house, and that you would readily consent to remove to it, It gives me pleasure now to be able to offer this agency to you.[32] The salary and subsistence money will be the same as heretofore allowed you at Mackinac—to wit $1000, and $365.

Mr. Charles Jouett the former military agent at Chicago has been appointed by the Secretary of war military agent for that post, he leaves the seat of government, tomorrow to prepare to embark at Erie Presque Isle on Lake Erie by the 16th of next month—there to embark in a public vessel which will be ordered by the Secretary of the navy to take him to Detroit, Mackinac, and to the bottom of Green Bay.

If you accept the appointment proposed and your affairs will permit you to sett of on your mission as soon, it would be usefull to the service, and very desirable to me, as you could assist with Mr. Jouett in selecting a proper place for a scite for the Post, with a view to the Interests of the factory and the convenience of communicating with the neighbouring tribes of Indians, and in prepareing the proper buildings for the Factory so as to be enabled to occupy them with the goods before winter.

---

[32] It will be seen by the following documents that Varnum did not accept this position, and that the position of first factor at Green Bay was filled by the appointment of Matthew Irwin.—ED.

In this case the assortment for trade and other articles could be sent to you and deposited at Mackinac so as to reach that place it is hoped by the last of September or the middle of October. I request to hear from you immediately on the reception of this letter, and to be informed first whether you accept the appointment, and next whether you can go on as speedily as proposed, if it can [not] be done with certainty so as to join Mr. Jouett at Erie by the 16th. July, it should not be attempted should you accept and not be able to make your arrangements so as to go with him, it will then be best that you go on with the goods, say from Erie about the 1st. of Sept: sooner than which I don't think they can be prepared and sent on, owing to the yet great scarcity and high prices of the proper articles.

In either case the commencement of your compensation will be dated from the time you take up your route from your present residence for your post.

In case you should accept and determine to go on with Mr. Jouett, and to save time I enclose you the form of the requisite bond and oath of office which you can execute, and return me the same securities given in your former bond will be deemed sufficient.

It was not in my power to have given you earlier information on this subject, as the arrangement was only determined by the Department of War yesterday.[33]

A strong military post and a Factory will be established this fall at Prarie des Chiens, the preperations for which in both Departments have been moved some time agoe. Mr. John Johnson the former factor at Fort Madison will have charge of the factory.[34]

---

[33] This gives with certainty the date that the United States government decided to build a post at Green Bay, where none had been established since the departure of the British in 1763. See *Wis. Hist. Colls.*, xviii, p. 254.—ED.

[34] John W. Johnson was a native of Maryland, who while quite young received the appointment as United States factor at Fort Madison, on the site of the present Iowa town of that name. This fort was built in 1808 as a protection for the newly-established factory. It was

It is intended to renew the post and factory at Chicago in which case Mr. Irwin will be reinstated there in his former agency. It is probable that this is all we shall be able to do previous to the next winter in the trade Department in the quarter of the Lakes.

If you determine to depart immediately with Mr. Jouett on hearing from you to that effect, I will write you some additional Instructions to meet you at Erie, or at Detroit or Mackinac, as I find I shall best be in time to do, and I request in such case that you will write me before you leave Erie a list of such articles as you may think will most properly constitute an assortment for the proposed trading house to be placed under your charge having reference to an amount of about $12 or 15,000$ in all which is about the amount I propose to supply you with this fall as also a list of such tools and materials say Ironmongery etc. as you may suppose necessary to enable you to put up, with the aid of the military the requisite buildings for a small factory establishment, which can be afterwards augumented if found necessary. I am etc. etc. etc.

J. M[ASON]

---

besieged in 1812, after the fall of Fort Dearborn; and the factory, which lay without the fort, was burned by the garrison to keep it from being plundered by hostile Indians. The following year, during July and August, the garrison endured an almost continuous siege, but skilfully escaped in the night of Sept. 3, 1813, burning the fort behind them. In all of these operations, Johnson seems to have had part, and to have continued trading with friendly Indians at St. Louis or vicinity—see *Amer. State Papers, Indian Affairs*, ii, pp. 39, 44, 49, 53. In 1816 he went to Prairie du Chien, where he established the factory, and in 1818 was chosen judge of the county court for Crawford. He remained in charge of the post until the close of the factory system, when he removed to St. Louis, where he was living as late as 1837. He married a Sauk woman, and by her had several children, whom he educated.—ED.

Fur-trade in Wisconsin

[Source, same as preceding document, but p. 379.]

INDIAN OFFICE WASHINGTON 28 July 1815

Mathew Irwin Esq

SIR—Your two letters of the 11th. March and 8th. April [from] White Hall N. York were received in due course, they were not replied to as it was not very certain when or how we should reestablish our Factories in the Lakes.

It has been lately decided to place a garrison and a Factory on the Green Bay of Lake Michigan, at or near where the Fox River or the streight of Lake Winebago falls into the Bay. Mr. Chas. Jouett the former military agent at Chicago, has been appointed by the Secretary of War military agent for this post. The Garrison and Mr. Jouett are already in motion for their destination by way of Detroit and Michilimackinac.

During an indisposition by which I was confined in the early part of this Month I requested Mr. Bronaugh[35] to write you and to inform you, that you would be reappointed to a factory and to request you to come here, we have not heard from you yet in reply. This then is to inform you that as in your letters of last spring you expressed a preference for the position at Green Bay, you will be appointed to that factory, provided you can go on immediately, your salary will be at the rate of $1000. per annum and allowance for subsistence money $365.

The goods intended for it are all here and now packing, they will be moved in a very few days in waggons via Pittsburg to Erie on Lake Erie, there to be embarked at any rate from that point not later than the 1st. Sept: by which time it will if you accept, be necessary that you be there to accompany the goods.

I have to request then that you let me hear from you with the least possible delay, and that you will inform, if you accept where I shall direct to you and in the meantime, if I can count with certainty—that you will be at Erie ready to embark by the 1st. Sept: should you take Philada. in your way, and be

---

[35] Jeremiah W. Bronough was chief clerk of the department of Indian trade, until its abolition in 1822.—ED.

able to be here by the first 5 or 6 days in august, I should be glad you would come on at once, but not otherwise, as after that time I shall probably be from home. You will necessarily see from the advanced stage of the season that there is not a moment to be lost. I am etc. etc. etc.

J. M[ASON]

[Source, same as preceding document, but p. 397.]

INDIAN OFFICE August 7, 1815

John W. Johnson Esq. U. S. F. at Prarie des Chiens.

SIR—I have received your letter of the 9 July from St. Louis, and am glad to find you had arrived safely with all your goods in so short a period.

I regret the mistake about your Tobacco, and hope you will be able to obtain it of Govr. Clarkes parcell. I will replace it as soon as possible. your draft for your quarters salary to 1 June will be paid.

In confirmation of the several conversations I had with you while here last spring as to the Factory to be established at Prarie des Chiens, You will if not already done proceed with the U. S. troops, or such detachment of them moving to Prarie des Chiens as will insure a safe convoy, with your assistant Mr. Belt,[36] and all the factory goods and implements remaining

---

[36] Robert B. Belt of Maryland became assistant factor to Johnson while the latter was in charge at Fort Madison, having been appointed in June, 1812. He must, therefore, have been a participant in the siege of Fort Madison (see *ante*, p. 383, note 34) and concerned in its evacuation and the destruction of the factory. Since his salary continued to be paid throughout the war, it is probable that he was connected with the peaceful Sauk and Foxes, who removed to Missouri on the outbreak of the War of 1812-15. Belt was at Prairie du Chien with Johnson for less than two years, when he was given charge of the new factory at Fort Edwards, on the Mississippi, below Rock Island. There Forsyth met him in 1819—see *Wis. Hist. Colls.*, vi, p. 190, where the name is erroneously printed "Bett." After the closing of the factories in 1822, nothing more is known by us concerning this person.—ED.

from the establishment at the River Le Moin,[37] and will establish yourself at or near the village of the Prarie des Chien, in the position which may in your opinion in conjunction with the Commanding officer or any other person authorised by the War Dept. for that purpose be found best to hold a communication in trade with the neighbouring tribes of Indians and at the same time, be sufficiently under the protection of the military force. if this should be at the village, it is presumed you will be able to occupy some of the houses there that are public property, or to rent of individuals on easy terms. If it should be not at the village, it will be requisite you should build the necessary houses; in which case you will be governed as nearly as

---

[37] The first factory on the Mississippi above the Des Moines was at Fort Madison, for which see *ante*, p. 383, note 34. In August, 1814, Maj. Zachary Taylor was sent up the Mississippi to re-inforce and provision the garrison left by Gen. William Clark at Prairie du Chien. He found that this place had been captured by the British under Maj. William McKay (see *ante*, p. 365, note 12). Taylor had a sharp skirmish near Rock Island, and having fallen back erected Fort Johnson, not far from the present Warsaw, Hancock County, Ill.—see *Niles' Register*, viii, suppl. p. 137; and *Wis. Hist. Colls.*, ix, pp. 243–245. This fort was burned and abandoned in October of the same year—*Ibid.*, p. 250; and *Life and Letters of Ninian Edwards* (Springfield, Ill., 1870), p. 82. There could have been no factory or factor's goods at this point. What was known as "Des Moines factory," whose reports were consecutively made from 1812 to 1815, must have temporarily been located near St. Louis, or within the protection of the American lines—for until 1816 there could have been no place near Des Moines River, where a factory of Indian goods might have been maintained. Johnson did not arrive at Prairie du Chien until May 26 of that year, for during all of 1815 the tribes on the Mississippi and Rock rivers were hostile—see *Amer. State Papers, Ind. Affs.*, ii, pp. 9, 11. Although the other hostile tribes made treaties at Portage des Sioux during the summer and autumn of 1815, the Rock River Sauk and Winnebago remained recalcitrant, and continued hostilities. Early in 1816 messages were sent to the disaffected tribes, who finally sent delegations to St. Louis, where on May 13 the Sauk of Rock River, and June 3, the Wisconsin Winnebago, bound themselves to keep the peace. In anticipation of this result, Johnson went to Prairie du Chien some months in advance of the military forces.—ED.

may be by the number of houses and kind of establishment you had at Le Moin, and in every case you will be governed by the strictest œconomy compatible with the public service.

In case of buildings or repairs as it is presumed labour of no other kind can be had in that quarter, you will apply to the Commanding officer to assist you by detaching from time to time such of the soldiers as may be necessary and can be spared from duty, to whom you will from the factory funds give the same allowance for fatigue duty in money and whiskey heretofore allowed on similar occasions at your Post, keeping and rendering accurate accounts of the same from time to time, and ultimately a complete [account] of the cost of your buildings, or repairs as the case may be. should the position chosen not be at the village, and should it be found that you will not have time to cover yourself at it this winter, it will be adviseable to establish yourself at the village untill you can compleat the intended buildings at the post. in such case if the military do not generally remain at the village you will apply to the Commanding officer for a sufficient guard to protect the public property in your charge while you remain there.

You will at the new establishment, open and carry on a fair and liberal trade with the neighbouring tribes of Indians, and make your returns of Peltries Furs and other things to the agt. of this office at Saint Louis, in the same manner and under the same general instructions as you have heretofore done at the former establishment, advising me as frequently as possible of all your movements and of your prospects, particularly of the tribes with which you will come in contact in that quarter of their dispositions toward the United States their location, numbers, hunting grounds, the produce of their hunts, and the articles most proper to furnish you with for trade with them. With best wishes for your health and success, I am etc. etc.

J. M[ASON]

P. S. Since you left us I have received three letters from your assist: Mr. Belt, informing me that by the advice of Gov: Clark he had furnished him with $600. worth of Goods intended for the Fox annuities,[38] which the Govt. had afterwards determined to give in presents to the Puttawatimies. in this last case you must get a bill on the Dept. of war for that sum and if requisite furnish anew for the Fox annuities. I have written to Mr. Belt and approve of this as well as some trafic he had made by the advice of Gov. Clark. [Word illegible] for Blankets and Tobacco.

J. M.

[Source, same as preceding document, but p. 402.]

INDIAN OFFICE 7th Aug: 1815

The Honbl. William H. Crawford Secretary of War

SIR—As has been heretofore customary (to shew which I beg leave to refer to my letter of the 13 May 1809 to the Secy. of War and to his reply of the 15 same month) and is really necessary under the peculiar circumstances of the case—I have to sollicit that you will be pleased to instruct the Commanding officers at the Posts nearest to the Factories about to be established at Prarie des Chiens and on the Missouri or Osage, at Green Bay at or near Chicago, to detach as occasion may require and place at the disposition of the United States factors respectively the requisite number of soldiers to erect for them suitable buildings for the factory establishment, from time to time to aid them in packing and beating furs and Peltries, The Factors making to the Men so employed a daily reasonable allowance for fatigue duty, which has been heretofore fixed at Ten Cents and a gill of whiskey per day (when this last can be

---

[38] The treaty of 1804 with the Sauk and Foxes, provided that an annuity of $1,000 should be paid—$600 for the former, $400 for the latter. For the payments in 1817 and 1819, see the Forsyth papers in *Wis. Hist. Colls.*, vi, p. 191; xiii, p. 347. The tribesmen were dissatisfied with these payments, refusing (in 1817) to accept them, and claiming that the treaty of 1804 was spurious. Later, their necessities induced the acceptance, but in 1821 they claimed that goods were not furnished that could be divided among the tribe. See Jedidiah Morse, *Report to the Secretary of War* (New Haven, 1822), p. 57, and app. p. 139.—ED.

had) during the time they are so engaged. The factors will be provided from this office with the requisite tools and materials.

The distance from the settlements at which the factories are established make it impossible to procure labour otherwise than from the military, and as the soldiers will have little else to do, it has been found that they chearfully engage in work of this kind for a small addition to their pay and comfort thus furnished from the factory fund.

As we have had at such posts too many instances of broils between the Commandants and the Factors, detrimental to the public service as well military as civil, I will take the liberty to suggest the propriety that both should receive strong injunctions to maintain harmony and keep up constantly an intercourse of reciprocal good offices, in their respective spheres. I have enjoined and shall continue to enjoin this course of conduct strictly on all the factors.

For your information I beg leave to enclose an extract of my instructions to John W. Johnson factor at Prarie des Chiens relative to the establishment under his charge. With great Respect etc. etc.

J. M[ASON]

[Source, same as preceding document, but p. 406.]

INDIAN OFFICE August 11th. 1815

The Honbl. Wm. H. Crawford Secretary of War

SIR—In consequence of the understanding on that subject with the Dept. of war, goods to the amount of $20.000 are now prepared at this office and will be moved in a very few days by way of Pittsburg to Erie on Lake Erie, intended for two factories one to be established at the Military post on Green Bay of Michigan and one at that which may be located at or near Chicago on Lake Michigan.

The uncertainty of getting the means of private transportation on the Lakes and the importance of a speedy conveyance at this late stage of the season, makes it very desireable to obtain this transportation by a public vessel, as I presume the navy

Department have vessels unemployed on that Lake, I will take the liberty to sollicit if in your opinion the measure be necessary, that you will be pleased to ask of the Navy Dept. a vessel to transport these Goods, and the two agents who will accompany them from Erie to Michilimackinac, and thence if necessary to Green Bay or Chicago, to be ready to take them in at Erie by the 10th. or at latest the 15th. Sept: I am etc. etc. etc.

J. M[ASON]

[Source, same as preceding document, but p. 416.]

INDIAN OFFICE WASHN. 20 aug. 1815

Mathew Irwin Esq. U. S. F. for Green Bay

SIR—This letter I presume will find you at Erie on your way to your Post. I enclose you herewith an Invo. of goods intended for the factory to be placed under your charge at *Green Bay* (Chicago)³⁹ containing *113* (65) Packages amo. *$15.738.06* ($9452.34). These goods are neither as well chosen or as advantageously bought as could be desired but the scarcity and present high prices of articles suitable for our purposes left us no choice in the desire, to have in the quarter of the country to which you are going some goods at least this winter to supply the wants of the Indians. you will find with the Post master at Erie a letter from Capt. Wooly at Pittsburg who conducts the transportation informing you who is his agent at Erie and who will place these Goods on board a public vessel the Schooner Ghent to your order. The Commander has directions to furnish you with a passage, your own stores you will lay in, he will proceed directly to Mackinac with you which will be garrisoned by our troops before you reach it. you will there apply to the Commanding officer for information, and enquire also for *Charles Jouett Esq* (Col: Boyer)⁴⁰ Military Indian agent who

---

³⁹ The words and figures enclosed in parentheses in the following document were supplied in the second letter (otherwise identical with this), intended for Jacob B. Varnum, who was going as Indian factor to Chicago.—ED.

⁴⁰ Col. John Bowyer belonged to a prominent family of Augusta

is to reside at the same place, and if in time to go with the troops and military stores, you will take your passage in company with them on this or some public vessel. if the troops and military stores should have gone on you will immediately follow and join them at the Post with your goods taking care not to move but in an armed vessel or under such protection of the public force, as well to ensure the protection of the property in your charge, and to this end you will apply to the Commanding Officer and the military agent will have fixed or in conjunction will fix on the particular scite at or near *Green Bay* (Chicago) deemed most proper to combine all the advantages for a military position, and for trade and intercourse with the neighbouring Indians. This done you will immediately set about erecting suitable buildings for the accomodation of yourself and the factory, it is presumed a dwelling house of about 20 by 30 feet, and a house for a store and warehouse of same dimensions will be sufficient with if necessary the aid of one or two small out houses. The Commanding officer at your Post has been instructed from the War Department to give you the requisite aid in putting up these buildings, and you will make to the Soldiers

---

County, Va., whose members took part in Dunmore's War (1774) and the Revolution. Inheriting military tastes, young Bowyer entered the regular army as lieutenant in 1792. Four years later, he was an officer of the 3d infantry, being promoted to a captaincy in 1799. By 1808 he had become major, and in 1812 lieutenant-colonel of the 2nd infantry; and in 1814, colonel of the 5th. In 1813, Colonel Bowyer was stationed on the Southern frontier, and in April of that year aided in the capture of Mobile. In the summer of the same year, a fort was built some miles below the city, and named for its commander, Fort Bowyer. Later it was dismantled, and the command removed. Colonel Bowyer had served with great efficiency, but upon the reduction of the army to a peace footing in 1815, he was discharged, and given instead an Indian agency. As shown by documents *post*. he arrived at Green Bay in the early summer of 1816, and for a home purchased the farm of Judge Charles Reaume. He was of Huguenot descent, spoke French, and made himself as popular with the unwilling inhabitants as any American Indian agent could. He subscribed to their schools, and brought his family to live at Green Bay, where he died in 1820, while still agent for the government.—Ed.

detached on this duty a fatigue allowance of 10 Cents and a gill of Whiskey to each man per day.

You will use every possible œconomy in putting up these buildings and when done render me accurate accounts of the whole cost. with your goods will be sent some tools and implements for building, and whiskey for the detached soldiers.

Should it happen that it be determined by the Military not to establish a Post this winter at the position described to you, or should it be that you arrive so late at Mackinac (which is to be avoided if it can possibly be) that it should not on account of the frost be in your power to get to that position before winter sets in, you will remain at Mackinac during winter and store your goods in some safe place untill you can proceed on the expedition in the spring; and in mean time if at or near that place you can with safety open any usefull traffic with the friendly Indians, and supply with goods for their skins furs etc., it will be best to do so to a certain extent and particularly if you find this is necessary to their real wants.

You will in all respects be governed by the general instructions, as to your conduct toward the Indians and the trade with them, given from this office to you while factor at *Chicago* (Sandusky)[41] and you will make return in Peltries furs etc. thro Mackinac and Erie to Capt. Abraham Wooly at Pittsburg, who will forward them to this office.

I beg thus early in forming a new establishment to recommend in the most particular manner to you that you will do all that may depend on you to preserve harmony, good understanding and an interchange of reciprocal good offices between the Military Commandant and yourself, as also with the military agent, the interest of the public service requires this and it is hoped that Gentlemen having all the same general object in charge, will unite each in his own sphere in producing the end desired by the Government.

---

[41] Varnum had been the government factor at Sandusky, as Irwin had been at Chicago; but the War of 1812-15 broke up their respective factories.—ED.

You will keep me constantly advised of your movements, and the general state of your business—be very particular in keeping your Inventories and accounts, and to make regular quarterly returns as heretofore in your former agency. Inform yourself as soon as you are able to give me detailed information with regard to all the Indian tribes within reach of you, their numbers, position, hunting grounds, produce of their hunts, articles suitable for their use etc. and their disposition toward the United States.

With best wishes for your speedy and safe arrival and the success of the establishment under your charge, I am etc. etc.

J. M[ASON]

P. S. As you will probably be some time in company with Capt. Varnum[42] who goes to Chicago, I beg you will give him all the information you may think usefull as to the tribes of

---

[42] Jacob B. Varnum was a younger brother of Joseph, who had formerly been factor at Mackinac; see *ante*, p. 326, note 69. He was born in Massachusetts in 1788, and in 1809 received his first appointment to an office in the militia. Two years later (Aug. 6, 1811), he was, through his father's influence, appointed factor at Sandusky, where the trading-house was broken up by hostile Indians (Oct. 31, 1812). During the war he served in the army, and being ordered to Maine, in command of a small coast fort, was captured (1813) by the officers of a British man-of-war, who released him upon parole. In August, 1815, having resigned from the army, Varnum was appointed factor for Chicago. He arrived there some time in the month of September, 1816, after a long delay at Mackinac, where he married Marianne Aikens. She died the year after her marriage, and in 1819 Captain Varnum married Catharine Dodimead of Detroit. The factory at Chicago was just south of the re-built Fort Dearborn. For a portion of the time Varnum boarded with Jean Baptiste Beaubien. His success in establishing trade with the Indians was very small, due to causes quite beyond his control. In the spring of 1820 he had exchanged but $25 worth of goods for furs—see letters in A. T. Andreas, *History of Chicago* (Chicago, 1884), i, pp. 88, 89, 93, 94. In 1822, the Chicago factory having been abolished, Varnum removed to Washington, whence in 1828 he made a home at Petersburg, Va. A non-combatant during the siege of that town in 1863, his home was burned and he finally returned to Washington, where he died in 1874.—ED.

Indians in that quarter and their trade intercourse etc. which your experience among them will enable you to do, and that you will give him your opinion at large as to the proper position in that quarter for a new Factory.

Should it happen that Capt. Varnum does not get up [in] time for the sailing of the vessel before mentioned you will take charge of all the goods, and deliver those for Chicago to the care of the Commanding officer at Mackinac to be held to the order of Capt. Jacob B. Varnum.

1815: USE OF LIQUOR PROHIBITED

[MS. in Wisconsin Historical Library. Pressmark: Wisconsin MSS., 3B42. Translated from the French.]

PRAIRIE DU CHIENS Oct. 22, 1815

SIR—Having learned from the account of Mr. bettelle that you wish me to know that you have suffered a Considerable loss since The War and that you are trying to recover since your loss has been Caused because you occupied a position under the Americans, I hope that you will be recompensed, if you make a representation and an estimate of your loss and send it with proper Certificates to Governor Edwards[43] at cahoux [Cahokia], and he can perhaps protect you. As for your place as magistrate I give you full power to exercise it since the treaty of peace, for he has invested me with these powers, until he sends you different orders. These orders are to prohibit liquor

---

[43] Ninian Edwards, territorial governor of Illinois, was born in Maryland in 1775. Early in life he removed to Kentucky, where he studied law and was judge of several courts, being in 1808 chief justice of the state. Upon the organization of the territory of Illinois, he was chosen governor, and served with vigor and effectiveness during the territorial period of that commonwealth. Being chosen first United States senator from Illinois, he was at the expiration of his term, appointed (1824) minister to Mexico, but resigned before visiting his post. From 1826–30 he served as governor of the state of Illinois, and died in 1833 at his home at Belleville.—ED.

among the nations especially at the post. I have asked Mr roy[44] to give you the notice that he Is to post at the portage of the Wisconsient in order that you may do the same at Labez If you discover that they refuse to obey write to the Governor and he will give you a force to see that it is Executed. I am Sir, your very humble servant

N. BOILVIN
agent & Judge of the peace

Mr. Raihome

If you have any news from Maquinac let me know it.

Addressed: A Monsieur Mons Rehome magistrat a Labez verte Favored by Mr. Roy

---

1815: DUTY ON FUR-TRADE MERCHANDISE

[Source, same as preceding document, but 3B44. Translated from the French.]

MICHILIMAKINAC Oct. 25, 1815.

MY DEAR SIR—The present is to Inform that I had the pleasure of seeing one of the desmoiselles Porlier at Montreal who was very well and had much pleasure in hearing of you,

---

[44] François Roy (or Le Roy) was a son of Joseph Roy, an early settler of Green Bay. Having married Thérèse Lecuyer—whose father had lived at the Fox-Wisconsin portage, where he was engaged in the transportation business—Roy himself settled at the portage about the beginning of the War of 1812–15. When Lockwood crossed in 1817, he found Roy engaged in portaging with teams, and charging $10 for each boat and fifty cents per hundred pounds for cargoes. Later, Roy seems to have given up the transportation business for the fur-trade, and had a home and trading house on the site where Fort Winnebago was built in after years. This location was purchased from him by the federal government, whereupon he removed to Wisconsin River, where he was living as late as 1831—see Juliette A. Kinzie, *Waubun;* Wis. Hist. Colls., xiv, pp. 165, 166. Not long after this, Roy removed to Green Lake, probably to the house of his son Pierre, who was found there in 1840 by the first American settlers—see Wis. Hist. Soc. Proc., 1909, p. 256. In 1856, Augustin Grignon had not heard of Roy's death.—ED.

as well as did the Messieurs Mailliot[45] who charged me to present to you their compliments. Mr. Rolette will give you the letter I brought with me. As it is at present possible to Communicate with the Gentlemen in Illinois you will Much oblige Me by writing to Monsieur Cabané or Monsieur Chenier[46] on the Subject of a letter of Exchange that your Sister has sent for a sum amounting to 165 Piastres. I have drawn by Monsieur Boilvin On General Clarck, in My favor for a power to receive the sum next year if possible.

My dear Sir, I am Charmed that you have had your Merchandise started from the Post before the disembarkment of the Americans[47] here For you would have had to pay the duty

---

[45] Jacques Porlier had two unmarried sisters, who at this time were living in Verchères, Canada. One of them, Louise, was his constant correspondent. In a letter preserved in the Wisconsin Historical Library (Wisconsin MSS., 3B29), she mentions her proposed visit to Montreal. Xavier and François Victor Malhiot were Porlier's cousins, and were likewise living at Verchères.—ED.

[46] These were two prominent merchants of St. Louis. John P. Cabanné, a native of Pau, France, emigrated first to New Orleans; but owing to his participation in a duel he was obliged to leave that place and settled (about 1804) at St. Louis. There he engaged in the fur-trade as a partner of the Chouteaus, and made a fortune in that business on the Missouri. For many years Cabanné was agent for the American Fur Company at Council Bluffs, where (in 1832) he had an affair with a rival trader, which caused him to return to St. Louis, where he had married Julie Gratiot, and maintained a fine home. He served as trustee (in 1806) for the village of St. Louis, and was in other directions a public-spirited citizen, dying there in 1841.

Antoine Chenier, of Canadian origin (1768), first ventured in the fur-trade in the neighborhood of Niagara. In 1796 he settled in St. Louis, where he married Marie Thérèse Papin, niece of the elder Chouteau. He owned much land and several buildings in old St. Louis, having a fine brick house, whose hospitality was proverbial. For his portrait see J. Thomas Scharf, *History of St. Louis* (Philadelphia, 1883), p. 358.—ED.

[47] Col. Anthony Butler, of the United States army, headed an expedition which left Detroit early in July, 1815, in a fleet of four vessels, he having been ordered to take formal possession of Mackinac. Having arrived July 18, and performed the necessary ceremonies of taking over

which is very high, as you may Judge, since it amounts to 31¼ Per Cent of the Montreal Price.

However I doubt whether you are yet Secure, having heard it said that the Collector received Instructions Three Days ago that all the merchandise which is in the Interior before his Arrival Would be Subject to the duties. I am happy to Inform you however that your trade is arranged for in any Case. I wish you Good Health and Much Success and Am awaiting your news Your very humble Servant And friend

J. B. BERTHELOT

Monseir Jacques Porlier La Bay verte

Addressed: Jacques Porlier Esq. La Bayverte Favored by Mr. J. Rolette.

Endorsed by Porlier: Berthelotte's letter 1815 recommendation of a note drawn on General Clark and announcing the high Duty at McKina

---

1815: ORDERS FROM ILLINOIS

[Source, same as preceding document, but 60B51. Translated from the French.]

According to The orders that I have Received from Governor Ninian Edwards, Governor of the Territory of the Illinois I have prohibited all Persons from carrying Liquors among the Nations under pain of Undergoing the punishment that The Law orders, and of being chased from the place if he is taken a second time. No License can be Granted to sell it and no Trader will be Permitted to conduct Trade who violates this injunction, and in default of a White, a Respectable Savage will be believed on his Declaration.

PRERIE DU CHIEN Oct. 29, 1815

N. BOILVIN
agent and judge of the peace

Endorsed: Ninian Edwards at Kaost.

---

the post, Butler departed with the fleet, leaving Capt. Willoughby Morgan in charge of the garrison. Morgan was (Aug. 31) superseded by Maj. Talbot Chambers; see *Mich. Pion. and Hist. Colls.*, xvi, pp. 177, 191, 200.—ED.

1815-1817] Fur-trade in Wisconsin

1815: INDIAN AGENT AT GREEN BAY

[MS. in Pension Office, Washington. Pressmark: Indian Office Letter Book "C," p. 289.]

DEPARTMENT OF WAR, Decemr. 30th. 1815.

SIR—Mr. Jewett [Jouett] has made an application to this department to exchange the agency of Green Bay for that of Chicago. As his previous residence at the latter place has given him a general knowledge of the Indians within that agency, this exchange would be acceptable to the government, provided you have no particular objection to it. The salary is the same, and it is believed that the Agency at Green Bay is the most eligible, and the one which you would have preferred.

Should you find it convenient to make this exchange, you will advise Mr. Jewett, as well as this department of your determination. I have the honor to be etc.

[GEORGE GRAHAM
Chief Clerk]

Addressed: Col. John Bowyer, In. Agt. Detroit.

1816: PROHIBITION OF LIQUOR

[MS. in Wisconsin Historical Library. Pressmark: Wisconsin MSS., 60B53. Translated from the French.]

For the United States.

By order of Governor Ninian Edwards, he enjoins me to post the notice at this place that all Traders and other citizens must Conform to the Prohibition made not to sell or have sold any Liquor to the Nations in any place whatsoever under pain of suffering under the Law and of being driven from this Place. Given and passed the Present, and put in force the eighth day of February of the year one thousand eight hundred and sixteen at la Baye verte.

CH^{les}. REAUME
Judge of the peace

By order of the Governor Ninian Edwards &c. at Kaost.

[Source, same as preceding document, but 54B24. Translated from the French.]

[written about 1816]

Charles Reaume, Esq.

The urgent Situation that our gentlemen at the Buttes des Mortes are in with regard to the prohibition of rum, puts me to the necessity of sending an express to secure your opinion as to what they can do. Consider yourself that they cannot resist a number of Savages resolved to go to extremes. We consider ourselves authorized by the danger that they will incur to beg you to lift that prohibition that came so late that our gentlemen were not able to carry it out. We await your immediate reply to transmit by the same express. You will notice, Sir, that liquor having once been allowed among the Savages it is not possible to restrain them from it, and that moreover there is not force enough here to sustain such a regulation. We have the honor to be with Consideration Your very humble Servants

JACQUES PORLIER
L^s. GRIGNON
JOHN LAWE.

Addressed: Chls. Reaume Esq.

1816: TRADERS AT MILWAUKEE

[Source, same as preceding document, but 3B50. Translated from the French.]

MILWAQUIS Feb. 25, 1816

SIR—After having made you my Compliments, if you will accept them from me I promise you to assist my Cousin Jaque Viaut[48] From this Place as far as the Portage of Sturgeon Bay

---

[48] For accounts of Jacques Vieau, the first permanent white settler on the site of Milwaukee, see the interesting narratives of his sons, Andrew J. and Peter J., in *Wis. Hist. Colls.*, xi, pp. 281–225; xv, pp. 458–469. A portrait of Andrew J. Vieau, in his twenty-first year, by the well-known artist, George A. P. Healey, is given herewith.—ED.

ANDREW JACQUES VIEAU

From oil portrait (Detroit, 1839) by George A. P. Healy, in possession of Wisconsin Historical Society

for the amount of a Fifty pound sack of Flour, if you will send it to me. I am sir your Very Humble Servant

JAMES MICHEL LEPALLIEUR[49]

Addressed: Louis Grignon   Bay Verte.

1816: BRITISH SUBJECTS IN WISCONSIN FUR-TRADE

[MS. in State Department, Washington. Bureau of Rolls and Library. Ninián Edwards to Monroe.]

KASKASKIA ILLINOIS TERRITORY March 3, 1816

SIR—Supposing it probable that the peculiar situation of this, and Missouri Territory, the extraordinary sensation excited in consequence of the Presidents proclamation, directing intruders upon public land to be removed by military force, and the various representations that have been made upon that subject, may produce some relaxation, or alteration of that measure, I beg leave to mention to you one description of intruders who are entitled to no favor, and against whom, the most rigid execution of the proclamation is in my opinion recommended by every dictate of policy in relation to the government, and of justice to its citizens—I mean those British subjects who have settled themselves at the village of La Bay, which is situated on Fox river, three miles above its confluence with Green Bay, and at the village of Prairie du Chien on the Mississippi, At both of which places, those intruders are not only engaged extensively in agriculture, but constantly carry on such an intercourse with the Indians, as is prohibited to our best citizens.

These villages are within the acknowledged limits of this Territory to the latter in particular, our laws have been specially extended, and if it be true that a Foreigner while residing in our country, and receiving its protection, owes a temporary allegiance to its Gov^t, and an obedience to its laws, there can be

---

[49] This is the clerk spoken of as "Mike le Pettéel" in *Id.*, xi, 220, 226. Nothing is known of him, save his services for Vieau. See likewise *Id.*, xv, p. 463.—ED.

nothing more certain than, that all those persons have violated the one, and infracted the other; for they have all without exception, been actively, and efficiently engaged in the war against us. They in fact constitute complete British establishments, and in that light must be so considered by that Gov^t, from the circumstance of its having already remunerated them, for one half of all the losses, which they sustained during the war—Of which I have been informed both officially, and by several of the individuals concerned. To permit them to remain under such circumstances, and to cultivate the lands from which our own citizens are excluded, would be, not only to cherish a set of unprincipled British spies, ever ready to communicate the measures of our gov^t, and to defeat, as far as possible, its endeavours to maintain the relations of peace, and friendly intercourse with the savages, but it would also continue to them evident advantages, in the prosecution of the fur trade, over our own traders.

Had it not been for the subsistence which their farms, and mills enabled them to afford the Indians in the late war, it would have been absolutely impossible to have rallied such a number against us, as were engaged in the battles of F^t Meigs[50] and other places, and therefore while the conduct of those people entitles them to no favor, the admonitions of experience seem to dictate precautions on our part, against the recurrence of similar evils, the more especially as at this very time, the conduct of the Indians (if concuring reports from different parts of their country can be relied upon) indicate great discontent, and disaffection towards our Gov^t. And although I am convinced that we need never expect entire tranquility on our frontiers, till some more efficient checks shall be imposed upon the machinations of British traders, or agents, yet I am greatly at a loss to comprehend the causes of the recent excitement, which from the reports of our public agents, as well as others,

---

[50] Fort Meigs was attacked May 1–5, 1813, by Gen. Henry Proctor, heading a force of nearly 2000 Indians, a large proportion of whom were from the region of Lake Michigan and the interior of Wisconsin.—ED.

seems very strongly to have manifested itself simultaneously, among several different Tribes, situated at distances very remote from each other.

Should the British subjects that I have mentioned be removed from the settlements they occupy, It might I think, be advisable to permit (under proper restrictions) their places to be supplied, by good American citizens, for the purpose of affording accomodation to our garrisons, to our traders, and to the Indians themselves. And indeed such a measure might be the most effectual means, of guarding against those casualties, to which the transportation of provisions to posts so remote from the settled parts of our country, must necessarily be exposed and of which we have heretofore had a monitory example in the necessary abandonment and distruction of F^t Madison.[51]

I discover from the newspapers, that a proposition has been made in congress, to exclude British subjects from all trade with the Indians within the limits of the United States, or those Territories. In consequence of which, though I have no knowledge whatever, of the views of the gov^t relative to that subject, I beg leave to suggest it as my opinion that a law predicated upon such an exclusion merely, without other auxilliary checks, would not produce the slightest change in their trade, nor correct any part of the evils, which it would be intended to remedy. The agents of the North West Company have long resided in this country, and of course can be naturalized, at any moment upon application to the competent Tribunal. Of which they will most certainly avail themselves, in order that they may carry on the same trade, and practise the same machinations in the character of American citizens.

This policy on their part has already commenced, and tomorrow one of the most distinguished of those gentlemen, will make application to the superior court at this place to be naturalized, that he may thereby be prepared for any change that may take place. I would here with great pleasure present the result of my own reflections as to the best means, or necessary

---

[51] See *ante*, p. 383, note 34.—ED.

expedients for correcting those evils & evasions, were I not under some apprehensions, that this uninvited communication may already be thought rather too obtrusive, and if that should be the case I hope an apology for me, will be found, in the only motives, by which I would possibly be influenced. I have the honor to be With very great respect Sir Y^r Mo Obd^t S^t

NINIAN EDWARDS

Honb^{le} James Monroe Sec. of State.

Addressed: The Honble James Monroe Sec. of State Washington City

---

[MS. in Wisconsin Historical Library. Pressmark: Wisconsin MSS., 3B52. Translated from the French.]

MICHILIMAKINAC Mar. 22, 1816

DEAR SIR—The present is to Inform you that I received the honor of your two last letters of the 22 and 28 of February, and Should have been pleased to have sent you the hyson Tea if I could have Found any. As I am expecting some from Drummond Island,[52] you will receive it by the Next Opportunity.

I Enquired about your Tobacco There are two Barrels that Mr. Daniel Mitchel[53] says he received for you without telling me the Number of Livres.

The Express which we expected from Detroit having arrived has brought me papers which announce a Treaty of Commerce between England and America by which no British Subject has the right to Trade with the Savages on the Territory of the United States. I do not know what to think of this.

As you probably have been Informed Mr. Astor's Company sent me at McKinac last fall 20000 Livres of Tobacco addressed to Mr. Saml. Abbot for the Trade of Next Year. You will learn presently that the Company of the North has succumbed

---

[52] For the British establishment on Drummond Island, see *ante*, p. 146, note 94.—ED.

[53] A son of Madame Mitchell, described in *Wis. Hist. Colls.*, xiv, pp. 35–38.—ED.

to Them And that it is Mr. Rocheblave under the Name of the Southwest Fur Company who has the money for it, Mr. Abbot having received a letter from Mr. Astor and Mr. Rocheblave on the Subject. Nothing more only wishing you Good Health and good Business. I am awaiting your reply, Sir, Your very humble and obedient servant and friend

J. B. BERTHELOT

Mr. Louis Grignon, La Baye Verte.

N. B. If I can procure for you by any Opportunity one of your Barrels of Tobacco, I will do it.

Addressed: Monsr Louis Grignon La Baye verte.

[MS. in Pension Office, Washington. Pressmark: Indian Office Letter Book "C," p. 344. Wm. H. Crawford to Gov. Cass and Indian Agents.]

DEPARTMENT OF WAR, 10th. May, 1816.

SIR—I have the honor of transmitting to you the copy of an act of Congress, passed on the 29th. of April last, intended to subject the right of foreign merchants, to trade with the Indian tribes within the limits of the United States, to the absolute control of the President.[54] It is deemed expedient that the power vested in the President by this act, shall be exercised with a view to secure to our savage neighbors a regular supply of those articles, which their wants and habits have rendered indispensable. This supply must be furnished by the government, by the individual enterprize of American citizens, or by foreigners. The fund hitherto employed by the government for this object is wholly incompetent for this supply. The tribes which have been usually supplied by the traders in the employ of the North West Company, reside far in the in-

---

[54] Act of 14th Cong., 1st sess., chap. clxv. Section one thereof forbids licenses for the Indian trade to any but United States citizens, save at the direction of the president. The following sections provide severe penalties for violations. The purpose of the act is set forth in this letter of Crawford.—ED.

terior to the North and to the West, and, as is generally understood, have had but little intercourse with our trading establishments, and have seldom, if ever, been visited by our licensed traders. It is therefore wholly improbable that the enterprize of American citizens will furnish an adequate supply to those remote tribes. The want of Capital in the hands of men accustomed to the trade, and who have enterprize to bear the fatigues, and brave the dangers incident to its prosecution, will, it is believed, render it necessary for the present to permit foreigners to carry on this trade, under such regulations as shall subject them to a strict observance of the laws of the United States upon this subject; secure their exertions in maintaining peace between the Indian tribes, and this government, and between themselves; and present additional inducements to respect the laws against smuggling. The more effectually to secure these results, the President has judged it expedient to vest in the Governor of the Michigan territory, and in the agents for Indian affairs at Michilimackinac, Green Bay, and Chicago, the exclusive right of granting licenses to foreigners to carry on this trade. In the execution of this trust, you will necessarily enquire into the character of those who apply for permission to embark in this commerce. Where the character of the applicant shall not be above suspicion, a license must be refused. The charge of having been concerned in smuggling supported by colourable evidence of its truth, will be a sufficient cause for a like refusal. Licenses when granted are to be revoked for any of the causes which would justify their refusal in the first instance. Previous to the delivery of any license, the applicant shall give bond and security in a sum equal to one fourth of the capital which he shall state upon oath, he intends to embark in the trade, which shall be forfeited to the use of the United States, upon the violation of the laws of the United States regulating trade with the Indian tribes. He shall at the same time give the description of the persons he intends to employ in the prosecution of his business. When any application for a license shall be refused, immediate notice of such refusal, and the grounds upon which it was made, shall be given to the agents to whom the execution of this law is specially entrusted by the President. It shall be the duty of the officer granting any license to give immediate notice to this department, to the Indian agents, the collectors of the customs, and to the commanding officers of posts and stations in and adjoining the Indian country, upon whom the execution of the act in question can, in any degree, possibly devolve. This notice shall contain the description of the person, his place of residence, and the amount of the capital which he intends to employ, and the number, names, and description of the persons, who will be employed in the transaction of his business with Indians.

Copies of the several acts regulating trade with the Indian tribes are forwarded, to be given to the persons to whom licenses shall be granted for the regulation of their conduct. I have the honor to be etc.

WM. H. CRAWFORD.

P. S. In communicating with this department, it is expected that the changes in the present system suggested by experience, will, from time to time, be presented, with a view to render it as perfect as the subject will permit.

W. H. C.

Endorsed: Lewis Cass, Gov. of Michigan Territory. Major Wm. H. Puthuff, I. Agt. Michilimackinac.[55] Charles Jouett, I. Agt. Chicago. John Bowyer, I. Agt. Green Bay.

---

[55] Maj. William Henry Puthuff was a native of Virginia, probably from Albemarle County. Having removed to Ohio, he enlisted (1812) as a volunteer, but was (May 20, 1813) made captain in the 26th infantry of the regular army. In February, 1814, he was promoted to a majority in the 2nd rifle regiment, being employed in the neighborhood of Detroit, where in the summer of 1815 he was in command, and received the thanks of the citizens for his spirited enforcement of their rights—see *Mich. Pion. and Hist. Colls.*, viii, p. 655. Having been honorably discharged from the army, at the reduction of its force, he was given an Indian agency and stationed at Mackinac, where he arrived in the late summer, or early autumn, of 1815. He was particularly suspicious of British influence, and his reports are stigmatized as untrue in the letters of the officers of Drummond Island—see *Id.*, xvi, pp. 369-401. He entered upon his duties with

[MS. in Pension Building, Washington. Pressmark: Indian Office Book 204. Letter Book 1, p. 204.]

MICHILLIMACKINAC AGENCY 14th. May 1816

DR. SIR—Discovering no provision to have been made for the supplying the post of Michillimackinac with goods destined for Indian Presents, or annuity's, Farming utensils, Mechanicks or agriculturalists for the promotion and encouragement of domestick pursuits, Industry and civilization among the neighbouring tribes of Indians, I hope I may be indulged in a few remarks on, what I conceive to be, the relative importance of that Post, and the necessity for the immediate attention of Government to so highly an interesting object.

In my communications, made to your Excellency upon the subject last autumn, I endeavoured to explain the British policy in their intercourse with the Indians living within the American limits say, in the neighbourhood of Michillimackinac, Chicago, Green Bay, Seaux St. Mary's, Lake Superior, etc.

It is a fact well known to your Excellency, that St. Joseph's now Drummond's Island, Is, and for many years has been, the grand depository for the receipt and distribution of most extensive annuities or Presents which the British Government have Semi-annually destributed with a liberal hand, to all who could be induced to attend, acknowledge the Supremicy of that Government, Pledge themselves to bring their furs to that place, or sell or trade them to none but British subjects etc., this Post is also the head Quarters of a vigorous, active, Enterprising, well informed and most Politick and designing company, who have long and almost Exclusively monopolized the trade of the North west. It is from thence that well instructed unprincipled agents are, and constantly have been, Employed and sent out among the many tribes of savages that inhabit the ex-

---

great zeal, and was president of the village (1817–21, 1823), justice of the county court (1818), and probate judge. In 1818, he was relieved from duties as an Indian agent, but continued to reside at Mackinac, where in 1822 Henry S. Baird found him exercising kindly hospitality—see *Wis. Hist. Colls.*, vii, p. 429. His death occurred Nov. 24, probably of the year 1823.—ED.

tensive Western and N. Western regions within the limits of the American Government, upon the Lakes Superior and Michigan and the head waters of the Mississippi and its tributary Streams, with small out-fits to give them the pretext and appearance of Indian traders This fact is clearly proven, and has been, as I conceive unquivocally established in the late war, when it was found to be, and is, an undeniable fact, that a very great proportion of those who were employed in trade within our limits prior to and at the commencement of the war, immediately thereafter were found to hold commissions under the British Government, and were found to be our most active inviterite and most dangerous Enemies.

The circumstances have drawn numerous hoards of savages from their respective hunting grounds, yearly to the Islands of St. Josephs and Michillimackinac for the purpose of hearing their Father in council, receiving their presents, disposing of their Furs, etc. etc.

The importance of supplying the post of Michillimackinac with the means of counteracting the effects resulting from the practise of the aforementioned policy, appears to me to be of the [utmost] necessity, to effect this desirable object it will require the most active and vigilent attention of Government.

The object and policy of the British Government in their Indian relations cannot be mistaken, It has but one Primary motive, one leading principle, one great and never to be forgotten design. It always has been thus actuated and Influenc'd, to alienate the Indians from the American Government and people, to attach them to the British Interests by every and by any the most insidious means.

To effect this purpose the hopes, the Fears, the ignorance, interest and cupidity of the unfortunate deluded savage, is most adroitly enlisted on the part of these politicians who whatever may be their professions, never loose sight of their favourite object, and in my opinion should be most narrowly watch'd and closely pursued throughout every the most distant ramifications of their trade or intercourse with the Indians residing within the limits of the American Government.

I am led Sir, to make these remarks from what has come to my knowledge of the character and conduct of the British Officer (Lt. Col. McDowell) commanding at Drummonds Island, and the Indian department there, from the *pretty* evident agency of certain British subjects (Mitchell and others),[56] living upon the Island of Michillimackinac, from certain *highly suspicious* persons, British pensioners, Interpreters and Commissioned Officers in their Indian Department, having actually came within our limits, and under the pretence of trading with the Indians, have destributed themselves throughout the Indian Country, and from a solemn conviction of the truth of the allegations which I have from a since of justice and duty to my Country taken the liberty thus to advance.

I am fully persuaded however that the result of the late war has effected a most fortunate and sensible change [in] the attachment and prejudices of the Indians toward the British Government and people, of this the British are perfectly sensible, and to restore and mantain their wonted influence, will leave no means in their power unattempted. previous to and at the commencement of the war the Indians as an additional motive whereby to induce their decided attachment, were promised the restoration of all that Country West and North west of the River Ohio then held by the American Government, to be put and left in the possession of all the Military posts within that extensive Country. The universal and undisturb'd Masacre, Plunder and Pillage of all its then Inhabitants The undisturbed occupancy of that country and enjoyments of its spoils, with a life of savage ease and Independance and a spontanious influx of goods, Ammunition, Arms, Provisions, Rum and Tobacco, to [be] effected and furnished by British power and munificence.

This and much more has been practised and promised by the agents employed on the part of the British Government.

---

[56] An acrimonious correspondence arose in the autumn of 1815 over the treatment of the Mitchells by the American soldiers and Indian officers; see *Mich. Pion. and Hist. Colls.*, xvi, pp. 298–401.—ED.

Prophets, Juglars, and persons professing to have supernatural powers and agency, have been imposed upon that deluded people and openly supported employed and used by that Government. Specious promises, Diabolical means; all have failed, the war has been terminated, and how differently from the promises held out to and consequent expectations of the savages.

The Indians have been deceived, grossly deceived. They have been deeply injured and imposed upon, they are sensible of it, they are mortified, disgusted and humbled, their eyes are opened to the base frauds which have been practised upon them by the British, nor will it be difficult, in my opinion by the practise of that humane candid and liberal policy which has ever characteris'd the American Government, to convince them of the[ir] true interests, and induce them to return to the peaceful pursuits of the chase and cultivation of their corn fields. They are sensible of the many and disastrous evils which they have suffered from a different line of conduct and are well disposed to return to their former habits of amity, friendship and trade with us, to take us by the hand, hold us fast and set themselves down under the protection of their great Father, the President of the United States.

Indulge me Sir, in urging to the consideration of Government the necessity for cultivating the present amicable disposition of the Indians in this section of the country, and vigilently counteracting the secret Machinations of the British agency, which, you may rest assured Sir, will be pratis'd to the utmost extent of their powers, in order to restore and maintain their wonted influence over that people. Their system has been already commenced and is in full operation, their agents have already gone into our Country, in the character of traders when the Indians shall see those who, during the late war, gave direction to their ruthless Tommahawks, and applauded the effects of their reeking scalping knives who openly encourag'd the waste of Blood, and received from their hands, with plaudits and rewards, the scalp fresh torn, alike from the hapless Father, defenceless tender and affectionate Mother, or innocent unoffending Babe, I repeat Sir, when the Indians shall see these people again sent and stationed among them, when they shall be told by them, that *they* are the only persons Enabled to supply the Indian wants, that were [it] not for them they the Indians would perish. That the Americans know it and dare not prevent their coming, That their British father, who sits upon the great waters, has taken pity on them and sent them goods etc. etc. when they see and hear this and much very much more, what effect may it not be presumed to have upon their unenlightened Minds, unless some discretionary power be extended to the agent, whereby to enable him to distinguish between the unprincipled blood thirsty assissin and the fair, honest, and Legal dealor who claim from him a license to trade with the Indians. It will be very difficult, or rather impossible to prevent or effectually counteract the influence, and effects of that policy, which ever has been and I do verily believe is now and will continue to be practised by the British in their intercourse with the Indians living within the American limits.

Michillimackinac for the reasons already assigned and from the additional circumstances of almost all the principle Indians from the Lakes Superior and Michigan, attending at [this] post in the course of each Summer, and that few or none of the Ottaways, or Chippeways, who reside near that post ever visit either of the other Agencies, Is in my opinion a post which requires the particular attention of Government.

The Ottaways residing at the River Shaboigan [Cheboygan] 3 Leagues [away] Lower and upper Larbré croche about 15 Leagues and at the Beaver Islands and Grand Traverse about 20 Leagues from Michillimackinac have progressed considerably in the arts of agriculture, their villages are populous and well setled they are supposed to dispose of about Twelve thousand bushels of corn and as many bushels of Irish potatoes per annum at the Island of Michillimackinac and the British post. Their corn is purchased principally for the use of the North west fur trade, with little encouragement they might be induced to locate themselves and much increase their agricultural labours, already do they supply our Market with considerable quantities of vegetables Cabbages, Turnips, Pumpkins,

Squashes, Cucumbers, Melons etc. etc., some of their chiefs have applied to me for cows, Hogs, Fowls, etc. etc. to be furnished them by their father the President of the U. States, For a blacksmith to make the repair their farming utensils, Traps, guns etc. etc and that he will instruct them to build houses and live as we whites live. I have promised them an answer from their great Father before the setting in of the next frosts. They have requested me to say to him that they used to draw those supplies from the red Coats, that the red Coats have told them lies, have deceived them, and that they will no more believe the red coats. They wish to settle down and make the road clear to Michillimackinac and hope their father will take pity upon them and supply their wants. I have the honour to Subscribe myself Your Excellency's mo. obt. hble. Servt.

WM. HY. PUTHUFF
Ind. Agt. Mackinaw.

His Excellency Lewis Cass Gov. Michigan Ty. etc. etc.

1816: AGENTS OF THE SOUTHWEST AND AMERICAN FUR COMPANIES

[MS. in Wisconsin Historical Library. Pressmark: Wisconsin MSS., 3B61.]

MONTREAL 15th May 1816

Mr. J. Porlier

SIR—We received your Letter of 16th July, and Mr. Rocheblave paid us Three hundred and ten pounds as you will see by the inclosed statement whereby you will find that the balance of the composition up to 1st October next, will be Four hundred and five pounds 1sh Currency.

It will afford us much pleasure to learn that you have been fortunate in Returns this season. We thank you for the preference given to Mr. Rocheblave in taking Goods from him, and are persuaded that he will allow you good prices for your Peltries. Muskrats however have greatly depreciated being scarcely worth half what they were. Beaver has also fallen off, and Swanskins fallen off, almost to nothing. Other articles have done well owing to the very small quantities at market.

We shall forever regret that at the late Treaty of peace more favorable terms had not been procured for the Indians. What the Americans may finally decide about the Indian Trade is unknown, as we do not perceive that any act has passed thereon at the last Session of Congress.

M^r. Rocheblave goes up again with Goods, and we hope will continue to have your Custom, but the excessive duties will now be a sad burthen to the Trade. We remain, Your most Obed^t Servants

FORSYTH RICHARDSON & Co.

Endorsed by Porlier: 1816 Forsyth Richardson's letter acknowledging the receipt of a certain sum.

[MS. in Pension Office, Washington. Pressmark: Indian Office Letter Book "C," p. 374.]

DEPARTMENT OF WAR, June 5th. 1816.

SIR—Mr. John Jacob Astor, of New-York, has engaged extensively in the Indian trade, and has appointed Mr. Varnum, Mr. Matthews, and Mr. Ramsay Crooks,[57] his agents. I am directed by the Secretary of War to request, that you will give to these gentlemen every possible facility and aid in the prosecution of their business, that may be compatible with your public duties. I have the honor to be, etc.

[GEORGE GRAHAM, chief clerk]

Addressed: Commanding officer at Michillimackinac, and to Wm. H. Puthuff, Indian agent at the same place.

---

[57] Joseph B. Varnum, for whom see *ante*, p. 326, note 69; for Ramsay Crooks, see *ante*, p. 347, note 91.

William W. Matthews enlisted in the Astorian enterprise as clerk, and went out to the Columbia River on the "Tonquin." While at Astoria he married the daughter of a Clatsop chief, and after the transfer of Astoria to the North West Company remained in the country until 1815. Coming back to New York, he entered Astor's service, becoming the forwarding agent at Montreal.—ED.

[1815–1817]   Fur-trade in Wisconsin

1816: SEIZURE OF FURS

[MS. in Pension Building, Washington. Pressmark: Indian Office Book 204. Letter Book 1, p. 225.]

MICHILLIMACKINAC June 6th. 1816.

D[EAR] SIR—I arrived on here on the evening of the 4th. inst. after a most tedious passage.

On my arrival I found every circumstance relating to my Agency in such state as to most imperiously require my presence. Such has been and yet is my extreme hurry of business as to preclude the possibility of furnishing you, by the Perry now about to get under way, with particulars. I can only observe that Lesley is in custody, his examination commenced yesterday and will require one or two days to complete. I have taken possession of twelve or fifteen thousand dollars worth of furs and goods on their way from the Indian Country to Drummonds Island which has been procured Contrary to the laws of the United States regulating trade and Intercourse with the Indians.

Two hundred and fifty two Fullsawwynyes [Folles Avoines: Menominee] were here on my arrival they are well disposed towards us.

As the vessel is weighing Anchor I hope you will pardon my not furnishing you a more circumstancial report until the next opportunity. I am Sir, Your most Obedt. Hble. Servt.

W. H. PUTHUFF
Ind. Ag. Mackinaw

His Excellency L. Cass Governor etc.

[MS. in Wisconsin Historical Library. Pressmark: Wisconsin MSS., 3B65. Translated from the French.]

MACKINAC 20th June, 1816.

MY DEAR FRIEND—This is the third time I have had the pleasure of writing you without however hoping that my letters have reached you. I have nothing very agreeable of which to inform you, on the contrary the vexations and troubles that await you here make me almost regret having given you the first advice, especially when I have no means of preventing them—as soon as people arrive here they are seized; at least their returns [in peltry] are, and I assure you it is not without trouble that matters are arranged, and possession is gotten with cautions about coming up. The law suit should begin at Detroit next September and God only knows how it will result. These seizures are made under pretext that the Packs have been secured by trading without a License etc.[58] I say nothing more about it only that I believe it is almost impossible that you should Save your Packs (I suppose that you will carry them elsewhere than here) the avenues being too well guarded. I believe that it will be better to bring them here and run the risk of a Law suit, than to run that of a seizure in trying to elude them. Moreover that will be the final result (if one should escape them) for a person who wishes to remain some time in this Country. I tell you this, but am far from believing you have need of my advice.

Take the precautions to put your Merchandise in a secure place if you have any, for fear of some domiciliary visits, and come as soon as possible to join one who is very sincerely Your Friend

P^r. ROCHEBLAVE

Jacques Porlier Esq.

Endorsed by Porlier: 1816 letter of Rocheblave reporting the difficulties of arriving at Makinac.

[Source, same as preceding document, but 1B36. Translated from the French.]

MAKINAC 20th June 1816

DEAR SIR—This is the third [letter] that I have addressed you without hoping that the other 2 reached you.

All your Packs were seized before arriving and it is only with great trouble that we have been able to recover them in

---

[58] On this point see the report of the British commandant at Drummond Island, in *Mich. Pion. and Hist. Colls.*, xvi, p. 465.—ED.

giving security for the value of the Peltries. These proceedings have taken place they say, because these people have had no license to trade with the Savages. The suit to decide the validity of these seizures will be tried in Detroit next September.

I believe that you would better come here immediately with your Packs and run the risk of a suit at law, rather than run the risk of a seizure at your place where they would pass the winter. If you have any merchandise you would better put it in a place of safety for fear of a visit. I give this as my opinion, but do not pretend to advise as to what is best. Hoping to see you I sign myself Sincerely, dear Sir Your very Humble Servant

[PIERRE ROCHEBLAVE][59]

Addressed: For Mr Louis Grignon, Green Bay.

[MS. in Pension Building, Washington. Pressmark: Indian Office Book 204. Letter Book 1, p. 239. William Henry Puthuff to Governor Lewis Cass.]

MICHILLIMACKINAC 20th. June 1816

DR. SIR—By return of the vessel Com. Perry, I gave you a hurried account of the situation of the agency here, my business has continued on the increase and kept me insessantly employed, on the 17 inst. I met 39 Ottaways from Green Bay 202 Chippeways from Lake Michigan, 584 Fallsawynes from Green Bay and its dependencies, 167 Wynabagoes from Green Bay or near that place and 141 Sieux from the Neighbourhood of Praire du Chéne in Council the pipe of peace was presented to the Orators of each tribe or nation respectively in the name of their nations and on behalf of the whole collectively.

The council opened on the part of the Fallsawyne by Tomah their principal chief who professed on behalf of his tribe and the whole present, the most amicable sentiments and feelings

---

[59] The signature in the original document has been destroyed; but the letter is in the same handwriting as the preceding one.—ED.

toward us, and asked that we would send them traders to reside among and with them. Charged the British with having induced them to embark in the late war, expressed his regret at having done so, and observed that he was now going [to] tell them so and demand his *discharge* from them, that he had now done with them and would never again quit his great father the President of the United States, he was followed by Ech Chaguin a young man so called, or private Orator for the Wynnebagoes a tribe of about 770 warriors living principally near Praire du Chéne and between there and Green Bay, who expressed the same wish in relation to the sending traders among them, but expressed no determined resolution to abandon the British acknowledged no wrong at the part of his people in the part they had taken during the late war nor made any promises or professions other than a wish to remain at peace and never again raise the Tomahawk. The Chippeway's expressed the same sentiments which had been advanced by the Falls-awynes, and the Sieux closed the council by a restoration of the sentiments, wishes, Professions and acknowledgements of the Falls and Chippeway's. I assured them that their Great Father the President of the United States, would comply with their request in sending traders among them, receive them under his protection and attend to their real wants etc. etc.

The Wynebagoes have no doubt many among them who are disaffected towards us, and cannot in my opinion be rely'd further than their weakness and want of support from the neighbouring tribes will justify. The Fallsawynes or a very decided majority of them, are decidedly favourably disposed to the Establishment of an American post at Green Bay, so are the Chippeways and Ottaway's in the vicinity of that place.

This day I have met in Council the Chiefs and head men of the Ottaways and Chippeways within my immediate agency, or near this Post. They have in the name of their respective tribes declared openly their determination forever to abandon the British Interest, have taken their American father by the hand, and have declared the determination never again to abandon us have acknowledged their error in having listened to other councils, stated that they were forced to take up the Tomahawk, were promised much and much disappointed, asked permission occasionally to visit Drummonds Island for the purpose of collecting their dues, and in a word, promised to conform strictly to our wishes in all things, and asked for advice, and orders. My answer was to assure them of our sincerity and the promises of protection we had accorded them, in the forgiveness of the past and necessity for their careful observance of their promises and professions for the future, this they most solemnly promised and pledged themselves it should be comply'd with.

I am sincerely of the opinion that no good grounds for a doubt of the sincerity of their professions exists, I think I can venture to pledge myself for them, that so long as a respectable force shall be kept at this post, they will decidedly adhere to us. I must beg leave again to repeat that they have been grossly deceived, they are sensible of it, and well disposed to return to their former habits of intimacy and friendship with us.

The issues here for the Indian Department have as will be seen by the subjoined report of Indians visiting this Post, far exceeded my expectation. I have been and shall continue to be as economical on that subject as possible. Many of the Indians from Lake Superior and its tributary streams may be expected to visit this Post shortly, several Canoes have this moment arrived, who report that many more may be immediately expected.

I expect to meet them collectively in Council in one or two days. the Potawatomies and neighbouring Indians from Chicagou and its vicinity will it is said soon visit us, by the next vessel I expect to be enabled to give you a particular account of their profession and requests, which I am inclined to believe will be similar to those of the Fallsawynes, Chippeways and Sieux. the Wynibagoes I am fully persuaded are the most hostile towards us of any tribes in this district of Country, and are encouraged in that hostility of feeling and disposition toward us, by certain traders Roulette, Grinois etc. who are now at the Green bay. I have good grounds for advancing this opinion and hope to succeed in arresting these fellows, who will be held to account for their ungenerous, Illiberal and Hostile conduct to an injured Country, who has but too long cherished reptiles of their description in its bosom in the character of traders, they will not easily escape the vigilence of this post. 4 Boats are almost constantly manned and cruising here for the purpose of intercepting all Boats, Canoes or other conveyances for Furs obtained without License in the Indian Country, my information on the subject of that trade, is general.

I am already apprized of every Trader who has thus gone into the Country and their place of trade, and the place where their Furs have been collected and probable time that they may be expected at the Foot of Lake Michigan. Colonel Chamber's[60] exertions to arrest them is unremitting, nor will any of them in my opinion be enabled to escape, the subjoined list of seizures made here, will inform you of our vigilence, the mode I have adopted, at the request of the respective owners, in releasing Goods, Wares and Merchandize thus seized, as will appear by Bonds herewith transmitted, will, I hope meet your approbation I was induced to adopt this mode from a belief that no injury would or could arise to the Country therefrom, and from a belief that the manner in which I have drawn up the Bonds (a copy of which I furnished Mr. Abbott—Notary Public and who has been employed to draw them up and have them signed pursuant to that Copy) will obviate any difficulty that might otherwise have arisen from the want of a regular process in releasing the goods so seized on this subject I wish for your opinion and advice by the first Opportunity.

---

[60] Col. Talbot Chambers, of the rifle regiment. His military history is given in detail in *Wis. Hist. Colls.*, xi, p. 393. In August, 1815, he was sent to command at Mackinac; the next July he accompanied the military expedition to Green Bay, and was during the winter left in command at Fort Howard. Early in 1817, Chambers was transferred to Prairie du Chien, where his tyrannies are related in *Id.*, ii, pp. 128, 129. His later history is told by Shaw, pp. 229, 230; see also his letters, *post.*—ED.

Lashley has been arrested and is now in confinement here he has requested permission to remain for a short time for the purpose of settling his Business here, in which request I have indulged him, he will be sent down probably in the next vessel for his trial.

John Dousman,[61] who has determined on remaining here has consented to command the company of Militia to be organized at this place, may I ask that you will forward his commission by the first Opportunity.

The Indians who have lately attended here in Council from Green Bay, Praire du Chéne etc., are now at Drummonds Island they have promised to call on their return and report what shall be said to them there, how sincere they may be in this promise, or how far their reports may be relied upon, is, perhaps in some degree doubtfull, Yet I am inclined to believe much important information may be collected from them. A party [of] Wynebagoes who had left this Post from [for] Drummonds Island the day or two previous to my arrival, have since returned here and proceeded on to their Summer residence near the Green Bay. They report that the British detained one Canoe of their Young Men, until they should hear from the King, when these young men, so detained are to return to their nation with the news. Many of the traders have been extremely active in the Chicago and Green Bay Countries, in souring the minds of the Indians, encouraging the disaffected, exciting their fears and preparing them to oppose the establishment of American posts at for one year longer in their Country.

---

[61] John Dousman was of Pennsylvania birth, and came West some time before 1808, being engaged as an army sutler. He lived for some time at Green Bay, married Rosalie Laborde, daughter of a resident of that place, and had much property there. Some time during the War of 1812–15, he removed to Mackinac, and seems to have remained on the island until about 1824, when he returned with his family to Green Bay. He was (in 1818) associate justice of the Mackinac county court, and his affidavits for the Green Bay land claims were made at the former place. See account of his return to Green Bay, in *Wis. Hist. Colls.*, xv, pp. 211, 212.—ED.

The Wynebago Orator Ech-cha-gun made this request in private council, he stated that though his chiefs would not permit him to do so in Public, yet that it was their real sentiments and that they would have asked or made the same request in Public, had they not feared a refusal, and that their father would be angry at them for doing so.

His reasons were that many of his Young Men were dissatisfied and might strike our young men if they came among them too soon, that by the next summer his Young men could be reconcil'd and there would then be no danger to be apprehended from them. That their Chiefs and great men were sincere in their professions of friendship towards us, that they had used every means in their power to satisfy and quiet their young men, but had not as yet entirely succeeded, but by the next summer he had no doubt, they would be enabled to quiet them and therefore asked his great Father the President not to send his soldiers among them until the next summer. Shortly after this request had been thus made, many of the same tribe, who had received information of its nature and my Answer, called upon me to request that I would pay no attention to their Orator, that he was himself one of the most disaffected among them and had with many others endeavoured to form a Coalition of all the Indians in that district of country against us but had failed, as not a single nation even their own the Wynebagoes, would consent to it or agree again to raise the Tomahawk they were tired of the War and sincerely wished for peace, that there were some among them hostile toward us but that it was only a few who would not dare to acknowledge their hostility when we did come among them. The small party who left this previous to my coming 30 or 40 in number, made the same request in council with Col. Chambers, from these different and conflicting accounts, little doubt exists of the unfriendly disposition of a part of this tribe at least, how far it may or will be evinced by their conduct on the establishment of a Milty. post at Green Bay, I am not prepared to venture a decided opinion, but am inclined to the belief that a respectable Military force will, the moment it appears among them, Quiet all murmering and produce the most happy effects in restoring an amicable intercourse between those Indians and our Government and People. They have been told by the restless unprincipalled traders who are yet with them, that it was the intention of our Government to take the lands from them and drive them still farther back upon the extensive Wilderness between them and Pacific Ocean. That we were determined to take their fur, skins etc. for a mere nothing and a thousand reports have been industrious circulated among them by the restless and designing men. at Drummonds Island the Indians are informed that presents cannot as Yet be made them to a large amount because of the determination of the American Government to prevent British Traders from living or residing with the Indians, and thus deprived of their best friends and natural protectors, the Americans will rob them of any valuable presents which they should receive.

I mentioned these reports merely to shew the spirit which is so industriously attempted to be raised and encouraged on the part of individuals attached to the British Government, among the Indians. there is no reason however to believe that any serious evil will grow out of this mode of procedure, as the Indians openly profess to believe it only calculated to evade the promises made them by that Government and call them Liars.

I have seen a letter addressed by J. J. Astor to a Mr. Franks a British trader now at this place in which Mr. Astor expresses surprise and regret at the passage of a law forbidding British subjects from trading with Indians, within the American limits etc. but observes that power is vested in the President to grant special license for that purpose and that he Astor has dispatched a messenger to the President from whom he entertains no doubt that some may be procured and will be immediately forwarded to Mr. Franks and Mr. Astor's friends in the North west trade. I wish to god the President knew this man Astor as well as he is known here. Licenses would not be placed at his descretion to be distributed among British subjects, Agents or Pensioners. I hope in god no such license will be granted, his British Friends here calculate confident on his success in this matter, that they may be disappointed is my most sincere wish, should they succeed incalculable evil will assuredly grow out of the measure.

I am Sir, Your most obt. and Hble. Servt.

WM. HENY. PUTHUFF
Ind. Agent Michillimackin[ac]

His Excellency L. Cass Gov. of M. Ty. etc.

The within despatch have been made up under the greatest possible pressure of business. Errors will I hope be excused.

1816: TROOPS AT PRAIRIE DU CHIEN

[MS. in Burton Library, Detroit, vol. 112, p. 138.]

PRAIRIE DU CHIEN 23d June 1816

SIR—On the 20th the United States Troops arrived here commanded by Brig^d. General Thomas A. Smith and accompanyed by Major Graham Indian Agent for the Territory of Illinoise,[62] on the 21st they commenced regulating the village

---

[62] Thomas A. Smith, of Virginia birth, enlisted in the regular army in 1803 as lieutenant in the artillery service. In 1808 he was promoted to a captaincy in the rifles, and became successively lieutenant-colonel and colonel of the same regiment. In 1814 he was brevetted brigadier-general, and served on the Lake Champlain frontier. After taking possession of Prairie du Chien, he retired, leaving a detachment, and in 1818 resigned from active service in the army.

Richard Graham was born in Virginia, but in early life emigrated to Kentucky, whence he entered the United States army (in 1801), serving through the regular grades until honorably discharged at the reduction of 1815. The same year, he was appointed Indian agent for Illinois, and assisted at the treaties of St. Louis, in the summers of 1817 and 1818. Later, he was transferred to the Osage agency, and in that capacity drew the treaty of 1822 with that nation. In 1825 he was transferred to the agency for the Delaware, Shawnee, and Kickapoo of Missouri, which he maintained until about 1828. His residence was principally at St. Louis, and there for his second wife, he married Catharine Mullanphy. He seems to have been an efficient and active agent.—ED.

by requireing of the Traders here to show their Licences. those who had not any, their goods were seized, your goods came under the Seizesure. They have taken possession of some Houses, Condemning them for public purposes. Those I live in are Seized and turned over to me for the United States Indian trading houses, forbidding me at the same time to pay no rent for them after that date. Thus you find how things are changed. Charges have been brought from St Louis against Mr M Brisbois he is arrested & will be sent to St Louis for Trial,⁶³ perhaps others here will accompany him. Mr Henery can inform you more particulary should you not return write me. in haist I remain your Hbl Svt

JNO W JOHNSON
U S A

Mr Francis Bouthilier now at Mackinack⁶⁴

1816: LICENSES FOR FOREIGNERS

[MS. in Pension Building, Washington. Pressmark: Indian Office Book 204. Letter Book 1, p. 271.]

MICHILLIMACKINAC 12th. July 1816

DR. SIR—In addition to the points on which I have felt myself bound to obtain your instructions before I should proceed farther, in relation to Indian Trade etc. as will appear from my former communications on that subject, many new and embarrassing principles have since arisen, from the nature and intention of the instructions from the Department of War of the 10th, of May 1816 combined with the very limited information I am in the possession of relating to that extensive District of Country West of the Mississippi River and above Praire du chien, embracing the Sieux etc. etc. etc.

How far that district of Country may be supplied with

---

⁶³ For this incident see *Wis. Hist. Colls.*, ii, p. 128, ix, p. 284. Brisbois is noted *ante*, p. 318, note 56. He had accepted an American commission before the war, and was thus liable to punishment.—ED.

⁶⁴ For this person see *Id.*, xviii, p. 463, note 85.—ED.

goods by American Citizens I am wholly uninformed. The South West Company have been in the habit of sending extensive supplies of goods, by way of Lake Michigan, Praire du Chien and Mississippi to that country and have applied to me for licenses, for that trade for the ensuing Year, and state that no American trading house, has ever heretofore been established there. the Sieux and other Indians from that quarter have been very importunate with me, to send them Traders. Under these circumstances I have proposed as the only means within my power to reconcile the supply of that Country, by foreigners, with the intention of the Instructions from the Department of War on that subject, That to such persons (foreigners) whose characters were unexpectionable, Licences would be given conditioned that they should be permitted to go into the Country with their Merchandize and should there be no American Establishments there, then to carry on their trade for one year; but not to open their goods or in any wise dispose of them to Indians at a village or hunting camp which they may find thus supplied by American Citizens; some two or three licenses will be taken on this condition, but the South West Company conceive the condition to be inadmissible. As I could not [feel] myself authorized to indulge them in erasing it, I have consequently referred Mr. Crooks, their agent, to your decision, have the goodness to write me particularly on this subject. the Interior Lakes will be amply supplied by american Citizens from this post [to] Lake Superior in part, and in part by foreigners. I have refused licenses in all cases to foreigners except the persons actually intended to go into the country, should himself, appear to support a character unexceptionable.

The Sieux, Foxes, Wynebagoes, Chippeways, and Potawatomies who some time since, visited Drummonds Island are now here on their return, they profess to be entirely pacific in their intentions and wishes towards us. while the Military force in this Country is respectable, I apprehend no danger from them nor do I believe any the most distant opposition will be made on their part, to the establishment of our posts at Chicago and Green Bay.

Fur-trade in Wisconsin

I unfortunately have a lame hand and can scarcely write intelligibly. Much matter which I should otherwise communicate, must necessarily be defered for a short time, as I write in the most excrutiating pain, from a bile on my wrist. I am Sir, Your most obt. Hble. Servt.

WM. HY. PUTHUFF
Ind. Agt.

His Excellency Lewis Cass Governor etc.

[Source, same as preceding document, but p. 278.]

DETROIT July 20th. 1816

DEAR SIR—Mr. Crooks arrived here yesterday bringing with him your letter.

Upon a view of the whole ground in relation to this subject, I have no doubt but it will be expedient to grant licenses without any condition to such Agents and traders of the Company to which you refer, as cannot from their character and conduct be suspected of a design to thwart the objects intended to be secured by the law.

Whether this law be wise and politick with a view to our Indian relations, or whether that necessity for the introduction of foreign traders, which appears to have produced the passage of the law in reality exists, are questions which we are not bound to determine.

In the execution of the trust reposed in us, we have nothing to do, but to ascertain as nearly as possible the views and objects of the Government, and to carry them into effect.

From all the information, which has reached [me] I have no doubt but the Government expect that the Country North and West of us will be supplied with goods by the Capital and enterprize of this Company, and I apprehend the question submitted to us as Agents under the law is not whether the Country shall be thus supplied by Foreigners, but whether the person applying for a license be one who can be safely admitted to trade in the Indian Country. In the resolution of this latter question is room for our discretionary powers. The character of the applicant, his former conduct, his present situation and connections, and his probable views must guide us in determining whether his admission into the Indian Country will be injurious to the United States.

But I apprehend the former question with respect to the course of the trade has been definitively determined by the Act of Congress and the Instructions of the Government.

Under this view of the subject I have no hesitation in advising you to grant licenses to applicants, whose characters are above suspicion.

With respect to Mr. Crooks, himself, I would grant him a license, but that he passes immediately through your Agency and I have a great aversion to making cyphers of any Officers.

I apprehend it would be improper to clog the licenses with any conditions, I doubt both its legality and expediency.

Upon the whole matter my opinion is that all the Agents and traders of this Company, to whose personal character and conduct, there can be no objections should be furnished with licenses. With much respect I am Dr. Sir, yo. obt. Servant

[LEWIS CASS]

Majr. Wm. Hy. Puthuff Indian Agent Michillimackinac

1816: GREEN BAY TRADERS AND PRICES

[MS. in Wisconsin Historical Library. Pressmark: Wisconsin MSS., 3B68. Translated from the French.]

MICHILLIMACKINAC July 24, 1816

MY DEAR BROTHER—As I find it necessary to go in the Washington[65] if the arrangement between us and M^r. Lawe is concluded you will take my Equipment according to the Memorandum that will be given you by our brother & Mr. Por-

---

[65] Both Lockwood and Augustin Grignon speak in their recollections of the voyage of the "Washington," that brought the troops from Mackinac to Green Bay. Grignon acted as pilot therefor. See *Wis. Hist. Colls.*, ii, p. 103, iii, p. 281.—ED.

[1815-1817] Fur-trade in Wisconsin

lier of the Merchandise of Messrs. Franks & Co. and you will adjust it as you think necessary as I would do myself.

N. B. if the arrangement that I mention to you above has not taken place you will do as our brother thinks best. Your brother

AGT. GRIGNON

Mr. Louis Grignon Present

[Source, same as preceding document, but Account Book 14. Translated from the French.]

Mka August 3 Southwest Company Dr for the Peltries of the invoice of Merchandize 1816

1100	deerskins	1.00	1100	
85	bearskins	5.50	467	50
20	bearcub skins	2.75	55	
4360	muskrats	15cts	651	50
267	do poor	6¼	16	68¾
220	lv of beaver	3 50	770	
361	Cats	62½	225	62½
40	Do poor	20	8	
141	Skunks	1 25	176	
8	Do poor	33⅓	2	66⅔
70	otters	4 50	315	
20	red foxes	1 25	25	
3	Do poor	20		60
5	Do virgin	50	2	50
9	Lynx	50	4	50
1	loup cervier			75
217	mink	66⅔	144	66⅔
20	Do poor	25cts	5	
516	marten	1.00	516	
24	bearskin covers	1.50	36	
			4582	99½

1816: TROOPS AT GREEN BAY

[MS. in Pension Building, Washington. Pressmark: Indian Office Book 204. Letter Book 1, p. 290.]

MICHILLIMACKINAC 4th. Augt. 1816

DEAR SIR—Nothing has transpired here since my last, relating to Indian matters worthy of communication, except the very extraordinary Issues of arms and ammunition made to the Indians at Drummonds Island, as many as 18 hundred have visited this post in one day, every *man* and *boy* has been furnished with arms and ammunition far exceeding the issues made at any one time during the late war. The Indians are told that the British and American Government are at Peace that they are included in that peace provided they wish it, that by the article including them it is provided that they shall be left in full possession of their lands, that the Americans never heretofore had a Post at Green Bay, But that they (the Indians) are now with the Americans and consequently may do as they think proper, if they choose to invite the Americans to come among them they may do so. But it is, I have good reason to believe, plainly insinuated that the Americans will impose upon them by fair promises until they obtain *Foot hold* that then their fate will be that of their red Brethren who have, as they are informed been thus driven by degrees from the lands they formerly inhabited.

I have however no cause to alter my former opinion, that however adverse the British Government may be to the Military occupation of Green Bay, Grand Portage, Praire du Chien, etc. by American troops, and however anxious they may be by indirect means, to prevent it, Yet there is no good grounds for a belief that they will succeed in the inducing open hostility on the part of the Indians of that district of Country, when we shall appear in respectable force. The Indians are not destitute of common sense, and certainly have more judgement, prudence and policy, than is generally believed to influence their political decisions. They are well appprised of the disastrous consequences that would ultimately result to them from a hostile

Fur-trade in Wisconsin

opposition to the landing or entre[n]ching our troops at those posts, there are however many of their more vicious and impolitic Young men that might and perhaps would proceed to open hostilities in opposition to the advice of their principal hereditary or Village Chiefs, should we appear in small force among them. Ambition for rule and power has made greater progress with that [them] than is generally believed, nor will the self and British created War Chief easily resign his powers and influence to the village Chiefs. it is upon the former that the insiduous policy of the Indian Agency at Drummonds Island is intended to operate, how far it may succeed is perhaps, measurably doubtful, but that open hostilities with the Indians will not take place, I feel pretty confident.

Under those circumstances Colo. Miller[66] ordered two companies of Infantry and a detachment of Artillery from the garrison here to cover the landing and aid in securing the encampment of the troops destined to garrison Green Bay, the Colo. commands the expedition in person. On the 29th. Ulto, the transports with the whole command were lying off the mouth of Green Bay at anchor, light winds and contratry. I entertain no doubt of their having reached their point of destination before this time.

By the next vessel I will furnish you a discriptive list of the persons, foreigners, who have obtained License for Indian Trade, there are as yet but three, Barthalott, Aird and Johnston. the S. W company's list is now before me, it contains many names that were of the British Indian Department, during the War, to them I have objected, my reasons with a list of their names and rank they held will be also forwarded to you by next vessel.

I am Sir, yo. mo. obt. Servt.

WM. HY. PUTHUFF
Indian Agent Mackinaw

His Excellency Lewis Cass Govr. etc. etc.

P. S. I have written most pressingly to Mr. Stockton to

---

[66] For a brief biographical sketch, see *Id.*, i, p. 51.—ED.

request Colo. McDougall to forward the Indian goods I left with him, those goods are much wanted here, nor can I obtain an answer or reason why they have not been forwarded. I sincerely hope goods may have arrived at Detroit for this Agency before this, when any may arrive will you have the goodness to direct Colonel McDougall to forward them immediately, he, I fear, is *slow* to act without a *spur*.

[Source, same as preceding document, but p. 303.]

MICHILLIMACKINAC 18th. August 1816

DEAR SIR—By the return of Colo. Miller from Green Bay we are informed of the result of the expedition under his command. The troops were landed without opposition, or even appearances of hostile feelings on the part of the Indians of that District of Country, with the particulars however, Colo. Bowyer has no doubt made you acquainted.

There are but few Indians at this place, those of the neighbouring villages only occasionally visit us. They are apparently perfectly reconcile[d] to our troops having occupied Green Bay and Chicago.

Herewith I send you a list of licenses issued to Foreigners. Applications for licenses within the districts of Green Bay and Chicago, have been referred to the respective agents at those posts.

I am now engaged collecting the most correct information of the different trading Posts visited by Foreigners, the number of Indians at those posts, and the amount of goods introduced, with a view to inform our Government of the true state of trade in this quarter, and the more effectually to enforce the opinion I formerly advanced, that there is not a necessity for the introduction of a *single foreigner,* except perhaps on Lake Superior, to furnish an ample supply of goods to our Indians. I will, this fall, furnish you with the result of my enquiries.

Such goods as you can spare me are much wanted here, by the Hunter I received goods for Green Bay and Chicago, those for Green Bay have been forwarded, those for Chicago shall go by the first vessel, Colo. McDougall writes me that he "had not time to put up the goods I left to forward by the Hunter." I am, Sir, your most obt. Hble. Servt.

WM. HY. PUTHUFF
Indian Agent.

His Excellency Govr. Cass

1816: FACTORY AT PRAIRIE DU CHIEN

[MS. in Pension Office, Washington. Pressmark: Indian Office Letter Book "D," pp. 126, 128.]

INDIAN OFFICE GEO:TOWN 30 aug: 1816

To John W Johnson Esq Prairie du Chien

SIR—Your several accounts and vouchers for the quarter ending with the 30 June 1st, I received in due course of mail. The expenditures are considerable, but I take for granted they have been made with all the ecconomy of which the case admitted. Having completed the buildings at P. du Chien, those will not recur; and from the stock of merchandize now on hand, added to the handsome supply now in motion, according to your last order, I anticipate with confidence, and pleasure, a very extensive display of profitable and harmonious operations. Your location at P. du Chien, from the best information, is of the very best for a large trade; and this together with your exertions, in which I am sure you will not be wanting, justify the hopes I entertain; and promise their ample realization.

* * * * * * * *

It appears to me to be proper in the present state of the property rented by you of the Mackinac company, to withold the price of the rent, *for the present.* the seizure of it by Genl. Smith, a Commanding officer in the United States army, and his assureance that it is the property of the United States, will justify this course. If the question of right shall occur; and if it shall be found to be in the Mackinac company, then of course you will pay the price agreed on for the rent of it.

It is exeedingly to be regretted that there should be any collissions between Gentlemen engaged in serving the interests of our common country. I know well the disposition of the War Department is to afford to the Indian factories as much aid from the military as is consistent with its regular duties. I sincerely hope Genl. Smith will not persist in denying reasonable aid, which is all that you would require, to the factory, and expecially so, as by the allowance made the soldiers, their consent would no doubt be voluntary.

I am happy to learn the pleasure of the Indians, on their satisfaction, much of your success will depend, as you well know.

I will write you further in reply to other parts of your letter, soon. Respectfully etc. etc.

T. L. Mc.Kenney[67]

INDIAN OFFICE GEO TOWN 2 Sept. 1816
To John W Johnson Esq

SIR—I addressed a letter to you on the 31 Ulto. in part answer to your of the 30. June last.

I have considered what remains, and particularly the desire

---

[67] Thomas Lorraine McKenney was born in Maryland in 1785, and during the War of 1812-15 acted as vidette and adjutant of the District of Columbia militia. For a year or more he was in business in Georgetown, where (April 2, 1816) he was appointed commissioner for Indian trade, to supersede Gen. John Mason, resigned. This position he held until the factory system was (in 1822) abolished. In 1824, upon the erecting of a bureau for Indian affairs in the war department, McKenney was placed in charge, and continued there until August, 1830. In 1826 he was made special commissioner to hold a treaty at Fond du Lac, Lake Superior; his experiences en route are embodied in his book, *Tour of the Lakes*. The following year he held an important treaty at Butte des Morts, and subsequently passed over the Fox-Wisconsin route to the Mississippi. Upon the latter river he visited the Indian tribes of the Southern states. After leaving the Indian office, Colonel McKenney devoted himself to publishing and lecturing in behalf of the Indian wards of the United States. In 1845 he published his *Memoirs*, and later (with a co-editor) three volumes of Indian biography. In his later years he lived in Brooklyn.

of the Sac Indians near the river St. Peters; and that also expressed by the Fox Indians near the lead mines, to be supplied with merchandize. It is entirely within the scope of our policy to extend every reasonable assistance to all the Indians within our limits, so far as that may be practicable, and consistent with the amount of our trading capital. At present however, I am unable to see how this can be done, to any considerable extent or at all unless you could send supplies from Prarie du Chien and out of your stock now in trade, which might be augmented, somewhat for this purpose. To make a depot at St. Louis, and supply Individuals from it, at cost and charges, however valuable the results might be in putting down the british traders, and in attaching the Indians to us, cannot be done at this time. This however may be done if congress shall accede to the plan of the Honbl. the Secy. of War, in augmenting the capital of this establishment—and under judicious regulations, much good would no doubt result from it. Meanwhile you can exercise your discretion, in pushing on occasional supplies from the factory at Prarie du Chien, which as I have said, shall be occasionally, and additionally replenished.

It is hardly necessary for me to call your attention to the risque that is involved in sending out traders. I am very sure that you will have an eye upon their honesty and fair dealings; and in case you shall be deceived, to have in your possession sufficient security, as a reserve to bring up their arrears, this point well guarded, and which must of course be left to you, I shall be gratified if those Indians on the river St. Peters, and at the lead mines could have their wants supplied, if but partially. It is but due to you to apprise you, that much is expected from the operation at Prairie du Chien, your own experience, your location there—perhaps the very best, your Forty thousand dollar capital, make a combination of points that afford just grounds for large expectations. To succeed well, and profitably, and to give entire satisfaction to the In-

---

and died in New York in 1859. He contributed to *Wis. Hist. Colls.*, v, pp. 178-204, a history of the Winnebago War.—ED.

dians with whom you will trade, will, I have no doubt, give much satisfaction to you. I need hardly assure you that I shall partake largely with you in this satisfaction. I hope ere this you have received the goods, as well as my letter of april last.

I franked, and forwarded your letter as you requested, to your brother. dont lose sight of Pryor and Butler. Respectfully etc. etc.

T. L. MC.KENNEY.

1816: POST BUILT AT GREEN BAY

[MS. in Library of Congress. McArthur Papers.]

MOUTH OF FOX RIVER GREEN BAY 24th. September 1816

MY DEAR SIR—Having received many instances of your friendship and believing that I am still honoured with its possession, I am emboldened to address you upon a subject of material consequence to me and depending much upon your approbation and support.

I have, my dear sir, lost all prepossessions for the army and determined to withdraw from it as soon as practicable;—a change of [se]ntement produced by the most substan[tial] reasons; among them may be cited the [con]duct evinced by my Cong Genl. to the [district] to which I belong, having employed i [MS. torn] intending still to employ it, in performi[ng] the duty of Pioneers to the other corps, [MS. torn] remain at a Post no longer than the com[ple]tion of the Fort. The loss next Spring of a large proportion of my Company by discharges, the only remaining tie that binds me to the Army and what is of the most serious concern to me finding, that, in these remote and inaccessible quarters of the world, my pay is entirely inadaquate to my support—Being poor, I as yet have no wish to return to the Country of my friends, altho I still and must ever retain for them the tenderest regard, and do often sigh for their society: But my pride and principles of

Fur-trade in Wisconsin

independence require a seperation till I possess greater means; and the longer I remain in the Army the greater will be the barriers to my return.

Weighing maturely all these facts, with others of equal consideration, have resolved me to make application for an [India]n or Factors Agency, To be situated [at] the Portage of this River and the Ousco[nsin w]here a Fort is to be erected next spring, I [sho]uld most prefer, but would be perfectly s[atisf]ied with a situation on the Mississippi or a[ny] of its waters. An Indian Agency, being reckoned the most responsible, would be my Choice.

We arrived here on the 8th of August last, in four vessels, without experiencing any difficulty in the navigation of this Bay, which was entirely unknown, or in crossing the Bar opposite the mouth of this river. Two companies of Riflemen and the same Infantry, commanded by Brevet Lieut Col Chambers, constitute the force intended for this Post, but an additional one, consisting of a detachment of Artillery and two companies of Infy with Col Jno Miller, accompanied the expedition hither,[68] as a precaution against any opposition from the Indians, it having been reported, tho most fa[lse]ly, that 800 warriors were embodied to [op]pose the Military establishment h[ere] but the few we found manifested [much] humility and friendship. Major [Graham who] is with us and often speaks of you with [much] regard, has selected for the Fort the pos[t], where the old French one once stood, [si]tuated about one mile up the river and one half mile below where commences a Mongrel French settlement that extends about five miles on both sides of the river and is occupied by about forty families, many of whom, in consequence of their extreme indolent habits and frequent Indian depredations upon their property, are reduced to the most distressing want. Prior to the war this settlement is represented to have been in a flourishing condition, being of itself completely capable of its sup-

---

[68] For another contemporary account of the American occupation of Green Bay, see *Wis. Hist. Colls.*, xiii, pp. 441–447.—ED.

port—having Grist, saw, horse mills and Distilerys, and abounding with cattle and horses and some hogs—but during the war the former were abandoned, the latter destroyed and their fields neglected.

The prospect of this country, to the extent of the settlement and in the direction of the Bay, is beautiful and interesting. The climate uniform, much milder than at [Detro]it, and experience has proved it to be [more] healthful. The soil as fertile as that of [MS. torn] and Kentucky, having observed in many p[laces] black light mold of fifteen inches deep. [with] garden productions in size larger than I h[ave] ever seen in any country, and vegetation, in [gen]eral, more luxuriant. This river, I would adjudge to be about four hundred yards wide, of a gentle current and sufficiently deep for the largest Vessels on the Lakes to the rapids, which is five miles from the mouth. This Bay is computed to be about 90 miles long, and from this place to Mackinac is calculated to be about 180 and to the Mississippi about 350 miles. The portage, which is half way to the Mississippi, is represented to be the most desirable part of this Country, and in time, from its peculiar position, must become a place of the first consequence. A Public trading House at that place would be profitable to Government and of the first import[ance] to the Indians, as it would, if prope[rly co]nducted, completely secure them from [the] monstrous impositions that are [being] practised upon them by British [an]d American Traders. And an India[n agen]cy as necessary for the control and Amer[can]izing the Winabagos who reside in its neigh[b]ourhood, a numerous mischievious and ungovournable people. Agreeable to the Opinion of the most reputable inhabitants of this country the place in question is more resorted to by Indians from the Lakes and the Mississippi than any other at which there is a Military establishment. Will you be pleased, my dear Sir, to de me the favour of communicating to me this winter by the way of Detroit, your opinion and advice upon the subject to which I have solicited your attention two [times] in the course of that season will

1815–1817]   Fur-trade in Wisconsin

pro[ceed] thence hither. W[ith] perfect respect Believe me your [si]ncere friend

JNO. O'FALLON[69]
Capt. Rifle Regt.

Addressed: Genl. Duncan Mc. Arthur[70] Chillicothe Ohio

Endorsed: John O'Fallon

---

[69] John O'Fallon was born in Louisville, Nov. 23, 1791, the son of Dr. James O'Fallon and the youngest sister of George Rogers Clark. He was practically the adopted son of his illustrious uncle, and spent most of his time with him until sent in 1803 to a boarding school. In 1811 he joined the army under Harrison, and was severely wounded at the battle of Tippecanoe. After convalescence at Vincennes, and a visit to St. Louis early in 1812, where he took part in Whiteside's Illinois expedition, he joined the army in October and was assigned to Harrison's staff. In that capacity he took part in the defence of Fort Meigs and the battle of the Thames. He remained with Harrison until the latter's resignation in May, 1814, and in 1815 was in station at Malden—for a short time, in command. As captain in the 1st rifles, he was sent first to Mackinac, then to Green Bay. He did not resign from the army until 1818, when he settled at St. Louis and entered a business career that proved successful. He was president of several banks and of an early railroad company, and aided much in building up the industries of Missouri and of the Mississippi valley generally. O'Fallon was a man of great philanthropy, and founded several institutions, such as the O'Fallon Polytechnic, St. Louis Medical College, and Home for the Friendless. His correspondence with Dr. Lyman Copeland Draper is a valued part of the Wisconsin Historical Society's collections. When he died in 1865, it was said of him that one "never knew a finer or nobler man."—ED.

[70] Gen. Duncan McArthur (1772–1839) was general of the Ohio militia during the War of 1812-15, and in 1814 succeeded Harrison in command of the Western army. He was a commissioner to negotiate Indian treaties (1815-17), and later a member of Congress (1823-25), as well as governor of Ohio (1830-32). His papers are in the Library of Congress.—ED.

1816: FACTORY AND LICENSES AT GREEN BAY

[MS. in Pension Building, Washington. Pressmark: Indian Office Book 204. Letter Book 1, p. 319.]

GREEN BAY AGENCY [Oct. 1, 1816][71]

SIR—I have seen most of the principal chiefs residing in this quarter. They all appear to be friendly disposed, and have generally expressed themselves well pleased with the establishments at this place. The Winnebagoes were opposed to the building of a Fort, when they first visited me, but after I held two or three talks with their Chiefs, they left me apparently well satisfied. I have had some trouble, from the want of Medals, Armbands, and small flags, believing these necessary articles would be here in a short time, I demanded from the Chiefs the medals etc. they had received from the British, promising to replace them with those of the United States, most of the Chiefs who have visited me since I made the demand, have delivered up their Medals etc. they had received, not having any to give in return, I considered myself bound to pay them well for what they gave up, and promised to replace them as soon as possible.

The whole of the goods intended for this Agency has gone to Chicago, and I have only received a few articles marked for that Agency, without Invoice or letter accompanying the packages I have made this statement to the Secretary of War, and have requested him to forward on Medals etc. in the Spring.

*   *   *   *   *   *   *   *

JNO. BOWYER
Ind. Agent.

His Excellency Governor Cass Detroit

---

[71] The following letter is undated in the original but the letters in the archives are inserted in chronological order, and this lies between one of Sept. 27 and another of Oct. 4, 1816.—ED.

Fur-trade in Wisconsin

[MSS. in Burton Library, Detroit, vol. 112, p. 224.]

GREEN BAY AGENCY October 3d. 1816

Received of Mr Peire Grignon fifty Dollars on Account of Mr Botillea [Bouthillier] for his Licence to trade with the Indians.

JN BOWYER
Indian Agent

GREEN BAY AGENCY October 3d. 1816

Received of Mr Peire Grignon on account of Mr Rolette for Licence to trade with the Indians. one hundred Dollars.

JN° BOWYER
Indian Agent

1816: LEGAL OPINION ON LICENSES

[MS. in Wisconsin Historical Library. Pressmark: Wisconsin MSS., 1D20.]

Opinion of Colonel Benton

Having carefully examined the Act of Congress passed 29th. April 1816 and also the Acts passed 30th March 1802, regulating the trade and intercourse with the Indian Tribes and have also Considered Other Acts on the same subject and the Provision of the Treaty of Ghent

I do therefore give it as my Opinion that Any Foreigner is at Liberty to introduce Goods into Any Part of the United States to which the Indian title has been extinguished without a Licence from Any Governor or Any Other Officer to trade with Indians Provided he has a Licence to sell Merchandize Generally under the several Laws of the United States as All Merchants Must have whether citizens or aliens.

And I also give it as my Opinion that no Goods [brought] By a foreigner into the United States According to Law And on which the Customary duties have been paid can be Seized by the Military or become forfeited or incur Any penalties which [while] kept or Vended Upon Any Teritory within the United States to which the Indian title has been extinguished.

BENTON
atty & Counseller at Law[72]

Given at my Office at ST LOUIS this 8 October 1816

1816: AFFAIRS AT GREEN BAY

[MS. in Pension Office, Washington. Pressmark: Indian Office Letter Book "D," p. 54.]

INDIAN OFFICE GEO TOWN 21 Oct. 1816

M. Irwin Esq

SIR—I am notified by your letter of the 30 aug: of your arrival off Green Bay on the 26th. of that month; and am gratified to learn that you have received favorable impressions of that place.

It seems to me that Col: Boyers testimony in the case of the plunder by the rifle corps, is sufficient to justify you in appealing to their commander for renumeraticn, which can be come at in a summary way, by ascertaining the amount stolen; and aportioning it amongst the parties concerned, and deducting it from their wages. I can see no reason why soldiers, more than other people, should steal with impunity. You will look to this affair. If you receive from the Commander of the rogues, the amount stolen by them, the mode and extent of chastisement will be with him to settle.

Let me hear from you as constantly as possible and when you look about you a little, give me some account of Green Bay with its relative position with other places of more note. Respectfully etc. etc.

T. L. MC.KENNEY.

---

[72]Thomas Hart Benton (1782–1858) came to St. Louis in 1815, and practiced law there until his election (1820) to the United States senate. His later career is a matter of national history—ED.

Fur-trade in Wisconsin

1816: LICENSES TO FOREIGNERS

[Source, same as preceding document, but Letter Book "C," p. 439.]

DEPARTMENT OF WAR, 29th. October, 1816.

SIR—I have the honor to enclose for your information and guidance, copies of the instructions which have been given to the several agents authorized to grant licenses to foreign traders. This authority was confined to the agents on the North Western frontier, because they were the only agents to whom it was probable that application would be made for original licenses. The agencies at Green Bay and Chicago were placed under the superintendence of the Governor of the Michigan territory, because the facilities of communication with Detroit were much greater than with Kaskaskias, and their supplies would necessarily take that direction; and because it was not absolutely certain in what territory those agencies would be, when a due North line from Post Vincennes should be accurately run; different maps lay down differently the relative situation of that place and Lake Michigan. I have the honor to be etc.

[GEORGE GRAHAM
Acting Secretary of War]

Addressed: *Ninian Edwards Gov. of Illinois Territory.*

[Source, same as preceding document, but p. 441.]

DEPARTMENT OF WAR, 30th. October, 1816.

SIR—The letter of the 10th. of May last, empowering certain agents to grant licenses to foreign traders, did not authorize any charge to be made on account of issuing such licenses, nor was it contemplated by the government that any agent would make such a charge; information has however been received at this department, founded, as it is represented, on the declarations of the traders who had obtained licenses at Michilimackinac, that they had paid fifty dollars for each license, and that they had paid for the release of certain cargoes of furs which had been seized at that place. Among others Rollette and Aird are stated to have paid a considerable sum on these accounts. It is believed that these representations are altogether unfounded, but it has become necessary to call on you for an explanation, which will no doubt be entirely satisfactory.

Should the fact however be satisfactorily established that any traders have made unfounded representations on this subject, they ought to be punished by recalling their licenses. I have the honor etc. etc.

[GEORGE GRAHAM
Act^g Secretary of War]

Addressed: Majr. William H. Puthuff, Ind. agent, Mackinac

[MS. in Wisconsin Historical Library. Pressmark: Wisconsin MSS., 55B71.]

United States of America }
District of Michilimackinac } ss   *To all whom it may Concern*

Whereas William Dixon a foreigner residing on the River St Peters[73] United States hath made application to trade with Indian Tribes at the River St Peters or in the Mississippi Country under the Law of Congress on that Subject passed 29th April 1816 and hath given the amount of goods he intends to embark in his Trade on Oath Viz Not exceeding Six thousand three hundred Dollars and 00 Cents

Now therefore he the said Wm Dixon being of good Reputa-

---

[73]William Dickson was the son of Col. Robert Dickson and a Sioux mother. He was educated by his father, and assisted him during the War of 1812–15. At this time, he was said to be still in the pay of the British government (*Wis. Hist. Colls.*, xi, 350); it does not therefore speak well for either the acumen or the integrity of Puthuff that he should grant him this license. Later Dickson continued the furtrade on Red River and vicinity, and in 1832 was on the Missouri, where Maximilian, Prince of Wied, met him. See Thwaites, *Early Western Travels*, xxiv, pp. 96, 97. In 1836, Dickson incited a halfbreed and Indian insurrection on Red River, and suicided two years later. See Edward D. Neill, *History of Minnesota* (St. Paul, 1882), p. 452; also *Wis. Hist. Colls.*, x, p. 141.—ED.

tion & having given Bond & Security agreeably to Law, is hereby licensed by authority of special powers, by the president of the United States of America to me for that purpose delegated, To Trade with Indian tribes on the waters of the Mississippi above prarie Duchien, for a term not exceeding one year from the date of these presents, Conditioned Specially that he the aforesaid William Dixon his clerks, interpreters or others employed by him in his trade or conveyance of goods in the Indian country Shall in all manner of things Strictly and literally conform to the Law above mentioned a copy of which is delivered to him with this licence

Given under my hand and Seal of my agency at Michilimackinac this 1st day of November One thousand Eight hundred & Sixteen

W^m. HENRY PUTHUFF
In Agent Michilimackinac

Endorsed: One of the $50 permits of which Mathew Irwin speaks off.[74]

1817: DIFFICULTIES OF WISCONSIN TRADERS

[Source, same as preceding document, but 4B51. Translated from the French.]

SIR AND FRIEND—It is without doubt a matter of indifference to you to receive news from this place where my ill fortune has brought me. I should have written you sooner but not being well informed my narration would have been incomplete.

The tribunal of a mercantile inquisition has not allowed me to go and winter with the Sacs as I had proposed. I was not clothed with the spotless robe, without which one could not be admitted to the number of the privileged ones. Far from it, I was found lacking in all ways as much for my self as for my men who no more than I were admissible. The season being too far advanced to allow me to turn back (even if they had been willing to permit it) I decided to winter at St Charles a

---

[74] For Matthew Irwin's report on the sale of these licenses, see *Wis. Hist. Colls.*, vii, p. 271.—ED.

little village on the Missoury 8 leagues from St. louis where for 100$ I found a shelter and warehouse for my goods for 6½ months which cost me more than double that in Capital. Alarmed at the difficulties, afraid that some would come up who would foil me I bought a half licence at the price of a whole one, for this place, dearly obtained, and I bargain daily for a shilling in thread and needles and am known throughout all the County as a merchant in these articles.

My store is on the 2nd floor where I have only a very steep stairway, so that it is frequented only by young people, the old having to remain at the foot; That is the most beneficial result of my licence.

Mr Bouteiller, that Sheep of the Good God, after so many hardships having been taxed with being at the head of the Savages during the war on a Great white horse with a great white plume and a long Saber and on the very point of having his scalp lifted and his neck cut, has succeeded in dissipating the prejudice against him with the aid of his purse. He has obtained at great expense a licence, and being admitted among the number of the elect, winters at the 2 rivers and informs me that he hopes to do a good business.

The Sacs have taken care of Lagotry[75] and have hidden him so well that no one can find him. it is to be presumed by the reports that he will do well. The Rumor runs that they sent to take him, but the contrary occurred. They were only troops who came down, as they say, trying to find him but could not. I await the result to know whether I did well or ill not to have followed him it having been impossible to undertake it by myself. All I can say is that the dispensors of favors must have carried a high head if they suffer such a check.

---

[75] Very little is known of this trader, Edward Lagoterie. He seems to have come out from Canada, and to have had a trading stand among the Sauk, especially at Black Hawk's village, at the mouth of Rock River. He was employed by Robert Dickson in 1812–14, to secure the Sauk allegiance; and by the United States commissioners in 1815 to invite the same tribesmen to the treaty of Portage des Sioux. For his arrest in 1817, see *post.*—ED.

Fur-trade in Wisconsin

Up to the time that I left the Bay they had received only good treatment from the Government the one in command [Col. Talbot Chambers] although violent and exacting showed himself just and sociable The agent [Col. John Bowyer] was all that could be asked, instructed at Mk^a that money accomplishes all, he proved to be accommodating enough, the factor [Matthew Irwin] is a Gentleman, not to him is the harm to commence to be imputed.

The arrangement we have made for a partnership will make trade succeed for us at La Baie in all probability. We must have 4 partners in the dependencies the opposition not appearing to be united, I believe that they will retire. The Store at la Bay is kept by Mr. Law & Mr. L. Grignon is there at the head of a contract with the government for a quantity of timber for the buildings of the government. This will be profitable if he can accomplish it.

I seriously regret having come here although I estimate that I can realize here either a loss or gain of at least 500£. All that I hope is to realize the first cost of my goods since only persons of means pay in currency, nor can I expect to recoup myself on the price of peltries they sell here for the same or less than at Mka. Deerskins sell these days at 40 sol per pound. If you have an opportunity let we know the prices at Mk^a so that I may make use of this information.

[JACQUES PORLIER]

Endorsed: to Pre. Rocheblave. 1817[76]

1817: FACTORY RECEIPTS

[MS. in Pension Office, Washington. Pressmark: Indian Office Letter Book "D," p. 476.]

OFFICE INDIAN TRADE GEO TOWN 6 Jany. 1817

Mathew Irwin Esq Green Bay

SIR—I received your letter and its accompanament—a Copy from your Journal. Since you have been at Green Bay your

---

[76] This letter is but a draft or copy of one sent to Rocheblave, and is undated, except for the year. It is not certain whether it refers to the winter of 1816–17, or of 1817–18—but probably the former.—ED.

returns have been very irregular and the business you have been doing, very limited. The whole amount of your sale appears to be only $5384. and of this sum it would seem about $1800. had been sold to Indians.[77]

I wish you to inform me with as little delay as possible the causes of the barren state of your factory, and whether the prospect is favorable for better business in future. Unless something in addition to present operations be done, I shall be compelled to recommend a breaking up of the Green Bay establishment.

Be pleased to give me all the information you can; and as soon as possible. I am etc. etc. etc.

T. L. Mc.K[ENNEY]

[Source, same as preceding document, but p. 226.]

OFFICE IN: TRADE, GEO. TOWN 22d. JANY. 1817

To James Kennerly Esq[78]

DEAR SIR—The contents of your letter of the 22d. ulto. have occasioned me much uneasiness, as well from the apprehensions of the final safety of the merch'ds. for Prarie du Chien; as from the incalculable disadvantage which will result to the Factory on account of its delay. "They are now, you say, in the mouth of Le Moin [Des Moines] River, and will remain there untill some rise of water, or untill some method is adopted to get them on." I sincerely hope you have been active in

---

[77] In view of the figures given for the Green Bay factory in the summary (*Amer. State Papers, Indian Affairs*, ii, p. 208), these figures and the admonition to Irwin seem extraordinary. The factor had but $4,617.28 worth of goods in all. Probably the sales aggregated only $538.40 and $180.00.—ED.

[78] James Kennerly (1792–1840) was of a Virginia family, related to Mrs. William Clark. He came to St. Louis about 1813, and entered the mercantile business, being associated with John O'Fallon, later with his brother George Kennerly. From 1827–37 he was sutler for the troops at Jefferson Barracks. At the time of this letter, he was forwarding agent at St. Louis for the United States Indian factories in that vicinity.—ED.

ascertaining what method was best; and that you have promptly adopted it. If so, the goods are before this at Prarie du Chien otherwise they are no doubt where you state them to have been, unless indeed some casuality, to which I should suppose them constantly liable, has put them out of our power to controul, in future.

Ferron and Connellys receipt being dated the 18th. of august, time enough in all conscience was at the disposal for *those* goods to have reached Prairie du Chien. There is nothing easier however, than to throw into the scale which is to balance that of *delay* and *indifference,* as much *"low water,"* as would make a River. And it happens unfortunately for the *public* business that this impediment is a standing apology with those Boatmen, when private individuals get along notwithstanding. I apprehend, Sir, that unless Boatmen can be had whose honesty will stand the test, our business will thus always drag. That some are more to be relied on than others, I take for granted—you would Do well to employ such men, *only.* I can see no possible advantage in having a Boat, if she is to be navigated by men who are indifferent about prosecuting the voyage; and who have as little concern, generally, when a Boat sinks, as when she swims. Still, however, some plan must be devised by which the public property can be made to keep pace at least with that belonging to private Traders. If to have a Boat at Saint Louis will do this, a Boat shall be had, but it must depend on the agent to select men for the voyage on whom some reliance can be placed. I am willing to put all necessary means in the hands of the agent, but at all hazards the merchandize *must go on.* I see, and am willing to make every allowance for the difficulties of the navigation; and for the delay consequent upon absence of boats and boatmen, but I must nevertheless believe that this is trifleing compared with the worthless character of the boatmen generally. You state yourself, that the delay of the Osage merchandize, was owing to the *faithlessness* of the undertaker, who left the packages about ⅔ rds. of the way from this to Ft. Osage.

I will suggest perhaps how this inexcusable evil may be

remedied, but really my dear Sir, this being so exactly within your province, I attempt it with reluctance, because the means, the prospects, the characters, being all there you only can judge of the best plan. I would suggest however—seeing that doubt must always hang upon a voyage, that you obtain security for the delivery of the Merchandize at the place of destination within stated periods, outside of such events as would forestall any human exertions, the existence of which, it should be obligatory on the undertaker to support by unquestionable testimony. To an undertaker of this sort pay an additional price. This may secure exertions, possibly, which without some such arrangement, I fear, I shall never witness.

I console myself in some measure with the hope that during the four weeks of spring like weather which prevailed here in December, the goods were progressed with, and reached Prarie du Chien. If not, I almost despair of their ever getting there.

I need not protract this communication by pronounceing upon the importance of promptitude in our remote agencies. It is known to you, I am sure, as an all important affair. Evils of an incalculable nature, growing out of a breach of the policy which the Government is sustaining thr'o this Department, towards the Indian tribes, are to be appprehended from proc[r]astination, and want of vigor in the prosecution of the public trust, far more to be dreaded than any losses in a Commercial point of view, however important it is to maintain also this branch of the subject. All this is known to you—and now my dear Sir let me hear from you, immediately if you please on the subject of those goods destined to Prarie du Chien, let me know what their fate is; and also suggest some plan by which such delay may be avoided in future. For some plan must be adopted, and I will sanction which ever may be best. Respectfully etc. etc. etc.

T L Mc.K[ENNEY]

Fur-trade in Wisconsin

1817: AMERICAN FUR COMPANY'S AGENTS

[Transcript in Burton Library, Detroit. Letter Book of Ramsay Crooks, p. 158.]

NEW YORK March 17, 1817

You know that I have bought out for account and on behalf of the American fur Company, all the interests which the gentlemen of Montreal held in the South West fur Company, consequently there will be wanted two Agents to conduct hereafter said business at Montreal, New York, Michilimacinac, and at all other places, who are to give their whole time and attention to said business, and not to trade for account of themselves or any other person whatsoever, except for the American fur Company—as I have great confidence in your ability and integrity, I have proposed you to be one of the two agents, and that you are to receive as a compensation, Two thousand Dollars per annum, and your expenses while absent on business of the company is to be paid by the company, in addition to which you are to have the profit or loss on five shares (out of one hundred shares in said business)

The profit or loss is to be declared after all interest and expenses are paid and deducted as well as two and a half per cent. commission which is to be charged by me, on the sale, or exportation on furs received as returns or otherwise.

You are to continue to be Agent for three years should the business be so long continued, it being understood that you are to receive and attend to all the goods comprehended in the outfit. [Those of] 1816, are included.

JOHN JACOB ASTOR
For American fur Com.

Mr. Ramsy Crooks

Endorsed: agreement with J. J. Astor Esq. 1817

1817: ABUSE OF LICENSING POWER

[MS. in Pension Office, Washington. Pressmark: Indian Office Letter Book "D," p. 258.]

INDIAN OFFICE GEO TOWN March 19th. 1817

To Geo Graham Esqr. Acting Secctry. War

DEAR SIR—Every Letter I receive from P. du Chein, confirms the fact, that licences to trade with the Indians are issued to an undue extent. I am aware of the broadness of the Law; and how easy it is to obtain this privilege, under its provisions—still, however, I apprehend, with all its extent of privilege, the use made of it, in many cases, is at War with its spirit, and certainly with the design of the Government.

The following is an extract from a Letter this day recd. from Jno. W. Johnson U. S. Factor at Prarie du Chien, dated 8th. Jany. last.

"How Major Puttoff, Indian Agent at Mackinac could licence Traders *for this Territory,* is surprising to all the Americans here. The blackest of characters were permitted, and are now trading with the Indians in every direction. Will you do me the favor to find out whether Mr. Puttoff received unlimited instructions from the President? Each (trader) paying 50$."

Our Trade must suffer under such pressure, and so must the Indians. Nor can any thing tend to the destruction of both more rapidly.

I submit it to the Dept. of War to provide suitable Checks for the evil, and hope some plan may be adopted that will correct the extent to which it is carried. Very respectfully etc.

T. L. McK[ENNEY]
S[uperintendent] I[ndian] T[rade].

Fur-trade in Wisconsin

1817: PRICES FOR FURS

[MS. in Burton Library, Detroit, vol. 113, p. 84.]

GREEN BAY April 13th 1817

Mr W Woodbridge[79]

D. SIR—Yours of the 6th of March last I received on the 9th Inst. and I am very sorry that not withstanding I have lived for near two years in this country I am not able to give you the particular information you require respecting the prices of the different kinds of Furs etc. The best season for making a purchase at Mackinac is in the Months of June & July & I suppose that Bear will be about $3, Otter 2, **Martin** 1.50 Muskrat $16 pr. 100. Letters rec^d. from the eastward by the last express state that Muskratt Sold last fall at Boston for $15. pr. 100. As to the currancy of the different Bank notes & places of deposit, I would advise Mr. Woodbridge to make his deposits in one of the pittsburgh Banks, and to procure as many N. Y. notes as possible there is now 25 pr. cent discount on Ohio money at this place. Owing to the small quantity of goods that are at this place I presume there will be very few Furs sold here this spring, they will all be taken to Michilimackinac and there is no person there that I could recommend as an agent to make the purchase unless Major Puthuff would be induced to do it for a handsome commission.

I expect to leave this about the first of June for Pittsburg, should I have an opportunity of procuring you a good Robe, you may rely on my taking it on with me to Detroit, where I hope to have the pleasure of seeing you & personally thanking you for relieving my friends anxiety respecting my safety.

---

[79] William Woodbridge (1780–1861) was born in Connecticut, but removed as a boy to Marietta, Ohio, where he began the practice of law, and was active in Ohio politics. At the close of the War of 1812–15, he was appointed secretary of Michigan Territory, and with his family removed to Detroit, of which he became a leading citizen. He was first the territorial delegate in Congress, then judge of the supreme court of the territory, served as a member of the state constitutional convention (1835), of the state senate (1837), was governor (1839–41), and finally was United States senator from Michigan (1851–47).—ED.

The letter from Gibbs that you mention in yours I have not rec^d. but expect to by the first vessel from Mackinac which we expect about the last of the Month.

Should you write to Mr. D. Woodbridge or any of the family, will you please to have the goodness to tender my warmest respects to Mrs. Woodbridge etc. believe me to be Sir, yours respectfully

L. MORGAN[80]

Address: Mr. Woodbridge Detroit, M. T.

1817: INSTRUCTIONS FOR SHIPPING FURS

[MS. in Pension Office, Washington. Pressmark: Indian Office Letter Book "D," p. 278.]

INDN. TRADE OFFICE Apl. 15th. 1817

To John W. Johnston Esq U S Factor P. du Chien

DEAR SIR—This is to request you to forward with as little delay as possible, the furs and Peltries you may now have on hand; and as many as you may receive in time to reach here by October, to James Kennerly Esqr. at St. Louis. The manner of securing them is important, and especially during the summer Months. I request with a view to their better security, in more ways than one, but especially as it relates to their preservation against the worm, that you prepared them well; sprinkle them with spirits of Turpentine, and pack them in Tierces, such as the Merchandize is sent in—I mean the fine and small furs. I request the favor of your particular attention to this.

Your Letter and its enclosures of the 31st. Decemr. came to hand in proper time, and shall have my reply soon.

---

[80] Probably Lewis Morgan, who had entered the army from Pennsylvania, and after serving in the artillery for four years, resigned in 1816 to enter the Indian trade. He was agent of fortifications at Green Bay in 1820, and perished there in 1824 during a winter storm— see *Wis. Hist. Colls.*, vii, pp. 258, 259. When he speaks of being in the country "near two years," he probably refers to his first station (in 1815) at Mackinac, and the next year at Green Bay.—ED.

Fur-trade in Wisconsin

You shall be served and well served with Goods of the best qualities and kinds. Very respectfully etc.

T. L. McK[ENNEY]

S. I. T.

1817: WINNEBAGO HOSTILE

[MS. in Pension Building, Washington. Pressmark: Indian Office Book 203. Letter Book 2, p. 33. C. Jouett to Lewis Cass.]

CHICAGO 29 April 1817.

SIR—The bearer who was sent to Green Bay, on his return gives accounts that the Winnebagoes are determined to do us mischief it seems that a small party have had their war dance, the object of which is to shed blood at or in the neighborhood of this post this information comes from a Mr. Boubia [Beaubien][81] corroborated by the Potawatomies of Milliwakee, it does not appear that is a national movement but confined to a few who have lost relations in the late war, I have sent to their village on Fox river, five respectable Indians, to ascertain the truth of the report and at the same time to use their influence to prevent any war party from setting out and should they fail in their object, they are to send me a runner with the earli-

---

[81] Probably Jean Baptiste Beaubien, one of the earliest permanent settlers of Chicago, and an early Milwaukee trader. Born at Detroit of the family of Cuillerier *dit* Beaubien (see *Wis. Hist. Colls.*, xviii, p. 235), he entered the fur-trade as a clerk for Joseph Bailly at Grand River, where he was located in 1808. Later he removed to Milwaukee, where (in 1814) the Potawatomi unsuccessfully planned to murder him and seize his goods. About 1818 he was removed from Milwaukee to Chicago by the American Fur Company, but seems to have established his family at the latter place at an earlier date. After the abolition of the United States factory, Beaubien bought the premises and lived thereon until 1840. He was chosen colonel of militia in 1834, and brigadier-general in 1850. He was usually known to early Chicagoans as Colonel Beaubien. In 1840, having lost his property in a government suit, he removed to a farm on the Des Plaines; later, he was again in Chicago for three years (1855-58), whence he removed to Naperville, Ill., where he died in 1863.—ED.

est intelligence. This nation must be done something with, they have been altogether unfriendly to our Government. I think a treaty of some kind should be made with them, by which we could have some little hold upon them.[82] Otherwise a drubing is indispensible, they threaten to cut off the communication to Green Bay. The Potawatomies, Chippewas and Ottawas are entirely friendly.

This Agency has suffered many inconveniences for want of the Blacksmith tools. I hope I shall have the honour of hearing from you by the first opportunity. I am Your Obedt. Servant,

C. JOUETT
Ind. Agt.

1817: PURPOSES OF PRIVATE TRADERS

[M.S. in Pension Office, Washington. Pressmark: Indian Office Letter Book "D," p. 294.]

OFFICE OF INDIAN TRADE GEO: TOWN May 2d. 1817
John W Johnson Esqr. U. S. F. P. du Chien.

SIR—I am very much in want of Wampum for the factory at Osage. No effort of mine, though they have extended to all the principal Cities, have been able to command it. There appears a total disappearance of the article. This is to ask you, (if you can spare it) to forward in suitable packages such portions of white and blue, as you may be able to part from, even tho' the quantity shall be small, by letter, under cover to Mr. Kennerly at St. Louis, with directions for him to forward it by the earliest conveyance to Fort Osage.

---

[82] The Winnebago were consistently opposed to the Americans, forming (in 1811) a large part of Tecumseh's army, and following Dickson's lead to the battles in northern Ohio and around Detroit. The bands on Rock River and its upper waters in Wisconsin refused to attend the treaties at Portage des Sioux and St. Louis (1815–17. In 1816, one band, residing on Wisconsin River, was induced to sign a treaty with the commissioners at St. Louis, but no other was concluded with the tribe until that of Prairie du Chien (1825).—ED.

Fur-trade in Wisconsin

Your supplies of of Merchandize will reach you in good time. The selections I hope will give you power over the private traders enterprize that surrounds you. What effect would it have on the surrounding tribes to send runners to anounce your means of serving them? Would its novelty awaken any additional attention to the Factory? And if so, the private traders must feel it in the same proportion.

Those traders are certainly at war with the interests and welfare of the Indians. Every advantage over them that can be fairly taken; and which includes the harmony of the tribes, and Justice, is within the limits of the duty we owe these unfortunate people, whose want of knowledge of what constitutes their happiness alone prevents them from putting to flight those speculators on their toils. Cherish these people, and as I am sure your own heart dictates, leave no means untried to impress them with the friendship of the Government; and of their interest in negotiating through its Agencies. Very respectfully etc.

T. L. McK[ENNEY]

S. I. T.

1817: FOREIGNERS NOT EXCLUDED

[Source, same as preceding document, but p. 35.]

DEPARTMENT OF WAR, 4th. May, 1817

His Excelly. Gov. Cass.

SIR—I am directed by the President to inform you, that the instructions dated the 10th: of May last, relative to the granting of licenses to foreigners are to be considered as still in force. The President thinks it probable that he shall be at Detroit himself, in the course of the ensuing summer, when he wishes this subject to be brought before him for final decision.

A letter has been received from Major Puthuff since I last wrote to you, referring to one dated in November, but which has not been received at this department, for an explanation of his conduct in relation to the fees taken for granting licenses to trade with the Indians. It is understood, that he has received on that account, at least three thousand dollars.

Mr. Astor having represented to this department, that he had purchased the whole of the interest in what is termed the South West Company, you will afford to him and his agents, every facility in your power, consistent with the laws and the regulations. I have the honor etc.

GEORGE GRAHAM,
A. S. W.

[MS. in Wisconsin Historical Library. Pressmark: Wisconsin MSS., 4B6.]

LA PRARIE DES CHIEN 10th May 1817

DEAR LAWE—The unexpected conveyance this moment presents itself which will hardly afford me time to say That we arrived Safely, enjoy good health, and estimate the many proofs of disinterested friendship, which we received from you, whilst at Green Bay, more highly than ever.

I can give you no news, there is still a talk of a rupture with the Indians, but I do not believe, at once that all British traders will be prohibited from having any intercourse with the Indians, but the truth of the matter is yet to be realized—do not take any steps, about making preparations for sending a party of men and boats into this country, until you hear from me again, I shall inform you as early as may be practicable. It is uncertain whether I remain in command here, the ensuing winter or not, but should I remain, you must certainly calculate on every exertion which I can make for you. The com^{dg} Officer here has a great deal in his power, it shall be exerted to the utmost in your behalf, but keep every thing which I write you, *quiet*.

O'Fallan is writing you. Dickson is well but in a [MS. torn]humour about a dance, which he has been prevented in going to by a Roman Chatholic Priest. You will see him probably in two or three weeks.

Fur-trade in Wisconsin

I am in great haste—farewell and believe me Sincerely and ever Your friend

T. CHAMBERS

Dont forget to write me a long letter by the first opportunity and tell me your wishes.

Addressed: Mr. John Lawe Green Bay
Endorsed: Letter from Colonel Chambers dated Prarie du Chien 10th May 1817 no answer.

[MS. in Pension Office, Washington. Pressmark: Indian Office Letter Book "D," p. 303.]

OFFICE IN: TRADE, GEO: TOWN 10th, May 1817

John W. Johnson Esq

SIR—Your letter of 10th. Feb is at hand, and I notice with regret the prevalence of an evil which it shall be my business to keep before the authorities, who, like myself, will be happy to see its consequences lessened—a final death can only be inflicted by the Congress. I refer to the extensive limits of the licence system. Extracts from your letter above referred to, I have laid before the Secretary of War. You will lodge your complaint against Nicholas Bolvoin, with the Governor of the Illinois Territory, and if on your statement, the Gov. can be satisfied of the impropriety of his conduct on such representation being made to the War office, by the Gov., Bolvoin will be removed; *or any other man* who can be fairly committed for any violation of the laws regulating Trade with, or for the better government of the Indian Tribes. The agent at Mackinac seems to have got himself into trouble. *I learn,* orders have been issued for him to refund the premiums received for licences. I hope this may be true. Be vigilant in your efforts to detect individuals who regardless of their duty, and of justice, go forth to peculate on the already too impoverished and miserable Indians, and make your reports direct to the Governor of the Illinois Territory, sending me copies of all your communications.

Rolette has been well informed no doubt; and the prices he

is giving for skins are justified by the foreign demand. But I have not thought it prudent to issue orders to rise in our price, for two reasons. *First,* This demand will cease when the scarcity is supplied which may be before we could make sales.

Second, Our fair dealings will not permit us to supply the chasm made by the high prices for Furs, by a correspondent increase on the cost of our goods. Justice forbids it, at least that *propriety of intercourse,* which it is desireable to keep up with the Indians. This is a sort of chicanery which suits very well the honor of tricky and low minded Men, whose avarice is always on the alert to *deceive,* if not by radically unjust means, yet by such as shall serve their ends as well. This however may not be Mr. Rolettes plan.

I shall afford you all the power that *good* goods, and *cheap* goods can impart; and will always second your efforts to rid the country of the swarms of private traders, whose regard for the Indians is measured by the profits of their intercourse with them. If you have any accumulation of bad goods which the scarcity during the War, forced upon my predecessor, get them off as well as you can. They will be more in the way as your stock increases by the supplies of last year, and of this year. write me as often as you can, and keep me constantly informed of whatever relates to the factory. I am etc. etc.

T. L. Mc.K[ENNEY]

[MS. in Pension Building, Washington. Pressmark: Indian Office Book 203. Letter Book 2, p. 69. Cass to W. H. Puthuff.]

DETROIT June 8, 1817

DEAR SIR—By a letter from the War Department dated May 4, 1817, I am informed that "Mr. Astor has purchased the whole of the interest, in what is termed the South West Company," and I am instructed to "afford to him and his agents every facility in my power consistent with the laws and the regulations."

To Mr. Crooks the Agent of Mr. Astor you will please to afford every assistance, which the nature of his business may require. From a correspondence, which Mr. Crooks has submitted to me, it is the intention of the Government that Mr. Crooks as the agent of Mr. Astor should have the selection of such persons to enter the Indian Country and conduct the business as he may require. To such persons therefore as Mr. Crooks may designate you will please to grant licenses, taking the security required by law or the regulations of May 10. 1816.

On mature reflection upon the subject I would recommend that as few licenses as may be consistent with those regulations be granted, rather reducing than exceeding the number.

I do not recommend Mr. Crooks to your hospitality. That I know he will receive. But I recommend to your aid and assistance the objects of his journey. With much esteem I am Dear Sir, Yo. obt. Servt.

[LEWIS CASS]

Maj. W. H. Puthuff Ind. Agent

1817: NEWS FROM MACKINAC

[MS. in Wisconsin Historical Library. Pressmark: Wisconsin MSS., 4B13.]

MICHILLIMACKINAC 18th June 1817

DEAR JOHN—I parted with your uncle Franks at Lachine on the 11th of May. He I suppose has informed you ere this, that by an arrangement he made with M^r. Stone[83] his goods come by way of New York; and consequently from Montreal he had but little to bring up, which I had imagined would con-

---

[83] David Stone was a New England capitalist, whose home was at Walpole, N. H. He had been in the fur-trade at Detroit before the War of 1812-15, in partnership with S. Conant. After the war, he continued under the name of David Stone & Company; later, Stone, Bostwick & Company, with a branch house at Cincinnati. This was the only large Eastern competitor of the American Fur Company, and received government encouragement; until, in 1824, an agreement was made to combine with the American Fur Company for three years. David Stone removed in 1828 to Dayton, Ohio, and appears to have retired from the fur-trade about that time.—ED.

[461]

sidering the number of men, and the lightness of his Boat, have enabled him to reach this place before me. He is however still absent, but by the arrival of M^r. Courselle[84] last evening I learn he was detained at the Portage of York much longer than he anticipated owing to the North West Boats having the preference of transportation. We look for him in a very few days.

You have no doubt heard before this of his having been joined in the holy bands of matrimony to Miss Solomon—the courtship you know having been uncommonly *short,* the consequences which naturally follow such *precipitate* matches, are verified in your case. He has beyond all doubt got an excellent wife—one who loves him with no ordinary affection, who seeks every opportunity to minister to his comfort, and who takes great pains by anticipating his wishes, to make him happy—to say all in a few words, He has obtained the *first prize* in this, *most hazardous* Lottery. I arrived here yesterday by way of New York, and the Lakes. I left Montreal the 12th May. Mr. Lemoine (Despins)[85] has gone up for Lord Selkirk, and strange as it may appear, our friend Mr. Robert Dickson has accompanied him with the intention of joining the Earl at Red River or elsewhere in the interior.[86]

---

[84] Michel Courselle was a British trader in the Michigan peninsula before 1812. In 1816 he was granted a lot on Drummond Island.—ED.

[85] Jean Baptiste Lemoine *dit* Despins had been trading in the Upper Country since the opening of the nineteenth century. In 1812 he married at St. Louis, Céleste Sanguinet, related to the Chouteau family.—ED.

[86] Thomas Douglas, earl of Selkirk (1771-1820), purchased in 1811 a large grant of land from the Hudson's Bay Company, on which to found a colony of Scotchmen. This proceeding was opposed by the members of the North West Company, and in 1816 a battle was fought, in which Robert Semple, governor of the colony, was killed. Selkirk thereupon proceeded to Fort William, and in his capacity of magistrate sent down to the colony under arrest, the principals of the North West Company. Selkirk proceeded in 1817 into the interior, where Dickson planned to join him. This portion of Dickson's career was not known, when the biographical sketch of that well-known trader appeared in *Wis. Hist. Colls.*, xii, pp. 133-153.—ED.

Fur-trade in Wisconsin

We have nothing new here. Provisions are abundant & cheap I hope you have passed a pleasant & prosperous winter. I am sorry to hear of Mr. Porlier's bad fortune, but I trust you will nevertheless make out pretty well. Wonders you could not expect to do. Hoping to have the pleasure of seeing you here at an early day I remain Dear John Yours truly

RAM^y CROOKS

Mr. John Lawe.

Your uncle reached Drumond Island last evening I suppose he will be here to-day.

R. C.

Addressed: Mr. John Lawe Green Bay Hon^d by Major Gratiot.
Endorsed: Letter from R. Crooks dated McKinac 18th June 1817 answered

---

1817: INSTRUCTIONS FOR WISCONSIN FACTOR

[MS. in Pension Office, Washington. Pressmark: Indian Office Letter Book "D," p. 346.]

INDIAN TRADE OFFICE 24th. June 1817

To *John W. Johnston Esqr U. S. F. P. du Chien*

SIR—Your letter of the 28th. April accompanied by your quarterly returns closing 31st. March preceding, arrived in due time.[87]

*   *   *   *   *   *   *   *

It will be necessary for you to use extreme caution in trustting out goods to traders. Boats may get upset, as in the case of Dorion[88]—and even if like him this should escape being drowned, the tommahawk may put them to rest, and releive you from the trouble of counting their returns. The very fact

---

[87] The omitted portions in this and some of the succeeding documents deal with financial accounts and errors, unnecessary to the present publication.—ED.

[88] There was in the Illinois settlements a considerable family by the name of Dorion. Pierre accompanied Lewis and Clark as interpreter, and his son was with the Astorian expedition; see Thwaites, *Early Western Travels*, v. p. 38.—ED.

you mention viz. the difficulty of traders giving security must render their access to the credit of the Factory more difficult. I wish you nevertheless to have all the chances that such aid can afford you, and authorize you to let out to discreet and honest men on the best security you can obtain, goods to limited amounts, to no one trader more than might be deemed a reasonable amount, not to be repeated 'till he settles for them when he is to have more.

I regret to notice the damage sustained by some of the goods, which remained so long at the rapids of De Moin. I have reported the transport agent (Mr. Bronaugh) your suggestion respecting a Column for the weights of each package, this will be attended to.

It affords me pleasure to learn that those goods are so very acceptable. It is surely high commendation you bestow, and it is the more welcome, because you certainly know how to estimate an entire suitableness of the articles to the tastes of Indians in your quarter.

I notice with pleasure that you are attracting by means of those goods the attention of the Indians, and that you took a thousand dollars worth of good furs in April. I hope the period is not distant when you will be rid of British traders. You should report Dixon to the Governor, he *cannot* have authority.[89] I wait daily to hear of your skins etc. being on the way to St. Louis. I presume we shall hold the property at P. d Chien I am not informed why we shall not. Very respectfully etc.

T. L McK[ENNEY]
S I T.

---

[89] See Forsyth's report of Dickson at Prairie du Chien in 1817, in *Wis. Hist. Colls.*, xi, p. 350.—ED.

Fur-trade in Wisconsin

[Source, same as preceding document, but p. 356.]

OFFICE OF INDIAN TRADE GEO TOWN July 10, 1817
M Irwin Esqr. U. S. F. Green Bay,

SIR—Your letters of the 15th and 17th May are received.[90]

* * * * * * * *

It is required that duplicate vouchers accompany the Contingent account. You have sent me none, nor have I received any *regular* accounts since your arrival at Green Bay. I must urge the necessity of some efforts to prepare the factory buildings. I suggest that you address a letter to the Commanding officer, asking for assistance. If he refuse it, let his answer come before me; and his scruples shall be adjusted by the War Department. In truth, Gentlemen mistake their duty exceedingly, when they manifest no interest for the operations of the *general* Government, outside the particular branch over which they preside, as well, in the language of the Patriotick Genl. Gains on this same subject, might the hand refuse its aid to the foot.

I cannot but flatter myself with the hope that the Commanding officer, influenced by a regard for whatever concerns the Government of his Country and its views, will unite in the accomplishment of its designs even tho' they be outside the special trust placed in his hands. The War Dept. could do no more than issue a *conditional* order: But of that condition the Commanding officer is constituted judge.

* * * * * * * *

You did well to sell the furs to preserve them from a loss on your hands. I do not wish sales made at either Green Bay or Mackinac, excepting under such circumstances. I am etc. etc.

T. L. McK[ENNEY]

---

[90] For other letters passing between Irwin and McKenney from 1817-21, see *Id.*, vii, pp. 270-282.—ED.

1817: PROCEEDS OF FACTORIES

[Source, same as preceding document, but p. 366.]

OFFICE INDIAN TRADE GEO TOWN 14th. July 1817

To James Kennerly Esq

DR. SIR—Your favor of the 15 Ulto. is before me, from which I learn that you have shipped from St. Louis, all the furs and Peltries that remained on hand, consisting of One hundred and fifty nine packages deer skins, Twenty eight of Beaver, and otter; Twenty one packs Rackoon, Cat, Rat and dressed Elk skins, 12 Packs of Bear skins—all from the Osage Trading house: also from Prarie des Chien—Twenty packs Deer 12 Bear 6 Racoon and 28 Muskrat, 7 Beaver four Packs otter, and three of Otter, Cat, Rat, Fishes, mink, wolves, Foxes and Rabit total 300 Packs. I am gratified to learn that those furs etc. left St. Louis in prime order; and that you provided in your contract for suitable inspections on their passage to Pittsburg. I wish you much happiness in the married state. I am etc. etc.

T L MC.K[ENNEY]

1817: PROHIBITION OF LIQUOR

[MS. in Pension Building, Washington. Pressmark: Indian Office Book 203. Letter Book 2, p. 147.]

GREEN BAY AGENCY 22d. July 1817

SIR—I have made the arrangements for this agency, so as if possible to keep the expenditures within the sum of five thousand Dollars, but this I fear will be impossible untill houses are built for this establishment, as it will require at least five hundred Dollars per annum for house rent, and the houses no better than hovels. Fuel will also require a considerable Sum, the price established by the troops for wood is five Dollars per Cord.

I wrote the Secretary of War last fall, I had taken from the Chiefs their British medals, arm bands and Flags, and had promised to replace them this summer. I have received no answer on this subject, I also requested a moderate supply of presents for the chiefs and their families. I may have acted improperly in taking those things from the chiefs and promising to give them others, but as I acted from the best of motives and my word is given, I hope you will have them forwarded as soon as convenient, I will thank you to forward to me a set of the laws of the United States, and if possible have the civil law established at this place.

The indians from fear more than from principle, appear friendly, it will for sometime require Strong Measures to destroy the British influence in this quarter, indeed so long as british subject[s] are suffered to have intercourse with the Indians, I feel confident British influence will continue, and it will be an expence without any advantage either to the United States or the indians to have agents or Factors in the Indian Country, unless positively ordered, I will give no Licences to British subjects this year.

I have prohibited the landing of every discription of spirits in this agency, for the purpose of trade or Barter, I hope this will meet yours and the President's approbation. I have taken the liberty of enclosing to you the Copy of a treaty made at St. Louis with the Menomenee Tribe of Indians. The fellows who have Signed this treaty, have no influence or character with the Indians, and I am confident this treaty has been made without the knowledge of the principle chiefs, and of nine tenths of the nation knowing or even hearing of the transaction.[91]

I would have written you by the General Jackson, but was on daily expectation of seing you at this place. I have the honor to be Sir, Very respectfully Your Obedt. Servt.

JNO. BOWYER
Indian Agent

Govr. Lewis Cass.

---

[91] None of the signatures to this treaty of St. Louis (made March 3, 1817) are those of prominent, well-known Menominee chiefs. See *United States Indian Treaties* (Washington, 1837), p. 306.—ED.

[MS. in Wisconsin Historical Library. Pressmark: Wisconsin MSS., 5B21.]

Sir—You have permission to trade with the Indians (whiskey) for Sturgeon not exceeding six Gallons at this time. Yours respectfully

Jn° Bowyer
Indian Agent

Green Bay 23d July 1817

Mr Louis Grignon

1817: BRITISH SUBJECTS AT GREEN BAY

[MS. in Pension Building, Washington. Pressmark: Indian Office Book 203. Letter Book 2, p. 165.]

Green Bay July 24, 1817

Sir—The Superintendent of Indian Trade directs me in his letter of the 28th. May last, to report to you, such of the British Traders, at this place, as are known to me, as having been hostile to the United States, during the late War with the British nations, for the purpose of enabling you to communicate their names to the War Department.

After a particular and strict enquiry, I learn that the following persons were Hostile to the United States during the late War, that they are British Subjects, in the practice of trading with the indian tribes, the most of whom have resided many years and hold landed and personal property here; that they were particularly active in exciting the Indians, residing in the Territories of the United States, to take up Arms against Michillimackinac, Detroit, Sandusky and La prairie du Chien, acting as their leaders in the several Capacities annexed to their Names (viz)

    James Porlear Senr. Capt. of Milita. and Commissary
    James Porlear Junr. Lieut of the Indn. Dept.
    Peter Grignon Captain of   ditto
    Lewis Grignon Lieut of   ditto

Augustus Grignon Interpr. and Commissary
Presch Grignon   ditto   ditto
John B. Grignon Serjt. of the Ind. Dept.
Paul Grignon Ensign of   ditto
Amable Grignon ditto of   ditto
Charles Grignon Interpreter of ditto
Jacob Franks Captain of ditto and Commissary
Joseph Rolette   ditto   of   ditto
Lawrence Filley Serjeant of ditto
Peter Powel Lieut of   ditto and
Robert Dickson Superint., and Agent of ditto.[92]

---

[92] All of the above-mentioned inhabitants of Green Bay have been sketched in previous notes in this volume, save the two youngest.

Joseph Jacques Porlier, Jr., was born at Green Bay about 1796. He was educated in Montreal, and returned to his Western home about the commencement of the War of 1812-15. He enlisted as a lieutenant in the Michigan Fencibles, and served with great credit on the Prairie du Chien campaign, receiving enconiums from his superior officers; see *Wis. Hist. Colls.*, x, p. 118; xiii, p. 58. At the close of the war, young Porlier was recommended for an ensigncy in the regular army (*Id.*, xiii, p. 93); but preferring civil to military life, he remained at Green Bay with his father, entering actively into the fur-trade—see documents *post*. He married Agatha Grignon, and was for some time on the upper Wisconsin. Finally, he settled at Grand Kaukauna, where in the spring of 1839 he died.

Amable Grignon was the youngest of that family, having been born in 1795, after his father's death. During the War of 1812-15, he acted as a corporal in the Green Bay detachment. In 1817 he went to St. Peter's River, under engagement with Duncan Graham (Wisconsin MSS., 5B4). The following spring, in the rendezvous at Lake Winnipeg, he had the fortune to please the governor of the Hudson's Bay Company, and was for the following year sent to Athabasca (*Ibid.*, 4B87, 1C25). The next year he renewed his engagement, and was stationed at Great Slave Lake (*Ibid.*, 5B13, 56B102). While there, because of his "well-known resolution" (*Ibid.*, 1C36) he received orders to arrest traders of the North West Company. The following year he was at Fort Wedderburn (*Ibid.*, 1C52), and in 1821 at Fort Chippewyan (*Ibid.*, 9B89). In 1823 he returned from the North, just too late to see his mother before her death, which occurred Oct. 25, 1823 (*Ibid.*, 15B49). At this time he brought with him as his wife, Marie

All the inhabitants here, except one, are British subjects, Consisting of about fifty families. They were actively opposed to the United States, during the late War.

It may be proper to remark that whilst these and other British subjects are suffered to enter and continue in this Country as traders, It will be useless in the Goverment to continue this factory here; principally from the ascendency which an interrupted intercourse of many years has enabled them to acquire over the minds of the Indians, supported by extensive families connections with them, and the advantage they might, and, in some places have made of it to the prejudice of the Factories. It would be unnecessary to detail to you the evils which have arisen and may yet arise, in case of another War with Great Britain, should those traders be suffered to reside at and enter this Country.

It may be sufficient to state, what I think you will readily admit, that this Factory, from the easy access to it, can supply the wants of the Indians, from the Mouth of this Bay to the portage of the Ouisconsin. I am very respectfully, Sir, Your Ob. Serv.

M. IRWIN
U. S. Factor

Col. John Bowyer, Indian Agent

1817: WISCONSIN INDIAN CENSUS

[Source, same as preceding document, but p. 163.]

GREEN BAY AGENCY August 12, 1817

SIR—I have the honor to transmit to you the following estimate of the probable number and residence (as far as I have

---

Judith Bourassa, whom he seems to have married at Mackinac. Having saved a small capital during his service with the Hudson's Bay Company, Amable went into partnership with his brother Paul, and secured an outfit for the Wisconsin trade. Later, they were located on the upper Wisconsin, where Amable made his home at what is now

Fur-trade in Wisconsin

been able to obtain information) of the Indian Tribes of this Agency.

The Minominees or Fullsavoines estimated at Five hundred Warriors, They reside during the summer on the Fullsavoine river, Kantong, Green Bay, Little Kackalin, Big Kackalin, Winabagoe Lake, River de Loup, But des Morts, Vermillion Island, an[d] Scattering villages, on the Islands and River of the Bay.

The Winabagoes, Estimated at, from Seven to Eight hundred, Their villages are on the Winabagoe Lake, Fox River, Green Lake, the portage Ouisconsin and the River au pins.

The Chippewas are intermixed with the Minominies and Ottawas, it is at present impossible to make a probable estimate of their numbers. They occupy the whole Country from Michillimackinac to the head Waters of the Mississippi River. Numbers visit this Agency in the Spring and fall.

The Indians in the vicinity of Millwakee are composed of Renigadoes from all the tribes around them (viz) The Sacques, foxes, Chippewas, Minominies, Ottawas, Winabagoes and Potawatamies, Estimated at Three hundred Warriors.

The tribes from the Lower and upper Mississippi pass this place on th[eir] Way to Michillimackinac.

It is believed that in the Summer Months fifteen hundred Warriors can be assembled at this place in fifteen days. I have not been able to get such information as can be depended upon, of the number of Woman and Children of the different tribes, but hope by middle of the next month, I shall accomplish it.

From every information I can get of the situation of the Indians in this quarter, The whole of the Indians on Green Bay and its islands and River and from thence to the Head Waters of the Mississippi, and from the mouth of Fox River, to the Portage Ouisconsin, and the Indians residing on the West side Millwackee (except the villages at the mouth of the Millwackee) should be attached to this agency. I am induced to be-

---

Grand Rapids. Two of his sons, Jean and Ignace, also lived recently at that place.—ED.

lieve this to be the natural Boundary, as all the indians residing within these limits can with ease bring all their Peltry by water to the factory at Green Bay.

I hav the honor to enclose to you a letter addressed to me by Mr. Irwin the United States Factor at this place, it will give you a correct idea of the Characters of the Inhabitants on the Bay. I have the honor to be Sir, Very respectfully Your Ob. Serv.

JNO. BOWYER
Indian Agent

His Excellency Lewis Cass Govr. of M. Territory

1817: WISCONSIN INDIANS VISIT BRITISH POST

[Source, same as preceding document, but p. 167.]

MICHILLIMACKINAC August 20, 1817

DEAR SIR—I should have written you sometime since but because of the very considerable number of Indians who have been passing and repassing this post for several Weeks. Considerable Bands of Sawks and foxes from the Lower Mississippi, Winabagoes from the Ouisconsin and near Prairie du Chien, Potawatamies and other tribes from the Illinois and Chippewas from Lake 'Superior and intervening Country bordering on the head Waters of the Mississippi, Ottawas from Lake Michigan, Menominees from Green Bay and Fox River, with many other scattering Bands of different tribes of Indians have visited this Post and Drummonds Island during the present Season. At Drummonds Island very extensive presents have been given them, and to the Sawks, Foxes, Winabagoes and Potawatamies particularly, large supplies of ammunition and Arms have been furnished.[93] It has been reported to me that the Sawks and Foxes, who left this Post a few days since on their return to the Mississippi, declared at Drummond's

---

[93] See account of the passing of the Indians in 1817 to Drummond's Island, in *Wis. Hist. Colls.*, i, pp. 54–57.

Island, their determination to prevent American Traders from going among them the ensuing Winter, stating that they had followed the surveyors who had been engaged as they said, in taking their Lands and had destroyed their marked trees, and they would not suffer them to return, or any settlers to remove to the Country, and would cut off or destroy all those who might have already settled within that district. How far these reports may deserve Credit is in my Opinion doubtful, or if true, how far they may have been intend[ed] merely to Illicit more presents deserves some consideration. The profession of all the Indians in Council, as they passed and repassed this Post, has been uniformly and decidedly friendly toward the United States. They [though] I am well aware that implecit confidence may not be given to Indian professions. Yet the issuing of such extraordinary quantity of arms and ammunition coupled with these reports, renders it as I conceive a duty on my part to apprize your Excellency of the facts so far as I have been able to develope them. The Prophet has lately sent an emmisary among the Ottawas and Chippewas of this Agency, who in a national Council with them, held out the idea of a Rupture's soon taking place between the Indians of the South Western part of the United States and the Americans, observing that all would be quiet for this year but sometime early in the next they would strike, that the Tomahawk was not entirely buried, a small part of the handle having been purposely left out, That all the Indians of that District of Country had promised their Cooperation and requested the Indians of the Lakes to join in a quarrel which equally Interested the whole. The Ottawas immediately gave me notice of the designs of the Prophet, and in Council tendered their assistance to the American Government in opposing his views, declaring their wish to remain at Peace with their American father, and determination to resist the Prophet or any other Indians who should dare with hostile, Tread upon their Lands to disturb their quiet.

This circumstance is probably only of importance to us in that, that it goes to evidence the attachment of the Indians of this Agency to the American Government and their sincere wish to remain in a state of peace at least for the present.[94]

* * * * * * * *

I am dear sir Yo Mo. Ob. H. Serv

WM. HEN. PUTHUFF

Ind. Agent

His Excellency Lewis Cass Gov of M. Territory

P. S. Enclosed I forward you a communication on the subject of Trade made by Mr. Morrison who was last and is this year engaged in Indian trade for the S. West Company on Lake Superior[95]

W. H. P.

1817: LOCKWOOD AT PRAIRIE DU CHIEN

[MS. in Wisconsin Historical Library. Pressmark: Wisconsin MSS., 4B25.]

PRABIE DE CHIEN Sept 2nd 1817

D^r. SIR—I arrived at this Place on the 30th of August. I had a verry disagreeable Passage being taken with the fever and ague at the But d. Mort I arrived at the Portage Wisconsin a day before any others but being Sick I was two & half days in the portage. I have had considerable difficulty to get Permission

---

[94] The omitted portion deals only with accounts.—ED.

[95] William Morrison came of fur-trading ancestors, being a grandson of Wadin, a Swiss killed in the Northwest in 1782; see *Wis. Hist. Colls.*, xviii, p. 315, note 39. He was probably a son of Charles Morison, noted *ante*, p. 249, note 62. Born in Montreal in 1783, William was an employee of the X Y Company in 1802, and the following winter visited the sources of the Mississippi. Later, he went into the North West Company, and was stationed at Fond du Lac, Lake Superior, and at inland posts. Pike heard of him, but did not meet him in 1805–06. In 1816, Morrison entered the South West Company, and was promoted rapidly; in time, he became one of the principal traders of the American Fur Company on Lake Superior. His station was for many years at L'Anse, on Keweenaw Bay; see *ante*, p. 208, note 98. After retirement he lived at Montreal, where he died Aug. 7, 1866.—ED.

JAMES H. LOCKWOOD
From oil portrait by Samuel M. Brookes, in possession of Wisconsin Historical Society

Fur-trade in Wisconsin

to Pass as Mr Ofallon is not here but have finally obtained Permission All the Equipments of Rolette are detained until the arrival of Mr Ofallan what the result will be I cannot say yesterday Col. Chambers was at my tent and in conversation asked if you was coming this way I told him that you had some idea of coming but was not sure that you could Pass he said that he thought you could Pass that were you to come that he would assist you in any thing that he could but for my Part I think that you may Pass with some difficulty I can give you no further information. I shall be off from this today I am gaining my health verry fast and none of my men have yet got the fever I have engaged an interpreter to whom I give two hundred dollars with his Equipment & gun. I am Sir Respectfully yours

J. H. LOCKWOOD[96]

John Lawe

1817: LICENSES AT GREEN BAY

[Source, same as preceding document, but 4B28. Translated from the French.]

BAYE VERTE 14 September 1817

DEAR SIR—I transmit to you the Information that I have reached here After a Passage of Twelve Days. I received from Captain Duncain the Goods according to the order I had given they are in as good condition as I could expect after the shipwreck he had the misfortune to endure in the Bay of Wachington. As your property I desire you to give me Instructions as to how you wish them Disposed of *on Your Account*.

In regard to the Licence After all the Trouble possible Col Boyer has decided to give them to every person who asks for them. He has said Openly that if the matter was at his option

---

[96] This is the well-known pioneer whose recollections of the Prairie du Chien neighborhood form so important a part of early volumes of these *Collections*. See vol. ii, pp. 98-196, wherein he has related almost all of his early history. Judge Lockwood died Aug. 24, 1857, at his Prairie du Chien home.—ED.

no one should obtain a Licence but Mr Rouse[97] Mr. Lawe & M[r]. James.[98] I have not been able to open my store here for eight days. The appearances are bad. I believe that there will be as many Traders as Houses. Nothing more to mention to you. I am dear Sir very Respectfully Your obedient Servant

L. GRIGNON.

Endorsed: Copy of a Letter to Mr. M. Dousman Michillimakinac.

[Source, same as preceding document, but 1D38.]

GREEN BAY the 16th. Septr. 1817

To Col¹ Boyer Indian Agent of the U. States

SIR—Having been informed by Major Puttuff the Indian Agent for the Port of McKinac to applie to you for Licence, I therefore request of you if you Would Grant me a Licence for the Port of Green Bay and Another for the Fox River.

I Will be oblige to Col¹. Boyer to have the Goodness as to Give me an answer as the Season is Getting much advanced I Remain With the highest regards Sir your very ob[t]. Serv[t]

F. O[LIVA.]

I Will Give Col¹. Boyer that Satisfaction that the Goods I

---

[97] Although born an American, Louis Rouse was of the same race as the majority of the Green Bay habitants. His father, Jacques Rouse, a refugee soldier (probably from Acadia), settled in 1783 in Clinton County, N. Y., on the site later known as Rouse's Point, on Lake Champlain, close to the Canadian boundary. There, Louis was born about 1792. He served in the American forces during the War of 1812–15, and at its close secured the suttling for the rifle regiment, which business brought him to Green Bay. There, the attraction of the fur-trade seized upon him, and for a few years he embarked extensively in that commerce, later becoming much embarrassed and a debtor to the American Fur Company. He owned and operated a farm at Green Bay, and was district judge during our pre-territorial regime. About 1836, Judge Rouse became interested in a mill in Manitowoc County, and finally removed to the city of that name, where he died April 19, 1855. See*Wis. Hist. Colls.*, ii, p. 100.—ED.

[98] Thomas P. James, an American trader, who about 1819 was selling goods for the factor at Menominee River.—ED.

1815–1817] Fur-trade in Wisconsin

have imported from Michil[a] Were purchased from the House of David Stone & C° Who have obtained the Same privilege as the American Fur Comp[y]

Endorsed: 1 for the Green bay 1 for fox River

1817: TRADERS ARRESTED ON THE MISSISSIPPI

[Transcript in Wisconsin Historical Library. Street Papers.]

FORT ARMSTRONG [CRAWFORD], 18 Septr, 1817

To Major Morgan

SIR—I have ordered two trading Boats from Mackinac, Messrs Farnham[99] and Darling traders to proceed to Bell fontain to report to Govr. Smith. They have on board in the capacity of clerks, the two celebrated characters E. Lagotherie and St. John.[1] Their object is to trade on the Demoin river this season, but to warrant such an act they must obtain Licence from Gen'l Clark[2] you will be pleased to examine their pass-

---

[99] Russell Farnham was a New Englander who joined the Astorian expedition, and went out as clerk on the "Tonquin." In Oregon, he had numerous adventures, being in the Indian fight at the Dalles; assisting in building a post near Spokane; and wintering (1812–13) among the Flatheads. After the sale of Astoria, Farnham left with Wilson Hunt on the "Pedlar," landed on the coast of Kamschatka, and made his way overland to Hamburg, whence he sailed for New York. Re-entering Astor's employ, this was one of his first trips to the West in the interest of the American Fur Company. He afterwards carried their trade into the Missouri Valley, and among the Sauk and Foxes, by whom he was awarded a payment in the treaty of 1832. He died of cholera at St. Louis, in October of that year.—ED.

[1] For Lagoterie, see *ante*, p. 446, note 75. Joseph la Perche *dit* St. Jean was a Canadian who had come to the Northwest before 1801. In that year he was trading below Prairie du Chien, on the Mississippi. During the War of 1812–15 he was one of Dickson's agents, being both lieutenant and interpreter in the Indian department. In 1816 he was at Mackinac, and as here shown joined the American Fur Company. As late as 1821 he was still trading among the Sauk and Foxes.—ED.

[2] According to H. H. Chittenden, *History of the American Fur Trade* (N. Y., 1902), p. 313, the inciting cause for this arrest was the jeal-

port and compell them to act conformably to their directions as far as may be practicable. I am respectfully

T. CHAMBERS,
Lieut [Colonel] Commanding

FORT CRAWFORD 18 Septr 1817

The Bearers Messrs. Farnham and Darling are permitted to visit St. Louis with their respective boats and crew for the purpose of procuring a license from Gov'r Clark to trade on the river Lemoine. They are positively ordered to make report at all the military posts situated between this and St. Louis and to Gen'l Smith commanding at military department previous to arriving at St. Louis during this passage they are positively prohibited from holding any intercourse or even converse with any Indians, save what may be absolutely indispensible to procure immediate wants or to land, deposit or dispose of any species of goods or merchandize or make any unnecessary halts or delays.

T. CHAMBERS
Lieut. [Colonel] Commanding

FORT CRAWFORD 19 Septr 1817

Major Morgan

SIR—I have this moment being informed that the masters of two Boats who I have ordered to St. Louis to obtain the permission of Gov. Clark, previous to opening a trade on the Lemoine viz Farland [Farnham] and Darling have declared prior to leaving this place that they were determined to open the cargoes below fort Armstrong on their way down the river

---

ousy which St. Louis traders felt for those from Mackinac. They were carrying licenses from the American agent at Mackinac, but Chambers arrested them because they had none from the governor either of Illinois or Missouri. Later, the American Fur Company sued Colonel Chambers for this action, and after a long legal contest obtained damages to the amount of $5,000.—ED.

they appeared to be hardened Raschels, particularly Lagoterie who declared that he would not visit St. Louis. I have thought it necessary to apprise you of this circumstance in order that the military might not be made the subject of derision by such named Raschels. the fellow St. John one of the clerks acknowledged here in the presence of Mr. Ofallon that those three american Sculps hoisted on his boat during the last war at this place.

T. CHAMBERS
Lieut. [Colonel]

FORT ARMSTRONG 27. Septr., 1817.

SIR—I send to Bell fontain under guard two mackinac Boats with their masters and crew

You will perceive by the enclosed papers that Lft. Col. Chambers has positively prohibited them from trading or even conversing with the Indians untill they shall have obtained licence from Govr. Clark yet they openly declared that it was their intention to commence trading two or three miles below this place. As an officer I have but one course to pursue, to enforce the orders of my superior officer, for any information connected with this command I beg permission to refer the Gen'l to Lt. Blair.[3] I have the honor to be

WILLOUGHBY MORGAN
Major

---

[3] Lieut. William Preston Smith Blair was a grand-nephew of Col. William Preston of Virginia, and a brother of Francis P. Blair, editor of the Washington *Globe*. He was born in Kentucky, and enlisted as ensign in 1813, becoming lieutenant in the 2nd rifles the following year. At the close of the war he returned to civil life, re-enlisting in 1817 as lieutenant in the rifles. In 1818 he was stationed in Arkansas, and resigned from the army in June, 1821. He died Aug. 3, 1828. His wife was Hannah Craig; and one son, Patrick M. Blair, became a well-known Illinois lawyer.—ED.

[4] Maj. Willoughby Morgan was a Virginian who entered the army as captain in 1812; during the war he was brevetted major, and at its close made an officer in the consolidated rifle regiment. In July, 1815, he was at Detroit, preparatory to taking over Mackinac from the

1817: LICENSES TO FOREIGNERS

[MS. in Pension Office, Washington. Pressmark: Indian Office Letter Book "D," p. 426.]

OFFICE INDIAN TRADE GEO TOWN 30 Sep 1817

Geo: Graham Esq acting Secy. of War

SIR—In prosecuting the trade with the several Indian Tribes in my capacity of Superintendent, I have endeavoared to ascertain the nature of those causes which I have perceived to interrupt, and injure it. I have also attempted through the agents who managed the concerns of the Factories; and whose opportunities to detect and apprehend evils are more directly at hand, to ascertain whether there are any lurking evils, or latent fires connected with those causes of interruption which it was likely to suspect might break out to the injury of our fronteer citizens in the event of British or Indian Wars. With a view to this I addressed a letter to Mathew Irwin the factor at Green Bay requiring first to inform himself on the subject of the extent to which licences had been issued by the Indian agent to foreigners, and 2dly. whether those foreigners now holding licences, and acting under them had been hostile to the U S. during the late War with England. I further instructed him that if on enquiry he should find these things to exist, to address a letter to Col: John Boyer, enumerating the

---

British. He commanded the latter post until relieved in the autumn by Colonel Chambers. In the summer of 1816, Morgan advanced with a detachment to Prairie du Chien, where he planned and began the first Fort Crawford. Early the following year (1817) he was again relieved by Colonel Chambers, being stationed during 1818 at Fort Armstrong, on Rock Island. In 1819 he was on the Missouri, near the present Fort Leavenworth, and two years later at Fort Harrison, in Indiana. The year 1822 found him again at Prairie du Chien, where he commanded during the Winnebago troubles of 1826–27. He appears to have continued in charge of that post until his death there in April, 1832. He was at this latter time colonel of the 1st infantry. Morgan was an efficient commander, and especially skilful in managing the Indians.—ED.

persons coming within the description specified[5]—they amount it seems to Eighteen in number and they are all, not only British subjects, but men who helped to kindle the fires of War in our Northern and Western territories, and even led on the savages to the conflict! the extent of mischeif that 18 Men (supposing them to be all) can do in estranging the Indians from our interests; and exciting them, as their avarice may dictate, to hostility, and blood, it is hard to estimate. Nor can it be known how difficult it is to compete with these men in the management of the Indian trade. Our agents are governed by certain specific instructions pointing directly to all the branches of their intercourse. These are known, as well to the British agents, no doubt, as to those who act under them. It is no hard matter so to vary the principles which govern this Trade on our part, as to realize a monopoly on theirs; and this too without any *real* advantage to the Indians. The nature of their location with their means of intercourse will preserve to them this power, nor is there any remedy in my opinion but a total restriction. As I have heretofore stated I am aware of the provision of the law; and the granting of licences is entrusted to the discretion of the agent. Indeed that on application, with a profer of surety there seems to be no power of refusal. But it appears to me the agt. might under instructions from the War Dept. at least reserve to himself the right to reject the application of notorious offenders, and enemies.

It is not at Green Bay only, where our trade is assailed by the license system, which appears to be so indiscreetly acted on, but at Prarie du Chien also. There, this evil reigns and without any controul.

It is but justice to Col: Boyer to state, that he promises to act in future; to countervail this evil. But there is no such assureance from Major Wm. H. Puthuff who, Mr. Irwin writes me he has been informed, and from a direct and respectable source, has received in one year from the British house of Bartlott [Berthelot] and Co. at Mackinac, $3.200. for issuing

---

[5] See Irwin's letter to Bowyer, *ante*, pp. 468–470.—Ed.

licences to their agents; and from other persons various sums supposed to amount to 4000$ and upwards. His plea is, so I have been informed, that by demanding 50$ per license, he should lessen the number of applications!

I make these communications with pain. I am always reluctant to present cases which tend to give trouble to the War Department to which this office is attached; and would prefer always to cure the evils that exist, than to complain of them. But where they cannot be destroyed by the power vested in me, it becomes my duty to represent them, and to hope for a speedy intervention of a superior authority. Otherwise the views of the Govt. in relation to Indian trade can be but partially met, the peacefull influence which it is designed to promote, will be always liable to disturbance; and the lives of our Citizens remain in continual jeopardy. I am etc. etc.

T L Mc.K[ENNEY]

[MS. in Pension Building, Washington. Pressmark: Indian Office Book 203. Letter Book 2, p. 186.]

MICHILLIMACKINAC 5 Oct. 1817.

William Woodbridge Esqr.

SIR—I have taken the liberty to address you as the only person to whom any individual undeserveignly ill treated can look to for redress. I shall now minutely give you my cause of Complaint.

I was last year in the employ of Mr. Bergin at Green Bay, and in May last Colo. Bowyer ordered me to leave that place without assigning any just cause for his so doing, although to the knowledge of Major Taylor, I did by letter request of him to have my Conduct strictly investigated and if there could be any proof then adduced of my having in any ways whatever violated the laws of the Country I was willing to be sent away or abide by any Verdict which a Court of Investigation might give, but this satisfaction was denied me. I nevertheless left Green Bay and shortly after my arrival here, I would have been employed to go into the interior in the Capacity of a Clerk for the New York furr Compy.

Fur-trade in Wisconsin

The Indian Agent here Major Puthuff objected to my going as being a British subject, was it a General Order that no British Subject should be allowed to go into the interior I consequently would have no room for Complaint, but when this priviledge is denied to one or two individuals only, is in my Humble opinion shewing too much partiality. I have been in the Country now 17 Years and in that space of time no person has ever had cause to Complain of my interfering with any Business which was out of the limits of the Trade, I might have been employed in, this restriction I mention being laid to me alone, altogether puts it out of my power to earn a Livelyhood, being brought up to the Indian Trade I would be unfit for any other occupation. Hoping you will take this into consideration I have the honor to be Sir, Respectfully Your Mo. Ob. Serv.

JOHN DREW.[6]

1817: MISSISSIPPI TRADERS ARRESTED

[Transcript in Wisconsin Historical Library. Street Papers. John O'Fallon to Gen. William Clark.]

BELLFONTAIN 6 October 1817

SIR—Enclosed you will receive statement from Lieut Col Chambers to Major Morgan on the Subject of the masters and clerks of two Mackinac boats which were destined to trade on the Lemoin river, your concurrence being deemed necessary preparatory to such a Step these traders were accordingly refused, but having declared notwithstanding intention to trade in the Missouri T'ry below Fort armstrong. without your authority as a certain precaution against the execution of such intention They are sent to you escorted by a military guard commanded by Lieut. Blair. I am instructed by the Gen'l to request you to return the inclosures as soon as they can be con-

---

[6] John Drew was a well-known merchant of Mackinac, who for many years was in the Indian trade. In 1836 he accompanied a number of chiefs to Washington, where he was witness to a treaty.—ED.

veniently spared. I have the honor to be with the highest respect Yr. Most Obt Servt,

JNO. O'FALLON.
Act. Asst Agt Gen'l.

1817: INSTRUCTIONS FOR GREEN BAY FACTOR

[MS. in Pension Office, Washington. Pressmark: Indian Office Letter Book "D," p. 429.]

OFFICE INDIAN TRADE GEO: TOWN 6 Octr. 1817

Mathew Irwin Esq U S. F. Green Bay

SIR—I duly received your communications of august 2d. and 3d.—together with a copy of the letter addressed by you to Col: Boyer. Considering, as I do, that the very spirit of the law authorizing the issues of licences to trade with the Indians, has been violated, and an undue use made of its provisions, equally prejudicial to the designs of the Govt. in its views of civilization, and to the success of the U. S trade, which is itself a branch of the same policy, I have reported the state of things in that country to the acting Secretary of War, at large; and am not without hope that if no good shall result from your investigation *immediately,* and which may be deferred from the looseness of the law, the Congress at its next session will apply a suitable corrective.

* * * * * * * *

I am averse to the risque which is involved in letting out goods to sub-traders. I question very much whether the advantages to the Indians, or to the factory, would not be counterbalanced by the losses which, from experience, I know wait upon the practise. Nor should any sub-agencies be exercised within the limits embraced by the suitable lines for the operations of the *main* factory: they destract the trade, and make it (the factory) uncertain as to its own business. Any adventures you may make must be made, *first,* on good security, 2d. The goods sent must not injure the assortment of the Factory, 3d. The sub agent must trade beyond the limits which include those Indians that deal with the factory, and 4th. those to whom the supplies are carried must be such as need them; and to serve whom it would be to serve the cause of humanity. A proper attention to those few particulars can only justify the practise.

* * * * * * * *

I am etc.

T. L. McK[ENNEY]

1817: LOCAL TRADING INCIDENTS

[MS. in Wisconsin Historical Library. Pressmark: Wisconsin MSS., 4B43. Translated from the French.]

KACALIN 23 november 1817

Mr. Lawe

SIR AND FRIEND—I Received the honor of your letter in which you advise me of the position of M[r]. Jacobs[7] and that he had not yet notified my brother. I believe that it will be Best for You to Send some one immediately to Recommend to Him not to Extend our credits for our Creditors have as much as they can pay.

In regard to M[r] Lusignan[8] you tell me that you have not been able to get a Reply from Colonel Boyer. I will send therefore some of my Men soon to the fond du Lac to see what is occuring there and on Their Return I will tell you what occurs there for about that time I mean to go to La Baye. It is certain from appearances that he is about to do us Much harm for the Savages draw more to his side than to Ours or to speak more accurately they do not come to us at all, especially those I expected.

I beg you not to be Rebuffed but to try again with Colonel Boyer for it is better to stop Him now than in the spring.

---

[7] For a note on this person, see *Wis. Hist. Colls.*, xi, p. 225.—ED.

[8] This trader was the one mentioned in *Id.*, vii, p. 277. Possibly he was a descendant of the French commandant of Green Bay from 1743-46; *Id.*, xviii, p. 6.—ED.

Nothing else to speak of except to beg you to believe me to be for life Your very humble Obedient Servant and friend

AUGT GRIGNON

pr. L. FILY

I beg you to assure M^r. Caron of my respects.

Addressed: Mr Lawe, Merchant at La Baye
Endorsed by Lawe: Grignon dated Kakalin 23^d Nov. 1817 an answer

---

[Source, same as preceding document, but 4B46.]

R DU S DU BOEUF 6 December 1817

To Mr John Law

SIR—This is to inform you that the last Letter I received from Mr P. Grignon mentions that he is sorrey of I being badley plassd on this River and that no Indians Winters on this River.

But for me to take courage and to send on Derouin[9] a la Foursh and Lac Ver and not make aney Credits save my Goods & number of Indians will be here this spring as well as to trade on shush prisess whish I keep his letter to be carefull to keep up shush Prisess as he mentions: I will strickley in all thinges act and do faithfully and Honestly according to his Orders and I am well pleased to be under his direction— he [h]as been polight to tell me and thank'd me of I drawing his Credits and making no C^r. and as been mush pleased he inteands to send Polite her[e] to bring me a few article to assort my goods. if you do not think this to be the fact I mention you Let me know by the first oppertunity I shall send you his letter at present I keep it to get acquaintead with shush prisess. Mr Rouse winters his Neighbour cells his goods the same Prise as M^r. Grignon all on C^r. Beauprey will do well, it seems that M^r. Dickson is gon to see his son on the River S^t. Peter and that Lord S^t. Carchel [Selkirk] went down the Mississipie pass'd the Prerie 2 Captⁿ. one Lieu^t. and 13 Solger dont know whare he is going This is all the Newes I got from the Ouiscosien.

---

[9] For significance of this expression see *ante*, p. 200, note 86.—ED.

Fur-trade in Wisconsin

I wish you and Familey well and Prosperitey and I wish my·sealf dead and your Propritey savead

J. B^{te} Jacobs

N. B. Mr Grignon did not keep my mean [men] he says I shall want them.

Addressed: Mr John Lawe Green Bay

1817: GREEN BAY AGENT'S REPORT

[MS. in Pension Building, Washington. Pressmark: Indian Office Book 203. Letter Book 2, p. 225.]

Green Bay Agency Dec: 15, 1817.

Sir—I have the honor to acknowledge the receipt of your letter of Oct. 12th. In consequence of the Jackson having left the Bay before I could send my letters on board, I could not answer you sooner. I received by the Jackson three large and four small medals, these I must hold, until I receive a further supply of these articles, if I deliver them I shall be called on in the Spring for Seven large and Twelve small medals and the same number of Arms and wrist bands.

I permitted Mr. Irwin to read the extract of your letter to Mr. Jouett, he made no remarks on the subject. I suppose a Copy of his letter to me, has been forwarded to the Superintendent of Indian Trade at the City of Washington.

On the subject of Joseph Rolette and the hundred Dollars I received for two Licences, I will forward to you in the Spring Mr. John Lawe's certificate with whom I transacted this business, which certificate I feel confident will satisfy you, I have acted correctly. And when Rolette arrives here in the Spring, I will make him give a certificate that will shew his conduct in this case; has been like every other transaction of his that has came to my knowledge that of a Scoundrel.

I am pleased you approve of my prohibiting the landing of spirituous liquors in this Agency, I think [it] will have a good effect; but could it be so arranged that the Collector at Mackinaw, should be directed not to give clearances for Spirituous

Liquors for this place, I then could command the Indians and traders, until this can be done the traders will run Whiskey into the Indian Country by the Indians and particularly Green Bay.

I have directed the traders to ascertain as near as possible the number of Men, Women and Children who reside in the Neighbourhood of their establishments, by this arrangement, I think I shall be able on the return of the traders to give you a tolerable correct estimate of the Indians residing within the limits of this Agency. The whole of the Indians left this about the 1st. of October for their hunting ground except a few families of old Women and Children who lost their husbands and Brothers in the late War, and are realy starving in consequence of the frost having destroyed their Corn, and the wild rice failing, not a tenth part of the latter, they formerly gathered has been made this fall and I am correct in saying not ten Bushels of Corn has been saved within Sixty Miles of this place. I shall be obliged to furnish those Women and Children with provisions from the public Store. I have the honor to be Sir, Very respectfully Yo. Ob. Serv.

JNO. BOWYER.

His Excellency Lewis Cass Gov. of M. T.

Index

[Names of Battles, Bays, Creeks, Forts, Islands, Lacs, Lakes, Portages, Points, Rapids, Rivers, Rivières, Treaties, and Wars are grouped under their respective heads, instead of their individual names.]

ABBOTT, James, Detroit merchant, 298.
Abbott, Samuel, Mackinac official, 340, 420; fur-trader, 404; sketch, 340.
Abitagowinan, children baptized, 148.
"Adams," fur-trade vessel, 322.
Adhemar, Angelique, witness, 96, 102; godmother, 100, 103-105, 110, 111, 116, 118, 121-124, 128, 129; teacher, 159.
Adhemar, Geneviève Blondeau, godmother, 97, 98, 104, 105, 107, 109, 113, 115, 117, 126; witness, 102, 103; marriage, 159.
Adhemar, Jean Baptiste, godfather, 65.
Adhemar, Josephe (Josette), godmother, 123, 129.
Adhemar, Marguerite, godmother, 121, 124, 125; witness, 121.
Adhemar, Patrice, godfather, 106, 107, 115, 116, 120, 125, 128; baptizes, 143; merchant, 307.
Adhemar, Toussaint Antoine. See St. Martin.
Agacouchin, Charles, child baptized, 117.
Agacouchin, Jean Baptiste, baptized, 117.
Agacouchin, Marguerite, ch ld baptized, 117.
Agassiz, Louis, *Lake Superior*, 172.
Agathe, a savage, baptized, 18.
Agnes, a slave, baptized, 32.
Aikens, Marianne, marr ed, 394.
Ailleboust, Sieur d'. See Coulonge, and La Magdeleine.
Ainse (Heins), Joseph Lou's, mother of 2; baptized, 11, 12; godfather, 47, 74, 78, 82, 90, 92, 93; baptizes, 77, 78; impresses provisions, 248. See also Heins.
Ainse, Pierre Joseph, godfather, 82.
Aird, James, Wisconsin trader, xvii, 358, 360, 367-369; arb trator, 270; licensed, 431, 444; letter from, 316, 317.
Aird, Robert, gives advice, 316.

Albany (N. Y.), settlers, 260; agent at, 329; battle near, 243.
Albert, François, godfather, 136, 137; witness, 136.
Albert, Marguerite Basile, godmother, 136, 137.
Alexandre Louis, a slave, baptized, 60.
Allen, Maj. Ebenezer, Revolutionary soldier, 282.
Allen, Ebenezer junior, Western trader, 282, 283.
American Fur Company, chartered, 337; founder, 291; organized, xvi, xx, 164; partner, 348; agents, 413, 414, 451, 477; traders for, 445, 474; employees, 162, 170, 171, 176, 190, 288; posts, 171, 173, 178, 208; creditor, 476; legal suit, 478; privileges, 414, 477; in War of 1812-15, 346-354; rival company, 461; buys South West Company, 451, 458.
American Historical Review, cited, 73.
American State Papers, cited, 314, 364, 384, 387, 448.
Amherst, Gen. Jeffrey, invades Canada, 294.
Amherstburg (Ont.), British post, xix; settlers, 253, 263, 292, 324; sheriff, 276; Indians visit, 314.
Amiot, Agathe Villeneuve, godmother, 26, 28; child baptized, 28, 29.
Amiot, Ambro se, baptized, 40.
Amiot, Augustin, godfather, 36.
Amiot, Blaise, baptized, 26.
Amiot, Jean Baptiste, children baptized, 2-6, 17, 26; godfather, 40, 49; slave baptized, 47, 64; sketch, 155.
Amiot, Louis I, baptized, 6.
Am ot, Louis II, baptized, 17; buried, 153.
Am ot, Marianne, children baptized, 17, 26; godmother, 31, 46, 47; buried, 155.

[489]

Amlot, Marie Anne, baptized, 4.
Amlot, Marie Louise, baptized, 3.
Amlot, Marie Ursule, baptized, 2.
Amlot, Nicolas, baptized, 3; son baptized, 40; wife baptized, 42; godfather, ⌣⊥.
Amʹot, Susanne, baptized, 42.
Amlot, Ursule, baptized, 5.
Anderson, John, trader, 277, 279, 286; sketch, 277.
Anderson, Col. John junior, militia officer, 277.
Anderson, Thomas, Wisconsin trader, 304, 305, 358-360; in War of 1812-15, 161; accounts, 345; in government employ, 368; sketch, 305.
Andreas, A. T., *Chicago*, 394.
"Angelica," fur-trade vessel, 241, 243, 252.
Angelique, a slave, baptized, 73.
Anne I, a slave, baptized, 13.
Anne II, a slave, baptized, 41, 42.
Antaya, Pierre Pelletier *dit*, founder of Prairie du Chien, xvii; letters to, 267-269.
Antaya. See also La Pointe, and Fraser.
Antoine I, a slave, baptized, 27.
Antoʹne II, a slave, baptized, 29.
Antoine III, a slave, baptized, 43.
Antoine IV, a slave, baptized, 49.
Antoine V, a slave, baptized, 66.
Antoine, fur-trade engagé, 313.
"Argus," naval vessel, 363.
"Ariadne," captured vessel, 278.
Arkansas Territory, officials, 340; army post in, 479.
Arundel, William, Illinois trader, 301.
Ashland, sites near, 174-176; postmaster, xxi.
Askin, Adelaide (Alice), married, 310; message for, 326.
Askin, Alexander, message for, 326.
Askin, Archange Barthe, child baptized, 77; godmother, 75; messages for, 273, 282, 287-289, 294, 297, 307, 324, 325, 337, 342, 374; messages from, 243, 245, 249, 251, 252, 254-256, 258; supplies for, 242, 248; daughter, 263.
Askin, Archange junior, baptized, 77.
Askʹn, Catharine (Kitty), wedding gown, 242, 248. See also Robertson, and Hamilton.
Askin, Charles, message for, 326.
Askin, Ellen (Nelly), message for, 326.
Askin, James, message for, 326.
Askin, John, child baptized, 77; early lʹfe, 298; at Mackinac, 323; letters, 263, 264, 273-275, 282, 283, 286, 287, 295-298; letters to, 260, 261, 264-266, 271, 272, 276, 277, 279-288, 291, 296, 298-300, 306-310, 336, 337, 372-374; land scheme, 282; sons, 306, 307; brother-in-law, 235, partners, 241, 254; sketch, 75, 234.

Askin, John junior, letters, 322-326, 342; letter to, 358; sketch, 324.
Askin, John III, employment, 342.
Askin, Madeleine, at Montreal, 263. See also Richardson.
Askin, Madeleine Pelletier, wife of John junior, 324, 325, 342.
Askin, Thérèse, letter for, 272. See also McKee.
Assumptʹon (Ont.), mission at, 147.
Astor, George Peter, at Montreal, 356; Detroit, 363.
Astor, John Jacob, organizes fur company, xvi, 164, 191; at Montreal, 290, 291; buys Mackinac Company, xvi, 336, 337; South West Company, 451, 458, 460; special privileges, xvii, 354, 355, 362, 423; censured, 423; characterized, 369-371; employees, 327, 371, 414, 461; brother, 363; letters, 348, 369, 451; letters to, 346-350, 352-354, 360-364; sends goods, 404, 405; befriends Wisconsin traders, xxi; sketch, 290.
Astoria (Ore.), plans for, 336, 337; founded, xvi, 291; expedition, 348, 371, 463, 477; events at, 365; clerks, 414; sold to British, 281, 477.
Athabasca, fur-traders in, 163, 290, 469.
Atten. See Bourassa.
Au Poste. See Vincennes (Ind.).
Auger, Etienne, godfather, 20.
Auger, Jean Marʹe, baptizes, 139.
Auger, René Bonaventure, godfather, 41, 67.
Augustin, a slave, baptized, 5.
Ayer, Edward E., aid acknowledged, xxi, 299; manuscripts, 300.

BADISHON, —, message for, 325.
Bailly, Angelique McGulpin, child baptized, 141.
Bailly, Joseph, child baptized, 141, godfather, 110, 111; fur-trader, 366; employee of, 455; sketch, 110, 366.
Bailly, Sophʹe, baptized, 141.
Bain, James, *Alexander Henry's Travels*, 170, 183, 194.
Baird, Mrs. Elizabeth Thérèse, mother of, 117; "Early Days at Mackinac," 233. See also Fisher.
Baird, Henry S., Green Bay settler, 139; at Mackinac, 408.
Baird, William, Buffalo merchant, 347.
Baker, —, Detroit carpenter, 308.
Balls Town, (Que.), springs at, 289.

Index

Bannerman, —, navigator, 240.
Baraga, Rev. Frederick, missionary, 208.
Barcellou, —, wife, 44.
Bardon, James, aid acknowledged, xxi, 173.
Baribeau, F., godfather, 21.
Barsaloux, Chippewa Indian, 200, 201, 217, 218, 220, 224.
Barthe, Antoine, godfather, 83, 86, 91; witness, 92.
Barthe, Archange, married, 234. See also Askin.
Barthe, Charles, son, 235.
Barthe, Felicité, godmother, 76, 77.
Barthe, Geneviève Beaubien Cuillerier, child baptized, 96, 97; godmother, 78, 79, 81-85, 87, 88, 91, 93.
Barthe, Jean Baptiste, children baptized, 96, 97; slaves baptized, 87, 88, 96; godfather, 95; witness, 156, 161; trader, 235, 239, 243, 260, 263; partner, 241; message for, 324, 325; sketch, 235.
Barthe, Louis, at Milwaukee, 253; message for, 326; sketch, 253.
Barthe, Thérèse Victoire, baptized, 96, 97.
Bartlett. See Berthelot.
Basile, Marguerite. See Albert.
BATTLES—
 Falsely reported, 248.
 Bennington, 282.
 Dalles of Columbia, 477.
 Fallen Timbers, 297.
 Lake Erie, 351, 361.
 Mackinac Island, 362.
 Nile, 281.
 Plattsburgh, 367.
 Seven Oaks, 462.
 Thames, 184, 214, 439.
 Tippecanoe, xviii, 322, 439.
 Yorktown, 273.
Batillot. See Clermont.
Baudion, Catherine Govreau, children baptized, 144.
Baudoin, François, children baptized, 144.
Baudoin, Pierre, baptized, 144.
Baudoin, Théotis, baptized, 144.
Bayfield, Admiral Henry W., charts, Lake Superior, 174, 215.
Bayfield County, sites in, 174.
BAYS—
 Aboukir, battle in, 281.
 Georgian, routes via, xv.
 Grand Traverse, Indians on, 412.
 Green, described, 438; navigation, 437; trade route, 378, 380, 385; affluents, 177, 187, 401; Indians near, 470-472.
 Keweenaw, 170, 208, 474. See also L'Anse.
 La Ronde, 360.
 Matchedash, 21, 58, 147; trade-route, 358, 359; war expedition to, 361, 367.
 St. Louis, 173.
 St. Therese. See Keweenaw.
 Sturgeon, portage, 400.
 Washington, shipwreck in, 475.
Bazinet, Jean Baptiste, voyageur, 184, 185, 189, 191, 192, 194, 195, 197-202, 204, 206, 212, 216-218, 220, 224; in charge of invoice, 225.
Bear's Oil. See Makometa.
Beaubassin, Pierre Joseph Hertel, sieur de commandant at Chequamegon, 175; godfather, 45, 46.
Beaubien, Angelique Cuillerier *dit*, married, 243, 244.
Beaubien, Charles, child baptized, 141.
Beaubien, Jean Baptiste, wife, 158; at Chicago, 394; Milwaukee, 455.
Beaubien, Jean Marie, reclaims anchor, 326.
Beaubien, Marguerite. See Nicole.
Beaubien, Marie, child baptized, 141; slave baptized, 33.
Beaubien, Marie junior, baptized, 141.
Beaujeu-Villemonde, Louis Liénard, sieur de, godfather, 33-35, 37, 52-56, 59-61; slave baptized, 56, 60; sketch, 33.
Beaulieu, —, voyageur, 185, 187, 209, 219.
Beaulieu, Catherine Brian *dit*, baptized, 35.
Beaulieu, Françoise, daughter baptized, 35.
Beaulieu, Jean Brian *dit*, daughter baptized, 35.
Beaupré, Louis, Wisconsin trader, 364, 367; wintering post, 486; sketch, 364.
Beaupré, Louis junior, at Helena, 364.
Beausoleille, —, trader, 239.
Beauvais, Marie Anne Viger, godmother, 72-74.
"Beaver," Astor's vessel, 348.
"Beaver," lakes vessel, 170.
Beaver Club, Montreal, described, 372, 373.
Beecroft, Daisy G., aid acknowledged, xxii.
Bellestre, Marie François Picoté, sieur de, commandant of Detroit, 13.
Bellestre, Françoise Marianne. See Quindre.
Belleville (Ill.), settlers, 395.
Bellfontaine (Mo.), military post, 477, 479, 483.
Belt, Robert B., factor, 386, 388, 389.

[491]

Bennett, Lieut. Thomas, sent to Grand Portage, 236, 237, 243, 248; accounts, 247, 259.
Benton, Thomas Hart, legal opinion, 441, 442.
Bergin, —, Green Bay, trader, 482.
Berthelot, Jean Baptiste, godfather, 129; power of attorney, 334; letters, 396-398, 404, 405; notes, 375; furs, 304, 318, 355, 357; goods, 341, 366; at St. Joseph's Island, 342; licenses, 431, 481; sketch, 304.
Bertrand, Barbe Felicité Pillet, godmother, 106, 107.
Bertrand, Eustache, baptized, 83.
Bertrand, Jean Baptiste, baptized, 75; child baptized, 138; wife, 129; witness, 99; godfather, 131.
Bertrand, Joseph, baptized, 83.
Bertrand, Joseph Laurent, children baptized, 75, 76, 83; baptizes, 117; godfather, 106, 107.
Bertrand, Josephe, baptized, 138.
Bertrand, Laurent, bapt'zed, 75.
Bertrand, Marguerite. See Bourassa.
Bertrand, Marguerite Kodeckoi, baptized 129.
Bertrand, Marguerite Ouigouisence, child baptized, 138.
Bertrand, Marie Therese Du Lignon, children baptized, 75, 76, 83.
Besnard, Jean Louis. See Carignan.
Betel —, messenger, 395.
Biauswa, Chippewa chief, 174.
Bichibichikoue, Marie, baptized, 50.
Biddle, Nicholas, edits Lewis and Clark's narrative, 313.
Billon, Bartholemi, trader, 271.
Bissonet,—, child, baptized, 65.
Bissonet, Michel, baptized, 65.
Bissonière, Geneviève, married, 158.
Black Hawk, village site, 446; *Autobiography*, 314.
Black Rock (N. Y.), lake port, 354.
Black Wolf. See Shounkchunk.
Blackwood, Thomas, Montreal merchant, 334, 335.
Blainville, Jean Baptiste Céleron junior, sieur de, slave, baptized, 7.
Blair, Francis P., editor, 479.
Blair, Patrick M., Illinois lawyer, 479.
Blair, William Preston Smith, army officer, 479, 483.
Bleakley, Josiah, fur-trader, 324; arbitrates dispute, 275.
Blondeau, —, witness, 44.
Blondeau, Anne Villeneuve, godmother, 18, 23, 36-38, 43, 47, 48; slave baptized, 51; buried, 154. See also Guillory.

Blondeau, Bartholemi, witness, 26, 27, 29, 30, 42-44, 47; godfather, 60.
Blondeau, Geneviève. See Adhemar.
Blondeau, Jean Marie, godfather, 13, 16, 18.
Blondeau, Joseph Bartholemi, baptized, 10, 11.
Blondeau, Josephe Marguerite, baptized, 18.
Blondeau, Marguerite, godmother, 60.
Blondeau, Mare Anne, baptized, 4.
Blondeau, Marie Josephe De Selle, children baptized, 11, 14, 18; godmother, 10, 11, 20, 21, 60.
Blondeau, Marie Josephe, baptized, 9, 10.
Blondeau, Michel, bapt'zed, 4.
Blondeau, Thomas, children baptized, 4, 9, 11, 14, 18.
Blondeau, Thomas junior, bapt'zed, 14.
Blot, Jerome, child baptized, 98.
Blot, Marie Magdeleine, baptized, 98.
Boilvin, Nicolas, Indian agent, xviii, 314-316, 339; in War of 1812-15, 345; letters, 395, 396; notes, 397; orders from, 398; complaints against, 459; sketch, 314.
Boiser, —, godfather, 62.
Boisguilbert, Agathe Villeneuve, godmother, 9, 14, 16, 18, 21, 26, 52. See also Souligny, and Roy.
Boisguilbert, François, wife, 2, 9, 14, 16; slave, 13; death, 52.
Bolon, Gabriel, children baptized, 3, 4, 14, 20.
Bolon, Jean Louis, bapt'zed, 4.
Bolon, Joseph, baptized 14.
Bolon, Louise, godmother, 23, 38.
Bolon, Marie Françoise, baptized, 20.
Bolon, Marie Louise. See Guillory.
Bolon, Philippe, bapt'zed, 3.
Bolon, Susanne Menard, children baptized, 14, 20; godmother, 21.
Bon Cœur, children baptized, 9.
Bonaparte, Napoleon, mentioned, xvii, 281, 285, 351, 372.
Bonasa umbellus See Grouse.
Bonga, Charlotte, baptized, 97.
Bonga, Jean, children bapt'zed, 83, 91; buried, 157.
Bonga, Marie Jeanne, children baptized, 83, 97.
Bonga, Rosalie, baptized, 83.
Bonneterre, Augustin, children baptized, 128, 129.
Bonneterre, Julie, baptized, 129.
Bonneterre, Marie, baptized, 128.
Boone, Daniel, captured, 265.
Boston, prices of furs in, 453.
Bostwick, —. See Stone, Bostwick & Co.

Bostwick, Henry, fur-trader, 254, 461; partner, 461; children baptized, 100; sketch, 100.

Bostwick, Henry junior, baptized, 100

Bostwick, Marie Josephe, baptized, 100.

Bouché, Joseph, child baptized, 91.

Bouché, Paul, baptized, 91.

Boucherville, Pierre Amable Boucher, sieur de, at Mackinac, 322.

Boucherville (Que.), voyageur from, 180; residents, 165.

Bouga. See Bonga.

Boulon,—, voyageur, 239.

Boundaries: Wisconsin-Michigan, 186, 187, 212.

Bourassa, Agathe, baptized, 121.

Bourassa Alexandre, baptized, 96, 97, 100; godfather, 132, 134, 138.

Bourassa, Amable, baptized, 133.

Bourassa, Angelique, baptized, 68, 69.

Bourassa, Anne Agnes, baptized, 47.

Bourassa, Anne Catherine, baptized, 19.

Bourassa, Anne Charlotte Veronique Chevalier, children baptized, 13, 19, 34, 39, 47, 55, 62, 63, 68, 69; godmother, 43, 58.

Bourassa, Archange, baptized, 80; godmother, 112, 116, 125, 132, 141.

Bourassa, Charles Louis, baptized, 39.

Bourassa, Charles Jean Baptiste, baptized, 62, 63.

Bourassa, Charlotte, godmother, 36-38 See also Langlade.

Bourassa, Daniel, baptized, 33, 34; children baptized, 79, 80, 96, 97, 100, 111, 112, 121, 133; slaves baptized, 97, 107, 109, 115; witness, 108; baptizes, 98; churchwarden, 160, 161; sketch, 33.

Bourassa, Daniel junior, baptized, 79

Bourassa, Eloy, baptized, 100; children baptized, 133; godmother, 133, 141; church warden, 162; sketch, 162.

Bourassa, Eusèbe, baptized, 133.

Bourassa, Ignace, dit La Ronde, child baptized, 28; godfather, 21, 27, 68.

Bourassa, Jean Baptiste, baptized, 80.

Bourassa, Léon, baptized, 111; godfather, 141.

Bourassa, Louis François Xavier, baptized, 55.

Bourassa, Magdeleine, baptized, 100. See also McGulpin.

Bourassa, Marguerite, baptized, 80; godmother, 111-113, 124.

Bourassa, Marguerite Bertrand, children baptized, 79, 80, 96, 97, 100, 111, 121, 133, 134; godmother, 81-85, 87, 88, 90, 92, 95, 147, 148.

Bourassa, Marie, baptized, 133.

Bourassa, Marie Atten, echildren baptized, 133; godmother, 133.

Bourassa, Marie Catherine Laplante de Lerigé, godmother, 10, 15, 17, 19, 20, 24, 25, 27, 29, 30, 32-35, 37, 41, 44-47, 49, 50, 53, 58.

Bourassa, Marie Judith, baptized, 111; godmother, 132, 141, 143; married, 469, 470.

Bourassa, Michel, baptized, 96.

Bourassa, René I, son, 28; slaves baptized, 25, 28, 29, 36, 60; witness, 23, 31, 45, 47; godfather 13, 22, 23, 28, 37, 43; slaves buried, 153, 154.

Bourassa, René II, children baptized, 12, 19, 33, 34, 39, 47, 55, 63, 68, 69; slaves baptized, 43; slaves buried, 153, 154; godfather, 21, 38, 45, 56, 64.

Bourassa, René III, baptized, 13; godfather, 69.

Bourassa, Thérèse, baptized, 133; godmother, 134, 138.

Bourbon, —, voyageur, 188.

Bourbonnière, Jean Baptiste, buried, 156.

Bourdon, Geneviève Plessey, godmother, 118.

Bourgouin, Marie Elizabeth. See Vaillancourt.

Bouriess, Louis de, child baptized, 106.

Bouriess, Magdeleine, baptized, 106.

Bouthillier, Elmire, married, 336

Bouthillier, François, merchant, 344, 345; goods seized, 425; licensed, 441, 446; godfather, 104, 110, 111; witness, 108; sketch, 104.

Boutin,—, slave baptized, 9.

Bowyer, Col. John, Indian agent, at Chicago, 391; Green Bay, 392, 399, 407, 432, 441, 447, 470, 481, 482; grants licenses, 468, 475, 476, 485; letters, 440, 466, 467, 470-472, 480, 484, 487, 488; letter to, 481; sketch, 391.

Boyd, Capt. E., vessel captured, 278.

Boyer, Charles, trader, 238; godfather, 63.

Boyer, Charles junior, baptized, 63.

Boyer, Josephe Marguerite du L'gnon, child baptized, 63; godmother, 65, 66, 72.

Boyer, Michel, child baptized, 63; witness, 66; godfather, 64, 65.

Bradstreet, Col. John, expedition, 276.

Brant, Joseph, correspondence, 202.

Brasse, (a measure), term explained, 216.

Brian See Beaulieu.

Brisbé, François, dit La Grandeur, children baptized, 41, 49, 56, 57, 62.

[493]

Brisbé, Josette Catherine, baptized, 62.
Brisbé, Marianne, baptized, 41.
Brisbé, Marianne Parent, children baptized, 41, 49, 56, 57, 62; godmother, 67, 72.
Brisbé, Marie Françoise, baptized, 49; buried, 152.
Brisbé, Pierre François, bapt'zed, 56.
Brisbois, Antoine, godfather, 106.
Brisbois, Michel, Wisconsin trader, 318, 345; arrested, 425.
Brit sh fur-traders, in American territory, xix, 376-379, 401-404; 441, 443; exclusion from fur-trade, 403-405, 423, 432, 457, 458, 467.
Bronaugh, Jeremiah W., transport agent, 385, 464.
Brookes, Samuel M., portrait by, 474.
Brown, Edward O., aid acknowledged, xxi.
Brown, McDonell & Co., Pittsburgh merchants, 372.
Bruce, —, trader on Assiniboin, 238.
Bruce Mines (Ont.), settlers, 132.
Brulé, Chippewa Indian, 216.
Brunot, —, voyageur, 219.
Brunson, Alfred, Indian agent, 184.
Brush, Elijah, Detroit merchant, 310; message for, 326, 337.
Buffalo (N. Y.), Indian agency, 340; port, 342, 354; letter from, 346, 347; H'storical Society *Publications*, 276.
Bunnell, —, fur-trader, 299.
Burlington Heights, British abandon, 349.
Burt, W. A., surveyor, 177, 187.
Burton, Clarence M., library, 234; aid acknowledged, xxi.
Butler, —, mentioned, 436.
Butler, Col. Anthony, retakes Mackinac, 397, 398.
Butte des Morts, Indian site, 417; fur-trade post, 90, 400, 474; settlers, 368; treaty at, 434.

CABANNÉ, John P., St. Louis merchant, 397.
Cadeau. See Cadotte.
Cadieu, —, wife, 22.
Cadieu, Catherine, slave baptized, 22; godmother, 23.
Cadott (Wis.), origin of name, 214.
Cadotte (Cadeau, Cadot), Athanase, children baptized, 60, 65, 70.
Cadotte, Augustin, child baptized, 144; sketch, 145.
Cadotte, Catherine, child baptized, 46, 47.
Cadotte, Charlotte, baptized, 60.
Cadotte, François, baptized, 144.
Cadotte, Jean Baptiste I, Henry's partner, 238; at La Po'nte, 175; children baptised, 46, 47, 60, 65, 66, 69, 70; daughters married, 70.
Cadotte, Jean Baptiste II, baptized, 65, 66; child baptized, 72; trader, 69, 171, 173, 174.
Cadotte, Jean Baptiste III, trader, 214.
Cadotte, Joseph, interpreter, 145.
Cadotte, l'Amainbile, child baptized, 144, 145.
Cadotte, Marguerite, baptized, 112.
Cadotte, Marie Mouet, child baptized, 72.
Cadotte, Marie Renée, bapt'zed, 46, 47.
Cadotte, Michel, baptized, 69; children baptized, 112, 113; wife, 175; son, 189, 190; son in-law, 190; rival, 190; trading posts, 171, 175, 176, 179, 184, 203, 214; employees, 168; letter, 212; sketch, 69.
Cadotte, Michel junior, baptized, 112; joins Malhiot, 189, 190; relatives, 207; commended, 205, 206; supplies for, 218, 227, 228; sketch, 184.
Cahokia (Ill.), court at, 264; governor, 398, 399; traders, 6; residents, 301, 303, 344, 345, 366, 395.
"Caledonia," fur-trade vessel, 308; in navy, 364.
Calhoun, John C., secretary of war, 140.
Cameron, Duncan, witness, 102.
Cameron, Murdock, trader, 140.
Campau, —, messenger, 253, 254.
Campbell, —, Mackinac resident, 294.
Campbell, Henry Colin, "Father Ménard," 187.
Campbell, John, Indian agent, xviii, 314, 323, 332; death in duel, 323, 325, 333, 342; sketch, 323.
Campbell, Marie. See Paquin.
Campbell, Robert, witness, 102.
Campeau, Hippolyte, godfather, 77.
Campion, Alexis, godfather, 84, 92.
Campion, Etienne, godfather, 71, 79, 81, 84, 85, 87, 91, 93, 100, 102; witness, 156, 161; baptizes, 96, 100, 106.
Campion, Thérèse. See Dubois.
Canada, divided into provinces, 272.
Canadian Pacific Railway, route, 270; stations, 167.
Canoes, described, 220; varieties, 204.
Canton. See Kantong.
Cape Girardeau (Mo.), Spanish grant at, 265.
Carbonneau, Archange, baptized, 135.
Carbonneau, Archange, baptized, 135.
Carbonneau, Joseph, bapt'zed, 135.
Carbonneau, Louis. See Provençal.
Carbonneau, Louis junior, baptized, 134.

Cardin, Charles Louis, baptized, 63.
Cardin, Charlotte, baptized, 37.
Cardin, Constante Chevalier, children baptized, 31, 32, 37, 43, 58, 63; godmother, 63, 65. See also Heins.
Cardin, François Louis, children baptized, 31, 37, 43, 58, 59, 63; slave baptized, 65, 70, 73; slave buried, 154; godfather, 83; notary, 75, 156; bur'ed, 155.
Cardin, Louis François, baptized, 58.
Cardin, Marianne. See La Fantaisie.
Cardin, Marie, baptized, 43.
Cardin, Mar'e Thérèse, godmother, 74.
Cardin, Veronique, baptized, 31, 32; godmother, 73; see also Sanguinet.
Cardinal, —, son baptized, 44.
Cardinal, Françoise, godmother, 32. See also Lacroix.
Cardinal, George, baptized, 44, 45.
Car gnan, Felicité Pillet, godmother, 79. 80, 82-95, 98-100, 102.
Carignan, Felicité junior, buried, 157.
Carignan, François Duclos *dit,* child baptized, 63.
Carignan, Jean Louis Besnard *dit,* godfather, 79, 82, 87, 94, 95; slave baptized, 79; baptizes, 95, 100, 102, 116; witness, 149, 156, 161; churchwarden, 160; drowned, 156, 157; sketch, 157.
Carignan, Marie Josephe Duclos *dit,* bapt'zed, 63.
Caris, Joseph de, godfather, 11, 14.
Carleton Sir Guy, governor of Canada, 262.
Caron, Claude, children baptized, 3, 12; slave baptized, 41; message for, 486.
Caron, Claude junior, baptized, 3.
Caron, Françoise Angelique, baptized, 12.
Caron, Joseph Gautier *dit,* children baptized, 120, 121; godfather, 132; married, 95.
Caron, Joseph Gautier *dit* junior, baptized, 120.
Caron, Louise Vasseur, child baptized, 120, 121; godmother, 122.
Caron, Marie, bapt'zed, 121.
Carp, in Lac du Flambeau, 188.
Carver, Jonathan, at Grand Portage, 169; names river, 313.
Cashaosha, Chippewa chief, 187.
Cass, Lewis, commission from, 142; on Lake Superior, 178, 183, 362; governor of Michigan Terr'tory, 350, 351, 381; superintendent of Indian affairs, 443; instructs Puthuff, 427, 428, 460, 461; letters, 376-379; letters to, 405-413, 415, 417-427, 430-432, 440, 457, 458, 467, 470-474, 487, 488; sketch, 350, 351, 379; portrait, 379.

Catherine I, baptized, 35.
Catherine II, a slave, baptized, 33.
Catherine III, a slave, baptized, 41.
Catherine IV, a slave, baptized, 56.
Catherine V, a slave, baptized, 115.
Catherine VI, a slave, child baptized, 59.
Catherine VII, a slave, child bapt.zed, 71.
Catherine VIII, a slave, buried, 153.
Catillan, —, baptizes, 116.
Catin, François, godfather, 118.
Catin, Nicolas, godfather, 73, 74.
Cauchois, Angelique Sejournée, *dit* Sans Chagrin, child baptized, 71; godmother, 70, 72, 76, 77.
Cauchois, Jean Bapt'ste, child baptized, 71; godfather, 70, 74.
Cauchois, Jean Baptiste George, baptized, 71.
Céloron, Pierre Joseph, godfather, 8.
Cerinaud, —, priest at Kingston, 136.
Cerré, Gabriel, godfather, 105.
Chaboillez (Chaboiller, Chaboyer), Augustin, baptized, 6; godfather 61.
Chabo'llez, Charles, children baptized, 4, 6, 9, 13, 17, 31, 34, 38; godfather, 11; slaves baptized, 22, 29, 32, 45; buried, 154.
Chaboillez, Charles (Charlotte) Domitelle, baptized, 34.
Chaboillez, Charles Jean Baptiste, of Mackinac, baptized, 4; godfather, 72, 75; churchwarden, 160, 161.
Chaboillez, Charles Jean Baptiste, of Three Rivers, in North West Company, 239, 245; wife sends supplies, 244, 245; sketch, 239.
Chaboillez, François, of Three Rivers, 239.
Chaboillez, François Hippolyte, baptized, 31; godfather, 77; trader, 241, 258.
Chaboillez, Jean Baptiste, godfather, 72, 73.
Chabo'llez, Louis Joseph, baptized, 6; godfather, 82; trader, 344.
Chaboillez, Marianne Chevalier, children baptized, 6, 9, 11, 13, 17, 31, 34, 38; godmother, 7, 12, 29, 43-45, 55, 59, 62.
Chaboillez, Marianne Marthe, baptized, 17; godmother, 59, 63, 64, 66. See also Farent.
Chaboillez, Marie Renée, baptized, 38.
Chaboillez, Paul Amable, baptized, 9; godfather, 34; witness, 45, 47.
Chaboillez, Pierre Louis, baptized, 13; baptizes, 75.
Chabo'llez family, at Mackinac, 239.
Chabot, Count, aids Askin, 325.
Chambele, child baptized, 51.
Chambers, Joseph, Indian agent, 303.

[495]

Chambers, Col. Talbot, commandant at Mackinac, 398, 420, 422, 480; at Green Bay, 437, 447; at Prairie du Chien, 459, 475, 480; arrests traders, 477-479, 483; characterized, 447; sketch, 420.
Champagne, Charles Michel, baptized, 122.
Champagne, Jean Baptiste Gourn *dit*, buried, 151.
Champagne, Marguerite Louise, baptized, 122. See also Rousseau.
Champagne, Simon, children baptized, 119, 122; godfather, 114.
Chandonnet, Charles, baptizes, 101, 118; godfather, 101, 128, 129; killed, 160; sketch, 305.
Chandonnet, Charlotte Marcot, buried, 159.
Chandonnet, Jean Baptiste, kills uncle, 306; sketch, 159, 160.
Chanteloups, Agnes Agathe Amiot Chartres *dit*, children baptized, 31, 36.
Chanteloups, Charles August n Chartres *dit*, baptized, 36.
Chanteloups, Charles Chartres *dit*, children baptized, 31, 36.
Chanteloups, Marianne Chartres *dit*, baptized, 31.
Chapoton, Alexis, godfather, 67, 68.
Chapoton, Marie, marriage, 160.
Chappu, Stanislaus, Wiscons n trader. 367.
Charlebois, André, child baptized, 115; child buried, 158; wife baptized, 94; buried, 158.
Charlebois, Josette junior, baptized, 115
Charlebois, Josette Hamelin, child baptized, 115; child and self buried, 158.
Charles I, a slave, baptized, 8, 9.
Charles II, a slave, baptized, 11.
Charles III, a slave, baptized, 29.
Charles IV, a slave, child baptized, 43.
Charles V, a slave, baptized, 43.
Charles, Ottawa chief, baptized, 85.
Charles Alexandre, baptized, 148.
Charles Joseph, a slave, baptized, 47.
Charlevoix, Pierre François Xavier de, traveller, 175.
Charlotte, a Ch ppewa, baptized, 102.
Charlotte, an Indian, child baptized, 66.
Charlotte, a slave, baptized, 42; buried, 154
"Charlotte," Lake Huron vessel, 286, 308.
Chartres. See Chanteloups.
Chauret. See Chorette.
Chauvin, Angelique, baptized, 119.
Chauvin, Jacques, wife baptized, 119
Chenier, Anto ne, St. Louis merchant, 397.
Chenier, Catherine. See Kimiouenan.

Chequamegon. See La Pointe.
Chesnier, Etienne, godfather, 29-31, wife bapt zed, 3.
Chevalier, Amable, children baptized, 93, 95, 101.
Chevalier, Angelique, baptized, 3; godmother, 22, 27, 31-33.
Chevalier, Anne Charlotte Veronique (Nanette), bapt zed, 3; godmother, 6, 7. See also Bourassa.
Chevalier, Anne Thérèse Esther, baptized, 3; godmother, 18, 21, 26, 27.
Chevalier, Archange, baptized, 125
Chevalier, Bartholemi, child baptized, 85.
Cheval er, Catherine, child baptized, 101.
Chevalier, Charles (L'avoine), baptized, 3.
Chevalier, Constance (Coussante), baptized, 2. See also Heins and Cardin.
Chevalier, Jean Baptiste I, voyageur, 8, 10, 12, 13; children baptized, 2-4; slaves, 5, 6, 18, 67; godfather, 19.
Chevalier, Jean Baptiste II, godfather, 85, 86.
Chevalier, Jean Baptiste III, baptized, 82.
Chevalier, Jean Baptiste IV, baptized, 124.
Cheval er, Joseph, baptized, 82.
Chevalier, Joseph Maurice, baptized, 3.
Chevalier, Josephe (Josephte), child baptized, 141.
Chevalier, Josephe junior, bapt zed, 141.
Chevalier, Josephe Marguerite, bapt zed, 2 See also Locat.
Chevalier, Louis, godfather, 12, 14.
Chevalier, Louis junior, children baptized, 124, 125.
Cheval er, Louis Pascal, bapt zed, 3; godfather, 18.
Chevalier, Louis Pascal junior, child baptized, 141.
Chevalier, Louis Thérèse, baptized. 2.
Chevalier, Luc, bapt zed, 4; godfather, 80; children bapt zed, 82, 83.
Chevalier, Marguerite, baptized, 82
Cheval er, Marguerite junior, baptized. 85; godmother, 99.
Chevalier, Mar anne. See Chaboillez.
Chevalier, Marie, baptized, 93.
Chevalier, Marie (Manon), baptized, 2. See also Dumée.
Chevalier, Marie (Manon) Françoise Alavoine, godmother, 8, 11-13, 15, 17, 32
Cheval er, Marie Louise, baptized, 95, 101.
Chévaré, Dominique, children baptized, 86, 87.
Chévaré, Etienne, baptized, 87.
Chévaré, Magde eine, baptized, 86.
Chevreaux, —, child baptized, 30.

Index

Chicago, site, 4, 17; on trade route, 387; massacre, 158, 159; Indians near, 408, 419; treaties at, 160; traders, xv, 421; Indian agency, 340, 379, 385, 399, 406, 407, 455, 456; post at, 384, 426, 432; fur-trade factory, xviii, 311, 389-392, 394, 395, 443, 455; goods for, 432, 440; factor, 326, 327, 331-333; residents, 158, 455; expedition (1832), 309. See also Fort Dearborn

Chicago and Northwestern Railway, station, 212.

Chichet, Ignace, adopts child, 128.

Chichet, Ignace junior, baptized, 128.

Chingwacok, child baptized, 148.

"Chippewa," trading vessel, 346.

Chippewa County, sites in, 214.

Chippewa Falls, trading post near, 184.

Chippewa (Saulteur, Sauteux) Indians habitat, xiv, 69, 471; villages, 173, 174, 181-183, 187, 194, 197; migrations, 171; camping ground, 174; handicraft illustrated, 174; food supply, 189; possess copper, 183; language, 208; religious rites, 194; married to whites, 85, 93, 149, 179, 361; baptized, 23, 54, 102, 108, 112, 118, 119; children baptized, 98, 99, 103-107, 112, 113, 116, 124, 125, 127, 129, 131, 140, 141, 144, 148; buried, 157; own slaves, 134; in War of 1812-15, 190; request truce, 350; visit Mackinac, 412, 420, 473; council, 417-422, friendly, 70, 456; visit Drummond Island, 472; portrait of chief, 208.

Chittenden, H. H., *American Fur-Trade*, 477.

Chopin, a slave, son baptized, 67.

Chopine, trade-term explained, 216.

Chorette (Chauret, Chaurette, Choret), Josephe, baptized, 140.

Chorette, Lizette, married, 375.

Chorette, Margeurite, children baptized, 140; godmother, 148, 149.

Chorette, Marguerite junior, baptized, 140.

Chorette, Simon, children baptized, 140; daughter married, 375; clerk for X Y Company, 170, 171, 178, 184, 185, 193, 202, 203, 209, 210; at portage, 190; fort, 192, 194, 198, 207, 211; visits Malhiot, 206; sketch, 206.

Choumen. See Kinonchamee.

Chouteau, Auguste, Indian agent, 315, 376; partner, 297.

Chouteau family, relatives, 462

Chovret, Marguerite, godmother, 145.

Christie, Gen. Gabriel, death, 281, 282.

Christine, daughter of Ouindigouich, baptized, 66.

Christy, Joseph Philippe, baptized, 139

Christy, Julie Moses, child baptized, 139.

Christy, Philippe, child baptized, 139.

Cincinnati (O.), troops at, 297; fur-trade, 461.

Ciscaouette. See Siskowit.

Claire, Marie Charlotte, baptized, 71.

Clark, Alexandre, baptized, 104.

Clark, Frances, married, 439.

Clark, George Rogers, expedition, 302, 366; employes Gibault, 73; relatives, 439.

Clark, James (Jacques), children baptized, 104.

Clark, Julienne, baptized, 104.

Clark, Louise, baptized, 104.

Clark, Gen. William, cited, 315, 317; Indian agent, 339, 448; superintendent, 379, 388, 389, 477-479; message to Indians, 376; letter to, 483, 484; notes 397, 398; in War of 1812-15, 387. See also Lewis and Clark expedition.

Clary, Robert E., on Mauvaise River, 176.

Clatsop Indians, chief's daughter, 414.

Claus, Col. William, in Indian department, 145.

Claves, Charlotte, baptized, 78.

Clayer, Sieur Rupalais, child baptized, 50; godfather, 9.

Clermont, Jeremie, child baptized, 147.

Clermont, Marie Anne, baptized, 147.

Clermont, Poncelet Batillot *dit*, godfather, 23, 30.

"Clermont," Gen. John Mason's estate, 331.

Clignancourt, Louis Matthieu Damours, sieur de, slave baptized, 4.

Clinton, Gen. Henry, in battle, 243.

Clinton County (N. Y.), settler, 476.

Clowes, ——, accounts of, 259.

Coates, John, notary, 78.

Colbert. See Cuthbert.

Collet, Charles Ange, godfather, 7.

Collin, ——, trader, 172.

Conant, Shubael, Detroit merchant, 461.

Condé, Marianne, married, 304.

"Congress," naval vessel, 363.

Connecticut, Western reserve, 284.

Connelly, ——, forwards goods, 449.

Conner's Point, Superior trading post, 173.

Connolly, ——, Detroit carpenter, 308.

Contrecoeur (Que.), Malhiot at, 166.

Cook, S. F., *Drummond Island*, 146.

Cook County (Minn.), sites in, 170-172.

Copper-mining, early development, 170; ore found, 182, 183.

Coquart, Claude Godefroy, missionary, 8, 10, 12, 13.

Corbin, —— report on mines, 183.

Corbin, Jean Baptiste, fur-trade clerk, 168, 171.
Cornucopia, site, 174.
Cornwallis, Gen. Lord, at Yorktown, 273.
Coton, Jean, fur-trader, 215.
Cotté, Agathe Desjardins, child baptized, 73; godmother, 77.
Cotté, Gabriel, child baptized, 73, 74; godfather, 87, 89; witness, 102, 161; letters to, 270, 271; sketch, 161.
Cotté, Gabriel junior, godfather, 121.
Cotté, Marianne, baptized, 73.
Cottenoire, Jean Baptiste, child baptized, 61.
Cottenoire, Marie, baptized, 61.
Cottenoire, Marie Josephe Ouagakouat, chi'd baptized, 61.
Cottrellsville (Mich.), early settlers, 308.
Couange, René, godfather, 47.
Coues, Elliott, zoological authority, 168; editor, 280; *New Light on Early History of Greater Northwest,* 167; *Pike's Expeditions,* 313.
Coulonge, Joseph d'Ailleboust, sieur de, godfather, 10, 15, 21, 24, 25, 27, 33; witness, 15; signature, 23.
Couroy, —, voyageur, 259.
Courselle, Michel, Michigan trader, 462.
Coursol, Jean, godfather, 128.
Courtois, Charles, godfather, 94.
Courtois, Joseph, chi'd baptized, 106.
Courtois, Marie Madeleine, baptized, 106.
Courts Oreilles Indians. See Ottawa.
Cousineau, Joseph, godfather, 12.
Cousineau, Marianne Cecile. See Monbrun.
Couterot, Hubert, godfather, 46.
Couvret, Charlotte, children baptized, 33, 39, 53.
Couvret, Joseph, children baptized, 33, 39, 53.
Couvret, Joseph Augustin, baptized, 39
Couvret, Marie Angel'que, baptized, 53.
Couvret, Therese Elizabeth, baptized, 33.
Cowen, Alexandre, baptized, 101.
Cowen, Amable, baptized, 138.
Cowen, Anne. baptized, 138.
Cowen, Elizabeth, baptized, 128.
Cowen, George, children baptized, 98, 101, 128.
Cowen, Jean Antoine, baptized, 98.
Cowen, Mar'anne Kinonchamut, child baptized, 128.
Cowen, Marianne (Nancy), baptized, 98; godmother, 101, 107, 110, 111, 115, 117, 128, 130.
Cowen, Marie Anne, baptized, 137.
Cowen, Pierre, children baptized, 137, 138; godfather, 144.
Craig, Hannah, married, 479.

Craig, Capt. John, raids Peoria, 366.
Cram, T. J., surveyor, 177, 187, 212; report, 213.
Crapets. See Sunfish.
Crawford, Lewis, Wisconsin trader, 342, 350, 357.
Crawford, Redford, in duel, 325, 342.
Crawford, William H., secretary of war, 389, 390; on exclusion of foreigners, 405–407.
Crawford County, officials, 384.
Credit system, in fur-trade, 178.
CREEKS—
  Audevie, identified, 313.
  Dutchman's early settlers on, 142.
  Laramie's, trading post on, 265.
Crenier, Josette de, mentioned, 375.
Crepeaux, Pierre, godfather, 144.
Crequé, Madeleine. See McGulpin.
Crevier, Joseph, priest, 147.
Crooks, Ramsay, on Astor'an expedition, 347, 371; in Astor's employ, xvi, 414, 426, 451, 4J0, 461; licensed, 428; on Mackinac expedition, 360–364; visits Cass, 427; letters, 346–350, 352–354, 461–463; letters to, 369–372; sketch, 347; portrait, 347.
Cruickshanks, R., merchant, 310.
Cruikshank, Ernest A., biography of Dickson, 307, 308, 462.
Cuillerier, Angelique. See Beaubien.
Cuthbert, Alexander, godfather, 101.

DALLAS, A. J., secretary of war, 379, 381.
Damours, Joseph, wife, 22.
Darling, Daniel, trader arrested, 477, 478.
Darnielle, Isaac, Illinois lawyer, 303.
David, David, of Montreal, 294.
David, Lazarus, in Montreal, 294.
David, Moses, Detroit merchant, 294.
Davidson, Judge —, daughter married, 365.
Davy, William, letter to, 311.
Dayton (Minn.), site, 313.
Dayton (O.), resident, 461.
Dearborn, Henry, secretary of war, 303, 311, 316; Boston merchant, 335.
Delaware Indians, agency for, 424; remove to Louisiana, 265.
Demais, Pierre, witness, 29.
De Peyster, Arent Schuyler, commandant at Mackinac, 237, 254; trials with Indians, 241; letters, 244, 257; accounts, 248.
Deschamps, Joseph, godfather, 138.
Deschenaux, Josette (Josephine) Legacé, baptizes, 141.
Deschenaux, Louis, wife, 141.

Index

Des Coteaux, Antoine, buried, 152.
Desfonts, Jean Baptiste, child baptized, 109.
Desfonts, Jean Baptiste junior, baptized, 109.
Des Hêtres, —, daughter baptized, 4.
Des Hêtres, Marie Catherine, baptized, 4.
Desjardins, Agathe. See Cotté.
Des Noyelles, Charles Joseph, godfather, 15–18, 20–22; sketch, 15.
Desnoyer, Jean Baptiste, godfather, 64. See also Marchetteau.
Despins. See Lemoine.
Desrivières, François, merchant, 334.
Desrivières, François junior, Montreal merchant, 334, 335, 366; legacy, 373.
Desroches. See Durocher.
Detour, passed, 146, 152; duel near, 325.
Detra'nville, Michel, child baptized, 125.
Detrainville, Michel junior, baptized, 125.
Detroit, route via, xv, 383–385, 397, 438, 497; commandants, 237, 274, 280, 298, 364; Pontiac's siege, 279; expedition to relieve, 276; British evacuate, 276, 277; surrendered to Proctor, 310, 327, 347; in War of 1812–15, 347, 349, 350, 355, 360, 363, 407, 456, 468, 469; early church, 132; priests, 132, 147; settlers, 13, 159, 253, 272, 277, 324, 379, 455; merchants, xvi, 243, 276, 278, 279, 291, 294, 304, 308, 310, 345, 453, 461; traders visit, 234, 241, 242, 266; goods, 262; prices, 235, 239; provisions, 236, 244–246, 257, 293, 294; detained at, 237, 239–244, 257; deserters at, 288; Indian council, 284; law-suit, 416, 417; fur-trade factory, 311; interpreter, 208; metropolis, 353, 443; Monroe to vis't, 457.
Dexter, Daniel S., naval officer, 363.
Dickson, Robert, early letter, 307; in duel, 325; acts as American official, 323; trader, 344–347, 351; post, 313; evades embargo, xviii, 342; in War of 1812–15, 160, 253, 306, 364, 456, 469; at Prairie du Chien, 458, 464; with Selk'rk, 462, 486; British Indian agent, 365; message for, 360; provisions, 352; subordinates, 446, 477; son, 444
Dickson, William, license for, 444; on St. Peter's River, 486.
Die, Jeanne. See Mata.
Dilhet, Father Jean, baptisms, 120–132; interments, 159.
Dinsmoor, Silas, Ind'an agent, 303.
Dion, —, child baptized, 22.
Dion, Louis René, baptized, 22, 23.
Dobie, Richard, Montreal merchant, 258, 259, 282.
Dodimead, Catherine, married, 394.

Dominicans, at Mackinac, 97.
Dorion, —, boatman, 463.
Dorion, Pierre, interpreter, 463.
Dorion, Pierre junior, on Astorian expedition, 463.
Doty, James D., on Lake Superior, 173, 175, 178, 181; map, 176, 187; describes sites, 186.
Dousman, George Smith, baptized, 146.
Dousman, John, children baptized, 146; godfather, 147; churchwarden, 162; commands militia, 421; trader, xvii; sketch, 421.
Dousman, Justin, witness, 162.
Dousman, Michael, Mackinac merchant, xvii, 345; letter to, 475, 476.
Dousman, Rosalie Laborde, children baptized, 146; godmother, 147.
Douville. See Quindre.
Draper, Lyman C., correspondent, 439.
Drew, John, Mackinac trader, 483.
Drouin, Manon, husband of, 156.
Drouine, term explained, 200; accounts for, 225; traders on, 312, 486.
Dubeau, Ambroise, clerk, 275.
Dubois, Agathe, godmother, 121.
Dubois, Elizabeth, godmother, 113.
Dubois, Etienne, godfather, 134, 135, 140, 142–144.
Dubois, Jean Baptiste, at Mackinac, 157.
Dubois, Louise. See Solomon.
Dubois, Pierre Ignace, wife, 73.
Dubois, Thérèse Campion, godmother, 73–75.
Du Braise, —, slave baptized, 4.
Dubuque, Catherine, married, 366.
Dubuque, Julien, lead-miner, xvii; letter, 318–320; kinswoman, 366.
Ducharme, Dominique, godfather, 100.
Ducharme, Jean Marie, son, 293.
Ducharme, Joseph, carries message, 355; sketch, 293.
Ducharme, Joseph Laurent, baptized, 53.
Ducharme, Laurent, children baptized, 53, 61, 68; slave baptized, 67; godfather, 70; witness, 161.
Ducharme, Lou's, baptized, 61.
Ducharme, Marguerite Metivier, children baptized, 53, 61, 68; godmother, 70.
Ducharme, Marie Marguerite, baptized, 68.
Ducharme, Pierre Augustin, baptized, 61.
Duclos, François. See Carignan.
Dufaux, Geneviève, bapt'zed, 85.
Dufaux, Louis, children baptized, 85, 88.
Dufaux, Marie Louise, children baptized, 85, 88.
Dufaux, Pierre, baptized, 62.
Duff, —, lake captain, 309.

Dufresne, Louis, blacksmith, 276.
Dufresne, Nicolas, godfather, 40, 42, 53, 56, 58.
Dugast, Pierre, godfather, 62.
Du Jaunay, Father Pierre, baptisms, 7-31, 33-35, 37, 42-44, 47, 49, 52, 53, 56, 58, 59, 63-71; last entry, 72.
Du Lignon, Angelique, baptized, 6.
Du Lignon, Françoise Marianne, baptized, 13.
Du Lignon, Françoise Michelle, baptized, 5.,
Du Lignon, Jean, children baptized, 4-6, 10, 13, 19, 20.
Du Lignon, Josephe (Josette) Marguerite, baptized, 19, 20; godmother, 60. See also Boyer.
Du Lignon, Louis Josué, baptized, 4.
Du Lignon, Marie Angelique, baptized, 5; children baptized, 10, 13, 19, 20; godmother, 15.
Du Lignon, Marie Thérèse, baptized, 6. See also Bertrand.
Du Lignon, Paul, baptized, 10.
Duluth, Daniel Greysolon, on Lake Superior, 164; names rivers, 177.
Dumée (Du May), Jacques, children baptized, 12, 24; son buried, 150.
Dumée, Jacques junior, baptized, 24; buried, 150.
Dumée, Marie, baptized, 12.
Dumée, Marie (Manon) Chevalier, children baptized, 12, 24; godmother, 21.
Dumouchel, Françoise, baptized, 76; children baptized, 76, 84.
Dumouchel, Jean, baptized, 76.
Dumouchel, Joachim, baptized, 84.
Dumouchel, Josephe, baptized, 84. See also Farly.
Dumouchel, Louis, children baptized, 76, 84; godfather, 57.
Dumouchel, Magdeleine, baptized, 84.
Duncain, Capt. —, messenger, 475.
Du Plassy, Charles Dominique, baptized, 4.
Du Plassy, Maurice, baptized, 4.
Du Plassy, Pierre, children baptized, 4.
Duplessis-Fabert, François Lefebre, sieur, godfather, 28, 29, 31.
Duplessis-Fabert, François junior, killed at Green Bay, 22.
Duplessis. See Morampont.
Dupré, Antoine, godfather, 123.
Dupuy, —, trader, 359.
Duquet, Louis, bapt'zes, 116.
Duquet, François, godfather, 87.
Durand, Jean, Illinois merchant, 263, 264.
Du Rivage, Ignace, son baptized, 2.
Du Rivage, Ignace junior, baptized, 2.
Du Rivage, Michel, baptized, 2.

Durocher, Urbain, voyageur, 188-190, 199, 203, 208, 218; sketch, 180.
Du Sable, Josephe. See Vieu.

EARLING, James, arbitrator, 275.
Eames, Wilberforce, aid acknowledged, xxii, 363.
Ech Chagu'n, Winnebago orator, 418, 422.
Edwards, Ninian, governor of Illinois Territory, 395; orders, 398, 399; letters, 401-404; letters to, 443; *Life and Letters*, 387; sketch, 395.
Eis, Rt. Rev. Frederick, aid acknowledged, xxi.
Elizabeth, an Indian, baptized, 18.
Elkswatawa. See Shawnee Prophet.
Ellice, Alexander, Montreal merchant, 259.
Ellice, Edward, English statesman, 259.
Ellice, Robert, at Montreal, 259.
Ellice. See Phyn, Ellice & Co.
Ell'en, Yve, godfather, 32.
Elliot, Jesse D., naval officer, 350, 351.
Embargo, affects fur-trade, xviii, 337-339; evaded, 342.
England, Col. Richard, British commandant at Detro't, 274, 277.
Épée, Angelique Fleurs d', baptised, 18.
Épée, Louis Fleurs d', daughter baptised, 18.
Erie (Presque Isle, Pa.), route via, 346, 363, 382-385, 390-393; traders at, 353.
Erie County (O.), boundary, 284.
Ernest, Matthew, Wayne County treasurer, 295.
Ethrington, Capt. George, commandant at Mackinac, 69.
Etienne, a slave, baptized, 96.
Eustis, William, secretary of war, 334; explains embargo, 339.
Ewing, William, agent for Sauk Indians, 315.

FABERT. See Duplessis.
Factory system for Indian trade, xviii, xx, 311, 326-335, 380-395, 433, 438, 444-454; crit'cized, 349, 350, 480-482; meagre results, 447, 448; directions for, 484-488; proceeds, 466; abolished, 434, 455.
Fafard, Alexis. See Laframboise.
Fairfax County (Va.), estate in, 331.
Farly, Albert, baptized, 42.
Farly, André Vital, baptized, 62.
Farly, Jacques Philippe (Charles), children baptized, 37, 42, 52, 62; slave baptized, 44, 57; godfather, 10, 52; wife buried, 154; sketch, 10.

Forts] # Index

Farly, Louis Joseph, baptized, 52; buried, 155.
Farly, Marie Charlotte, baptized, 37.
Farly Marie Josephe (Josette) Dumouchel, children bapt zed, 37, 42, 52, 62; godmother, 38, 41, 42, 44, 46, 48, 49, 55, 57; buried, 154.
Farnham, Russell, trader arrested, 477, 478.
Ferron, ——, forwards goods, 449.
Fifield, Samuel S., aid acknowledged, xxi, 174.
F gured Stone. See Shinaabaw'osin.
Fillon, Jean W., godfather, 138, 144.
Fily, Constant, child baptized, 70; godfather, 68.
Fily, Jean Marie, godfather, 41.
F ly, Laurent Constant, baptized, 70; in War of 1812–15, 469; clerk for Grignon, 486; sketch, 70.
Fily, Marie Angelique Metivier, child baptized, 70; godmother, 61, 62, 68.
Fily de Kerigou, Michel, grandson baptized, 70.
Findlay, James, trader, 266.
Fiolles, term expla ned, 217.
Fisher (*mustela pennanti*), fur-bearing animal, 231.
Fisher, Elizabeth Thérèse, baptized, 139, 140; godmother, 148. See a so Baird.
Fisher, Henry Monroe, Wisconsin trader, xvi; child baptized, 139; wife, 78, 117; sketch, 139.
Fisher, Jane. See Rolette.
Fisher, Madele ne Gautier, married, 78.
Fisher, Marianne Lasalière, child baptized, 139; godmother, 134–137, 140, 142, 144.
Flamand, Jean Baptiste, child baptized, 120.
Flamand, Joseph, bapt zed, 120.
Flamand, Marie, child baptized, 120.
Flathead Indians, traders w th, 477.
Flower, Frank A., *Eye of the Northwest*, 179.
Folle Avoine, a Chippewa, 198, 218.
Folles Avoines Indians. See Menominee.
Folles Avoines Sauteurs. See Chippewa.
Fond du Lac (Lake Superior), 172, 174, 179; wintering place, 35; post near, 173; traders at, 288, 474; Malhiot, 215; treaty, 434; sketch, 173.
Fond du Lac (W s.), fur-trade post, 304, 485.
Forester, Pierre, godfather, 76.
Forest, ——, Montreal trader, 351, 359, 362.
Forster, John Adam, mining expert, 183.
Forsyth, John, Montreal merchant, xvi n 9.

Forsyth, Thomas, visits Wisconsin, 386; report, 464; papers, 389.
Forsyth, William, removes from Quebec, 379.
Forsyth, Richardson & Co., Montreal merchants, 280, 285, 309; buy out traders, 337, 338; equip traders, 356; letter, 414.
FORTS—
Armstrong, commandant, 478, 480; traders near, 479, 483.
Bourbon, trading post, 163.
Bowyer, named, 392.
Chequamegon, sketch, 175. See also La Pointe.
Ch ppewyan, trading post, 469.
Crawford, built, xx, 140, 480; letter from, 477.
Crown Point, officer, 27.
Dearborn, massacre, 159, 379, 381. See also Chicago.
Edwards, fur-trade factory at, 386.
Erie, described, 276; vessels at, 277.
Harrison, officer at, 480.
Howard, built, xx; commandant, 420. See also Green Bay.
Johnson, built, 387.
Kaministiquia, commandant, 15, 19; headquarters, 190, 191, 194, 196, 200, 204; Malhiot at, 189; vessel for, 172; Indians at, 32; sketch, 166.
Leavenworth, officer at, 480.
Madison, fur-trade factory at, 383, 386, 387; destroyed 403; sketch, 383.
Malden. See Malden.
Meigs, siege, 346, 368, 402, 439.
Miami, location, 274.
Nelson, fur-trade post, 374.
Nigigon, commandant, 12; traders at, 152; settlers, 66.
Osage, fur-trade factory at, 449, 456, 466.
Pitt. See Pittsburgh.
Recovery, on boundary line, 295.
St. Joseph (Mich.), 2, 4, 19, 24, 25, 117; traders at, 160, 161.
St. Joseph (Ont.). See Islands: St. Joseph.
Shelby, captured, 140.
Stephenson, besieged, 346.
Ticonderoga, soldier at, 282.
Vermilion, built, 238.
Wayne, supplies at, 350; commandant, 298; fur-trade factory, 311; Indian agent, 340.
Wedderburn, fur-trade post, 469.
William, fur-trade rendezvous, 167, 170, 362, 366, 462. See also Kaministiquia.

Wisconsin Historical Collections [Forts

FORTS (continued)—
William Henry, siege, 153.
Winnebago, site, 396.
Fox (Outagami) Indians, habitat, 435, 471; hostile to Ch ppewa, 174; lead mines, 320; visit Mackinac, 426; Drummond Island, 472; annuities, 389; friendly, 386; traders for, 477; marry whites, 267; chief's portrait, 420.
Franchère, Gabriel, "Narrative," 226, 362.
François, baptized, 131.
François, a voyageur, 247, 248, 253.
François Regis, a slave, baptized, 107.
François Renard, a slave, baptized, 4.
François Xavier I, a slave, baptized, 59.
François Xav er II, a slave, baptized, 86.
Françoise, an Indian, baptized, 17.
Françoise, daughter baptized, 18.
Franks, Jacob, British trader, xvii, 292, 423, 429; I censed, 295; provisions for, 294; in War of 1812-15, 499; deta ned by war expedition, xix, 358-360; letters, 365-369; letters to, 316, 317; at Sandwich, 346; Lachine, 461; married, 462; employees, 305, 306; sketch, 292.
Franks, Rebecca, at Toronto, 368.
Fraser, —, Mackinac settler, 294.
Fraser, Alexander, child baptized, 136.
Fraser, Alexander junior, baptized, 136.
Fraser, Simon, explorer, 136.
Fraser, Ursule Leblanc, ch ld baptized, 136; godmother, 138, 141, 144, 145.
Fraser family, at Prairie du Chien, 267.
Freer, Noah, secretary, 355.
Freraux (Freraut), Josette, baptized, 102, 106.
Freraux, Marie Josephe Poitras, children baptized, 102, 106, 111; godmother, 100, 101, 112.
Freraux, Nicolas, children baptized, 102, 106, 111; godfather, 100, 101, 113, 117.
Freraux, Nicolas junior, bapt zed, 111.
Frobisher, Benjamin, Montreal trader, 336, letters to, 235, 243, 249; money for, 248; sketch, 235.
Frobisher, Benjamin junior, death, 235.
Frobisher, Joseph, Montreal trader, 235; letters, 244; letter to, 245, 246.
Frobisher, Thomas, Montreal trader, 235.
Frobisher Brothers, fur-traders, xvi, 163. See also McTavish, Frobisher & Co.

GAILLARD, Jacques, child baptized, 59; godfather, 62.
Gaillard, Louis Jacques, baptized, 59.
Gaillard, Marie Jbeau, child baptized, 59; godmother, 62.

Gallard, —, pays debt, 250.
Gamelin, Pierre, baptizes, 102.
Gansevoort, Gen. Peter junior, United States agent, 329.
Gates, Gen. Horatio, in battle, 243.
Gatien, Jean Baptiste, godfather, 112.
Gausselin Pierre, godfather, 127.
Gautier (Gattris, Gauthier, Gotiez, Gotrie), Agathe, godmother, 138.
Gautier, Charles de Verville, mother of, 2; baptized, 5; ch ldren baptized, 78, 79; adopts child, 79; sons, 179; baptizes, 96, 98, 99; godfather, 85; leads Indians to war, 251; sketch, 5.
Gautier, Charles junior, at Lac du Flambeau, 165, 185-188, 190, 193, 194, 196, 199, 208, 211, 227; proposals to, 182-184; alarmed, 181; improves, 204; w fe, 207; supplies for, 216-220; on drouine, 229-233; sketch, 179.
Gautier, Claude de Verville, children baptized, 5-8; 16; slave baptized, 6; wife, 2, 11.
Gautier, Domitelle, baptized, 78, 79. See also Brisbois.
Gautier, Jean Baptiste, baptized, 6; godfather, 113, 115.
Gautier, Joseph Augustin, baptized, 16. See also Caron.
Gautier, Madeleine, baptized, 78. See also Fisher.
Gaut er, Madeleine Pascal Chevalier, children baptized, 78, 79; godmother, 79-84, 86, 88, 89, 91, 92, 94, 99, 100, 106.
Gautier, Marie, baptized, 7, 8.
Gautier, Marie Louise Thérèse Villeneuve, children baptized, 8, 16; godmother, 11.
Gendron, —, wife of, 2.
Gendron, Marie Judith, baptized, 2.
"General Hunter," vessel on Lake Huron, 322, 324.
"General Jackson," lake vessel, 467.
Généreux, Louis, godfather, 148.
Geneviève, a slave, baptized, 60.
Georgetown (D. C.), headquarters for Indian trade, 434.
Germain, Claude, godfather, 10.
Gervais, Louis, godfather, 39, 40.
Gete Kitigan. See Lacs: Vieux Désert.
"Ghent," vessel on Lake Erie, 391.
Giasson, Jacques, godfather, 41, 61, trader, 155.
Giasson, Jacques junior; godfather, 118, 119, 121, 124; witness, 118, 119; Mackinac merchant, 307, 327; arbitrator, 275; letters. 285, 286, 288, 295, 296; accounts, 286, 298, 304; sells furs, 286, 299; sends witnesses, 300; sketch, 276.

Gibault, Father Pierre, vicar-general of Illinois, 72; baptizes, 73-77; sketch, 73.
Gibault, Marie Louise, godmother, 73, 74.
Gibbs, —, letter from, 454.
Gillespie, George, Montreal merchant, 337, 342.
Girardin, Clotilde. See L'Eveillé.
Gitshee Migeesee. See L'Aigle.
Godefroy, Jean Baptiste, godfather, 27.
Gonneville, —, godfather, 32.
Gordon, Col. —, son of, 146.
Gordon, Agathe (Agnes) Landry, child baptized, 146.
Gordon, Eleanor Lytle Kinzie, *John Kinzie*, 379.
Gordon, George, child baptized, 146.
Gordon, William d'Alcantura, baptized, 146.
Gore, Francis, governor of Upper Canada, 273.
Gotiez. See Gautier.
Gouin, Charles, trader, sketch, 279.
Govreau, Catherine. See Baudoin.
Gould, Charles Henry, aid acknowledged, xxi.
Gourn. See Champagne.
Graham, Maj. —, locates Green Bay post, 437.
Graham, Duncan, fur-trader, 469.
Graham, George, in war department, 414, 443, 444, 452, 458, 480.
Graham, Richard, Indian agent, 424.
Grand Marais (Minn.), Malhiot at, 172.
Grand Portage (Minn.), fur-trade rendezvous, xvi, 69, 163, 166, 196, 213, 214, 236, 239, 240, 244, 263, 365; provisions for, 258; post recommended for, 378, 430; officer guards, 240-243; vessel at, 226; in War of 1812-15, 190; present conditions, 170; sketch, 169, 170.
Grand Rapids (Mich.), early settlers, 109, 471. See also Grand River.
Granger, Erastus, Indian agent, 339, 340.
Granger, Gideon, postmaster-general, 340.
Grant, —, trader, 255, 256.
Grant, Com. Alexander, message to 282; sketch, 273.
Grant, Charles, trader, 256.
Grant, James, outfitter, 256.
Grant, John, trader, 256.
Grant, John junior, witness, 335.
Grant, William, trader, 256; witness, 78.
Gratiot, Maj. Charles, messenger, 463.
Gratiot, Julie, married, 397.
Gravelle, Joseph, daughter baptized, 129.
Gravelle, Josette St. Raisin, daughter baptized, 129.

Gravelle, Louis, Green Bay settler, 376.
Gravelle, Marie Angelique, baptized, **129**. See also Grignon.
Great Eagle. See L'Aigle.
Green Bay (La Baye), site of French post, 437; lessee of, 4, 12, 41; French commandant, 22, 36, 38, 42, 46, 485; interpreter, 48; Pontiac's conspiracy at, 68; American post recommended, 378, 380, 383; Indians favor post, 418, 422, 426, 430, 432; oppose, 440; post built, xx, 420, 436-439, 454; American troops at, 428, 430-432; officers, xviii, 142, 458, 482; Indian agents at, 379-381, 399, 406, 407, 442, 443, 466, 467, 487, 488; fur-trade factory, 311, 380-386, 389-392, 440, 447, 448, 465, 470-472, 480-484; liquor prohibited at, 396, 398, 466, 467, 487, 488; letters from, 267-271, 368; letter for, 355; engagement contract at, 292, 293; goods for, 340, 358, 432; trading license, 476, 477; early residents, xvii, 20, 25, 27, 35, 46, 55, 66, 69, 90, 98, 105, 117, 122, 127, 134, 139, 248, 293, 299, 300, 352, 364, 365, 376, 421, 439, 468, 469, 476; neighboring Indians, 408, 417, 418, 421, 455, 456; partnership at, 447; British subjects, 401-404, 420, 467-470, 481; sales at, 464; settlement, xi, xv; librarian, xxii.
Green Lake, early settlers, 396. See also Lakes: Green.
Greenville (O.), treaty at (1814), 160.
Gregory, John, in North West Company, 256, 266.
Gregory & McLeod, Montreal merchants, 290.
Grignon, Agatha, married, 469.
Grignon, Amable, baptized, 93; at Montreal, 271.
Grignon, Amable junior, partner, 375, 470; in War of 1812-15, 469; sketch, 469-471.
Grignon, Antoine, aid acknowledged, xxi.
Grignon, Augustin, baptized, 90; in War of 1812-15, 469; pilots troops, 428, 429; gives information, 396; letter from, 485, 486; letter to, 317, 318; sketch, 90.
Grignon, Charles, baptized, 89; at Montreal, 271; in War of 1812-15, 469.
Grignon, David H., aid acknowledged, xxi.
Grignon, Domitelle, baptized, 88.
Grignon, Fanfan. See Pierre Antoine Grignon.
Grignon, François, child baptized, **129**; godfather, 132.

[503]

Grignon, Hippolyte (Paul), trader, 375, 376; clerk, 486; partner, 470; in War of 1812–15, 469; sketch, 376.
Grignon, Ignace, at Grand Rapids, 471.
Grignon, Jean, at Grand Rapids, 471.
Grignon, Jean Baptiste, baptized, 91; in War of 1812–15, 469.
Grignon, Joseph, mentioned, 375.
Grignon, Louis, baptized, 90; adopted, 248; merchant, 345; license, 468; meets Pike, 306; post, 314; contract, 447; at Mackinac, 429; clears cargo, 340; furs seized, 416, 417; in War of 1812–15, 468; receives news of peace, 350–352; letters, 475, 476; letters to, 375, 376, 401, 404, 405; protest, 400.
Grignon, Louise Domitelle Langlade, children baptized, 88, 89, 90, 91; godmother, 94; messenger, 271; death, 469.
Grignon, Marie Angelique Gravelle, child baptized, 129.
Grignon, Marie Archange, baptized, 129.
Grignon, Perische, merchant, 368; in War of 1812–15, 469.
Grignon, Pierre, children baptized, 88–91, 93; son, 368; nephew, 129; wife, 56; godfather, 73, 74, 79, 81, 94; witness, 161; letters, xvi', 267–271.
Grignon, Pierre Antoine (Fanfan), baptized, 89; at Montreal, 271; in War of 1812–15, 468; trader, 485–487; at Mackinac, 352, 428, 429; license for, 441; censured, 419; letters, 375, 376; sketch, 89.
Grignon, Simon, mentioned, 375.
Grignon family, tutor for, 313; letters, 304; in War of 1812–15, 469; traders, 170.
Gros Puant, Indian debtor, 312.
Grosseilliers, Medart Chouart, sieur de, on Lake Superior, 166, 175, 215.
Grosse Pointe (Mich.), settlers of, 278.
Grouse (*canachites canadensis canace*), in Wiscons'n, 187.
Guigère, Anto'ne, child baptized, 92.
Guigère, Antoine junior, baptized, 92.
Guillory, Anne Villeneuve, godmother, 9, 10. See also Blondeau.
Guillory, Antoine, wife, 2, 9, 10, 161; godfather, 8.
Guillory, Antoine II, bapt'zed, 49; children baptized, 81, 88, 89, godfather, 111, 112.
Guillory, Antoine III, baptized, 88.
Guillory, Jean Bapt ste, baptized, 89; witness, 161.
Guillory, Joseph, children baptized, 45, 46, 49; godfather, 136; married, 161.
Guillory, Marie, baptized, 81.

Guillory, Marie Catherine, baptized, 45, 46.
Guillory, Marie Louise Bolon children baptized, 45, 49.
Guillory (Guyari) family, 161.
Guion, —, slave baptized, 152.
Gull Prairie (Mich.), early settler, 148.
Gunston Hall, home of George Mason, 330.
Guyari. See Guillory.

HALDIMAND, Sir Frederick, commands in Canada, 275.
Halstead, Jonathan, Indian agent, 303.
Hamelin, Awaci, son married, 149.
Hamelin, Augustin, baptized, 95; godfather, 116, 121.
Hamelin, Catherine (Marie Athanase), baptized, 23, 24; children baptized, 23, 25.
Hamelin, Catherine junior, baptized, 94.
Hamelin, Charles, children bapt zed, 5, 6, 23, 25; wife baptized, 5, 24; slaves baptized, 7, 15; slave buried, 150; residence, 7; son married, 149.
Hamelin, Charlotte, baptized, 94.
Hamelin, François Marie, godfather, 49; slave bapt'zed, 49, 50.
Hamelin, Madame Hyacinthe, slave baptized, 86.
Hamelin, Jacques Michel, baptized, 5; godfather, 36; grandchild baptized, 60; buried, 154.
Hamelin, Jean Baptiste, baptized, 6.
Hamelin, Jean Baptiste junior, baptized, 94.
Hamelin, Josephe le Sable, baptized, 93; children baptized, 94, 95.
Hamelin, Josette, baptized, 60.
Hamelin, Josette junior, baptized, 94. See also Charlebo's and Hogan.
Hamelin, Louis Charles, baptized, 5; wife baptized, 93, 118; married, 149; children baptized, 94, 95; godfather, 98, 100.
Hamelin, Marianne, baptized, 5.
Hamelin, Marie Athanase, baptized, 5; slave baptized, 15; sister, 14, 15; death, 15.
Hamelin, Marie Françoise, baptized, 6.
Hamelin, Marie Josephe, baptized, 25.
Hamelin, Marie Louise, baptized, 118.
Hamelin, Pierre Charles, bapt zed, 23.
Hamelin, Pierre Pascal, baptized, 5.
Hamilton, Henry, commandant at Detroit, 237, 243, 244, 257.
Hamilton, Robert, Queenston merchant, 242, 276, 306.
Hamtramck, John Francis, at Detroit, 297.

Index

Hancock County (Ill.), historic sites in, 387.
Hands, Williams, Detroit merchant, 276.
Harkness, Peter, registrar at Montreal, 335.
Harmon, Daniel W., *Voyages and Travels*, 166.
Harrison, Gen. William H., proclamation, 302; governor of Indiana Territory, 303; commissions, 142, 159; O'Fallon with, 439; in War of 1812-15, 347, 350; treats with Indians, 315.
Harrow, Alexander, lake captain, 308, 309.
Hattnas, Gabriel. See La Violette.
Hawkins, Benjamin, Indian agent, 303.
Hay, Jehu, at Detroit, 242.
Hay, John, Indian trader, 242, 250, 251.
Hazen, Moses, Revolutionary officer, 297.
Heald, Mrs. Nathan, at Fort Dearborn, 159, 160.
Heald family, in Missouri, 160.
Healy, George A. P., portraits by, 379, 400.
Heins (Ainse, Hins), Constance (Coussante) Chevalier, children baptized, 8, 11, 26, 30, 31; godmother, 9. See also Cardin.
Heins, Joseph, children baptized, 8, 11, 12; wife baptized, 2; godfather, 6, 7.
Heins, Joseph Louis. See Ainse.
Heins, Marie Angelique, baptized, 30, 31.
Heins, Marie Conssante, baptized, 8; buried, 150.
Helena, shot-tower at, 364.
Hennepin, Father Louis, among Sioux, 313.
Henry, —, messenger, 425.
Henry, Alexander, in Northwest fur-trade, xvi, 245; partner, 238, 255; at Grand Portage, 169; explores for copper, 183; at La Pointe, 175; describes church, 150; slave baptized, 67; letters, 234, 280-285, 289-291, 309, 310, 336, 337, 372-374; letters to, 253, 282; *Travels*, 170, 219; sketch, 238.
Henry, Mrs. Alexander, message, 337, 373.
Henry, Alexander junior, career, 373, 374.
Henry, Alexander, cousin of foregoing, enters fur-trade, 281; meets trader, 215; *Journal*, 167; sketch, 280.
Henry, James, Detroit merchant, 296.
Henry, Julia, mentioned, 373.
Henry, Capt. William, sailor, 296, 297.
Henry, William, in Northwest trade, 337, 373, 374.
Herbin, Louis, godfather, 38.
Hesse, district of Upper Canada, 272; officials, 278.

Hins. See Heins.
Hirbour, Susanne, godmother, 98, 113. See also Pelletier.
Hoffman, Walter J., "Midewinin, or Grand Medicine Society of the Ojibwa," 194.
Hogan, Josette Hamelin, child baptized, 130.
Hogan, Marie Isabelle, godmother, 142.
Hogan, Marie Vaillancourt, child baptized, 135.
Hogan, Stephen, child baptized, 130.
Hogan, Thomas, baptized, 130.
Holland, Maj. S., surveyor, 367.
Holland Land'ng (Ont.), naval station, 368.
Holliday, William, Lake Superior trader, 208.
Holmes, Maj. Arthur H., killed at Mackinac, 361.
Holmes, William, Northwest trader, 255, 256; sells out, 267.
Honoré, Louis, interpreter, 315.
Hooker, John W., Indian agent, 303.
Hough, F. B., *Journals of Major Robert Rogers*, 153.
Houghton, Douglass, geologist, 176, 183.
Howard, Don Carlos, Spanish commissioner, 314.
Howard, Joseph, fur-trader, 174, 238, 246, 249; sketch, 238.
Howard, William, draft on, 341.
Howard, Capt. William, commandant at Mackinac, 69.
Hubbard, Gurdon, *Autobiography*, 165
Hubert, Joseph Amable. See Marantot.
Hudon, Clement, godfather, 136.
Hudson's Bay Company, rendezvous for, 469; post, 270; land-grant, 462; rivalry with, 235; unites with North West Company, 163, 210, 259, 309, 366, 371; goods for, 221; employes, 139, 146, 351, 469, 470.
Hughs, Maj —, at Montreal, 282.
Hull, Gen. William, governor of Michigan Territory, 327, 339; surrenders Detroit, 327.
Hunt, Wilson, on Astorian expedition, 348, 477.
Hunter, Gen. Peter, governor of Upper Canada, 273.
"Hunter," vessel on Lake Huron, 432, 433.
Hurley, on boundary line, 212.
Huron County (O.), boundary of, 284.
Huron Indians, mission for, 147; guide, 187.

Ignace I, an acolyte, baptized, 6.
Ignace II, a slave, baptized, 36, 37.

Ignace III, a slave, buried, 154.
Illinois, fur-trade in, 295; traders, 142, 264, 317, 397; sites in, 315; post, 378; during Revolution, 366; early residents, 22, 151, 267, 301, 306, 463; Indians from, 472.
Illinois Indians, neophyte from, 22.
Illinois Territory, boundary, 443; governor, 395, 398, 459, 478; Indian agent, 424; intruders expelled, 401.
Inaououoiskamoquoy, baptized, 108.
Indiana Historical Society, *Publications*, 302.
Indiana Territory, boundaries, 295, 323; assembly, 296; officials, 139, 142, 159, 301, 302; regulations for fur-trade, 301, 302; *Executive Journal*, 302, 307.
Inglis. See Phyn, Inglis and Co.
Ionia County (Mich.), early settler, 148.
Iowa, first settler, xvii, 320; *Annals*, 320.
Iowa Indians, villages, 315.
Iron County, streams in, 212.
Iroquois Indians, agent for, 340.
Irving, Washington, *Astoria*, 167, 291.
Irwin, Matthew, factor at Chicago, 326, 331-333, 384, 393; at Green Bay, 382, 385, 386, 442, 445, 447, 480, 487; letters, 468-470, 472, 481; journal, 447; orders for, 390-395, 448, 465, 484, 485; sketch, 326.
ISLANDS—
  Beaver, Indian village on, 412.
  Bois Blanc, near Mackinac, 354.
  Chenaux, priest from, 147.
  Deer, vessel at, 246.
  Drummond, post at, xix, 404, 408; officers, 407, 410, 416; Indian agency, 365, 431; Indians v'sit, 419, 421, 423, 426, 430, 472, 473; fur-market, 415, 463; residents, 141, 145-147, 304, 462; captive at, 366; removal from, 351; sketch, 146.
  Encampment, Malhiot at, 215.
  Grand Portage, Malhiot passes, 215.
  La Cloche, trader on, 162.
  Mackinac, post removed to, xii, 241, 254, 323; purchased, 237; map of, 234; view on, 362. See also Mackinac.
  Madela'ne, origin of name, 175; residents, 69, 175, 176.
  Rock, fort at, 386, 480; skirmish near, 387.
  St. Joseph, British post on, 145, 160, 161, 322, 323, 337, 342, 408; officials at, 145, 376, 324, 351; in War of 1812-15, 361-363; fur-trade rendezvous, 307, 334, 343-345, 349.
  St. Michel. See Madelaine.

Twelve Apostles, site, 175.
Vermilion, Indian site, 471.
Ives, Louis T., portrait by, 379.

"JACKSON," vessel on Lake Michigan, 487.
Jacobs, Jean Baptiste, Wisconsin trader, 485-487.
James, —, accident to, 256.
James, Edwin, *Narrative of John Tanner*, 134.
James, Thomas P., American trader, 476.
Jameson, J. Franklin, aid acknowledged, xxi.
Janis, Antoine, godfather, 26, 42, 46, 50, 55, 57-60; slave baptized, 60.
Janis, Bartholemi, godfather, 57.
Janis, Hppolyte, godfather, 17.
Jarrot, Nicolas, St. Louis merchant, 344, 345.
Jasmin. See La Fetière.
Jauvan Angelique Roy, baptized, 127; children baptized, 126.
Jauvan, Jacques, children baptized, 126; w fe baptized, 127.
Jauvan, Madeleine, baptized, 126.
Jauvan, Paul, baptized, 126.
Jbeau, Marie. See Gaillard.
Jean, a slave, baptized, 43.
Jean Baptiste I, a slave, wife baptized, 5.
Jean Baptiste II, a slave, baptized, 10.
Jean Bapt'ste III, a slave, bapt'zed, 22.
Jean Baptiste IV, a slave, baptized, 37.
Jean Baptiste V, a slave, buried, 152.
Jean Baptiste VI, son of Letourneau, 131.
Jean Baptiste François, a slave, baptized, 7.
Jefferson, Thomas, favors factory system, 311; cabinet officer, 340.
Jefferson Barracks (Mo.), troops at, 448.
Jenks, Albert E., "Wild Rice Gatherers," 189.
Jerosme, François, godfather, 18.
Johnson, John W., factor at Prairie du Chien, 383, 386-390; letters, 424, 425, 452; letters to, 433-436, 454, 455-457, 459, 460, 463, 464; sketch, 383, 384.
Johnston, Jane, married, 361.
Johnston, John, Indian agent at Fort Wayne, 303, 339, 340.
Joonston, John, Lake Superior trader, 208; at Chequamegon, 175; Sault Ste. Marie, 120, 431; place burned, 361; wife's influence, 362; "Lake Superior," 176; sketch, 361.
Jolifour, Pierre, godfather, 131.
Jolliet, François, godfather, 8.
Jones, John Rice, attorney-general of Indiana, 302.

Index

Jones, Peter, Christian Ind an, 208.
Joseph I, a slave, baptized, 7.
Joseph II, a slave, baptized, 37, 38.
Joseph III, a slave, baptized, 48.
Joseph IV, a slave, baptized, 64.
Joseph V, baptized, 66.
Josette, a slave, baptized, 60.
Jouett, Charles, Indian agent, 339; for Green Bay, 378-380, 382-385, 391; at Chicago, 390, 407, 456, 487; orders for, 381; sketch, 339, 340.
Jourdain, Jean Baptiste, children baptized, 20, 27, 46, 61.
Jourdain, Jean Baptiste junior, baptized, 26, 27.
Jourdain, Marie Angelique, baptized, 61.
Jourdain, Marie Josephe, baptized, 20.
Jourdain, Marie Josephe junior, baptized, 46.
Jourdain, Marie Josephe Reaume, children baptized, 20, 27, 46, 61.
Jourdain, Marie Magdeleine, baptized, 46.
Joutras, Catherine l'Archevêque, godmother, 25.

KACKALIN. See Kaukauna.
Kahpukmekah. See Siskowit River.
Kakigiguam, Joseph, children baptized, 73, 74.
Kakigiguam, Marie, baptized, 74.
Kakigiguam, Marie Josephe, baptized, 74.
Kakigiguam, Marie Louise, baptized, 73.
Kakigiguam, Marie Nanjoiquoy, children baptized, 73, 74.
Kalamazoo (Mich.), former name of, 14.
Kalamazoo County (Mich.), early settler, 148.
Kantong, Indian village site, 471.
Kaokitte, Indian debtor, 312.
Kaouchmagan, died of smallpox, 51.
Kaskaskia, Illinois territorial capital, 401, 443; residents, 301, 302.
Katakitakon, Indian village, 187.
Kaukauna, letter from, 485; Indian site, 471; settlers, 90, 469.
Kawasidijiwong, Indian name for Montreal River, 176.
Kay, —, merchant, 310.
Kay, Alexander, trader, 173.
Keeotuckkee, Potawatomi chief, portrait. 256.
Keeshkenum. See La Pierre à Affiler.
Kellogg, Louise P., aid acknowledged, xxii.
Kemble, —, paymaster, 368.
Kennerly, George, St. Louis merchant, 448.

Kennery, James, forwarding agent, **448**, 454, 456; letter to, 466.
Kentucky, Jouett in, 340.
Ker goufili. See Fily.
Keshena, Indian school at, 105.
Ketchinape, Angelique Nekikkoue, child baptized, 40.
Ketchinape, Pierre, child baptized, 40.
Ketchinape, Joseph, baptized, 40.
Kickapoo Indians, agency for, 424.
Kigesse, brother buried, 153.
Kikkanamazoo, traders' wintering place, 14.
Kim noucane (La Pluie), grandson baptized, 131.
Kimiouenan, Catherine Chenler, children baptized, 93, 95.
Kingston (Ont.), priest, 136; merchant, 305.
Kinicona, child baptized, 113.
Kininchioue, child baptized, 50; buried, 153.
Kiniouichatoun, Marie, child baptized, 65.
Kiniouichatoun, Pierre, baptized, **43**; child baptized, 65.
Kiniouichatoun, Pierre Ignace, baptized, 65.
Kinonchamee (Kinonchamek), —, granddaughter baptized, 44.
Kinonchamee, Augustin, baptized, **57**.
Kinonchamee *dit* Choumen, Hippolyte, children baptized, 52, 57, 72.
Kinonchamee, Jean Baptiste, baptized, 72.
Kinonchamee, Marianne, child baptized, 57.
Kinohchamee, Thomas, baptized, 52.
Kinonchamon, baptized, 52.
Kinoncheton, Antoine, baptized, 57.
Kinoncheton, Pierre, children baptized, 57, 58.
Kinoncheton, Pierre junior, baptized, 58.
Kinzie, John, recommended for Indian agent, 379; employee of, 159.
Kinzie, Juliette A., *Waubun*, 396.
Kinzie family, at Chicago, 158.
Kiotom, Indian debtor, 312.
Kioueiatchiouenoukoue, Charlotte, baptized, 59.
Kitchinapé, Angelique, son baptized, **48**.
Kitchinapé, Augustin, baptized, 48.
Kitchinapé, Pierre, son baptized, 48.
Knaggs, Mrs. James, mentioned, 375.
Kourseur, Manitou, daughter baptized, 129.

LA BAPTISTE, —, witness, 30.
Labat, Michel, child baptized, 81.
Labat, Michel junior, baptized, 81.

[507]

La Baye. See Green Bay.
La Biche, Indian debtor, 313.
Laborde, Catherine, baptized, 123.
Laborde, Elizabeth, baptized, 122.
Laborde, Jean Bapt ste *dit* Sans Regret, children baptized, 103, 105, 122, 123; godfather, 99; baptizes, 141.
Laborde, Jean Baptiste junior, baptized. 122.
Laborde, Marguerite Machar Chevalier, children baptized, 103, 105, 122, 123; godmother, 99, 114, 115.
Laborde Rose (Rosalie), baptized, 105; marr ed, 421.
La Branche, Antoine, wife, 139.
La Branche, Charlotte Parent, godmother, 139.
La Bruyere, Michel, wife baptized, 108.
La Chêne, André, godfather, 113, 123, 125; baptizes, 142.
Lachine (Que.), settlers, 265.
La Chouette, a Chippewa, 185, 188, 198, 201, 202, 207, 209, 216, 217, 219. 220, 224, 229; characterized, 203; wife, 185, 192.
La Corne, Louis, sieur de, commandant at Mackinac, 17.
La Corneille, a Chippewa, 224.
La Crémaillère, a Chippewa, 185, 216. 224.
Lacroix, André, baptized, 123.
Lacroix, Françoise Card'nal, godmother, 12, 20.
Lacroix, Hubert, godfather, 112, 120, 122.
Lacroix, Isadore, child baptized, 130; godfather, 106, 109, 123, 124.
Lacroix, Joseph Amable Hubert. See Marantot.
Lacroix, Louis, baptized, 130.
Lacroix, Magdeleine, baptized, 123.
Lacroix, Marie Françoise Hubert de. See La Fetière.
Lacroix, Marie McGulpin, children baptized, 123; godmother, 114; 126.
Lacroix, Michel, godfather, 117, 130. 131; trader, 366, 369.
Lacroix, Paul Hubert, godfather, 86; buried, 158.
Lacroix, P erre, children baptized, 123; godfather, 114, 122, 126; witness. 129.
Lacroix, Pierre junior, bapt'zed, 123.
Lacroix, P erre Ignace, Montreal merchant, 358.
LACS (see also Lakes)—
Courts Oreilles, origin of name, 171; Indians of, 207; traders, 69.
Du Flambeau, Indians of, 193-198. 201, 202, 206, 216; village, 224; reservation, 181; traders, xiv, 69.

342; post, 164, 178, 180, 181; new fort, 209; equipment, 182, 216, 224; rivalry, 169, 170, 196; hardships, 191; employees, 171, 188; settlers, 179; sketch, 181, 186.
Folle Avo ne (La Folle). See Wild Rice Lake.
La Pluie. See Rainy Lake.
La Truite. See Trout Lake.
Ver. See Green Lake.
Vieux Désert, on boundary, 177, 212; outlet, 181; Indian band, 199, 207, 209, 224; trading on, 226, 230; sketch, 186, 187.
La Culote, granddaughter baptized, 50.
La Douceur, Jean Baptiste, godfather, 54.
La Fantaisie, Marianne Card n, children bapt'zed, 77, 78; godmother, 76.
La Fetière, Augustin Jasmin *dit*, baptized, 32; buried, 151.
La Fetière, Basile Jasmin *dit*, bapt'zed, 28.
La Fetière, Jean Baptiste Jasm'n *dit*, children baptized, 28, 30, 32; godfather, 28.
La Fetière, Louis Poncelet Jasmin *dit*, baptized, 30.
La Fetière, Marie Françoise Hubert de Lacroix, children baptized, 30, 32; godmother, 30.
La Feuille, a Chippewa, 217, 218, 224.
La Fond, Catherine Personne *dit*, bapt'zed, 25.
La Fond, Charles Fersonne *dit*, children baptized, 25, 46.
La Fond, Hubert Personne *dit*, baptized, 46.
La Fond, Jean Simon Personne *dit*, baptized, 46.
La Fond, Susanne Reaume Personne *dit*, children baptized, 25, 46.
La Fontaine, François, godfather, 76.
La Fontaine, Marion *dit*, brothers, desert employers, 288.
La Fortune, Antoine Tellier *dit*, baptized, 3; children baptized, 40, 41, 45, 54, 58, 62, 68, 71, 72; servant, 66; godfather, 66.
La Fortune, Antoine Tellier junior *dit*, baptized, 71.
La Fortune, Charles Tellier *dit*, bapt'zed, 54.
La Fortune, Charlotte Ouetokich Tellier *dit*, children baptized, 40, 41, 45, 54, 58, 62, 68, 71; godmother, 66.
La Fortune, François Tellier *dit*, baptized, 72.
La Fortune, François Xavier Tellier *dit*, baptized, 21; buried, 152.

La Fortune, Françoise Tellier *dit*, baptized, 107.
La Fortune, Ignace Tellier *dit*, baptized, 21.
La Fortune, Ignace (junior) Tellier *dit*, baptized, 68.
La Fortune, Jean Baptiste Tellier *dit*, children baptized, 3, 21, 35; godfather, 46, 66; witness, 41; slave baptized, 41, 59.
La Fortune, Jean Baptiste (junior) Tellier *dit*, baptized, 40, 41.
La Fortune, Joseph Tellier *dit*, baptized, 21; buried, 151.
La Fortune, Joseph (junior) Tellier *dit*, bapt zed, 62; child baptized, 107.
La Fortune, Joseph Marie Tellier *dit*, buried, 151.
La Fortune, Josette Kiouittakigir, godmother, 40.
La Fortune, Marie Josephe (I) Tellier *dit*, baptized, 20, 21; children baptized, 21, 35; godmother, 39, 58, 63, 66; buried, 151.
La Fortune, Marie Josephe (II) Tellier *dit*, baptized, 21.
La Fortune, Marie Josephe (III) Tellier *dit*, baptized, 35.
La Fortune, Nicolas Tellier *dit*, baptized, 58.
La Fortune, Pierre Antoine Tellier *dit*, bapt zed, 45.
La Fortune, René François Tellier *dit*, baptized, 21; son baptized, 72; godfather, 59, 60.
La Fourche, Indian site, 486.
Laframboise, Alexis (I) Fafard *dit*, children baptized, 96, 102, 103, 105, 106, 108, 110, 119, 121; slaves baptized, 96; witness, 96, 97, 118, 161; godfather, 88, 90, 93, 97, 103, 104, 108, 113, 115, 116; sketch, 158.
Laframboise, Alexis II, baptized, 96, 105.
Laframboise, Alexis III, early Chicago settler, 158.
Laframboise, Claude, godfather, 110.
Laframboise, Claude junior, Chicago settler, 158.
Laframboise, François, at M lwaukee, 158, 305, 306; children baptized, 108; godfather, 103-105; witness, 102.
Laframboise, Geneviève, baptized, 102, 105.
Laframboise, Jean Baptiste I, son of, 158.
Laframboise, Jean Baptiste II, godfather, 80, 87; adopts child, 81.
Laframboise, Jean Baptste III, baptized, 106.

Laframboise, Joseph I, child baptized, 109; wife, 86; godfather, 105; witness, 102.
Laframboise, Joseph II, baptized, 106.
Laframboise, Joseph III, Chicago settler, 158.
Laframboise, Josephe, baptized, 105.
Laframbo se, Josette, baptized, 109.
Laframboise, Josette junior, marries, 158.
Laframboise, Josette Blondeau Adhemar, married, 158, 159; children baptized, 96, 102, 103, 105, 108, 110, 119, 121; witness, 96; godmother, 100, 103-106, 109, 110, 116, 118, 120, 121, 130.
Laframboise, Madeleine Marcot, child baptized, 109; godmother, 133, 140, 146; gives to church, 150.
Laframboise, Marguerite, baptized, 109, 110.
Laframboise, Marie, baptized, 119.
Laframboise, Marie Marguerite, bapt zed, 121.
Lagacé, Elizabeth, child baptized, 110.
Lagacé, Joachim, ch'ld baptized, 110.
Lagacé, Josette, baptized, 110; baptizes, 141. See also Deschenaux.
Lagoterie, Edward, trader with Sauk, 446; arrested 477, 479.
La Grande Loutre, a Chippewa, 195, 217, 218, 224.
La Grandeur. See Brisbé.
La Grue Blanche, a Chippewa, 201, 220.
La Guereche, Antoine, godfather, 29.
La Haie, Claude Pelletier (Pellé) *dit*, ch'ld baptized, 48; buried, 154.
La Haie, Marie Anne Pelletier *dit*, baptized, 48.
La Haie, Marie Meghissens Pelletier *dit*, child baptized, 48.
L'Aigle (Egle), Chippewa chief, 200, 207, 218, 219, 224.
La Jeunesse, Jean Baptiste, at Milwaukee, 306.
La Jeunesse family, 306.
La Joye, —, child bapt zed, 70, 71.
La Joye, Marie, baptized, 70, 71.
La Joye, P erre, godfather, 65.
Lake County (Minn.), s tes in, 215.
LAKES (see also Lacs)—
Cass (Minn.), traders at, 174.
Champlain, site on, 476; exped ton, (1757), 153; in War of 1812-15, 424; settlers, 139; Henry visits, 336.
Erie, route via, 348, 349; shipping, 354, 381, 382, 390; in War of 1812-15, 351, 363; land-sales near, 284.
Great, route v a, xv, 234, 236, 241, 242, 253, 255, 462; fur-trade, **xv**,

LAKES: Great (continued)—
xvi, 348; Indians on, 438; shipping, 262; entrepot for, xi; in War of 1812-15, xvii.
Great Slave, fur-trade post on, 469.
Green (Wis.), Indians on, 471; trading, 486.
Huron, route via, 162, 352; shipping on, 170, 235, 236, 240, 296, 308, 354; duel on, 325; expedition, 357-364; naval vessels, 367; post on, xi.
Island, on boundary, 212.
Leech, posts on, 173, 174.
Little Rice, site of, 198.
Long (Wis.), on portage path, 178, 181, 213.
Michigan, maps, 443; affluents, 285; Indians near, 401, 409, 417, 472; drowning in, 235; wreck, 134; naval force on, 381; shipping, 241, 420; route via, 426; posts on, xi, 390.
Mille Lac, outlet, 313.
Ontario, navy on, 275; route via, xv.
Ottawa. See Lac Courts Oreilles.
Pelican (Wis.), Indians from, 202; trading on, 232.
Portage (Wis.). See Long Lake.
Rainy, route via, 23; post on, 214.
Red Cedar (Minn.), posts on, 173.
St. Clair, shipping on, 241.
Sandy (Minn.), posts on, 173.
Simcoe, on portage route, 367.
Superior, 163, 165, 168, 173, 180, 434; chart, 174, 177; described, 176; surveyed, 215; affluents, 166, 176, 182, 378; copper near, 183; fish in, 172; pigeons cross, 177; Indians from, 408, 409, 419, 473; route via, 426; traders on, 160, 161, 208, 214, 215, 234, 238, 245, 249, 258, 342, 432, 474; posts, xv, 69, 270; shipping on, 169, 170, 239, 262, 362; fur-trade department, 168, 170.
Tomahawk (Wis.), trading near, 184.
Torch. See Lacs: Du Flambeau.
Trout (Wis.), location, 198; village on, 197; trading on, 200, 216, 218, 231.
Turtle (Wis.), location, 181; Indian village on, 198.
Wauswaginng. See Lac: Du Flambeau.
Wild Rice (Wis.), identified, 198; trading on, 233.
Winnebago, outlet, 382, 385; Indian site on, 471; Dickson at, 364.
Winnipeg, fur-trader at, 469.
Lalancette, Antoine, at Lac du Flambeau, 169, 184, 190, 192, 205-207, 209; sketch, 170.
La Loche, a Chippewa, 198, 204, 224.

La Magdeleine, Sieur d'Ailleboust de, godfather, 13.
La Marche, —, trader, 190.
La Moitié du Chef, a Ch'ppewa, 217, 229.
Lamorandière, Etienne, godfather, 124..
La Morinie, Father Jean Baptiste, missionary, 7, 22, 23, 31, 32.
La Mothe, —, child baptized, 67.
La Mothe, Guillaume, witness, 103; godgather, 104; k'nsman, 358.
La Mothe, Joseph, baptized, 67.
Lamotte, Joseph Maurice, Montreal merchant, 358.
Landroche, André Skayamick dit, child baptized, 16.
Landroche, Anne Parent, child baptized, 16.
Landroche, Marianne, baptized, 16.
Landry, Agathe. See Gordon.
Langlade, Agathe. See Lusignan.
Langlade, Angelique, recollections, 142.
Langlade, Augustin Moras, s'eur, son baptized, 3; slaves baptized, 4, 8, 33, 37, 52; churchwarden, 43; godfather, 10, 12, 14, 16, 23, 25, 32, 35, 39, 41, 43, 44, 47, 48, 55-57, 59; step-daughter, 248.
Langlade, Charles (I) Michel, baptized, 3; children baptized, 44, 56; slave baptized, 51; servant, 118; godfather, 9, 22, 29, 37, 54, 63, 94; nephew, 5; relatives, 161; descendants, 146; commandant at Mackinac, 54, 69; in Revolution, 251, 264; at Green Bay, 69; land grant, 299, 300, sketch, 3.
Langlade, Charles II, child baptized, 82; godfather, 80, 89; daughter, 142; sketch, 82.
Langlade, Charles III, baptized, 82.
Langlade, Charlotte Bourassa, children bapt'zed, 44, 56; godmother, 39-42, 44, 46, 47, 49, 53, 54, 60, 61, 63, 64, 67, 68, 71; letter from, 300.
Langlade, Charlotte (Lalotte) Catherine, baptized, 44.
Langlade, Domitelle Villeneuve, children baptized, 1-3; slaves baptized, 33, 42; godmother, 8, 13, 19, 24, 28, 33, 34, 43, 52, 56, 59, 60. See also Villeneuve.
Langlade, Louise Domitelle, bapt'zed, 56. See also Grignon.
Langlade, Marguerite, marries, 146.
La Noue, Zacherie Robutel, sieur de, builds post, 166.
L'Anse (Mich.), trading post, 220, 227; reservation, 187; traders at, 209, 474; sketch, 208.
La Palme, —, godfather, 43, 44.

[510]

Index

La Perche. See St. Jean.
La Perrière, Claude Marin de, slave baptized, 22.
La Perrière, Magdeleine Villiers de, godmother, 22.
La Petite Racine, a Chippewa, 210, 216, 224.
La Pierre à Affiler (Keeshkenum), Chippewa chief, 185, 193, 216, 220, 224; identified, 206; son, 201, 210; plot, 206; in War of 1812-15, 184.
La Plante, —, son baptized, 32; godfather, 27.
La Plante, Louis, baptized, 32.
La Pluie. See Kiminoucane.
La Pointe family, at Prairie du Chien, 267.
La Pointe du Chequamegon, French post, 12; commandant, 30, 45, 175, 183; missions, 176; fur-trade post, 175, 176, 179, 190, 203, 208, 214, 215; settlement at, xi; agency, 181; treaty, 187; goods for, 171; traders at, 2, 12, 27, 45, 65, 67, 69, 70, 168, 361; boundary, 173; point, 176. See also Islands : Madelaine.
La Porcelaine Claire. See Ouassimigueso.
La Porceline, a Chippewa, 179.
La Puise, a Chippewa, 227.
Laramie. See Lorimier.
L'Arbre Croche, Ottawa village, 68, 322, 412.
L'Archevêque, Augustin, children baptized, 4, 24.
L'Archevêque, Augustin junior, baptized, 24.
L'Archevêque, Marie Catherine. See Joutras.
L'Archevêque, Marie Esther, baptized, 4
L'Archevêque, Marie Reaume, child baptized, 24, 25.
La Roche Debout, on Lake Superior, 172.
La Ronde, a slave, baptized, 52.
La Ronde, Ignace *dit*. See Bourassa.
La Ronde, Louis Denis, sieur de, commandant at Chequamegon, 175; finds copper, 182; owns vessel, 170.
Larrivée, Hippolyte, child baptized, 91.
Larrivée, Magdeleine, baptized, 91.
Lasalière, Marianne, baptized, 117, 118; godmother, 128, 131; sketch, 117. See also Fisher.
Lasalière, Pierre, child baptized, 117; wife, 86.
Lasalière Thérèse Marcot, child baptized, 117. See also Schindler.
Lashley. See Lesley.
Lasselay, François Samuel, baptized, 148. 148.
Lasselay, Samuel, child baptized, 148.
La Tête Grise, a Chippewa, 207, 224.

La Tortue, Chippewa chief, 198, 200; village, 212, 217.
Latour, Charles, death, 214.
Laurent, Alexandre, baptized, 125; child baptized, 148.
Laurent, Pierre, child baptized, 125.
Laurent, Pierre junior, baptized, 148.
Laventure, François, godfather, 126.
La Vérendrye, Pierre Gautier de junior, in Northwest, 29; slave, 37, 38.
La Vielle Française, a Chippewa, 216.
La Vigne, Urbain Texier *dit*, slave baptized, 27.
La Violette, Gabriel Hattinas *dit*, child baptized, 84.
La Violette, Gabriel (junior) Hattinas *dit*, baptized, 84.
La Voine, —, voyageur, 239.
Lavoin, —, witness, 37.
Lawe, John, Wisconsin trader, 400, 428, 447; post, 364, witness, 293; letters to, 346, 357-360, 458, 459, 461-463, 474, 475, 485-488; license for, 476; certificate, 487; accounts, 345; employees, 367.
"Lawrence," naval vessel, 363.
Lead mines, Indians near, 435.
Leath. See Leith.
Lebeau, —, voyageur, 179.
Leblanc, Ursule. See Fraser.
Le Bruié, a Chippewa, 209.
Le Canard, a Chippewa, 224.
Le Chef des Oiseaux, a Chippewa, 207, 218, 220, 224.
Le Cioux, a Chippewa, 220, 224.
L'Ecuyer, —, adopts child, 12.
L'Ecuyer, Blondeau, godmother, 12.
L'Ecuyer, Thérèse, married, 396.
Le Dru, F., Dominican friar, baptisms, 97-102.
Le Duc, Pierre. See Souligny.
Lee, Gen. Fitzhugh, mother of, 331.
Lefebre, Jean Baptiste, godfather, 46, 48; slave baptized, 48; at Green Bay, 55.
Lefevre, —, trader, 248.
Le Franc, Father Marie Louis, baptisms, 33-42, 44-63; interments, 150-156, sketch, 34.
Légal. See Sans Quartier.
Le Genou, Chippewa chief, 177, 178, 209, 224, 228.
Le Grand Canard, a Chippewa, 195, 219, 229.
Leith (Leath), George, Detroit merchant, 291.
Lemoine, Jean Baptiste, godfather, 118, 125, 131.
Lemoine, Jean Baptiste, *dit* Despins, St. Louis trader, 462.
Lemoine, Joseph, godfather, 139.

[511]

Le Muffle d'Orignal, identified, 193; Chippewa chef, 207, 218, 224.
Lepallieur, James Michel, Milwaukee trader, 401.
L'Epaule de Canard, a Chippewa, 197, 199, 202, 213, 217, 219, 220, 224; commended, 203.
Le Petit Canard, a Chippewa, 217.
Le Petit Forgeron, a Chippewa, 186, 224.
Le Petit Jour, a Chippewa, 218.
Le Petit Tonner, a Chippewa, 224.
Le Pettéel. See Lepallieur.
Le Pic, trading post at, 270.
L'Epiphanie (Que.), voyageur from, 180.
Le Porcipique, a Chippewa, 224.
Lerige, Marie Catherine. See Bourassa.
Le Roy. See Roy.
Le Sable, Josette, married, 149. See also Hameln.
Les Grandes Oreilles, Chippewa chief, 177, 178, 224, 228.
Lesley, —, arrested at Mackinac, 415, 421.
L'Esperance, Alexis Manian *dit*, baptized, 28.
L'Esperance, Anne Esther, baptized, 27.
L'Esperance, Antoine, baptized, 2.
L'Esperance, Christine, godmother, 66.
L'Esperance, Jean Manian *dit*, baptized, 2; children 12, 27, 28, 30.
L'Esperance, Marie Josephe, baptized, 12.
L'Esperance, Marie Josephe junior, baptized, 27.
L'Esperance, Marin Manian *dit*, baptized, 30.
L'Esperance, Rose Manian *dit*, baptized, 28; children baptized, 28, 30.
L'Étang (Le Temps), —, Wisconsin trader, 192, 193.
Letard, Joseph, godfather, 120.
Le Taureau, a Chippewa, 194, 217.
Le Teller. See La Fortune.
Letourneau, child baptized, 131.
Levadoux, Father Michel, American priest, 103–107, 157.
Levasseur. See Vasseur.
L'Éveillé, Augustin, children baptized, 35, 36.
L'Éveillé, Clotilde, baptized, 36.
L'Éveillé, Clotilde Girardin, children baptized, 35, 36.
L'Éveillé, Daniel Augustin, baptized, 35.
Le Vieux Sorcier, a Chippewa, 224, 230.
Levy, Misses, Montreal housekeepers, 369.
Lewis, James Otto, portraits by, 208, 256, 320.
Lewis and Clark, expedition, xvii, 239, 240, 280, 313, 317, 463.

Licenses, for foreigners, xvii, 480–482, 484; purchased, 452, 487; speculation in, 459; number decreased, 461.
Lincoln, Gen. Benjamin, commissioner, 275.
Lincoln County, sites in, 202.
Linctot family. See Godefroy.
Lindsay, Col. Crawford, notes by, 186, 188, 199, 205, 214, 222, 224; aid acknowledged, xxi.
Liquors, prohibited in fur-trade, 396, 398, 466, 467, 487, 488.
L'Isle, Guillaume de, map by, 187.
Little Kaukauna, Indian site, 371; early settler, 143.
Little York. See Toronto.
Locat, Elizabeth Louise, baptized, 15.
Locat, Josette Chevalier, children baptized, 15, 19.
Locat, Pierre, children baptized, 15.
Locat, Thérèse, baptized, 19.
Lockwood, Benjamin, child baptized, 121.
Lockwood, James H., Wisconsin pioneer, 428; at Portage, 396; letter, 474, 475; portrait, 490; sketch, 475.
Lockwood, Marianne Pelletier, child baptized, 121.
Lockwood, Mathilde, baptized, 121.
Loisel, Nicolas, godfather, 99.
London, fur-sales in, 281, 284; shipments to, 291.
Long, J., "Voyages," 196.
Longueuil, Charles Jacques le Moyne, baron de, godfather, 34.
Lorimier, Louis, removes to Louisiana, 265.
Lorimier, Peter, trader, 265.
Lorty, —, news of, 257.
Louis Hubert, a slave, baptized, 36.
Louis Joseph, a Potowatomi, baptized, 118.
Louis Joseph, a slave, baptized, 57.
Louise I, a slave, baptized, 56.
Louise II, a slave, child baptized, 115.
Louisiana province, under Spanish control, 265, 314; vicar general of, 72–74; cession to United States, 265; fur-trade factory in, 311; Indian agent, 339.
Louisville (Ky.), early settler, 302.
L'Ours, a Chippewa, 210.
Louson, Joseph, child baptized, 137.
Louson, Joseph junior, baptized, 137.
Louson, Nancy Pilot, child baptized, 137.
L'Outarde, Chippewa chief, 194, 195, 202, 217, 219, 220, 224, 229; aids Malhiot, 197, 200, 209, 218; commended, 192; characterized, 203.
Lusignan, —, Wisconsin trader, 485.

[512]

Lusignan, Agathe Langlade, children baptized, 142, 143.
Lusignan, François, ch'ldren baptized, 142, 143.
Lusignan, Marie Judith, baptized, 142.
Lusignan, Paul Louis Dazenard, sieur de, descendant of, 485.
Lusignan, Pierre, bapt zed, 143.
Lyons, Benjamin, Mackinac trader, 254–257, 259.
Lytle, Eleanor, married, 379.

MCARTHUR, Gen. Duncan, commandant at Detroit, 350; letter to, 436–439; sketch, 439; *Papers*, 354.
McBeath, George, witness, 78; trader, 236, 259; messenger, 245, 246; sketch, 236.
Maccatemicoueoue, child baptized, 72.
McClellan, Robert, fur-trader, 347.
McCrae, D., witness, 78.
McDonald, —, messenger, 240.
McDonald, El'zabeth. See Maillet.
McDonald, Geneviève, child baptized, 119.
McDonnell, —, clerk, 237, 238.
McDonnell, Madame, message to, 237.
McDonnell, John, fur-trader 165, 238; *Journal*, 165.
McDouall, Col. Robert, goes to Mackinac. 351, 352; commandant, 364; superintendent of Indians, 365; at Drummond's Island, 410; sketch, 364.
McDougall, —, Detroit merchant, 432, 433.
McDougall, Mrs. —, Montreal housekeeper, 369.
McGill, Andrew, letters, 279, 280, 298–300, 306, 307; letters to, 286, 287; death, 334.
McGill, James, Montreal merchant, 234, 245, letters, 261–263; 277–280, 298–300, 306, 307, 334, 335; letters to, 234, 235, 240, 246, 286, 287; stepson, 334, 373; forwards supplies, 244, 271; characterized, 336; bequest, 373; sketch, 235. See also Todd & McG ll.
McGill, Mrs. James, messages, 263; messages for, 249, 252, 255; property, 373.
McGill, John, at Sault Ste. Marie, 249; letters to, 245, 246; accounts, 248; sketch, 245.
McG.ll Brothers, Montreal traders, xvi: letters from, 234.
McGill University, founded, 373; manuscripts in l brary, 216.
McG llevray, William, fur-trade partner. xvi. 167, 185, 188, 195, 196, 200, 212, 213; consults Astor, 337; letter,

181; sketch, 167. See also McTavish, McGillevray & Co.
McGregor, Gregor, Detroit merchant, 278, 298.
McGulpin, Angelique. See Bailly.
McGulpin, Elizabeth, baptized, 114.
McGulpin, Giles, baptized, 114, 115.
McGulpin, Guillaume. See Will am McGulpin.
McGulpin, Henry, baptized, 114.
McGulpin, Madeleine, signature, 62; godmother, 123, 124, 127, 131.
McGulpin, Madele ne Bourassa, children baptized, 132, 133.
McGulpin, Madeleine Crequé, children baptized, 114.
McGulpin, Marie, baptized, 132; godmother, 131. See also Lacroix.
McGulpin, Patrick, children baptized, 114, 115.
McGulpin, Ursule, baptized, 133.
McGulpin, William (Guillaume), children baptized, 132, 133; godfather, 143, 146, 147; churchwarden, 162.
McIntosh, —, trader, 374.
McIntosh, James, at Detroit, 309.
McKay, Alexander, death, 365.
McKay, Donald, trader, 365.
McKay, Robert, judge, 365.
McKay, William, in War of 1812–15, 148; expedition to Prairie du Chien, 356, 368, 387; superintendent of Indians, 365; sketch, 365.
McKee, Col. Alexander, son of, 272; post, 274.
McKee, Capt. Alexander junior, wife, 272; n Montreal, 374.
McKee, Thérèse Askin, message to, 285; in Montreal, 374.
McKenney, Thomas L., supersedes Mason, 331; superintendent of Indian trade, 433, 442, 448–450, 452, 455, 457, 460, 464–466, 480–482, 484, 485, 487; *Tour of Lakes*, 175, 177, 434; sketch, 434.
Mackenzie, Sir Alexander, explorations, 164; kinsmen, 370; forms new company, 169; *Voyages*, 170; sketch, 290.
McKenzie, Donald, at Astoria, 281; in fur-trade, 370, 371.
McKenz'e, John, surgeon, 379.
McKenzie, Margaret, captured, 379.
McKenzie, Robert, witness, 102.
McKenzie, Roderick, explorer, 166, 167; bro'her of, 370; collects manuscripts, 182.
McKillip, Capt. Dan'el, British officer, 379
Mack'nac (Mackinaw, Michilimackinac), described, 233; map, 234; climate 287, 294; view, 362; neighboring Indians,

MACKINAC (continued)—
408, 409, 412, 471; council at, 417–422, 473; church, xi, xii, 1, 150; mission, xi, 1, 6; Protestant mission, 371; hotels, 150, 156; cemetery, 156; old fort, 149; post, 6; commandants, xii, 8, 11, 15, 17, 18, 20–22, 24–26, 29, 33, 35, 37, 38, 51–55, 61, 69, 78, 83, 90, 237, 241, 242, 351, 355, 380, 420; interpreter, 10, 85, 120; Indian agents, xix, 365, 379, 406, 407, 459, 476; factor, 341; collector, 340, 487; custom house, 294; commissary, 243; local official, 408; militia, 421; early residents, 235, 249, 296, 305, 306, 410; fur-trade rendezvous, xv, 234, 235. 238, 241, 267, 270, 293, 297, 319, 322, 343, 349, 383, 451; merchants, xvii, 236, 298, 307, 320, 345, 454, 461, 477, 483; goods for, 262, 285, 286, 306. 348, 356. 366, 367, 370; provisions, 322; licenses and seizures, 443–445. 452, 478, 481; prices, 452; fur-trade factory, xvi'i, 311, 327, 331–335, 394. 465; Astor's furs at, 353–355, 362, 363; Pontiac's conspiracy, 68; American Revolution, 264; captured by British (1812), 140, 184; in War of 1812–15, xvii, xviii, 321–324, 342, 345. 352, 355, 357–364, 468; Americans retake, xv, xix, 397, 398; troops at, 439, 479, 480; in Indiana Territory, 295; duel near, 323, 324; smallpox at, 153; real-estate, 271; shipping at. 342; route via; 383–385, 391, 393; view of British Landing, 362. See also Islands: Mackinac.

Mackinac County (Mich.), officers, 421.

Mackinac (Michilimackinac) Fur Company, members. 275; posts, 301; property, 433; operations, xvi. 191; employee, 343, 344; purchased by Astor, 291. 334–338.

Mackinac Register, loaned, xxi; described, xi, xii, 1; facsimiles, *frontispiece*. 8, 26. 75; baptisms, 1–149; marriage, 149; interments, 150–159; parish meeetings, 160–162.

Mackinaw City (Mich.), old house at. 323.

McKinsay, —, messenger. 286.

McLeod. See Gregory & McLeod.

Macnamaa, John L, witness, 78.

Macomb, Alexander, Detroit merchant, 260.

Macomb, Gen. Alexander junior, army officer. 260.

Macomb, William. Detroit merchant, 260.

McTavish, Simon, fur-trader, 163, 169.

McTavish, Frobisher & Co., Montreal merchants, 266, 290.

McTavish, McGillevray & Co, agents for North West Company, 309, 354, 356.

Mador, Basile, godfather, 73.

Madeleine I, a slave, child baptized, 22.

Madeleine II, a slave, baptized, 45.

Madeleine III, a slave, child baptized, 67.

Madison, President James, des'res peace, 351; signs document, 381.

Magee, —, message from, 372.

Maillet, Charles, child baptized, 119.

Maillet, Charles junior, baptized, 119.

Maillet, Elizabeth McDonald, child baptized, 119.

Mainard. See Menard.

Maitland. See Seaton, Maitland & Co.

Makometa (Bear's Oil), Menominee chief, portrait, 208.

Malden (Ont.), Ind'an councils at, 377; notary, 300; evacuated by British, 347; American commandant, 439.

Malhiot, François Victor (Erambert), letters, 166, 199; supplies for, 216–224; kinsman, xiv, 320; at Verchères, 397; *journal*, xiv, 163–215; broadside from, 224.

Malhiot, Franço's Xavier Ignace, educated, 166.

Malhiot, Lieut Col. Pierre Ignace, in Canadian army, 165.

Malhoit, Xavier, in Canadian parliament, 165; merchant, 397.

Malhiot fam ly, relatives, 320.

Mandan Ind'ans. baptized, 118; Lewis and Clark with, 240.

Manian. See L'Esperance.

Manistique (Mich.), trading site, 8.

Manitowa, child baptized, 112.

Manitowoc, resident, 476

Manitowoc County, mill built, 476.

Maouemkouens, child baptized, 40.

Maps, Lewis and Clark's, mentioned, 313; of Mackinac Island, 234.

Maranda, Jean Baptiste, godfather, 130.

Marantot, Joseph Amable Hubert Lacroix *dit*, godfather, 30. 40, 42.

Marchenaux, Nicolas, godfather, 106, 107; witness, 161.

Marchesseau, Nicolas, godfather, 72, 89.

Marchetteau, Jean Baptiste, godfather, 64.

Marchetteau, Marie Anne, baptized, 69.

Marchetteau, Michel Joseph, *dit* Desnoyer, child baptized. 69

Marchetteau, Thérèse Parent, child baptized, 69.

Marcot, Charlotte. See Chandonnet.

Marcot, Jean Baptiste, children baptized, 59, 65, 77, 86; wife baptized, 44; godfather, 18.
Marcot, Jean Baptiste junior, baptized, 65.
Marcot, Magdeleine, baptized, 86. See also Laframboise.
Marcot, Marguerite, baptized, 77; child baptized, 101.
Marcot, Mar anne, baptized, 77.
Marcot, Marie, baptized, 59.
Marcot, Marie Mighissen, child baptized, 59, 65.
Marcot, Marie (Marianne) Neskeek, children baptized, 77, 86.
Marcot, Thérèse, bapt zed, 86. See also Lasalière and Sch ndler.
Marguerite I, daughter baptized, 9.
Marguerite II, an Ottawa, child baptized, 118.
Marguerite III, a slave, baptized, 96.
Marianne I, a slave, baptized, 5.
Marianne II, a slave, bapt zed, 25.
Marianne III, a slave, child baptized, 28
Marianne IV, a slave, baptized, 54.
Marie I, an Ottawa, baptized, 44.
Marie II, a slave, baptized, 3.
Marie IV, a slave, baptized, 33.
Mar e V, a slave, child baptized, 43.
Marie Anne I, baptized, 104
Marie Anne II, a slave, baptized, 41.
Marie Athanase, a slave, baptized, 15; buried, 150.
Marie Catherine I, a slave, baptized, 34
Marie Catherine II, a slave, bapt zed, 49, 50.
Marie Charlotte I, an Indian, baptized, 14, 15.
Marie Charlotte II, an Indian, daughter baptized, 18.
Marie Charlotte III, a slave, baptized, 39, 40.
Marie Françoise I, a slave, bapt zed, 4.
Marie Françoise II, a slave, baptized, 30
Marie Jeanne, an Indian, baptized, 53.
Marie Josephe, baptized, 75; buried, 155.
Marie Lou se, daughter of Manitowa, baptized, 112; bur'ed, 157.
Marie Madeleine I, a slave, baptized, 4.
Marie Madeleine II, a slave, baptized, 6.
Marie Xavier, a slave, baptized, 57.
Mar etta (O.), resident, 453.
Mar n, Claude See La Perrière.
Marin, Joseph la Malgue, sieur, godfather, 30, 36, 38.
Marin, Pierre Paul, commandant in Wisconsin, 22.
Marion. See Lafontaine.
Marly, Charles, children bapt zed, 143; godfather, 121.

Marly, Charles junior, baptized, 143.
Marly, Josephe Vaillancourt, children baptized, 143.
Marly, Luc, baptized, 143.
Marquette (Mich.), bishop of, xxi
Marsollete, Jean Baptiste, godfather, 9.
Martin, Anto ne, dit Soud, ch ldren baptized, 99, 107, 113, 127; baptizes, 110.
Martin, Antoine junior, dit Soud, baptized, 99.
Martin, Catherine, baptized, 107.
Martin, Charles, bapt zed, 127.
Martin, Deborah M., aid acknowledged, xxii.
Martin, Louis, baptized, 113.
Martin, Marie Magdeleine, dit Soud, baptized, 99.
Martin, Philippe, dit Soud, godfather, 99.
Martineau, Ambrose, voyageur, 179, 205, 209, 218, 233.
Maskalonge. See Muskallunge.
Maskinonge (Can.), voyageur from, 343.
Mason, George, son of, 330.
Mason, James, Confederate commissioner, 331.
Mason, Gen. John, superintendent of Indian trade, 330-336, 380-395; resigns, 434; sketch, 330.
Massachusetts Historical Collections, 275.
Masson, L. R., finds material, 182, 216; notes by, 203, 205-207; *Les Bourgeois de la Compagnie du Nord-Ouest*, 61, 164, 165, 169, 176, 178, 238, 373.
Mata, Jeanne Die, child baptized, 138.
Mata, Julie, baptized, 138.
Mata, Maurice, child baptized, 138; godfather, 145.
Matchiougakouat, Marie, bapt zed, 38; ch ld baptized, 38.
Matthews, William W., in Astor's employ, 414.
Maugres, ——, a slave, baptized, 10.
Maur, Louis, child baptized, 87.
Maur, Louis jun'or, baptized, 87.
Maur, Marie Moran, child bap zed, 87.
Maximilien, prince of Wied, travels in America, 444.
Mayamo, child bapt zed, 147.
Mayet, Charles, godfather, 104.
Meghissens, Mar e. See La Hale
Megonojan. See Paccacona.
Meigs, Return J., Indian agent, 303.
Meldrum, George, witness, 78.
Meldrum & Park, Detroit merchants, 278, 287.
Memanghiouinet, children baptized, 51, 52; bur'ed, 154.
Menard (Mainard), Anne, baptized, 5
Menard, Antoine, baptized, 1; godfather, 148.

Menard, François, daughter baptized, 5.
Menard, Maurce, child baptized, 1; slave baptized, 3, 4.
Ménard, Father René, in Wisconsin, 187, 208.
Menard, Susanne. See Bolon.
Menominee (Folles Avoines) Indians, marry whites, 375; children baptized, 127, 144, 147; reservation, 105; school, 105; traders among, 313; numbers, 471; in War of 1812–15, 316; message for, 376; visit Mackinac, 415–418; treaty, 467; visit Drummond Island, 472; chief's portrait, 208.
Mercier (Mersier), Jacques, baptized, 124.
Mercier, Joseph Marie, children baptized, 80. 81, 98, 124.
Mercier, Joseph Marie junior, baptized, 80.
Mercier, Marie, baptized, 81.
Mercier, Marie Angel que, baptized, 124.
Mercier, Ursule, baptized, 98.
Methodists, missions for Indians, 208.
Metivier, Gabriel, baptized, 67.
Metvier, Jean Baptiste, children baptized, 58, 64, 67; buried, 156.
Metivier, Jean Baptiste junior, baptized, 58.
Metivier, Joseph Jean Baptiste, baptized, 64.
Metiv er, Josette Parent, child baptized, 58, 64, 67.
Metivier, Marguerite. See Ducharme.
Metivier, Marie Angelique, godmother, 53–55. 58; witness, 60. See also Fily.
Michel, a slave, baptized, 6.
Michigan, boundaries, 177, 186, 187, 212; early settlements in, xii; territorial governor, 339, 350. 379. 443; other territorial officials, 453; senator from, 453; treasurer, 372; *Historical and Pioneer Collections*, 133, 145, 177, 258, 279, 351, 398, 407, 410, 416.
Michigan Fencibles, officers, 365, 469.
Michilimackinac. See Mackinac.
Migouanounjan, Mare, baptized, 38, 39.
Migouanounjan, Pierre, child baptized, 38, 39; godfather, 45.
Mikisinensa, relatives baptized, 51, 52.
Miller, Col. John, builds Green Bay post, 431, 437; returns to Mackinac, 432.
Mills, Capt. —. lake captain, 309
Milwaukee, Indian village, 455; band. 471; traders, xv, 158, 253, 254, 305, 306, 375, 400, 401; provisions at. 230; early settler, 146.
Minanaconaton, child baptized, 109.
Mine à Breton. See Potosi.

"Mink," naval vessel, 363; burned, 361.
Minnesota, Indian sites in, 173; *Historical Collections*, 194, 207..
Minot, term explained, 225.
Misoumanitou, child baptized, 42.
Missouri Territory, Indians of, 386; governor, 478; traders in, 483; mines, 302; intruders expelled, 401.
Missoussicoue, grandson baptized, 72.
Mitchell, Madame, Mackinac resident, 404, godmother, 108, 119.
Mitchell, Daniel, at Mackinac, 404.
Mitchell, Dr. David, son, 323; accounts, 259.
Mitchell, David junior, sketch, 323.
Mitchell, Samuel, Indian agent, 303.
Mitchell family, Mackinac residents, 410.
Mobile (Ala.), in War of 1812–15, 392.
Mocock, term explained, 232.
Moith, E., witness, 108.
Monbrun, Marianne Cecile Cousineau, godmother, 39, 40, 42, 49, 53.
Monbrun, Perre. godfather, 39, 40, 53; slave baptized, 39; buried, 152.
Mongulpine. See McGulpin.
Monroe, James, secretary of state, 404.
Montgomery, Gen. Richard, at Quebec, 297.
Montreal, siege (1760), 27; growth, 336; visited, 397; merchants, xvi, 234, 238, 240, 243, 245, 258, 259, 271, 276, 280, 282, 290, 291, 294, 309, 323, 334, 335, 337, 351, 358, 359, 366, 377, 451; contracts, 343, 344; prices, 289, 365, 366; canoes from, 249, 251, 287, 322, 342, 352; goods from, xviii, xix. 257, 461; furs shipped to, 297; trial at, 241; children educated, xvii, 271, 469; Beaver Club, 373; McGill University, xxi. 216. 373.
Montressor, Capt. John, builds Fort Erie, 276.
Montrose (Ia.), site, 314.
Montvert, trading site, 5.
Mooney, James, "Ghost Dance Religion," 322.
Moran, Marie. See Maur.
Morampont, Charles Denis Duplessis, sieur, godfather, 15, 19.
Moravians, as missionaries, 301.
Morgan, Lewis, Wisconsin trader, 453, 454.
Morgan, Willoughby, at Mackinac, 398; at Fort Armstrong, 477, 479, 483.
Morison, Charles, Northwest trader, 249, 251; son, 474; letters, 287, 289, 294, 297.
Mormons, in Illinois, 315.
Morrison, James, at Montreal, 282.
Morrison, William, Lake Superior trader, 215, 474.

Morse, Jedidiah, *Report to the Secretary of War,* 389.
Mouet, Marie. See Cadotte.
Mougrain, Maurice, godfather, 101.
Mountains, Rocky, crossed, 163, 290.
Mouus, a Chippewa, 23.
Mozoboddo. See Le Muffle d'Orignal.
Mullanphy, Catharine, married, 424.
Munroe, Robert, Indian agent, 303.
Murray, Samon & Co., merchants, 310.
Muskallunge (*esox nabilior*) in Lac du Flambeau, 187, 207; bought, 218.
Mustela pennanti. See F.sher.

NADEAU, Julie, baptized, 125.
Nadeau, René, child baptized, 125.
Nahshawagaa (White Dog's Son), Potawatomi chief, portrait, 256.
Nanchoukaché, lodge, 51; relatives baptized, 52.
"Nancy," fur-trade vessel, 308, 309.
Naperville (Ill.), resident, 455.
Nattamanisset, Elizabeth, child baptized, 65.
Nauvoo (Ill.), site, 315.
Navarre, Catherine, married, 260.
Neagles, John, Montreal merchant, 282.
Neill, Edward D., *Minnesota,* 170, 444.
Nekikkoue. See Ketch nape.
Nelson, —, Detroit carpenter, 308.
Nelson, Admiral Horatio, wins battle, 281.
Neoukima, baptized, 50; child baptized, 52.
Neskeek, Marianne. See Marcot.
Nekses, an Ottawa, daughter baptized, 44.
New York, fur-trade emporium, xvi, 451, 461, 462.
New York Fur Company, trader, 482.
Niagara, on trade route, 234, 243, 249, 255, 257, 284, 288; traders at, 397; seat of government, 275; residents, 241, 242; in War of 1812-15, 276, 327.
Nicole, Isabelle, baptized, 137.
Nicole, Jean, child baptized, 137.
Nicole, Marguerite Beaubien, child baptized, 137.
Niles' Register, cited, 387.
Nipissing Indians, marry whites, 21, 46, 47, 60.
Nolin, Jean Baptiste, witness, 149.
North West Fur Company, precursor, 236; history, 163, 164; partners, 167, 174, 192, 196, 235, 238, 239, 241, 245, 256, 267, 323, 342, 365, naturalized, 403; importance, 234, 248; rivalry with, xvi, 169, 170, 191, 235, 280, 285, 289, 290, 463, 469; headquarters, 167, 170, 408; posts, 166, 173, 209,

270, 337; agents, 69, 70; employees, 136, 139, 165, 168, 170, 176, 214, 281, 347, 371, 474; departments, 168, 173; vessels, 170, 262, 462; supplies for, 247, 248, 252, 267, 285; during American Revolution, 240; unites with X Y Company, xvi, 163, 169, 210, 267, 308-310, 366; in War of 1812-15, xix, 361, 362, 366; Astor's connection with, 336, 337; secures Astoria, 414; union with Hudson's Bay Company, 289, 309, 366, 371; letter to, 257.
Northwest Territory, laws, 295.
Nova Scotia, governor, 355.
Noyaux porceline, term explained, 222.
Numainville, Jean Baptste, children baptized, 126.
Numainville, Joseph, baptized, 126.
Numainville, Marie, baptized, 126.
Nunns, Annie A., aid acknowledged, xxii.

OCEANS—
Arctic, discovered, 163; visited, 290.
Pacific, overland route to, 163, 290.
Odanah, Indian settlement, 176.
O'Fallon, Dr. James, at Louisville, 439.
O'Fallon, John, at Green Bay, 436; Prairie du Chien, 475, 477; partner, 448; letters, 436-439, 458, 483, 484; sketch, 439.
Ohio, traders in, 277; militia, 439; reserves, 284; money from, 453; in War of 1812-15, 456.
Ojibwa Indians. See Chippewa.
Okondokon, Chippewa chief, 183.
Oliva, Frederic, in South West Company, 344; requests license, 476; letter, 351, 352; accounts, 321; sketch, 321.
Olivier, —, baptizes, 109.
Oneida County, sites in, 202.
Ontario, crown-lands department, 367; Historical Society *Papers,* 120, 132, 141, 142, 145, 161, 249, 308.
Ontonagon (Mich.), location, 183.
Opost. See Vincennes (Ind.).
Oregon, adventures in, 477.
Osage Indians, agency, 424.
Oshkosh, early settler, 89.
Otchipwa Indians. See Chippewa.
Ottawa (Courts Oreilles) Indians, habitat, 412; migrations, 171; baptized, 44, 53, 85, 100, 115; marry whites, 86; children baptized, 98-101, 109, 110, 113, 116, 117, 128, 130, 131, 137, 138, 147, 148; in Revolution, 242, 243; follow the Prophet, 322; ask for truce, 350; council with Americans, 417; visit Drummond Island, 472; Mackinac, 473; friendly to Americans, 456, 471.

Ouabeno, Achaka, son baptized, 40.
Ouabikeki, baptized, 51; lodge, 52.
Ouakkouaouagan, Marie, ch ld baptized, 38, 39.
Ouassimigueso (La Porcelaine Claire), child baptized, 131.
Ouechibisse, Angelique, slave baptized, 66.
Ouech'poussé, godmother, 40.
Ouichema, buried, 153; child bur'ed, 153.
Ouicheina, Lou, child baptized, 50.
Ouigouisence, Marguerite. See Bertrand.
Ouindigouich, child baptized, 66.
Ou ouiskoin, Madeleine. See Vasseur.
Ouiskentcha *dit* Teleiprieoue, child baptized, 66.
Oukimakoue, child baptized, 40.
Oulaoue, niece baptized, 66.
Outagami Indians. See Foxes.
Outeskouiabano, baptized, 50.

PACIFIC FUR COMPANY, founded, xvi, 291; partners, 347, 348, 371.
Pacoacona, Françoise Marie Megonojan, child baptized, 74.
Pacoacona, Jean Baptiste, child baptized, 74.
Pac¨acona. Marie Louise, baptized, 74.
Paget, François, wife baptized, 144, godfather, 144, 145, 147-149.
Papin. Marie Thérèse, married, 397.
Paquin. Catherine, baptized, 145.
Paquin. Louis, baptized, 145.
Paquin, Marie Campbell, children baptized, 145.
Paqu'n, Pierre, children baptized, 145.
Parent, Angelique, baptized, 28.
Parent, Anne Catherine, baptized, 8; godmother, 57, 62, 64, 67.
Parent, Anne Domitille (Nanette), baptized, 3; godmother, 8, 10. See also Landroche.
Parent, Anne Josephe (Josette), baptized, 6. See also Metivier.
Parent, Charles Antoine. baptized, 11.
Parent. Charlotte, baptized, 3; godmother, 14. 21, 24, 28, 29. See a'so La Branche.
Parent, Ignace, baptized, 5; buried, 154.
Parent. Joseph, baptized, 4; buried, 153.
Parent, Marianne Chaboillez, children baptized, 8, 11, 16, 28; godmother, 16, 39-41. 64, 65, 69.
Parent. Marie Anne, baptized, 4. See also Brisbé.
Parent, Marie Françoise (Manon), baptized, 3; godmother, 16. See also Pelletier.
Parent, Pierre, children baptized, 3-6, 8. 11, 16, 28; slave baptized, 39, 64;

slave buried, 156; godfather, 49, 57, 58, 65; commandant at Mackinac, 69.
Parent, Pierre Coussant, baptized, 3.
Parent, Thérèse, baptized, 16; godmother, 68. See also Marchetteau.
Park, William, Detroit merchant, 278, 308. See also Medrum & Park.
Parkman Club, *Papers,* 187.
Partridges, identified, 187, 188.
Patterson, Charles, trader, 235, 256.
Patt nson, —, message for, 326.
Pauquette, Pierre, death, 375.
Pause, term explained, 180.
Payet, Father Louis, in Mackinac Register, baptisms, 78-95; other entries, 149, 156, 161; sketch, 78.
Pecan. See Fisher.
"Pedlar," fur-trade vessel, 477.
Pellé. See La Haie.
Pelletier, —, wife, 180.
Pelletier, Angelique, baptized, 24.
Pelletier (Pellé), Claude. See La Haie.
Pelletier (Peltier), Jacques, Detroit settler, 325.
Pelletier, Madeleine. See Askin.
Pelletier, Marianne. See Lockwood.
Pelletier, Marie Françoise (Manon) Parent, child baptized, 24.
Pelletier, Pierre, ch ld baptized, 24.
Pelletier, Pierre II. See Antaya.
Pelletier, Susanne Hirbour, godmother, 79, 80, 86.
Pembina (N. Dak.), post at, 239.
Pemmican, described, 226.
Penetanguishene (Ont.), naval station, 368; settlers, 120, 132, 141, 145, 146, 305, 351; settlement begun, 147.
Peoria (Ill.), early trader, 366; letter from, 301-303.
Perinault. —, trader, 258, 259.
Perinault, Joseph, godfather, 75, 76.
Perrault, Jean Baptiste, trader, 173, 174.
Perry, Oliver, naval officer, 263, 351; retires, 363.
"Perry," vessel on Lake Huron, 415, 417.
"Perservance," schooner burned, 361.
Personne. See La Fond.
Peterkin, Thomas, Indian agent, 303, 310.
Petersburg (Va.), siege, 394.
Petit, Elias, godfather, 105.
Petit Bled, a Chippewa, 216.
Petit Jour, a Chippewa, 217.
Petit Pêche, on Lake Superior, 172.
Philipson, —, St. Louis merchant, 354.
Phyn, Ellice & Co., London merchants, 241.
Phyn. Inglis & Co., London merchants, 169.

Index

Pichet, William J., witness, 128, 129.
Pichipieca, Indian debtor, 312.
Pierce, Capt. Benjamin K, wife, 109.
Pierre, a negro, baptized, 64.
Pierre, son of Ouabeno, bapt'zed, 40.
Pierre, a slave, baptized, 79.
Pierre Augustin, a slave, baptized, 10.
Pierre François, a slave, baptized, 39.
Pierre Louis, a slave baptized, 4.
Pigeons (*ectopistes migratorius*), on Lake Superior, 177.
Pike, Lieut. Zebulon M, visits Wisconsin, xviii, 139, 267, 306, 313, 323, 345, 474; map, 313; journey, 315, 320; chooses fort site, 315.
Pike-perch (*stizostedion vitreum*), 168.
Pillet, Felicité. See Carignan.
Pilot, Nancy. See Louson.
Piquet, Noel, godfather, 17.
Pitatchaouanon, relatives baptized, 51, 52.
Pittsburgh, letter from, 352; bank at, 453; early traders, 277; route via xviii, 342, 390-393.
Plat Coté, a Chippewa, 184, 216, 224.
Platt, —, Montreal merchant, 369.
Playing Fox. See Waapalaa.
Plessy, Geneviève. See Bourdon.
Plomondone, Jacques, child baptized, 128.
Plot, G., Montreal merchant, 359, 360.
Plus, term explained, 178.
POINTS—
Au Sable, near Mackinac, 56.
Detour, on Lake Superior, 174.
Patterson, drowning near, 235.
St. Ignace, site, 5; mission at, 1, 6, 66.
Poison Doré (*stizostedion vitreum*), in Lake Superior, 168.
Poitras, Marie Josephe. See Freraux.
Pompey, Askin's servant, 238.
Pond, Peter, fur-trader, 163; sells out, 167; describes Mackinac church, 150.
Porlier, Jacques, Wisconsin fur-trader, 170; godfather, 128; power of attorney, 299, 334; tutor, 313; accounts, 304, 305; sales, 357, 413, 414; furs seized, 416; protest, 409; on Mississippi, 276, 313; Missouri, 445-447; at Mackinac, 428, 429; in War of 1812-15, 468; partner, 366; kinsman, 166, 320, 396, 397; meets Pike, 313; buys factory goods, 341; bad fortune, 463; a messenger, 376; letters, 311-313, 317, 318; letters to, 304, 318-320, 337, 338, 355, 356, 396-398; sketch, 313.
Porlier, Joseph Jacques, in War of 1812-15, 356, 468; sketch, 469.
Porlier, Louise, in Canada, 166; letter, 397.

Porlier, Marianne, in Canada, 166; visits Montreal, 397.
Portage des Sioux, treaties at, 160.
Portage la Prairie, trader at, 365.
PORTAGES—
Brulé-St. Croix, described, 171.
Fox-Wiscons'n, route via, 90, 368, 474; described, 438; Indians near, 470, 471; agency for, 437; settlers, 127, 375, 396.
Grand, 169. See also Grand Portage.
Keweenaw, 208.
La Tortue. See Turtle.
Maumee-Miami, 265.
Mauvaise River-Namekagan, 176.
Montreal River, length, 180; described, 177, 178, 181, 186, 198, 199; traversed, 184, 212-214.
St. Louis River-Sandy Lake, 173.
Sturgeon Bay, 400.
Toronto, described, xv, 367, 462.
Turtle, 232, 233.
Portelence, Louis, w'tness, 43.
Port Hope (Ont.), Indian agent at, 305.
Pot, French measure, described, 216.
Potawami Indians, baptized, 117, 118; marry whites, 158; smallpox among, 150; at Milwaukee, 471; visit Mackinac, 419, 426; Drummond Island, 472; friendly, 456; hostile, 455; presents for, 389; chief's portrait, 256.
Pothier, Toussaint, witness, 96; godfather, 104, 122.
Pothier, Toussaint junior, agent of North West Company, 337, 338, 342-344, 351, 354, 358-360; buys furs, 357; letter, 355, 356; sketch, 323.
Potosi (Mo.), mine at, 302.
Pouchot, François, *War in America*, 153.
Poulain, Pierre. See Sans Gêne.
Powell, Peter, Wisconsin trader, 368; in War of 1812-15, 469; sketch, 368.
Prairie du Chien, founders, xvii, 267; council at (1783), 237; arbitration, 275; fur-trade rendezvous, 191, 301, 304, 315, 318, 329, 344, 345, 353, 425, 426, 445, 475, 477; Indians near, 417, 418, 421, 472; in War of 1812-15, xvi', xviii, 140, 161, 253, 356, 365, 367, 368, 387, 468; post planned, 378, 383; Indians favor post, 430; post built, xx, 424, 425, 480; American officials at, xviii, 308, 398, 420, 458, 459, 480; Indian agents, 314, 323, 333; fur-trade factory, 384, 386-390, 433, 436, 463, 464, 481; furs from, 451, 466; goods for, 448-450; wampum at, 456; licenses, 452; British subjects, 401-404, 464; settlement,

PRAIRIE DU CHIEN (continued)—
xi; settlers, xvii, 78, 104, 139, 140;
Selk'rk passes, 486. See also Forts:
Crawford.
Presque Isle. See Erie (Pa.).
Preston, William C., plans Wisconsin
boundary, 177.
Preston, Col. William, relative of, 479.
Prevost, Sir George. orders from, 351,
354, 355; aide-de-camp, 322; recalled,
367; sketch, 355.
Proctor, Gen. Henry, in War of 1812-15,
272, 367; beseiges Fort Meigs, 402;
evacuates Malden, 347, 350; paroles
prisoner, 379.
Provancher, René, godfather, 24, 63.
Provençal, Louis Carbonneau dit, children baptized, 134, 135.
Pryor, —, mentioned, 436.
Puthuff, Maj. William Henry, Indian
agent at Mackinac, xix, 407, 414, 463,
476; seizes furs, 415-417, 420; issues
licenses, 444, 445, 452, 457, 458; refuses license, 483; councils with Indians. 417-423, 473; descr'bes British
policy, 408-413, 423, 424, 430; requests instructions, 425-427; instructed by Cass, 428, 460, 461; censured, 443, 444, 459, 481; letters, 430-433, 472-474; sketch, 407.

QUEBEC, besieged (1776), 297; furprices at, 298.
Queenston (Ont.), founder, 276; settlers, 272; route via, 342.
Quierigoufili. See Fily.
Quindre, Antoine de. godfather. 133.
Quindre, Cæsar de, sieur d'Ouville,
child baptized, 19, 26; commandant at
Detroit.
Quindre, Charles Stanislas de, baptized,
19.
Quindre, Françoise Marianne Bellestre
de, child baptized, 19; godmother, 13.
Quiquanamoso. See Kikkanamazoo.

RACICOT, Jacques, voyageur, 179, 180,
184, 190, 199, 201, 221; on drouine,
225; sketch, 180.
Radisson, Pierre Esprit, in Lake Superior, 166, 175, 215.
Ramezav, Jean Baptiste, sieur de, commandant at Nipigon, 12.
Rankin, David, trader, 236; sketch, 237.
Rapids, Des Moines, in Mississ'ppi,
464.
Rassade, term explained, 217.
Rastel. See Rocheblave.
Rayshay mekoquan, an Indian, brings
information, 326.

Reaume, Alexis, merchant, 345.
Reaume, Charles, Green Bay magistrate,
xviii, 142; *dispute with engagé*, 275;
proh'bits liquor-selling, 399, 400; sells
land, 392; nephew, 345; letter to,
395, 396; sketch, 142.
Reaume, Jean Baptiste, children baptized, 2, 38, 48, 49.
Reaume, Jean Baptiste junior, baptized,
38.
Reaume, Joseph, baptized, 48, 49.
Reaume, Judith, baptized, 2.
Reaume, Marie. See L'Archeveque.
Reaume, Marie Josephe, children baptized, 48, 49.
Reaume, Marie Josephe junior. See
Jourda'n.
Reaume, Susanne. See La Fond.
Reed, Celeste, baptized, 144.
Reed, N., child baptized, 144.
Reeves, Jean. godfather, 80, 83, 84, 88,
104; witness, 161.
Regis, a slave, baptized, 97.
Regis, Jean François, a slave, baptized,
29.
Reid, James, Mackinac merchant, 345.
Reilhe. Antoine, godfather, 103.
Rémond, Indian gives 'nformation, 177.
René, a slave, baptized, 67.
René Michel, a slave, baptized, 3.
Repentigny. Louis le Gardeur, cheval'er
de, godfather, 26, 39, 42, 54; slaves
baptized, 36, 47; sketch, 26.
Reynolds, Gov. John, wife, 366.
Rhinelander, lakes near, 202.
R'card, Joseph, godfather, 126.
Richard, Father Gabriel, baptisms, 109-
118, 132-149; describes church, 150;
presides at meeting, 162; interments,
157, 158; note by, 161; sketch, 109.
Richardson, John. Montreal merchant,
xvi, 308, 337, 338; sketch, 309.
Richardson, Maj. John, traveller, 263.
Richardson, Dr. Robert, of Sandwich,
263, 324.
Richardson. Forsyth & Co., Montreal
merchants. 169.
Richot, Pierre, godfather, 12.
Rigaud, François Vandreuil, marqu's de,
at Crown Point, 27.
RIVERS—
Assiniboine. fur-traders on, 165, 196,
239, 366; Indians hostile, 238.
Athabasca. fur-traders on, 366.
Aux Pleines. See Des Plaines.
Bad. reservation on, 176. See also
Rivières: Mauvaise.
Balsam, described, 212, 213.
Baraboo, origin of name, 21.
Bois Brulé (Wis.), 171.
Bons Secours. See Chippewa.

Index

Boyer, origin of name, 238.
Brulé (Minn.), Malhiot at, 171.
Cheboygan, Indians at, 412.
Chippewa (Wis.), map, 187; portage to, 176; Indians on, 189; fur-traders 69, 184, 190, 191, 193, 202, 203; trading posts, 171; sketch, 171.
Churchill, trader on, 245.
Clearwater (Minn.), fort on, 215.
Columbia, fur-traders on, 136, 281, 371; expedition to, xvi', 348, 414; dalles of, 477.
Crow, post on, 313.
De Loup. See Wolf.
Des Moines, mouth, 314; Indians on, 319; villages, 315; traders at, 477, 478, 483; fur-trade factory near, 387, 388; goods, 448.
Des Plaines, significance of name, 17; resident, 455.
Detroit, mouth, 277; as boundary, 234.
Du Bœuf, letter from, 486.
Du Lac. See Rum.
English, trading on, 290.
Flambeau, route via, 181; described, 186.
Fox (Ill.), Indian village on, 455.
Fox (Wis.), route via, xv, xviii, 378; Indians on, 471, 472; settlement, 293, 401; fort, 436; land-claims, 364, 368, 376; traders on, 283; trading license for, 476, 477; agency on, 380-382, 385.
Fraser, discovered, 136.
French, trade route, xv, 358, 359, 362; post at mouth, 242, 248, 249, 257.
Gogogashugum. See Middle River.
Gooseberry (Minn.), described, 215.
Grand (Can.). See Ottawa.
Grand (Mich.), trading site on, xv, 9, 28, 44, 65, 148, 295, 455.
Grand (Mo.), land grant on, 314.
Grand (Oh'o), port at, 363.
Great Miami, portage to, 265.
Holland, portage route, 367.
Illinois, trade route, 378.
Indian Camp, identified, 215.
Issati. See Rum.
Kalamazoo, trading site, xv, 14.
Kaministiquia, significance of name, 166; outlet, 168; fur-trade route, 169.
Lemoin. See Des Moines.
Lemonweir (Wis.), traders on, 364.
Liard, post on, 374.
Mackenzie, discovered, 290.
Manitowish, on Montreal River portage, 181.
Maumee, portage to, 265; rapids, 274.

Mauvaise (Bad, Muskego), Malhiot at, 176; Indians, 213; fish from, 215.
Menominee, as boundary line, 177; source, 187; Indians on, 471; traders, 365, 367, 476.
M ddle, identified, 213.
Milwaukee, Indian villages on, 471.
Minnesota. See St. Peters.
Mississippi, headwaters, 471, 474; watershed, 182; route via, xviii, 342, 426; route to, xv, 434; navigation, 449; Ind ans on, xviii, 189, 314, 472; hostile, 387; traders on, xvi, xvii, 48, 69, 71, 214, 276, 306, 307, 323, 343, 345, 353, 378, 409, 445, 477; posts, 173, 174, 386; expedition, 387; Indian agent, 333, 365, 437; settlement, 401; Selkirk descends, 486.
Missouri, Indians of, 424; fur-trade on, xvii, 317, 343, 353, 378, 397, 477; British traders, 239, 240; ncident of fur-trade, 347; trapping expedition, 318; traveller, 444; fur-trade factory, 389; mil'tary post, 480; town, 446; industr es, 439
Montreal, route via, 171, 214; tributaries, 212, 213; fur-trade department, 167, 168; described, 177. See also Portages.
Muskeego. See Mauvaise.
Niagara, fort on, 276; early settlers, 347.
Namekagan, portage to, 176.
Ohio, as boundary, 410; hostilties on, 280; route via, xviii, 342.
Ontonagon, Indian band on, 200; described, 182.
Osage, fur-trade factory on, 389.
Ottawa (Grand), fur-trade route, xv, 167, 234, 236, 241, 242, 244, 245, 252, 255, 366
Peace, post near, 238.
Petite, Malhiot at, 21.
Pic, post on, 270.
Pigeon, portage to, 169.
Pine (des Pins), Indians on, 471; described, 212.
Platte, traders on, 348; Aird visits, 317.
Qu'appelle, trading post on, 165.
Raspberry (Minn.), 215.
Raspberry (W s), Malhiot at, 174.
Red (of the North), Indians on, 134; traders, 136, 165, 219, 444; colony, 139, 371, 462; posts, 280; riot, 174.
Red Lake (Minn.), fort on, 215.
Rock (Ill.), Indians on, 353, 387, 446, 456.

[521]

RIVERS (continued)—
Rum (Minn.), letter from, 313, 314.
St. Clair (Mich.), settlers on, 308.
St. Croix, Indians on, 189; fur-trade route, 171; portage to, 176; traders on, 69, 142, 313.
St. François. See Rum.
St. Joseph, trading on, 295.
St. Louis (Minn.), posts on, 173.
St. Peters (Minnesota), Indians near, 435; traders visit, 275, 444, 469, 486.
Saskatchewan, posts on, 281.
Savanna, portage route, 173.
Sioux, charted, 175.
Siskowit, Malhiot at, 174, 215.
Talon See Ontonagon.
Thames (Ont.), battle on, 184, 214.
Vermilion (S. Dak.), post on, 317.
Winnipeg, fort on, 166.
Wisconsin (Ouisconsin), source, 182, 187; mouth, 71; Indians of, 189, 387, 471, 472; fur-traders on, 184, 191, 201, 221, 224, 225, 318, 470, 486; fur-trade route, xv, xviii, 301, 378; Ménard on, 187; at the portage, 396. See also Portages: Fox-Wisconsin, and Routes.
Wolf. Indians on, 471.
RIVIÈRES—
A la Framboise. See Raspberry.
A l'Eau de Vie, identified, 313.
Aux Groseilles. See Gooseberry.
Des Pins. See Pine.
Des Sapins. See Balsam.
Des Sauteux. See Chippewa.
Du Milieu. See Middle River.
De Vasynagan, wintering place, 30
Rivières, Amable de, godfather, 53, 66.
Rivières, Hippolyte de, son baptized, 66; godfather 85, 91.
Rivières, Hippolyte junior de, baptized, 66.
Rivières, Marie de, child baptized. See also Des Rivières.
Robertson, Catherine Askin, messages from, 243, 245, 254; at Detroit, 258
Robertson. Capt. Daniel, commandant at Mackinac, 83, 90, subordinate, 236.
Robertson, Capt. Samuel, navigator, 248; trader, 241, 249, 252, 254; marriage, 242, 248, 254; brother, 272; sketch, 241.
Robertson, William, identified, 284; sketch, 272.
Robertson, William junior, inherits property, 272.
Robinson, William, mentioned, 284, 291
Roc, Angelique, baptized, 92.
Roc, Charlotte, baptized, 92.
Roc, Joseph, children baptized, 91, 92.
Roc, Joseph junior, baptized, 92.
Roc, Louise, baptized, 91.
Rocambole. See Pierre Louis.
Rocheblave, Charlotte, baptized, 130.
Rocheblave, Noel, trader, xvii; child baptized, 130; godfather, 125, 130; father of, 366; power of attorney for, 299, 300; accounts, 304, 305, letter to, 315, 320.
Rocheblave, Philippe François Rastel, sieur de, commandant in Illinois, 366.
Rocheblave, Pierre, in South West Company, xvii, 366, 405; buys furs, 413; imports goods, 414; letters, 415–417; letter to, 447.
Rocheloi, Jean Baptiste, buried, 151.
Rocheveau, Catherine, baptized, 4; godmother, 18.
Rocheveau, Françoise, baptized, 4, 5; sister baptized, 17; died, 5.
Rocheveau, Françoise Veronique, baptized, 5.
Rocheveau, Jean Baptiste, baptized, 6.
Rocheveau, Jean Baptiste junior, baptized, 54.
Rocheveau, Marie Josephe, baptized, 54.
Rocheveau, Marie Tiennotte, children baptized, 54.
Rocheveau, Michel, children baptized, 4–6; wife, 5; slave buried, 152; godfather, 19.
Rocheveau, Michel junior, wife baptized, 54; children baptized, 54, 55.
Rolette, Jane Fisher, married, 140.
Rolette, Joseph, godfather, 140; churchwarden, 162; in War of 1812-15, 469; trader, 345, 459, 460, 475; carries message, 397, 398; licenses, 441, 443, 487; censured, 419; letters to, 304; sketch, 140.
Romain, Jean, baptized, 147.
Romain, Jean Baptste. See Sans Crainte.
Rose, Nicolas, godfather, 9.
Rouse, Jacques, refugee, 476.
Rouse, Louis, Wisconsin trader, 476, 486; sketch, 476.
Rouse's Point (N. Y.), site, 476.
Rousseau, Charles, godfather, 137; in Hudson's Bay Company, 351.
Rousseau, Dominique, children baptized, 136; godfather, 137.
Rousseau, Marguerite Champagne, child baptized, 136.
Rousseau, Marie Bourassa, baptized, 136.
Rousseau, Jean Baptiste, Northwest trader, 351.
Rousseau, Jean Baptiste junior, in Hudson's Bay Company, 351.
Rousseau, Sophie, baptized, 136.
Routes, for fur-trade, xv, xviii, 173, 378, 434.

Index

Roy, Agathe Villeneuve, at Green Bay, 248. See also Bo'sguilbert, and Souligny.
Roy, Amable, Wisconsin trader, 248.
Roy, André, child baptized, 100.
Roy, Angelique, baptized, 99, 127; godmother, 132. See also Jauvan.
Roy, Angelique junior, baptized, 103.
Roy, Charlotte, baptized, 127; godmother, 130.
Roy, François I, child baptized, 85.
Roy, Franço s II, baptized, 85.
Roy, François III, trader at L'Anse, 208, 219, 220; letter from, 212.
Roy, François IV, at Portage, 127, 396; sketch, 396.
Roy, Geneviève, baptized, 103.
Roy, Joseph, children baptized, 99, 127, 128; son, 396; sketch, 127.
Roy, Louis, children baptized, 103.
Roy, Louis junior, baptized, 103.
Roy, Marguerite, children bapt zed, 127, 128.
Roy, Marie, baptized, 100.
Roy, Pierre, baptized, 99.
Roy, Pierre junior, at Green Lake, 396.
Roy, Pierre Amable, godfather, 71; baptizes, 72.
Royal Americans (60th British infantry), officers, 281.
Rupala's. See Clayer.

"SAGINAW," fur-trade vessel, 285-287, 299, 307.
Saintain, E., portrait by, 347.
Ste. Anne, parish church at Mackinac, xi, 1, 6, 109; described, 150; slaves for neophytes, 29, 34, 64; wardens, 160-162; treasurer, 161; new lot for, 162.
St. Antoine. See Vacher.
St. Amand, Antoine, buried, 155.
St. Aubin, Joseph, godfather, 62.
St. Charles (Mo.), trader at, 445-447.
St. Clair, Arthur, governor, 303.
St. Clair County (Ill.), officers, 345.
St Clair County (Ind.), officials, 314.
St. Clair County (Mich.), early settlers, 308.
St. Cyr, —, fur-trade clerk, 243, 245.
St. Cyr, Hélène, married, 314.
St Cyr, Hyacinthe, daughter married, 314.
Ste. Geneviève (Mo.), settlers, 267, 314.
St. Germain, Antoine, godfather, 21, 48-50; slave baptized, 49.
St. Germain, Jacques, buried, 159.
St Germain, Joseph, godfather, 65.
St. Germa'n, Léon, trader, 190; visits Malhoit, 210; sketch, 190.

St. Ignace. See Point St. Ignace.
St. Jean, Joseph la Perche dit, trader arrested, 477, 479.
St. Louis, expedition of 1780, 174; Spanish at, 314; in War of 1812-15, 314; residents, 302, 384, 397, 424, 442, 477; merchants, xvi, 103, 304, 320, 347, 448, 478; voyageurs at, 353; fur-trade centre, 354; depot for factories, 435, 448-450, 454, 456, 464, 466; Astorians at, 348, 371; trial at, 425; route via, xviii, 386; Indian treaty at, 467; charitable institutions, 439.
Ste. Marie de Lanaudière, Canadian seignoiry, 323.
St. Martin, Toussaint Antoine Adhemar, sieur de, royal notary, 98; justice, 157, 158; witness, 102; godfather, 97-100, 105, 109; baptizes, 96-100, 102, 103, 106-110, 117-119; son, 307; letter to, 300; buried, 159; sketch, 159.
St. Mary's. See Sault Ste. Marie.
St. Medard, Nicolas, buried, 156.
St. Pierre, Jacques le Gardeur, sieur de, godfather, 24-26.
St. Pierre and St. Paul, settlement, 17.
St. Rais'n, Josette. See Gravelle.
Samon. See Murray, Samon & Co.
San Domingo, officials, 273.
Sand Rock (Wis.), location, 212.
Sandusky, in War of 1812-15, 468; fur-trade factory at, 393; trading post, 266; trader, 301.
Sandwich (Ont.), mission near, 147; settlers, 263, 272; traders, 346; in War of 1812-15, 350.
Sanguinet, Céleste, married, 462.
Sanguinet, Charles, St. Louis merchant, 304, 305.
Sanguinet, Veronique Cardin, child baptized, 75.
Sans Chagrin, Alexis Sejourné dit, child baptized, 26; slaves baptized, 34, 51, 71; godfather, 16, 28, 32, 55, 63, 67, 71.
Sans Chagrin, Angelique Sejourné dit, baptized, 26. See also Cauchois.
Sans Chagrin, Marie Angel que Taro Sejourné dit, child baptized, 26; godmother, 31, 34, 35, 46, 48, 50, 54, 57, 65, 69, 71.
Sans Crainte, Jacques Romain dit, baptized, 61, 62.
Sans Crainte, Jean Baptiste Romain dit, child baptized, 61, 62.
Sans Gêne, Pierre Poulain dit, godfather, 33.
Sans Peur, Catherine, baptized, 57.
Sans Peur, Joseph, child bapt zed, 57, 67.

[523]

Sans Peur, Michelle, child baptized, 57, 67.
Sans Peur, Thérèse, baptized, 67, 68.
Sans Quartier, Eustache Légal *dit*, buried, 159.
Sans Regret. See Laborde.
Sarasin, Augustin, child baptized, 79.
Sarasin, Augustin junior, baptized, 79.
Sarasto, a slave, baptized, 51.
Sauk County, river in, 21.
Sauk Indians, villages, xviii, 314, 435, 446; in Spanish alliance, 314; hostile, 387; lead mines, 320; treaty with, 315; annuities, 389; at Milwaukee, 471; visit Drummond Island, 472; traders among, 304, 353, 445, 446, 477; marry whites, 384.
Sault Ste. Marie, neighboring Indians, 206, 408; commandant, 39; interpreter, 134; early settlers, 5, 7, 10, 15, 19, 20, 23, 33, 35, 39, 46, 47, 65, 67, 70, 120, 208; baptism at, 208; shipping for, 170, 239; provisions, 244, 246, 254, 256; traders, xv, 235, 241, 244, 246, 249, 355, 356; in War of 1812–15; 357, 361-364.
Sauteux Indians. See Chippewa.
Sayer, Guillaume, at Red River, 174.
Sayer, John, Lake Superior trader, 173, 174, 238; letter, 181; partner, 190; sketch, 173.
Scharf, J. Thomas, *St. Louis*, 397.
Schindler, George, wife, 86.
Schindler, Thérèse Marcot, adopts child, 134. See also Lasalière.
Schoolcraft, Henry R., on Lake Superior, 173, 175, 176, wife, 361; *Indian Tribes*, 176, 300; *Narrative Journal*, 173, 183, 220.
Schoolcraft, James, murdered, 134.
Scotch, as fur-traders, xiii.
Seaton, Maitland & Co., China merchants, 290.
Sejourné. See Sans Chagrin.
Selkirk, Thomas Douglas, earl, founds colony, 366, 462; on Mississippi, 486; sketch, 462.
Selle, Marie Josephe de. See Blondeau
Semple, Robert, governor of Red River colony, 136, 462.
Shadawish, Chippewa chief, 206.
Shantytown, near Green Bay, 293. See also Green Bay.
Sharp, George, trader, 280; death, 291.
Shaw, Alexander, witness, 102.
Shaw, Col. John, narrative, 420.
Shawneeawkee. See John Kinzie.
Shawnee Indians, remove to Louisiana, 265; agency for, 424.

Shawnee Prophet, influence, xviii, 322, 323; later activity, 473.
Sheipland, —, accompanies Indians, 281.
Shounkchunk (Black Wolf), Winnebago chief, portrait, 320.
Shinaabaw'osin (Figured Stone), Chippewa chief, portrait, 208.
Simcoe, Sir John Graves, governor of Upper Canada, 273–275, 307.
Sinclair, Capt. Arthur, naval officer, 362, 363.
Sinclair, Patrick, commandant at Mackinac, 78, 150, 241, 254; subordinate, 236.
Sioux Indians, habitat, 69, 319, 425, 426; hostile, 5, 313; traders among, 191, 342; visit Mackinac, 417, 419, 426; as Indian slaves, 23, 30; marry whites, 444; children baptized, 119, 124, 134, 135. See also Teton Indians, and Yankton Indians.
Siskowit (*christivomer namycush siscowit*), in Lake Superior, 172.
Six Nations. See Iroquois.
Skayamick, André. See Landroche.
Slavery, Indians in, 3–5, 8–10, 13, 15, 22, 29, 33, 34, 36, 39, 42, 47–49, 51, 54, 57, 59, 60, 64, 66, 67, 70, 73, 86–88, 96, 97, 107, 150, 152, 240.
Smallpox, at Mackinac, 50–52, 153.
Smith, Gen. Thomas A., at Prairie du Chien, 424, 433, 434; Bellfontaine, 477, 478; sketch, 424.
Smithsonian Institution, copper boulder in, 183.
Solomon, Miss —, married, 462.
Solomon, Agibicocona, children baptized, 110.
Solomon, Alexis, baptized, 113.
Solomon, Elizabeth, godmother, 100.
Solomon, Ezekiel, son, 120; godfather, 110; trader, 252.
Solomon, Ezekiel junior, godfather, 127.
Solomon, Guillaume, children baptized, 104, 110, 120.
Solomon, Henri, baptized, 110.
Solomon, Hubert, baptized, 120.
Solomon, Louis, recollections, 120.
Solomon, Louise Dubois, godmother, 101, 103, 106, 110, 112, 120, 122, 125, 127, 128; witness, 113, 121; baptizes, 110.
Solomon, Marguerite, baptized, 127.
Solomon, Marie, child baptized, 113.
Solomon, Marie Louise, baptized, 110.
Solomon, Samuel, child baptized, 113.
Solomon, Sophie, baptized, 104, 105; godmother, 104, 106.
Sommers, Rev. M. C., aid acknowledged, xxi.

Index

Soud. See Martin.

Souligny, Agathe Villeneuve, godmother, 55, 57, 59, 61. See also Boisguilbert and Roy.

Souligny, Apolline, baptized, 101.

Souligny, Charlotte, baptized, 55.

Souligny, François, child baptized, 95; godfather, 95.

Souligny, Franeois Lou's, baptized, 95.

Souligny, Marie, godmother, 89.

Souligny, Philippe François, child baptzed, 100; godfather, 98.

Souligny, Pierre le Duc, *dit,* child baptized, 55; slave baptized, 55; godfather, 38, 45, 55, 61; sketch, 38.

South West Fur Company, founded, xvi, 291, 337; partners, 280, 324; agents, 351, 363, 413, 414, 426, 431; employees, 176, 474; territory supplied, 426; goods, 355; accounts, 344; buys furs, 429; affected by embargo, 342; relation to Astor, 405, 451, 458, 460.

Spanish, control Louisiana, 265; allied with Indians, 314; land-grants, 320.

Spinard, Charles, son buried, 157.

Spokane (Wash.), post near, 477.

Squirrels, damage from, 188.

Steadman, —, merchant, 247.

Sterling, James, Detroit merchant, 243, 244, 278.

Stock Leo F., aid acknowledged, xxi.

Stockton, —, letter to, 431.

Stone, Bostwick & Co., fur-merchants, 461.

Stone, David, fur merchant, 461, 477.

Strabane, Askin's estate, 324, 326.

Street, Joseph, papers of, 477, 483.

Stuart, Betsy, message from, 371.

Stuart, David, fur-trader, 371.

Stuart, Robert, letter, 368-372.

Sturgeon, in Lake Superior, 183, 214, 215.

Sunday, John, a Chippewa, 200.

Sunfish, in Lac du Flambeau, 188.

Superior, trading post at, 173; Historical Society, 173.

Susanne, a slave, baptized, 43.

Tabeau, Antoine, godfather, 93.

Tabeaux, Baptiste, witness, 161.

Tabeaux, P., witness, 161.

Taillefer, Joseph, children baptized, 116.

Taillefer, Josette, baptized, 130

Taillefer, Louise, children baptized, 116.

Taillefer, Louise junior, baptized, 116.

Taillefer, Marie, baptized, 116; godmother, 126; mother baptized, 130.

Tallier, Charles Chevalier, child baptized, 23

Tallier, Pierre, baptized, 23.

Talon, Jean, river named for, 183.

Tanner, John, child baptized, 134.

Tanner, Lucille (Lucy), baptized, 134.

Taro, Marie Angelique. See Sans Chagrin.

Tason, Charles, engagement contract, 292, 293.

Taxier, Charles, adopts child, 12.

Taylor, Maj. Zachary, at Green Bay, 482; expedition on Mississppi, 387.

Tecumseh, alliance with Chippewa, 207; confederacy, xviii, 322, 323; army, 456.

Teleiprioue. See Ouiskentcha.

Tellier. See La Fortune.

Ten Eyck, Conrad, fur-trader, 347-349, 360; sketch, 347.

Ten Eyck, Jeremiah, Detroit merchant, 347.

Tenier, Paul, godfather, 88, 91.

Tenkswatawa. See Shawnee Prophet.

Terrebonne (Que.), retired traders at, 240.

Teton Indians, hostile, 347.

Texier, Urbain. Se La Vigne.

Thierry, Pierre, canoe conductor, 256; godfather, 83, 88, 92, 115, 121, 123, 130; witness, 161; sketch, 256.

Thimotée, an Ottawa, children baptized, 86.

Thomas. See Tomah.

"Thomas," Lake Huron vessel, 288.

Thomas, Paul, godfather, 67.

Thwaites, Reuben G., *Early Western Travels,* 196, 226, 362, 444, 463; *Original Journals of Lewis and Clark Expedition,* 317.

Tiennotte, Marie, baptized, 54; children baptized, 54, 55. See also Rocheveau

Todd, Isaac, Montreal trader, 280, 282, 285, 286; in England, 261, 263; returns, 260, 264; ill, 310; visits springs, 289, 372; at New York, 336; Philadelphia, 281; Niagara, 284; letters, 271, 272, 276, 277; letters to, 234, 240, 246.

Todd, Mrs. Isaac, in England, 249.

Todd Brothers, traders, xvi, 139.

Todd & McGill, Montreal traders, 250; letters, 261, 264-266; letters to, 251-256, 258.

Tomah (Thomas), Menominee chief, 346, 376; defends Mackinac, 362; speech in council, 417, 418.

"Tonquin," fur-trade vessel, 365, 371, 414, 477.

Toronto (Little York), fur-trade rendezvous, 358, 359; portage route, xv, 367; mail route via, 351; residents, 368; provisions at, 368, 369.

TREATIES—
Paris (1763), 234.
Greenville (1795), 284.
Sauk and Fox (1804), 389.
Ghent (1814), xix, 146, 395, 414, 441
Greenville (1814), 160.
Portage des Sioux (1815), 160, 387, 446, 456.
General Indian (1815–17), 439.
Great Britain, commercial (1816), 404.
Winnebago (1816), 435.
St. Louis (1816), 387.
St. Louis (1817), 424, 467.
Menominee (1817), 467.
Prairie du Chien (1825), 456.
Chippewa (1826), 200.
Fond du Lac (1826), 434.
Butte des Morts (1827), 434.
Chicago (1832), 160.
Sauk and Fox (1832), 477.
Chicago (1833), 160.
Washington (1836), 483.
La Pointe (1854), 187.
Tremblé, Rémie, voyageur, 179, 218, 226; deserts, 208, 209, 227; returns, 211, 212
Trempealeau, resident, xxi.
Tiny (Ont), settlers, 161.
Trout (*cristivomer namycush*), in Lake Superior, 172.
Turcotte, Pierre, deserted engagé, 288.
Turpin, Amable, godfather, 138.
Two Rivers, trader at, 446.

"UNION," fur-trade vessel, 355.
United States, cession of Louisiana, 265; Bureau of Ethnology *Report*, 189, 197, 322; *Indian Treaties*, 467.
Upper Canada, organized, 272, 278; officials, 273, 368; capital, 275; governor, 367; early settlers, 235; removal to, xx.
Upper Piqua (Ohio), Indian agent at, 340.
Urtubize, Marin, slave baptized, 5.

VACHER, Charles St. Antoine *dit*, engagement contract, 343, 344.
Vacher, Joseph St. Antoine *dit*, contract, 343.
Vaillancourt, Angelique, baptized, 102, 103.
Vaillancourt, Elizabeth, baptized, 142.
Vaillancourt, Hariette, baptized, 135.
Vaillancourt, Jean Baptiste, baptized, 112.
Vaillancourt, Joseph, children baptized, 102, 108, 111, 112, 142.
Vaillancourt, Joseph junior, baptized, 111.
Vaillancourt, Josephe, godmother, 122, 123, 126. See also Marly.
Vaillancourt, Marie. See Hogan.
Vaillancourt, Marie Elizabeth Bourgoin, children baptized, 102, 108, 111, 112, 142.
Valé, Charles, child baptized, 92, 93.
Valé, Pierre, baptized, 92, 93.
Van Buren, President Martin, appointments, 347.
Varin, Guillaume, wife baptized, 80.
Varnum, Jacob B., factor at Chicago, 391, 394, 395; at Sandusky, 393, 394; sketch, 394.
Varnum, Gen. Joseph Bradley, speaker of House of Representatives, 326.
Varnum, Joseph Bradley junior, factor at Mackinac, 326, 327, 330–334, 339, 341; chosen for Green Bay, 382–384; in Astor's employ, 414; brother, 394; sketch, 326.
Vasseur, André le, baptized, 131, 132.
Vasseur, Geneviève le, baptized, 117.
Vasseur, Jacques le, children baptized, 95, 113, 116, 117, 131, 132; wife baptized, 115.
Vasseur, Jacques le junior, baptized, 116.
Vasseur, Jean Baptiste le, baptized, 132.
Vasseur, Joseph le, baptized, 113.
Vasseur, Louis le, baptized, 116, 117.
Vasseur, Louise le, baptized, 95; godmother, 120, 131, 132. See also Gautier *dit* Caron.
Vasseur, Madeleine Ouiouiskoin le, baptized, 115; children baptized, 113, 116, 117, 131, 132.
Vaudette, Angelique, baptized, 108.
Vaudette, Hippolyte, children baptized, 108, 131
Vaudette, Marie, baptized, 131.
Verchères, Jean Jarret, sieur de, commandant at Mackinac, 11.
Verchères (Que.), residents, 166.
Vérendrye. See La Vérendrye.
Verge, French measure, explained, 223.
Veronique I, a slave, baptized, 9.
Veron que II, a slave, child baptized, 96.
Verville, Claude de. See Gautier.
Vieau, Andrew Jacques, portrait, 400.
Vieau, Jacques, Milwaukee trader, 400, 401.
Vieau, Peter J., narrative, 400.
Vieu, Indian debtor, 312.
Vieu, Angelique du Sable, son baptized, 2.
Vieu, Catherine Angelique, baptized, 3.
Vieu, Coussant, baptized, 2.
Vieu, Ignace, children baptized, 2, 3; son died, 2.
Vieu, Louis Thérèse, baptized, 2; died, 2.

Index

Viger, Marie Anne. See Beauvais.
V go, François, trader at Vincennes, 264, 266.
Vilas County, streams in, 181; sites, 197.
Villebon, Charles René Desjordy, sieur de, commandant at Green Bay, godfather, 42.
Villeneuve, Agathe, baptized, 2; signature, 13. See also Boisguilbert, Souligny, and Roy.
Villeneuve, Anne (Nanette), baptized, 2; signature, 8; married, 161; buried, 154; sketch, 2. See also Guillory and Blondeau.
Villeneuve, Charlotte, baptized, 56.
Villeneuve, Constant (Coussant) Stanislaus, baptized, 3; children baptized, 56, 65.
Villeneuve, Daniel, children baptized, 2.
Villeneuve, Daniel junior, baptized, 2; child baptized, 22.
Villeneuve, Domitelle, children baptized, 2, 3. See also Langlade.
Villeneuve, Jean Bapt ste, baptized, 2.
Villeneuve, Marie Louise Thérèse, baptized, 2. See also Gautier.
Villeneuve, Pierre Louis, baptized, 65.
Vi'liers, Magdeleine de. See La Perrière.
Vill ers, Nicolas Antoine Coulon de, k lled, 22.
Vincennes (Ind.), on boundary, 443; capital of Indiana Territory, 295, 296; early residents, 159, 302, 439.
Volant, Nicolas, godfather, 35.

WAAPALAA (Playing Fox), portrait, 320.
Wadin, —, trader killed, 474.
Wagacoucher, Charles, child baptized, 101.
Wagacoucher, Charlotte, baptized, 101.
Wagner, Prof. George, a d acknowledged, xxii, 172, 188.
Walpole (N. H), fur-trade at, 461.
Warren, John, Fort Erie commissary, 276.
Warren, Admiral John B., wins battle, 281.
Warren, Lyman M., Wisconsin trader, 70, 171, 176.
Warren, Truman, Wisconsin trader, 70, 176.
Warren, William, Wisconsin trader, 184.
WARS—
French and Indian (1754-63), partic pants, 27, 243.
Pontiac's consp racy (1763), xii, 68, 279.
Lord Dunmore's (1774), participant, 392.

American Revolution (1775-82), in Northwest, xvii, 166, 234, 264; Canada, 238; Illinois, 366; participants, 273, 282, 297, 308, 314, 392; American sympathizers, 244, 301; loyalists, 259, 260, 272, 3 5; British agents, 265; British post, 276; sufferers from, 284; naval officer, 275; Indians employed, 242, 243, 251, 252.
1812-15, declaration, xviii, 348; partic pants, 145, 214, 272, 304-306, 310, 321, 368, 379, 407, 424, 433, 444, 454, 479; surgeon, 263; interpreters, 184, 190, 208, 253; comm s-sary, 330; fur-traders in, 366, 367, 446, 468, 469, 476, 477; Indian allies, 322, 347, 386, 468; vessels employed, 308, 351; in the West, xvii, 439, 456; the South, 392; on Niagara frontier, 276, 327; at Detroit, 294, 350; Mackinac, xix, 139, 140, 146, 184, 323, 324, 327, 345, 355, 357-364, 421; on Lake Super or, 190; in Wisconsn, 148, 160, 161, 314, 345, 356, 365, 368, 387, 402, 469, 481; destroys fur-trade, 393, 394; peace declared, 369; boundaries adjusted, 167 See also Treaties: Ghent.
Winnebago (1827), history. 435, 480.
Warsaw (Ill), site, 387.
Washington, George, favors factory system, 311; first executive mansion, 260; death mentioned, 291.
Washington (D. C.), arch ves. xx ; Library of Congress collections, 436-439; Globe, editor of, 479.
"Washington," vessel on Lake Michigan, 428
Waters, Marie Magdeleine, baptized, 81.
Waubajeeg, Chippewa chief, 175.
Wayne, Gen. Anthony, officers, 297, 347.
Wayne County (Mich.), offic'n s, 296, 347; trading l cense, 295.
'Weasel," vessel wrecked, 326.
Wells, William, Indian agent, 303
Wheeler, L. H., missionary, 176.
Wheeling (W. Va.), Indian agent at, 310.
Whe y, —, chi'd baptized, 119.
White, David, Montreal merchant, 310
White Crane, Ch'ppewa chief, 70.
White Crow. Chippewa chief, 193.
White Dog's Son. See Nahshawagaa.
Whitefish (coregonus clupeiformis), in Lake Superior, 172, 176, 214, 324
W ed, prince of. See Maximilien.
Wild Goose (bernicle Canadensis), purchased, 219

[527]

Wild rice (*zizania aquatica*) Indian food, 184; described, 189; gathered, 197; purchased, 189, 190, 193, 198, 200, 216, 217.
Wilkinson, Gen. James, cited, 315.
Williams, John R., Detroit merchant, 309, 310.
Williams, Thomas, fur-trader, 309.
Wilt, —, Crooks's agent, 854
Winnebago County, trading village in, 90.
Winnebago Indians, habitat, 418; census, 471; characterized, 438; hostile to Americans, 158, 387, 419, 422, 455, 456, 480; oppose post at Green Bay, 440; visit Mackinac, 417; council with, 417-422; visit Drummond Island, 421, 426, 472; trade with, 353; marry whites, 179, 368; chief's portrait, 320; village pictured, 300.
Winnipeg (Man.), site, 165.
Wisconsin, boundaries planned, 177, 186, 187, 212; geological survey, 178; early settlements, xi, xii; early saw mills, 140; territorial growth, 379; fur-trade in, 163-233, 267-269, 275, 282, 283, 292, 293, 305, 306, 311-318, 340, 344-346, 375-488. See also the several captions.
Woodbridge, Dudley, message for, 454.
Woodbridge, William, Detroit merchant, 453; letter to, 482, 483.

Woodbridge, Mrs. William, message for, 454.
Wooly, Capt. —, transportation agent, 391, 393.
Wormers, term explained, 221.
Wright, Dr. —, in English army, 282.
Wright, Archange Grant, message from, 282.

X Y FUR COMPANY, organized, 280-282, 290; partner, 366; employees, 170, 219, 474; vessels, 169, 170; Indians attached to, 184, 196, 206; rivalry with, xvi, 169-171, 178, 179, 185, 192, 285, 289; posts, 185, 192, 200; union with North West Company, xvi, 210, 267, 308-310, 366; sketch, 169.

Yankton (Sioux) Indians, traders among, 317, 368.
Yarns, George, voyageur, 184, 202, 220, 227-230, 232.
Yonge Street (Toronto), laid out, 367.
York (Ont.), route via, 342, 351. See also Toronto, and Portages.
Young, G. E., justice of peace, baptizes, 108; witness, 96, 108.

Zizania aquatica. See Wild Rice.

Day of month	Names of Savages	Rum by large Kegs	Rum by the Pot	Rum by the chopine	Rum by the half chopine	Chiefs' Coats	Chiefs' Shirts	Chiefs' Plumes	Chiefs' Hats	Laced Capots	Carrots of Tobacco	Tobacco by the Brasse	Tobacco by the half brasse	Tobacco by the foot	Tobacco by the pouce	Powder by double handfuls	Bullets	Shot by the handful	Flints	Wormers	Steels for striking fire	Awls	Needles	Small sleigh-bells	Vermillion by the pinch	Braid by the Fathom	Large Knives	Small Knives	Combs
	Totals	7	196	107 [117]	30	4	11	4	4	5	1	25	34	50	61	43	1127 [1190]	31	161	46	42	60	154	78	99	57	29	24	33
	Brought forward	7	171	105	24	4	11	4	4	5	1	24	29	47	58	38	1007	31	145	39	39	52	130	54	87	52	27	20	28
1805 April 11	Le Vien cloux & Band												1																
17	Old La Chouette and Band		5										1		1	2			6	2			12	12	4	4			
21	La Feuille												1	1	1														
23	To the young men of L'Outarde		8	2															4	2									
24	L'Egle's brother																					6	6						
25	The son of La Pierre à siffler												1	1	1						2		4		4	1			1
	L'Outarde			4											1				4			1			2				
May 1	To le Chef des Oiseaux & Band		8									1				3	60				1	1	2	10	2		1	2	2
8	The war-party																												
10	The war-party		6		6								1				60		2						2		1	2	
May 19	Old La Chouette and Band			6																1		1	2						2
21	To le Petit Oiseau and Band																												1

STATEMENT OF THE GOODS GIVEN TO THE SAVAGES FOR NOTHING

Day of the month	Names of Savages	Rum by large kegs	Rum by the Pot	Rum by the chopine	Rum by the half-chopine	Chiefs' coats	Chiefs' shirts	Chiefs' plumes	Chiefs' hats	Laced capots	Carrots of Tobacco	Tobacco by the brasse	Tobacco by the half-brasse	Tobacco by the foot	Tobacco by the pouce	Powder by double handfuls	Bullets	Beaver shot by the handful	Flints	Wormers	Steels for striking fire	Awls	Needles	Small sleigh-bells	Vermillion by the plich	Braid by the brasse	Large common knives	Small common knives	Horn combs	Box-wood combs	Thread
1804																															
July 25	Les Grandes Oreilles		8	12									1	4	6	2	30	2	12	2	2	3	6		4	4	4	3	1		1
August 3	Le Genou & Band		1				2					3		1			120		12	2	2		12	12	8	6	4		4	2	1
4	La pierre à suffler & band	2			5							1	1	1	3		90		15				5								
7	Le Plat côté		4							1		1		1		3	60	1	6			1	6		8	8	1	1	4		1
8	Latcramallière		2		6					1		1		1		3	60	2	4	3	3	2	5		4	4	2				1
9	La chouette		4				2					1	1	1		3	30	1	24	2	2	12	24	3	4	8	2	2	6	2	1
11	La chouette Fogerou											1		2		2	30					1	2			4	1				
20	La chouette & band											2		1				2		1	1	1			1		2	1	2		
21	La Petite Roche	1	4			1	1	1	1	1	1	1	1	2			30		4							2	2	2		2	1
25	L'Outarde's young men		4										1												12				6		
	La Chief des Oiseaux & band		4									2				2															
	L'aigle d'Original & band		4		3							3	2	2		3	60	2								2	2	2	1	2	1
	La Feuille													1																	
	La Tête grise										1			1																	
	La Loche																														
	La Corneille		4																												
	L'Outarde & Band																														
	The Brother of La Feuille		4									2																			
September 3rd	L'Outarde & Band		8								1			1			30			1	1	1			1	2		1			
5	La Grande Loutre & Band		4										1	2		1	30	1				1							1		
8	La Lapière & Band		4										1	1		1	60	20	4	1	1					2	1	2	2		1
11	Canard & Band		4									2										1									
15	To The people of Lac du Plumbeau		4																												
18	The two young men of Vieux Désert																									13	3				
24	La Petite Roche																														
27	Le Petit Tonner																														
	To Lachouette's young men																														
	To the people of le Vieux Désert																														
28	L'aigle de Canard																60	1					8								
October 3	L'Égle and Band		4			1	1	1	1	1		3	1	2		2	30	1	2	1	1	4	8		4	3			1		
4	Barotoux and band																														
29	L'épaule de canard & band		2																												
	Barotoux and band																														
	The son of La pierre à suffler																														
	La Chouette & Band																20														
	To Barnet's Brothers-in-law & some other young men																														
	Le Mulle d'Original and Band																														
Totals		7	79	43	14	4	11	4	4	5	1	19	13	28	20	22	590	21	87	27	27	37	70	24	60	34	22	17	20	7	7

Day of month	Names of Savages	Rum by large Keg	Rum by the Pot	Rum by the chopine	Rum by the half-chopine	Chiefs' Coats	Chiefs' Shirts	Chiefs' Plumes	Chiefs' Hats	Laced Capots	Carrots of Tobacco	Tobacco by the brasse	Tobacco by the half brasse	Tobacco by the foot	Tobacco by the pouce	Powder by double handfuls	Bullets	Shot by the handful	Flints	Wormers	Steels for striking fire	Awls	Needles	Small sleigh-bells	Vermillion by the pinch	Braid by the brasse	Large Knives	Small Knives	Horn combs	Box-wood combs	Thread
	Brought forward	7	171	105	24	4	11	4	4	5	1	24	29	47	59	38	1007 [1070]	31	145	39	39	59	130	54	87	52	27	90	28	10	9
1834 October 13	La Feuille		2	3	1								1	1																	
	La Grande Loutre & band		6		3								1	2	4	1	30		4	2	2	2	4								
	La Feuille's brother			12									1	1		1							13	13							
	Old Cioux & band		4	6									1	2	4	1	30	1	6	3	3	3	6	6							1
	La Tête Grise		2	3	2								1		1	1							1	1		6	4				
November 17	Bareloux & Band		4	4								2					30			1	1	1	13	13	6	3	3	1	1		1
November 26	La chouette		4	4									1		8		30						6	6		6					
December 10	Old La chouette																30														
December 19	Le Genou		14	10													30														
1835 February 15	To the people of Lake Superior		15																2												
February 19	To Legrotron's son		8																												
	to old La Chouette & Band																														
February 20	To L'outarde, L'epaud de Canard & Bands											2			6	1	60	1	4	1	1	1	2		6	3		1			
	old La Chouette & Band		2	6								1	1	1	6	2	30	1	3	1	1		4	6	2		1	1	1		1
February 25	To La outarde, L'gaud de Canard & Bands		4		3							1	1		6	3	30	2	10	1	1	1	16		3		1	1	2		
	To La Chouette & Band		4	6								1	1	1		1	30	2	20	2	2	2	8		8	6	3	1			1
	To L'Outarde & band		4										1	1	6	1	60	2	4	2	2	2	2		1	2					
	To La Loche				3								1	1		2	30	1	4				16	6	8	3		2			
	To La Porcpique		4										1	3		3	30	3	24	1	1	1	2							3	
	to le vieux Sorcier & band		4																4												
March 3	to La Chouette's son		4																												
March 10	To L'Egle and Band																														
March 14	Old La Chouette & Band																														
March 16	To L'outarde & band																														
March 19	To le Petit Tonner and band																														
	La Chef des Oiseaux & band																														
April 27	Bareloux & band																														
April 29	Bareloux, L'Egle and Bands																														
April 9	To le Chef des Oiseaux and Bands		79	43	14	4	11	4	4	5	1	19	13	28	29	23	590	21	87	27	27	37	70	24	60	34	22	77	20	7	7

www.ingramcontent.com/pod-product-compliance
Lightning Source LLC
Chambersburg PA
CBHW060218230426
43664CB00011B/1475